Encyclopedia of
Dinosaurs
The Sauropods

Encyclopedia of
Dinosaurs
The Sauropods

Rubén Molina-Pérez and Asier Larramendi
Illustrated by Andrey Atuchin and Sante Mazzei

Translated by Joan Donaghey

Published by the Natural History Museum, London

Rubén Molina-Pérez and Asier Larramendi are the founders and scientific directors of Eofauna, a company that creates scientifically accurate representations of prehistoric fauna. Molina-Pérez specialises in biogeography, biometrics, and palaeontology. Larramendi's work focuses on the comparative anatomy and morphology of extinct vertebrates.

Also available
Encylopedia of Dinosaurs: The Theropods

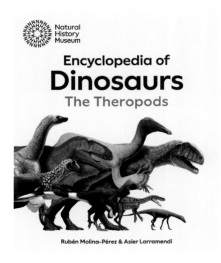

First published in the United Kingdom by the Natural History Museum, Cromwell Road, London SW7 5BD

Reprinted 2024

ISBN 978 0 565 09518 5

10 9 8 7 6 5 4 3 2

A catalogue record for this book is available from the British Library

Editorial: Robert Kirk and Abigail Johnson
Production Editorial: Kathleen Cioffi
Jacket Design: Lorraine Doneker
Production: Steven Sears
Copyeditor: Patricia Fogarty
Printed in China by Toppan Leefung Limited

Prologue

In the first volume of this series, on theropod dinosaurs, readers were able to appreciate the surprising variety of forms and sizes in which this group of animals developed, from just a few grams to heavier than an African elephant. Some species are believed to have run very fast, some had incredibly powerful bite forces, and across all species there was extreme diversity in diet (most were carnivores, although others were phytophagous, pescivorous, insectivorous, or omnivorous) as well as modes of locomotion (on land, in water, and even in the air). And as we now know, dinosaurs are still among us; modern-day birds are the direct descendants of non-avian theropods.

This new volume is perhaps even more astounding, as it allows us to admire the largest land animals ever to walk the Earth. Some of them were almost as heavy as the largest whales in our oceans today, and a few were almost four times as tall as a giraffe. Even the most primitive of this group of dinosaurs, sauropodomorphs, were genuine record-breakers.

From the time sauropods were first discovered by humans, as early as 2000 years ago in ancient China, people have been fascinated by their enormous bones, which in the distant past were mistaken for the skeletons of enormous dragons or other mythological beasts. It was only later, in the 19th century, that these remains were first identified scientifically. The first sauropod genera to be created included the celebrated *Cetiosaurus*, *Apatosaurus*, *Brontosaurus*, and *Camarasaurus*, among other lesser-known ones. Early investigators and scientists were stunned by the incredibly long necks and tails of these animals, as well as their seemingly impossible size. Since then, people have sought to discover just how heavy these creatures could have been, and which was the largest of them all. In the latter case, there was no shortage of candidates to bring into the debate. Through the 19th and into the 20th century, the extremely famous Brontosaurus was popularly considered the largest land animal of all time, despite the fact that remains had been found of several other species that were clearly larger (e.g., *Brachiosaurus*). In the late 20th century, rivalries among countries such as Argentina, Australia, China, South Korea, Spain, the United States, France, India, Morocco, Mexico, and Tanzania emerged to see which could claim the largest of all the dinosaurs. Since then, every so often, a new publication will appear, claiming the discovery of the largest sauropod of all time in a different part of the world. In this book, we will examine the validity of some of those claims.

We, the authors, have been waiting a long time, with much anticipation, for the publication of this book. Indeed, we met each other while attempting to discover the exact sizes that the largest (and not so large) dinosaurs reached. Since then, it has been raining data, and we have compiled a huge amount of information from scientific articles, museums, and our own research, to enable us to estimate the size of these fossil vertebrates, including estimations based entirely on footprints. Thanks to some hard work, we can show our readers how large the most gigantic dinosaurs were, as well as the size of each of the species and ichnospecies identified to date.

In general, this book is organized in the same way as the first volume, although here we have included some new features, such as a section focusing specifically on the plants that these gigantic herbivores ate, as well as the kinds of teeth they had, and how these teeth were linked to their diet.

Asier Larramendi and Rubén Pérez-Molina, April 2018

Contents

Comparing species

Mesozoic calendar

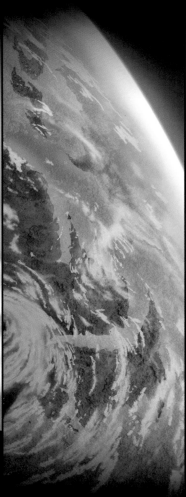

The world of dinosaurs

Prehistoric puzzle

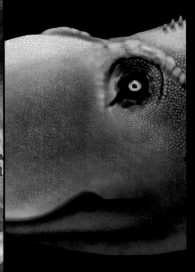

Sauropod life

Testimony in stone

Chronicle and dinomania

Sauropod list

How to use this book

The book begins with an introductory section that explains how the size and appearance of each dinosaur have been determined. It should be noted that each record-holding dinosaur species shown in this book is the largest or smallest specimen discovered for that species; size can vary considerably within a given species.

The book is divided into eight main chapters: "Comparing Species," "Mesozoic Calendar," "The World of Dinosaurs," "Prehistoric Puzzle," "Sauropod Life," "Testimony in Stone," "Chronicle and Dinomania," and "List of Sauropodomorphs," with each chapter including all pertinent records and information. The identification of footprints presented in this book is part of an as-yet unpublished study (Molina-Pérez et al. manuscript in preparation). The final section presents a complete list of all sauropods discovered up to the time this book went to press. The final pages of the book include a glossary, index, bibliography, and an appendix with additional facts and figures.

Each record holder is classified into a size class by weight. Weights have been used for statistics in the online appendix.

The dinosaurs are compared to the following present-day animals: white rhinoceros, giraffe, and African elephant.

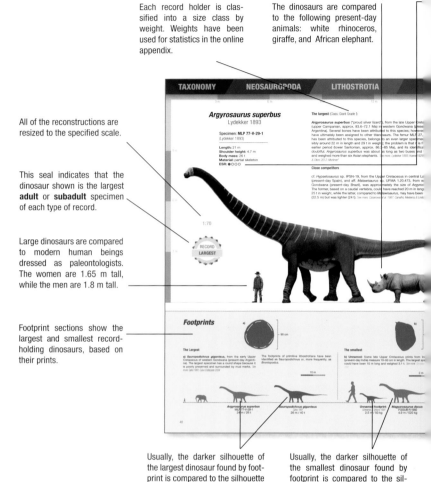

All of the reconstructions are resized to the specified scale.

This seal indicates that the dinosaur shown is the largest **adult** or **subadult** specimen of each type of record.

Large dinosaurs are compared to modern human beings dressed as paleontologists. The women are 1.65 m tall, while the men are 1.8 m tall.

Footprint sections show the largest and smallest record-holding dinosaurs, based on their prints.

Usually, the darker silhouette of the largest dinosaur found by footprint is compared to the silhouette of the largest dinosaur found by bone.

Usually, the darker silhouette of the smallest dinosaur found by footprint is compared to the silhouette of the smallest dinosaur found by bone.

Animals frequently used for comparison in this book

Animal		Size	Weight
Sparrow		15 cm long	30 g
Common pigeon		35 cm long	350 g
Housecat		45 cm long (without tail)	4.5 kg
Emperor penguin		1.2 m high	30 kg
Human		1.8 m high	75 kg
Brown bear		1.25 m shoulder height	400 kg
Fighting bull		1.4 m shoulder height	600 kg
Saltwater crocodile		5 m long	600 kg
Great white shark		5 m long	1000 kg
Giraffe		5.3 m high	1.2 t
Hippopotamus		1.5 m shoulder height	1.5 t
White rhinoceros		1.75 m shoulder height	2.5 t
Asian elephant		2.75 m shoulder height	4 t
African elephant		3.2 m shoulder height	6 t
Orca		8 m long	7 t
Sperm whale		16 m long	40 t
Blue whale		26 m long	110 t

Other objects used for comparison

Object		Dimensions	Weight
Car		4 m long	-
City bus		12 m long and 3 m high	-

Dinosaur lengths employed in this book

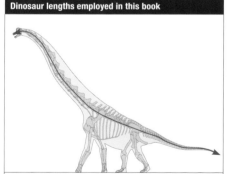

Length ◄——►
Approximate length of the animal when alive, from the tip of the snout to the tip of the tail along the **vertebral centra.**

Most books and scientific publications do not explain how the lengths presented were obtained. For vertebrates, the length usually taken is from the tip of the snout to the tip of the tail, along the animal's dorsal side (along the back or vertebrae). This means that animals with very prominent vertebrae (e.g., *Amargasaurus* or *Rebbachisaurus*) would yield a very large length, which makes it difficult to compare them with animals with less prominent vertebrae. For this reason, the lengths presented in this book represent the distance from the tip of the snout to the end of the tail, along the **vertebral centra**.

Abbreviations used in this book

Ma	millions of years
mm	millimeters
cm	centimeters
m	meters
km	kilometers
km²	square kilometers
g	grams
kg	kilograms
t	metric ton (1000 kg)
~	approximately
cc	cubic centimeters
N	North
S	South
°C	degrees centigrade
CO₂	Carbon dioxide

Estimated Size Reliability (ESR)

ESR	Description
●○○○ / ●●○○	When the size of the specimen is based on very poor material, such as bones that do not directly support the animal's weight or whose size varies greatly between individuals: *teeth, phalanges, broken bones, etc.*
●●○○	When the size of the specimen is based on isolated bones, but these can be compared to more complete specimens or can be used relatively reliably to estimate their size: *skulls, appendicular bones, vertebrae, etc.*
●●●○	When the size of the specimen is based on a partial skeleton.
●●●●	When the size of the specimen is based on a nearly complete skeleton.

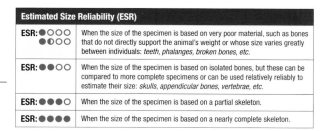

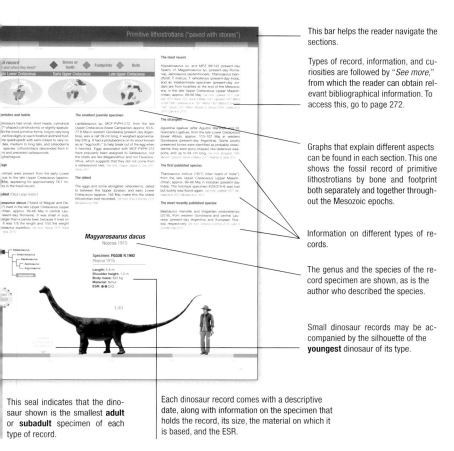

This bar helps the reader navigate the sections.

Types of record, information, and curiosities are followed by "*See more,*" from which the reader can obtain relevant bibliographical information. To access this, go to page 272.

Graphs that explain different aspects can be found in each section. This one shows the fossil record of primitive lithostrotians by bone and footprint both separately and together throughout the Mesozoic epochs.

Information on different types of records.

The genus and the species of the record specimen are shown, as is the author who described the species.

Small dinosaur records may be accompanied by the silhouette of the **youngest** dinosaur of its type.

This seal indicates that the dinosaur shown is the smallest **adult** or **subadult** specimen of each type of record.

Each dinosaur record comes with a descriptive date, along with information on the specimen that holds the record, its size, the material on which it is based, and the ESR.

The pages with lists of records in small type are records and curiosities ordered chronologically.

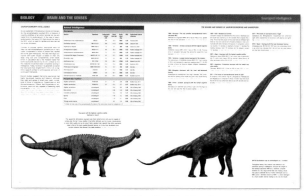

Each chapter contains numerous tables, in which interesting comparative information is summarized. This table shows a list of current and extinct animals with their bite force.

Record samples (animal, footprint, or egg) are grouped by their size class. This helps classify them and generate statistics.

SIZE CLASSES (by weight)

MINUSCULE		TINY	
Grade I	0–3 g	Grade I	+12–24 g
Grade II	+3–6 g	Grade II	+24–50 g
Grade III	+6–12 g	Grade III	+50–100 g
DWARF		**VERY SMALL**	
Grade I	+100–200 g	Grade I	+0.8–1.5 kg
Grade II	+200–400 g	Grade II	+1.5–3 kg
Grade III	+400–800 g	Grade III	+3–6 kg
SMALL		**MEDIUM**	
Grade I	+6–12 kg	Grade I	+50–100 kg
Grade II	+12–25 kg	Grade II	+100–200 kg
Grade III	+25–50 kg	Grade III	+200–400 kg
LARGE		**VERY LARGE**	
Grade I	+400–800 kg	Grade I	+3–6 t
Grade II	+0.8–1.5 t	Grade II	+6–12 t
Grade III	+1.5–3 t	Grade III	+12–25 t
GIANT			
Grade I			+25–50 t
Grade II			+50–100 t
Grade III			+100 t

SIZE CLASSES (by footprint length)

MINUSCULE	0–15 mm
TINY	+15–30 mm
VERY SMALL	+30–60 mm
SMALL	+60–120 mm
MEDIUM	+120–250 mm
LARGE	+250–500 mm
VERY LARGE	+50–100 cm
GIANT	+100–200 cm

SIZE CLASSES (by egg weight)

VERY SMALL		SMALL	
Grade I	0–0.25 g	Grade I	+1–2 g
Grade II	+0.25–0.5 g	Grade II	+2–4 g
Grade III	+0.5–1 g	Grade III	+4–8 g
MEDIUM		**LARGE**	
Grade I	+8–15 g	Grade I	+60–120 g
Grade II	+15–30 g	Grade II	+120–240 g
Grade III	+30–60 g	Grade III	+240–500 g
VERY LARGE		**GIANT**	
Grade I	+0.5–1 kg	Grade I	+4–8 kg
Grade II	+1–2 kg	Grade II	+8–16 kg
Grade III	+2–4 kg	Grade III	+16 kg

Methodology and calculations

Size, shape, and appearance of sauropodomorphs

As in the first volume, *Dinosaur Facts and Figures: The Theropods and Other Dinosauriformes*, the appearance and size of each of the dinosaurs presented in this book have been obtained on the basis of volumetric estimates and the most rigorous and up-to-date reconstructions carried out by various authors.

Although a good number of sauropodomorphs are known from relatively complete skeletons, most species are known from very fragmentary evidence, which makes it quite difficult to represent many of them accurately. In order to interpret the size and shape of the worst-preserved species, phylogenetic studies are a great aid, as they help situate these species among their closest, best-preserved relatives.

Regarding the body size of sauropodomorphs in particular, it is important to note that the cartilages on their appendicular skeletons were enormous, even larger than in theropods and ornithischians. Furthermore, unlike the bones of modern mammals, dinosaur bones lacked an epiphysis (the larger rounded end of a long bone), and so these creatures developed cartilages of notable proportions. Most reconstructions do not take this into account, so size estimations tend to be on the conservative side.

For the lengths and weights presented in this book, we have also attempted to take into account ontogenetic factors relevant to each animal. For example, most sauropods had very long necks, but not during all stages of their lives. Newborns had very different proportions from adults, with large heads and relatively short tails, and relatively more gracile bodies, and their proportions changed as they grew. Their bodies, for example, tended to become more robust and their necks became longer, but once the animals reached one-third to one-half of their adult size, their necks grew isometrically.

How much did a sauropodomorph dinosaur weigh?

As in the previous volume on theropods, weight estimations in this book have been obtained from volumetric calculations, using the graphic double integration (GDI) method.

Some of the latest volumetric methods, such as those proposed by W. I. Sellers et al. (2012) and Brassey and Gardiner (2015), which are based, respectively, on the minimal convex hulling and on the alpha shapes of complete mounted skeletons, are problematic, mainly because the skeletons of prehistoric animals are not often mounted in an anatomically correct way, which distorts the proportions of the animals when alive.

Worth special mention are the masses estimated from the skeleton of *Giraffatitan brancai* mounted in the Für Naturkunde Museum in Berlin. Studies conducted in the 21st century on this skeleton have attributed volumes to the living animal that vary from 29 to 87 m³. These quite divergent results depend on how massive the animal's musculature was estimated to have been and on the skeletal reconstruction itself. Another problem derives from the inexact reconstruction of the skeleton. W. I. Sellers et al. (2012), using the new method based on the minimal convex hulling of complete mounted skeletons, obtained a result of 29 m³ in volume for the living animal. This estimate was based on a complete scan of the mounted skeleton in Berlin. The problem is that the most voluminous part of the animal, the rib cage, is not correctly restored. The ribs of this skeleton are positioned too vertically, creating a very narrow body (the ribs barely stand out from the pelvis). However, the preserved fossilized ribs are straighter than they would have been in life, as they have lost all of their flexibility. This same issue can be observed in present-day elephants, in which the curvature of the ribs is very pronounced, producing the characteristic round, broad body. The broadest part of an elephant is the posterior part of the belly, which is slightly wider or as wide as the pelvis, but as with the skeleton of *Giraffatitan*, most skeletons of modern elephants mounted in museums have their ribs mounted relatively straight, creating an abdomen considerably narrower than the pelvis. The pelvis of *Giraffatitan* is proportionately much narrower than that of an elephant, and the ribs are much longer, so the abdomen of *Giraffatitan* would have stuck out considerably more beyond its pelvis. Taking into account the preserved material used to create this composite individual, a correct reconstruction of the abdomen suggests a minimum width of 2.6 meters while living, around 35% more than the width of the pelvic region. The calculated total volume obtained from GDI on a correct reconstruction of *Giraffatitan brancai* HMN SII is 37 m³.

Specific gravities

According to some recent studies, the specific gravity (SG) or body density of sauropods may have been very low. According to Wedel (2005), *Diplodocus* had an SG as low as 0.8, taking into account air in the trachea, the respiratory system, the air sacs, the intraosseous diverticulum, and in the pneumatic bones, especially the vertebrae. This means that the density of different parts of a sauropod varied significantly. The neck was always the least dense part of the animal, followed by the body (excluding the limbs), then finally the tail. Thus, it is ideal to estimate the SGs of the different parts, in order to obtain the most precise overall density possible.

In principle, an SG of 0.8, which is possibly even lower than that of most of today's flying birds, particularly for an animal the size of two African elephants, could be too conservative. The key may be that in these kinds of studies, it is usually, if not always, assumed that the respiratory system of the animals examined was completely full of air. However, if we analyze animals living nowadays, we see that this is not the case. In modern-day birds, for example, the lungs and air sacs are not completely full when the animal is in a normal, relaxed state. Also, when the air in the vertebrae of *Diplodocus* was estimated, taking into account the air space proportion (ASP), which refers to the proportion of the bone volume (the area of a section of bone) occupied by these air spaces, the volume of the vertebral bodies was calculated assuming that they were cylindrical in shape. But since the vertebrae have many concave parts, the results yielded are much higher than the true volume, and thus the quantity of air contained is overestimated. Lastly, the soft tissue that would have replaced the air system volume, as well as the whole animal without air, were estimated with an SG of 1.0. But this figure is conservative, because all soft tissue (excluding fat) and long bones have an SG well above 1.0. In summary, taking these factors into account and assuming that the body of *Diplodocus* without air would have had an SG of at least 1.05, the total SG of *Diplodocus* may have been more like 0.9. It should be clarified that these kinds of estimates are always approximate, as it is not possible to obtain 100% accuracy. Another complication specific to sauropods is the need to apply the SG of their necks separately from the rest of their bodies. It is also worth noting that the pneumatic adaptations found on sauropodomorph skeletons are quite variable within different taxonomic groups and species, making it impossible to calculate the SG for each one. We know that the skeletons of the most primitive sauropods had fewer pneumatic adaptations than the more derived ones, so the densities of the former would have been somewhat higher. Nevertheless, because estimating each species precisely, one by one, is not possible, when calculating the body masses of the sauropods in this book, we have employed an SG of 0.9 for all.

Lastly, it should be mentioned that, despite the fact that certain indications suggest that primitive sauropodomorphs had air sacs, these would have been considerably smaller among their more advanced relatives, so the body density of these dinosaurs would have been considerably higher than that of sauropods. Tentatively, their SGs would have been around 0.95.

See more: Colbert 1962; Jerison 1973; Hurlburt 1999; Wedel 2004, 2005, 2007; Murray & Vickers-Rich 2004; Gunga et al. 2008; Sellers et al. 2012; Brassey & Gardiner 2015; Larramendi 2016; Larramendi et al. in prep.

Figure 1. Rigorous reconstruction of the skeleton of *Giraffatitan* HMN SII. The total volume estimated by means of GDI is 37 m³, which yields a body mass of some 33 t, applying a specific gravity of 0.9.

How big can a land animal get?

One of the most notable characteristics of sauropods is their great size, which averaged 11.5 t (in a range of 500 kg to 80 t). The fact that 40% of potential species weighed more than 10 t leads us to question what advantage that giant size gave them over other dinosaurs. Did it protect them from predators? Allow them to take advantage of food sources out of reach of the competition, or to defend a territory, preserve heat, or consume large quantities of food of low nutritional quality? The problem is that, to maintain such an enormous weight, the body has to change in ways that ultimately make the animal a slow, clumsy creature incapable of leaping and forced to spend much of its time eating; it would also have had more difficulty adapting to sudden changes in the environment.

Small sauropods seem to have been relatively defenseless animals, given their lack of armor and slow speed, so they may have been very vulnerable to predation until reaching a certain size. If so, they may have laid large numbers of eggs. But this situation is not that simple, either, as the presence of small species living alongside large carnivorous dinosaurs means they may have had defensive strategies we are unaware of today.

The largest of the sauropods that we know of with certainty reached a weight of 80 t. This seems to be an impossible size for a land animal, although we must consider that one calculation has suggested that the size limit for a land animal is much larger, around 140 t. Surpassing this theoretical limit, the legs would have to be too wide and heavy for the muscles. This is because as the animal's size increases, the muscles' cross-sectional areas grow more slowly than the volumes of bone and body.

The largest quadrupedal animals on Earth today, elephants, weigh up to 6 t, although the largest extinct species reached maximum masses of around 20 t. Considering that an African elephant requires many hours each day to feed itself and has developed adaptations to offset the problems associated with maintaining a weight of 6 t, it is difficult to imagine how an animal 10 times that size could accomplish the same thing. However, the sizes that sauropods achieved were the result of a combination of many factors, such as metabolism, food sources, anatomical innovations, and biomechanics, among others. See more: *McGowan 1991; Gould 1993; Carpenter 2006; Sander et al. 2011; Woodruff & Forster 2014; Larramendi 2016*

Definitions

The innovative sauropodomorphs

Sauropodomorphs are a group of animals that includes sauropods and their close relatives, formerly known as "prosauropods." According to phylogenetic analyses, the most primitive of the group is the dinosaur *Buriolestes*, although in other studies *Eoraptor*, *Guaibasaurus*, and similar creatures may be included as well. In fact, the fossil record is still incomplete enough to prevent us from understanding just how closely related the first dinosaurs, which shared many characteristics, were to each other.

Most primitive sauropodomorphs were bipedal animals that tended to consume plants, although the possibility that they were omnivores has not been ruled out, as the shape of their teeth is very similar to that of some present-day lizards and iguanas with a mixed diet. Some of these animals developed teeth similar to those of sauropods. Over time, they became quadrupeds, perhaps because they became increasingly larger and needed larger stomachs to digest their food, which they hardly chewed at all. These animals managed to outcompete, and ultimately replace, other phytophagous animals of their time. See more: *Galton 1990; McIntosh 1990; Heerden 1997; McIntosh, Brett-Surman & Farlow 1997; Wilson & Curry-Rogers 2012; Yates 2012; Cabreira et al. 2016; Norman & Barrett 2017a, 2017b*

The gigantic sauropods

The best known sauropodomorphs are the sauropods, a group of dinosaurs that was not only very large, but also included evolutionary innovations that enabled these creatures to prosper in the Jurassic and Cretaceous periods. Their most outstanding anatomical feature was the long neck that most species developed; this feature is also a bit of a mystery, as in some cases those necks were impossibly elongated. They may have managed to achieve such enormous size because they had air sacs for breathing, like birds. The most advanced species had vertebrae that were spongy or partially hollow, which would have reduced their weight significantly.

Some sauropods reached sizes that seem impossible for a land animal. At least a few species are estimated to have weighed more than 55 t. Some of these were identified on the basis of footprints and include *Malakhelisaurus mianwali* of the Middle Jurassic in Hindustan (present-day Pakistan), *Breviparopus taghbaloutensis* from the Upper Jurassic in south-central Neopangea (present-day Morocco), an unnamed species from the Upper Jurassic in north-central Neopangea (present-day Spain), and *Ultrasauripus ungulatus*, from the Lower Cretaceous in eastern Laurasia (present-day South Korea). Others were estimated from bones, including *Hudiesaurus sinojapanorum* from the Upper Jurassic in Paleoasia (present-day China), *Barosaurus lentus* from the Upper Jurassic in

northwestern Neopangea (present-day USA), and *Argentinosaurus huinculensis* from the early Upper Cretaceous in western Gondwana (present-day Argentina), among others.

Eighty tons may be a size limit for a land animal; although reports of two sauropods that may have been even bigger do exist, they are very doubtful. These two are *Maraapunisaurus fragillimus*, from the Upper Jurassic in northwestern Neopangea (present-day USA), and *Bruhathkayosaurus matleyi*, from the late Upper Cretaceous in Hindustan (present-day India).

No other group of land animals has managed to reach even 25 t in weight; the closest are the hadrosaurid dinosaurs *Magnapaulia laticaudus* of the Upper Cretaceous in western Laurasia (present-day Mexico) and *Amblydactylus* sp. from the Upper Cretaceous in eastern Laurasia (present-day Mongolia), as well as the proboscidean *Palaeoloxodon namadicus* from the Middle Pleistocene in southern Asia (present-day India), which reached nearly 20 t. See more: *Falconer & Cautley 1846; Morris 1981; Ishigaki et al. 2009; Prieto-Márquez, Chiappe & Joshi 2012; Larramendi 2016*

The origin and extinction of sauropodomorph dinosaurs

Sauropodomorphs descended from primitive saurischians, carnivorous animals that lived in the Middle and Upper Triassic. They survived the mass extinction that occurred between the Upper Triassic and Lower Jurassic, thriving in both periods. However, they declined to the point that only two or three reports of their presence exist for the Middle Jurassic.

Sauropods appeared in the Lower Jurassic, although some remains from the Upper Triassic may also have belonged to this kind of dinosaur. Although they coexisted with several other groups of phytophagous animals at the time, sauropods were so successful that the larger species prevailed over their competitors and were virtually unrivaled in the Jurassic, until another group of dinosaurs, the ornithischians, began to prosper and also develop into very large animals with a great capacity for consuming plants.

Sauropods thrived during the Jurassic and Cretaceous periods on almost all land masses on Earth, except in the early Upper Cretaceous in North America, where they seem to have become extinct until recolonizing the region in the late Mesozoic era. Like 70% of all other species alive at the time, these dinosaurs did not survive the mass extinction that ushered in the Cenozoic era.

The most primitive sauropodomorph?
Buriolestes schultzi
Specimen: JVP 16:728

This was the only species to have entirely knife-shaped teeth (zyphodonts), indicating that it was a carnivore. These early sauropodomorphs were very similar to theropods. See more: *Cabreira et al. 2016*

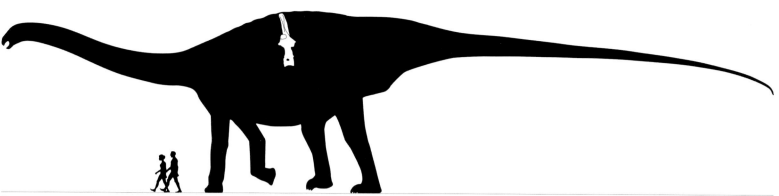

Most enigmatic Jurassic sauropod
Maraapunisaurus fragillimus

As the fossils we have seen of this enormous sauropod consisted of mudstone, unfortunately they were so fragile that they disintegrated, so doubts have emerged about the actual size of the bones. The exact dimensions of this species are impossible to ascertain without the original material. However, some authors have attempted to offer more precise estimations. See more: *Cope 1878; Osborn & Mook 1921;Cope et al. 1987; Paul 1997; Carpenter 2006; Woodruff & Forster 2014; Carpenter 2018*

1:200

Most enigmatic Cretaceous sauropod
Bruhathkayosaurus matleyi

These remains were first described as theropod bones, were later recognized as those of a sauropod, and are now suspected to have actually been fossil tree trunks. To add to the mystery, the fossils were lost in a flood. The largest specimen was identified as a tibia, although it looks like a fibula. Informally, it has been estimated that this sauropod could have been up to 45 m long and weighed up to 220 t, although it may also have been much smaller in size, 37 m long and weighing 95 t.
See more: *Yadagiri & Ayyasami 1989; Krause et al. 2006; Mortimer**

Strangest sauropod
Isisaurus colberti

Sauropods came in a wide variety of forms, so there were notable differences among different species. The most renowned case is that of *Isisaurus*, which had some anatomical features that gave it an extraordinary appearance. A combination of long legs and very short forelegs, atypical caudal vertebrae, a short neck, and a very broad body made this creature unique among sauropods.
See more: *Jain & Bandyopadhyay 1997; Wilson & Upchurch 2003; Naish**

Classification

Possible sauropodomorph phylogenies

A heated debate is currently raging about which is the most reliable phylogenetic model for basal dinosaur groups. It is difficult to resolve this dispute with the information currently available, because primitive dinosaurs share several anatomical features as well as some convergent evolutionary innovations. Here we present the most well-known models, while noting that any of them could be validated or discredited as new evidence is obtained from the always-expanding fossil record.

Harry Govier Seeley model 1888

This is the most traditional model, as it remained in use for 130 years, although it was not the only model that was proposed during that time. It divides dinosaurs, primarily on the basis of their hips, into two groups: "lizard hipped" saurischians and "bird hipped" ornithischians. This division has been reinforced over time, with other anatomical features added along the way, although it is now strongly suspected to be incorrect.

Robert Thomas Bakker model 1986

This model brings together sauropodomorphs and ornithischians in the Phytodinosauria clade, as the two have several anatomical similarities, although these may have been convergent owing to their diet. Recently, an analysis (Parry et al. 2017) revalidated it as one among several possible models.

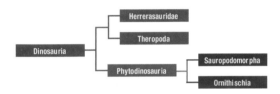

Baron, Norman & Barrett model 2017

The rigorous anatomical review of various basal dinosaurs has had a great impact on the traditional Seeley model of 1888, leading to some revisions. This new model resuscitates the Ornithoscelida clade that contains ornithischians and theropods, while sauropodomorphs and Herrerasauridae are seen as part of a second Dinosauria group. This model is not supported by all scientists, but it is just as valid as all other models proposed to date.

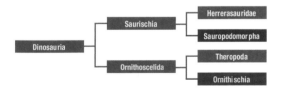

Ferigolo & Langer model 2006

This alternative proposal departs from those mentioned above, proposing that ornithischians were close relatives of silesaurids, while saurischians were a separate group altogether. This would make silesaurids, traditionally considered dinosauromorphs, part of the Dinosauria group. It is worth considering that *Pisanosaurus*, considered the most primitive among the ornithischians, could have been a silesaurid dinosauromorph. This model was analyzed in the studies of Cabreira et al. (2016) and Baron et al. (2017).

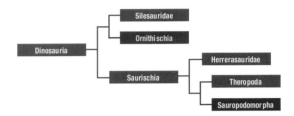

When Richard Owen coined the term Dinosauria (dinosaurs) in 1842, it was based on a mere three genera, the theropod *Megalosaurus* and two ornithischians, *Hylaeosaurus* and *Iguanodon*. Sauropodomorphs were not included, despite the fact that *Cardiodon*, *Cetiosaurus*, *Plateosaurus*, and *Thecodontosaurus* were all known at the time, because they had not yet been identified as dinosaurs. Instead, they were considered terrestrial or marine reptiles or even geological curiosities, as in the case of "*Rutellum*." In any case, any current phylogeny would include sauropodomorphs in the Dinosauria group, as this clade has been redefined to always include the three main groups—Theropoda, Sauropodomorpha, and Ornithischia.

First sauropod fossil with 17 cervical vertebrae
Euhelopus zdanskyi

The classification of Asian sauropods was not an easy task, as different species had similar anatomical forms and features that were also shared with other, less related groups. *Euhelopus, Klamelisaurus, Mamenchisaurus, Omeisaurus*, and their close relatives had very long necks with numerous cervical vertebrae (17, 16, 19, and 17, respectively). See more: *Wiman 1929; Young 1954; Romer 1956; Zhao 1993*

Evolutionary history of sauropodomorph dinosaurs

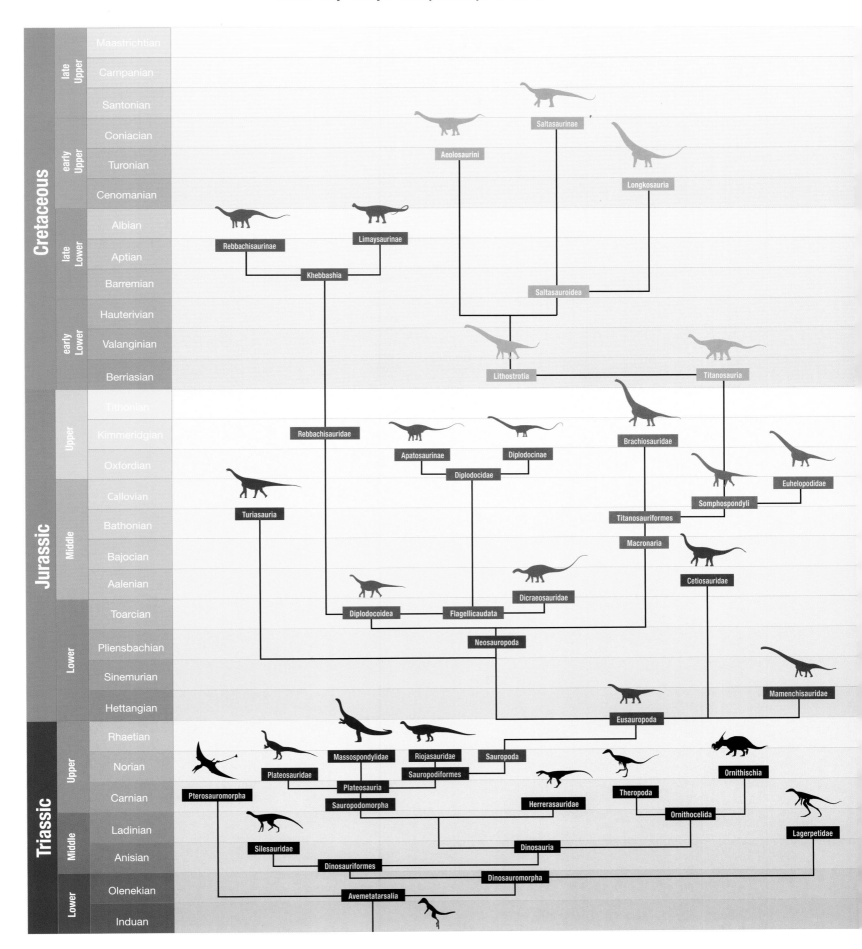

Comparing species
Sauropodomorpha taxonomy

Records: the largest and smallest by taxonomic group

Sauropodomorphs comprise a group of primarily saurischian dinosaurs that were specialized as phytophages. The most primitive forms were obligate bipeds that were similar in appearance to theropods, while the most derived (advanced) were very large creatures that were graviportal quadrupeds that consumed only plants. Some time ago, sauropodomorphs were classified into two groups: prosauropods and sauropods. This division is no longer considered valid, however, as sauropods are now considered direct descendants of sauropodomorphs. The concept of "sauropod" has changed over the years, and so some primitive species are now considered not to belong to this clade.

2 m   4 m

Efraasia minor
Huene 1908

RECORD
LARGEST

4 m

1:25

2 m

The largest (Class: Large I)

Efraasia minor ("Eberhad Fraas's smaller one") lived in the Upper Triassic (Middle Norian, approx. 215.6–212 Ma) in north-central Pangea (present-day Germany). It was a bipedal omnivore or phytophage as heavy as four people. Its original name was *Teratosaurus minor*. See more: *Huene 1908, 1932; Fraas 1912; Galton 1973; Yates 2003, 2004*

The same species, or relatives?

Plateosauravus stormbergensis, Gigantoscelus molengraaffi, Plateosauravus cullingworthi and *Euskelosaurus africanus* are all contemporaries of *Euskelosaurus browni*, and as they are all based on incomplete material, they may belong to the same species. See more: *Huxley 1866; Broom 1915; Hoepen 1916; Haughton 1924; Durand 2001; Yates 2003, 2004, 2006; Yates & Kitching, 2003*

Specimen: SMNS 12843
(Huene 1932)

Length: 5.3 m
Hip height: 1.2 m
Body mass: 365 kg
Material: partial skeleton and cranium
ESR: ●●●○

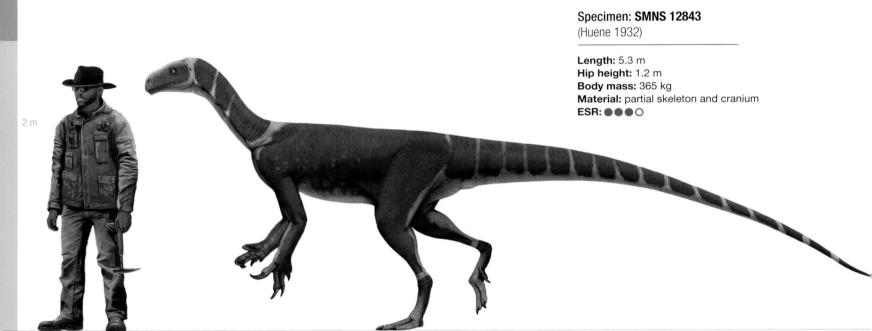

Footprints

a)   ~22 cm

b)   1.8 cm

The largest

a) *Cridotrisauropus unguiferus*: Dated to the Upper Triassic of north-central Pangea (present-day France). Similar to Jurassic or Cretaceous theropods but could have been a basal sauropodomorph as it is similar to the footprint of *Efraasia*. It had very prominent claws. *See more: Ellenberger 1965*

The prints known as *Anatrisauropus, Senqutrisauropus, Sillimanius, Trichristolophus, Trisaurodactylus, Trisauropodiscus*, and some species assigned to *Cridotrisauropus* are enigmatic. However, their similarity to bird prints and the length of the big toe (hallux), coincide with the feet of primitive sauropodomorphs, which were contemporary and entirely bipedal.

The smallest

b) *Trisauropodiscus aviforma passer*: Some small footprints from the Upper Triassic in south-central Pangea (present-day Lesotho). Their diminutive size indicates they would have been produced by very young individuals, as another contemporary variety known as *Trisauropodiscus aviforma vanellus* reached 4 cm in length. *See more: Ellenberger 1972*

2 m

80 cm

Cridotrisauropus unguiferus
Ellenberger 1965
3.5 m / 110 kg

Efraasia minor
SMNS 12843
5.3 m / 365 kg

Trisauropodiscus aviforma passer
Ellenberger 1972
29 cm / 30 g

Pampadromaeus barberenai
ULBRA-PVT016
1.4 m / 3 kg

8 m   10 m

Characteristics and habits

These creatures had small to large leaf-shaped heads with denticles in phytophagous types (lance-olate foliodont), knife-shaped (zyphodont) in carnivorous types, or mixed in omnivorous types, with a medium-length neck, five digits on each foreleg and hind leg, and forelegs with large claws. They were bipedal, with light to semi-robust bodies, and long tails. They were more suited to running than any other group of sauropodomorphs, and that ability may have allowed them to escape from predators or to hunt small prey. Primitive sauropodomorphs descended from primitive saurischians and preceded plateosaurs and sauropodiforms (the three groups formerly known as "prosauropods"). See more: *Galton 1985; Upchurch 1997a, 1997b; Galton & Upchurch 2004; Martinez & Alcober 2009; Sereno et al. 2013*

Diet: small game carnivorous, omnivorous, and/or phytophagous.

Time range

From the Upper Triassic to the Middle Jurassic (approx. 232–167.2 Ma), appearing for 64.8 million years in the fossil record.

The smallest (Class: Very small Grade II)

Pampadromaeus barberenai ("Mário Costa Barberene's pampas runner") lived in the Upper Triassic (lower Carnian, approx. 237–232 Ma) of southwestern Pangea (present-day Brazil). Fossil CAPPA/UFSM 0027, known as cf. *Pampadromaeus barberenai*, is probably a larger-sized individual, 1.65 m long and weighing 4.8 kg. *Pampadromaeus* was 1/4 the length and 1/120 the weight of *Efraasia minor*. *Alwalkeria maleriensis*, from Hindustan (present-day India), was even smaller, with a length of 1.3 m and weight of 2 kg; however, its classification as a primitive sauropodomorph is still in dispute. See more: *Chatterjee 1986; Cabreira et al. 2011; Martinez et al. 2011; Sereno et al. 2013; Baron et al. 2017*

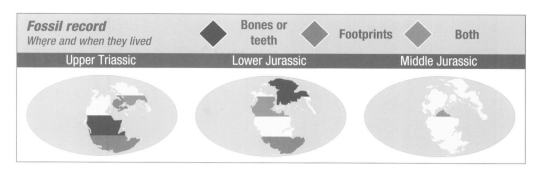

The smallest juvenile specimens

Pantydraco caducus ("ancient dragon of the Pantyffynnon quarry"), from the Upper Triassic (Rhaetian, approx. 208.5–201.3 Ma) in north-central Pangea (present-day Wales, United Kingdom), is known only from two specimens, partial skeleton P65/24, 85 cm long and weighing 790 g, and teeth P65/42, which belonged to another individual of similar size. They were considered juvenile *Thecodontosaurus antiquus*. See more: *Kermack 1984; Yates 2003, Galton et al. 2007*

The oldest

Buriolestes schultzi (present-day Brazil), *Pampadromaeus barberenai*, and *Panphagia protos*, from southwestern Pangea (present-day Argentina) are the oldest, dating to the early Upper Triassic (middle Carnian, approx. 232 Ma). The oldest mistaken report is "*Thecodontosaurus*" sp. of the Lower Triassic in Russia, which was actually a protorosaurid (a pseudosuchian). There is doubt, however, as to whether the Middle Triassic species *Nyasasaurus parringtoni* and *Thecodontosaurus alophos* were basal dinosaurs or sauropodomorphs. See more: *Haughton 1932; Yakovlev 1923; Charig 1957; Martinez & Alcober 2009; Cabreira et al. 2011; Müller et al. 2015; Cabreira et al. 2016; Baron et al. 2017*

The most recent

It is suspected that some remains identified as the theropod *Sarcosaurus woodi* from the Lower Jurassic (Sinemurian, approx. 199.3–190.8 Ma) of north-central Pangea (present-day England), actually belonged to a sauropodomorph similar to *Saturnalia*. The footprint *Trisauropodiscus* sp. from Morocco dates to the Middle Jurassic (upper Bajocian or lower Bathonian, approx. 169.3–167.2 Ma). See more: *Huene 1932; Gierlinski et al. 2017; Mortimer**

The strangest

Xixiposaurus suni ("lizard of Professor Sun Ge's town of Xixipo") is from the Lower Jurassic of northeastern Pangea (present-day China). Its feet were different from those of all other sauropodomorphs, as toe IV was slightly longer than toe III (III was usually the longest). See more: *Sekiya 2010*

The first published species

Thecodontosaurus (1836) ("alveolar-toothed lizard"), from the Upper Triassic of north-central Pangea (present-day England). Discovered in 1834 and reported in 1835, it was the first sauropodomorph species to be named, receiving the species name of *T. antiquus* seven years later. See more: *Williams 1835; Riley & Stutchbury 1836; Morris 1843; Galton 1985*

The most recently published species

Bagualosaurus agudoensis (2018) ("bagel lizard of Agudo municipality"), from the Upper Triassic (lower Carnian, approx. 237–232 Ma) in southwestern Pangea (present-day Brazil). See more: *Pretto et al. 2018*

Pampadromaeus barberenai
Broom 1915

RECORD
SMALLEST

Specimen: ULBRA-PVT016
(Cabreira et al. 2011)

Length: 1.4 m
Hip height: 28 cm
Body mass: 3 kg
Material: partial skeleton
ESR: ●●●○

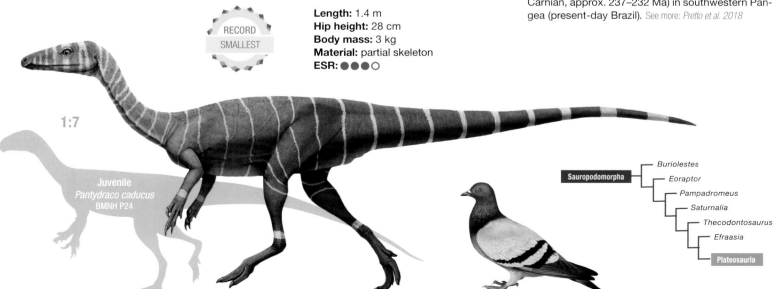

1:7

Juvenile
Pantydraco caducus
BMNH P24

Sauropodomorpha
— Buriolestes
— Eoraptor
— Pampadromeus
— Saturnalia
— Thecodontosaurus
— Efraasia
Plateosauria

30 cm   60 cm   90 cm   120 cm

2 m   4 m   6 m   8 m

6 m

Plateosaurus engelhardti
Meyer 1837

4 m

1:40

Specimen: Uncatalogued
(Wellnhofer 1993)

Length: 9.4 m
Hip height: 2.3 m
Body mass: 2.6 t
Material: femur
ESR: ●●○○

2 m

The largest (Class: Large Grade III)

Plateosaurus engelhardti ("broad lizard of Dr. Johann Friedrich Engelhardt") lived during the Upper Triassic (Norian, approx. 221.5–208 Ma) in north-central Pangea (present-day Germany). Although in some reconstructions it appears in a quadrupedal posture, this was not possible for this animal, as it could not use its forefeet to move on the ground. The specimen "Ellingen" is the largest one known. It was about as long as two saltwater crocodiles placed end to end and as heavy as a white rhino. See more: *Wellnhofer 1993; Moser 2003; Sander & Klein 2005; Bonnan & Senter 2007*

The second largest

Plateosaurus longiceps ("flat, long-headed lizard") was more recent than *P. engelhardti* and of similar size, although its tail was proportionately longer, making it 9.3 m in length and weighing 2.1 t. See more: *Fraas 1896; Jaekel 1914; Moser 2003*

RECORD
LARGEST

Footprints

a)

— 60 cm

— 8.5 cm

b)

The largest

a) *Pseudotetrasauropus mekalingensis,* the largest bipedal sauropodomorph print from the Upper Triassic in south-central Pangea (present-day Lesotho). See more: *Ellenberger 1972; Porchetti & Nicosia 2007*

The morphology of the bipedal footprints of *Evazoum*, *Pengxiangpus*, and *Pseudotetrasauropus* and the quadrupedal prints of *Tetrasauropus*, from the Lower Triassic to the Lower Jurassic, coincides with tracks of Plateosauria.

The smallest

b) *Evazoum* **sp.:** A small print that dates to the Upper Triassic in north-central Pangea (present-day Poland). Given its small size, it may have been a young individual. See more: *Gierlinski 2009*

4 m

2 m

Pseudotetrasauropus mekalingensis
Ellenberger 1972
9.1 m / 2 t

Plateosaurus engelhardti
Uncatalogued
9.4 m / 2.6 t

Evazoum sp.
Gierlinski 2009
1.33 m / 3.5 kg

"Gripposaurus" sinensis
IVPP V.27
2.9 m / 58 kg

0 m   12 m   14 m   16 m   18 m

Characteristics and habits

These small-headed dinosaurs had leaf-shaped (lanceolate foliodont) or conical (conodont) teeth, medium-length necks, five digits on each forefoot and hindfoot and large claws on the forefeet. They were bipeds with semi-robust bodies and long tails. Their diet was primarily plant-based, but they likely consumed small prey or even carrion. They developed large cheeks to improve their ability to obtain food. It has been suggested that some had keratin beaks on the lower jaw. Plateosaurs descended from basal sauropodomorphs. See more: *Galton 1985; Upchurch 1997; Galton & Upchurch 2004; Martinez 2009*

Diet: omnivorous and/or phytophagous.

Time range

Present from the Upper Triassic to the Lower Jurassic (approx. 232–174.1 Ma), a span of 57.9 million years in the fossil record.

The smallest (Class: Small Grade III)

"Gripposaurus" sinensis ("gryphon lizard of China"), from the Lower Jurassic of northeastern Pangea (present-day China), weighed about as much as a human adult and was 1/3 as long and 1/45 the weight of *Plateosaurus engelhardti*. See more: *Apaldetti et al. 2011*

The smallest juvenile specimens

Both embryos and newborns of some Plateosauria species have been discovered. The smallest of all is specimen BP/1/5347A, a *Massospondylus carinatus* (present-day South Africa) just 13 cm long and weighing 7 g. It was very similar in size to *Lufengosaurus* sp. (present-day China), 13.5 cm long and weighing 8 g. See more: *Kitching 1979; Reisz et al. 2005, 2010, 2013*

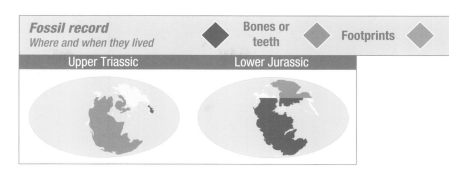

Fossil record
Where and when they lived

◆ Bones or teeth   ◆ Footprints   ◆ Both

Upper Triassic   Lower Jurassic

The oldest

Specimens NMMNH P 26400 and NMMNH P-18405 have been identified as having teeth similar to *Plateosaurus*, which dates to the Upper Triassic (upper Carnian, approx. 232–227 Ma) in northwestern Pangea (present-day New Mexico and Texas, USA). The footprint *Prosauropodichnus bernburgensis*, from the Middle Triassic (Anisian, approx. 247.2–242 Ma), does not seem to have belonged to a sauropodomorph, as its shape is similar to prints left by large archosaurs such as *Chirotherium*. See more: *Heckert 2001, 2004; Diedrich 2009, 2012*

The most recent

A claw from toe II of cf. *Lufengosaurus huenei* dates to the Lower Jurassic (Toarcian approx. 182.7–174.1 Ma). It was discovered in northeastern Pangea (present-day China). Some suspected that it was actually from the Middle Jurassic See more: *Wang & Sun 1983; Dong et al. 1984; Weishampel et al. 2004*

The strangest

Macrocollum itaquii (2018) ("José Jerundino Machado Itaqui's long-necked lizard"), from the Upper Triassic (Norian, approx. 227–208.5 Ma) in southwestern Pangea (present-day Argentina), was a close relative of *Unaysaurus* and had a proportionately longer neck. See more: *Temp-Muller et al. 2018*

The first published species

Plateosaurus engelhardti (1837): Discovered in 1834, it is the type species for several species that emerged over time. Today only the first is accepted, along with *P. longiceps* and *P. gracilis*. See more: *Meyer 1837; Huene 1908; Jaekel 1913*

The most recently published species

Macrocollum itaquii (2018). See more: *Temp-Muller et al. 2018*

Plateosauria — Plateosaurus
Massopoda — Massospondylus / Lufengosaurus / Sauropodiformes

Specimen: IVPP V.27
(Young 1941)

Length: 2.9 m
Hip height: 60 cm
Body mass: 58 kg
Material: incomplete femur
ESR: ●●○○

"Gripposaurus" sinensis
Young 1941

1:15

RECORD SMALLEST

Embryo
Massospondylus carinatus
BP/1/5347A

50 cm   100 cm   150 cm   200 cm   250 cm   300 cm

2.5 m   5 m   7.5 m   10 m

7.5 m

The largest (Class: Very large Grade II)

The enormous caudal vertebra Meet BP/1/5339, from the Upper Triassic (Rhaetian, approx. 208.5–201.3 Ma) in south-central Pangea (present-day South Africa), was first presented on a blog by Adam Yates three years before being formally presented, in association with a radius. The piece is similar to the vertebrae of *Aardonyx* and so could belong to the largest of the bipedal sauropodomorphs, which weighed about as much as an African and Asian elephant combined and was as long as a sperm whale. See more: *Wedel & Yates 2011; Yates*

Largest quadruped of the group

Camelotia borealis ("from the woods of Camelot") lived in the Upper Triassic (Rhaetian, approx. 208.5–201.3 Ma) of north-central Pangea (present-day England) and has been considered a derived sauropodiform or a primitive sauropod. It was 10 m long and weighed 2.75 t. Some bones contemporary with *Camelotia* were from an even larger animal that was more than 11 m in length and weighed 4.7 t, although some suggest they belong to ornithischian dinosaurs, which is doubtful. See more: *Reynolds 1946; Galton 1985; Galton 2005*

Unnamed
Wedel & Yates 2011

5 m

RECORD
LARGEST

Specimen: Meet BP/1/5339
(Wedel & Yates 2011)

Length: 16 m
Hip height: 3.55 m
Body mass: 10 t
Material: ulna and caudal vertebra
ESR: ●●○○

2.5 m

1:50

Footprints

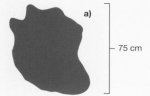

a)

— 75 cm

b)

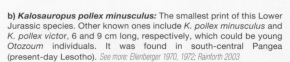

— 6 cm

The largest

a) *Otozoum* sp.: The largest sauropodomorph footprint could have been made by a species similar to *Aaardonyx* but is larger and was found in what was then south-central Pangea (present-day Morocco). See more: *Ishigaki & Haubold 1985; Ishigaki 1988*

The footprints belonging to Sauropodiforms are often bipedal (*Kalosauropus*), quadripedal (*Barrancapus, Eosauropus, Lavinipes* and *Tetrasauropus*) or mixed (*Navahopus* and *Otozoum*).

The smallest

b) *Kalosauropus pollex minusculus*: The smallest print of this Lower Jurassic species. Other known ones include *K. pollex minusculus* and *K. pollex victor*, 6 and 9 cm long, respectively, which could be young *Otozoum* individuals. It was found in south-central Pangea (present-day Lesotho). See more: *Ellenberger 1970, 1972; Rainforth 2003*

6 m

80 cm

***Otozoum* sp.**
Ishigaki & Haubold 1985
12.4–15 m / 4.5–8.5 t

Unnamed
Meet BP/1/5339
16 m / 10 t

Kalosauropus pollex minusculus
Ellenberger 1970
78 cm / 590 g

Anchisaurus polyzelus
YPM 1883
2.4 m / 25 kg

2.5 m | 15 m | 17.5 m | 20 m | 22.5 m

Characteristics and habits

These dinosaurs had small heads, leaf-shaped (lanceolate foliodont), cylindrical (cylindrodont) or conical (conodont) teeth, medium-length necks, five digits on each forefoot and hind foot, and large claws on the forefeet. They were bipedal or quadrupedal, with semi-robust bodies and long tails. The most primitive were omnivores, although some species had very advanced specializations for plant eating. Sauropodiforms descended from Plateosauria. See more: *Galton 1985; Upchurch 1997; Galton & Upchurch 2004; Yates 2007*

Diet: omnivorous or phytophagous.

Time range

Present from the Upper Triassic to the Middle Jurassic (approx. 237–170.3 Ma), a duration of 66.7 million years.

The smallest (Class: Small Grade II)

Anchisaurus polyzelus ("much-coveted near-lizard"), from the Lower Jurassic (Hettangian, approx. 201.3–199.3 Ma) in northwest Pangea (present-day Connecticut and Massachusetts, USA). This small dinosaur weighed about as much as an emperor

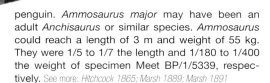

penguin. *Ammosaurus major* may have been an adult *Anchisaurus* or similar species. *Ammosaurus* could reach a length of 3 m and weight of 55 kg. They were 1/5 to 1/7 the length and 1/180 to 1/400 the weight of specimen Meet BP/1/5339, respectively. See more: *Hitchcock 1865; Marsh 1889; Marsh 1891*

The smallest juvenile specimen

Holotype specimen PVL 4068 of *Mussaurus patagonicus* ("rat-lizard of Patagonia") was a calf some 30 cm long and weighing 50 g. Adults were estimated to be 3 meters long and 70 kg in weight, until some adult remains were discovered that were 8 m long and weighed 1.35 t, so the name does not accurately reflect its size. See more: *Bonaparte & Vince 1979; Casamiquela 1980; Montague 2006; Otero & Pol 2013*

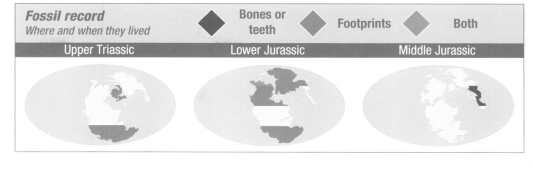

Fossil record Where and when they lived | ◆ Bones or teeth | ◇ Footprints | ◈ Both

| Upper Triassic | Lower Jurassic | Middle Jurassic |

The oldest

Despite being advanced species, *Melanorosaurus readi* and *Meroktenos thabanensis* are the oldest recorded specimens in the group and may even have appeared some time earlier. They date to the Upper Triassic (upper Norian, approx. 218–208.5 Ma) in south-central Pangea (Lesotho and South Africa). The footprints of "*Tetrasauropus*" *jaquesi*, similar in appearance to those of *Otozoum*, are currently considered to be *Lavinipes jaquesi*. They may be Sauropodiform prints. They date to the Carnian (approx. 237–227 Ma) in south-central Pangea (present-day Lesotho). See more: *Haughton 1924; Ellenberger 1970; Gauffre 1993; Porchetti & Nicosia 2007; Peyre de Fabrègues & Allain 2016*

The strangest

Aardonyx celestae ("Celeste Yates' earth-claw"), from the Lower Jurassic in south-central Pangea (present-day South Africa), had a very high forehead, so its nose may have been broad. Other adaptations allowed it to walk on two or four legs, so it represents an intermediate form between the two modes of mobility. See more: *Yates et al. 2010*

Anchisaurus polyzelus
Hitchcock 1865

Specimen: YPM 1883
(Marsh 1891)

Length: 2.4 m
Hip height: 47 cm
Body mass: 25 kg
Material: partial skeleton
ESR: ●●●○

The most recent

Yunnanosaurus youngi ("lizard of Yunnan province and paleontologist Yang Zhongjian, also known as Chung Chien Young") dates to the Middle Jurassic (Aalenian approx. 174.1–170.3 Ma) in eastern Paleoasia (present-day China). It was a large species comparable in length to a city bus and weighing as much as a white rhino. It was the last bipedal sauropodomorph. The teeth of *Yunnanosaurus* were smooth, with a slightly rough texture, and as a result of convergence were similar to those of primitive sauropods (circular-tipped spatulate foliodonts), so much so that the two were often confused. See more: *Young 1942; Simmons 1965; Wang & Sun 1983; Dong et al. 1983; Barrett 1999; Weishampel et al. 2004; Lu et al. 2007*

The first published species

Anchisaurus polyzelus (1865) has a complicated history, as the remains were discovered in 1818, then published two years later, identified as a human skeleton; then, in 1855, they were recognized as belonging to a dinosaur. Ten years later, a species with the name *Megadactylus* was created, but as the name was already in use, it was changed to *Amphisaurus*, and then later changed to *Anchisaurus* for the same reason. See more: *Smith 1818; Smith 1820; Hitchcock 1865; Cope 1869; Marsh 1882, 1885; Baur 1883*

The most recently published species

Ingentia prima, Ledumahadi mafube, and *Yizhousaurus sunae* (2018). The last was an informal name created eight years previously. See more: *Chatterjee et al. 2010; Zhang & You 2017; Apaldetti et al. 2018; McPhee et al. 2018; Zhang et al. 2018*

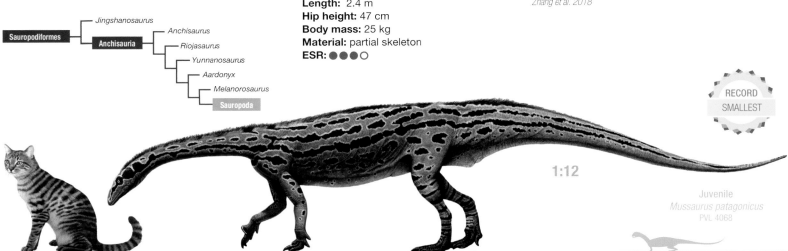

Sauropodiformes — Jingshanosaurus — Anchisauria — Anchisaurus — Riojasaurus — Yunnanosaurus — Aardonyx — Melanorosaurus — Sauropoda

RECORD SMALLEST

1:12

Juvenile
Mussaurus patagonicus
PVL 4068

50 cm | 100 cm | 150 cm

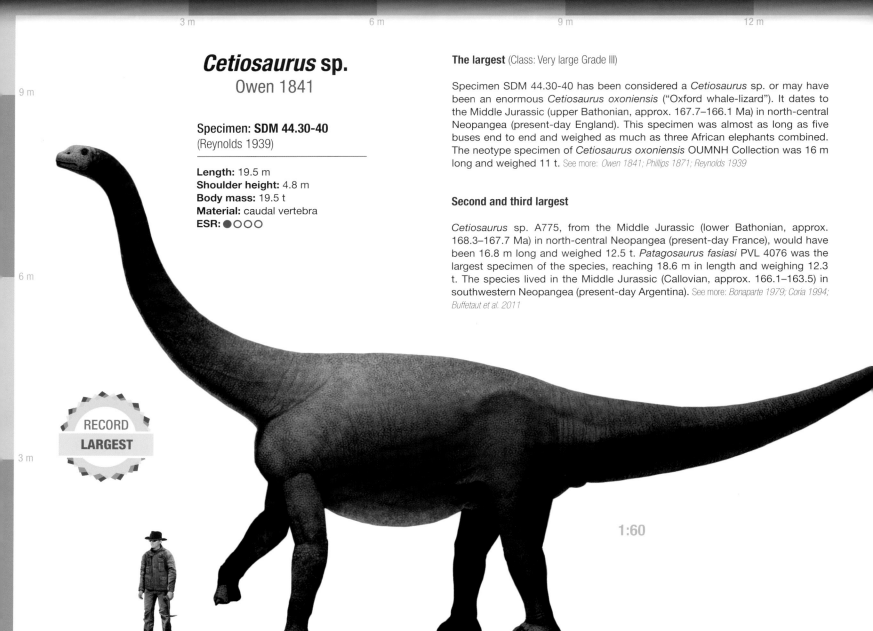

3 m | 6 m | 9 m | 12 m

9 m

6 m

3 m

Cetiosaurus sp.
Owen 1841

Specimen: SDM 44.30-40
(Reynolds 1939)

Length: 19.5 m
Shoulder height: 4.8 m
Body mass: 19.5 t
Material: caudal vertebra
ESR: ●○○○

RECORD
LARGEST

1:60

The largest (Class: Very large Grade III)

Specimen SDM 44.30-40 has been considered a *Cetiosaurus* sp. or may have been an enormous *Cetiosaurus oxoniensis* ("Oxford whale-lizard"). It dates to the Middle Jurassic (upper Bathonian, approx. 167.7–166.1 Ma) in north-central Neopangea (present-day England). This specimen was almost as long as five buses end to end and weighed as much as three African elephants combined. The neotype specimen of *Cetiosaurus oxoniensis* OUMNH Collection was 16 m long and weighed 11 t. See more: *Owen 1841; Phillips 1871; Reynolds 1939*

Second and third largest

Cetiosaurus sp. A775, from the Middle Jurassic (lower Bathonian, approx. 168.3–167.7 Ma) in north-central Neopangea (present-day France), would have been 16.8 m long and weighed 12.5 t. *Patagosaurus fasiasi* PVL 4076 was the largest specimen of the species, reaching 18.6 m in length and weighing 12.3 t. The species lived in the Middle Jurassic (Callovian, approx. 166.1–163.5) in southwestern Neopangea (present-day Argentina). See more: *Bonaparte 1979; Coria 1994; Buffetaut et al. 2011*

Footprints

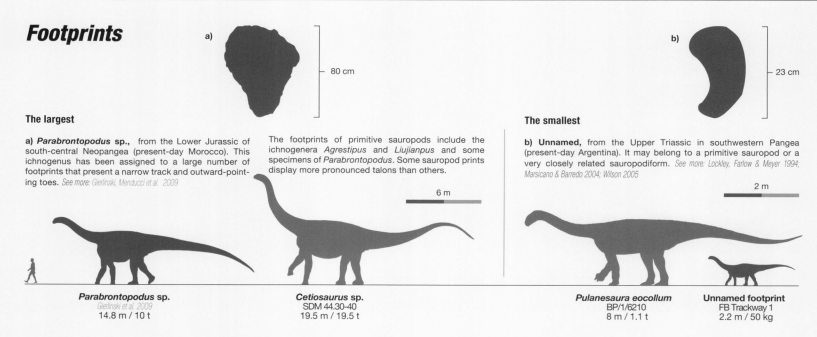

a) 80 cm

b) 23 cm

The largest

a) *Parabrontopodus* **sp.**, from the Lower Jurassic of south-central Neopangea (present-day Morocco). This ichnogenus has been assigned to a large number of footprints that present a narrow track and outward-pointing toes. See more: *Gierlinski, Menducci et al. 2009*

The footprints of primitive sauropods include the ichnogenera *Agrestipus* and *Liujianpus* and some specimens of *Parabrontopodus*. Some sauropod prints display more pronounced talons than others.

6 m

The smallest

b) **Unnamed,** from the Upper Triassic in southwestern Pangea (present-day Argentina). It may belong to a primitive sauropod or a very closely related sauropodiform. See more: *Lockley, Farlow & Meyer 1994; Marsicano & Barredo 2004; Wilson 2005*

2 m

Parabrontopodus sp.
Gierlinski et al. 2009
14.8 m / 10 t

Cetiosaurus sp.
SDM 44.30-40
19.5 m / 19.5 t

Pulanesaura eocollum
BP/1/6210
8 m / 1.1 t

Unnamed footprint
FB Trackway 1
2.2 m / 50 kg

5 m   18 m   21 m   24 m   27 m

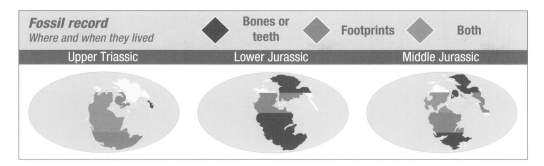

Fossil record Where and when they lived	◆ Bones or teeth	◆ Footprints	◆ Both

Upper Triassic	Lower Jurassic	Middle Jurassic

Characteristics and habits

These dinosaurs had small- to medium-sized heads, leaf-shaped teeth with or without denticles (triangular-crowned, spoon-shaped spatulate foliodonts) with serrated edges, along with some zyphodonts as in *Shunosaurus*. They had medium-length necks, five digits on each forefoot and hind foot, and forefeet with large claws, and were quadrupedal with semi-robust to robust bodies and long tails. They ate plants and were the first terrestrial animals to weigh more than 10 t. Their large size would be a useful strategy for escaping from predators and for dominating other species. Sauropods descended from sauropodiforms and predated mamenchisaurids, turiasaurs, and neosauropods. See more: *Upchurch, Barrett & Dodson 2004; McIntosh 1997*

Diet: phytophagous.

Time range

They are known to have existed from the Upper Triassic to the Upper Jurassic (approx. 232–148.5 Ma), a span of 83.5 million years.

Pulanesaura eocollum
McPhee et al. 2015

Specimen: BP/1/6210
(McPhee et al. 2015)

Length: 8 m
Hip height: 1.8 m
Body mass: 1.1 t
Material: partial hind limb
ESR: ●◑○○○

The smallest (Class: Large Grade I)

Pulanesaura eocollum, from the Lower Jurassic (upper Hettangian, approx. 200.3–199.3 Ma) in south-central Pangea (present-day South Africa), was the smallest primitive sauropod to be confirmed as an adult, having a length of 8 m and weighing about as much as a giraffe, 1.1 t. It was less than half as long and 1/18 the weight of *Cetiosaurus oxoniensis*. Some authors consider it an advanced sauropodiform, as the incomplete remains cannot be used to verify all of its characteristics. If true, then *Ohmdenosaurus liasicus* (present-day Germany) would be the smallest of the sauropods, as it measured 6.2 m in length and weighed 1.1 t. See more: *Wild 1978; McPhee et al. 2015; McPhee & Choiniere 2017; Mortimer**

The smallest juvenile specimen

Specimen To2-112 belonged to a calf of *Tazoudasaurus naimi* (Tazouda's thin-lizard), measuring just 3.2 m in length and 200 kg in weight. It lived in the Lower Jurassic (Pleinsbachian 190.8–182.7 Ma). See more: *Peyers & Allain 2010*

The oldest

The unnamed sauropod PULR 136 dates to the Upper Triassic (Norian, approx. 227–208.5 Ma). Some prints discovered in the Portezuelo Formation (upper Carnian, 232–227 Ma) are even older, and one investigation has suggested they were sauropods. See more: *Ezcurra & Apaldetti 2011; Marsicano & Barredo 2004; Wilson 2005*

The most recent

The oldest primitive sauropod identified was dated to the Upper Jurassic (Tithonian, approx. 152.1–148.5 Ma) and lived in southwestern Neopangea (present-day Argentina). Specimen MCF-PVPH-379 consists of two fragmented hindfoot bones belonging to a juvenile individual. See more: *García, Salgado & Coria 2003*

The strangest

Shunosaurus lii ("lizard of Sechuan Province and Li Bing"), from the Middle Jurassic of northeastern Paleoasia (present-day China). In appearance, it differed from other primitive sauropods, having especially long feet and a relatively short trunk, while the tip of its tail sported a bone club (from thickened, fused final caudal vertebrae) with pointed osteoderms. See more: *Dong, Zhou & Zhang 1983*

The first published species

The name *"Rutellum implicatum"* (1699) was given to a sauropod tooth that was catalogued in a collection as No. 1352. The name is considered invalid as it was assigned 59 years before Carl Linnaeus proposed his zoological nomenclature system. Because it was not used for more than 60 years, it became a *nomen oblitum* ("disused name"). *Cetiosaurus oxoniensis* (1841) is the first valid species but was preceded by another six: *C. brachyurus, C. brevis, C. epioolithicus, C. hypoolithicus, C. longus*, and *C. medius*, all of which are now considered invalid or belonging to another kind of dinosaur. See more: *Lhuyd 1699; Linnaeus 1758; Owen 1841, 1842; Melville 1849; Huxley 1870; Phillips 1871; Hulke 1874; Sauvage 1874; Sauvage 1880; Woodward 1905; Lapparent 1955; Delair & Sarjeant 2002*

The most recently published species

Pulanesaura eocollum (2015) ("ancient-necked rainmaker lizard"), from the Lower Jurassic in south-central Pangea (present-day South Africa). See more: *McPhee et al. 2015*

1:40

RECORD SMALLEST

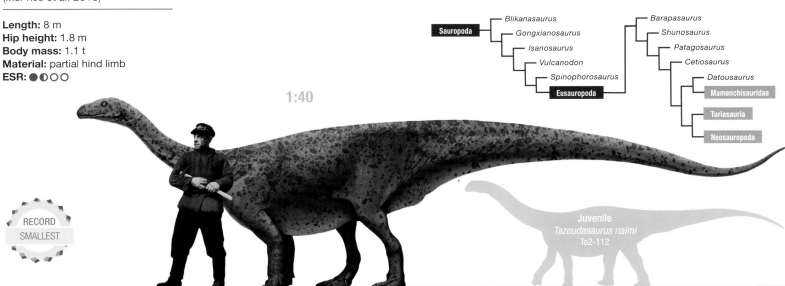

Juvenile
Tazoudasaurus naimi
To2-112

		Blikanasaurus		Barapasaurus
Sauropoda		Gongxianosaurus		Shunosaurus
		Isanosaurus		Patagosaurus
		Vulcanodon		Cetiosaurus
		Spinophorosaurus		Datousaurus
	Eusauropoda			**Mamenchisauridae**
				Turiasauria
				Neosauropoda

2 m   4 m   6 m   8 m

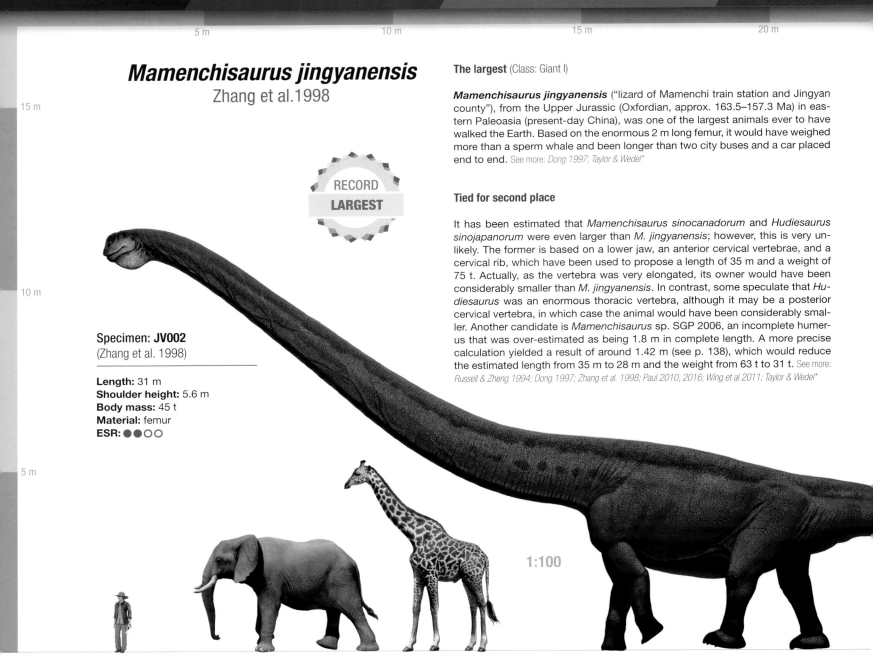

5 m   10 m   15 m   20 m

15 m

Mamenchisaurus jingyanensis
Zhang et al.1998

The largest (Class: Giant I)

Mamenchisaurus jingyanensis ("lizard of Mamenchi train station and Jingyan county"), from the Upper Jurassic (Oxfordian, approx. 163.5–157.3 Ma) in eastern Paleoasia (present-day China), was one of the largest animals ever to have walked the Earth. Based on the enormous 2 m long femur, it would have weighed more than a sperm whale and been longer than two city buses and a car placed end to end. See more: *Dong 1997; Taylor & Wedel**

Tied for second place

It has been estimated that *Mamenchisaurus sinocanadorum* and *Hudiesaurus sinojapanorum* were even larger than *M. jingyanensis*; however, this is very unlikely. The former is based on a lower jaw, an anterior cervical vertebrae, and a cervical rib, which have been used to propose a length of 35 m and a weight of 75 t. Actually, as the vertebra was very elongated, its owner would have been considerably smaller than *M. jingyanensis*. In contrast, some speculate that *Hudiesaurus* was an enormous thoracic vertebra, although it may be a posterior cervical vertebra, in which case the animal would have been considerably smaller. Another candidate is *Mamenchisaurus* sp. SGP 2006, an incomplete humerus that was over-estimated as being 1.8 m in complete length. A more precise calculation yielded a result of around 1.42 m (see p. 138), which would reduce the estimated length from 35 m to 28 m and the weight from 63 t to 31 t. See more: *Russell & Zheng 1994; Dong 1997; Zhang et al. 1998; Paul 2010, 2016; Wing et al 2011; Taylor & Wedel**

RECORD LARGEST

10 m

Specimen: JV002
(Zhang et al. 1998)

Length: 31 m
Shoulder height: 5.6 m
Body mass: 45 t
Material: femur
ESR: ●●○○

5 m

1:100

Footprints

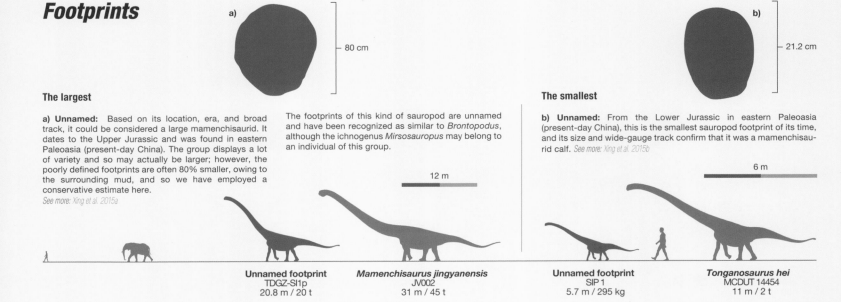

a)

— 80 cm

b)

— 21.2 cm

The largest

a) Unnamed: Based on its location, era, and broad track, it could be considered a large mamenchisaurid. It dates to the Upper Jurassic and was found in eastern Paleoasia (present-day China). The group displays a lot of variety and so may actually be larger; however, the poorly defined footprints are often 80% smaller, owing to the surrounding mud, and so we have employed a conservative estimate here.
See more: Xing et al. 2015a

The footprints of this kind of sauropod are unnamed and have been recognized as similar to *Brontopodus*, although the ichnogenus *Mirsosauropus* may belong to an individual of this group.

The smallest

b) Unnamed: From the Lower Jurassic in eastern Paleoasia (present-day China), this is the smallest sauropod footprint of its time, and its size and wide-gauge track confirm that it was a mamenchisaurid calf. *See more: Xing et al. 2015b*

12 m

6 m

Unnamed footprint
TDGZ-SI1p
20.8 m / 20 t

Mamenchisaurus jingyanensis
JV002
31 m / 45 t

Unnamed footprint
SIP 1
5.7 m / 295 kg

Tonganosaurus hei
MCDUT 14454
11 m / 2 t

25 m   30 m   35 m   40 m   45 m

Characteristics and habits

These dinosaurs had small to very small heads, leaf- or broadleaf-shaped teeth (triangular-crowned, spoon-shaped spatulate foliodont), long to very long necks, five digits on each forefoot and hind foot, and large claws on the forefeet. They were quadrupeds with semi-robust to very robust bodies and long tails. The long-necked, short-bodied form is repeated in several distantly related Asian sauropods (neosauropods similar to *Klamelisaurus*, euhelopodids, and some somphospondylids), and so it may have been a convergent adaptation to similar ecosystems. Mamenchisaurids descended from primitive sauropods.

Diet: phytophagous or durophagous-phytophagous.

Time range

They are known to have existed from the Lower Jurassic to the early Lower Cretaceous (approx. 201.3–139.8 Ma), a span of 61.5 million years.

The smallest (Class: Large Grade III)

Tonganosaurus hei ("He's Tongan lizard"), from the Lower Jurassic (Hettangian, approx. 201.3–199.3 Ma) in eastern Paleoasia (present-day China), was as long as a bus but quite light, weighing as much as two great white sharks. It was just 1/3 the length and 1/22 the weight of *Mamenchisaurus jingyanensis*. See more: *Li et al. 2010*

The smallest juvenile specimen

aff. *Mamenchisaurus* sp., from the Upper Jurassic (Tithonian,

Fossil record
Where and when they lived

◆ Bones or teeth   ◆ Footprints   ◆ Both

Lower Jurassic   Middle Jurassic   Upper Jurassic

Early Lower Cretaceous

approx. 152.1–145 Ma). This animal from eastern Paleoasia (present-day Mongolia) was 8.7 m long and weighed 1 t, so it may have been a juvenile. It is the first Jurassic sauropod reported in Mongolia. See more: *Graham et al. 1997*

The oldest

Tonganosaurus hei dates to the early Lower Jurassic (Hettangian, approx. 201.3–199.3 Ma) and lived in eastern Paleoasia (present-day China). It was similar to *Omeisaurus*, which had a very light body compared to other mamenchisaurids. See more: *Li et al. 2010*

The most recent

Mamenchisaurus sp. has been found in the Phu Kradung Formation (present-day Thailand) at the Upper Jurassic–early Lower Cretaceous boundary (Titho-

nian-Berriasian, approx. 152.1–139.8 Ma). Other reports assigned to the late Lower Cretaceous in China and Japan are doubtful and are possibly euhelopodids. See more: *Hasegawa & Manabe 1991; Jerzykiewicz & Russell 1991; Le Loeuff et al. 2008; Racey & Goodall 2009*

The strangest

Xinjiangtitan shanshaensis ("lizard of Xinjiang autonomous region and the kingdom of Shanshan"). From the Middle Jurassic (Bathonian, approx. 168.3–166.1 Ma) in northeastern Paleoasia (present-day China), it had short, robust limbs compared to those of other mamenchisaurids. See more: *Wu et al. 2013*

The first published species

Cetiosaurus epioolithicus (1842), *Gigantosaurus megalonyx* (1869) and *Cetiosauriscus glymptonensis* (1871), from north-central Neopangea (present-day England), are of uncertain classification, although they may have been mamenchisaurids. *Omeisaurus junghsiensis* (1939), from China, is the oldest species that undoubtedly belonged to this family. See more: *Owen 1842; Seeley 1869; Phillips 1871; Fraas 1908; Haughton 1928; Young 1939; Wilson 2002; Whitlock 2011*

The most recently published species

Anhuilong diboensis (2018) ("Dragon of Anhui Province"), from the Middle Jurassic of northeastern Paleoasia (present-day China). The article describing this animal was in review when this book went to press. See more: *Ren et al. 2018*

Mamenchisauridae
├─ *Omeisaurus*
├─ *Chuanjiesaurus*
└─ *Mamenchisaurus*

Specimen: MCDUT 14454
(Li et al. 2010)

Length: 11 m
Shoulder height: 2.3 m
Body mass: 2 t
Material: partial skeleton
ESR: ●●●○

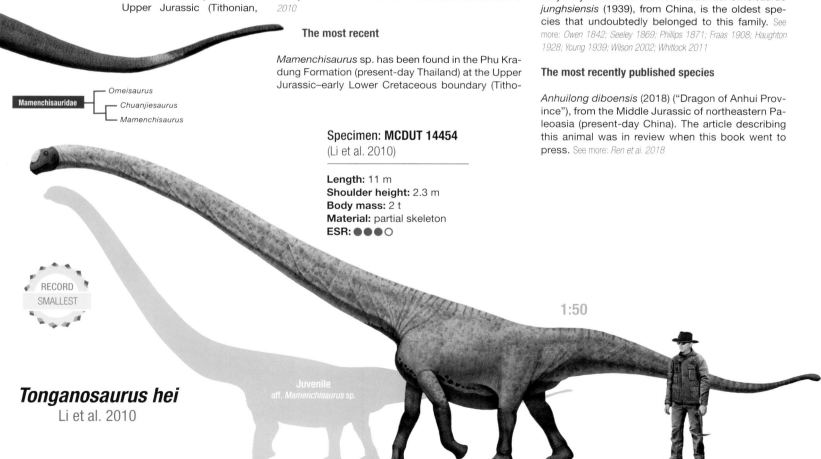

RECORD SMALLEST

1:50

Tonganosaurus hei
Li et al. 2010

Juvenile
aff. *Mamenchisaurus* sp.

2.5 m   5 m   7.5 m   10 m

3 m   6 m   9 m   12 m   15 m

Neosodon praecursor
Sauvage 1876

9 m

RECORD
LARGEST

The largest (Class: Great Grade I)

Neosodon praecursor ("new-tooth precursor") lived in the Upper Jurassic (Kimmeridgian, approx. 157.3–152.1 Ma) in north-central Neopangea (present-day France and Portugal). It has teeth that are similar to *Turiasaurus riodevensis*, just 8% larger. It weighed almost as much as a sperm whale and was as long as two city buses placed end to end. See more: *Sauvage 1876; Moussaye 1885*

Third place goes to *Turiasaurus*

cf. *"Pelorosaurus" humerocristatus,* from the Upper Jurassic (Kimmeridgian, approx. 157.3–152.1 Ma) in north-central Neopangea (present-day England and Portugal), are teeth from a sauropod up to 21.5 m long and weighing 32 t. In contrast, *Turiasaurus riodevensis* ("lizard of the Turia River and Riodeva village"), sometimes considered the largest sauropod of Europe, is a partial skeleton that tells us this creature was 21 m long and weighed 30 t. It is the best-known turiasaur and had teeth very similar to those of *Neosodon*, although smaller in size. See more: *Lydekker 1893; Royo-Torres et al. 2006; Mocho et al. 2013*

6 m

1:70

3 m

Specimen: BHN2R 113
(Moussaye 1885)

Length: 22.5 m
Shoulder height: 5.9 m
Body mass: 35 t
Material: tooth
ESR: ●○○○

Footprints

— 1.08 m

b)

— 54 cm

The largest

a) Unnamed: The footprints of this group have a wide-gauge track, although some exceptions are semi-wide or narrow. In this specimen, the forelimbs were held out to the side as the animal walked along. It dates to the Middle Jurassic and was found in north-central Neopangea (present-day England). See more: *Day et al. 2004*

The footprints of Turiasauria often had a very characteristic shape that is identified with the ichnogenus *Polyonyx*. Two unofficial names have been assigned to prints of these kinds of sauropods—"Opisthonyx" and "Transonymanus."

b) aff. *Polyonyx*: These are prints of the Upper Jurassic from central Neogondwana (present-day Spain). The individual may have been a juvenile, as others also exist. It is from a track that includes prints ranging from 54 cm to 66 cm in length. See more: *Torcida Fernández-Baldor et al. 2015*

8 m

3 m

Neosodon praecursor
BHN2R 113
22.5 m / 35 t

Unnamed footprint
Day et al. 2004
25 m / 45 t

"Ornithopsis" greppini
MH 342
6.3 m / 1 t

aff. *Polyonyx*
LS7A
12.5 m / 6.5 t

18 m   21 m   24 m   27 m   30 m   33 m

Characteristics and habits

These dinosaurs had medium-sized heads, leaf-shaped teeth (triangular-crowned spatulate folio-donts), long necks, five digits on each forefoot and hind foot, and large claws on the forefeet. They were quadrupeds with robust bodies and long tails. They were identified by their heart-shaped teeth and have only been found in western Europe and southern Africa. See more: Royo-Torres et al. 2006; Royo-Torres & Cobos 2009; Mocho et al. 2015

Diet: phytophagous

Time range

They are known to have existed from the Middle Jurassic to the late Lower Cretaceous (approx. 170.3–113 Ma), appearing for approximately 57.3 million years in the fossil record.

The smallest (Class: Large Grade II)

"Ornithopsis" greppini ("Jean-Baptiste Greppin's bird-likeness") from the Upper Jurassic (Kimmeridgian, approx. 157.3–152.1 Ma) in north-central Neopangea (present-day Switzerland). Better known as "Cetiosauriscus" greppini, this creature was longer than a saltwater crocodile and weighed almost as much as a giraffe. Despite its size, it was an adult 1/3 as long and 1/35 the weight of *Neosodon praecursor*. See more: Huene 1922; Schwarz, Wings & Meyer 2007

The smallest juvenile specimen

Several specimens of *Bellusaurus sui* ("Youling Sui's beautiful lizard") exist that have been dated to the Middle Jurassic (Callovian, approx. 166.1–163.5 Ma) in eastern Paleoasia (present-day China). The smallest of all is IVPP V17768, 4.4 m long, and weighing 310 kg. It has been suggested that *Klamelisaurus gobiensis* was an adult of this species; however, it is not from the same era; the latter is from the early

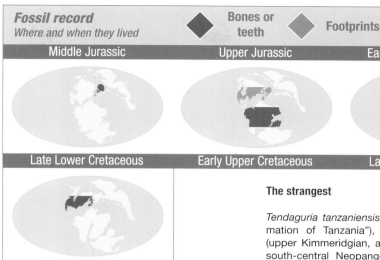

Fossil record — Where and when they lived · Bones or teeth · Footprints · Both

Middle Jurassic · Upper Jurassic · Early Lower Cretaceous · Late Lower Cretaceous · Early Upper Cretaceous · Late Upper Cretaceous

Upper Jurassic (Oxfordian, approx. 163.5–157.3 Ma). Recently it has been proposed as a Turiasauria calf. See more: Dong 1990; Zhao 1993; Mannion 2019

The oldest

Cardiodon rugolosus (present-day Scotland and England), from the Middle Jurassic (Bathonian, approx. 168.3–166.1 Ma), is the oldest, except for *Polyonyx gomesi*, a series of tracks attributed to a turiasaur (Bajocian, approx. 170.3–168.3 Ma) from north-central Neopangea (present-day Portugal). See more: Owen 1841, 1844; Santos et al. 2004, 2009; Barrett 2006; Mocho et al. 2012

The most recent

Moabosaurus utahensis ("lizard of Moab city and the state of Utah"), from the late Lower Cretaceous (upper Aptian, approx. 125–119 Ma) in western Laurasia (present-day Utah, USA). More than 5,500 bones have been found, broken, crushed, and ravaged by necrophagous insects. See more: Gervais 1852; Lydekker 1893; Royo-Torres & Cobos 2007

The strangest

Tendaguria tanzaniensis ("from the Tendaguru Formation of Tanzania"), from the Upper Jurassic (upper Kimmeridgian, approx. 154.1–152.1 Ma) in south-central Neopangea (present-day Tanzania). Although little is known about this animal, it is a highly derived species, as the axial musculature was differently positioned in this species. See more: Marsh 1888; Mateus et al. 2014

The first published species

Cardiodon rugolosus (1841, 1844) ("wrinkled heart-shaped tooth") was given a species name three years after being named *Cardiodon*. See more: Owen 1841, 1842, 1844

The most recently published species

Mierasaurus bobyoungi (2017) ("scientists Bernardo de Miera y Pacheco and Robert Young's lizard"), from the early Lower Cretaceous in Utah, USA. See more: Young 1960; Britt et al. 2017

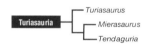

Turiasauria — Turiasaurus · Mierasaurus · Tendaguria

1:40

"Ornithopsis" greppini
Huene 1922

Specimen: MH 342
(Huene 1922)

Length: 6.3 m
Shoulder height: 1.8 m
Body mass: 1 t
Material: partial skeleton
ESR: ●●●○

Juvenile
"Pelorosaurus" sp.

2 m

RECORD SMALLEST

3 m · 6 m · 9 m · 12 m · 15 m

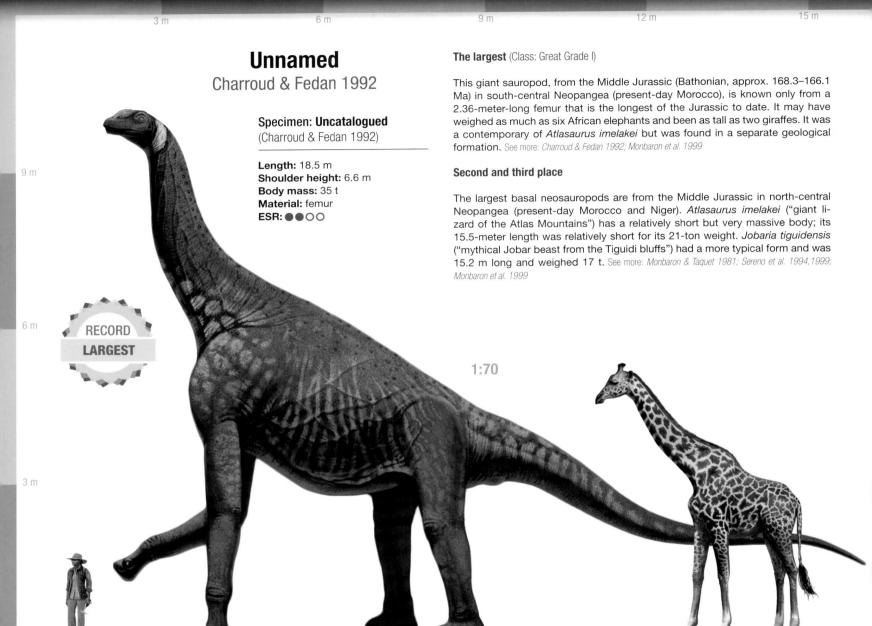

Unnamed
Charroud & Fedan 1992

Specimen: Uncatalogued
(Charroud & Fedan 1992)

Length: 18.5 m
Shoulder height: 6.6 m
Body mass: 35 t
Material: femur
ESR: ●●○○

RECORD
LARGEST

1:70

9 m · 6 m · 3 m

The largest (Class: Great Grade I)

This giant sauropod, from the Middle Jurassic (Bathonian, approx. 168.3–166.1 Ma) in south-central Neopangea (present-day Morocco), is known only from a 2.36-meter-long femur that is the longest of the Jurassic to date. It may have weighed as much as six African elephants and been as tall as two giraffes. It was a contemporary of *Atlasaurus imelakei* but was found in a separate geological formation. See more: *Charroud & Fedan 1992; Monbaron et al. 1999*

Second and third place

The largest basal neosauropods are from the Middle Jurassic in north-central Neopangea (present-day Morocco and Niger). *Atlasaurus imelakei* ("giant lizard of the Atlas Mountains") has a relatively short but very massive body; its 15.5-meter length was relatively short for its 21-ton weight. *Jobaria tiguidensis* ("mythical Jobar beast from the Tiguidi bluffs") had a more typical form and was 15.2 m long and weighed 17 t. See more: *Monbaron & Taquet 1981; Sereno et al. 1994,1999; Monbaron et al. 1999*

Footprints

a)

⌐ 1.3 m

b)

⌐ 18 cm

The largest

a) *Malakhelisaurus mianwali*: This gigantic print from the Middle Jurassic in south-central Neopangea (present-day Pakistan) was originally known as *Malasaurus mianwali*. Its shape, wide-gauge track, and semi-circular forefoot suggest that the animal that made it was similar to *Atlasaurus*. See more: *Malkani 2007, 2008*

There are some footprints that present intermediate features between primitive sauropods and their derivatives, which here are considered probable neosauropods. The only one that has been given a name is *Malakhelisaurus* (previously known as *Malasaurus*).

The smallest

b) Unnamed: This is a single footprint from the Upper Jurassic in northwest Neopangea (present-day Colorado, USA). It is different from the prints of Diplodocoidea and Macronaria, as the digits point forward, and so may have been produced by a neosauropod calf. See more: *Lockley et al. 1986*

12 m

Unnamed species
Charroud & Fedan 1992
18.5 m / 35 t

Malakhelisaurus mianwali
Malkani 2007, 2008
21.5 m / 55 t

4 m

Unnamed footprint
Lockley et al. 1986
2.2 m / 6.7 kg

Ferganasaurus verzilini
PIN N 3042/1
9.1 m / 3.6 t

18 m   21 m   24 m   27 m   30 m   33 m

Characteristics and habits

These dinosaurs had medium-sized heads, leaf-shaped teeth with or without denticles (triangular-crowned spatulate foliodonts), medium-length necks, five digits on each forefoot and hind foot, and large claws on the forefeet. They were quadrupeds with semi-robust bodies and long tails. Neosauropods descended from primitive sauropods and preceded diplodocoids and macronarians. Some researchers have identified the different neosauropod species as turiasaurs (*Atlasaurus*), diplodocoids (*Haplocanthosaurus*), macronarians (*Bellusaurus, Dashanpusaurus, Jobaria, Klamelisaurus*), or titanosauriforms (*Daanosaurus, Lapparentosaurus, Volkheimeria*). See more: *Bonaparte 1979, 1986; Dong 1990; Zhao 1993; Monbaron, Russell & Taquet 1999; Upchurch et al. 2004; Taylor & Naish 2005; Peng, Ye, Gao et al. 2005; Ye et al. 2005; Salgado & Coria 2005; Whitlock 2011*

Diet: phytophagous

Time range

They are known to have existed from the Middle to the Upper Jurassic (approx. 172.2–148.5 Ma), a period of approximately 23.7 million years.

The smallest (Class: Large Grade III)

Ferganasaurus verzilini ("lizard of the Ferganá Valley and Professor Nikita N. Verzilin"), from the Middle Jurassic (Callovian, approx. 166.1–163.5 Ma) in western Paleoasia (present-day Kyrgyzstan). It was longer than a killer whale and weighed as much as two hippopotamuses, making it 1/2 as long and 1/10 the weight of the largest neosauropod. See more: *Rozhdestvensky 1969; Alifanov & Averianov 2003*

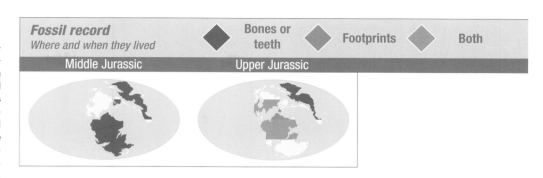

Fossil record
Where and when they lived

◆ Bones or teeth   ◆ Footprints   ◆ Both

Middle Jurassic   Upper Jurassic

The smallest juvenile specimen

Several specimens of *Bellusaurus sui* ("Youling Sui's beautiful lizard") exist, dated to the Middle Jurassic (Callovian, approx. 166.1–163.5 Ma) in eastern Paleoasia (present-day China). The smallest of all is IVPP V17768, 4.4 m long and weighing 310 kg. It has been suggested that *Klamelisaurus gobiensis* was an adult of this species; however, they are not from the same era. The latter is from the early Upper Jurassic (Oxfordian, approx. 163.5–157.3 Ma) See more: *Dong 1990; Zhao 1993*

The oldest

Some remains from the Middle Jurassic (upper Aalenian, approx. 172.2–170.3 Ma) in north-central Neopangea (present-day England) have been identified as belonging to a neosauropod after being examined under a microscope. The pubis is similar to *"Apatosaurus" minimus*. See more: *Reid 1984; Hunt et al. 1994*

The most recent

Apatosaurus minimus ("lesser deceptive-lizard"), from the Upper Jurassic (upper Kimmeridgian, approx. 157.3–152.1 Ma) in northwestern Neopangea (present-day Wyoming, USA). See more: *Mook 1917*

The strangest

Atlasaurus imelakei had a peculiar shape in comparison to other sauropods, with a short neck, long feet, and a very wide body. The remains were believed to be another large *Cetiosaurus mogrebiensis* individual when they were discovered. See more: *Lapparent 1955; Monbaron & Taquet 1981; Monbaron et al. 1999*

The first published species

Bothriospondylus madagascariensis (1895) was thought to be a very old brachiosaurid but was actually an indeterminate neosauropod, possibly similar to *Atlasaurus*. Another specimen discovered in France was assigned to this species, although it is now considered a titanosauriform. See more: *Lydekker 1895; Lapparent 1943; Mannion 2010*

The most recently published species

Daanosaurus zhangi and *Dashanpusaurus dongi* (2005); the former is a juvenile. See more: *Peng et al. 2005; Ye, Gao, & Jiang 2005*

Neosauropoda
— Atlasaurus
— Jobaria
— Diplodocoidea
— Klamelisaurus
— Macronaria

Ferganasaurus verzilini
Alifanov & Averianov 2003

Specimen: PIN N 3042/1
(Alifanov & Averianov 2003)

Length: 9.1 m
Shoulder height: 2.8 m
Body mass: 3.6 t
Material: teeth and partial skeleton
ESR: ●●●○

RECORD SMALLEST

1:50

Juvenile
Bellusaurus sui
IVPP V17768

2 m   4 m   6 m   8 m   10 m

5 m   10 m   15 m   20 m

15 m

Maraapunisaurus fragillimus
Cope 1877

Specimen: AMNH 5777
(Cope 1877)

Length: 35 m
Hip height: 7.7 m
Body mass: 70 t
Material: Partial thoracic vertebra and femur
ESR: ◐○○○

Mythical giant (Class: Giant Grade II)

Maraapunisaurus fragillimus ("enormous, very fragile lizard"), from the Upper Jurassic (Tithonian, approx. 152.1–145 Ma) in northwestern Neopangea (present-day Colorado, USA). An incomplete thoracic vertebra and a fragment of a femur that, unfortunately, was lost have cast significant doubt about the veracity of the measurements. Its length was estimated at 60 m and weight at 150 t when it was believed to be a diplodocid. It may have weighed almost as much as two sperm whales and could easily been longer than a blue whale. See more: *Cope 1877; Osborn & Mook 1921; Gillette 1996a, 1996b; Tschopp, Mateus & Benson 2015; Carpenter 2018*

Largest diplodocoides of the Cretaceous

Rebbachisaurus garasbae ("Ait Rebbach and Gara Sba's lizard") lived in the early Upper Cretaceous (upper Cenomanian, approx. 97.2–93.9 Ma) in central Gondwana (present-day Morocco). It was as heavy as a sperm whale and as long as a blue whale. Another great diplodocoid was *Rayososaurus* sp. UFMA 1.20.418 (present-day Brazil), measuring 21 m in length and weighing 20 t. See more: *Lavocat 1954; Russell 1996; Medeiros & Schultz 2004; Carvalho et al. 2007*

10 m

5 m

1:100

RECORD LARGEST

Footprints

a)

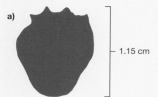

— 1.15 cm

b)

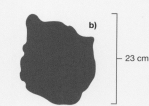

— 23 cm

The largest

a) *Breviparopus taghbaloutensis*: This footprint has been mistaken for that of a giant brachiosaurid. However, its narrow-gauge track, the position of the claws, and the era all indicate that it belonged to an enormous diplodocoid. From the Middle Jurassic of south-central Neopangea (present-day Morocco). See more: *Dutuit & Ouazzou 1980*

Breviparopus and some footprints identified as *Parabrontopodus*, from the Middle Jurassic to the early Upper Cretaceous, belong to this group. The forefoot prints are kidney-shaped

10 m

The smallest

b) Unnamed: A footprint, dating to the early Lower Cretaceous from central Laurasia (present-day Croatia), was similar to *Breviparopus*, and so was likely from a diplodocoid. In that geographic zone, sauropods were smaller, in terms of both bones and footprints. See more: *Mezga et al. 2007*

3 m

Breviparopus taghbaloutensis
Dutuit & Ouazzou 1980
33.5 m / 62 t

Maraapunisaurus fragillimus
AMNH 5777
35 m / 70 t

Unnamed footprint
Mezga et al. 2007
7.2 m / 850 kg

Nigersaurus taqueti
Pv-6127-MOZ
10 m / 1.9 t

25 m   30 m   35 m   40 m   45 m

Characteristics and habits

These dinosaurs had medium-sized heads, cylindrical teeth (cylindrodonts with a circular cross-section), medium to long necks, five digits on each forefoot and hind foot, and large claws on the forefeet. They were quadrupeds with light to robust bodies and long tails. Diplodocoids descended from neosauropods and preceded the flagellicaudata, which are divided into dicraeosaurids and diplodocids. **Diet:** phytophagous

Time range

They are known to have existed from the Middle Jurassic to the early Upper Cretaceous (approx. 174.1–98.1 Ma), a span of 82.3 million years, but they may have lived until the end of the late Upper Cretaceous (approx. 66 Ma), a period of 108.1 Ma.

The smallest (Class: Large Grade III)

Nigersaurus taqueti ("lizard of Niger and paleontologist Philippe Taquet") lived in the late Lower Cretaceous (Aptian, approx. 125–113 Ma) of central Gondwana (present-day Niger). It was 1/3 to 1/4 the length and 1/37 the weight of *Maraapunisaurus fragillimus*. See more: *Sereno et al. 1999*

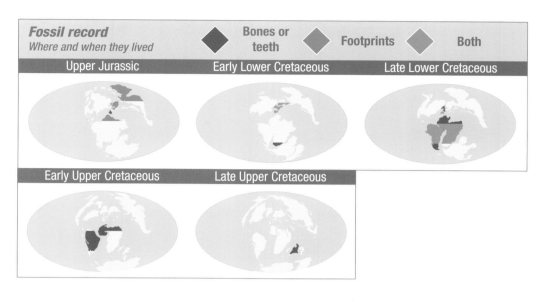

The smallest juvenile specimen

Several remains of small cf. *Zapalasaurus* were found in association with an adult individual. The smallest of all may have been 2.9 m long and weighed 65 kg. Another notable calf is *Nopcsaspondylus alarconensis*, which would have been 3.6 m long and 120 kg in weight. See more: *Nopcsa 1902; Apesteguía 2007; Salgado et al. 2012*

The oldest

The footprints of *Breviparopus* have been identified as those of large brachiosaurids; however, their narrow width and feet with four pointed claws (unlike diplodocids) suggest that they belonged to large primitive diplodocoids. The oldest of all is from the Middle Jurassic (Aalenian, approx. 174.1–170.3 Ma) in north-central Neopangea (present-day England). See more: *Romano et al. 1999*

The most recent

Specimens UNPSJB-PV 1004 and UNPSJB-PV 1005 date to the late Upper Cretaceous (upper Cenomanian-lower Turonian, approx. 97.2–91.8 Ma) in western Gondwana (present-day Argentina). It is possible that *"Titanosaurus" rahioliensis*, from the late Upper Cretaceous (upper Maastrichtian, approx. 69–66 Ma), was a diplodocoid. See more: *Mathur & Srivastava 1987; Martinez 1998; Lamanna et al. 2001; Wilson & Upchurch 2003; Ibiricu et al. 2012*

The strangest

Nigersaurus taqueti had a very broad snout, with the teeth positioned at the tip. Its teeth were also very numerous (they numbered around 500) and replaced themselves very quickly. The animal's head faced downward. See more: *Sereno et al. 1999, 2007; Weishampel et al. 2007; Marugán-Lobón et al. 2013*

The first published species

It has also been suggested that *Ischyrosaurus manseli* (1869) was a rebbachisaurid; however, it also could have been a titanosauriform, *Xenoposeidon proneneukos* (2007), which was discovered in 1893. See more: *Hulke 1869; Hulke in Lydekker 1888; Lydekker 1893; Nopcsa 1902; Apesteguía 2007; Taylor & Naish 2007; Barrett, Benson & Upchurch 2010; Taylor & Wedel**

The most recently published species

Lavocatisaurus agrioensis (2018) from the late Lower Cretaceous (Aptian, approx. 125–113 Ma) in western Gondwana (present-day Argentina). There is evidence that it had a keratin sheath on its snout. See more: *Canudo et al. 2018*

Specimen: MNN GAD517
(Sereno et al. 1999)

Length: 10 m
Hip height: 2.15 m
Body mass: 1.9 t
Material: cranium and partial skeleton
ESR: ●●●●

Nigersaurus taqueti
Sereno et al. 1999

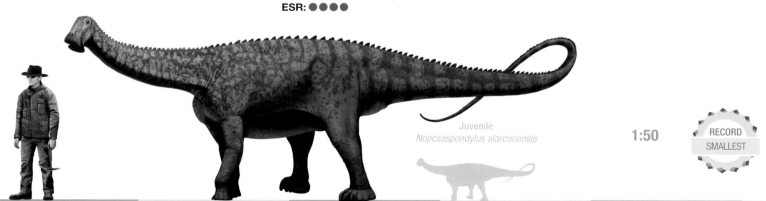

Juvenile
Nopcsaspondylus alarconensis

1:50

RECORD SMALLEST

2 m   4 m   6 m   8 m   10 m

3 m   6 m   9 m   12 m   15 m

9 m

6

3

"*Morosaurus*" *agilis*
Marsh 1889

Specimen: USNM 5371
(Marsh 1889)

Length: 22 m
Hip height: 4.8 m
Body mass: 17 t
Material: metacarpal
ESR: ●◑○○○

The largest (Class: Very Large Grade III)

"*Morosaurus*" *agilis* ("stupid, agile lizard"), from the Upper Jurassic (Kimmeridgian, approx. 157.3–152.1 Ma) in northwestern Neopangea (present-day Colorado, USA), was considered a primitive neosauropod or a basal macronarian. It was as long as two city buses and weighed more than three African elephants combined. See more: *Marsh 1889; Gilmore 1907; Whitlock & Wilson 2015, 2018*

The second largest

Morinosaurus typus ("common lizard of the town of Morini"), from the Upper Jurassic (Kimmeridgian, approx. 157.3–152.1 Ma) in north-central Neopangea (present-day France), is known from a single tooth that was similar to *Dicraeosaurus* but larger, so its length was inferred to be 19 m, with a weight of 11 t. See more: *Sauvage 1874; Upchurch et al. 2004*

RECORD
LARGEST

1:70

Footprints

a)
— 59 cm

b)
— 23 cm

The largest

a) Unnamed: Found in what was then north-central Neopangea (present-day Croatia) and dated to the early Lower Cretaceous. The species in this family are often smaller in size compared to other sauropods. *See more: Mezga et al. 2007*

Footprints of dicraeosaurids are not easy to identify; however, a distinctive type of small diplodocoid left horseshoe-shaped prints of the front forefoot.

The smallest

b) Unnamed: From a print dating to the early Upper Cretaceous in central Laurasia (present-day Croatia), we can deduce that it belongs to a dicraeosaurid, given the horseshoe-shaped forefoot. *See more: Mezga et al. 2006*

6 m

4 m

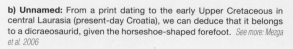

Unnamed footprint
Mezga et al. 2007
17.4 m / 8.7 t

"*Morosaurus*" *agilis*
MPEF-PV 1716
22 m / 17 t

Unnamed footprint
Mezga et al. 2006
10 m / 970 kg

Unnamed species
MLL-003
9 m / 1 t

18 m 21 m 24 m 27 m 30 m 33 m

Characteristics and habits

These dinosaurs had medium-sized heads, cylindrical teeth (transversally circular cylindronts), short necks, five digits on each forefoot and hind foot, and large claws on the forefeet. They were quadrupeds with light to semi-robust bodies and long tails. Dicraeosaurids descended from diplodocoids. Their teeth were different from those of other contemporary diplodocoids and titanosaurs, indicating that they may have eaten different kinds of plants to avoid direct competition.
Diet: phytophagous

Time range

Present from the Lower Jurassic to the early Upper Cretaceous (approx. 174.1–93.9 Ma). Together they appear for approximately 80.2 million years in the fossil record.

The smallest (Class: Very large Grade II)

A braincase of a possible Dicraeosaurid was reported from the Mulichinco Formation (present-day Argentina), dating to the early Lower Cretaceous (Valanginian, approx. 139.8–132.9 Ma). It belonged to a subadult or adult specimen that was approximately 65% the size of the holotype specimen of *Amargasaurus cazaui*. It would have been longer than a killer whale and as heavy as a great white shark. It was 2.5 the length and 1/17 the weight of *"Morosaurus" agilis*. See more: *Carabajal et al. 2017*

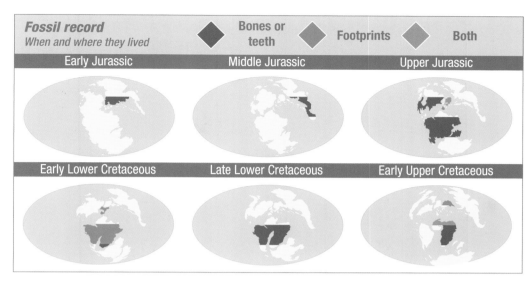

Fossil record
When and where they lived

◆ Bones or teeth   ◇ Footprints   ◇ Both

Early Jurassic | Middle Jurassic | Upper Jurassic
Early Lower Cretaceous | Late Lower Cretaceous | Early Upper Cretaceous

Unnamed

Carabajal et al. 2017

Specimen: **MLL-003**
(Carabajal et al. 2017)

Length: 9 m
Hip height: 2 m
Body mass: 1 t
Material: endocranium
ESR: ●●●○

The smallest juvenile specimen

cf. *Dicraeosaurus* sp. has been reported from the early Upper Cretaceous (Cenomanian, approx. 100.5–93.9 Ma) in central Gondwana (present-day Sudan). The largest specimens were barely 7 m long and weighed 600 kg. It is not known whether they were adults or juveniles. See more: *El-Khashab 1977; Rauhut 1999*

The oldest

Lingwulong shenqi ("surprising dragon of Lingwu") is unexpected, as it dates to the lower and Middle Jurassic (Toarcian-Aalenian, approx. 174.1 Ma). It is also the only diplodocoid ever found in Asia. See more: *Xu et al. 2018*

The strangest

Amargasaurus cazaui ("lizard of geologist Luis B. Cazau's La Amarga Formation"), from the late Lower Cretaceous (Barremian, approx. 129.4–125 Ma) in western Gondwana (present-day Argentina), had some extremely high, pointed cervical vertebrae (with keratin sheaths) that formed a double crest, which would have made it appear larger and more aggressive to its predators and competitors. See more: *Salgado & Bonaparte 1991; Paul 2000; Salgado & Coria 2005; Schwarz et al. 2007*

The most recent

cf. *Dicraeosaurus* sp. from the early Upper Cretaceous (Cenomanian, approx. 100.5–93.9 Ma) in Central Gondwana (present-day Egypt and Sudan). It was suspected that *Dyslocosaurus polyonichius* was from the late Upper Cretaceous, but it more likely belonged to the Upper Jurassic. See more: *Stromer 1832; El-Khashab 1977; McIntosh et al.1992; Rauhut 1999; Tschopp et al. 2015*

The first published species

Morinosaurus typus (1874). Unfortunately, the piece has been lost. See more: *Sauvage 1874*

The most recently published species

Pilmatueia faundezi (2018) ("from Pilmatué plain and Ramón Faúndez") lived in the early Lower Cretaceous (Valanginian, approx. 139.8–132.9 Ma) in western Gondwana (present-day Argentina. The final paginated version dates to 2019. See more: *Coria et al. 2018*

Flagellicaudata — Dicraeosauridae — *Dicraeosaurus* / *Amargasaurus*
Diplodocidae

1:50

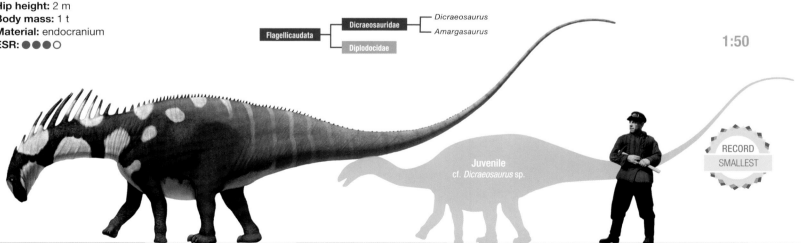

Juvenile
cf. *Dicraeosaurus* sp.

RECORD SMALLEST

2 m 4 m 6 m 8 m 10 m

24 m

16 m

8 m

8 m   16 m   24 m   32 m

RECORD
LARGEST

cf. *Barosaurus lentus*
Marsh 1890

Specimen: BYU 9024
(Jensen 1985)

Length: 45 m
Hip height: 6.4 m
Body mass: 60 t
Material: cervical vertebrae
ESR: ●◐○○○

The largest (Class: Giant Grade II)

cf. *Barosaurus lentus* ("slow, heavy lizard"), from the Upper Jurassic (upper Kimmeridgian–lower Tithonian, approx. 154.7–148.5 Ma) in northwestern Neopangea (present-day Colorado, USA). The cervical vertebra BYU 9024, which had been considered a posterior piece of *Supersaurus vivianae*, has recently been recognized as a middle piece of *Barosaurus lentus* (perhaps a second species). This was the longest of all the sauropods, longer than a blue whale and sperm whale combined. Its neck was longer than any other dinosaur's, measuring more than 15 m; if it could have stood on its hind legs, this animal would have been 22 m high. It was as heavy as 10 African elephants. If, as some suggest, its cervical vertebra BYU 9024 was really a C9 instead of a C11, this animal would have weighed more than 80 tons, equal to two sperm whales. Some enormous vertebrae housed in the AMNH collection were around the same size as BYU 9024. *See more: Jensen 1985, 1987; Lovelace, Scott & William 2007; Taylor & Wedel 2016, Taylor**

Return of the mythical giant?

Other diplodocids believed to be enormous in size, such as *Seismosaurus* (now *Diplodocus*) and *Supersaurus*, were revised to the smaller sizes of 30 and 33 m in length and 21 and 35 t in weight, respectively. Previous estimates had given *Seismosaurus* a length of 58 m and a weight of 100 t. *See more: Jensen 1985; Gillette 1991; Lucas et al. 2004, 2006; Lovelace et al. 2007*

1:150

Footprints a)

~8.3 cm

1.23 m

The largest

a) Unnamed: From the Upper Jurassic in southwestern Neopangea (present-day Uruguay). The same track contains footprints 95 and 123 cm long; some of the prints are poorly preserved and include the marks of the surrounding mud. *See more: Mesa & Perea 2015*

The type footprints of *Parabrontopodus* and *Gigantosauropus* represent those of diplodocidae.

The smallest

b) Unnamed: These prints were found in the Upper Jurassic of northwest Neopangea (present-day Colorado, USA). It has been suggested that they belong to *Apatosaurus* calves. *See more: Mossbruckert 2010*

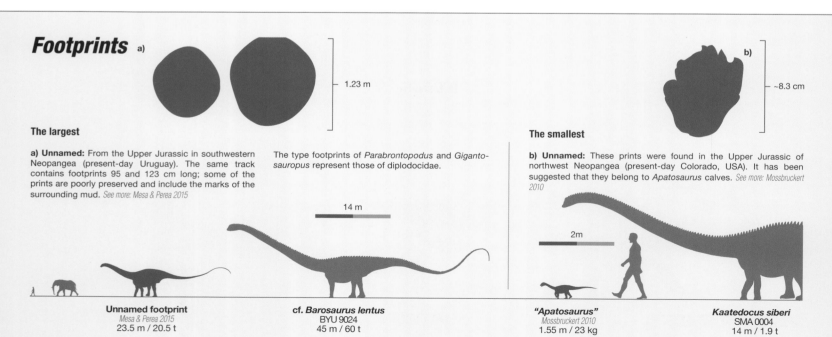

14 m

2 m

Unnamed footprint
Mesa & Perea 2015
23.5 m / 20.5 t

cf. Barosaurus lentus
BYU 9024
45 m / 60 t

"Apatosaurus"
Mossbruckert 2010
1.55 m / 23 kg

Kaatedocus siberi
SMA 0004
14 m / 1.9 t

40m   48 m   56 m   64 m

Characteristics and habits

These dinosaurs had medium-sized heads, cylindrical teeth (cylindrodonts with a circular cross section), medium to long necks, five digits on each forefoot and hind foot, and large claws on the forefeet. They were quadrupeds with light or robust bodies and long tails. Diplodocids descended from diplodocoids.
Diet: phytophagous.

Time range

Present from the Upper Jurassic to the early Lower Cretaceous (approx. 163.5–139.8 Ma), appearing for approximately 23.7 million years in the fossil record.

The smallest (Class: Large Grade III)

Kaatedocus siberi ("Hans-Jakob 'Kirby' Siber's small-beam"), from the Upper Jurassic (upper Kimmeridgian, approx. 157.3–152.1 Ma) in northwestern Neopangea (present-day Wyoming, USA). It may have been the smallest, although it has a rival—*Leinkupal laticauda* ("thick-tailed, from a vanishing family") from the early Lower Cretaceous (upper Berriasian, approx. 142.4–139.8 Ma) in south-central Gondwana (present-day Argentina). The latter was just 11 m long and weighed 1.65 t, but it is not known whether it was an adult or not. They were 1/3 to 1/4 the length and 1/31 to 1/36 the weight of cf. *Barosaurus lentus*. See more: *Tschopp & Mateus 2012; Gallina et al. 2014*

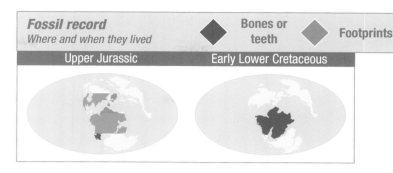

Fossil record Where and when they lived

◆ Bones or teeth   ◆ Footprints   ◆ Both

Upper Jurassic | Early Lower Cretaceous

The smallest juvenile specimens

The smallest calf of *Brontosaurus excelsus* ("mighty thunder lizard") was OMNH 1251, which was merely 3.1 m in length and 100 kg in weight. It dates to the Upper Jurassic (Kimmeridgian, approx. 157.3–152.1 Ma) in northwestern Neopangea (present-day Oklahoma, USA). The juvenile *Brontosaurus parvus* ("small thunder lizard") from Wyoming, USA was a similar size and from the same period. See more: *Peterson & Gilmore 1902; Carpenter & McIntosh 1994*

The oldest

Several informally described fossils known as "Amphicoelias brontodiplodocus" date to the Upper Jurassic (Oxfordian, approx. 163.5–157.3 Ma) in northwestern Neopangea (present-day Wyoming, USA). This species is based on the assumption that *Brontosaurus* and *Diplodocus* are immature *Amphicoelias altus* individuals; however, "A. brontodiplodocus" has been discarded by the entire scientific community. See more: *Galiano & Albersdörfer 2010; Taylor**

The strangest

Amphicoelias altus ("tall biconcave"), from the Upper Jurassic (Kimmeridgian, approx. 157.3–152.1 Ma) in northwestern Neopangea (present-day Oklahoma, USA), had a femur that was unique among sauropods, as the medial part was cylindrical instead of broad and flat. See more: *Cope 1877; Cope 1878; Osborn & Mook 1921*

The most recent

Leinkupal laticauda ("thick-tailed from a vanishing family"), from western Gondwana (present-day Argentina), and another nameless one from central Gondwana (present-day South Africa). The two date to the early Lower Cretaceous (Berriasian, approx. 145–139.8 Ma). Even more recent is cf. *Barosaurus* sp. from the late Lower Cretaceous (upper Albian, approx. 113–100.5 Ma) in western Laurasia (present-day Utah, USA). However, it is based on some vertebrae that are similar to those of the somphospondylid sauropod *Sauroposeidon*. See more: *Tschudy et al. 1984; Weishampel et al. 2004; Gallina et al. 2014; McPhee et al. 2015*

The first published species

Amphicoelias altus, *Apatosaurus ajax* and *Atlantosaurus montanus* (1877). Described in the same year, the first two are currently valid species, while the third is doubtful. See more: *Cope 1877; Marsh 1877*

The most recently published species

Galeamopus pabsti (2017) ("Dr. Ben Pabst's need-helmet), from the Upper Jurassic in northwestern Neopangea (present-day Wyoming, USA). The genus name alludes to the fact that the neurocranium was uncovered, but is also a nod to William Holland and William Utterback, whose first names are derived from "Wil-helm," which also means "need-helmet." It was created to separate it from *Diplodocus hayi*, then was given a new species name two years later. See more: *Tschopp et al. 2015; Tschopp & Mateus 2017*

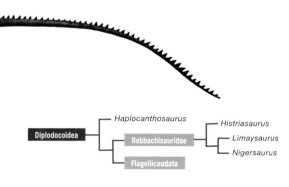

Diplodocoidea — Haplocanthosaurus
Rebbachisauridae — Histriasaurus
— Limaysaurus
— Nigersaurus
Flagellicaudata

RECORD SMALLEST

Kaatedocus siberi
Tschopp & Mateus 2012

Specimen: SMA 0004
(Tschopp & Mateus 2012)

Length: 13 m
Hip height: 2.15 m
Body mass: 1.9 t
Material: cranium and partial skeleton
ESR: ●●●○

1:60

Juvenile
Brontosaurus excelsus
OMNH 1251

2 m   4 m   6 m   8 m   10 m   12 m

3 m   6 m   9 m   12 m   15 m

9 m

6 m

3 m

RECORD
LARGEST

Camarasaurus supremus
Cope 1877

AMNH 5760 (Cope 1877)

Length: 20 m
Shoulder height: 5 m
Body mass: 30 t
Material: tibia
ESR: ●●○○

1:70

The largest (Class: Very large Grade III)

Camarasaurus supremus is known from several individuals dated to the Upper Jurassic (upper Kimmeridgian, approx. 154.7–152.1 m. a.) that lived in northwestern Neopangea (present-day Colorado, USA). This sauropod was as long as five buses end to end and weighed as much as six African elephants combined. It had a powerful jaw compared to other sauropods, suggesting that it consumed tougher plants than those eaten by the diplodocids and titanosauriforms it lived alongside. It also seems to have been more abundant than other contemporary species, perhaps because of its feeding capacity, which allowed it to take advantage of more food sources. See more: *Cope 1877; Osborn & Mook 1921*

Mistaken identity

Lourinhasaurus alenquerensis ("lizard of the towns of Lourinha and Alenquer"), from the Upper Jurassic (upper Kimmeridgian, approx. 154.7–152.1 Ma) in north-central Neopangea (present-day Portugal). It is known from several postcranial remains that were originally thought to belong to *Apatosaurus*. It was also very large, with a length of 17.5 m and a weight of approximately 19 t. It is sometimes confused with the contemporary theropod *Lourinhanosaurus*, as they were both named the same year. See more: *Lapparent & Zbyszewski 1957; Dantas et al. 1998; Mateus 1998; Upchurch et al. 2004; Mocho et al. 2014*

Footprints

a)

— 87 cm

The largest

a) *Rotundichnus munchehagensis* dates to the early Lower Cretaceous in central Laurasia (present-day Germany). It has been considered a doubtful name, with similarities to *Brontopodus*; however, its tracks are proportionally narrower. See more: *Hendricks 1981; Wright 2005; Hornung et al. 2012; Wings, Lallensack & Mallison 2016*

The medium-gauge tracks characteristic of basal macronarians (*Elephantophoides*, *Rotundichnus*, and some reported as *Brontopodus*) have been found only outside of Paleoasia and eastern Laurasia.

b)

— 47.2 cm

The smallest

b) Unnamed, from the late Lower Cretaceous in western Gondwana (present-day Brazil). They were identified as possible titanosaur prints, but do not differ in any way from those of primitive macronarians. See more: *Leonardi & dos Santos 2004*

8 m

5 m

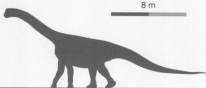

Camarasaurus supremus
AMNH 5760
20 m / 30 t

Rotundichnus munchehagensis
Hendricks 1981
21.5 m / 36.5 t

Unnamed footprint
Romano et al. 1999
5.5 m / 1.1 t

Camarasaurus sp.
QG59
12.9 m / 7.5 t

18 m   21 m   24 m   27 m   30 m   33 m

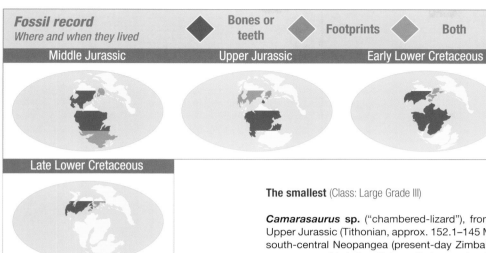

Fossil record
Where and when they lived

◆ Bones or teeth   ◆ Footprints   ◆ Both

Middle Jurassic   Upper Jurassic   Early Lower Cretaceous

Late Lower Cretaceous

dongi, from eastern Paleoasia (present-day China), is from the same period; however, it is not yet known whether it was a primitive neosauropod or a macronarian. See more: *Moser et al. 2004; Peng et al. 2005*

The most recent

Specimens RIN/1, MPZ 2004/2 (present-day Spain) and SV7 (present-day France) seem to be the last primitive macronarians, as they date to the late Lower Cretaceous (Albian, approx. 145–139 Ma). See more: *Buffetaut 2001; Buffetaut & Nori 2012*

The strangest

Several strange sauropods, such as *Janenschia*, were considered macronarians, but over time were classified within other groups. The bones of *Lourinhasaurus alenquerensis* (present-day Portugal), from the Upper Jurassic (Kimmeridgian, approx. 157.3–152.1 Ma) in north-central Neopangea, were similar to those of *Apatosaurus*. See more: *Lapparent & Zbyszewski 1957*

The first published species

Camarasaurus grandis and *C. supremus*, from northwestern Neopangea (present-day Colorado, New Mexico, and Wyoming, USA), were described in 1877 along with *Caulodon diversidens*, which consists of some teeth from the second species mentioned. The famous antagonists of the "Bone Wars" independently described two different *Camarasaurus* species the same year. See more: *Cope 1877; Marsh 1878*

The most recently published species

Cathetosaurus lewisi (1988) presents evidence of a possible keratinous beak, which might have been present in all sauropods. See more: *Jensen 1988; Ikejiri 2005; Mateus & Tschopp 2013; Wiersma & Sander 2016*

The smallest (Class: Large Grade III)

Camarasaurus sp. ("chambered-lizard"), from the Upper Jurassic (Tithonian, approx. 152.1–145 Ma) in south-central Neopangea (present-day Zimbabwe), was comparable in length to a city bus and weighed more than an African elephant. It was 2/3 the length and 1/4 the weight of *C. supremus*. See more: *Mantell 1852; Upchurch, Mannion & Taylor 2015*

The smallest juvenile specimens

The teeth MPZ 96/111 and MPZ 96/112 belong to small macronarians from the late Lower Cretaceous (Barremian, approx. 129.4–125 Ma). From the size of the pieces, which range from 2.6–2.9 mm long and 2–2.33 mm wide, they may have been calves 1.35–1.7 m long and weighing 16–32 kg. Because some of the teeth display wear from consuming plants, it has been suggested that they were not embryos. See more: *Ruiz-Omeñaca, Canudo & Cuenca-Bescós 1995*

The oldest

Specimen RUC 19991 dates to the Middle Jurassic (Bajocian, approx. 170.3–168.3 Ma) in south-central Neopangea (present-day India). *Dashanpusaurus*

Characteristics and habits

These dinosaurs had relatively large, short heads, broad spatula-shaped teeth (circular-crowned spatulate foliodonts), medium-length necks, five digits on each forefoot and hind foot, and large claws on the forefeet. They were quadrupeds with robust to very robust bodies and long tails. Macronarians descended from neosauropods and preceded titanosauriforms.
Diet: durophagous-phytophagous

Time range

Present from the Middle Jurassic to the late Lower Cretaceous (approx. 170.3–100.5 Ma), they appear for approximately 69.8 million years in the fossil record.

Camarasaurus sp.
Cope 1877

Specimen: QG59
(Raath & McIntosh 1987)

Length: 12.9 m
Hip height: 3.2 m
Body mass: 7.5 t
Material: femur
ESR: ●●○○

RECORD SMALLEST

Macronaria
Camarasaurus
Galvesaurus
Aragosaurus
Titanosauriformes

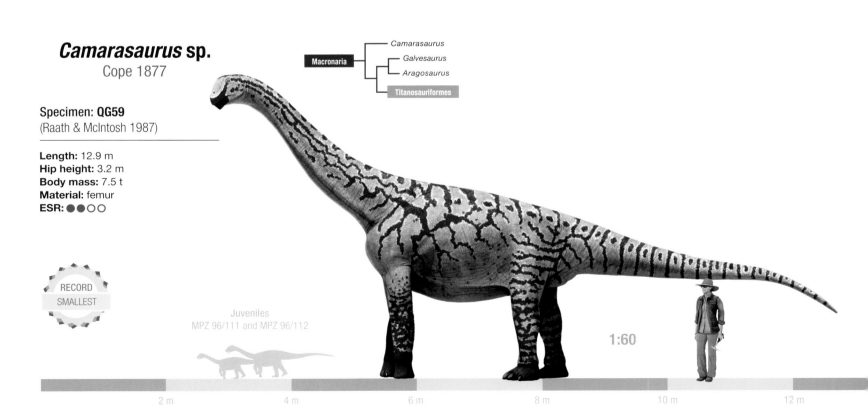

Juveniles
MPZ 96/111 and MPZ 96/112

1:60

2 m   4 m   6 m   8 m   10 m   12 m

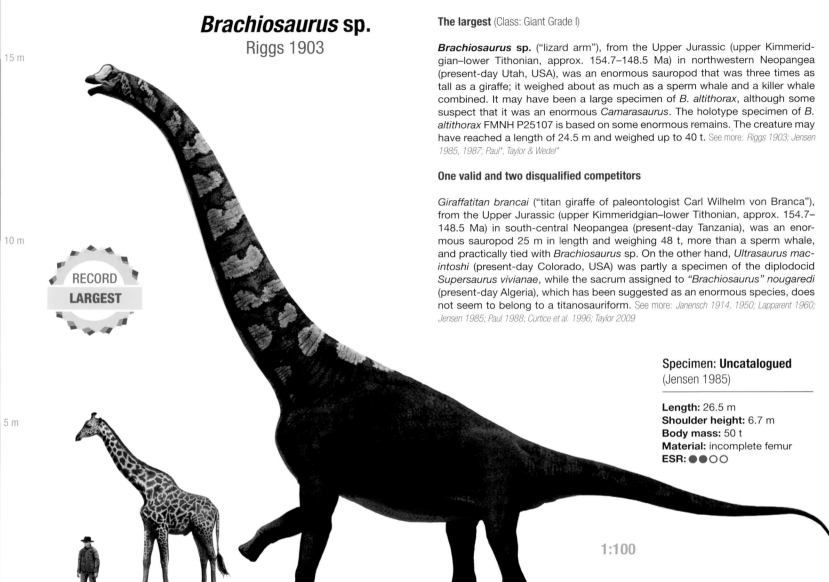

Brachiosaurus sp.
Riggs 1903

RECORD
LARGEST

The largest (Class: Giant Grade I)

***Brachiosaurus* sp.** ("lizard arm"), from the Upper Jurassic (upper Kimmeridgian–lower Tithonian, approx. 154.7–148.5 Ma) in northwestern Neopangea (present-day Utah, USA), was an enormous sauropod that was three times as tall as a giraffe; it weighed about as much as a sperm whale and a killer whale combined. It may have been a large specimen of *B. altithorax*, although some suspect that it was an enormous *Camarasaurus*. The holotype specimen of *B. altithorax* FMNH P25107 is based on some enormous remains. The creature may have reached a length of 24.5 m and weighed up to 40 t. See more: *Riggs 1903; Jensen 1985, 1987; Paul*, Taylor & Wedel**

One valid and two disqualified competitors

Giraffatitan brancai ("titan giraffe of paleontologist Carl Wilhelm von Branca"), from the Upper Jurassic (upper Kimmeridgian–lower Tithonian, approx. 154.7–148.5 Ma) in south-central Neopangea (present-day Tanzania), was an enormous sauropod 25 m in length and weighing 48 t, more than a sperm whale, and practically tied with *Brachiosaurus* sp. On the other hand, *Ultrasaurus macintoshi* (present-day Colorado, USA) was partly a specimen of the diplodocid *Supersaurus vivianae*, while the sacrum assigned to *"Brachiosaurus" nougaredi* (present-day Algeria), which has been suggested as an enormous species, does not seem to belong to a titanosauriform. See more: *Janensch 1914, 1950; Lapparent 1960; Jensen 1985; Paul 1988; Curtice et al. 1996; Taylor 2009*

Specimen: Uncatalogued
(Jensen 1985)

Length: 26.5 m
Shoulder height: 6.7 m
Body mass: 50 t
Material: incomplete femur
ESR: ●●○○

1:100

Footprints

a) ~95 cm

b)
12 cm

The largest

a) Unnamed: This enormous natural cast of a forefoot dates to the Upper Jurassic in central Neopangea (present-day Spain). The largest fossil forefoot ever discovered. If it belonged to a type similar to *Brachiosaurus*, it would have weighed 70 t, although this form has only been discovered in North America and Portugal, which were connected at the time. *See more: García-Ramos et al. 2006*

The prints of this group are known as *Brontopodus* but differ from somphospondylian footprints, in which claw II is more prominent than claw I.

The smallest

b) Unnamed: Some prints from the Upper Jurassic in central Neopangea (present-day Spain) measure 12–16 cm in length. The largest specimen may have been 2.1 m long and 43 kg in weight. *See more: García-Ramos et al. 2005; García-Ramos et al. 2006*

12 m

3m

Brachiosaurus sp.	Unnamed footprint	Unnamed footprint	*Europasaurus holgeri*
Riggs 1903	García-Ramos et al. 2006	García-Ramos et al. 2005	DFMMh/FV 157
26.5 m / 50 t	28 m / 70 t	2.8–3 m / 93–115 kg	6 m / 800 kg

25 m   30 m   35 m   40 m   45 m

Characteristics and habits

These small-headed dinosaurs had spatula-shaped (circular-crowned spatulate foliodonts), broad-spatulate or semi-cylindrical teeth, medium to long necks, five digits on each forefoot and hind foot, fore-feet with very long metacarpals, and large claws. They were quadrupeds with robust to very robust bodies and medium-length or relatively long tails. Titanosauriforms descended from macronarians and preceded somphospondylids.
Diet: phytophagous

Time range

Present from the Middle Jurassic to the late Upper Cretaceous (approx. 167.2–66 Ma), this group of sauropods lived for the longest time, appearing for 101.2 million years in the fossil record.

The smallest (Class: Large Grade I)

Europasaurus holgeri ("Holger Lüdtke's European lizard"), from the Upper Jurassic (Kimmeridgian, approx. 157.3–152.1 Ma) in north-central Neopangea (present-day Germany), was a truly small sauropod that would barely have been able to peer above a basketball hoop. It was less than 1/4 the length and 1/62 the weight of *Brachiosaurus* sp. and was the smallest Jurassic sauropod, as it inhabited islands. See more: *Windolf 1998; Sander et al. 2004, 2006; D'Emic 2012; Mannion et al. 2013*

The smallest juvenile specimens

Of the several *Europasaurus holgeri* calves known, specimen DFMMh/FV 291.9 was the smallest, approximately 1.45 m in length and weighing 15 kg. In contrast, the *Brachiosaurus* sp. calf SMA 0009 measured 2.45 m in length and weighed 55 kg and was originally considered a diplodocid. See more: *Carpenter & McIntosh 1994; Mateus, Laven & Knotschke in Sander et al. 2006; Carballido 2010; Carballido et al. 2012; Carballido & Sander 2013*

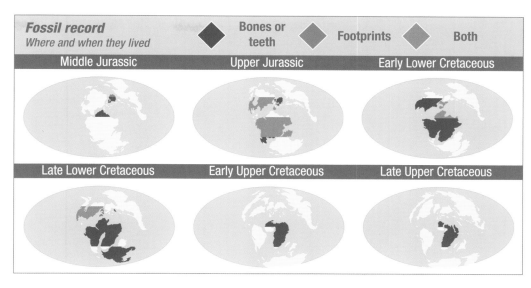

Fossil record Where and when they lived

◆ Bones or teeth   ◆ Footprints   ◆ Both

Middle Jurassic | Upper Jurassic | Early Lower Cretaceous

Late Lower Cretaceous | Early Upper Cretaceous | Late Upper Cretaceous

The most recent

Specimens Vb-646 (present-day Egypt) and OCP-DEK/GE 31 (present-day Morocco) are titanosauriforms that survived to the end of the Mesozoic Era, as both date to the late Upper Cretaceous (upper Maastrichtian, approx. 69–66 Ma). The most recent record after these reports is that of *Sonorasaurus thompsoni* ("Sonora Desert lizard") from the late Lower Cretaceous (upper Albian, approx. 106.7–100.5 Ma) in western Laurasia (present-day Arizona, USA). See more: *Rauhut & Werner 1997; Ratkevich 1998; Pereda-Suberbiola et al. 2004; Weishampel et al. 2004; D'Emic et al. 2016*

The oldest

Specimen NMS G 2004.31.1 dates to the Middle Jurassic (upper Bathonian, approx. 167.2–166.1 Ma) in north-central Neopangea (present-day Scotland, UK). It consists of a tooth similar to that of the primitive sauropod *Shunosaurus* or those of titanosauriformes. cf. *Ornithopsis leedsii* BMNH R1716 is another discovery from a later time (Callovian 166.1–163.5 Ma). See more: *Barrett 2006; Evans et al. 2006*

The strangest

Abydosaurus mcintoshi ("Abidos and paleontologist John S. McIntosh's lizard"), from the late Lower Cretaceous (middle Albian, approx. 106.7 Ma) in western Laurasia (present-day Utah, USA). Its teeth were much narrower than those of all other brachiosaurids, which may reflect a convergence with cylindrical-toothed sauropods that occurred because of a gradual change in the flora. It also displays a smaller nasal foramen. See more: *Chure, Britt, Whitlock & Wilson 2010*

The first published species?

Cetiosaurus brevis (1842) and *Pelorosaurus conybearei* (1849) may be somphospondylids, and if so, then the oldest report would be *Oplosaurus armatus*. All are from the early Lower Cretaceous (Valanginian, approx. 139.8–132.9 Ma) in central Laurasia (present-day England). See more: *Owen 1842; Melville 1849; Gervais 1852; Radley & Hutt 1993*

The most recently published species

Soriatitan golmayensis (2017) ("titan of Soria city and the Golmayo Formation") dates to the early Lower Cretaceous (Hauterivian, approx. 132.9–129.4 Ma) in central Laurasia (present-day Spain) and is similar to the North American brachiosaurids *Abydosaurus*, *Cedarosaurus*, and *Venenosaurus*. The informal name "Biconcavoposeidon" (2017) refers to some strange vertebrae from the Upper Jurassic (present-day Wyoming, USA). See more: *Royo-Torres et al. 2017; Taylor & Wedel 2017*

RECORD SMALLEST

Specimen: DFMMh/FV 157
(Sander et al. 2006)

Length: 6 m
Shoulder height: 1.7 m
Body mass: 800 kg
Material: fibula
ESR: ●●○○

Europasaurus holgeri
Sander et al. 2006

1:40

Juvenile
Europasaurus holgeri
DFMMh/FV 291.9

Titanosauriformes — Europasaurus
— Padillasaurus
— Giraffatitan
— Brachiosaurus
Somphospondyli

2 m   4 m   6 m   8 m

15 m

10 m

5 m

5 m   10 m   15 m   20 m

Unnamed

-

RECORD
LARGEST

Specimen: Uncatalogued

-

Length: 28 m
Shoulder height: 6.5 m
Body mass: 47 t
Material: incomplete femur
ESR: ●◗○○○

1:100

The largest (Class: Giant Grade I)

These unpublished remains, from the early Lower Cretaceous (Hauterivian, approx. 132.9–129.4 Ma) in central Laurasia (present-day France), are from an animal as long as a blue whale, or two buses and a car placed end to end; it weighed as much as a sperm whale and killer whale combined. The species, known informally as "Francoposeidon," has the longest femur ever found in Europe—2.2 m long—and includes another incomplete piece from a larger individual (see p. 144). It had not yet been published when this book went to press. See more: *Néraudeau et al. 2012*

Second place (tie)

Sauroposeidon proteles ("lizard earthquake god, perfect before the end"), from the late Lower Cretaceous (Aptian, approx. 125–113 Ma) in western Laurasia (present-day Oklahoma and Texas, USA). Its neck was extremely long, allowing it to reach food up to 16 m off the ground and making it one of the tallest dinosaurs. It was about 29 m long and weighed 40 t. Weighing nearly the same, but perhaps less long (25 m), *Fusuisaurus zhaoi* was a species from the early Late Cretaceous (Cenomanian, approx. 112.6–125.45 Ma) in eastern Laurasia (present-day China). See more: *Ostrom 1970; Wedel, Cifelli & Sanders 2000; Mo et al. 2006; D'Emic & Foreman 2012*

Footprints

a)

⊢ 1.75 m

The Largest

a) Unnamed: Found in a remote zone, it is the longest footprint known. There is another that was apparently larger; however, that was because the print was surrounded by mud marks. They date to the early Lower Cretaceous of eastern Gondwana (present-day Australia). See more: *Thulbom 2012; Salisbury et al. 2017*

The original prints of *Brontopodus* and *Oobardjidama* represent this group. *Chuxiongpus* is considered a junior synonym of *Brontopodus*.

b)

⊢ 5.8 cm

The smallest

b) Brontopodus sp.: Identical to those of *Brontopodus birdi*, although smaller in size, which suggests that they were from very young individuals of the species. They date to the late Lower Cretaceous of western Laurasia (present-day Texas, USA). See more: *Stanford 1998*

12 m

Unnamed species
ANG
28 m / 47 t

Unnamed footprint
BSM ?A
31 m / 72 t

4 m

***Brontopodus* sp.**
Standford 1998
1 m / 4 kg

"*Pleurocoelus*" cf. *valdensis*
MMM815/99
9 m / 2.4 t

25 m   30 m   35 m   40 m   45 m

Characteristics and habits

These dinosaurs had small heads, spatulate- or semi-cylindrical (circular-crowned spatulate folio-dont) or semi-cylindrical (cylindrodont) teeth, long to very long necks, five digits on each forefoot and hind foot, and large claws on the forefoot. They were quadrupeds with semi-robust to very robust bodies and medium-length tails. Somphospondylids descended from titanosauriforms and preceded euhelopodids and Titanosauria.
Diet: phytophagous

Time range

Present from the Upper Jurassic to the late Upper Cretaceous (approx. 152.1–66 Ma), appearing in the fossil record for 101.2 million years.

The smallest (Class: Large Grade III)

"Pleurocoelus" cf. valdensis ("hollow rib of Weal-den district") dates to the late Lower Cretaceous (Barremian, approx. 129.4–125 Ma) in central Laurasia (present-day Spain, England, and Portugal). Although unconfirmed, it has been suggested that it may be a valid species. It was 1/3 the length and 1/20 the weight of the largest somphospondylids. See more: *Ruiz-Omeñaca & Canudo 2005*

The smallest juvenile specimens

It is suspected that *Astrodon* sp. SMU 72146 were teeth of a sauropod calf or perhaps an ornithischian. It could have reached 2 m in length and weighed 47 kg. *Pleurocoelus nanus* specimens USNM 2263, USNM 5656, and USNM 5567 were juveniles of similar size, 3.8 m long and 175 kg in weight. See more: *Marsh 1888; Winkler et al. 1999*

The oldest

An unnamed species from the northwest area of Neopangea (present-day Cuba) dates from the Upper Jurassic (Oxfordian, approx. 163.5–157.3 Ma) See more: *de la Torre & Callejas 1949; Gasparini & Iturralde-Vinent 2006; Iturralde-Vinent & Ceballos-Izquierdo 2015; Apesteguía et al. 2019*

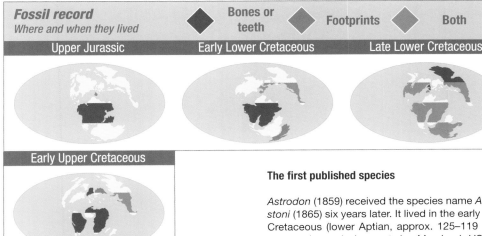

Fossil record *Where and when they lived*		Bones or teeth	Footprints	Both
Upper Jurassic		Early Lower Cretaceous		Late Lower Cretaceous

Early Upper Cretaceous

The strangest

Brontomerus mcintoshi ("thunder thighs of physicist/mathematician John 'Jack' Stanton McIntosh"), from the late Lower Cretaceous (Aptian, approx. 125–113 Ma) in western Laurasia (present-day Utah, USA). Like specimen BMNH R12713 (present-day England), this creature had a well-developed ilium, so its legs were presumably very strong, perhaps allowing it to defend itself or move through rugged terrain. See more: *Blows 1995; Taylor, Wedel & Cifelli 2011*

The most recent

Angolatitan adamastior ("mythological adamastor titan of Angola") lived in the early Upper Cretaceous (upper Turonian, approx. 91.8–89.8 Ma) in central Gondwana (present-day Angola). The last somphospondylids lived in a very arid desert. See more: *Mateus et al. 2011*

The first published species

Astrodon (1859) received the species name *A. johnstoni* (1865) six years later. It lived in the early Lower Cretaceous (lower Aptian, approx. 125–119 Ma) in western Laurasia (present-day Maryland, USA). See more: *Johnston 1859; Leidy 1865*

The most recently published species

Europatitan eastwoodi (2017) ("actor/director Clint Eastwood's European titan") and *Sibirotitan astrosacralis* ("Siberian titan with star-shaped sacrum") date to the late Lower Cretaceous (Albian, approx. 113–100.5 Ma) in central Laurasia (present-day Spain and Russia, respectively). See more: *Averianov et al. 2017; Fernández-Baldor et al. 2017*

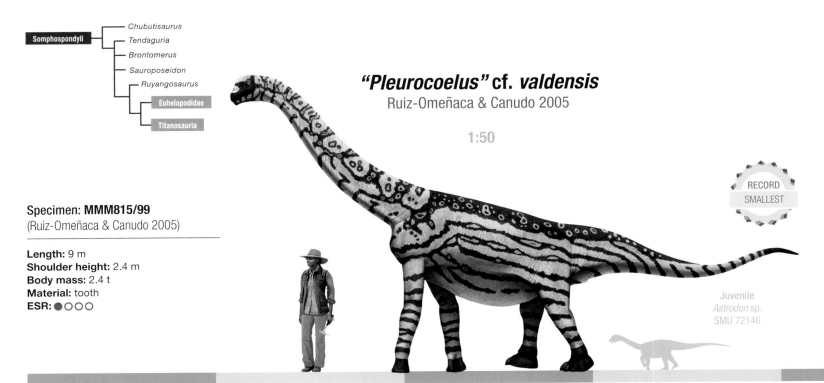

Somphospondyli
— Chubutisaurus
— Tendaguria
— Brontomerus
— Sauroposeidon
— Ruyangosaurus
— Euhelopodidae
— Titanosauria

"Pleurocoelus" cf. *valdensis*
Ruiz-Omeñaca & Canudo 2005

1:50

RECORD SMALLEST

Specimen: MMM815/99
(Ruiz-Omeñaca & Canudo 2005)

Length: 9 m
Shoulder height: 2.4 m
Body mass: 2.4 t
Material: tooth
ESR: ●○○○

Juvenile
Astrodon sp.
SMU 72146

2.5 m   5 m   7.5 m   10 m

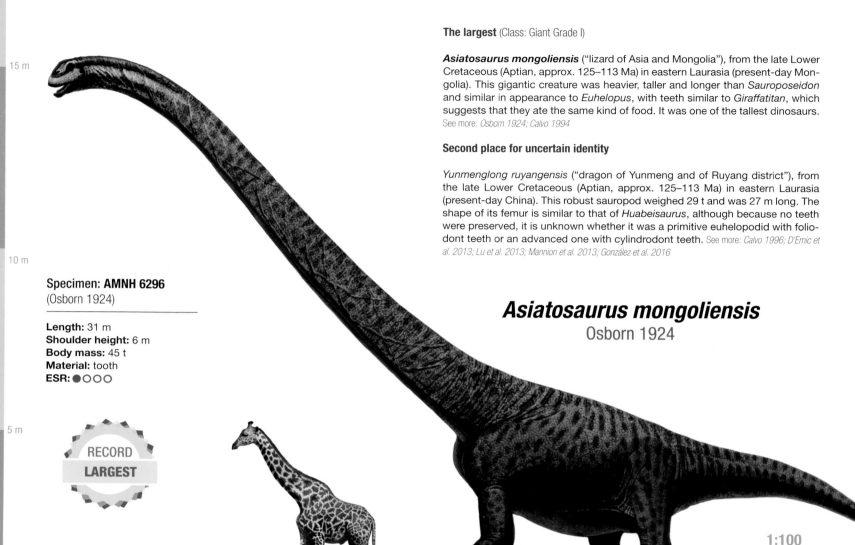

The largest (Class: Giant Grade I)

Asiatosaurus mongoliensis ("lizard of Asia and Mongolia"), from the late Lower Cretaceous (Aptian, approx. 125–113 Ma) in eastern Laurasia (present-day Mongolia). This gigantic creature was heavier, taller and longer than *Sauroposeidon* and similar in appearance to *Euhelopus*, with teeth similar to *Giraffatitan*, which suggests that they ate the same kind of food. It was one of the tallest dinosaurs. See more: *Osborn 1924; Calvo 1994*

Second place for uncertain identity

Yunmenglong ruyangensis ("dragon of Yunmeng and of Ruyang district"), from the late Lower Cretaceous (Aptian, approx. 125–113 Ma) in eastern Laurasia (present-day China). This robust sauropod weighed 29 t and was 27 m long. The shape of its femur is similar to that of *Huabeisaurus*, although because no teeth were preserved, it is unknown whether it was a primitive euhelopodid with foliodont teeth or an advanced one with cylindrodont teeth. See more: *Calvo 1996; D'Emic et al. 2013; Lu et al. 2013; Mannion et al. 2013; González et al. 2016*

Specimen: **AMNH 6296**
(Osborn 1924)

Length: 31 m
Shoulder height: 6 m
Body mass: 45 t
Material: tooth
ESR: ●○○○

RECORD
LARGEST

Asiatosaurus mongoliensis
Osborn 1924

1:100

Footprints

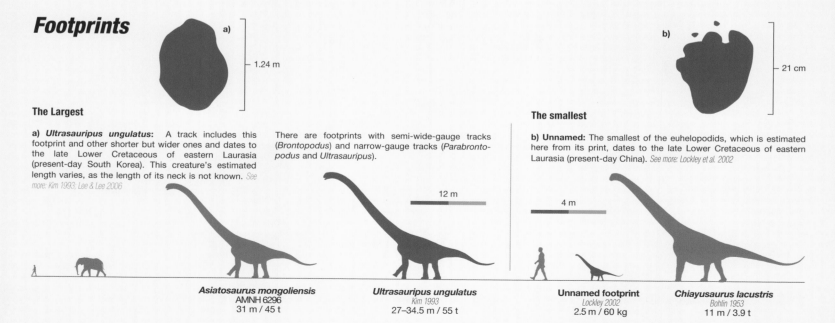

a) — 1.24 m

b) — 21 cm

The Largest

a) *Ultrasauripus ungulatus*: A track includes this footprint and other shorter but wider ones and dates to the late Lower Cretaceous of eastern Laurasia (present-day South Korea). This creature's estimated length varies, as the length of its neck is not known. *See more: Kim 1993, Lee & Lee 2006*

There are footprints with semi-wide-gauge tracks (*Brontopodus*) and narrow-gauge tracks (*Parabrontopodus* and *Ultrasauripus*).

The smallest

b) Unnamed: The smallest of the euhelopodids, which is estimated here from its print, dates to the late Lower Cretaceous of eastern Laurasia (present-day China). *See more: Lockley et al. 2002*

12 m

4 m

Asiatosaurus mongoliensis
AMNH 6296
31 m / 45 t

Ultrasauripus ungulatus
Kim 1993
27–34.5 m / 55 t

Unnamed footprint
Lockley 2002
2.5 m / 60 kg

Chiayusaurus lacustris
Bohlin 1953
11 m / 3.9 t

25 m   30 m   35 m   40 m   45 m

Characteristics and habits

These dinosaurs had short, medium-sized heads, spatulate- or broad-spatulate (circular-crowned spatulate foliodont) or cylindrical (cylindrodont) teeth with or without serrated denticles, long to very long necks, five digits on each forefoot and hind foot, and large claws on the forefeet. They were quadrupeds with robust to very robust bodies and medium-length tails. Euhelopodids descended from somphospondylids

The three types of euhelopodid teeth were comparable to those of *Brachiosaurus*, *Camarasaurus*, and *Diplodocus*, possibly because they occupied different ecological niches than macronarians, titanosauriforms, and diplodocoidea, all of which were absent in Asia, which was relatively isolated from the Middle Jurassic to the early Lower Cretaceous.
Diet: phytophagous or durophagous-phytophagous

Fossil record
Where and when they lived

◆ Bones or teeth   ◆ Footprints   ◆ Both

Middle Jurassic	Upper Jurassic	Early Lower Cretaceous
Late Lower Cretaceous	Early Upper Cretaceous	Late Upper Cretaceous

Time range

Present from the Middle Jurassic to the late Upper Cretaceous (approx. 166.1–66 Ma), appearing in the fossil record for 100.1 million years.

The smallest (Class: Very large Grade I)

Chiayusaurus lacustris ("lake-lizard of Chiayuquan city"), from the late Lower Cretaceous (Aptian, approx. 125–113 Ma) in eastern Laurasia (present-day China), was similar in size to an Asian elephant. The species is based on teeth alone, including some pieces from the Upper Jurassic. The largest specimens were nearly 1/3 the length and 1/11 the weight of *Asiatosaurus mongoliensis*. See more: *Bohlin 1953; Dong 1992*

The smallest juvenile specimen

Numerous *Phuwiangosaurus sirinhornae* ("lizard of Phu Wiang and Princess Maha Chakri Sirindhorn") calves of different sizes date to the late Lower Cretaceous (Barremian, approx. 129.4–125 Ma) and lived in the paleocontinent Cimmeria (present-day Thailand). The smallest may have been 1.7 m in length and weighed 23 kg. See more: *Martin 1994; Martin et al. 1994*

The oldest

cf. "*Camarasaurus*" sp. from the Middle Jurassic (Callovian, approx. 166.1–163.5 Ma) in eastern Paleoasia (present-day Russia). They consist of some teeth similar to those of *Euhelopus*, which, like the mamenchisaurids *Omeisaurus* and the macronarians *Camarasaurus*, had broad, spatula-shaped teeth and strong jaws, perhaps because they consumed tougher plants than other sauropods. See more: *Calvo 1994; Kurzanov, Efimov & Gubin 2003; Button, Barrett & Rayfield 2016*

The most recent

Gannansaurus sinensis ("lizard of Gannan county in China"), from the late Upper Cretaceous (Maastrichtian, approx. 72.1–66 Ma) in eastern Laurasia (present-day China). It was an enormous dinosaur almost 26 m long and weighing 25 t. See more: *Lu et al. 2013*

The strangest

Erketu ellisoni ("lizard of the god Erketu and of paleontologist Mick Ellison"), from the early Upper Cretaceous (Cenomanian, approx. 100.5–93.9 Ma) in eastern Laurasia (present-day Mongolia). It had the proportionately longest neck relative to its body of any neosauropod, because its cervical vertebrae were extremely elongated. It was 16 m long and weighed 5.6 t approximately.

Mongolosaurus haplodon ("Mongolian single-tooth"), from the late Lower Cretaceous (Aptian-Albian, approx. 125–100.5 Ma) in eastern Laurasia (present-day Mongolia). It had unique cylindrical but serrated teeth. Some authors consider it an euhelopodid, others a lithostrotian. See more: *Gilmore 1933; Calvo 1996; Ksepka & Norell 2006, 2010; Mannion 2011; D'Emic et al. 2013; Mannion et al. 2013*

An enigmatic tooth known informally as "Oharasisaurus," from the late Lower Cretaceous in eastern Laurasia (present-day Japan), was from a small sauropod no longer than 4.5 m and weighing 160 kg. The origin of the name is a mystery, although there is a Japanese paleontologist named Masaaki Ohara, so they may be related. See more: *Ohara 2008*

The first published species

Asiatosaurus mongoliensis (1924) was the first sauropod reported in eastern Asia; however, Otto Zdansky apparently uncovered the remains of *Euhelopus zdanskyi* (1929) in 1922, so it may have been discovered first. See more: *Osborn 1924; Wiman 1929; Romer 1956*

The most recently published species

Tambatitanis amicitiae (2014) ("friendly titan of Tamba province"), from the late Lower Cretaceous (lower Albian, approx. 106.7–100.5 Ma) in eastern Laurasia (present-day Japan). This is the sauropod with the largest chevrons in proportion to its size. See more: *Saegusa & Ikeda 2014*

Chiayusaurus lacustris
Bohlin 1953

Specimen: uncatalogued
(Bohlin 1953)

Length: 11 m
Shoulder height: 2.75 m
Body mass: 3.9 t
Material: tooth
ESR: ●○○○

RECORD SMALLEST

1:70

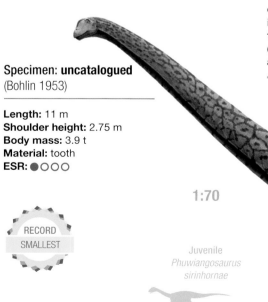

Juvenile *Phuwiangosaurus sirinhornae*

Euhelopodidae	Euhelopus
	Asiatosaurus
	Huabeisaurus

3.5 m   7 m   10.5 m   14 m

5 m   10 m   15 m   20 m

15 m

10 m

5 m

Unnamed
McLachlan & McMillan 1976

Specimen: PEM
(McLachlan & McMillan 1976)

Length: 25 m
Shoulder height: 5.5 m
Body mass: 30 t
Material: incomplete femur
ESR: ●○○○

RECORD LARGEST

The largest (Class: Giant Grade I)

An unnamed titanosaur from the early Lower Cretaceous (Berriasian, approx. 145–139.8 Ma) in central Gondwana (present-day South Africa), it is known solely from an incomplete femur. The piece is very large, with a circumference of 92.1 cm. The animal may have been as long as two city buses end to end and weighed as much as five African elephants combined. If we calculate the weight based on the minimum circumference of its femur, we arrive at 55 t; however, this method is not reliable, as it yields a result that is nearly double the result produced by the volumetric method. *Dreadnoughtus*, for example, was estimated to have weighed 59 t but probably weighed just 35 t. See more: *McLachlan & McMillan 1976; Anderson et al. 1985; Paul 1988; Lacovara et al. 2014; Bates et al. 2015*

The largest sauropods?

Bruhathkayosaurus matleyi from the late Upper Cretaceous (Maastrichtian, approx. 72.1–66 Ma) in Hindustan (present-day India). At first, the larger specimen was interpreted as a theropod tibia, but it appears more like a sauropod fibula. Informally, the animal was estimated to have been 45 m long and to have weighed 139–220 t, but it may have been 37 m long and weighed 95 t. However, its true nature is very much in doubt, and some now speculate that the pieces were fossilized tree trunks that unfortunately disintegrated in a flood. See more: *Yadagiri & Ayyasami 1989; Anonymous 2000; Krause et al. 2006; Hone, Farke & Wedel 2016; Mortimer*; Taylor & Wedel**

1:90

Footprints

a)

— 80 cm

~24.2 cm

b)

The Largest

a) *Brontopodus* sp., from the early Lower Cretaceous in eastern Gondwana (present-day Australia). The shape is different from that of a somphospondyl and so may have belonged to a primitive titanosaur. See more: *Thulborn et al. 1994*

Primitive titanosaurs left prints with very large forefeet and semi-wide- or wide-gauge tracks. The only named ichnogenus in this group is known as *Titanosaurimanus*.

The smallest

b) Unnamed: A print from the early Lower Cretaceous in central Laurasia (present-day Spain) has been identified as a possible titanosaur. See more: *Canudo et al. 2008*

4 m

12 m

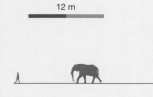

Unnamed species
PEM
25 m / 30 t

Brontopodus sp.
Thulborn et al.1994
26.5 m / 34 t

Unnamed footprint
Canudo et al. 2008
7.5 m / 1 t

Unnamed species
MLP 46-VIII-21-2
8 m / 1.2 t

25 m   30 m   35 m   40 m

Characteristics and habits

These dinosaurs have small, short heads, spatulate (circular-crowned foliodont) teeth, long to very long necks, five digits on each forefoot and hind foot, and large claws on the forefeet. They were quadrupeds with robust to very robust bodies and medium to long tails. Titanosaurs descended from somphospondylids.
Diet: phytophagous

Time range

They were present from the early Lower Cretaceous to the late Upper Cretaceous (approx. 145–66 Ma), appearing for 79 million years in the fossil record.

The smallest (Class: Large Grade II)

Specimen MLP 46-VIII-21-2 was an adult individual that weighed about as much as a giraffe and belongs to an as-yet-unnamed species. It lived in the early Lower Cretaceous (Coniacian, approx. 89.8–86.3 Ma) in western Gondwana (present-day Argentina). It was 1/3 as long as and weighed 1/25 as much as UFMA 1.10.246. *Clasmodosaurus spatula* may have been even smaller, but as it was identified from teeth alone, it is difficult to establish a record. See more: *Ameghino 1898; Bonaparte 1996; Filipinni, Otero & Gasparini 2016*

The smallest juvenile specimen

Some teeth dating to the late Lower Cretaceous (upper Albian, approx. 106.7–100.5 Ma) in western Gondwana (present-day Argentina) may have belonged to a small sauropod measuring 4.9 m in length and weighing 310 kg. See more: *Otero & Pol 2013*

Titanosauria
— Andesaurus
— Diamantinasaurus
— Xianshanosaurus
— Yongjinglong
— Lithostrotia

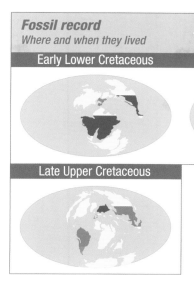

Fossil record
Where and when they lived

◆ Bones or teeth   ◆ Footprints   ◆ Both

Early Lower Cretaceous | Late Lower Cretaceous | Early Upper Cretaceous
Late Upper Cretaceous

The oldest

Triunfosaurus leonardii and specimen DGEO-CTG-UFPE 7517 date to the early Lower Cretaceous (Berriasian, approx. 145–139.8 Ma) in western Gondwana (present-day Brazil). The two are known to be different species because the former was large, approximately 20.8 m long and weighing 17 t, while the latter was a subadult specimen 9 m long and weighing 1.5 t, although the adult is estimated as having been 40–50% larger. A large femur from the same period, but from South Africa, has been referred to as a titanosaur, but it is not certain whether or not it is one. See more: *McLachlan & McMillan 1976; Paul 1988; Ghilardi et al. 2016; de Souza-Carvalho et al. 2017*

The most recent

Specimen MNHN 1972-3 is a caudal vertebra that dates to the late Upper Cretaceous (Maastrichtian, approx. 72.1–66 Ma) and lived in central Laurasia (present-day Spain). See more: *Pereda-Suberbiola & Ruiz-Omeñaca 2001*

The strangest

Yongjinglong datangi ("dragon of Yongjing country, the Tang Dynasty, and Zhi-Lu Tang"), from the late Lower Cretaceous (Aptian-Albian, approx. 125–100.5 Ma) in eastern Laurasia (present-day China), had a very strange shape, with very short forearms and an extremely long, robust scapula, making it appear very different from any other known sauropod. It is difficult to classify, as in addition to being incomplete, it displays some characteristics similar to euhelopodids and the saltasauroid *Opisthocoelicaudia*. Here it is considered a primitive titanosaur, owing to its foliodont teeth. See more: *Saegusa & Ikeda 2014; Averianov & Sues 2017*

The first published species

Aepisaurus elephantinus (1852) ("tall, elephant-like lizard"), from the late Lower Cretaceous (Albian, approx. 113–100.5 Ma) in central Laurasia (present-day France). It is based on an incomplete humerus. See more: *Gervais 1852*

The most recently published species

Liaoningotitan sinesis (2018) ("titan of China's Liaoning Province") dates to the early Lower Cretaceous (Cenomanian, approx. 100.5–93.9 Ma) in eastern Laurasia (present-day China). Earlier, the name was used informally for several years. See more: *Zhou et al. 2018*

Unnamed
Filipinni et al. 2016

Specimen: MLP 46-VIII-21-2
(Filipinni et al. 2016)

Length: 8 m
Shoulder height: 1.9 m
Body mass: 1.2 t
Material: Ilium and sacral vertebrae
ESR: ●○○○

1:50

RECORD SMALLEST

Juvenile titanosaur

2.5 m   5 m   7.5m   10 m

3 m   6 m   9 m   12 m   15 m

Argyrosaurus superbus
Lydekker 1893

Specimen: MLP 77-V-29-1
(Lydekker 1893)

Length: 21 m
Shoulder height: 4.7 m
Body mass: 26 t
Material: partial skeleton
ESR: ●○○○

9 m

6 m

1:70

3 m

RECORD
LARGEST

The largest (Class: Giant Grade I)

Argyrosaurus superbus ("proud silver lizard"), from the late Upper Cretaceous (upper Campanian, approx. 83.6–72.1 Ma) in western Gondwana (present-day Argentina). Several bones have been attributed to this species; however, most have ultimately been assigned to other titanosaurs. The femur MLP 27, which has been attributed to this species, belongs to an even larger specimen (possibly around 22 m in length and 29 t in weight); the problem is that it is from an earlier period (lower Santonian, approx. 86.3–85 Ma), and its identification is doubtful. *Argyrosaurus superbus* was about as long as two buses end to end and weighed more than six Asian elephants. See more: *Lydekker 1893; Huene 1929; Mannion & Otero 2012, Mortimer**

Close competitors

cf. *Hypselosaurus* sp. IPSN-19, from the Upper Cretaceous in central Laurasia (present-day Spain), and aff. *Malawisaurus* sp. UFMA 1.20.473, from western Gondwana (present-day Brazil), were approximately the size of *Argyrosaurus*. The former, based on a caudal vertebra, could have reached 20 m in length and 25 t in weight, while the latter, compared to *Malawisaurus*, may have been longer (22.5 m) but was lighter (24 t). See more: *Casanovas et al. 1987; Carvalho, Medeiros & Lindoso 2007*

Footprints

a)
— 90 cm

b)
— 10 cm

The Largest

a) *Sauropodichnus giganteus*, from the early Upper Cretaceous of western Gondwana (present-day Argentina). The largest specimen has a round shape because it is poorly preserved and surrounded by mud marks. See more: *Calvo 1991; Calvo & Mazzeta 2004*

The footprints of primitive lithostrotians have been identified as Sauropodichnus or, more frequently, as *Brontopodus*.

The smallest

b) Unnamed: Some late Upper Cretaceous prints from Hindustan (present-day India) measure 10–50 cm in length. The largest specimen could have been 10 m long and weighed 3.1 t. See more: *Ghevariya & Srikami 1991*

10 m

2 m

Argyrosaurus superbus
MLP 77-V-29-1
21 m / 26 t

Sauropodichnus giganteus
Calvo 1991
26 m / 40 t

Unnamed footprint
Ghevariya & Srikami 1991
2.5 m / 50 kg

Magyarosaurus dacus
FGGUB R.1992
4.9 m / 520 kg

18 m   21 m   24 m   27 m   30 m   33 m

Fossil record
Where and when they lived

◆ Bones or teeth	◆ Footprints	◆ Both

Late Lower Cretaceous	Early Upper Cretaceous	Late Upper Cretaceous

Characteristics and habits

These dinosaurs had small, short heads, cylindrical teeth ("D"-shaped cylindrodonts) or slightly spatulate teeth in the most primitive forms, long to very long necks, and five digits on each forefoot and hind foot. They were quadrupeds with semi-robust to very robust bodies, medium to long tails, and osteoderms in some species. Lithostrotians descended from titanosaurs and preceded saltasauroids.
Diet: phytophagous

Time range

These animals were present from the early Lower Cretaceous to the late Upper Cretaceous (approx. 145–66 Ma), appearing for approximately 78.1 million years in the fossil record.

The smallest (Class: Large Grade I)

Magyarosaurus dacus ("lizard of Magyar and Dacia town") lived in the late Upper Cretaceous (upper Maastrichtian, approx. 69–66 Ma) in central Laurasia (present-day Romania). It was small in size, slightly larger than a panda bear, because it lived on islands. It was 1/5 the length and 1/50 the weight of *Argyrosaurus superbus*. See more: *Nopcsa 1915; Huene 1932; Stein et al. 2010*

The smallest juvenile specimen

Laplatasaurus sp. MCF-PVPH-272, from the late Upper Cretaceous (lower Campanian, approx. 83.6–77.8 Ma) in western Gondwana (present-day Argentina), was a calf 39 cm long; it weighed approximately 230 g. It had a protuberance on its snout known as an "egg tooth," to help it break out of the egg when it hatched. Eggs associated with MCF-PVPH-272 have popularly been assigned to *Saltasaurus*, but the shells are like *Megaloolithus* and not *Faveoloolithus*, which suggests that they did not come from a saltasauroid nest. See more: *Chiappe, Salgado & Coria 2001; Garcia 2007*

The oldest

The eggs and some elongated osteoderms, dated to between the Upper Jurassic and early Lower Cretaceous (approx. 145 Ma), make this the oldest lithostrotian ever recorded. See more: *Bond & Bromley 1970; Munyikwa et al. 1998*

The most recent

Hypselosaurus sp. and MPZ 99/143 (present-day Spain), cf. *Magyarosaurus* sp. (present-day Romania), *Jainosaurus septentrionalis*, *Titanosaurus blandfordi*, *T. indicus*, *T. rahioliensis* (present-day India), and an indeterminate specimen (present-day Jordan) are from localities at the end of the Mesozoic era, in the late Upper Cretaceous (upper Maastrichtian, approx. 69–66 Ma). See more: *Lydekker 1877, 1879; Huene 1932; Huene & Matley 1933; Lapparent 1947; Mathur & Pant 1986; Casanovas et al. 1987; Mathur 1987; Mathur & Srivastava 1987; Canudo 2001; Wilson, Mustafa & Zalmout 2006; Codrea et al. 2010; Csiki et al. 2010*

The strangest

Agustinia ligabuei (after Agustin Martinelli and Dr. Giancarlo Ligabue), from the late Lower Cretaceous (lower Albian, approx. 113–107 Ma) in western Gondwana (present-day Argentina). Some poorly preserved bones were identified as probable osteoderms; they were spiny-shaped, like defensive weapons, and up to 64 cm long. See more: *Bonaparte 1999; Mannion et al. 2013; Bellardini & Cerda 2016*

The first published species

Titanosaurus indicus (1877) ("titan lizard of India"), from the late Upper Cretaceous (upper Maastrichtian, approx. 69–66 Ma) in Hindustan (present-day India). The holotype specimen K20/315–6 was lost but luckily was found again. See more: *Lydekker 1877; Mohabey et al. 2012, Mohabey et al. 2013*

The most recently published species

Baalsaurus mansillai and *Volgatitan simbirskiensis* (2018), from western Gondwana and central Laurasia (present-day Argentina and European Russia), respectively. See more: *Averianov & Efimov 2018; Calvo & Gonzalez-Riga 2018*

Magyarosaurus dacus
Nopcsa 1915

Lithostrotia
— Malawisaurus
— Antarctosaurus
— Rapetosaurus
— Aeolosaurus
— Argyrosaurus
Saltasauroidea

RECORD SMALLEST

Specimen: FGGUB R.1992
(Nopcsa 1915)

Length: 5.4 m
Shoulder height: 1.2 m
Body mass: 520 kg
Material: femur
ESR: ●●○○

1:40

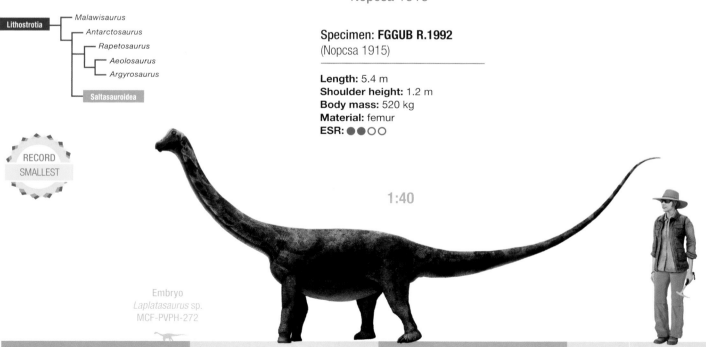

Embryo
Laplatasaurus sp.
MCF-PVPH-272

2 m   4 m   6 m   8 m

6 m   12 m   18 m   24 m

RECORD
LARGEST

Specimen: MLP-DP 46-VIII-21-3
(Mazzetta et al. 2004)

Length: 36 m
Shoulder height: 7 m
Body mass: 80 t
Material: incomplete femur
ESR: ●●○○○

1:130

The largest (Class: Giant Grade II)

cf. *Argentinosaurus* ("Argentina lizard from the Huincul Formation"), from the early Upper Cretaceous (upper Cenomanian, approx. 97.2–93.9 Ma) in western Gondwana (present-day Argentina). Specimen MLP-DP 46-VIII-21-3 is an incomplete femur measuring 1.75 m in length that would have been 2.7 m when complete (see p. 144). This indicates that it would have been slightly larger than the holotype of *Argentinosaurus huinculensis*. It was as long as three city buses placed end to end and weighed as much as two sperm whales combined. It may have been up to 17 m tall, which would make it one of the tallest four-legged dinosaurs. See more: *Bonaparte & Coria 1993; Bonaparte 1996; Mazzetta et al. 2004*

The fight for second place

The holotype of *Argentinosaurus huinculensis* ("Argentinean lizard of the Huincul Formation"), from the early Upper Cretaceous (upper Cenomanian, approx. 91.85 Ma) in western Gondwana (present-day Argentina). Measuring 35 m in length and weighing 75 t, it was significantly larger than *Patagotitan mayorum* and *Puertasaurus reuili*, which at the time were believed to surpass *Argentinosaurus* in size. See more: *Novas et al. 2005; Carballido et al. 2017*

cf. *Argentinosaurus*
Bonaparte & Coria 1993

Footprints

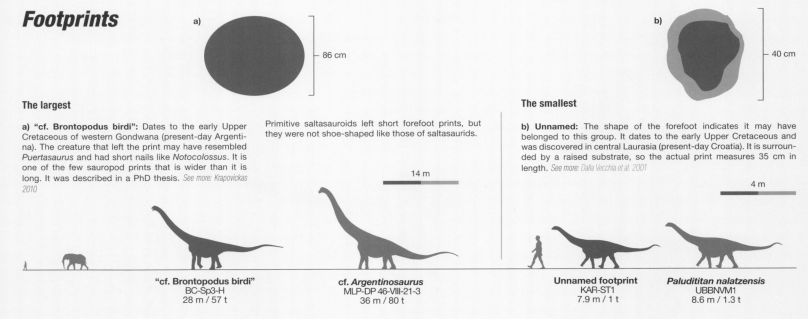

a)

├─ 86 cm

b)

├─ 40 cm

The largest

a) "cf. Brontopodus birdi": Dates to the early Upper Cretaceous of western Gondwana (present-day Argentina). The creature that left the print may have resembled *Puertasaurus* and had short nails like *Notocolossus*. It is one of the few sauropod prints that is wider than it is long. It was described in a PhD thesis. *See more: Krapovickas 2010*

Primitive saltasauroids left short forefoot prints, but they were not shoe-shaped like those of saltasaurids.

The smallest

b) Unnamed: The shape of the forefoot indicates it may have belonged to this group. It dates to the early Upper Cretaceous and was discovered in central Laurasia (present-day Croatia). It is surrounded by a raised substrate, so the actual print measures 35 cm in length. *See more: Dalla Vecchia et al. 2001*

14 m

4 m

"cf. Brontopodus birdi"
BC-Sp3-H
28 m / 57 t

cf. *Argentinosaurus*
MLP-DP 46-VIII-21-3
36 m / 80 t

Unnamed footprint
KAR-ST1
7.9 m / 1 t

Paludititan nalatzensis
UBBNVM1
8.6 m / 1.3 t

Characteristics and habits

These dinosaurs had medium to large heads, cylindrical teeth (D-shaped cylindrodont), short to long necks, five digits on each forefoot and hind foot, with more phalanges in the feet than saltasaurids, and no claws on the forefeet. They were quadrupeds and had semi-robust to very robust bodies and medium to long tails; some species had osteoderms as well. Saltasauroids descended from primitive lithostrotians and preceded saltasaurids.
Diet: phytophagous

Time range

They were present from the late Lower Cretaceous to the late Upper Cretaceous (approx. 129.4–69 Ma), appearing for 60.4 million years in the fossil record.

The smallest (Class: Large Grade III)

Paludititan nalatzensis ("swamp titan of Nalat-Vad") lived in the late Upper Cretaceous (upper Maastrichtian, approx. 69–66 Ma) in central Laurasia (present-day Romania). As long as two cars and slightly heavier than a giraffe, it was 1/4 the length and 1/60 the weight of cf. *Argentinosaurus*. See more: *Csiki et al. 2010*

The smallest juvenile specimen

Specimen UNPSJB-Pv 581, from the late Upper Cretaceous (upper Cenomanian, approx. 97.2–89.6 Ma) in western Gondwana (present-day Argentina), was similar to *Argentinosaurus* and more derived than *Epachthosaurus*. It may have been 7.1 m long and weighed some 790 kg. It is known as "Taxon B." See more: *Sciutto & Martinez 2001; Ibiricu et al. 2011*

The oldest

Rukwatitan bisepultus ("twice-buried titan of Lake Rukwa") dates to the late Lower Cretaceous (Aptian, approx. 129.4–127.2 Ma) in central Gondwana (present-day Tanzania). See more: *Gorscak et al. 2014*

The most recent

Puertasaurus reuili ("Pablo Puerta and Santiago Reuil's lizard") dates to the late Upper Cretaceous (lower Maastrichtian, approx. 72.1–69 Ma) and lived in western Gondwana (present-day Argentina). Its vertebrae were wider than those of any other sauropod. A femur recorded as MPM-Pv.39 was contemporary and, based on its size (2.22 m long, with a 99-cm minimum shaft circumference), may have belonged to the same species. See more: *Lacovara et al. 2004; Novas et al. 2005*

The first published species

"Antarctosaurus" giganteus ("giant southern lizard") (1929), from the early Upper Cretaceous (upper Coniacian, approx. 88.5–83.6 Ma) in western Gondwana (present-day Argentina). It is uncertain whether it belonged to this group; if not, the first to be named would have been *Epachthosaurus sciuttoi* (1990). See more: *Huene 1929; Powell 1990*

The strangest

Futalognkosaurus dukei ("giant chief lizard of Duke Energy Argentina"), from the early Upper Cretaceous (Turonian, approx. 91.85–89.8 Ma) in western Gondwana (present-day Argentina). Its appearance was unlike that of any other titanosaur, so estimating its size was a challenge, despite the discovery of a rather complete skeleton. Its pelvis was proportionately very wide and its vertebrae very similar to those of *Alamosaurus*, so the two would have been similar in appearance. Its relative, *Puertasaurus reuili*, may have been even stranger, but is known only from some bone fragments. See more: *Novas et al. 2005; Calvo et al. 2007, 2008*

The most recently published species

Mansourasaurus shahinae and *Choconsaurus baileywillisi* (2018): present-day Egypt and Argentina, respectively. See more: *Sallam et al. 2018; Simón et al. 2018*

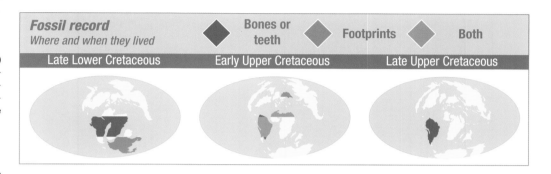

Fossil record — Where and when they lived. Bones or teeth / Footprints / Both. Late Lower Cretaceous / Early Upper Cretaceous / Late Upper Cretaceous

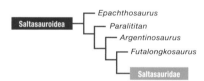

Saltasauroidea — Epachthosaurus, Paralititan, Argentinosaurus, Futalongkosaurus, Saltasauridae

Paludititan nalatzensis
Csiki et al. 2010

Specimen: UBBNVM1
(Csiki et al. 2010)

Length: 8.6 m
Shoulder height: 1.7 m
Body mass: 1.3 t
Material: partial skeleton
ESR: ●●●○

1:50

Juvenile GSI/GC/2901-2904

RECORD SMALLEST

2.5 m 5 m 7.5 m 10 m

5 m   10 m   15 m   20 m

Alamosaurus sanjuanensis
Gilmore 1922

RECORD
LARGEST

15 m

10 m

1:100

5 m

The largest (Class: Giant Grade I)

Alamosaurus sanjuanensis ("lizard of the Ojo Álamo Formation and San Juan County"), from the late Upper Cretaceous (upper Campanian and lower Maastrichtian, approx. 77.8–69 Ma) in western Laurasia (present-day New Mexico, Texas, and Utah, USA). Numerous individuals exist, but specimen SMP VP-1850 was the largest of all; it was longer than two city buses end to end and must have weighed as much as six African elephants combined. An incomplete femur (present-day Mexico) that was mistaken for a tibia was thought to be a much larger individual, but the piece is now under review. See more: *Rivera-Sylva et al. 2009; Fowler & Sullivan 2011; Ramírez-Velasco & Molina-Pérez manuscript in prep.; Hartmann**

Close rivals

Notocolossus gonzalezparejasi and *Dreadnoughtus schrani* (present-day Argentina) were very similar in size to *Alamosaurus*, the first measuring 28 m in length and 40 t in weight, and the second 24 m in length and 35 t in weight. Also very similar is FSAC-KK 7000 (present-day Morocco), 24.5 m long and weighing 34 t, as well as an unnamed titanosaur (present-day Honduras), at 25 m long and weighing 33 t. See more: *Fowler & Sullivan 2011; Lacovara et al. 2014; Gónzalez-Riga et al. 2016; Ibrahim et al. 2016; Zuñiga 2015*

Specimen: **SMP VP-1850**
(Fowler & Sullivan 2011)

Length: 26 m
Shoulder height: 6 m
Body mass: 38 t
Material: cervical vertebrae
ESR: ●○○○

Footprints

a)

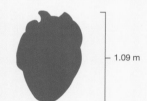

— 1.09 m

b)

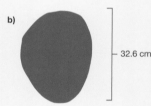

— 32.6 cm

The Largest

a) Unnamed: Dates to the early Upper Cretaceous of eastern Laurasia (present-day Mongolia). The saltasaurids of Asia were similar to Opisthocoelicaudia. It is a natural cast that has only been mentioned, not described. See more: *Ishigaki 2016; Nakajima et al. 2017*

Saltasauroids left forefoot prints that resembled a shoe print. The ichnogenus *Titanopodus* represents this group.

The smallest

b) Unnamed: Because this print dates to the early Upper Cretaceous and was discovered in western Laurasia (present-day Mexico), it was likely left by a saltasaurid similar to *Alamosaurus*. It was presented in a thesis. See more: *Servín Pichardo 2013*

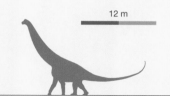

12 m

4 m

Unnamed footprint
Ishigaki et al. 2009
24 m / 32 t

Alamosaurus sanjuanensis
SMP VP-1850
26 m / 38 t

Bonatitan reigi
MACN RN 821
6 m / 600 kg

Unnamed footprint
Servín Pichardo 2013
7.2 m / 1.25 t

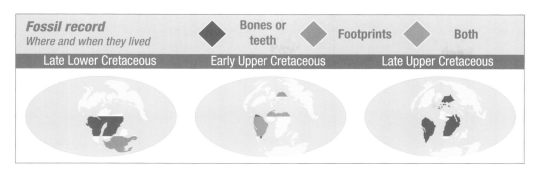

Fossil record
Where and when they lived

Bones or teeth ◆   Footprints ◆   Both ◆

Late Lower Cretaceous | Early Upper Cretaceous | Late Upper Cretaceous

Characteristics and habits

These dinosaurs had medium to large heads, cylindrical teeth (D-shaped cylindrodont), short to long necks, five digits on each forefoot and hind foot, fewer phalanges in the feet, and no claws on the forefeet. They were quadrupeds with semi-robust to very robust bodies and medium to long tails; some species also had osteoderms. Saltasaurids descended from primitive saltasauroids.
Diet: phytophagous

Time range

They were present from the late Lower Cretaceous to the late Upper Cretaceous (approx. 129.4–66 Ma), appearing for 63.4 million years in the fossil record.

The smallest (Class: Large Grade I)

Bonatitan reigi ("paleontologists José Bonaparte and Osvaldo Reig's titan") lived in the late Upper Cretaceous (upper Campanian, approx. 77.8–72.1 Ma) in western Gondwana (present-day Argentina). It was comparable in size to a saltwater crocodile and was 1/4 the length and 1/63 the weight of *Alamosaurus sanjuanensis*. It was the smallest non-island-dwelling sauropod of the Cretaceous. See more: *Martinelli & Forasiepi 2004; Gallina & Carabajal 2015*

The smallest juvenile specimen

Specimen NSM60104403-20554450 from the late Lower Cretaceous (upper Aptian, approx. 119–113 Ma) in eastern Laurasia (present-day Mongolia) was an embryo 30 cm long and weighing 125 g. It has been identified as a saltasaurid, as the egg found in association was the *Faveoloolithus* type. See more: *Grellet-Tinner et al. 2011; Kim, Sim, Kim & Grellet-Tinner 2012*

The oldest

Some remains known as "the Smokejacks sauropod" (MPEF V 1698) have been identified as a saltasaurid dating to the late Lower Cretaceous (lower Barremian, approx. 129.4–127.2 Ma) in central Laurasia (present-day England). See more: *Rivett 1953; Rivett 1956; Benton & Spencer 1995; França et al. 2016*

The most recent

P-35957, SMP VP-1625, and SMP VP-1494 are remains attributed to *Alamosaurus sanjuanensis* that date to the late Upper Cretaceous (upper Maastrichtian, approx. 66 Ma) in central Laurasia (present-day New Mexico, USA). Some researchers suspect that these pieces may even date to the early Paleocene, but not all paleontologists agree, as the materials may have been transported to the site and deposited, then covered over by more recent sediment. See more: *Lucas 1981; Fassett, Zielinski & Budahn 2002; Fassett 2009; Lucas et al. 2009*

The strangest

Isisaurus colberti ("lizard of the Indian Statistical Institute and Edwin Harris Colbert"), from the late Upper Cretaceous (upper Maastrichtian, approx. 69–66 Ma) in Hindustan (present-day India). It had a very strange appearance, with a short neck, long legs, and disproportionately long forearms, and was also one of the broadest sauropods in proportion to its size. Interestingly, two reconstructions of this animal exist: one based on the scale bars of the published paper and another on the skeletal measurements, each yielding different proportions. Another interesting case is that of *Ampelosaurus atacis* ("impossible vine lizard"), from the late Upper Cretaceous (upper Campanian, approx. 77.8–72.1 Ma) in eastern Laurasia (present-day France). Its teeth were different from those of other saltasauroids, as they were broader than those of its relatives and grew more slowly than those of other titanosaurs. See more: *Sanz & Buscalioni 1987; Le Loeuff et al. 1994; Le Loeuff 1995; Jain & Bandyopadhyay 1997; Wilson & Upchurch 2003; Headden*, Taylor & Wedel**

The first published species

Microcoelus patagonicus, *Titanosaurus australis* and *T. nanus* (1893) are synonyms of *Nequensaurus australis* (1992) that date to the late Upper Cretaceous (Santonian and lower Campanian, approx. 86.3–77.8 Ma) in western Gondwana (present-day Argentina and Uruguay). Several other individuals assigned to this species are more recent (upper Campanian and lower Maastrichtian, approx. 77.8–69 Ma). See more: *Lydekker 1893; Huene 1929; Bonaparte & Powell 1980; Powell 1992; Salgado et al. 2005; Otero 2010; D'Emic & Wilson 2011*

The most recently published species

Zhuchengtitan zangjiazhuangensis ("titan of Zucheng county and Zangjiazhuang locality"), from eastern Laurasia (present-day Mongolia). It is known only from an almost complete humerus and was a contemporary of the tyrannosaurid *Zhuchengtyrannus magnus*. See more: *Mo et al. 2017*

Bonatitan reigi
Csiki et al. 2010

RECORD
SMALLEST

Notocolossus
Dreadnoughtus
Alamosaurus
Ampelosaurus
Opisthocoelicaudia
Saltasauridae
Isisaurus
Saltasaurus

Specimen: MACN RN 821
(Martinelli & Forasiepi 2004)

Length: 6 m
Hip height: 1.35 m
Body mass: 600 kg
Material: partial skeleton
ESR: ●●●○

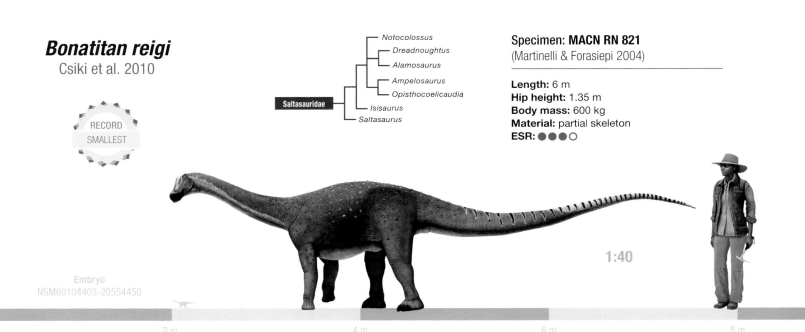

Embryo
NSM60104403-20554450

1:40

15 m

10 m

1:100

5 m

5 m   10 m   15 m   20 m

Asiatosaurus
Length: **31 m**
Weight: **45 t**

Sauroposeidon
Length: **29 m**
Weight: **40 t**

Mamenchisaurus
Length: **31 m**
Weight: **45 t**

Giant sauropodiform
Length: **16 m**
Weight: **10 t**

Efraasia
Length: **5.3 m**
Weight: **365 kg**

"Thotobolosaurus"
Length: **11 m**
Weight: **3.6 t**

African elephant
Height: **3.2 m**
Weight: **6 t**

Camarasaurus
Length: **20 m**
Weight: **30 t**

Apatosaurus
Length: **30 m**
Weight: **33 t**

RECORD: The heaviest

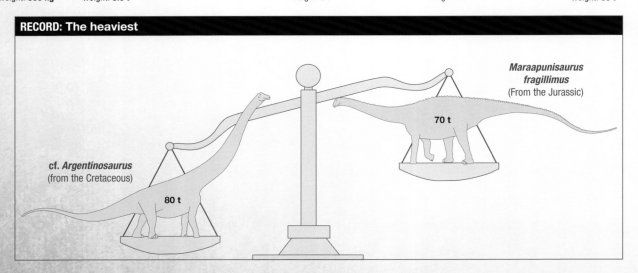

cf. *Argentinosaurus*
(from the Cretaceous)

80 t

Maraapunisaurus fragillimus
(From the Jurassic)

70 t

25 m   30 m   35 m   40 m   45 m

Giraffatitan
Length: **25 m**
Weight: **48 t**

Brachiosaurus
Length: **26.5 m**
Weight: **50 t**

Puertasaurus
Length: **28 m**
Weight: **50 t**

"Antarctosaurus" giganteus
Length: **30.5 m**
Weight: **45 t**

Giant neosauropod
Length: **18.5 m**
Weight: **35 t**

cf. **Barosaurus**
Length: **45 m**
Weight: **60 t**

Rebbachisaurus
Length: **26 m**
Weight: **40 t**

"Morosaurus"
Length: **22 m**
Weight: **17 t**

"Seismosaurus" - Diplodocus hallorum
Length: **31 m**
Weight: **21 t**

Masai giraffe
Height: **5.3 m**
Weight: **1.2 t**

RECORD: The tallest

Estimating the height of sauropods is difficult, as a lot depends on the flexibility of their necks. Here, we show the approximate greatest heights of the largest species. The graphic shows *Barosaurus* in a bipedal posture, which would make it the record holder, but it is not certain whether an animal this enormous could actually have maintained such a posture.

a *Asiatosaurus mongoliensis* - 17.5 m
b *Sauroposeidon proteles* - 16.5 m
c cf. *Barosaurus lentus* - 22 m
d *Xinjiangtitan shanshanesis* - 17 m
e cf. *Argentinosaurus* - 17 m

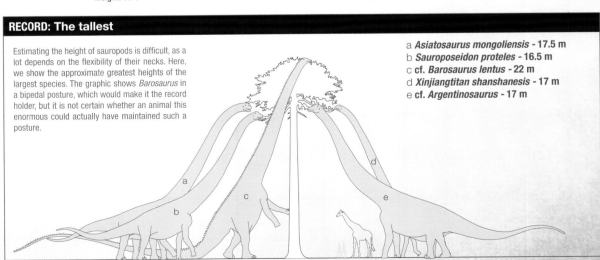

50 m 55 m 60 m 65 m 70 m

cf. *Argentinosaurus*
Length: **36 m**
Weight: **80 t**

1:100

Patagotitan
Length: **31 m**
Weight: **55 t**

"Francoposeidon"
Length: **28 m**
Weight: **47 t**

Neosodon
Length: **22 m**
Weight: **35 t**

Supersaurus
Length: **33 m**
Weight: **35 t**

Maraapunisaurus
Length: **35 m**
Weight: **70 t**

African elephant
Height: **3.2 m**
Weight: **6 t**

Futalognkosaurus
Length: **24 m**
Weight: **30 t**

Barapasaurus
Length: **14 m**
Weight: **8.5 t**

Blue whale
Length: **26 m**
Weight: **110 t**

75 m   80 m   85 m   90 m

15 m

10 m

Xinjiangtitan
Length: **27 m**
Weight: **25 t**

Alamosaurus
Length: **26 m**
Weight: **38t**

Cetiosaurus
Length: **19 m**
Weight: **18 t**

Magyarosaurus
Length: **5.4 m**
Weight: **540 kg**

Masai giraffe
Height: **5.3 m**
Weight: **1.2 t**

Amargasaurus
Length: **13.5 m**
Weight: **4 t**

Bothriospondylus
Length: **15 m**
Weight: **16 t**

Isisaurus
Length: **11 m**
Weight: **11.5 t**

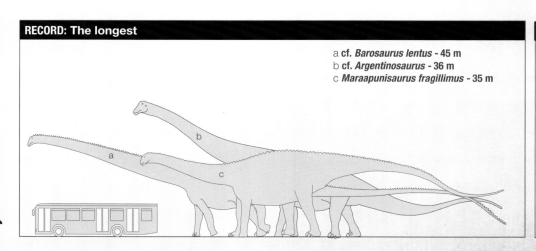

RECORD: The longest

a cf. *Barosaurus lentus* - 45 m
b cf. *Argentinosaurus* - 36 m
c *Maraapunisaurus fragillimus* - 35 m

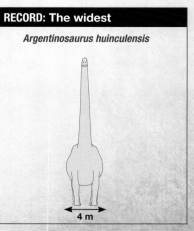

RECORD: The widest

Argentinosaurus huinculensis

← 4 m →

50 cm

1 m

1 m

1:6

50 cm

Leyesaurus
Length: **2.4 m**
Weight: **31 kg**

Thecodontosaurus minor
Length: **1.45 m**
Weight: **3.8 kg**

Pampadromaeus
Length: **1.4 m**
Weight: **3 kg**

Alwalkeria
Length: **1.3 m**
Weight: **2 kg**
A possible primitive
saurischian

Common pigeon
Length: **25 cm** (35 cm with feathers)
Weight: **350 g**

Anchisaurus
Length: **2.4 m**
Weight: **25 kg**

.5 m

2 m

2.5 m

Magyarosaurus
Length: **5.4 m**
Weight: **520 kg**

It was the smallest sauropod

Asylosaurus
Length: **2.25 m**
Weight: **14 kg**

"Gripposaurus"
Length: **2.9 m**
Weight: **58 kg**

House cat
Length: **45 cm** (without tail)
Weight: **4.5 kg**

59

TAXONOMIC HISTORY OF PRIMITIVE SAUROPODOMORPHS AND SAUROPODS

1699—England—First sauropod published
A sauropod tooth known as "Rutellum implicatum" was found in a collection that had been reported and illustrated. At that time, no one knew what it actually was. See more: *Lhuyd 1699; Gunther 1945; Delair & Sarjeant 2002*

1699—England—First binomial sauropod name
"Rutellum implicatum" is an invalid name because it preceded, by 59 years, the binomial nomenclature system proposed by Carl Linnaeus in 1758. See more: *Lhuyd 1699; Linnaeus 1758; Gunther 1945; Delair & Sarjeant 2002*

1818—USA—First sauropodomorph discovered
It was named *Megadactylus polyzelus* 47 years after being discovered, but is now known as *Anchisaurus polyzelus*, as the name *Megadactylus* was already in use. See more: *Smith 1820; Hitchcock 1865; Marsh 1882, 1885; Baur 1883*

1818—USA—First sauropodomorph not identified as a dinosaur
The remains of *Anchisaurus polyzelus* were believed to be human remains until they were reclassified as dinosaur remains in 1855. See more: *Smith 1820; Hitchcock 1865; Galton 1976*

1836—England—First genus name assigned to a sauropodomorph
Thecodontosaurus was the first genus, but it did not receive a species name when it was created. The names *Palaeosaurus cylindricum* and *P. platyodon* came to be considered sauropodomorphs, but they were really archosaurs. See more: *Riley & Stutchbury 1836*

1837—Germany—First species name assigned to a sauropodomorph
Plateosaurus engelhardti preceded *Thecodontosaurus antiquus* by six years. See more: *Meyer 1837; Morris 1843*

1841—England—First genus names assigned to sauropods
Cardiodon and *Cetiosaurus* did not receive species names when they were created. See more: *Owen 1841*

1842—England—First sauropod chimera with an ornithischian dinosaur
The species *Cetiosaurus brevis* was based on remains of the sauropod *Pelorosaurus conybearei* and an *Iguanodon*. See more: *Owen 1842*

1842—England—First species names assigned to sauropods
Cetiosaurus had several species names assigned to it a year after it was created—*C. brachyurus, C. brevis, C. epioolithicus, C. hypoolithicus, C. longus,* and *C. medius.* However, all of these species are considered doubtful, invalid, or as belonging to other genera. See more: *Owen 1841, 1844*

1842—England—First invalid sauropod names
"*Cetiosaurus epioolithicus*" and "*C. hypoolithicus*" were not correctly described and so are not deemed valid. See more: *Owen 1844*

1846—Germany—First attempted sauropodomorph name change
The reasoning behind the name *Plateosaurus* ("flat lizard") is not known; some believe it was a spelling mistake and should rather have been *Platysaurus* ("broad lizard"), but this name was not successfully adopted. See more: *Meyer 1837; Agassiz 1846; Geinitz 1846*

1852—England—First sauropods mistaken for carnivorous dinosaurs

The spatulate tooth *Oplosaurus armatus* was believed to be from a carnivore, as it has a pointed tip. See more: *Gervais 1852*

1877—India, USA—First replacement sauropod name
Titanosaurus indicus kept its name because it was described before *T. montanus*, so the latter name was changed to *Atlantosaurus*, all in the same year. See more: *Lydekker 1877; Marsh 1877*

1877—USA—First sauropod families created
"*Atlantosauridae*" encompassed *Atlantosaurus, Pelorosaurus, Ornithopsis,* and other similar species. It is now considered a synonym of Diplodocidae. The family "Camarasauridae" included *Camarasaurus* and *Caulodon*, which are now considered synonyms. See more: *Cope 1877; Marsh 1877, 1884; Lydekker 1888*

1877—USA—A prophetic sauropod name
Apatosaurus which means "deceptive lizard," has coincidentally been involved in several disputes related to the most famous sauropod of all—*Brontosaurus* (considered a synonym). Furthermore, despite the fact that the skull of the species *A. louisae* was discovered in 1909, it took some time for researchers to discover that it was very similar to that of *Diplodocus*. See more: *Marsh 1877; Riggs 1903; Holland 1915; McIntosh & Berman 1975; Tschopp, Mateus & Benson 2015*

1878—USA—The term "sauropoda" is coined
Based on the Latin *sauros*, meaning "lizard," and *podus*, meaning "foot." See more: *Marsh 1878*

1879—USA—Sauropod name that has inspired the most other sauropod names
Different names have been created based on *Brontosaurus*, including some invalid or informal sauropods like "*Brontodiplodocus*" ("thunder double beam"), *Brontomerus* ("thunder thigh"), *Eobrontosaurus* ("ancient *Brontosaurus*"), "*Amphicoelias brontodiplodocus*," and the less subtle *Suuwassea* ("first spring thunder"); added to these are the two sets of footprints *Brontopodus* and *Parabrontopodus*; curiously, the latter was the same kind of print as *Brontosaurus*. See more: *Marsh 1879; Farlow, Pittman & Hawthorne 1989; Lockley, Farlow & Meyer 1994; Harris & Dodson 2004; Taylor, Wedel & Cifelli 2011*

1882—USA—First sauropodomorph family created
"*Amphisauridae*" was the first, but had to change its name to "Anchisauridae" as the name *Amphisaurus* was already in use. See more: *Marsh 1882, 1885; Baur 1883*

1883—Russia—First sauropod chimera with a theropod
Poekilopleuron schmidti is based on cervical ribs, gastralia, and one metacarpal IV from a titanosauriform sauropod, as well as some theropod remains. See more: *Kiprijanow 1883; Nesov 1995*

1884—USA—First sauropod taxonomic group
The concept of "Diplodocoidea" emerged in 1884, but it took 111 years to define all the relatives of *Diplodocus*. See more: *Marsh 1884; Upchurch 1995*

1890—England—First family of sauropodomorphs from the Triassic
"*Thecodontosauridae*" includes *Thecodontosaurus* and its close relatives, some of which have been discovered to be juveniles of other distantly related species. The family is not currently active, although the type genus is still accepted. See more: *Lydekker 1890*

1893—India—First family of sauropods from the Cretaceous
"*Titanosauridae*" encompasses *Titanosaurus* and its close relatives. It is not currently valid, however, as it is based on procoelous vertebrae, a feature that several sauropods display, so the name of the type species *T. indicus* is doubtful. See more: *Lydekker 1893;*

Salgado 2003

1896—USA—First sauropod chimera with another sauropod
The reconstructed *Brontosaurus excelsus* skeleton used the skull of a *Brachiosaurus* sp., as no other material was available at the time. The reconstructed skeleton remained on display for more than 64 years (from 1931 to 1995), until it was exchanged for a skull similar to that of *Apatosaurus*. See more: *Marsh 1896; Norell, Gaffney & Dingus 1995.*

1898—England—First chimera sauropodomorph
The teeth of the archosaur *Avalonia sanfordi* were thought to belong to the bones of *Gresslyosaurus* and so were considered a carnivore with a long neck and body similar to *Plateosaurus*. See more: *Seeley 1898; Galton 1985*

1913—Germany—First sauropodomorph taxonomic groups
"Plateosauria" is now revalidated after the disappearance of "Prosauropoda." See more: *Tornier 1913*

1913—Germany—First sauropodomorph to include a second species
Plateosaurus longiceps was described 76 years after the type species *P. engelhardti*. Between these two species, several species were discovered and found to be valid, synonyms, doubtful, or belonging to other kinds of dinosaurs: *P. poligniensis* (*Dimodosaurus*), *P. obtusus* ("*Megalosaurus*"), *P. plieningeri* (*Zanclodon*), *P. quenstedti* (*Zanclodon*), *P. erlenbergiensis, P. reinigeri, P. ornatus, P. elizae, P. robustus* (*Gresslyosaurus*), *P. ajax* (*Pachysaurus*), *P. magnus* (*Pachysaurus*), *P. gracilis* (*Sellosaurus*), *P. trossingensis* ("*Teratosaurus*"), *P. torgeri* (*Gresslyosaurus*), and *P. integer*. Furthermore, during this time lapse, *Anchisaurus* received the new species *A. major, A. colurus,* and *A. solus*, but they are synonyms or belong to *Ammosaurus*. During this time, *Thecodontosaurus* had new species added, *T. indicus* (*Ankistrodon*), *T. gibbidens* (*Galtonia*), *T. latespinatus* (*Tanystropheus*), and *T. primus* (*Tanystropheus*); however, none of them turned out to be a dinosaur. See more: *Riley & Stuchbury 1836; Meyer 1837; Morris 1843; Pidancet & Chopard 1862; Hitchcock 1865; Huxley 1865; Henry 1876; Cope 1878; Marsh 1889, 1891, 1892; Fraas 1896; Koken 1900; Huene 1905; Sauvage 1907; Huene 1908; Fraas 1913, Jaekel 1913; Hunt & Lucas 1994*

1920—Germany—The term "Prosauropoda" is coined
This clade is currently inactive but was very popular in its time. It included all primitive sauropodomorphs that were not sauropods, but as it was a paraphyletic group, it had to be discarded. See more: *Huene, 1920*

1923—India—Most recent sauropod chimera
The dinosaur *Lametasaurus indicus* is based on the osteoderms of a sauropod, crocodile teeth, and the bones of the theropod *Rajasaurus narmadensis*. It dates to the late Upper Cretaceous (upper Maastrichtian, approx. 69–66 Ma). See more: *Matley 1923*

1932—Germany—The term "Sauropodomorpha" is coined
The name means "having a sauropod-like shape." It includes a wide variety of species, ranging from bipedal carnivores in the most basal taxa to herbivorous quadrupeds (the vast majority). See more: *Huene 1932; Cabreira et al. 2016*

2001—USA, Switzerland—Sauropod with the shortest nickname
A specimen of *Apatosaurus* found in the Sauriermuseum Aathal (Aathal Dinosaur Museum) is known as "Max." See more: *http://www.swissinfo.ch*

2005—Algeria—Sauropod with the longest nickname
Chebsaurus algerensis is known as "the Giant of Ksour." See

more: *Mahammed et al. 2005*

2007—Most recent sauropod family
"Huanghetitanidae" (Huanghetitanids) is the last family created before this issue went to press. The two species of *Huanghetitan* may belong to different genera. See more: *You et al. 2006; Lu et al. 2007; Mannion et al. 2013*

2007—Most recent sauropodomorph taxonomical group
When this book went to press, "Riojasauridae" (Riojasaurids) was the most recent clade created to date, although it has been called into doubt. See more: *Yates 2007; McPhee et al. 2015*

2009—Australia—Sauropod with the most nicknames
Several specimens identified as *Austrosaurus* have received different nicknames, although it is not certain that they belong to the same species, as some have turned out to be *Wintonotitan watsi*. Those nicknames include "Cooper," "Elliot," "George," and "Mary." See more: *Longman 1933; Hocknull et al. 2009*

2013—Most recent sauropod taxonomic group
As this book went to press, "Khebbashia" ("Kebasia") was the most recent clade created, for some derived rebbachisaurids. See more: *Fanti et al. 2013*

2018—Most recent sauropodomorph families created
Lessemsauridae and Unaysauridae were the most recent when this book went to press. The former has been considered a sauropod or primitive sauropodomorph. See more: *Apaldetti et al. 2018; Müller et al. 2018*

NOMENCLATURE RECORDS OF
SAUROPODOMORPH DINOSAURS

1699—England—First forgotten sauropod name
"Rutellum implicatum" is the earliest name given to a dinosaur, but it fell into disuse for nearly 250 years. See more: *Lhuyd 1699; Gunther 1945; Delair & Sarjeant 2002*

1836—England—First primitive archosaur mistaken for a sauropodomorph
Palaeosaurus cylindricum and *P. platyodon* are teeth of a phytosaurian archosaur that were considered sauropodomorph teeth and were even used as the basis for the two species, *Thecodontosaurus cylindrodon* and *T. platyodon*. See more: *Riley & Stutchbury 1836; Huene 1908*

1836—Germany—Name most often used for a sauropodomorph
Palaeosaurus was changed to *Palaeosauriscus* and to *Paleosaurops*, as 28 years previously the name had been used for the extinct reptile *Palaeosaurus* (now a synonym of *Aeolodon*). It was later used for *Palaeosaurus sternbergii* (now a synonym of *Sphenosaurus*). See more: *Saint-Hilaire 1833; Riley & Stutchbury 1836; Meyer 1830; Fitzinger 1840*

1837—Germany—First binomial sauropodomorph name
Plateosaurus engelhardti was discovered in 1834 and described three years later. See more: *Meyer 1837*

1837—Germany—First commemorative sauropodomorph species name
Plateosaurus engelhardti was named in honor of physicist Johann Friedrich Engelhardt. See more: *Meyer 1837*

1844—Germany—First spelling mistake in a sauropodomorph name
Plateosaurus is mentioned as "*Platysaurus*." See more: *Agassiz 1846*

1847—Massachusetts, USA—First species name based on a sauropodomorph print
Edward Hitchcock named *Otozoum moodii* ("Pliny Moody's giant creature") in honor of the first person to discover and preserve footprints in the area where it was found. The footprint *Sillimanius adamsanus*, described two years earlier, may have been of a sauropodomorph or a primitive saurischian, owing to the shape of its toes, including the hallux (big toe), and their width. See more: *Hitchcock 1845, 1847; Lull 1953; Lockley 1991*

1847—USA—Simplest name for a sauropodomorph footprint
Otozoum means "giant animal." See more: *Hitchcock 1847*

1849—England—First sauropodomorph name to be discarded
A name proposed for *Pelorosaurus conybearei* was "Colossosaurus"; however, as "colossus" means "statue" and not "large," it was not chosen. See more: *Mantell 1849 in Torrens 1997; Mantell 1850*

1849—England—First commemorative species name for a sauropod
"*Cetiosaurus conybearei*" (now *Pelorosaurus*) was named in honor of geologist/paleontologist William Daniel Conybeare. See more: *Melville 1849; Mantell 1850*

1849—England—First sauropod to be identified as a dinosaur
Pelorosaurus conybearei (formerly *Cetiosaurus*) was identified as a large land animal thanks to the discovery of a humerus. *Cetiosaurus* had previously been considered a marine animal. See more: *Melville 1849; Mantell 1850*

1849—England—First sauropod with a second name
Cetiosaurus conybearei was renamed *Pelorosaurus conybearei* the year after it was published. See more: *Melville 1849; Mantell 1850*

1852—England—First binomial sauropod name
Before *Aepisaurus elephantinus* and *Oplosaurus armatus*, sauropod names had been created in publications other than those in which their species names had been assigned. Although "Rutellum implicatum" preceded it, that name is not valid as it was given before Linnaeus's classification system was established. See more: *Lhuyd 1699; Gervais 1852*

1852—England—Sauropod with identical genus and species meanings
Oplosaurus armatus is a redundant name, as both terms mean "armored lizard." See more: *Gervais 1852*

1854—South Africa—First sauropodomorph name to refer to a place
Leptospondylus capensis is named after the city of Cape Town. It is now a synonym of *Massospondylus carinatus*. See more: *Owen 1854*

1855—Germany—First discarded sauropodomorph name
One publication referred to *Plateosaurus engelhardti* as "Riesensaurus." See more: *Meyer 1855*

1856—Switzerland—First previously occupied sauropodomorph name
Dinosaurus gresslyi was created without any description, but as the name *Dinosaurus* was already in use, it was changed the following year to *Gresslyosaurus ingens*. But the name was invalid (because it included no description), and so the combination "*Gresslyosaurus gresslyi*" could not be used. See more: *Fischer 1847; Rutimeyer 1856*

1859—France—First spelling mistake in reference to a sauropod

Aepisaurus elephantinus was referred to as "*Aepysaurus*" by its own creator, seven years after it was named. See more: *Gervais 1852, 1859*

1865—USA—Sauropod name most frequently changed for the same reason
The name *Megadactylus* had to be changed to *Amphisaurus*, as the same name had been used for another animal 22 years earlier. But the name *Amphisaurus* had also been taken 12 years previously, and so the creature was again renamed, to *Anchisaurus*. See more: *Fitzinger 1843; Hitchcock 1865; Barkas 1870; Marsh 1877, 1885*

1867—South Africa—Sauropodomorph name with the simplest meaning
Orosaurus means "mountain lizard" but is considered a doubtful name. See more: *Huxley 1867*

1869—England—Sauropod name with the simplest meaning
Gigantosaurus, meaning "giant lizard," was used by two different authors. There are other sauropod names just as simple, but this one would work for any species of this group of enormous animals. See more: *Seeley 1869; Fraas 1908*

1870—England—First sauropod mistaken for a pterosaur
Because of the very large chambers (pleurocoels) inside *Ornithopsis hulkei*'s vertebrae, these remains were thought to belong to a large pterosaur. Its name means "geologist John Whitaker Hulke's bird-likeness." See more: *Seeley 1870*

1874—France—First sauropod named after a tribe
Morinosaurus is named after the ancient Celtic tribe Morini, from the historical Gaul. See more: *Sauvage 1874*

1875—England—First unjustified sauropod name change
The pieces known as *Ornithopsis hulkei* were separated into two new species—*Bothriospondylus magnus* and *B. elongatus*—without respecting the precedence of the original name. See more: *Seeley 1870; Owen 1875*

1875—England—First sauropod with two names in the same publication
Bothriospondylus robustus was also referred to as *Marmarospondylus* in the same article. See more: *Owen 1875*

1877—India—First sauropod named after an Asian country
Titanosaurus indicus was the first to be described from Hindustan. See more: *Lydekker 1877*

1877—USA—Most similar sauropod names
Amphicoelias altus and *A. latus* are almost exactly the same in spelling, except for the transposition of two letters; the latter name refers to a crushed femur of *Camarasaurus supremus*. See more: *Cope 1877*

1877—India—First Asian sauropod named after a mythological being
Titanosaurus ("titan lizard") was named after beings in Greek mythology who rebelled against Zeus. See more: *Lydekker 1877*

1877—USA—First North American sauropod named after a mythological being
Atlantosaurus ("Atlas lizard") was named after the giant from Greek mythology who held the world on his shoulders. See more: *Marsh 1877*

1878—France—First species epithet reused for a sauropod
In *Diplodocus longus*, *longus* refers to the elongated form of its vertebrae, as it does in *Cetiosaurus longus*. See more: *Owen 1842; Marsh 1878*

1888—England—First sauropod name previously occupied

Ischyrosaurus manseli is a genus first coined in an unpublished work in 1874 and entered into a catalogue of fossil species 14 years later, but another discovery named *Ischyrotherium* had been changed to *Ischyrosaurus* two years before that unpublished paper. See more: *Cope 1869, 1871; Hulke in Lydekker 1888*

1889—South Africa—First sauropod name mistakenly changed

Orosaurus was mistakenly changed to *Orinosaurus* 22 years after the former was created, but as there was a reptile known as *Oreosaurus*, the researcher Richard Lydekker mistakenly considered that the name was taken, and so the change was not adopted. See more: *Peter 1862; Huxley 1867; Lydekker 1889*

1895—Madagascar—First sauropod species name referring to an African country

Bothriospondylus madagascariensis was also reported in France, but it was actually another kind of sauropod. See more: *Lydekker 1895; Dorlodot 1934; Mannion 2010*

1901—USA—First sauropod named after a philanthropist

Diplodocus carnegii is named in honor of Andrew Carnegie, who financed paleontological studies focused on dinosaurs. See more: *Hatcher 1901*

1902—South Africa—First corrected sauropodomorph name

Euskelosaurus browni was first named *Euskelesaurus* but was corrected 36 years later. See more: *Huxley 1866; Huene 1902*

1908—Tanzania—First species epithet of a sauropod named after the African continent

Gigantosaurus africanus (now *Tornieria africana*) was also known as *Barosaurus africanus*. See more: *Fraas 1908*

1915—USA—First sauropod named after a woman

Apatosaurus louisae was named in honor of Louise Whitfield Carnegie (the wife of philanthropist Andrew Carnegie), who made several charitable donations to the field and was awarded a gold medal by the Pennsylvania Society. See more: *Holland 1915*

1922—USA—First sauropod name with a mistaken meaning

Alamosaurus was named after the Ojo Álamo Formation, although some sources say it is named after the Alamo fort or the famous battle that took place there. See more: *Gilmore 1922*

1924—South Africa—First sauropodomorph species epithet to refer to the African continent

Euskelosaurus africanus is a synonym of *Plateosauravus stormbergensis*. See more: *Broom 1915; Haughton 1924*

1924—China—First sauropod named after the Asian continent

Asiatosaurus mongoliensis is the first sauropod from eastern Asia to be described. See more: *Osborn 1924*

1924—South Africa—First primitive sauropodomorph mistaken for a sauropod

Melanorosaurus readi is so much like a sauropod it was believed to be one for many years. See more: *Haughton 1924*

1926—Australia—First sauropod in Oceania named after a mythological being

Rhoetosaurus ("Rhoetus lizard") is named after one of the titans of Greek mythology. See more: *Longman 1926*

1929—China—First sauropod to receive a name used twice previously

Helopus was changed to *Euhelopus* because the former had been used for the bird *Helopus caspius* (now a synonym of *Hydroprogne caspia*). The plant *Helopus annulatus* (now a synonym of *Eriochloa procera*) also precedes it; however, botanical and zoolo-

gical nomenclature maintain a certain independence. See more: *Pallas 1770; Wagler 1832; Fluggé 1829; Wiman 1929; Romer 1956*

1929—China—First sauropod name similar to that of a plant species

Helopus is written the same as the grass species *Panicum* or *Urochloa helopus* (presently a synonym of *Urochloa panicoides*). See more: *Beauv 1812; Fluggé 1829; Wiman 1929*

1929—Argentina—First mistaken combination used in citing a sauropod name

"*Laplatasaurus wichmannianus*" is a combination that emerged from the mistaken fusion of *Antarctosaurus wichmannianus* and *Laplatasaurus araukanicus*. See more: *Huene 1929*

1932—Egypt—First sauropod named after an African country

Aegyptosaurus was destroyed in 1944, during World War II. See more: *Stromer 1932*

1932—Hungary—First sauropod named after a European country

Magyarosaurus hungaricus might be a variety of *M. dacus*. See more: *Huene 1932*

1939—Kazakhstan—Sauropod with the most confusing genus and species names

Antarctosaurus jaxarticus ("southern lizard of the Yaxartes River") is named after the Yaxartes (now Syr Darya) River in northern Asia, the opposite of what its name implies. See more: *Riabinin 1939*

1941—Poland—First invertebrate mistaken for a sauropod

Succinodon putzeri ("Putzer's narrow-jaw") was believed to be a jawbone with sauropod teeth but was actually a decomposed piece of wood perforated by clams. See more: *Huene 1941; Pozaryska & Pugaczewska 1981*

1948—China—First sauropodomorph name referring to the Triassic

Sinosaurus triassicus is a chimera that includes remains of large theropods and sauropodomorphs that actually date to the Lower Jurassic. The name is currently in use for a theropod similar to *Dilophosaurus*. See more: *Young 1948; Walker 1964; Galton 1999*

1951—China—Sauropodomorph with the most confusing genus and species name

Pachysuchus imperfectus ("imperfect thick crocodile") was mistakenly identified as a phytosaur archosaur similar to a present-day crocodile. A later review revealed that it was actually a skull fragment of an unknown species of sauropodomorph. See more: *Young 1951; Barrett & Xing 2012*

1953—China—First sauropod to have its name corrected

Chiayusaurus lacustris was originally named *Chiayüsaurus* but had to be changed, as the rules of nomenclature do not allow punctuation (commas, dashes, etc.) or linguistic marks. See more: *Bohlin 1953*

1954—China—First sauropod name cited correctly and misspelled in the same publication

Mamenchisaurus is referred to as *Manenchisaurus*, as well as its correct name, in the same publication. See more: *Young 1954*

1954—China—First sauropod named after a fortuitous circumstance

Mamenchisaurus constructus was discovered during construction work. See more: *Young 1954*

1970—Lesotho—First sauropodomorph footprint referring to a place

Tetrasauropus seakaensis was named after the locality of Seaka. Other species described the same year also referring to places

(*Parasauropodopus corbesiensis*, *Paratetrasauropus corbensiensis*, *Pentasauropus morobongensis*, and *Pseudotetrasauropus andusiensis*) are not dinosaurs. See more: *Ellenberger 1970*

1971—South Africa—Strangest typographical error in a sauropodomorph name

Euskelosaurus is referred to as "*Entelosaurus*." See more: *Huxley 1866; Russell 1971*

1972—Zimbabwe—First sauropod name based on a mythological being

Vulcanodon ("Vulcan tooth") was named after the god of fire and volcanoes in Roman mythology. See more: *Raath 1972*

1972—Brazil—First sauropod species named after a country in South America

Antarctosaurus brasiliensis. See more: *Arid & Vizotto 1972*

1972—Lesotho—Sauropod footprint with the most confusing name

Pseudotetrasauropus bipedoida ("bipedal almost-Tetrasauropus") is a curious name, because all *Pseudotetrasauropus* species are bipedal. See more: *Ellenberger 1972*

1972—Zimbabwe—Sauropod with the most confusing name

Vulcanodon karibaensis ("Vulcan tooth from Lake Kariba") is a strange name, as the fossil included no teeth. See more: *Raath 1972*

1974—USA—First species name for a footprint attributed to a sauropod

Elephantopoides barkhausensis ("Barkhaus's elephant skin") was discovered in 1921 on an almost vertical cliff. See more: *Kaever & Lapparent 1974; Lockley & Meyer 2000*

1974—Germany—First sauropod footprint name to refer to a place

Elephantopoides barkhausensis is named after the locality of Barkhausen. See more: *Kaever & Lapparent 1974*

1976—China—First sauropod fossil egg named after a place

Faveoloolithus ningxiaensis is named after the city of Ningxiang. See more: *Zhao & Dong 1976*

1977—China—Sauropodomorph name with the most typographical errors

Chiayusaurus has the most incorrect names. It has been referred to alternately as "*Chiayasaurus*," "*Chiayausaurus*," "*Chiayiisaurus*," "*Chiayuesaurus*," and "*Chiryuesaurus*" in different publications. Notably, its original name was *Chiayüsaurus*. See more: *Bohlin 1953; Young 1958; Rozhdestvensky & Tatarinov 1964; Dong 1977*

1979—Argentina—Sauropodomorph with the most confusing name

Mussaurus ("mouse lizard"). The first specimen was a juvenile but was mistaken for an adult of a small species. It is now known that the adults were up to 8.6 m in length and weighed up to 1.55 t. See more: *Bonaparte & Vince 1979; Otero & Pol 2013*

1980—South Africa—Sauropodomorph name with the most typographical errors

Euskelosaurus has accumulated the most incorrect spellings. In different publications it is referred to as "*Enskelosaurus*," "*Ensklosaurus*," "*Entelosaurus*," "*Euscelesaurus*," "*Euscelidosaurus*," "*Euscellosaurus*," "*Euscelosaurus*," "*Euskelesaurus*," and "*Euskelosaurus*." See more: *Huxley 1866, 1867; Cope 1867; Sauvage 1883; Lydekker 1890; Lydekker in Nicholson & Lydekker 1889; Nopcsa 1929; Russell 1971; Heerden 1979*

1980—Uruguay—First sauropod fossil egg named after a person

Sphaerovum erbeni was named in honor of Dr. Heinrich K. Erben.

See more: *Mones 1980*

1983—South Korea—Sauropod name that expresses the largest size
Many sauropod names refer to size, as these creatures tended to be very large. In etymological terms, *Ultrasaurus* ("ultra lizard") refers to the greatest size possible, surpassing *Atlantosaurus*, *Atlasaurus*, *Austroposeidon*, *Gigantosaurus*, *Notocolossus*, *Pelorosaurus*, *Sauroposeidon*, *Seismosaurus*, *Supersaurus*, and others. See more: *Kim 1983; Jensen 1985*

1984—China—First sauropod mistaken for a primitive sauropodomorph
The lower jaw of *Kunmingosaurus wudingensis* was believed to belong to the sauropodomorph *Lufengosaurus magnus*. See more: *Dong 1984; Zhao 1985*

1985—Japan—First chironym sauropod names
"Hisanohamasaurus" and "Sugiyamasaurus" are derived from informal names such as "Hisanohama-ryu" and "Sugiyama-ryu." Although they were latinized, both are currently deemed invalid. See more: *Hisa 1985, Lambert 1990*

1986—China—First typographical error in a sauropod species epithet in the same publication
Chinshakiangosaurus zhongheensis is also referred to as *Chinshakiangosaurus zhonghonensis*. See more: *Zhao 1986*

1986—USA—First erroneous citation referring to a sauropodomorph footprint
Navahopus is mentioned as "*Navajopus*" in a symposium summary. See more: *Baird 1980; Morales & Colbert 1986; Ford**

1986—India—Oldest sauropodomorph fossil chimera
Alwalkeria maleriensis is based on a crocodylomorph skull, protosaurus cervical vertebrae, and sauropodomorph thoracic vertebrae, femur, and talus. All of them date to the Upper Triassic (lower Carnian, approx. 242–237 Ma). See more: *Chatterjee 1986; Chatterjee & Creisler 1994; Remes & Rauhut 2005*

1987—Argentina—First South American sauropod named after a mythological being
Aeolosaurus ("lizard of the wind god Aeolus") is named after the god of Greek mythology who controlled the wind. This sauropod's vertebrae are steeply sloped, as though they had been pushed over by the wind—hence its name. See more: *Powell 1987*

1991—Argentina—Sauropod footprint name with the simplest meaning
Sauropodichnus giganteus means "giant sauropod footprint." The names *Brontopodus birdi* ("Roland T. Bird's brontosaurus-foot") and *Titanopodus mendozensis* ("titanosaur-foot of Mendoza city") are similar in this regard. See more: *Farlow, Pittman & Hawthorne 1989; Calvo 1991; Gónzalez Riga & Calvo 2009*

1991—South Africa—First sauropod named after two peoples
Seismosaurus halli was corrected to *S. hallorum* (presently *Diplodocus*) to honor not only James W. Hall, but also his wife, Ruth. See more: *Gillette 1991; Olshevsky 1998*

1993—Argentina—First sauropod named after a South American country
Argentinosaurus is one of the largest known sauropods. See more: *Bonaparte & Coria 1993*

1994—South Korea—Strangest typographical error in a sauropod name
Ultrasaurus is referred to as "Hltrasurus" by the author who created the name. See more: *Kim 1983, 1994*

1994—Thailand—First sauropodomorph named after a princess

Phuwiangosaurus sirindhornae was named in honor of Princess Maha Chakri Sirindhorn, for her interest in geology and paleontology. See more: *Martin 1994*

1994—Uruguay—First attempted name change of a fossil sauropod egg
It was suggested that *Sphaerovum erbeni* change its name to *Sphaeroolithus erbeni*, but the change was unsuccessful. See more: *Mones 1980; Carpenter & Alf 1994*

1995—India—Sauropod egg with the most confusing name
Megaloolithus cylindricus ("large petrified cylindrical egg") was spherical in shape, like all other sauropod eggs, but it refers to the internal structure of the egg and not its outward appearance. See more: *Kholsa & Sahni 1995*

1999—Brazil—First sauropod named after a paleocontinent
Gondwanatitan refers to the ancient supercontinent Gondwana, which existed during the Mesozoic. See more: *Kellner & Azevedo 1999*

1999—Brazil—First sauropodomorph named after a festival
Saturnalia makes reference to the ancient Roman festival of the same name. See more: *Langer et al. 1999*

2000—China—Quickest sauropod name correction
Chuanjiesaurus a'naensis was corrected to *Chuanjiesaurus anaensis* immediately in the publication where the former was mentioned, as the rules of nomenclature do not allow divided words, dashes, or punctuation marks. See more: *Fang et al. 2000a, 2000b; Olshevsky**

2001—Madagascar—First Madagascan sauropod named after a mythological being
Rapetosaurus ("Rapeto lizard") is named after an evil giant in Malagasy mythology. See more: *Curry Rogers & Forster 2001*

2001—Thailand—First sauropod named to mark a special occasion
The species epithet of *Pukyongosaurus millenniumi* commemorates the new millennium. See more: *Dong, Paik & Kim 2001*

2001—South Africa—First sauropodomorph named after two people
Arcusaurus pererabdalorum was named in honor of Lucille Pereira and Fernando Abdala, who discovered the fossils. See more: *Yates, Bonnan & Neveling 2011*

2001—Argentina—The genus *Sauropodus* is created
Its name was informally announced in a newspaper and has not yet been formalized. See more: *Simón in Anonymous 2001*

2002—Portugal—First sauropod footprint named after a European country
"*Transonymanus portucalensis*" named after Portugal, is not a valid name as it only appears in a thesis. See more: *Santos 2002*

2002—Portugal—First sauropod footprint names coined in a thesis
"*Digitichnus zambujalensis*" and "*Transonymanus portucalensis*" have not been formalized to date. See more: *Santos 2002*

2002—Argentina—First sauropodomorph name coined in a thesis
"*Jachalsaurus milanensis*" was published informally 15 years before being officially presented as *Adeopapposaurus mognai*. See more: *Martínez 1998, 1999, 2002, 2009*

2003—China—First sauropodomorph name coined in a thesis
"*Yibinosaurus zhoui*" was mentioned in a museum guide two

years before it was presented. It has not been formally described. See more: *Ouyang in Anonymous 2001; Ouyang 2003*

2003 (1969)—Kyrgyzstan—Sauropod name that took the longest to be formalized
The name "*Ferganasaurus*" existed informally 34 years before it was formalized. See more: *Rozhdestvensky 1969; Alifanov & Averianov 2003*

2003—Portugal—First European sauropod name based on a mythological being
Lusotitan ("titan of Lusitania province") refers to its enormous size. See more: *Telles-Antunes & Mateus 2003*

2004—Portugal—First citation error referring to a sauropod footprint
"*Polyonyx*" was referred to as "Polyonichnus" when the name was informal; five years later it appeared in a scientific publication. See more: *Azevedo & Santos 2004; Santos, Moratalla et al. 2004; Santos et al. 2009*

2005—Spain—First dispute over the contemporary nature of a sauropod name
The name "*Galveosaurus*" had been cited informally in manuscripts and had also appeared in a museum exhibition, where the name had been assigned to a sauropod and even a small ornithopod by mistake. Bárbara Sánchez-Hernández formalized the name on August 11, 2005, while another publication also printed the name *Galvesaurus* in the July–December issue that same year in an article written by Barco, Canudo, Cuenca-Bescós, and Ruiz-Omeñaca. This incited a problem that has caused confusion to date, as different sources give priority to one citation over the other or include one as a lesser synonym of the other. See more: *Barco et al. 2005; Sánchez-Hernández 2005a, 2005b; Barco & Canudo 2012*

2005—Argentina—Sauropod name that includes the name of another species
Cathartesaura includes the name of the turkey vulture (*Cathartes aura*), which is very abundant in the region where the specimen was found. See more: *Linnaeus 1758; Gallina & Apesteguia 2005*

2006—Most sauropods named in a single year
Thirteen new names and one invalid name were created that year, for a total of fourteen.

2006—Germany—First sauropod name to refer to the European continent
Europasaurus holgeri. See more: *Sander, Mateus, Laven & Knotschke 2006*

2007—Most sauropodomorph genera named in a single year
Three new genera were created.

2007—Wales, United Kingdom—First European sauropodomorph name based on a mythological being
Pantydraco caducus ("fallen dragon of Pantyffynnon town"); the name of the locality means "dry valley." See more: *Yates 2003; Galton, Yates & Kermack 2007*

2007 (1909)—Tanzania—Sauropodomorph with the longest time lapse between its discovery and its scientific naming
Australodocus bohetii was discovered in 1909 and received its name 98 years later. See more: *Remes 2007*

2007 (1972)—South Africa—Sauropodomorph footprint that took the longest time to change genus
Pseudotetrasauropus jaquesi was changed to *Lavinipes jaquesi* after 35 years. See more: *Ellenberger 1972; Olsen & Galton 1984; D'Orai et al. 2007*

2008—USA, England—First dinosauromorph named after an academic institution

Asylosaurus yalensis was named after Yale University; the remains were saved from destruction because they were on loan to that institution. See more: *Galton 2007*

2008—South Korea—Sauropod footprint with the most confusing name

"*Elephantosauripus metacarpus*" ("elephant footprints") is an informal name of unknown origin.

2009 (1854)—Longest time lapse between two sauropodomorph species of the same genus

Massospondylus carinatus was created 155 years before *M. kaalae*. See more: *Owen 1854; Barrett 2009*

2010—USA—First North American sauropodomorph name based on a mythological being

Seitaad is named after a sand monster in the Diné culture that buried its victims alive. The animal seems to have died under a layer of sand. See more: *Sertich & Loewen 2010*

2010—Argentina—First sauropod named after a corporation

Panamericansaurus schroederi is named in honor of the company Pan American Energy, which funded the investigations. See more: *Calvo & Porfiri 2010*

2010 (1998)—China—Longest time elapsed for a fossil egg to change genus

Youngoolithus xipingensis was changed to *Parafaveoloolithus xipingensis* after 12 years. See more: *Xiaosi et al. 1998; Zhang 2010*

2011 (1939)—Longest time elapsed between two sauropod species of the same genus

Omeisaurus junghsiensis was created 72 years before *O. jiaoi*. Even more time elapsed (120 years) between *Titanosaurus indicus* and *T. colberti*; however, the latter is now considered part of the *Isisaurus* genus. See more: *Lydekker 1877; Young 1939; Jain & Bandyopadhyay 1997; Jiang et al. 2011*

2013 (1941)—China—Country most often appearing in sauropod and sauropodomorph names

The People's Republic of China appears in five species names—*Dongyangosaurus sinensis, Gannansaurus sinensis, Gripposaurus sinensis, Hudiesaurus sinojapanorum* and *Mamenchisaurus sinocanadorum*) See more: *Young 1941; Russell & Zheng 1994; Dong 1997; Lu et al. 2008; Lu et al. 2013*

2014—Most sauropod species named in a single year

Twelve new species names were created that year, while in 2010, 11 accepted and 3 invalid species were named.

2014—Argentina—Most complicated sauropod name

Dreadnoughtus ("fearless one") one of the most difficult to pronounce and memorize. See more: *Lacovara et al. 2014*

2014—China—Sauropod name most resembling one of its authors' names

Huangshanlong ("dragon of Huangshang") is often believed to refer to paleontologist Jian-Dong Huang, who described it. See more: *Huang et al. 2014*

2014—Pakistan—First acronym used in a sauropod name

Gspsaurus is named after the acronym of the Geological Survey of Pakistan (GSP). See more: *Malkani 2014*

2014—Portugal— Shortest sauropod name

Zby ("abbreviation for geologist/paleontologist Georges Zbyszewski") is the shortest name of any sauropod. See more: *Mateus et al. 2014*

2015—Spain—First reptile with a name inspired by a contemporary sauropod

The name of *Riodevemys inumbragigas* ("La Rioja turtle in the shadow of the giant") indicates that it was contemporary with *Turiasaurus*. See more: *Pérez-Garcia, Royo-Torres & Cobos 2015*

2015 (1852)—England—Sauropod name with the most time elapsed for a change of genus

Pelorosaurus becklesii was changed to *Haestasaurus becklesii* after 163 years. See more: *Mantell 1852; Upchurch et al. 2015*

2016—Spain—First European sauropod named after a fictitious character

The species epithet of *Lohuecotitan pandafilandi* refers to the fictitious character of Pandafilando de la Fosca Vista in the novel *Don Quixote* by Miguel Cervantes. See more: *Cervantes Saavedra 1605; Díez-Díaz et al. 2016*

2017—Most sauropodomorph species named in a single year

Four new species were named.

2018—Brazil—Most recent sauropodomorph family created

The family Unaysauridae, based on species found in Brazil and India. See more: *Temp-Muller et al. 2018*

–Sauropod names with the simplest meaning

Cathartesaura literally means "turkey" (*Cathartes aura*). *Clasmodosaurus* means "tooth fragment." *Erketu* is a god from Mongolian mythology. See more: *Gallina & Apesteguia 2005; Ksepka & Norell 2006*

–Sauropodomorph species with the most synonyms

Massospondylus carinatus—**12 formal synonyms** (*Aetonyx palustris, Aristosaurus erectus, Dromicosaurus gracilis, Gyposaurus capensis, Hortalotarsus skirtopodus, Leptospondylus capensis, Massospondylus browni, Massospondylus harriesi, Massospondylus schwarzi, Pachyspondylus orpenii, Thecodontosaurus browni,* and *Thecodontosaurus dubius*).

–Sauropod species with the most synonyms

Neuquensaurus australis—**4 synonyms. 3 formal** (*Loricosaurus scutatus, Microcoelus patagonicus,* and *Titanosaurus nanus*) and 1 **informal** ("*Thyreophorus*").

–Sauropod species with the greatest number of informal synonyms

Giraffatitan brancai—**7 synonyms. 1 formal** (*Brachiosaurus fraasi*) and **6 informal** ("*Abdallahsaurus*," "*Blancocerosaurus*," "*Ligomasaurus*," "*Mtapaisaurus*," "*Salimosaurus*," and "*Wangonisaurus*").

–Sauropodomorph species with the most alternative names

Plateosaurus longiceps—**14 combinations**: (*Dimodosaurus poligniensis, Gresslyosaurus plieningeri, Gresslyosaurus torgeri, Plateosaurus erlenbergiensis, Plateosaurus fraasianus, Plateosaurus integer, Plateosaurus plieningeri, Plateosaurus poligniensis, Plateosaurus torgeri, Plateosaurus trossingensis, Smilodon laevis, Teratosaurus suevicus,* and *Teratosaurus trossingensis*).

–Sauropodomorph species with the most name combinations

Camarasaurus grandis—**8 additional alternative names** (*Apatosaurus grandis, Astrodon montanus, Camarasaurus impar, Camarasaurus robustus, Morosaurus grandis, Morosaurus impar, Morosaurus robustus,* and *Pleurocoelus montanus*).

–Sauropodomorph with the most species assigned

Plateosaurus was used to define multiple sauropodomorphs, which turned it into a catchall genus. The genus *Plateosaurus* actually includes only three valid species: *P. engelhardti, P. gracilis,* and *P. longiceps. Plateosaurus*—**24:**

Valid—**3** (*P. engelhardti, P. gracilis,* and *P. longiceps*).

Synonyms—**13** (*P. bavaricus, P. erlenbergiensis, P. fraasi, P. fraasianus, P. giganteus, P. integer, P. plieningeri, P. poligniensis,* *P. quenstedti, P. reinigeri, P. robustus, P. torgeri,* and *P. trossingensis*).

Do not belong—**8** ("*P.*" *ajax,* "*P.*" *cullingworthi,* "*P.*" *elizae,* "*P.*" *ingens,* "*P.*" *magnus,* "*P.*" *ornatus,* "*P.*" *stormbergensis,* and "*P.*" *wetzelianus*).

–Sauropod with the most species assigned

Titanosaurus is a doubtful genus, but it came to include a number of species that were later Identified as belonging to different taxa.

Titanosaurus—**14:**

Doubtful—**2** (*T. blansfordi* and *T. indicus*).

Do not belong—**12** ("*T.*" *australis,* "*M.*" *colberti,* "*M.*" *dacus,* "*M.*" *falloti,* "*M.*" *hungaricus,* "*M.*" *lydekkeri,* "*T.*" *madagascariensis,* "*T.*" *nanus,* "*M.*" *rahioliensis,* "*M.*" *septentrionalis,* "*T.*" *transsylvanicus* and "*T.*" *valdensis*).

–Sauropod with the greatest number of valid species

Omeisaurus—**7:**

Valid—**5** (*O. changshouensis, O. jiaoi, O. junghsiensis, O. luoquanensis,* and *O. tianfuensis*).

Different genus?—**2** (*O. fuxiensis* and *O. maoianus*).

–Sauropod with the greatest number of invalid species

Mamenchisaurus—**12:**

Valid—**4** (*M. constructus, M. hochuanensis, M. jingyanensis,* and *M. sinocanadorum*)

Different genus?—**2** (*M. anyuensis* and *M. youngi*).

Invalid—**6** ("*M. chuanjieensis*," "*M. guangyanensis*," "*M. gonjianensis*," "*M. jiangshanensis*," "*M. yaochinensis*," and "*M. yunnanensis*").

–Sauropod egg with the greatest number of valid species

Megaloolithus—**19:**

Valid—**9** (*M. cylindricus M. dhoridungriensis, M. jabalpurensis, M. maghrebiensis, M. mammilare, M. megadermus, M. mohabeyi, M. petralta,* and *M. siruguei*).

Synonyms—**10** (*M. baghensis, M. balasinorensis, M. khempurensis, M. matleyi, M. patagonicus, M. phensaniensis, M. pseudomamillare, M. rahioliensis, M. trempii,* and *M. walpurensis*).

–Sauropodomorph footprint with the greatest number of valid species

Otozoum—**6:**

Valid—**4** (*O. caudatum O. minus, O. moodii,* and *O. parvum*).

Doubtful—**1** (*O. lineatus*).

Synonyms—**1** (*O. grandcombensis,* and *O. swinnertoni*).

–Sauropodomorph footprint with the greatest number of invalid species

Otozoum—**6:**

Valid—**4** (*O. caudatum, O. minus, O. moodii,* and *O. parvum*).

Not sauropodomorphs—**1** ("*O.*" *lineatus*).

Synonyms—**1** (*O. grandcombensis* and *O. swinnertoni*).

–Sauropodomorph footprint with the greatest number of invalid species

Pseudotetrasauropus— **11:**

Valid—**5** (*P. actunguis, P. andusiensis, P. bipedoida, P. grandcombensis,* and *O. mekalingensis*).

Not sauropodomorphs—**5** ("*P.*" *angustus,* "*P.*" *curtus,* "*P.*" *dulcis,* "*P.*" *elegans,* and "*P.*" *francisci*).

Synonyms—**1** (*O. jaquesi*).

–Sauropod footprint with the greatest number of valid species

Brontopodus—**4:**

Valid—**3** (*B. birdi, B. changlingensis,* and *B. pentadactylus*)

Erroneous—**1** ("*P. jenseni*")

–Species name most frequently used for sauropods

madagascariensis —**Valid 3:** (*Bothriospondylus, Lapparentosaurus,* and *Titanosaurus*).

–Species name most frequently used for sauropodomorphs
robustus —**Valid 2:** (*Lufengosaurus* and *Gresslyosaurus*).

–Sauropod footprint with the most synonyms
Lavinipes —**1:** (*Pseudotetrasauropus* in part)

–Sauropod footprint with the most synonyms
Brontopodus —**1:** (*Chuxiongpus*)

–Sauropod egg with the most synonyms
Fusioolithus baghensis—**4:** (*Megaloolithus balasinorensis, M.
pseudomamilare, M. trempii,* and *Patagoolithus salitralensis*)

RECORDS AND CURIOSITIES IN SAUROPODOMORPH AND SAUROPOD NOMENCLATURE

LONGEST AND SHORTEST BINOMIAL AND TRINOMIAL NAMES

Sauropodomorphs with the longest and shortest names: ***Plateosauravus stormbergensis*** — **28**, ("Kholumolumosaurus ellenbergerorum" — **32**, is an invalid name), ***Seitaad ruessi***—**13**

Sauropods with the longest and shortest names: ***Bothryospondylus madagascariensis, Chinshakiangosaurus chunghoensis,*** **and *Lapparentosaurus madagascariensis***—**32** ("*Chinshakiangosaurus zhonghonensis*" and "*Chinshakiangosaurus
chuanghoensis*" — **34**, are invalid names), ***Zby atlanticus***—**13**
(*Astrodon altus* and *Astrodon nanus*—**13** are invalid combinations).

Sauropods with the longest and shortest names: ***Pseudotetrasauropus grandcombensis*** — **33** and ***Evazoum sirigui*** — **14**

Sauropod footprints with the longest and shortest names:
Elephantopoides barkhausensis—**28, *Brontopodus birdi***
and *Brontopodus zheni* (*Chuxiongpus zheni* is currently an inactive combination)— **16**

Sauropod eggs with the longest and shortest names: ***Similifa-
veoolithus gongzhulingensis*** — **36, *Sphaerovum erbeni***—**17**

LONGEST AND SHORTEST GENUS NAMES

Sauropods with the longest and shortest species names: ***Chinshakiangosaurus***— **21, *Seitaad***— **7**

Sauropods with the longest and shortest names: ***Archaeodontosaurus* & *Opisthocoelicaudia***— **18** ("*Lancangjiangosaurus*"
and "*Lanchanjiangosaurus*" — **19** are invalid names), ***Zby***— **3**

Sauropodomorph footprints with the longest and shortest
names: ***Pseudotetrasauropus***— **19, *Otozoum***—**6**

Sauropod footprints with the longest and shortest names:
***Elephantophoides* and *Titanosaurimanus*— 16, *Polyonyx*—**
8

Sauropod eggs with the longest and shortest names: ***Similifa-
veoolithus*— 20, *Sphaerovum*— 10**

LONGEST AND SHORTEST SPECIES NAMES

Sauropods with the longest and shortest species names: ***madagascariensis***—**17** (*Bothryospondylus, Lapparentosaurus* and
Titanosaurus), ***saihangaobiensis***—**17, *lii*— 3** (*Shunosaurus*) .

Sauropodomorphs with the longest and shortest species names:
dharmaramensis—**14** (*Lamplughsaura*), ***pererabdalorum***—**14**

(*Arcusaurus*), ***roychowdhurtii***—**14** (*Nambalia*), ***stormbergensis*
—14** (*Plateosauravus*), ***erlenbergiensis***—**15** (*Plateosaurus* currently an inactive combination), ***suni***—**4** (*Xixiposaurus*).

Sauropodomorph footprints with the longest and shortest species names: ***grandcombensis***—**14** (*Pseudotetrasauropus*), ***minor*** — **5** (*Kalosauropus*).

Sauropod footprints with the longest and shortest species
names: ***muenchehagensis***—**15** (*Rotundichnus*), ***taghbaloutensis*** – **15** (*Breviparopus*), ***nana***—**4** (*Titanosaurimanus*).

Sauropod eggs with the longest and shortest species names:
dhoridungriensis—**16** (*Megaloolithus*), ***microtuberculata***
—**16** (*pseudomamillare*), ***atlasi***— **6** (*Pseudomegaloolithus*),
jiangi—**6** (*Protodictyoolithus*), ***zhangi***—**6** (*Faveoloolithus*).

SAUROPOD ALPHABET

If we place the scientific names on an alphabetic list in different
categories, these are the first and last names on that list.

BINOMIAL NAMES

Sauropodomorphs: ***Aardonyx celestae* —*Yunnanosaurus
youngi***

Sauropods: ***Abrosaurus dongpoi*** ("*Abdallahsaurus*" is not a
valid name)—***Zizhongosaurus chuangchengensis*** ("*Zizhongosaurus huangshibanensis*" is not a valid name)

Sauropodomorph footprints: ***Agrestipus hottoni* — *Trisauropodiscus superavipes***

Sauropod footprints: ***Breviparopus taghbaloutensis*—*Titanosaurimanus nana*** ("*Ultrasauripus ungulatus*" is not a valid name)

Sauropod egg: ***Faveoloolithus ningxiaensis***, (*Dictyoolithus
lishuiensis* a sauropod egg?), (*Dendroolithus guoqingsiensis* actually is now *Parafaveoloolithus*)—***Pseudomegaloolithus atlasi***
(*Stromatoolithus pinglingensis* a sauropod egg?, ***Youngoolithus
xipingensis*** is now *Parafaveoloolithus*)

GENUS NAMES

Sauropodomorphs: ***Aardonyx—Yunnanosaurus***

Sauropods: ***Abrosaurus—Zizhongosaurus***

Sauropodomorph footprints: ***Agrestipus—Trisauropodiscus***

Sauropod footprints: ***Breviparopus—Titanosaurimanus*** ("*Ultrasauripus*" is not a valid name)

Sauropod eggs: ***Faveoloolithus,*** (*Dictyoolithus* a sauropod
egg?)—***Pseudomegaloolithus*** (*Stromatoolithus* a sauropod
egg?).

SPECIES NAME (SPECIES EPITHET)

Sauropodomorphs: ***antiquus*** (*Thecodontosaurus*), ***zastronensis***
(*Sefapanosaurus*)

Sauropods: ***africana*** (*Tornieria*), ***affinis*** (*Barosaurus*, is a doubtful name) —***yulinensizhaoi*** (*Fusuisaurus*), ***zhoui*** ("*Yibinosaurus*" is an invalid name)

Sauropodomorph footprints: ***acutunguis*** (*Pseudotetrasauropus*)
—***yulinensis*** (*Pengxianpus*)

Sauropod footprints: ***asturiensis*** (*Gigantosauropus*)—***zheni***
(*Brontopodus*)

Sauropod eggs: ***aureliensis*** (*Megaloolithus*)—***zhangi*** (*Faveoloolithus*)

SIMILAR NAMES

We know that ***Zigongosaurus—Zizhongosaurus*** are very similar names, but look at these other ones:

Most similar sauropod names:
Fukuititan—Fusuititan (90%), *Galveosaurus—Galvesaurus*
(91.7%) are synonyms

Most similar sauropodomorph names:
Eucnemesaurus—Euskelesaurus: 13 letters, 3 different
(76.9%) ***Euskelesaurus*** was corrected to ***Euskelosaurus***: 4
different letters (69.2%)

Most similar sauropodomorph and sauropod names:
Jiangshanosaurus—Jingshanosaurus: 16 letters—1 different (93.75%)

Most similar theropod and sauropod names:
Giganotosaurus—Gigantosaurus: 14 letters—1 different
(92.86%)

Most similar sauropod and ornithischian names:
Isanosaurus—Pisanosaurus: 14 letters—1 different (92.86%)

Most similar sauropodomorph and ornithischian names:
Gripposaurus—Gryphosaurus 12 letters—2 different (83.3%)

Most similar sauropodomorph footprint names:
Pseudotetrasauropus—Tetrasauropus: 19 letters—6 different (68.4%), ***Paratetrasauropus*** is not a sauropodomorph footprint.

Most similar sauropod footprint names:
Eosauropus—Neosauropus: 11 letters—1 different (90.9%)

Most similar sauropod oolite species names:
Parafaveoloolithus—Faveoloolithus: 18 letters—4 different
(77.8%)

INTEGRATED SPECIES NAMES

Sauropod names with the highest degree of integration:
Eobrontosaurus—Brontosaurus: 14 letters—12 integrated
(85.7%)
Hoplosaurus—Oplosaurus: 10 letters—9 integrated (90.9%)
The first name is an error that has remained over time.

Sauropod and sauropodomorph names with the highest degree
of integration:
Morosaurus—Orosaurus: 10 letters—9 integrated (90%)
Pelorosaurus—Orosaurus: 12 letters—9 integrated (75%)

Sauropod and theropod names with the highest degree of integration:
Calamosaurus—Alamosaurus: 12 letters—11 integrated
(91.67%)

Sauropod and ornithischian names with the highest degree of
integration:
Pisanosaurus—Isanosaurus: 12 letters—11 integrated (91.7%)
Panoplosaurus—Oplosaurus: 13 letters—11 integrated (76.9%)

Sauropodomorph and ornithischian names with the highest degree of integration:
Torosaurus—Orosaurus: 10 letters—9 integrated (90%)
Tianchisaurus—Anchisaurus: 13 letters—11 integrated
(84.6%)

Sauropod egg names with the highest degree of integration:
Parafaveoloolithus—Faveoloolithus: 18 letters—14 integrated (77.8%)
Similifaveoloolithus—Faveoloolithus: 20 letters—14 integrated (70%)

Sauropodomorph footprints names with the highest degree of integration:
Pseudotetrasauropus—Tetrasauropus: 19 letters—13 integrated (68.4%)

Sauropod footprint names with the highest degree of integration:
Eosauropus—Neosauropus: 11 letters—10 integrated (90.9%)
Parabrontopodus—Brontopodus: 15 letters—10 integrated (73.3%)

Sauropod name most often integrated with other dinosaur names:
Elosaurus (7 occasions): The name occurs in two different sauropods: **Ampelosaurus** and **Hypselosaurus** and in a sauropodomorph: **Euskelosaurus**. Also in one theropod: **Coelosaurus** and in two ornithischians: **Othnielosaurus** and **Thescelosaurus** as well as a species that was once considered a dinosaur: **Macroscelosaurus.**

Sauropod egg name most often integrated among other dinosaur names:
Faveoloolithus (two occasions): It is repeated in **Hemifaveoloolithus** and **Parafaveolollithus**.

Full sauropod footprint name occurring as part of another:
Malakhelisaurus—Malasaurus: 15 letters—10 integrated (66. 7%)

Full sauropod footprint name occurring as part of another:
Galveosaurus—Galvesaurus: 12 letters—11 integrated (91.7%)
Plateosauravus—Plateosaurus: 14 letters—11 integrated (85.7 %)

Full sauropod name occurring sectioned in another dinosaur name:
Gigantosaurus is divided in **Giganotosaurus**: 14 letters—13 integrated (92.85%)

**Most complete sauropod with
heart-shaped teeth**
Turiasaurus riodevensis

The teeth of this sauropod, and of others such as *Turiasauria*, are heart-shaped. This feature may be a specialization adapted to the consumption of a certain type of plant. Almost all species in this group are based on fragmentary specimens or single teeth. See more: *Royo-Torres, Cobos & Alcalá 2006; Mocho et al. 2015; Hallett & Wedel 2016; Mocho et al. 2017*

1 m

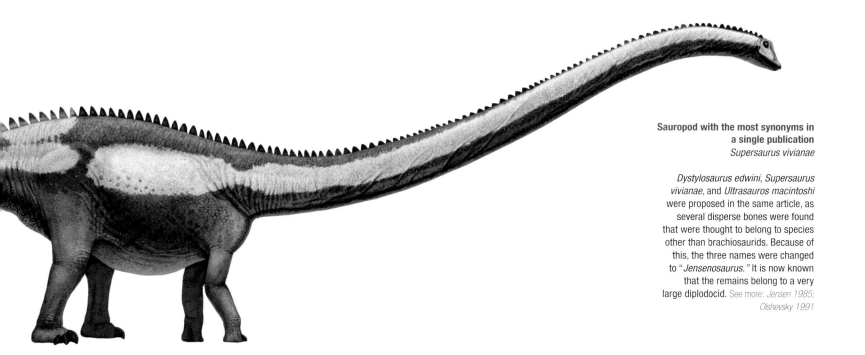

Sauropod with the most synonyms in a single publication
Supersaurus vivianae

Dystylosaurus edwini, *Supersaurus vivianae*, and *Ultrasauros macintoshi* were proposed in the same article, as several disperse bones were found that were thought to belong to species other than brachiosaurids. Because of this, the three names were changed to "*Jensenosaurus.*" It is now known that the remains belong to a very large diplodocid. See more: *Jensen 1985; Olshevsky 1991*

Largest Jurassic sauropod skeleton of Europe
Lusotitan atalaiensis

It weighed up to 34 t; however, *Neosodon precursor* may have been a larger sauropod but is based on teeth alone. *Turiasaurus* is usually named as the largest European dinosaur; however, *Lusotitan* was probably taller, longer and heavier. See more: *Sauvage 1888, 1896; Moussaye 1885; Mannion et al. 2013; D'Emic et al. 2016; Poropat et al. 2016*

1 m

Chronology of the largest sauropods throughout history

Year	Species and specimen	Actual size (length - weight)	Interesting facts and country	Reference
1841	*Cardiodon rugolosus* BMNH R1527	18 m - 19.5 t	The first sauropod tooth known (except for "Rutellum implicatum"). England, UK.	Owen 1841, 1844
1842	*Cetiosaurus epioolithicus* SCAWM 4G	24 m - 32 t	Known solely from metatarsals, its size has not been estimated. England, UK.	Owen 1842
1849	*Pelorosaurus conybearei* BMNH 28626	14 m - 9 t	The enormous size of its humerus, 1372 mm, was astounding. England, UK.	Melville 1849; Mantell 1850
1852	*Oplosaurus armatus* NHMUK R964	15.6 m - 12.4 t	Traditionally considered similar in size to *Giraffatitan brancai*. England, UK.	Gervais 1852
1869	*Cetiosaurus?* J230 05	13 m - 5.9 t	Discovered in 1809. It was believed to be of enormous size. England, UK.	Seeley 1869; Delair & Sarjeant 1975
1870	*Cetiosaurus giganteus*	-	Synonymous with *Cetiosaurus oxoniensis*. England, UK.	Owen in Huxley 1870
1870	*Ornithopsis hulkei* BMNH 28632	17.4 m - 15.5 t	Also known as *Bothriospondylus magnus*. England, UK.	Seeley 1870; Owen 1875
1877	*Apatosaurus ajax* YPM 1860	23 m - 20 t	The species type specimen. USA.	Marsh 1877
1877	*Atlantosaurus immannis* YPM 1840	23 m - 20 t	Originally called *Titanosaurus montanus*. USA.	Marsh 1877a, 1877b
1877	*Camarasaurus supremus* AMNH 5760	20 m - 30 t	Several different specimens of similar size are known and are identified with the same museum number. USA.	Cope 1877
1878	*Diplodocus longus* YPM 1920	26 m - 13 t	For a long time, it was considered the longest sauropod. USA.	Marsh 1878
1878	*Maraapunisaurus fragillimus* AMNH 5777	35 m - 70 t	It was estimated to be up to 60 m in length and up to 150 t in weight. USA.	Cope 1878; Paul 2010
1893	*Argyrosaurus superbus* MLP 77-V-29-1	21 m - 26 t	An estimated length of up to 40 m was mentioned. Argentina.	Lydekker 1893
1898	"Brontosaurus giganteus"	22 m - 17 t	The *New York Journal and Advertiser* published the name "Brontosaurus giganteus," found in Wyoming, with exaggerated measurements; the total femur length, estimated from a fragment, was mistakenly given as 2.4 m when it was actually 1.76 m. The creature was introduced as "the most collosal animal on earth," believed to be 40 m long and weighing 54 t.	Anonymous 1898; Breithaupt 2013
1903	*Brachiosaurus altithorax* FMNH P25107	24.5 m - 40 t	The first sauropod identified as being higher at the front than the back. USA.	Riggs 1903
1914	*Giraffatitan brancai* HMN XV2	25 m - 48 t	Presented to the public in the media as "*Gigantosaurus*." Its estimated weighted was up to 100 t. Tanzania.	Janensch 1914
1929	*Antarctosaurus giganteus* MLP 26-316	30.5 m - 45 t	Its maximum estimated length was 40 m and its weight was 80 t. Argentina.	Huene 1929
1960	"*Brachiosaurus*" *nougaredi*	29.5 m - 25 t	The narrow sacrum suggests it may have been a diplodocus. Algeria.	Lapparent 1960
1972	*Supersaurus vivianae* BYU 12962	33 m - 35 t	Includes *Dystylosaurus edwini* and *Ultrasaurus macintoshi*. USA.	Jensen 1972, 1985
1985	*Ultrasaurus macintoshi* BYU 9044	33 m - 35 t	It was believed to be a brachiosaurus weighing up to 180 t. USA.	Jensen 1985
1985	cf. *Barosaurus lentus* BYU 9024	45 m - 60 t	The piece was thought to belong to a *Supersaurus vivianae*. USA	Jensen 1985, 1987
1989	*Bruhathkayosaurus matleyi*	37 m - 95 t?	The bones are likely fossilized tree trunks. It was estimated at up to 44 m long and 220 t in weight. India.	Yadagiri & Ayyasami 1989
1991	*Diplodocus hallorum* NMMNH-P3690	30 m - 21 t	It was believed to be 54 m in length and 113 t in weight. It was known as *Seismosaurus halli*. USA.	Gillette 1987, 1991
1993	*Argentinosaurus huinculensis* PVPH-1	35 m - 75 t	It was thought to be 45 m in length and up to 100 t in weight. Argentina.	Bonaparte & Coria 1993
1994	*Mamenchisaurus sinocanadorum* IVPP V10603	25 m - 24 t	It was mistakenly estimated as being 35 m in length and and 75 t in weight. China.	Russell & Zheng 1994
1997	*Hudiesaurus sinojapanorum* IVPP V. 11120	30.5 m - 44 t	It was believed to rival *Argentinosaurus* in size. China.	Dong 1997
2000	"Giant of Río Negro"	29 m - 40 t	Nonprofessional publications mentioned a length of 51 meters and a weight of 110 t. Argentina.	Anonymous 2000
2001	*Futalognkosaurus dukei* MUCPv-323	24 m - 30 t	It was estimated to be 30 m in length and 50 t in weight. Argentina.	Calvo 2001a, 2001b, 2002; Calvo et al. 2007
2004	cf. *Argentinosaurus* MLP-DP 46-VIII-21–3	36 m - 80 t	Some consider it as *A. huinculensis*, but it is more recent.	Mazzetta et al. 2004
2005	*Puertasaurus reuili* MPM 10002	28 m - 50 t	In some estimates it is larger than *Argentinosaurus*. Argentina.	Novas et al. 2005
2009	Unnamed	22.5 m - 24.5 t	It is considered a huge tibia belonging to a giant *Alamosaurus* of up to 32 m in length, but the specimen actually is not a tibia.	Rivera-Sylva et al. 2009; Ramírez-Velasco & Molina-Pérez, in prep.
2014	*Dreadnoughtus schrani* MPM-PV 1156	24 m - 35 t	Its weight was estimated at 59 t. Argentina.	Lacovara et al. 2014
2017	*Patagotitan mayorum* MPEF PV 3399	31 m - 55 t	There is a skeletal reconstruction of 37.2 meters in length. It was ultimately thought to be larger than an *Argentinosaurus*.	Carballido et al. 2017

Chronology of sauropods considered the smallest historically

Year	Species and specimen	Actual size (length - weight)	Interesting facts and country	Reference
1842	*Cetiosaurus medius* OUMNH J13721	10.8 m - 3.3 t	It was older than *Cetiosaurus oxoniensis*. England.	Owen 1842
1852	*Haestasaurus becklesii* NHMUK R1868-1870	8.3 m - 2.5 t	It is not known whether it was an adult or a juvenile. England.	Mantell 1852
1888	*Pleurocoelus nanus* USNM Col.	3.75 m - 175 kg	It was thought to be a small species but was in fact a juvenile. USA.	Marsh 1888
1915	*Magyarosaurus dacus* BMNH R.3861a	5.4 m - 520 kg	This was an adult individual, although there may have been populations of large and small individuals. Romania.	Nopcsa 1915
1985	*Blikanasaurus cromptoni* SAM K403	5.4 m - 420 kg	It is not known whether it was an adult or a juvenile. South Africa.	Galton & Van Heerden 1985
2006	*Europasaurus holgeri* DFMMh/FV 157	6 m - 800 kg	The smallest sauropod of the Jurassic. Germany.	Sander et al. 2006

Chronology of early sauropodomorphs considered the smallest historically

Year	Species and specimen	Actual size (length - weight)	Interesting facts and country	Reference
1818	*Anchisaurus polyzelus* MT 6928/29	1.95 m - 15 kg	It was not identified as a dinosaur until 1855. USA.	Smith 1818
1836	*Thecodontosaurus* BMNH 37001	2.5 m - 20 kg	It was an adult more than a year old. England.	Riley & Stutchbury 1836; Morris 1843
1891	*Anchisaurus polyzelus* YPM 1883 (YPM 2128)	2.4 m - 25 kg	It was known as *Anchisaurus solus*. USA	Marsh 1891
1986	*Alwalkeria maleriensis* ISI R 306	1.2 m - 2 kg	It was similar to *Eoraptor*, so was possibly a primitive sauropodomorph. India.	Chatterjee 1986; Chatterjee & Creisler 1994
1993	*Eoraptor lunensis* LACM 33213	1.65 m - 5 kg	Identified as a sauropodomorph in 2011. Argentina.	Sereno et al. 1993
2013	*Pampadromaeus barberenai* ULBRA-PVT016	1.4 m - 1.8 kg	Possibly not an adult. Brazil.	Elzanowski 1981; Kurochkin et al. 2013
2016	cf. *Pampadromaeus barberenai* CAPPA/UFSM 0027	1.65 m - 2.9 kg	An adult *Pampadromaeus barberenai*? Brazil.	Muller et al. 2016

Chronology of the largest early sauropodomorphs in history

Year	Species and specimen	Actual size (length - weight)	Interesting facts and country	Reference
1837	*Plateosaurus engelhardti* UEN	6.1 m - 690 kg	Discovered in 1834. Germany.	Meyer 1837
1855	*"Riesensaurus"*	-	It is mentioned as a creature larger than *Plateosaurus*. Germany.	Meyer 1855
1862	*Plateosaurus engelhardti* POL 76	7.7 m - 1.48 t	It was known as *Dimodosaurus poligniensis* or *Plateosaurus* cf. *plieningeri*. France.	Pidancet & Chopard 1862
1896	*Plateosaurus longiceps* SMNS 80664	8.8 m - 2.1 t	It was known as *Gresslyosaurus plieningeri* or *Smilodon laevis*. Germany..	Fraas 1896
1916	*Gigantoscelus molengraaffi* MT 65	9 m - 1.6 t	It was probably similar to *Plateosauravus stormbergensis*. South Africa.	Hoepen 1916
1924	*Melanorosaurus readi* SAM 3450	5.6 m - 450 kg	According to popular belief, it was 12 m in length. South Africa.	Haughton 1924
1969	*Riojasaurus incertus* PVL 3808	6.8 m - 800 kg	It has been presented as a creature 11 m in length. Argentina.	Bonaparte 1969
1985	*Camelotia borealis* BMNH R2870-R2874	10.2 m - 2.75 t	Some authors consider it a primitive sauropod. England.	Galton 1985
1993	*Plateosaurus engelhardti* IFG uncatalogued	9.4 m - 2.6 t	The largest known *Plateosaurus* specimen. Germany.	Wellnhofer 1993; Moser 2003
2011	Unnamed Meet BP/1/5339	16 m - 10 t	Older than *Aardonyx celestae*. South Africa.	Yates 2008*; Wedel & Yates 2011
2018	*Lessemsaurus sauropoides* CRILAR-PV 302	10.3 m - 2.9 t	Its weight was calculated at 10 t, based on the circumference of its limb bones. Argentina.	Apaldetti et al. 2018

The longest estimated lengths of any sauropod

The longest length published in a pop science book
Maraapunisaurus fragillimus 60 m - *Paul 2010*
The longest length reported in a formal publication
Maraapunisaurus fragillimus 58–60 m - *Paul 1997; Carpenter 2006*
(may have been 35 m in length)

The largest estimated weights of any sauropod

In non-peer-reviewed online publications
Bruhathkayosaurus matleyi 220 t (it is uncertain whether they are sauropod bones)
The largest weight published in a pop science book
Maraapunisaurus fragillimus 150 t - *Paul 2010*
The highest estimated body mass reported in a formal publication
Maraapunisaurus fragillimus 122.4–125 t - *Paul 1997; Carpenter 2006*
(it actually was about half of that weight)

Mesozoic calendar
The chronology of the sauropodomorphs

Records: The oldest and most recent
The largest and smallest by era

The oldest sauropodomorphs known are from the Upper Triassic, 232 million years ago, meaning that they lived on Earth for 166 million years. Sauropods disappeared completely in the extinction that took place at the end of the Mesozoic era and ushered in the Cenozoic era.

These animals ate plants, which adapted and diversified over time, taking new forms, and we see this reflected especially in sauropodomorph teeth. They initially consumed gymnosperms, ferns, and small prey, then began eating the abundant angiosperm plants that surrounded them.

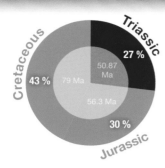

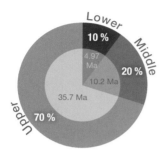

Earth's rotation reduced the area over geological time. As a result, days are becoming longer at a rate of 1.79 milliseconds every 100 years. Among the forces that led to this deceleration, the primary one was the stoppage of the tides owing to the moon's proximity.

Sauropodomorphs lived exclusively during the Mesozoic era, from the Middle or Upper Triassic onward. Before they appeared, other life-forms were consuming the resources—mostly plants—that the sauropods would later feed upon. Large ancient phytophagous creatures did not exceed 3 m in height, and so the canopies of the highest plants were not eaten by large vertebrates but instead were eaten by several species of insects and some tree-dwelling species.

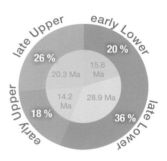

Volcanoes of the Lower Triassic

The Mesozoic was an era of intense volcanic activity, and some of the most important volcanic events of each period are presented below. Volcanic activity in the Mesozoic lasted for the entire Permian and Triassic periods in what is known today as the Ochoco Mountains (present-day Oregon, USA, approx. 300–200 Ma). It lasted for some 100 Ma, half of that time spanning the entire Triassic. The largest volcanic zone of the Lower Triassic was the Siberian Traps (present-day Russia, 252.17–251.2 Ma). The zone covered 7 million km², although today only 2 million km² remain. See more: *Beebee et al. 2002; Sahney & Benton 2008; McClaughry et al. 2009; Sun et al. 2013*

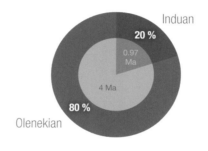

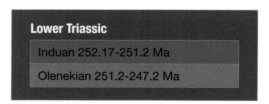

The first part of the Triassic was the shortest, lasting some 4.97 million years, or 10% of the duration of the Triassic and 3% of the Mesozoic era.

General paleoclimatology 30–40° C (Holtz 2015)
Sea temperature at the equatorial zone 40° C (Sun et al. 2012)
Length of day: 22.8 hours.

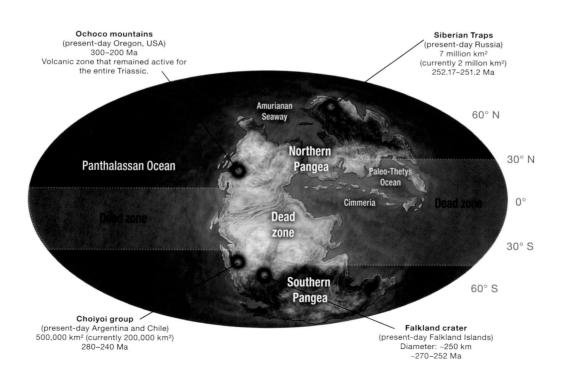

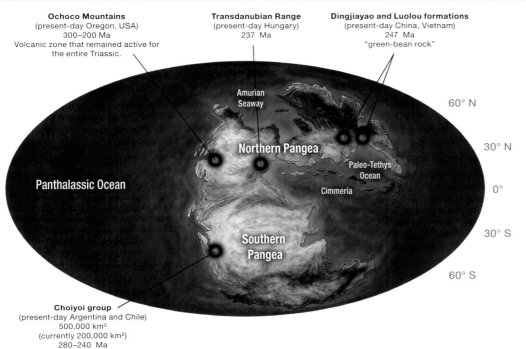

Ochoco Mountains
(present-day Oregon, USA)
300–200 Ma
Volcanic zone that remained active for
the entire Triassic.

Transdanubian Range
(present-day Hungary)
237 Ma

Dingjiayao and Luolou formations
(present-day China, Vietnam)
247 Ma
"green-bean rock"

Amurian
Seaway

Northern Pangea

Paleo-Tethys
Ocean

Panthalassic Ocean

Cimmeria

Southern
Pangea

60° N

30° N

0°

30° S

60° S

Choiyoi group
(present-day Argentina and Chile)
500,000 km²
(currently 200,000 km²)
280–240 Ma

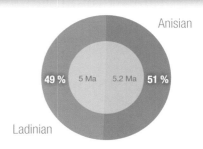

Anisian

49 %   5 Ma   5.2 Ma   51 %

Ladinian

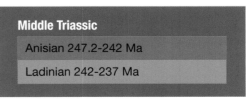

Middle Triassic

| Anisian 247.2-242 Ma |
| Ladinian 242-237 Ma |

The second part of the Triassic lasted some 10.2 million years, or 20% of the duration of the Triassic and 5% of the Mesozoic era.

General paleoclimatology 20–30° C
Length of day: 22.8 hours.

Volcanoes

The oldest volcanic resurgence of the Middle Triassic occurred in the Dingjiayao, Luolou, Napanjiang, and Xinyuan formations (present-day China and Vietnam, approx. 247 Ma). Volcanic tuff ("green-bean rocks") is a kind of porous volcanic ash that formed from the rapid cooling of volcanic rock. The greatest zone of volcanic activity in the Middle Triassic was the Choiyoi Group (present-day Argentina and Chile, 280–240 Ma). It covered an area of 500,000 km², although today only 200,000 km² remain. The most recent volcanic zone of the Middle Triassic was the Transdanubian Range (present-day Hungary, approx. 237 Ma). See more: *Stipanicic et al. 1968; Qin et al. 1989; Jiayong & Enos 1991; Llambías 1999; Llambías et al. 2003; Xiao & HU 2005; Kleiman & Japas 2009; Martinez & Giambiagi 2010; Vallecillo et al. 2010; Yan et al. 2015; Ma et al. 2016; Farics et al. 2017*

Sauropodomorphs of the Middle Triassic?

Some authors believe it is possible that *Nyasasaurus* was a derived dinosauromorph, while others suspect that it could have been the oldest known dinosaur, whether a very primitive form, similar to an Eoraptor, or even a massospondylid sauropodomorph. The latter is surprising for the age of the remains, as it dates to the Anisian (approx. 247.2–242 Ma). The problem is that it is very difficult to verify, because the fossils are very fragmented and incomplete. Some speculate that *Thecodontosaurus alophos*, also known as "Teleocrater rhadinus," was synonymous with this species, although other investigators believe it was likely a neotheropod. The silhouette represents the potential size of *Nyasasaurus*, if it was similar to *Massospondylus*. See more: *Charig 1967; Nesbitt et al. 2013; Baron et al. 2017; Baron 2018*

There are reports of footprints that were originally assigned to sauropodomorphs of the Middle Triassic; however, both cases were ruled out as such. *Prosauropodichnus bernburgensis*, from the Anisian (present-day Germany, approx. 247.2–242 Ma), 35 cm in length, does not seem to belong to a dinosaur. Another report refers to *Tetrapodosaurus* sp. some 30 cm in length, that had been dated to the Ladinian (present-day Argentina, approx. 242–237 Ma), although they are now known to be footprints from the Upper Triassic (Lower Carnian, approx. 237–232 Ma). See more: *Diedrich 2009; Melchor & De Valais 2006; Marsicano et al. 2016*

Nyasasaurus parringtoni
Nesbitt et al. 2013

1:10

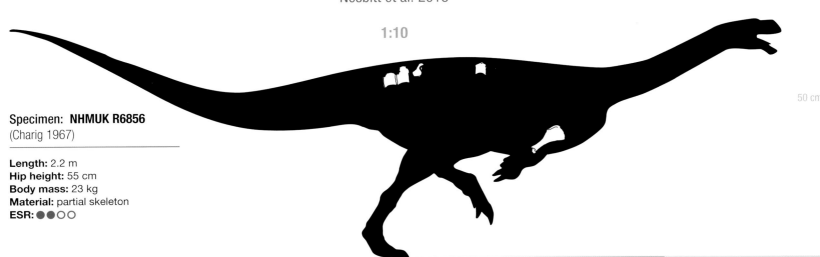

50 cm

Specimen: NHMUK R6856
(Charig 1967)

Length: 2.2 m
Hip height: 55 cm
Body mass: 23 kg
Material: partial skeleton
ESR: ●●○○

50 cm   100 cm   150 cm   200 cm

Volcanoes

The Upper Triassic zone that had the greatest volcanic activity was situated in what is now North America (present-day Canada and the USA [New Jersey, New York, Oregon, and Pennsylvania], approx. 237 Ma). The Central Atlantic magmatic province emerged (present-day Brazil, France, Mali, Texas, USA, approx. 201.3 Ma); it ultimately covered an area of more than 7 million km² and was part of the Pangea fragmentation. This magmatism coincided with a mass extinction at the Triassic-Jurassic boundary. See more: *Armstrong & Besancon 1970; Muller 1980; Kodama 1983; Jungen 1985; Houghton 1988; Bertrand 1991; Caroff et al. 1995; Baksi 1997; Dostal et al. 1999; Marzoli et al. 1999; McHone 2000; Greene et al. 2005; Jones et al. 2007; Glenn 2008; Zurevinski et al. 2008*

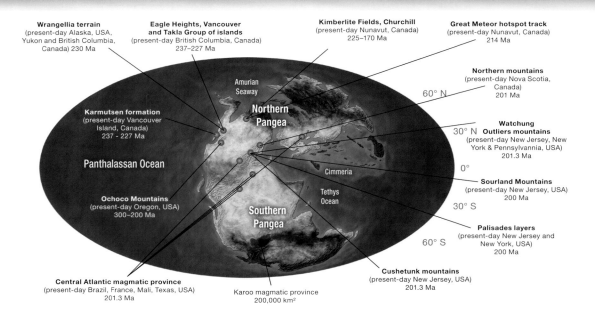

Wrangellia terrain (present-day Alaska, USA, Yukon and British Columbia, Canada) 230 Ma

Eagle Heights, Vancouver and Takla Group of islands (present-day British Columbia, Canada) 237–227 Ma

Kimberlite Fields, Churchill (present-day Nunavut, Canada) 225–170 Ma

Great Meteor hotspot track (present-day Nunavut, Canada) 214 Ma

Karmutsen formation (present-day Vancouver Island, Canada) 237 - 227 Ma

Northern mountains (present-day Nova Scotia, Canada) 201 Ma

Watchung Outliers mountains (present-day New Jersey, New York & Pennsylvania, USA) 201.3 Ma

Sourland Mountains (present-day New Jersey, USA) 200 Ma

Ochoco Mountains (present-day Oregon, USA) 300–200 Ma

Palisades layers (present-day New Jersey and New York, USA) 200 Ma

Cushetunk mountains (present-day New Jersey, USA) 201.3 Ma

Central Atlantic magmatic province (present-day Brazil, France, Mali, Texas, USA) 201.3 Ma

Karoo magmatic province 200,000 km²

Amurian Seaway · Northern Pangea · Panthalassan Ocean · Cimmeria · Tethys Ocean · Southern Pangea

60° N · 30° N · 0° · 30° S · 60° S

General paleoclimatology 38° C
Length of day: 22.8–23 hours.

The smallest of the Upper Triassic (Class: Very small Grade II)

Pampadromaeus barberenai ("Mário Costa Barberena's pampa runner") (Carnian approx. 237–232 Ma), from southwestern Pangea (present-day Brazil). It was perhaps the smallest sauropodomorph of all, weighing as much as a ferret. Specimen CAPPA/UFSM 0027 is suspected to be an adult of the species known as cf. *Pampadromaeus barberenai*. This specimen was larger, measuring 1.65 m in length and weighing 4.8 kg. In contrast, *Alwalkeria maleriensis*, from south-central Pangea (present-day India), was 1.3 m long and weighed 2 kg, but may have been a primitive saurischian. The smallest quadruped sauropodomorph was *Meroktenos thabanensis* (present-day Lesotho), 4.8 m in length and weighing 300 kg. The smallest sauropod of this period was *Isanosaurus attavipachi*, 8.3 m in length and weighing 1.3 t. See more: *Galton & van Heerden 1985; Chatterjee 1987; Gauffre 1993; Yates 2008; Cabreira et al. 2011; McPhee et al. 2014, 2015; Muller et al. 2016.*

The smallest juvenile

Mussaurus patagonicus ("rat-lizard of Patagonia") (Norian, approx. 227–208.5 Ma) from southwestern Pangea (present-day Argentina). It was mistakenly identified as a likely adult because it was accompanied by some small spheres of doubtful identification that were mistakenly thought to be eggs. They were calves 30 cm long and weighing 40 g. See more: *Bonaparte & Vince 1979*

The first published species of the Upper Triassic

Thecodontosaurus (1836)) ("socket-toothed lizard"), from north-central Pangea (present-day England). It was discovered in 1834 and reported in 1835; the genus was named in 1836 and assigned a species in 1843. *Anchisaurus polyzelus* was thought to be from the Triassic, but we now know it dates to the Lower Jurassic, and although it was named later, the remains were announced in 1820. See more: *Smith 1820; Williams 1835; Riley & Stutchbury 1836; Morris 1843; Hitchcock 1865; Galton 1985*

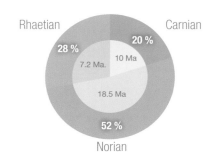

Rhaetian · Carnian · Norian

20 % 10 Ma
28 % 7.2 Ma.
18.5 Ma
52 %

Upper Triassic	
Carnian 237-227 Ma	
Norian 227-208.5 Ma	
Rhaetian 208.5-201.3 Ma	

The final part of the Triassic was the shortest, lasting just 35.7 million years, or 70% of the entire Triassic and 20% of the duration of the Mesozoic era.

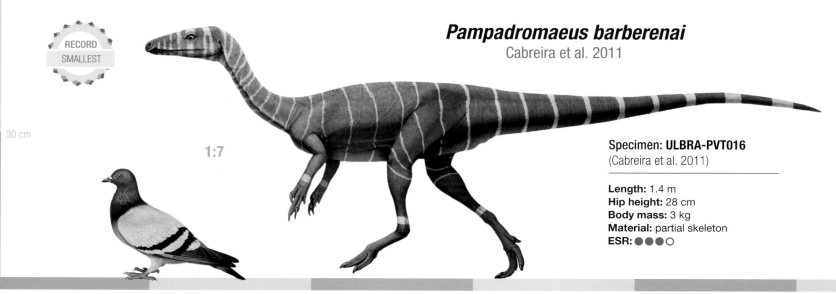

RECORD SMALLEST

30 cm

1:7

Pampadromaeus barberenai
Cabreira et al. 2011

Specimen: ULBRA-PVT016
(Cabreira et al. 2011)

Length: 1.4 m
Hip height: 28 cm
Body mass: 3 kg
Material: partial skeleton
ESR: ●●●○

30 cm · 60 cm · 90 cm · 120 cm · 150 cm

Unnamed
Wedel & Yates 2011

RECORD
LARGEST

1:70

Specimen: Meet BP/1/5339
(Wedel & Yates 2011)

Length: 16 m
Hip height: 3.55 m
Body mass: 10 t
Material: ulna and caudal vertebra
ESR: ●●○○

The largest of the Upper Triassic (Class: Very large Grade II)

Specimen Meet BP/1/5339 (Rhaetian, approx. 208.5–201.3 Ma), from south-central Pangea (present-day South Africa), was one of the largest bipedal sauropodomorphs, as long as a sperm whale and weighing about as much as an African and Asian elephant combined. The largest quadrupedal sauropodomorph was an animal similar to *Riojasaurus* (Norian, approx. 227–208.5 Ma), from southwestern Pangea (present-day Argentina), 14.5 m in length and weighing 7.8 t. The largest sauropod of this time was *Isanosaurus* sp. (Rhaetian, approx. 208.5–201.3 Ma), from the paleocontinent Cimmeria (present-day Thailand), measuring 13.8 m in length and weighing 6 t. See more: *Buffetaut et al. 2002; Martínez et al. 2004; Wedel & Yates 2011*

Most recently published species of the Upper Triassic

Bagualosaurus agudoensis ("strapping lizard of Agudo municipality") from southwestern Pangea (present-day Brazil), *Ingentia prima* ("first huge one") from south-central Pangea (present-day Argentina), and *Ledumahadi mafube* ("giant thunderclap at dawn") from south-central Pangea (present-day South Africa) were described in 2018. See more: *Apaldetti et al. 2018; McPhee et al. 2018; Pretto et al. 2018*

Footprints

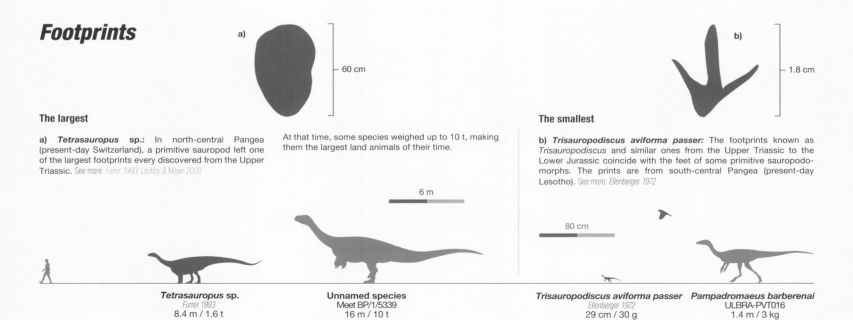

a) — 60 cm

b) — 1.8 cm

The largest

a) *Tetrasauropus* sp.: In north-central Pangea (present-day Switzerland), a primitive sauropod left one of the largest footprints every discovered from the Upper Triassic. See more: *Furrer 1993; Lockley & Meyer 2000*

At that time, some species weighed up to 10 t, making them the largest land animals of their time.

The smallest

b) *Trisauropodiscus aviforma passer:* The footprints known as *Trisauropodiscus* and similar ones from the Upper Triassic to the Lower Jurassic coincide with the feet of some primitive sauropodomorphs. The prints are from south-central Pangea (present-day Lesotho). See more: *Ellenberger 1972*

6 m

80 cm

Tetrasauropus sp.
Furrer 1993
8.4 m / 1.6 t

Unnamed species
Meet BP/1/5339
16 m / 10 t

Trisauropodiscus aviforma passer
Ellenberger 1972
29 cm / 30 g

Pampadromaeus barberenai
ULBRA-PVT016
1.4 m / 3 kg

Volcanoes

The largest volcanic zone of the Lower Jurassic was the Central Atlantic magmatic province (present-day Algeria, Brazil, Canada, Cameroon, USA, France, Guinea, Mauritania, Morocco, Mali, and Senegal, approx. 201.3 ± 4 Ma). It ultimately covered an area of more than 7 million km². Other notable volcanic events of the time occurred in what are now Canada, Chile, Lesotho, the USA (Massachusetts), and South Africa. See more: *Truswell 1977; Raymo & Raymo 1989; Caroff et al. 1995; Kramer & Ehrlichmann 1996; Baksi 1997; Barboza-Gudiño et al. 1999; Dostal et al. 1999; Marzoli et al. 1999; McHone 2000; Miller 2001; Fastovsky et al. 2005; Hautmann 2012; Bull et al. 2015; Elliot et al. 2016*

The smallest of the Lower Triassic (Class: Very small Grade III)

Thecodontosaurus minor ("lesser socket-toothed lizard") (Hettangian, approx. 201.3–199.3 Ma) from south-central Pangea (present-day South Africa). It was believed to be a juvenile *Massospondylus carinatus* but was actually an adult specimen that weighed barely as much as a domestic cat. The smallest sauropod of this period was *Pulanesaura eocollum* (present-day South Africa), 8 m in length and weighing 1.1 t. See more: *Haughton 1918; McPhee et al. 2015; Yates*

The smallest juvenile

The calves *Massospondylus carinatus* (present-day South Africa) were 13 cm long and weighed 7 g at birth, which is 2.6% of the length and 0.2% of the weight of the largest adult specimen. See more: *Owen 1854; Kitching 1979; Reisz et al. 2005, 2010*

The first published species of the Lower Jurassic

Leptospondylus capensis and *Pachyspondylus orpenii* (1854): Probably vertebrae from the same species as *Massospondylus carinatus* (1854). They were discovered in south-central Pangea (present-day South Africa). See more: *Owen 1854*

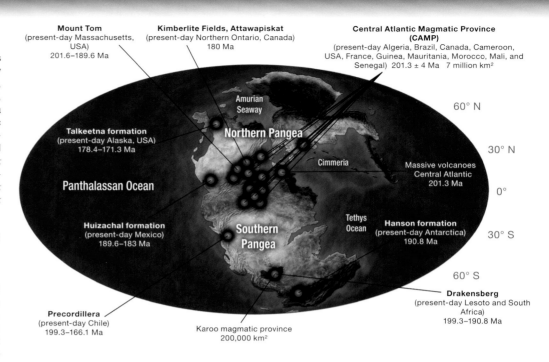

Mount Tom
(present-day Massachusetts, USA)
201.6–189.6 Ma

Kimberlite Fields, Attawapiskat
(present-day Northern Ontario, Canada)
180 Ma

Central Atlantic Magmatic Province (CAMP)
(present-day Algeria, Brazil, Canada, Cameroon, USA, France, Guinea, Mauritania, Morocco, Mali, and Senegal) 201.3 ± 4 Ma   7 million km²

60° N

Amurian Seaway

Northern Pangea

Talkeetna formation
(present-day Alaska, USA)
178.4–171.3 Ma

Cimmeria

30° N

Massive volcanoes Central Atlantic
201.3 Ma

Panthalassan Ocean

0°

Huizachal formation
(present-day Mexico)
189.6–183 Ma

Southern Pangea

Tethys Ocean

Hanson formation
(present-day Antarctica)
190.8 Ma

30° S

60° S

Precordillera
(present-day Chile)
199.3–166.1 Ma

Karoo magmatic province
200,000 km²

Drakensberg
(present-day Lesoto and South Africa)
199.3–190.8 Ma

General paleoclimatology 35° C
High concentrations of CO_2
Length of day: 23–23.1 hours.

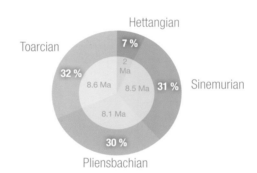

Hettangian
7 %
2 Ma
Toarcian
32 %
8.6 Ma
8.5 Ma
31 %
Sinemurian
8.1 Ma
30 %
Pliensbachian

Lower Jurassic
Hettangian 201.31–199.3 Ma
Sinemurian 199.3–190.8 Ma
Pliensbachian 190.8–182.7 Ma
Toarcian 182.7–174.1 Ma

The first part of the Jurassic lasted for 27.2 million years, or 48% of the entire Jurassic period and 15% of the entire Mesozoic.

Thecodontosaurus minor
Haughton 1918

Specimen: uncatalogued
(Haughton 1918)

Length: 1.45 m
Hip height: 26 cm
Body mass: 3.8 kg
Material: partial skeleton
ESR: ●●●○

1:10

50 cm

RECORD
SMALLEST

50 cm   100 cm   150 cm   200 cm

3 m   6 m   9 m   12 m

6 m

Barapasaurus tagorei
Jain et al. 1975

Specimen: ISIR Coll.
(Bandyopadhyay et al.2010)

Length: 14 m
Hip height: 3.7 m
Body mass: 8.5 t
Material: ulna
ESR: ●●○○

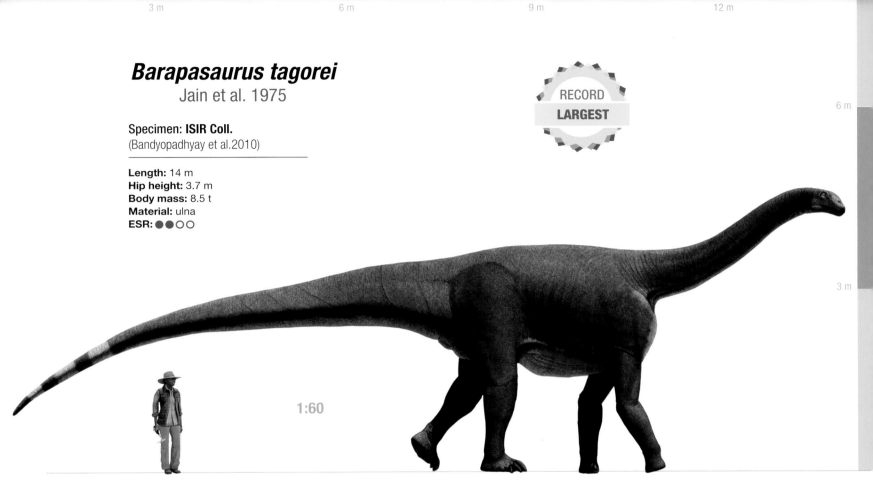

1:60

3 m

The largest of the Lower Jurassic (Class: Very large Grade II)

Barapasaurus tagorei ("poet Rabindranath Tagore's big-footed lizard") (Sinemurian, approx. 199.3–190. Ma) from south-central Pangea (present-day India). It was the largest of the quadruped sauropodomorphs, longer than a city bus and weighing as much as two Asian elephants combined. "Damalasaurus laticostalis" (present-day China) is another sauropod that appears to be of similar size, although it has not been formally described. It is possible that *Patagosaurus fariasi* belonged to the Lower Jurassic, which would make it the largest sauropod for this era. The largest sauropodomorph of the time was cf. *Yunnanosaurus* sp. (present-day China), 12 m long and weighing 3.6 t. See more: *Jain et al. 1975; Xing et al. 2013*

Most recently published species of the Lower Jurassic

Lingwulong shenqi (2018) is from the boundary between the Lower and Middle Jurassic (Toarcian-Aalenian, approx. 174.1 Ma); this is unexpected, as the neosauropods had only become prevalent during the Middle Jurassic. For its part, the last sauropodomorph of the Lower Jurassic to be described is *Yizhousaurus sunae* (2018). Both are from northeastern Pangea (present-day China). See more: *Kramer & Ehrlichmann 1996; Haxel et al. 2005; Bull et al. 2015; Xu et al. 2018; Zhang et al. 2018*

Footprints

a)

80 cm

b)

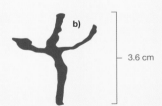

3.6 cm

The largest

a) Unnamed: From south-central Pangea (present-day Morocco). This animal may have been larger than *Barapasaurus* and *Damalasaurus*. It lived in the same area where the largest sauropodomorphs and sauropods of its time also lived. See more: *Jenny & Jossen 1982; Ishigaki & Haubold 1985; Ishigaki 1988*

Sauropodomorphs and sauropods were very diverse, and included small and large species, bipedal, quadrupedal, and mixed ones, omnivores and phytophages, and medium- and long-necked animals. The largest of all weighed more than 10 t.

6 m

The smallest

b) *Saurichnium tetractis*: This enigmatic footprint is similar to *Trisauropodiscus* and was found in south-central Pangea (present-day Namibia). Its size indicates that it likely belonged to a very young calf. See more: *Gurich 1926*

1.5 m

Barapasaurus tagorei
ISIR col.
14 m / 8.5 t

Parabrontopodus sp.
Gierlinski et al. 2009
14.8 m / 10 t

Saurichnium tetractis
Gurich 1926
30 cm / 35 g

Thecodontosaurus minor
Haughton 1918
1.45 m / 3.8 kg

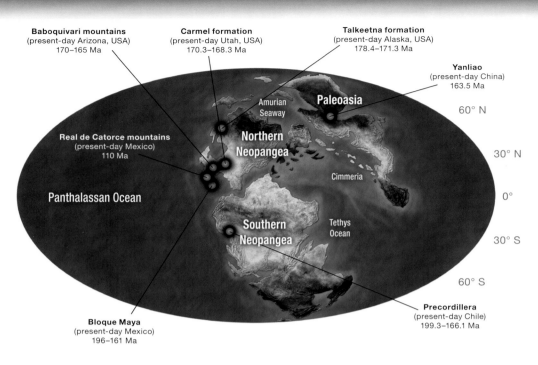

Baboquivari mountains
(present-day Arizona, USA)
170–165 Ma

Carmel formation
(present-day Utah, USA)
170.3–168.3 Ma

Talkeetna formation
(present-day Alaska, USA)
178.4–171.3 Ma

Yanliao
(present-day China)
163.5 Ma

Paleoasia

Amurian
Seaway

60° N

Real de Catorce mountains
(present-day Mexico)
110 Ma

Northern
Neopangea

Cimmeria

30° N

0°

Panthalassan Ocean

Southern
Neopangea

Tethys
Ocean

30° S

60° S

Bloque Maya
(present-day Mexico)
196–161 Ma

Precordillera
(present-day Chile)
199.3–166.1 Ma

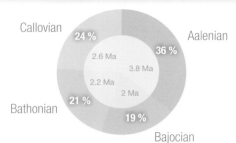

Callovian
24 %
2.6 Ma

Aalenian
36 %
3.8 Ma

2.2 Ma
2 Ma

Bathonian
21 %

Bajocian
19 %

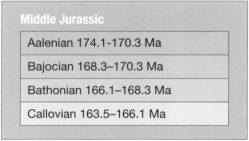

Middle Jurassic	
Aalenian 174.1-170.3 Ma	
Bajocian 168.3–170.3 Ma	
Bathonian 166.1–168.3 Ma	
Callovian 163.5–166.1 Ma	

The Middle Jurassic lasted for some 10.6 million years, accounting for 19% of the entire Jurassic period and 6% of the Mesozoic.

General paleoclimatology 26–30° C
Length of day: 23.2 hours.

Volcanoes

The intense volcanic activity of the Middle Jurassic presaged the end of Pangea, which broke apart in the Middle Jurassic into two zones—Paleoasia and Neopangea. The dinosaurs of Paleoasia had a different evolutionary history, with forms convergent with those found in other parts of the globe. The notable volcanic events of the time took place in what are currently the USA (Alaska, Arizona, and Utah), Chile, and Mexico. See more: *Kramer & Ehrlichmann 1996; Haxel et al. 2005; Bull et al. 2015; Xu et al. 2016; Yang et al. 2018*

The smallest juvenile

The smallest calves of *Tazoudasaurus naimi* ("Tazouda's thin-lizard") were just 3.2 m long and weighed 200 kg. This species lived in what is now China (Pliensbachian 190.8–182.7 Ma). See more: *Peyers & Allain 2010*

First published species of the Middle Jurassic

"Rutellum implicatum" (1699): The name is invalid and predates *Cardiodon* and *Cetiosaurus* (1841) by 143 years. See more: *Lhuyd 1699; Owen 1841*

Nebulasaurus taito
Xing et al. 2015

Specimen: LDRC-v.d.1
(Xing et al. 2015)

Length: 8 m
Hip height: 1.95 m
Body mass: 1.7 t
Material: incomplete cranium
ESR: ●●○○

The smallest of the Middle Jurassic (Class: Large Grade III)

Nebulasaurus taito ("Taito Corporation's cloudy lizard") (Aalenian, approx. 174.1–170. Ma) from eastern Paleoasia (present-day China). Comparable in size to a hippopotamus, it was smaller than the only bipedal sauropodomorph of the Middle Jurassic, *Yunnanosaurus youngi* (present-day China), which measured 10.8 m in length and weighed 2.6 t. See more: *Xing et al. 2015*

RECORD
SMALLEST

2 m

1:40

2 m   4 m   6 m   8 m

4 m   8 m   12 m   16 m

1:80

8 m

4 m

RECORD
LARGEST

Unnamed
Charroud & Fedan 1992

Specimen: uncatalogued
(Charroud & Fedan 1992)

Length: 18.5 m
Shoulder height: 6.6 m
Body mass: 35 t
Material: femur
ESR: ●●○○

The largest of the Middle Jurassic (Class: Giant Grade I)

A sauropod similar to *Atlasaurus*, but larger in size and weighing as much as five African elephants combined. Another great dinosaur was "Cetiosaurus epioolithicus," which at 24 m was even longer than the former but had a similar weight of 32 t. The two were contemporary (Bathonian, approx. 168.3–166.1 Ma), although the former lived in south-central Neopangea (present-day Morocco), and the latter lived in the north-central zone (present-day England). *See more: Owen 1842; Charroud & Fedan 1992; Upchurch 1995; Upchurch & Martin 2003; Whitlock 2011*

Most recently published species of the Middle Jurassic

Anhuilong diboensis (2018) ("dragon of Anhui Province"), from the Middle Jurassic (Aalenian-Callovian, approx. 170.3 Ma), was similar in appearance to Omeisaurus but smaller in size. It may have been 17.5 m long and weighed more than an African elephant. The article at the end of this book is still in review, so it officially is from 2019. *See more: Ren et al. 2019*

Footprints

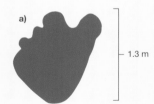
— 1.3 m

b)

— 7 cm

The largest

a) *Malakhelisaurus mianwali*: These prints were found in what was south-central Neopangea (present-day Pakistan). The shape indicates that it was not a diplodocoid, macronarian, or primitive sauropod, so it may have been similar to *Atlasaurus*. *See more: Malkani 2007, 2008*

The first sauropods to reach 55 t in weight, the neosauropods, appeared in this period. Bipedal sauropodomorphs gradually disappeared, as the lack of fossil footprints attests.

The smallest

b) *Trisauropodiscus* sp.: The last footprints of this type were found in what was south-central Neopangea (present-day Morocco). The largest individuals were 9.1 cm in length. *See more: Gierlinski et al. 2017*

2 m

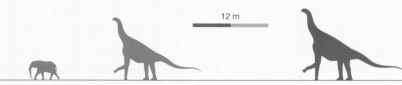

12 m

Unnamed species
Charroud & Fedan 1992
18.5 m / 35 t

Malakhelisaurus mianwali
Malkani 2007, 2008
21.5 m / 55 t

Trisauropodiscus sp.
Gierlinski et al. 2017
1.35 m / 1.45 kg

Nebulasaurus taito
LDRC-v.d.1
9.1 m / 1.7 t

Volcanoes

The largest volcano of the Upper Jurassic, Tamu Massif, is 4,460 m high and 650 km in diameter. It was submerged in the great ocean Panthalassa (present-day Pacific Ocean, approx. 145 Ma). Notable volcanic events of this period occurred in what are now Chile, China, South Korea, Cuba, Holland, Japan, and Russia. See more: *Cottencon et al. 1975; Pszczolkowski & Albear 1983; Segura-Soto et al. 1985; Perrot & van der Poel 1987; Herngreen et al. 1991; Chen et al. 1993; Mahoney et al. 2005; Wang et al. 2006; Prokopiev et al. 2009; Witze 2013; Rossel et al. 2014*

The smallest of the Upper Jurassic   (Class: Large Grade I)

Europasaurus holgeri ("Holger Lüdtke's European lizard"), from the Upper Jurassic (Kimmeridgian, approx. 157.3–152.1 Ma) in north-central Neopangea (present-day Germany), was a small sauropod that was half as tall as a giraffe. It may have become extinct because the island it inhabited fused with the mainland, which may have allowed large predators to invade the area. See more: *Sander et al. 2006; Lallensack et al. 2015*

The smallest juvenile

Camarasaurus sp. calves BYUVP 8967 (present-day Colorado, USA), from the Kimmeridgian (approx. 157.3–152.1 Ma), were 76 cm long and weighed 1.7 kg. See more: *Britt & Naylor 1994*

First published species of the Upper Jurassic

Gigantosaurus megalonyx (1869) ("Large-clawed giant lizard"), of north-central Neopangea (present-day England), is known solely from an incomplete foot, a cervical vertebra, and an osteoderm. It was considered synonymous with *Pelorosaurus* or *Ornithopsis*, so the name was reused for the species that are now *Janenschia* (*G. robustus*), *Malawisaurus* (*G. dixeyi*) and *Tornieria* (*G. africanus*). See more: *Seeley 1869; Fraas 1908; Haughton 1928*

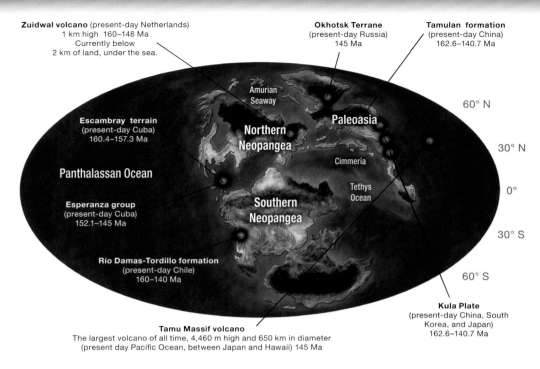

Zuidwal volcano (present-day Netherlands)
1 km high 160–148 Ma
Currently below
2 km of land, under the sea.

Okhotsk Terrane
(present-day Russia)
145 Ma

Tamulan formation
(present-day China)
162.6–140.7 Ma

Amurian Seaway

Paleoasia

Escambray terrain
(present-day Cuba)
160.4–157.3 Ma

Northern Neopangea

Cimmeria

Panthalassan Ocean

Tethys Ocean

Esperanza group
(present-day Cuba)
152.1–145 Ma

Southern Neopangea

Río Damas-Tordillo formation
(present-day Chile)
160–140 Ma

60° N

30° N

0°

30° S

60° S

Kula Plate
(present-day China, South Korea, and Japan)
162.6–140.7 Ma

Tamu Massif volcano
The largest volcano of all time, 4,460 m high and 650 km in diameter
(present day Pacific Ocean, between Japan and Hawaii) 145 Ma

General paleoclimatology 15–38° C
Length of day: 23.2 hours.

Tithonian   38 %   7.1 Ma.   6.2 Ma   34 %   Oxfordian

5.2 Ma

28 %

Kimmeridgian

Upper Jurassic	
Oxfordian 157.3–163.5 Ma	
Kimmeridgian 152.1–157.3 Ma	
Tithonian 145–152.1 Ma	

The final part of the Jurassic lasted some 18.5 million years, or 33% of the length of the Jurassic and 8% of the duration of the Mesozoic era.

Europasaurus holgeri
Sander et al. 2006

Specimen: DFMMh/FV 157
(Sander et al. 2006)

Length: 6 m
Shoulder height: 1.7 m
Body mass: 800 kg
Material: fibula
ESR: ●●○○

2 m

RECORD
SMALLEST

1:40

2 m   4 m   6 m   8 m

6 m 12 m 18 m 24 m 30 m

18 m

Maraapunisaurus fragillimus
Cope 1877

RECORD
LARGEST

Specimen: AMNH 5777
(Cope 1877)

Length: 35 m
Hip height: 7.7 m
Body mass: 70 t
Material: incomplete thoracic vertebra and femur
ESR: ◑○○○

1:150

12 m

6 m

The largest of the Upper Jurassic (Class: Giant Grade II)

Maraapunisaurus fragillimus (previously known as *Amphicoelias*) from the Upper Jurassic (present-day Colorado, western USA) was somewhat heavier than cf. *Barosaurus lentus* BYU 9024 (present-day Colorado, USA) but not as long, as it, at 45 m, was the longest of all known animals, except for the bootlace worm *Lineus longissimus*; its longest reported individuals measured up to 55 m in length. See more: *Jensen 1985, 1987; Carwardine 1995; Taylor & Wedel 2016; Carpenter 2018; Taylor & Wedel**

Most recently published species of the Upper Jurassic

Galeamopus pabsti (2017) is the last species described before this edition went to press. *Maraapunisaurus* (2018) is a name change of *Amphicoelias fragillimus*. See more: *Tschopp & Mateus 2017; Carpenter 2018*

The largest number of sauropod fossils found have been dated to the Upper Jurassic.

A recount of these finds indicates 301 reports from the Tithonian. See more: *Mannion & Upchurch 2009*

Footprints

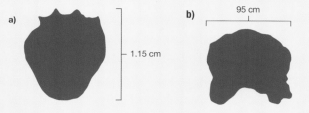

a)

b) 95 cm

1.15 cm

c)

12 cm

The largest

Two animals seem to be tied for the largest Upper Jurassic sauropod based on hindprint and foreprint: **a)** *Breviparopus* (present-day Morocco) and **b)** an unnamed impression (present-day Spain). See more: *Dutuit & Ouazzou 1980; García-Ramos et al. 2006*

As in the previous period, the largest sauropods of the Upper Jurassic weighed more than 70 t. *Maraapunisaurus fragillimus* may have been larger, but this is difficult to verify.

The smallest

c) Unnamed: The smallest footprints, made by calves of brachiosaurid sauropods, were found in central Neopangea (present-day Spain). See more: *García-Ramos et al. 2005, 2006*

12 m

3m

Breviparopus taghbaloutensis
Dutuit & Ouazzou 1980
33.5 m / 62 t

Unnamed footprint
García-Ramos et al. 2006
28 m / 70 t

Maraapunisaurus fragillimus
AMNH 5777
35 m / 70 t

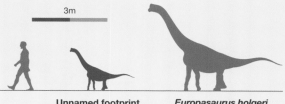

Unnamed footprint
García-Ramos et al. 2005
2.8–3 m / 93–115 kg

Europasaurus holgeri
DFMMh/FV 157
6 m / 800 kg

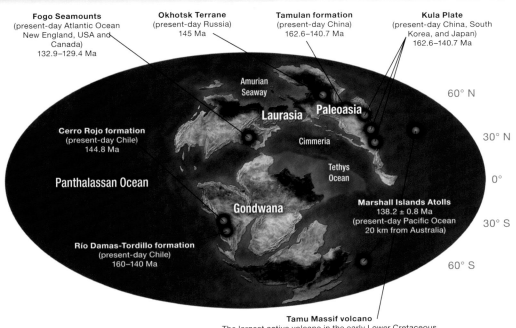

Fogo Seamounts
(present-day Atlantic Ocean
New England, USA and
Canada)
132.9–129.4 Ma

Okhotsk Terrane
(present-day Russia)
145 Ma

Tamulan formation
(present-day China)
162.6–140.7 Ma

Kula Plate
(present-day China, South
Korea, and Japan)
162.6–140.7 Ma

Amurian
Seaway

Laurasia   Paleoasia

60° N

Cerro Rojo formation
(present-day Chile)
144.8 Ma

Cimmeria

30° N

Tethys
Ocean

Panthalassan Ocean

0°

Marshall Islands Atolls
138.2 ± 0.8 Ma
(present-day Pacific Ocean
20 km from Australia)

Gondwana

30° S

Río Damas-Tordillo formation
(present-day Chile)
160–140 Ma

60° S

Tamu Massif volcano
The largest active volcano in the early Lower Cretaceous
(present-day Pacific Ocean, between Japan and Hawaii) 145–140 Ma

General paleoclimatology 26–30° C
Length of day: 23.3–23.4 hours.

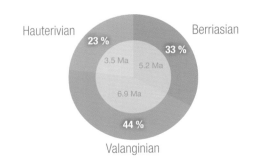

Hauterivian   Berriasian
23 %   33 %
3.5 Ma   5.2 Ma
6.9 Ma
44 %
Valanginian

Volcanoes

The largest volcano in the early Lower Cretaceous, the Tamu Massif, was active between 145 and 140 Ma. It was submerged in the great ocean Panthalassa (present-day Pacific Ocean). Notable volcanic events of this period occurred in what are now Canada, Chile, China, South Korea, Japan, Russia, and the Marshall Islands. See more: *Chen et al. 1993; Pe-Piper et al. 2003; Lincoln et al. 1993; Wang et al. 2006; Prokofiev et al. 2006; Mahoney et al. 2005; Witze 2013; Rossel et al. 2014; Sepúlveda & Vásquez 2015*

The smallest of the early Lower Cretaceous (Class: Large Grade II)

Remains of dicraeosaurids were found in Argentina (Valanginian, approx. 139.8–132.9 Ma), but a description is still pending. An endocranium of a subadult or adult specimen could be that of a dicraeosaurid similar in weight to a white shark and as long as a killer whale. See more: *Carabajal et al. 2017*

The smallest juvenile

Teeth of cf. *Pleurocoelus* sp. (Upper Hauterivian, approx. 142.4–139.8 Ma) from central Laurasia (present-day Denmark) belonged to a young sauropod 5.9 m long and weighing 680 kg. See more: *Bonde & Christiansen 2003*

First published species of the early Lower Cretaceous

Cetiosaurus brevis (1842) is now an invalid species from central Laurasia (present-day England). It consists of bone remains of an iguanodontid and *Pelorosaurus conybearei* (1849). See more: *Owen 1842; Melville 1849; Mantell 1850; Taylor & Naish 2007; Upchurch et al. 2011*

Early Lower Cretaceous

Berriasian 145-139.8 Ma
Valanginian 139.8-132.9 Ma
Hauterivian 132.9-129.4 Ma

The early Lower Cretaceous lasted some 15.6 million years, or 20% of the length of the Cretaceous and 8% of the entire duration of the Mesozoic era.

Unnamed
Carabajal et al. 2017

1:50

Specimen:
(Carabajal et al. 2017)

Length: 9 m
Hip height: 2 m
Body mass: 1 t
Material: endocranium
ESR: ●○○○

2,5 m

RECORD
SMALLEST

2.5 m   5 m   7.5 m   10 m

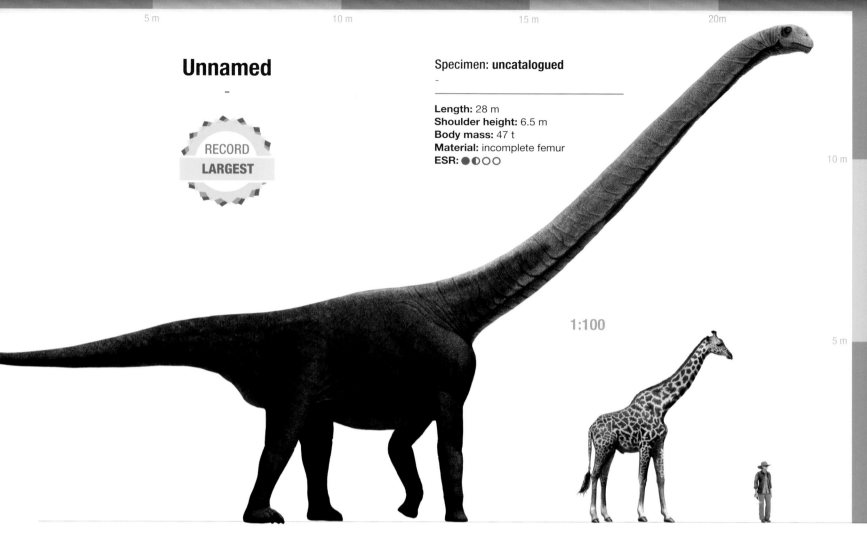

5 m   10 m   15 m   20m

Unnamed

-

RECORD
LARGEST

Specimen: uncatalogued

-

Length: 28 m
Shoulder height: 6.5 m
Body mass: 47 t
Material: incomplete femur
ESR: ●◐○○○

1:100

10 m

5 m

The largest of the early Lower Cretaceous (Class: Giant Grade I)

An enormous sauropod (Hauterivian, approx. 132.9–129.4 Ma), known informally as "Francoposeidon," was found in what was central Laurasia (present-day France). It weighed about as much as a sperm whale and killer whale combined and was longer than a blue whale. It has not yet been described in detail but is based on several bones, some of which are the largest bones ever found in Europe. See more: *Néraudeau et al. 2012*

Most recently published species of the early Lower Cretaceous

*Pilmatueia faundez*i (Valanginian, approx. 139.8–132.9 Ma) from western Gondwana (present-day Argentina) and *Volgatitan simbirskiensis* (upper Hauterivian, approx. 131–129.4 Ma) from central Laurasia (present-day European Russia). Both were described in 2018, although the former will be published in a paginated issue in 2019. See more: *Averianov & Efimov 2018; Coria et al. 2019*

Footprints

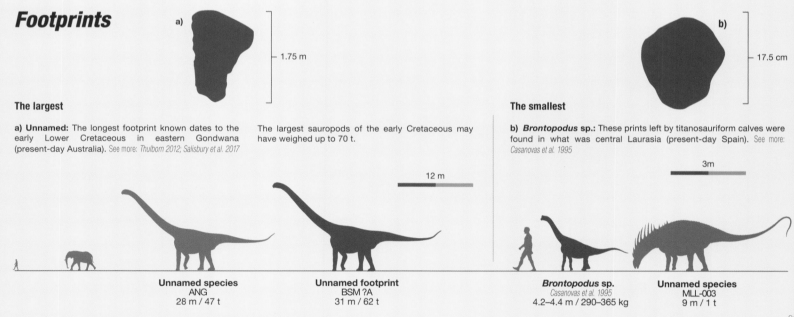

a)

- 1.75 m

The largest

a) Unnamed: The longest footprint known dates to the early Lower Cretaceous in eastern Gondwana (present-day Australia). See more: *Thulborn 2012; Salisbury et al. 2017*

The largest sauropods of the early Cretaceous may have weighed up to 70 t.

b)

- 17.5 cm

The smallest

b) *Brontopodus* sp.: These prints left by titanosauriform calves were found in what was central Laurasia (present-day Spain). See more: *Casanovas et al. 1995*

12 m

3m

Unnamed species
ANG
28 m / 47 t

Unnamed footprint
BSM ?A
31 m / 62 t

***Brontopodus* sp.**
Casanovas et al. 1995
4.2–4.4 m / 290–365 kg

Unnamed species
MLL-003
9 m / 1 t

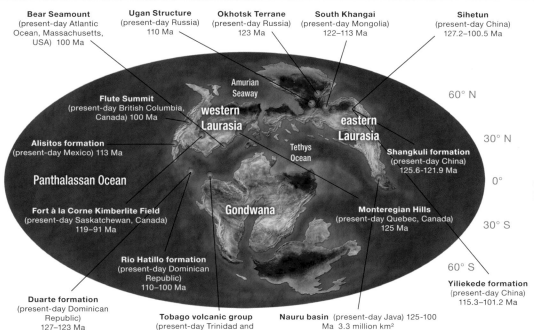

Bear Seamount
(present-day Atlantic
Ocean, Massachusetts,
USA) 100 Ma

Ugan Structure
(present-day Russia)
110 Ma

Okhotsk Terrane
(present-day Russia)
123 Ma

South Khangai
(present-day Mongolia)
122–113 Ma

Sihetun
(present-day China)
127.2–100.5 Ma

Amurian
Seaway

Flute Summit
(present-day British Columbia,
Canada) 100 Ma

western
Laurasia

eastern
Laurasia

60° N

Alisitos formation
(present-day Mexico) 113 Ma

Tethys
Ocean

Shangkuli formation
(present-day China)
125.6–121.9 Ma

30° N

Panthalassan Ocean

0°

Fort à la Corne Kimberlite Field
(present-day Saskatchewan, Canada)
119–91 Ma

Gondwana

Monteregian Hills
(present-day Quebec, Canada)
125 Ma

30° S

Rio Hatillo formation
(present-day Dominican
Republic)
110–100 Ma

60° S

Yiliekede formation
(present-day China)
115.3–101.2 Ma

Duarte formation
(present-day Dominican
Republic)
127–123 Ma

Tobago volcanic group
(present-day Trinidad and
Tobago)

Nauru basin (present-day Java) 125-100
Ma 3.3 million km²

General paleoclimatology 26–30° C
Length of day: 23.4–23.5 hours.

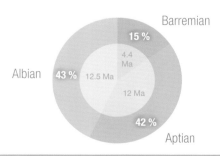

Barremian
15 %
4.4
Ma
Albian **43 %** 12.5 Ma
12 Ma
42 %
Aptian

Volcanoes

A large number of volcanic events occurred during this period, some of them in parts of what are now Canada, China, Java, the USA (Massachusetts), Mexico, Mongolia, the Dominican Republic, Russia, Trinidad and Tobago, and the Atlantic Ocean. The most extensive volcanic zone of the late Lower Cretaceous was in the Nauru Basin (present-day Java, approx. 125–100 Ma), which stretched over 3.3 million km². The Sihetun Area (present-day China, approx. 127.2–100. Ma) is especially favorable for the study of paleontology, as volcanic activity enabled the preservation of the Jehol biota. The fossils in that place were exceptionally well preserved and include remains as delicate as feathers and filaments. See more: *Kesler et al. 1977; Almazan-Vázquez 1988; Sleep 1990; Gutierrez & Lewis 1996; Smith et al. 1998; Snoke & Noble 2001; Moore et al 2003; Payne et al. 2004; Souther 2004; Mochizuki et al. 2005; Wang et al. 2006; Doubrovine et al. 2009; Prokopiev et al. 2009; Jiang et al. 2011; Sorokin et al. 2012; Yarmolyuk et al. 2015*

The smallest of the late Lower Cretaceous (Class: Large Grade II)

Nigersaurus taqueti was a small sauropod with dental batteries. It lived in the late Lower Cretaceous (upper Aptian, approx. 119–113 Ma), in central Gondwana (present-day Niger). See more: *Sereno et al. 1999*

The smallest juvenile

Specimen NSM60104403–20554450 (Upper Aptian, approx. 119–113 Ma) from central Laurasia (present-day Spain) was an embryo 31 cm long and weighing 125 g. See more: *Grellet-Tinner et al. 2011; Kim, Sim, Kim & Grellet-Tinner 2012*

First published species of the late Lower Cretaceous

Aepisaurus elephantinus (1852). From central Laurasia (present-day France), it is a lost fossil that is sometimes mistakenly cited as *Aepysaurus*. See more: *Gervais 1852, 1859*

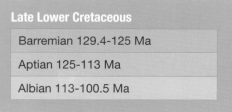

Late Lower Cretaceous
Barremian 129.4-125 Ma
Aptian 125-113 Ma
Albian 113-100.5 Ma

The late Lower Cretaceous lasted for 28.9 million years, or 36% of the entire duration of the Jurassic and 15% of the length of the Mesozoic.

Nigersaurus taqueti
Sereno et al. 1999

Specimen: MNN GAD517
(Sereno et al. 1999)

Length: 10 m
Hip height: 2.15 cm
Body mass: 1.9 t
Material: skull and partial skeleton
ESR: ●●●●

2,5 m

1:50

RECORD
SMALLEST

2.5 m   5 m   7.5 m   10 m

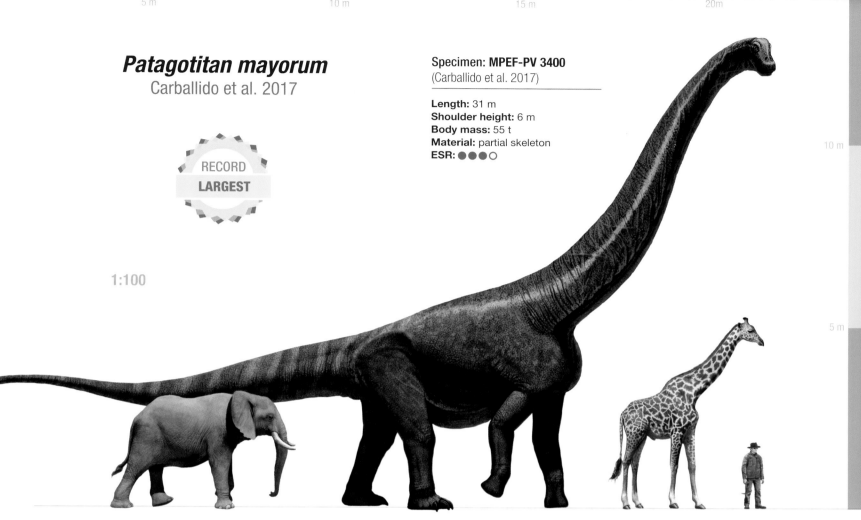

5 m   10 m   15 m   20m

Patagotitan mayorum
Carballido et al. 2017

RECORD
LARGEST

Specimen: MPEF-PV 3400
(Carballido et al. 2017)

Length: 31 m
Shoulder height: 6 m
Body mass: 55 t
Material: partial skeleton
ESR: ●●●○

10 m

5 m

1:100

The largest of the late Lower Cretaceous (Class: Giant Grade II)

Patagotitan mayorum ("greater titan of the Patagonian region") (Upper Albian, approx. 106–100.5 Ma) from western Gondwana (present-day Argentina). It was as heavy as nine African elephants and longer than a blue whale. It is one of the most complete skeletons known for the large sauropods. See more: *Carballido et al. 2017*

Most recently published species of the late Lower Cretaceous

Lavocatisaurus agrioensis (present-day Niger) and *Liaoningotitan sinensis* (present-day China) are species described in 2018. The former was first known as cf. *Zapalasaurus* in 2012. See more: *Salgado et al. 2017; Canudo et al. 2018; Zhou et al. 2018*

Most recently published species of the late Lower Cretaceous

A recount of these finds indicates 168 reports from the Albian. See more: *Mannion & Upchurch 2009*

Footprints

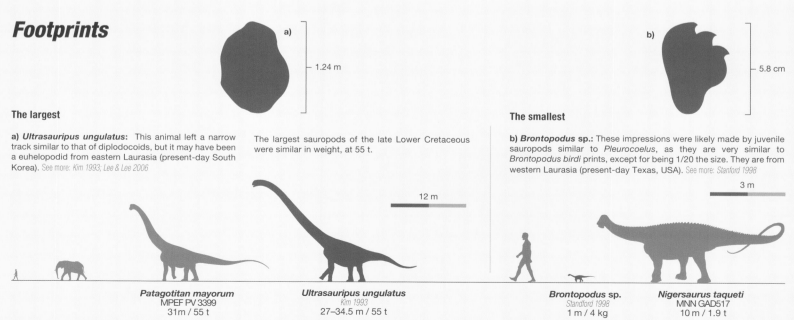

a)
— 1.24 m

b)
— 5.8 cm

The largest

a) *Ultrasauripus ungulatus:* This animal left a narrow track similar to that of diplodocoids, but it may have been a euhelopodid from eastern Laurasia (present-day South Korea). See more: *Kim 1993; Lee & Lee 2006*

The largest sauropods of the late Lower Cretaceous were similar in weight, at 55 t.

The smallest

b) *Brontopodus* sp.: These impressions were likely made by juvenile sauropods similar to *Pleurocoelus*, as they are very similar to *Brontopodus birdi* prints, except for being 1/20 the size. They are from western Laurasia (present-day Texas, USA). See more: *Stanford 1998*

12 m

3 m

Patagotitan mayorum
MPEF PV 3399
31m / 55 t

Ultrasauripus ungulatus
Kim 1993
27–34.5 m / 55 t

Brontopodus sp.
Standford 1998
1 m / 4 kg

Nigersaurus taqueti
MNN GAD517
10 m / 1.9 t

Volcanoes

Notable volcanoes of this period are found in what is now the USA (Arkansas), Canada, Java, Mongolia, Russia, and the Dutch Antilles. The most extensive volcanic zone of the early Upper Cretaceous, the Nauru Basin (present-day Java, approx. 100–80 Ma), was reactivated, covering 3.3 million km². See more: *MacDonald 1968; Smith et al. 1998; Aulbach et al. 2004; Mochizuki et al. 2005; Doubrovine et al. 2009; Sorokin et al. 2012; Yarmolyuk et al. 2015*

Smallest of the early Upper Cretaceous (Class: Large Grade II)

Specimen MLP 46-VIII-21–2 (Coniacian, approx. 89.8–86.3 Ma), from western Gondwana (present-day Argentina), was a small titanosaur similar in weight to a hippopotamus. See more: *Filipinni et al. 2016*

The smallest juvenile

Specimen Vb 719 (Cenomanian, approx. 100.5–93.9 Ma) in central Gondwana (present-day Sudan) may have been a titanosaur calf 1.35 m long and weighing 7 kg. See more: *Werner 1994*

First published species of the early Upper Cretaceous

Aegyptosaurus baharijensis (1932), from central Gondwana (present-day Egypt). A previous report was *Argyrosaurus superbus* (present-day Argentina), which for a long time was believed to be from that era; however, we now know that this sauropod was more recent (upper Campanian, approx. 83.6–72.1 Ma). See more: *Lydekker 1983; Stromer 1932*

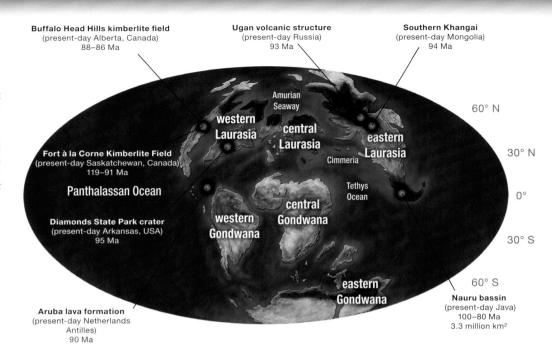

Buffalo Head Hills kimberlite field (present-day Alberta, Canada) 88–86 Ma

Ugan volcanic structure (present-day Russia) 93 Ma

Southern Khangai (present-day Mongolia) 94 Ma

Amurian Seaway

western Laurasia

central Laurasia

eastern Laurasia

Cimmeria

Fort à la Corne Kimberlite Field (present-day Saskatchewan, Canada) 119–91 Ma

Panthalassan Ocean

Tethys Ocean

Diamonds State Park crater (present-day Arkansas, USA) 95 Ma

western Gondwana

central Gondwana

eastern Gondwana

Aruba lava formation (present-day Netherlands Antilles) 90 Ma

Nauru bassin (present-day Java) 100–80 Ma 3.3 million km²

60° N

30° N

0°

30° S

60° S

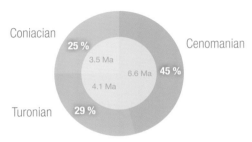

Coniacian 25 % 3.5 Ma

Cenomanian 45 % 6.6 Ma

Turonian 29 % 4.1 Ma

General paleoclimatology 28–45° C
Length of day: 23.5–23.6 hours.

The early Late Cretaceous spanned 14.2 million years, or 18% of the duration of the Cretaceous and 8% of the length of the Mesozoic era.

Early Late Cretaceous		
Cenomanian 100.5-93.9 Ma		
Turonian 93.9-89.8 Ma		
Coniacian 89.8-86.3 Ma		

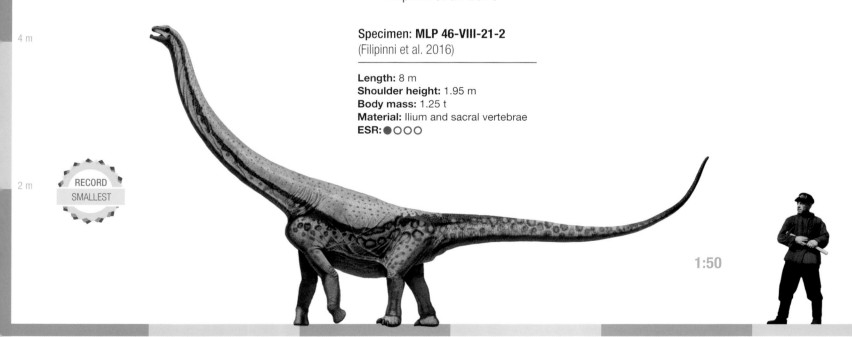

Unnamed
Filipinni et al. 2016

Specimen: MLP 46-VIII-21-2
(Filipinni et al. 2016)

Length: 8 m
Shoulder height: 1.95 m
Body mass: 1.25 t
Material: Ilium and sacral vertebrae
ESR: ●○○○

RECORD SMALLEST

1:50

4 m

2 m

2 m   4 m   6 m   8 m   10 m

cf. *Argentinosaurus*
Bonaparte & Coria 1993

RECORD
LARGEST

1:150

Specimen: MLP-DP 46-VIII-21-3
(Mazzetta et al. 2004)

Length: 36 m
Shoulder height: 7 m
Body mass: 80 t
Material: incomplete femur
ESR: ●◑○○

The largest of the early Upper Cretaceous (Class: Great Grade II)

cf. *Argentinosaurus* huinculensis (Middle Turonian, approx. 91.85 Ma), from western Gondwana (present-day Argentina), was somewhat larger and more recent than the type material of the famous *Argentinosaurus huinculensis* (upper Cenomanian, approx. 97.2–93.9 Ma) in western Gondwana (present-day Argentina). Its weight has been estimated between 55 and 100 t; however, it is most likely that its weight was in between, around 80 t. It was the largest dinosaur based on solid evidence. See more: *Bonaparte & Coria 1993; Bonaparte 1996; Lamanna 2004; Mazzetta et al. 2004; Paul 2010*

Most recently published species of the early Upper Cretaceous

Choconsaurus baileywillisi (2017) ("lizard of Villa El Chocón and of geologist Bailey Willis"), from western Gondwana (present-day Argentina), was a titanosaur contemporary to the great predatory dinosaur, *Giganotosaurus carolinii*. The online version is from 2017, but the paginated issue is from 2018. See more: *Simón et al. 2018*

Footprints

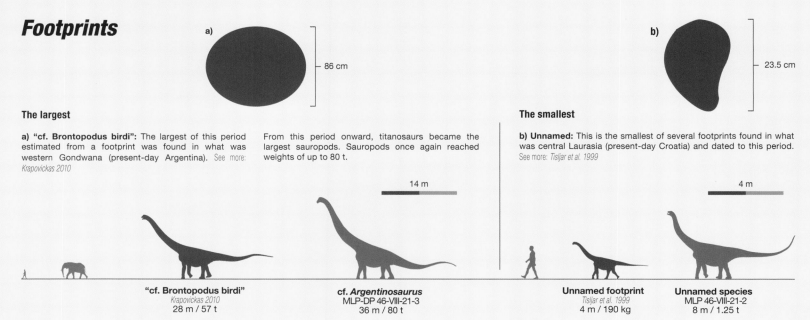

a)

— 86 cm

The largest

a) "cf. Brontopodus birdi": The largest of this period estimated from a footprint was found in what was western Gondwana (present-day Argentina). See more: *Krapovickas 2010*

From this period onward, titanosaurs became the largest sauropods. Sauropods once again reached weights of up to 80 t.

b)

— 23.5 cm

The smallest

b) Unnamed: This is the smallest of several footprints found in what was central Laurasia (present-day Croatia) and dated to this period. See more: *Tisljar et al. 1999*

14 m

"cf. Brontopodus birdi"
Krapovickas 2010
28 m / 57 t

cf. *Argentinosaurus*
MLP-DP 46-VIII-21-3
36 m / 80 t

4 m

Unnamed footprint
Tisljar et al. 1999
4 m / 190 kg

Unnamed species
MLP 46-VIII-21-2
8 m / 1.25 t

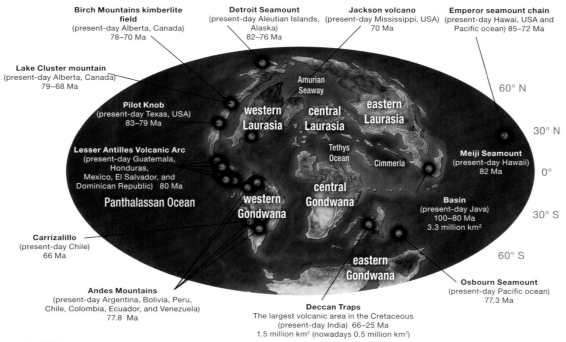

Birch Mountains kimberlite field
(present-day Alberta, Canada)
78–70 Ma

Detroit Seamount
(present-day Aleutian Islands, Alaska)
82–76 Ma

Jackson volcano
(present-day Mississippi, USA)
70 Ma

Emperor seamount chain
(present-day Hawai, USA and Pacific ocean) 85–72 Ma

Lake Cluster mountain
(present-day Alberta, Canada)
79–68 Ma

Pilot Knob
(present-day Texas, USA)
83–79 Ma

Lesser Antilles Volcanic Arc
(present-day Guatemala, Honduras, Mexico, El Salvador, and Dominican Republic) 80 Ma

Meiji Seamount
(present-day Hawaii)
82 Ma

Carrizalillo
(present-day Chile)
66 Ma

Basin
(present-day Java)
100–80 Ma
3.3 million km²

Andes Mountains
(present-day Argentina, Bolivia, Peru, Chile, Colombia, Ecuador, and Venezuela)
77.8 Ma

Osbourn Seamount
(present-day Pacific ocean)
77.3 Ma

Deccan Traps
The largest volcanic area in the Cretaceous
(present-day India) 66–25 Ma
1.5 million km² (nowadays 0.5 million km²)

Amurian Seaway, western Laurasia, central Laurasia, eastern Laurasia, Tethys Ocean, Cimmeria, Panthalassan Ocean, western Gondwana, central Gondwana, eastern Gondwana

60° N, 30° N, 0°, 30° S, 60° S

General paleoclimatology 28–45° C
Length of day: 23.6–23.7 hours.

Volcanoes

The most extensive volcanic zone of the late Upper Cretaceous was the Nauru Basin (present-day Java, approx. 100–80 Ma), which covered 3.3 million km². The zone with the most intense volcanic activity in the late Upper Cretaceous was the Deccan Traps (present-day India, approx. 66.5–63 Ma, in the first intensely active stage). Covering 1.5 million km², the zone was so vast in scale that its activity is believed to be one of the causes of the extinction of non-avian dinosaurs. An enormous quantity of volcanic material released by the traps formed a 2-km-thick layer of deposits. Other notable volcanoes of the time were located in what are now the USA (Alaska, Mississippi, Texas), Argentina, Bolivia, Canada, Chile, Colombia, Ecuador, Guatemala, Hawaii, Honduras, Mexico, El Salvador, the Dominican Republic, Venezuela, and the Pacific Ocean. See more: *Sager & Keating 1984; Pindell & Barret 1990; Jaillard 1993; Rivera & Mpodozis 1994; Dockery III et al. 1997; Scholl & Rea 2002; Eccles et al. 2003; Archibald & Fastovsky 2004; Clouard & Bonneville 2005; Garcia et al. 2005; Kerr et al. 2005; Mochizuki et al. 2005; Parker 2006; Doubrovine et al. 2009; Keller 2014; Schoene et al. 2014*

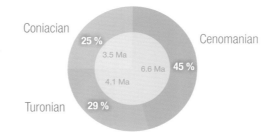

Coniacian 25 % — 3.5 Ma
Cenomanian 45 % — 6.6 Ma
Turonian 29 % — 4.1 Ma

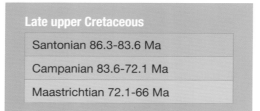

Late upper Cretaceous

| Santonian 86.3-83.6 Ma |
| Campanian 83.6-72.1 Ma |
| Maastrichtian 72.1-66 Ma |

The early Upper Cretaceous lasted some 14.2 million years, or 18% of the length of the Cretaceous and 8% of the entire duration of the Mesozoic era.

The smallest of the late Upper Cretaceous (Class: Large Grade I)

Magyarosaurus dacus ("Magyar and Dacian lizard") (Upper Maastrichtian, approx. 69–66 Ma), from central Laurasia (present-day Romania), was the smallest sauropod of the Cretaceous, with a weight comparable to a fighting bull, although its relative, *Magyarosaurus hungaricus*, 11.3 m long and 3.3 t in weight, may have been a variety of the same species. See more: *Nopcsa 1915; Huene 1932; Stein et al. 2010*

The smallest juvenile

Laplatasaurus sp. MCF-PVPH-272 (Lower Campanian, approx. 83.6–77.8 Ma), from western Gondwana (present-day Argentina), was 39 cm long and weighed 230 g. See more: *Chiappe et al. 2001; Garcia 2007*

First published species of the late Upper Cretaceous

Argyrosaurus superbus and *Neuquensaurus australis* (previously *Titanosaurus*) were the first reports assigned to this era. Other species, such as *Microcoelus patagonicus* and *T. nanus*, were juvenile *Neuquensaurus australis* individuals (present-day Argentina). See more: *Lydekker 1823*

Magyarosaurus dacus

Nopcsa 1915

Specimen: FGGUB R.1992
(Nopcsa 1915)

Length: 5.4 m
Shoulder height: 1.2 m
Body mass: 520 kg
Material: femur
ESR: ●●○○

2 m

1:40

RECORD SMALLEST

2 m   4 m   6 m   8 m

5 m   10 m   15 m   20 m

10 m

Puertasaurus reuili
Novas et al. 2005

Specimen: MPM 10002
(Novas et al. 2005)

Length: 28 m
Shoulder height: 6 m
Body mass: 50 t
Material: vertebrae
ESR: ●○○○

RECORD
LARGEST

1:100

5 m

The largest of the late Upper Cretaceous (Class: Giant Grade II)

Puertasaurus reuili ("Pablo Puerta and Santiago Reuil's lizard") (Lower Maastrichtian, approx. 72.1–69 Ma), from western Gondwana (present-day Argentina). It was similar to *Futalognkosaurus dukei*, but its vertebrae were very low rather than high. It was one of the most gigantic dinosaurs, weighing about as much as eight African elephants and as long as a blue whale. *Bruhathkayosaurus matleyi* (Maastrichtian, approx. 72.1–66), from Hindustan (present-day India), may have been even larger, with a probable length of 37 m and weight of 95 t. The problem is that the bones have been lost, and some suspect that they were actually the

trunks of a palm or other trees. See more: *Yadagiri & Ayyasami 1989; Anonymous 2000; Novas et al. 2005; Krause et al. 2006; Hone et al. 2016*

The most recently published of the late Upper Cretaceous

Baalsaurus mansillai (present-day Argentina) and *Mansourasaurus shahinae* (present-day Egypt). See more: *Calvo & Riga 2018; Sallam et al. 2018*

Footprints

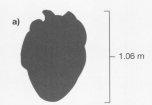

a)

— 1.06 m

The largest

a) Unnamed: This footprint from eastern Laurasia (present-day Mongolia), not yet formally described, is the largest of its time. See more: *Ishigaki 2016*

Since sauropods became extinct, no other land animal has reached the same gigantic sizes. Their closest rivals are elephants, with some extinct species reaching up to 20 t. See more: *Larramendi 2016*

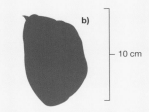

b)

— 10 cm

The smallest

b) Unnamed: They may belong to Eutitanosaur calves from a zone that was isolated at the time: Hindustan (present-day India). See more: *Ghevariya & Srikarni 1991*

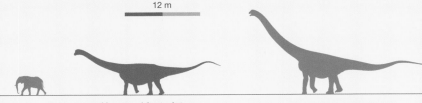

12 m

Unnamed footprint
Ishigaki et al. 2009
24 m / 32 t

Puertasaurus reuili
MPM 10002
28 m / 55 t

2 m

Unnamed footprint
Ghevariya & Srikarni 1991
2.5 m / 50 kg

Magyarosaurus dacus
FGGUB R.1992
5.4 m / 520 kg

JANUARY—252.17 to 236.36 Ma

M	T	W	T	F	S	S
Induan 1 — The Lower Triassic begins at 1:00 a.m.	**Induan** 2 — Oldest sturgeon *Errolichthys mirabilis* Lehman 1952	**Olenekian** 3 — Oldest phyloceratid *Monophyllites wengensis* Klipstein 1843	**Olenekian** 4 — Oldest aquatic reptiles of the Triassic *Agkistrognathus campbelli & Paralonectes merriami* Nicholls & Brinkman 1993	**Olenekian** 5 — Impact of the Gow Lake, Canada, and Kursk, Russia, meteorites	**Olenekian** 6 — Oldest ceratodontiform *Ptychoceratodus donensis* Vorobyeva & Minikh 1968	**Olenekian** 7 — Oldest placodontiform *Placodus* sp. Brotzen 1956
Olenekian 8 — Oldest tanystropheid *Augustaburiania vatagini* Sennikov 2011	**Olenekian** 9 — Oldest ichthyosaurs *Chaohusaurus, Grippia & Utatsusaurus* Young & Dong 1972; Shikama & Kamei 1978; Wiman 1929	**Olene/Anisian** 10 — Middle Triassic begins at 5:00 p.m.	**Anisian** 11 — Oldest floating crinoid *Pentacrinites carolinensis* Eagle 2003	**Anisian** 12 — Oldest lobster *Yunnanopalinura schrami* Feldmann et al. 2012	**Anisian** 13 — Oldest pistosauroid *Pistosaurus longaevus* Meyer 1839	**Anisian** 14 — Oldest phytophagous aquatic reptile *Atopodentatus unicus* Cheng et al. 2014
Anisian 15 — Largest placodontiform *Placodus gigas* Agassiz 1833	**Anisian** 16 — Most dominant aquatic predator of the Middle Triassic *Thalattoarchon saurophagis* Fröbisch et al. 2013	**Anisian** 17 — Largest ichthyosaur of the Middle Triassic *Chonespondylus grandis* Leidy 1868	**Anisian** 18 — Oldest aquatic archosaur *Qianosuchus mixtus* Li et al. 2006	**Anisian** 19 — Largest amphibian of the Middle Triassic in Gondwana *Chernina megarhina* Chernin & Cosgriff 1975	**Anisi/Ladin** 20 — Largest amphibian of Antarctica *Kryostega collinsi* Sidor et al. 2008	**Ladinian** 21 — Smallest notosauroid *Neusticosaurus pygmaeus* Fraas 1896
Ladinian 22 — Largest volcanic zone of the Middle Triassic becomes inactive Choyoi group Jourdan et al. 2005	**Ladinian** 23 — Oldest glypheoids *Pemphix sueri & P. malladai* Meyer 1840; Via 1971	**Ladinian** 24 — Oldest marine archosauriform *Litorosuchus somnii* Li et al. 2016	**Ladinian** 25 — Oldest proterochampsid Unnamed Kischlat 2000	**Ladinian** 26 — Oldest nautilid *Cenoceras trechmanni* Kummel 1953	**Ladinian** 27 — Oldest bivalve-perforating snail *Ampullina* sp. Busse 1974	**Ladinian** 28 — Largest notosauroid *Lariosaurus calcagnii* Peyer 1931
Ladinian 29 — Oldest pachycormid fish *Prohalecites porroi* Bellotti 1857	**Carnian** 30 — Upper Triassic begins at 1:00 a.m.	**Carnian** 31				

FEBRUARY—236.36 to 222.08 Ma

M	T	W	T	F	S	S
			Carnian 1	**Carnian** 2	**Carnian** 3 — Oldest "water boatman" insect (Corixidae) Zheng et al. 2018	**Carnian** 4 — Oldest euechinoid sea urchin *Hemipedina incipiens* Bather 1990
Carnian 5 — Oldest orectolobiform shark Unnamed Murry 1986	**Carnian** 6 — Longest animal of the Triassic *Traumatocrinus* sp. Hagdorn, Wang & Wang 2007	**Carnian** 7 — Oldest proterochampsid *Proterochampsa barrionuevoi* Reig 1959	**Carnian** 8 — Largest thalattosauroid *Miodentosaurus brevis* Cheng, Wu & Sato 2007	**Carnian** 9 — Oldest aquatic pantelstudine *Odontochelys semitestacea* Li et al. 2008	**Carnian** 10 — Oldest carnivorous sauropodomorph of South America *Buriolestes schultzi* Cabreira et al. 2016	**Carnian** 11 — Oldest omnivorous sauropomorphs *Pampadromaeus & Panphagia* Martínez & Alcober 2009; Cabreira et al. 2011
Carnian 12 — Oldest and smallest sauropodomorph of Asia? *Alwalkeria maleriensis* Chatterjee 1987	**Carnian** 13 — Largest brachiopod of the Triassic *Orbiculoidea* sp. Dagys 1965	**Carnian** 14 — Oldest Plateosauria Unnamed Heckert 2001; Diedrich 2009	**Carnian** 15 — Oldest sauropod prints Unnamed Marsicano & Barredo 2004; Wilson 2005	**Carnian** 16 — Oldest sauropodomorph of Africa cf. *Saturnalia* sp. Raath 1996	**Carnian** 17 — Impact of the Saint Martin meteorite, Canada	**Carnian** 18 — Largest marine amphibian *Hyperokynodon keuperinus* Plieninger 1852
Carni/Norian 19 — Largest Plateosauria (estimated from a print) *Pseudotetrasauropus mekalingensis* Ellenberger 1972	**Norian** 20 — Oldest sauropodiform (identified from a print) *Lavinipes jaquesi* Ellenberger 1970	**Norian** 21 — Smallest Plateosauria (estimated from a print) *Evazoum* sp. Gierlinski 2009	**Norian** 22	**Norian** 23	**Norian** 24	**Norian** 25
Norian 26	**Norian** 27	**Norian** 28 — Oldest quadrupedal sauropodomorph of North America *Agrestipus hottoni* Weems 1987				

On this scale, each day represents 510,000 years, each hour 21,000 years, each minute 350 years, and each second 5.8 years.

The "Mesozoic Calendar" presented here offers a model that compresses the 186.17 Ma of the Mesozoic era into a 365-day year, just as we presented in the book *Dinosaur Facts and Figures: The Theropods and Other Dinosauriformes*. In this calendar we include sauropodomorphs as well as other aquatic organisms to examine some major events that occurred over time. The concept was originally used by geologist Don L. Eicher in his book *Geologic Time*, which examined the period extending from Earth's creation to the present day. See more: *Eicher 1976; Sagan 1978; Wilford 1985; de Grasse-Tyson 2014; Molina-Pérez & Larramendi 2016*

Up to the beginning of the Jurassic era, sauropodomorphs were not always the largest dinosaurs of their time, as during the Triassic some aquatic animals superseded them—in mass, for example, giant ichthyosaurs like *Himalayasaurus*, *Shastasaurus*, and *Shonisaurus*, and in height, the enormous crinoid *Traumatocrinus*, which reached 11 m in height.

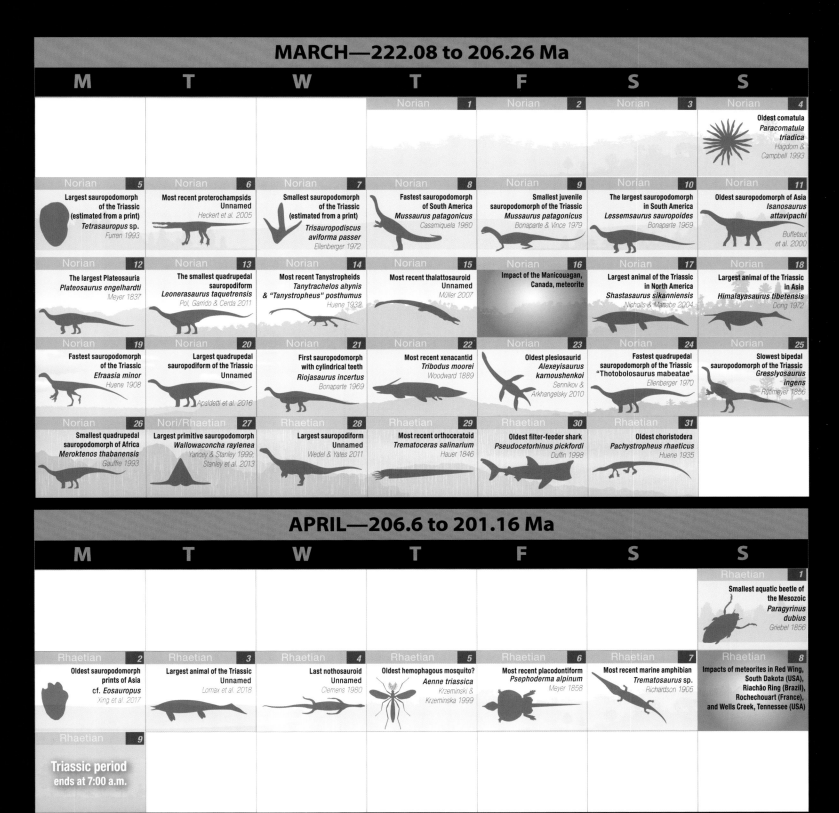

MARCH—222.08 to 206.26 Ma

M	T	W	T	F	S	S
			Norian **1**	Norian **2**	Norian **3**	Norian **4** Oldest comatula *Paracomatula triadica* Hagdorn & Campbell 1993
Norian **5** Largest sauropodomorph of the Triassic (estimated from a print) *Tetrasauropus* sp. Furren 1993	Norian **6** Most recent proterochampsids Unnamed Heckert et al. 2005	Norian **7** Smallest sauropodomorph of the Triassic (estimated from a print) *Trisauropodiscus aviforma passer* Ellenberger 1972	Norian **8** Fastest sauropodomorph of South America *Mussaurus patagonicus* Casamiquela 1980	Norian **9** Smallest juvenile sauropodomorph of the Triassic *Mussaurus patagonicus* Bonaparte & Vince 1979	Norian **10** The largest sauropodomorph in South America *Lessemsaurus sauropoides* Bonaparte 1969	Norian **11** Oldest sauropodomorph of Asia *Isanosaurus attavipachi* Buffetaut et al. 2000
Norian **12** The largest Plateosauria *Plateosaurus engelhardti* Meyer 1837	Norian **13** The smallest quadrupedal sauropodiform *Leonerasaurus taquetrensis* Pol, Garrido & Cerda 2011	Norian **14** Most recent Tanystropheids *Tanytrachelos ahynis* & "*Tanystropheus*" *posthumus* Huene 1932	Norian **15** Most recent thalattosauroid Unnamed Müller 2007	Norian **16** Impact of the Manicouagan, Canada, meteorite	Norian **17** Largest animal of the Triassic in North America *Shastasaurus sikanniensis* Nicholls & Manabe 2004	Norian **18** Largest animal of the Triassic in Asia *Himalayasaurus tibetensis* Dong 1972
Norian **19** Fastest sauropodomorph of the Triassic *Efraasia minor* Huene 1908	Norian **20** Largest quadrupedal sauropodiform of the Triassic Unnamed Apaldetti et al. 2016	Norian **21** First sauropodomorph with cylindrical teeth *Riojasaurus incertus* Bonaparte 1969	Norian **22** Most recent xenacantid *Tribodus moorei* Woodward 1889	Norian **23** Oldest plesiosaurid *Alexeyisaurus karnoushenkoi* Sennikov & Arkhangelsky 2010	Norian **24** Fastest quadrupedal sauropodomorph of the Triassic "*Thotobolosaurus mabeatae*" Ellenberger 1970	Norian **25** Slowest bipedal sauropodomorph of the Triassic *Gresslyosaurus ingens* Rütimeyer 1856
Norian **26** Smallest quadrupedal sauropodomorph of Africa *Meroktenos thabanensis* Gauffre 1993	Nori/Rhaetian **27** Largest primitive sauropodomorph *Wallowaconcha raylenea* Yancey & Stanley 1999; Stanley et al. 2013	Rhaetian **28** Largest sauropodiform Unnamed Wedel & Yates 2011	Rhaetian **29** Most recent orthoceratoid *Trematoceras salinarium* Hauer 1846	Rhaetian **30** Oldest filter-feeder shark *Pseudocetorhinus pickfordi* Duffin 1998	Rhaetian **31** Oldest choristodera *Pachystropheus rhaeticus* Huene 1935	

APRIL—206.6 to 201.16 Ma

M	T	W	T	F	S	S
						Rhaetian **1** Smallest aquatic beetle of the Mesozoic *Paragyrinus dubius* Griebel 1856
Rhaetian **2** Oldest sauropodomorph prints of Asia cf. *Eosauropus* Xing et al. 2017	Rhaetian **3** Largest animal of the Triassic Unnamed Lomax et al. 2018	Rhaetian **4** Last nothosauroid Unnamed Clemens 1980	Rhaetian **5** Oldest hemophagous mosquito? *Aenne triassica* Krzeminski & Krzeminska 1999	Rhaetian **6** Most recent placodontiform *Psephoderma alpinum* Meyer 1858	Rhaetian **7** Most recent marine amphibian *Trematosaurus* sp. Richardson 1905	Rhaetian **8** Impacts of meteorites in Red Wing, South Dakota (USA), Riachão Ring (Brazil), Rochechouart (France), and Wells Creek, Tennessee (USA)
Rhaetian **9** **Triassic period ends at 7:00 a.m.**						

In the Jurassic, sauropods dominated terrestrial ecosystems, competing only with the other two large dinosaur groups—the ornithischians and the phytophagous theropods. Very few animals rivaled the greatest sauropods in size, such as the 15-meter-tall *Seirocrinus* and the 16.5-meter-long *Leedsichthys*.

Different explanations have been proposed for the beginning of the Jurassic period, but what is certain is that there was massive volcanic activity in what is now the **Atlantic Ocean.** See more: *Hautmann 2012*

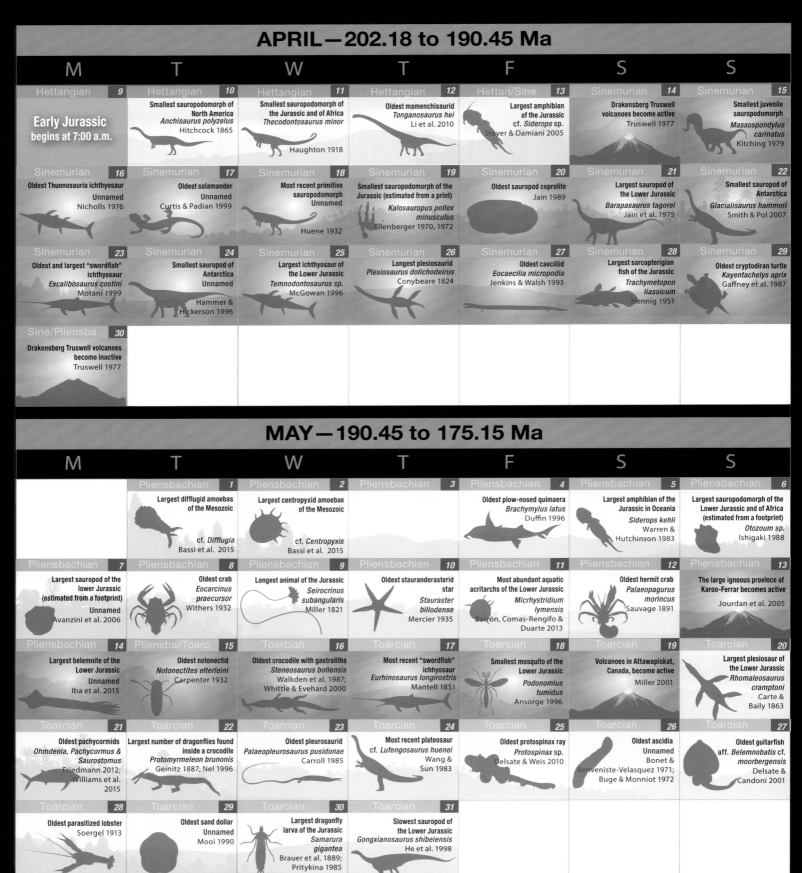

APRIL—202.18 to 190.45 Ma

M	T	W	T	F	S	S
Early Jurassic begins at 7:00 a.m.	Hettangian 10 — Smallest sauropodomorph of North America *Anchisaurus polyzelus* Hitchcock 1865	Hettangian 11 — Smallest sauropodomorph of the Jurassic and of Africa *Thecodontosaurus minor* Haughton 1918	Hettangian 12 — Oldest mamenchisaurid *Tonganosaurus hei* Li et al. 2010	Hettan/Sine 13 — Largest amphibian of the Jurassic cf. *Siderops* sp. Steyer & Damiani 2005	Sinemurian 14 — Drakensberg Truswell volcanoes become active Truswell 1977	Sinemurian 15 — Smallest juvenile sauropodomorph *Massospondylus carinatus* Kitching 1979
Sinemurian 16 — Oldest Thunnosauria ichthyosaur Unnamed Nicholls 1976	Sinemurian 17 — Oldest salamander Unnamed Curtis & Padian 1999	Sinemurian 18 — Most recent primitive sauropodomorph Unnamed Huene 1932	Sinemurian 19 — Smallest sauropodomorph of the Jurassic (estimated from a print) *Kalosauropus pollex minusculus* Ellenberger 1970, 1972	Sinemurian 20 — Oldest sauropod coprolite Jain 1989	Sinemurian 21 — Largest sauropod of the Lower Jurassic *Barapasaurus tagorei* Jain et al. 1975	Sinemurian 22 — Smallest sauropod of Antarctica *Glacialisaurus hammeri* Smith & Pol 2007
Sinemurian 23 — Oldest and largest "swordfish" ichthyosaur *Excalibosaurus costini* Motani 1999	Sinemurian 24 — Smallest sauropod of Antarctica Unnamed Hammer & Hickerson 1996	Sinemurian 25 — Largest ichthyosaur of the Lower Jurassic *Temnodontosaurus sp.* McGowan 1996	Sinemurian 26 — Longest plesiosaurid *Plesiosaurus dolichodeirus* Conybeare 1824	Sinemurian 27 — Oldest caeciliid *Eocaecilia micropodia* Jenkins & Walsh 1993	Sinemurian 28 — Largest sarcopterigian fish of the Jurassic *Trachymetopon liassicum* Hennig 1951	Sinemurian 29 — Oldest cryptodiran turtle *Kayentachelys aprix* Gaffney et al. 1987
Sine/Pliensba 30 — Drakensberg Truswell volcanoes become inactive Truswell 1977						

MAY—190.45 to 175.15 Ma

M	T	W	T	F	S	S
	Pliensbachian 1 — Largest difflugid amoebas of the Mesozoic cf. *Difflugia* Bassi et al. 2015	Pliensbachian 2 — Largest centropyxid amoebae of the Mesozoic cf. *Centropyxis* Bassi et al. 2015	Pliensbachian 3	Pliensbachian 4 — Oldest plow-nosed quimaera *Brachymylus latus* Duffin 1996	Pliensbachian 5 — Largest amphibian of the Lower Jurassic in Oceania *Siderops kehli* Warren & Hutchinson 1983	Pliensbachian 6 — Largest sauropodomorph of the Lower Jurassic and of Africa (estimated from a footprint) *Otozoum sp.* Ishigaki 1988
Pliensbachian 7 — Largest sauropod of the lower Jurassic (estimated from a footprint) Unnamed Avanzini et al. 2006	Pliensbachian 8 — Oldest crab *Eocarcinus praecursor* Withers 1932	Pliensbachian 9 — Longest animal of the Jurassic *Seirocrinus subangularis* Miller 1821	Pliensbachian 10 — Oldest stauranderasterid star *Stauraster billodense* Mercier 1935	Pliensbachian 11 — Most abundant aquatic acritarchs of the Lower Jurassic *Micrhystridium lymensis* Barrón, Comas-Rengifo & Duarte 2013	Pliensbachian 12 — Oldest hermit crab *Palaeopagurus morincus* Sauvage 1891	Pliensbachian 13 — The large igneous province of Karoo-Ferrar becomes active Jourdan et al. 2005
Pliensbachian 14 — Largest belemnite of the Lower Jurassic Unnamed Iba et al. 2015	Pliensba/Toarc 15 — Oldest notonectid *Notonectites elterleini* Carpenter 1932	Toarcian 16 — Oldest crocodile with gastroliths *Steneosaurus bollensis* Walkden et al. 1987; Whittle & Evehard 2000	Toarcian 17 — Most recent "swordfish" ichthyosaur *Eurhinosaurus longirostris* Mantell 1851	Toarcian 18 — Smallest mosquito of the Lower Jurassic *Podonomius tumidus* Ansorge 1996	Toarcian 19 — Volcanoes in Attawapiskat, Canada, become active Miller 2001	Toarcian 20 — Largest plesiosaur of the Lower Jurassic *Rhomaleosaurus cramptoni* Carte & Baily 1863
Toarcian 21 — Oldest pachycormids *Ohmdenia, Pachycormus & Saurostomus* Friedmann 2012; Williams et al. 2015	Toarcian 22 — Largest number of dragonflies found inside a crocodile *Protomyrmeleon brunonis* Geinitz 1887; Nel 1996	Toarcian 23 — Oldest pleurosaurid *Palaeopleurosaurus pusidonae* Carroll 1985	Toarcian 24 — Most recent plateosaur cf. *Lufengosaurus huenei* Wang & Sun 1983	Toarcian 25 — Oldest protospinax ray *Protospinax* sp. Delsate & Weis 2010	Toarcian 26 — Oldest ascidia Unnamed Bonet & Benveniste-Velasquez 1971; Buge & Monniot 1972	Toarcian 27 — Oldest guitarfish aff. *Belemnobatis* cf. *moorbergensis* Delsate & Candoni 2001
Toarcian 28 — Oldest parasitized lobster Soergel 1913	Toarcian 29 — Oldest sand dollar Unnamed Mooi 1990	Toarcian 30 — Largest dragonfly larva of the Jurassic *Samarura gigantea* Brauer et al. 1889; Pritykina 1985	Toarcian 31 — Slowest sauropod of the Lower Jurassic *Gongxianosaurus shibeiensis* He et al. 1998			

JUNE—175.15 to 159.85 Ma

M	T	W	T	F	S	S
				Toarcian **1**	Toarcian **2** The oldest dicraeosaurid *Lingwulong shenqi* Xu et al. 2018	Toar/Aaleni **3** **Middle Jurassic** **begins at 1:00 a.m.**
Aalenian **4** Smallest sauropod of the Middle Jurassic *Nebulasaurus taito* Xing et al. 2015	Aalenian **5** Largest sauropodiform of the Middle Jurassic *Yunnanosaurus youngi* Lu et al. 2007	Aalenian **6** Oldest diplodocoid *Breviparopus* sp. Romano et al. 1999	Aalenian **7** Largest belemnite *Megateuthis* sp. Weis & Mariotti 2007	Aalenian **8** Oldest neosauropod Unnamed Reid 1984	Aalenian **9** Baboquivari volcanoes become active Haxel et al. 2005	Aaleni/Bajo **10** Oldest metriorynchus crocodile *Metriorhynchus* sp. Gasparini et al. 2000
Bajocian **11** Impacts of the Obolon (Ukraine) and Upheaval Dome, Utah (USA) meteorites	Bajocian **12** Oldest macronarian Unnamed Moser et al. 2004	Bajocian **13** Smallest sauropod of the Middle Jurassic (estimated from a footprint) Unnamed Ferrusquia-Villafranca et al. 2007	Bajo/Batho **14** Most recent sauropodomorph print *Trisauropodiscus* sp. Sierlinski et al. 2017	Bathonian **15** Oldest turiasaur *Cardiodon rugolosus* Owen 1841, 1844	Bathonian **16** Impacts of the Puchezh-Katunki (Russia) and Zapadnaya (Ukraine) meteorites	Bathonian **17** Largest sauropod of the Middle Jurassic Unnamed Charroud & Fedan 1992
Batho/Callo **18** Largest sauropod of the Middle Jurassic (estimated from a footprint) *Malakhelisaurus* *mianwali* Malkani 2007, 2008	Callovian **19** Largest brachiopod of the Jurassic *Lessinirhynchia* *benettii* Vörös 1993, 1995	Callovian **20** Largest fish of the Jurassic *Leedsichthys problematicus* Woodward 1889	Callovian **21** Oldest sea turtle *Eileanchelys* *waldmani* Anquetin et al. 2009	Callovian **22** Oldest euhelopodid cf. *"Camarasaurus"* sp. Kurzanov et al. 2003	Callo Oxfor **23** **Late Jurassic** **begins at 9:00 p.m.**	Oxfordian **24** The oldest filter elasmosaur *Tatenectes laramiensis* Knight 1900
Oxfordian **25** The largest sauropod of the Jurassic and Asia *Mamenchisaurus* *jingyanensis* Zhang et al. 1998	Oxfordian **26** Oldest angelshark *Squatina* sp. Thies 1983	Oxfordian **27** Largest sauropod of Africa (estimated from a footprint) (tie) *Breviparopus* *taghbaloutensis* Dutuit & Ouazzou 1980	Oxfordian **28** Largest ammonite of the Jurassic Unnamed Poulton 1989	Oxfordian **29** Oldest diplodocid "*Amphicoelias* *brontodiplodocus*" Galiano & Albersdörfer 2010	Oxfordian **30** Impact of the Vepriai, Lithuania meteorite	

JULY—159.85 to 145.06 Ma

M	T	W	T	F	S	S
						Oxfordian **1** Oldest sawfish *Pristis dubius* Münster 1846
Oxfordian **2** Largest fish of the Upper Jurassic *Leedsichthys notocetes* Martill et al. 1999	Oxfordian **3** Largest sauropod of the Antilles Unnamed de la Torre & Callejas 1949	Oxfordian **4** Last toothed turtle *Sichuanchelys* *palatodentata* Joyce et al. 2016	Oxfordian **5** Oldest stingray Unnamed Buffetaut et al. 1985	Kimmeridgian **6** Largest ammonite of Oceania *Lytoceras* *taharoaense* Stevens 1985; Grulke 2014	Kimmeridgian **7** Oldest sauropod embryo *Camarasaurus* sp. Britt & Naylor 1994	Kimmeridgian **8** Largest sauropod of Europe *Neosodon praecursor* Sauvage 1876
Kimmeridgian **9** Smallest sauropod of the Upper Jurassic and North America *Europasaurus holgeri* Sander et al. 2004	Kimmeridgian **10** Smallest sauropod of North America *Kaatedocus siberi* Tschopp & Mateus 2013	Kimmeridgian **11** Largest sea turtle of the Jurassic Unnamed Lapparent & Brown 1996; Gaillard et al. 2003	Kimmeridgian **12** Largest sauropod of Europe (estimated from a footprint) (tie) Unnamed García-Ramos, Piñuela & Lires 2006	Kimmeridgian **13** Largest pliosaur "Aramberri monster" Knutsen et al. 2012	Kimmer/Titho **14** Largest aquatic crocodile of the Jurassic *Plesiosuchus manselli* Hulke 1870	Tithonian **15** Largest sauropod of Africa *Giraffatitan brancai* Janensch 1914
Tithonian **16** Largest sauropod of North America cf. *Barosaurus lentus* Jensen 1985	Tithonian **17** Largest sauropod of North America *Pleurosaurus ginsburgi* & *P. goldfussi* Meyer 1831; Fabre 1974	Tithonian **18** Oldest picnodon with serrated teeth *Piranhamesodon pinnatomus* Kölbl-Ebert et al. 2018	Tithonian **19** Largest aquatic bug of the Mesozoic *Scarabeides* *deperditus* Germar 1839	Tithonian **20** Largest arachnid of the Mesozoic *Mesolimulus* *walchi* Demarest 1822	Tithonian **21** Oldest somphospondylid *Australodocus* & *Tendaguria* Bonaparte, et al. 2000; Remes 2007	Tithonian **22** The largest sauropod of the Jurassic and North America *Maraapunisaurus fragillimus* Cope 1877
Tithonian **23** Largest pliosaurus? *Pliosaurus rossicus* Tarlo 1959	Tithonian **24** Largest crocodile of the Upper Jurassic *Chalawan thailandicus* Buffetaut & Ingavat 1980	Tithonian **25** Largest snail of the Jurassic *Leviathania gigantea* Makowsky 1874	Tithonian **26** Largest sauropod of Cimmeria *Mamenchisaurus* sp. Suteethorn et al. 2013	Tithonian **27** Tamu Massif, the largest volcano of all time, emerges Mahoney et al. 2005; Witze 2013	Tithonian **28** Impact of the Morokweng (South Africa) meteorite	Tithonian **29** **The Jurassic** **ends at 12:00 p.m.**

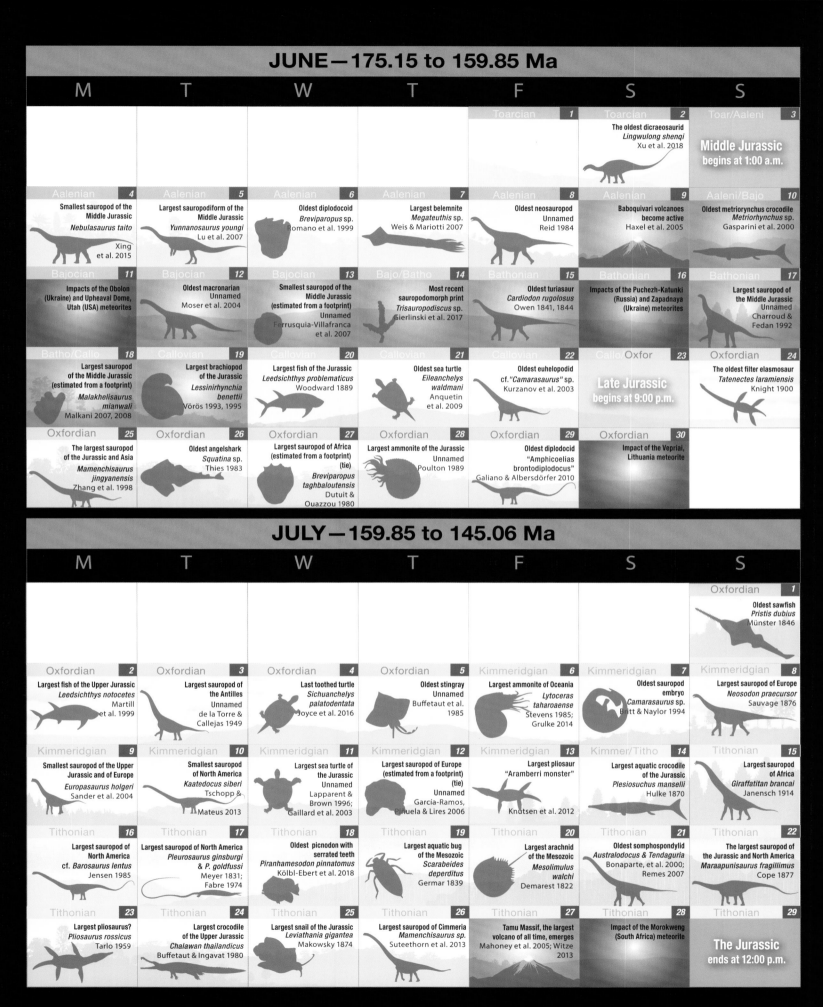

The continents began breaking up, provoking large-scale changes in the climate; some geographic zones were left isolated, although there were some periods when the fauna intermingled.

At the time, no animal grew as large, as long, or as heavy as the largest sauropods. Only the enormous trees of the time, including araucarias and sequoias, were larger. One thing that impacted the sauropods was the domain of angiosperm plants, which gradually replaced the gymnosperms; that shift could have led to the disappearance of some groups and have favored diversity among others. In the early days of the Lower Cretaceous, sauropods had predominantly foliodont teeth; at the end of this period, however, cylindrodont teeth became more prevalent.

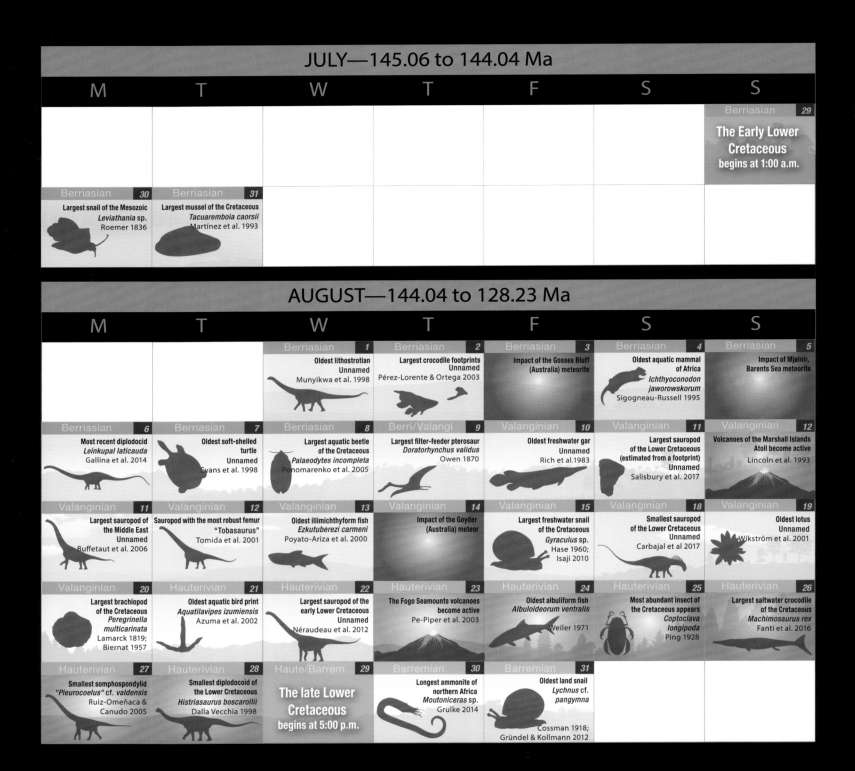

JULY—145.06 to 144.04 Ma

M	T	W	T	F	S	S
						Berriasian 29 — **The Early Lower Cretaceous** begins at 1:00 a.m.
Berriasian 30 — Largest snail of the Mesozoic *Leviathania* sp. Roemer 1836	Berriasian 31 — Largest mussel of the Cretaceous *Tacuaremboia caorsii* Martínez et al. 1993					

AUGUST—144.04 to 128.23 Ma

M	T	W	T	F	S	S
		Berriasian 1 — Oldest lithostrotian Unnamed Munyikwa et al. 1998	Berriasian 2 — Largest crocodile footprints Unnamed Pérez-Lorente & Ortega 2003	Berriasian 3 — Impact of the Gosses Bluff (Australia) meteorite	Berriasian 4 — Oldest aquatic mammal of Africa *Ichthyoconodon jaworowskorum* Sigogneau-Russell 1995	Berriasian 5 — Impact of Mjølnir, Barents Sea meteorite
Berriasian 6 — Most recent diplodocid *Leinkupal laticauda* Gallina et al. 2014	Berriasian 7 — Oldest soft-shelled turtle Unnamed Evans et al. 1998	Berriasian 8 — Largest aquatic beetle of the Cretaceous *Palaeodytes incompleta* Ponomarenko et al. 2005	Berri/Valangi 9 — Largest filter-feeder pterosaur *Doratorhynchus validus* Owen 1870	Valanginian 10 — Oldest freshwater gar Unnamed Rich et al.1983	Valanginian 11 — Largest sauropod of the Lower Cretaceous (estimated from a footprint) Unnamed Salisbury et al. 2017	Valanginian 12 — Volcanoes of the Marshall Islands Atoll become active Lincoln et al. 1993
Valanginian 11 — Largest sauropod of the Middle East Unnamed Buffetaut et al. 2006	Valanginian 12 — Sauropod with the most robust femur "Tobasaurus" Tomida et al. 2001	Valanginian 13 — Oldest illimichthyform fish *Ezkutuberezi carmeni* Poyato-Ariza et al. 2000	Valanginian 14 — Impact of the Goyder (Australia) meteor	Valanginian 15 — Largest freshwater snail of the Cretaceous *Gyraculus* sp. Hase 1960; Isaji 2010	Valanginian 18 — Smallest sauropod of the Lower Cretaceous Unnamed Carbajal et al 2017	Valanginian 19 — Oldest lotus Unnamed Wikström et al. 2001
Valanginian 20 — Largest brachiopod of the Cretaceous *Peregrinella multicarinata* Lamarck 1819; Biernat 1957	Hauterivian 21 — Oldest aquatic bird print *Aquatilavipes izumiensis* Azuma et al. 2002	Hauterivian 22 — Largest sauropod of the early Lower Cretaceous Unnamed Néraudeau et al. 2012	Hauterivian 23 — The Fogo Seamounts volcanoes become active Pe-Piper et al. 2003	Hauterivian 24 — Oldest albuliform fish *Albuloideorum ventralis* Weiler 1971	Hauterivian 25 — Most abundant insect of the Cretaceous appears *Coptoclava longipoda* Ping 1928	Hauterivian 26 — Largest saltwater crocodile of the Cretaceous *Machimosaurus rex* Fanti et al. 2016
Hauterivian 27 — Smallest somphospondylid "*Pleurocoelus*" cf. *valdensis* Ruiz-Omeñaca & Canudo 2005	Hauterivian 28 — Smallest diplodocoid of the Lower Cretaceous *Histriasaurus boscarollii* Dalla Vecchia 1998	Haute/Barrem 29 — **The late Lower Cretaceous** begins at 5:00 p.m.	Barremian 30 — Longest ammonite of northern Africa *Moutoniceras* sp. Grulke 2014	Barremian 31 — Oldest land snail *Lychnus* cf. *pangymna* Cossman 1918; Gründel & Kollmann 2012		

SEPTEMBER—128.23 to 112.92 Ma

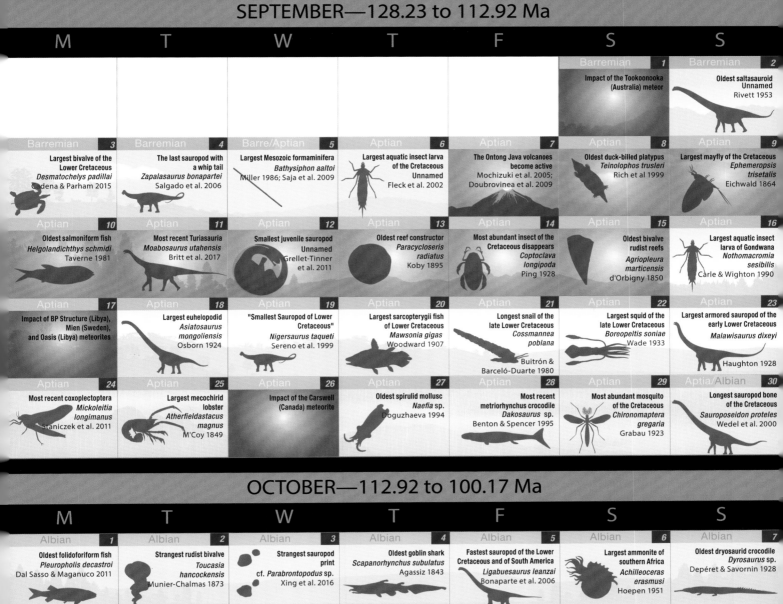

M	T	W	T	F	S	S
					Barremian **1** Impact of the Tookoonooka (Australia) meteor	Barremian **2** Oldest saltasauroid Unnamed Rivett 1953
Barremian **3** Largest bivalve of the Lower Cretaceous *Desmatochelys padillai* Cadena & Parham 2015	Barremian **4** The last sauropod with a whip tail *Zapalasaurus bonapartei* Salgado et al. 2006	Barre/Aptian **5** Largest Mesozoic formaminifera *Bathysiphon aaltoi* Miller 1986; Saja et al. 2009	Aptian **6** Largest aquatic insect larva of the Cretaceous Unnamed Fleck et al. 2002	Aptian **7** The Ontong Java volcanoes become active Mochizuki et al. 2005; Doubrovinea et al. 2009	Aptian **8** Oldest duck-billed platypus *Teinolophos trusleri* Rich et al 1999	Aptian **9** Largest mayfly of the Cretaceous *Ephemeropsis trisetalis* Eichwald 1864
Aptian **10** Oldest salmoniform fish *Helgolandichthys schmidi* Taverne 1981	Aptian **11** Most recent Turiasauria *Moabosaurus utahensis* Britt et al. 2017	Aptian **12** Smallest juvenile sauropod Unnamed Grellet-Tinner et al. 2011	Aptian **13** Oldest reef constructor *Paracycloseris radiatus* Koby 1895	Aptian **14** Most abundant insect of the Cretaceous disappears *Coptoclava longipoda* Ping 1928	Aptian **15** Oldest bivalve rudist reefs *Agriopleura marticensis* d'Orbigny 1850	Aptian **16** Largest aquatic insect larva of Gondwana *Nothomacromia sesibilis* Carle & Wighton 1990
Aptian **17** Impact of BP Structure (Libya), Mien (Sweden), and Oasis (Libya) meteorites	Aptian **18** Largest euhelopodid *Asiatosaurus mongoliensis* Osborn 1924	Aptian **19** "Smallest Sauropod of Lower Cretaceous" *Nigersaurus taqueti* Sereno et al. 1999	Aptian **20** Largest sarcopterygii fish of Lower Cretaceous *Mawsonia gigas* Woodward 1907	Aptian **21** Longest snail of the late Lower Cretaceous *Cossmannea poblana* Buitrón & Barceló-Duarte 1980	Aptian **22** Largest squid of the late Lower Cretaceous *Boreopeltis soniae* Wade 1933	Aptian **23** Largest armored sauropod of the early Lower Cretaceous *Malawisaurus dixeyi* Haughton 1928
Aptian **24** Most recent coxoplectoptera *Mickoleitia longimanus* Staniczek et al. 2011	Aptian **25** Largest mecochirid lobster *Atherfieldastacus magnus* M'Coy 1849	Aptian **26** Impact of the Carswell (Canada) meteorite	Aptian **27** Oldest spirulid mollusc *Naefia* sp. Doguzhaeva 1994	Aptian **28** Most recent metriorhynchus crocodile *Dakosaurus* sp. Benton & Spencer 1995	Aptian **29** Most abundant mosquito of the Cretaceous *Chironomaptera gregaria* Grabau 1923	Aptia/Albian **30** Longest sauropod bone of the Cretaceous *Sauroposeidon proteles* Wedel et al. 2000

OCTOBER—112.92 to 100.17 Ma

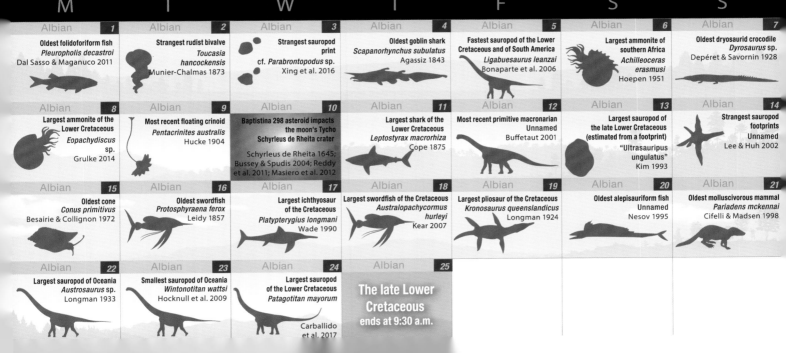

M	T	W	T	F	S	S
Albian **1** Oldest folidoforiform fish *Pleuropholis decastroi* Dal Sasso & Maganuco 2011	Albian **2** Strangest rudist bivalve *Toucasia hancockensis* Munier-Chalmas 1873	Albian **3** Strangest sauropod print cf. *Parabrontopodus* sp. Xing et al. 2016	Albian **4** Oldest goblin shark *Scapanorhynchus subulatus* Agassiz 1843	Albian **5** Fastest sauropod of the Lower Cretaceous and of South America *Ligabuesaurus leanzai* Bonaparte et al. 2006	Albian **6** Largest ammonite of southern Africa *Achilleoceras erasmusi* Hoepen 1951	Albian **7** Oldest dryosaurid crocodile *Dyrosaurus* sp. Depéret & Savornin 1928
Albian **8** Largest ammonite of the Lower Cretaceous *Eopachydiscus* sp. Grulke 2014	Albian **9** Most recent floating crinoid *Pentacrinites australis* Hucke 1904	Albian **10** Baptistina 298 asteroid impacts the moon's Tycho Schyrleus de Rheita crater Schyrleus de Rheita 1645; Bussey & Spudis 2004; Reddy et al. 2011; Masiero et al. 2012	Albian **11** Largest shark of the Lower Cretaceous *Leptostyrax macrorhiza* Cope 1875	Albian **12** Most recent primitive macronarian Unnamed Buffetaut 2001	Albian **13** Largest sauropod of the late Lower Cretaceous (estimated from a footprint) "*Ultrasauripus ungulatus*" Kim 1993	Albian **14** Strangest sauropod footprints Unnamed Lee & Huh 2002
Albian **15** Oldest cone *Conus primitivus* Besairie & Collignon 1972	Albian **16** Oldest swordfish *Protosphyraena ferox* Leidy 1857	Albian **17** Largest ichthyosaur of the Cretaceous *Platypterygius longmani* Wade 1990	Albian **18** Largest swordfish of the Cretaceous *Australopachycormus hurleyi* Kear 2007	Albian **19** Largest pliosaur of the Cretaceous *Kronosaurus queenslandicus* Longman 1924	Albian **20** Oldest alepisauriform fish Unnamed Nesov 1995	Albian **21** Oldest molluscivorous mammal *Pariadens mckennai* Cifelli & Madsen 1998
Albian **22** Largest sauropod of Oceania *Austrosaurus* sp. Longman 1933	Albian **23** Smallest sauropod of Oceania *Wintonotitan wattsi* Hocknull et al. 2009	Albian **24** Largest sauropod of the Lower Cretaceous *Patagotitan mayorum* Carballido et al. 2017	Albian **25** **The late Lower Cretaceous ends at 9:30 a.m.**			

In the Upper Cretaceous there were many species of sauropods with osteoderms and/or cylindrodont teeth, and some species became larger than sauropods in previous periods. Several groups became extinct, with sauropodomorphs disappearing in North American until they later recolonized the continent, possibly from Paleoasia. This may have been caused by the replacement of gymnosperm plants by angiosperms and/or by increasing competition with ornithischian dinosaurs.

As the new angiosperm plants came to predominate, sauropods evolved new feeding strategies, and those adaptations are evident in species such as *Bonitasaura*, which had a beak; *Brasilotitan*, with its square jaw; *Rapetosaurus* and *Rinconsauria*, with their distinctive teeth; and Ampelosaurus, with its strange teeth; they are also evident in the voluminous stomachs of *Futalognkosaurus* and saltasaurids.

In terms of mass, only a few animals managed to reach even one-quarter of the mass of the largest sauropods; these include some hadrosaurids of the Mesozoic and a few perissodactyls and proboscideans in the Cenozoic. Even the largest theropods barely reached one-tenth the weight of *Argentinosaurus*.

OCTOBER—100.68 to 97.11 Ma

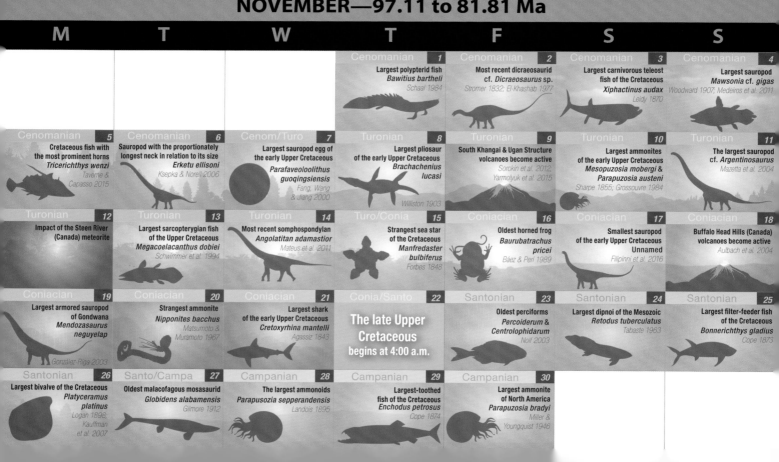

M	T	W	T	F	S	S
			Cenomanian 25 — The Early Upper Cretaceous begins at 9:30 a.m.	Cenomanian 26 — Most recent ichthyosaurs *Platypterygius americanus* & *Pervushovisaurus bannovkensis* Nace 1939; Arkhangel'skii 1998	Cenomanian 27 — Impact of the Sierra Madera, Texas (USA), and Deep Bay (Canada) meteorite. Ontong Java volcanoes become active	Cenomanian 28 — Largest sauropod of the early Upper Cretaceous (estimated from a footprint) "Brontopodus birdi" Krapovickas 2010
Cenomanian 29 — Oldest sea snake Unnamed Rage & Werner 1999	Cenomanian 30 — Largest sawfish *Onchopristis numidus* Haug 1905	Cenomanian 31 — Largest elasmosaurid of the early Upper Cretaceous *Thalassomedon hanningtoni* Welles 1943				

NOVEMBER—97.11 to 81.81 Ma

M	T	W	T	F	S	S
			Cenomanian 1 — Most recent polypterid fish *Bawitius bartheli* Schaal 1984	Cenomanian 2 — Most recent dicraeosaurid cf. *Dicraeosaurus* sp. Stromer 1832; El-Khashab 1977	Cenomanian 3 — Largest carnivorous teleost fish of the Cretaceous *Xiphactinus audax* Leidy 1870	Cenomanian 4 — Largest sauropod *Mawsonia* cf. *gigas* Woodward 1907; Medeiros et al. 2011
Cenomanian 5 — Cretaceous fish with the most prominent horns *Tricerichthys wenzi* Taverne & Capasso 2015	Cenomanian 6 — Sauropod with the proportionately longest neck in relation to its size *Erketu ellisoni* Ksepka & Norell 2006	Cenom/Turo 7 — Largest sauropod egg of the early Upper Cretaceous *Parafaveoloolithus guoqingsiensis* Fang, Wang & Jiang 2000	Turonian 8 — Largest pliosaur of the early Upper Cretaceous *Brachachenius lucasi* Williston 1903	Turonian 9 — South Khangai & Ugan Structure volcanoes become active Sorokin et al. 2012; Yarmolyuk et al. 2015	Turonian 10 — Largest ammonites of the early Upper Cretaceous *Mesopuzosia mobergi* & *Parapuzosia austeni* Sharpe 1855; Grossouvre 1984	Turonian 11 — The largest sauropod cf. *Argentinosaurus* Mazetta et al. 2004
Turonian 12 — Impact of the Steen River (Canada) meteorite	Turonian 13 — Largest sarcopterygian fish of the Upper Cretaceous *Megacoelacanthus dobiei* Schwimmer et al. 1994	Turonian 14 — Most recent somphospondylan *Angolatitan adamastior* Mateus et al. 2011	Turo/Conia 15 — Strangest sea star of the Cretaceous *Manfredaster bulbiferus* Forbes 1848	Coniacian 16 — Oldest horned frog *Baurubatrachus pricei* Báez & Peri 1989	Coniacian 17 — Smallest sauropod of the early Upper Cretaceous Unnamed Filippini et al. 2016	Coniacian 18 — Buffalo Head Hills (Canada) volcanoes become active Aubach et al. 2004
Coniacian 19 — Largest armored sauropod of Gondwana *Mendozasaurus neguyelap* González-Riga 2003	Coniacian 20 — Strangest ammonite *Nipponites bacchus* Matsumoto & Muramoto 1967	Coniacian 21 — Largest shark of the early Upper Cretaceous *Cretoxyrhina mantelli* Agassiz 1843	Conia/Santo 22 — The late Upper Cretaceous begins at 4:00 a.m.	Santonian 23 — Oldest perciforms *Percoiderum* & *Centrolophidarum* Nolf 2003	Santonian 24 — Largest dipnoi of the Mesozoic *Retodus tuberculatus* Tabaste 1963	Santonian 25 — Largest filter-feeder fish of the Cretaceous *Bonnerichthys gladius* Cope 1873
Santonian 26 — Largest bivalve of the Cretaceous *Platyceramus platinus* Logan 1898; Kauffman et al. 2007	Santo/Campa 27 — Oldest malacofagous mosasaurid *Globidens alabamensis* Gilmore 1912	Campanian 28 — The largest ammonoids *Parapusozia sepperandensis* Landois 1895	Campanian 29 — Largest-toothed fish of the Cretaceous *Enchodus petrosus* Cope 1874	Campanian 30 — Largest ammonite of North America *Parapuzosia bradyi* Miller & Youngquist 1946		

Planet Earth is approximately 4.55 billion years old, or 24.4 times the length of the Mesozoic era.

The Paleozoic era lasted approximately 318 million years, 1.7 times as long as the Mesozoic.

The present era, the Cenozoic, began 66 million years ago and to date has lasted about as long as the middle Pliensbachian age (May 9 on this chronological calendar).

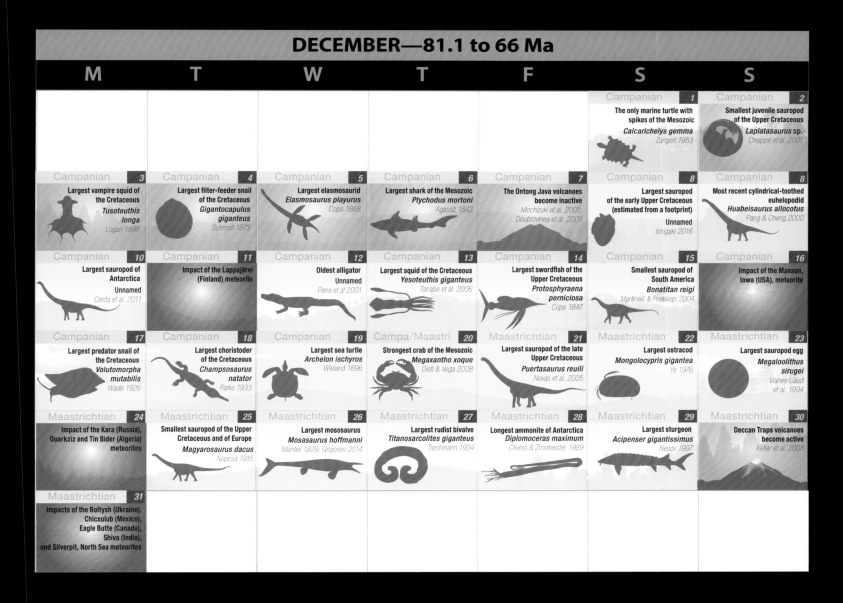

DECEMBER—81.1 to 66 Ma

M	T	W	T	F	S	S
					Campanian 1 — The only marine turtle with spikes of the Mesozoic — *Calcarichelys gemma* — Zangerl 1953	Campanian 2 — Smallest juvenile sauropod of the Upper Cretaceous — *Laplatasaurus* sp. — Chiappe et al. 2001
Campanian 3 — Largest vampire squid of the Cretaceous — *Tusoteuthis longa* — Logan 1898	Campanian 4 — Largest filter-feeder snail of the Cretaceous — *Gigantocapulus giganteus* — Schmidt 1873	Campanian 5 — Largest elasmosaurid — *Elasmosaurus playurus* — Cope 1868	Campanian 6 — Largest shark of the Mesozoic — *Ptychodus mortoni* — Agassiz 1843	Campanian 7 — The Ontong Java volcanoes become inactive — Mochizuki et al. 2005; Doubrovinea et al. 2009	Campanian 8 — Largest sauropod of the early Upper Cretaceous (estimated from a footprint) — Unnamed — Ishigaki 2016	Campanian 8 — Most recent cylindrical-toothed euhelopodid — *Huabeisaurus allocotus* — Pang & Cheng 2000
Campanian 10 — Largest sauropod of Antarctica — Unnamed — Cerda et al. 2011	Campanian 11 — Impact of the Lappajärvi (Finland) meteorite	Campanian 12 — Oldest alligator — Unnamed — Pena et al 2001	Campanian 13 — Largest squid of the Cretaceous — *Yesoteuthis giganteus* — Tanabe et al. 2006	Campanian 14 — Largest swordfish of the Upper Cretaceous — *Protosphyraena perniciosa* — Cope 1847	Campanian 15 — Smallest sauropod of South America — *Bonatitan reigi* — Martinelli & Forasiepi 2004	Campanian 16 — Impact of the Manson, Iowa (USA), meteorite
Campanian 17 — Largest predator snail of the Cretaceous — *Volutomorpha mutabilis* — Wade 1926	Campanian 18 — Largest choristoder of the Cretaceous — *Champsosaurus natator* — Parks 1933	Campanian 19 — Largest sea turtle — *Archelon ischyros* — Wieland 1896	Campa/Maastri 20 — Strongest crab of the Mesozoic — *Megaxantho xoque* — Dietl & Vega 2008	Maastrichtian 21 — Largest sauropod of the late Upper Cretaceous — *Puertasaurus reuili* — Novas et al. 2005	Maastrichtian 22 — Largest ostracod — *Mongolocypris gigantea* — Ye 1976	Maastrichtian 23 — Largest sauropod egg — *Megaloolithus sirugei* — Vianey-Liaud et al. 1994
Maastrichtian 24 — Impact of the Kara (Russia), Ouarkziz and Tin Bider (Algeria) meteorites	Maastrichtian 25 — Smallest sauropod of the Upper Cretaceous and of Europe — *Magyarosaurus dacus* — Nopcsa 1915	Maastrichtian 26 — Largest mosasaurus — *Mosasaurus hoffmanni* — Mantell 1829; Grigoriev 2014	Maastrichtian 27 — Largest rudist bivalve — *Titanosarcolites giganteus* — Trechmann 1924	Maastrichtian 28 — Longest ammonite of Antarctica — *Diplomoceras maximum* — Olivero & Zinsmeister 1989	Maastrichtian 29 — Largest sturgeon — *Acipenser gigantissimus* — Nesov 1997	Maastrichtian 30 — Deccan Traps volcanoes become active — Keller et al. 2008
Maastrichtian 31 — Impacts of the Boltysh (Ukraine), Chicxulub (Mexico), Eagle Butte (Canada), Shiva (India), and Silverpit, North Sea meteorites						

Geological dating of fossils covers an enormous time frame as the formations studied were shaped over millions of years. This means that species can occupy several "days" in our Mesozoic Calendar model, and so they have been situated between the oldest and most recent probable times; thus their assignment to precise days is relative.

HOW DID SAUROPODS BECOME EXTINCT?

Like all other dinosaurs, sauropods were present for two of the five largest mass extinctions of all time—one in the Triassic-Jurassic and the other in the Cretaceous-Paleogene. It should be noted, however, that there were other major extinction events in the Mesozoic era in which the fauna present on Earth changed dramatically, including that of the Lower-Middle Jurassic, that of the Upper Jurassic-Lower Cretaceous, and that of the early Upper Cretaceous–late Upper Cretaceous.

The last sauropodomorphs survived until approximately 66 Ma and thus lived for some 166 Ma, inhabiting all the continents of Earth. Bipedal forms lived from the Upper Triassic to the Middle Jurassic (approx. 232–167.2 Ma), a period of 64.8 million years in the fossil record, while quadrupeds were present from the Upper Triassic to the end of the Cretaceous, existing for some 161 Ma.

THE GREATEST MASS EXTINCTIONS OF THE MESOZOIC ERA

Permian-Triassic Extinction

This was one of the most significant mass extinctions in Earth's history, with close to 96% of all marine species and 70% of terrestrial ones ceasing to exist. It has not been easy to determine the cause of this global cataclysm; however, some studies suggest that methane and other gases provoked a greenhouse gas effect that led to extreme global warming. Those gases may have originated in coal deposits or volcanism or were released from the ocean floor. See more: *Olsen et al.1987*

Triassic-Jurassic Extinction

The fifth-largest mass extinction of all time occurred during the transition from the Triassic to the Jurassic and affected close to 20% of all biological families on Earth. This enabled dinosaurs, which already dominated most terrestrial niches, to become the only phytophagous creatures and the largest carnivores in all terrestrial ecosystems, as they were left with virtually no competition. The causes of this event have not been confirmed, although evidence that meteorites struck Earth at the time is growing. We do know that some groups of sauropodomorphs disappeared at this time and others took their place. See more: *Olsen et al.1987*

Jurassic-Cretaceous Extinction

Although it was a moderate extinction event, many animal species did disappear, including large groups of sauropods, such as mamenchisaurids and diplodocids, while the number of turiasaurs, primitive macronarians, and primitive titanosauriforms diminished drastically.

Early Upper–late Upper Cretaceous Extinction

In this event, known as the Cenomanian-Turonian anoxic boundary event or the Bonarelli event, the ocean lost much of its oxygen over nearly half a million years, and the global climate became extremely cold or hot for periods on both land and sea. It is believed to have been caused by sub-oceanic volcanism, and led to the disappearance of many kinds of dinosaurs, including the sauropods that tended to inhabit coastal and continental zones (rebbachisaurids, euhelopodids, and primitive somphospondylians), while sauropods inhabiting inland environments and fluvio-lacustrine systems (titanosaurs) thrived. See more: *Karakitsios et al. 2007; Mannion & Upchurch 2009; Wan, Wignall & Zhao 2003; Omaña, Centeno-García & Buitrón-Sánchez 2012*

Cretaceous-Tertiary Extinction

The second-largest mass extinction of all time occurred during the transition from the Cretaceous to the Tertiary periods, and thus is known as the K/T Boundary Event (from the German Kreide/Tertiär Grenze). During this event, 50% of all biological genera disappeared from the planet, including all non-avian dinosaurs, while very few marine birds inhabiting the polar regions managed to survive. See more: *Alvarez et al. 1980; McLean 1985; Donovan et al. 1988; Hallam 1989; Marshall & Ward 1996; MacLeod et al. 1997; Toon et al. 1997; Li & Keller 1998; Keller 2001; Sarjeant & Currie 2001; Molina 2007; Zhao et al. 2009; Schulte et al. 2010; Bryant 2014; Brusatte et al. 2014; Sakamoto et al. 2016; Kaiho & Oshima 2017; Sellès et al. 2017*

POST-METEORITE IMPACT: WHAT WAS LIFE LIKE FOR THE LAST SAUROPODS?

- Many plants and animals on land and sea were frozen to death by the strong winds that resulted from the meteor's impact, while others were incinerated or crushed by the force of the impact itself. The material from the impact dispersed around the globe and was ejected into the atmosphere, even reaching the moon and perhaps even Mars.
- The rise in temperature caused fires that burned at 700–800°C for several hours over 70% of the continental land mass and were accompanied by earthquakes measuring up to 11 on the Ritcher scale.
- Enormous waves rose up for distances of more than 300 km, causing tsunamis 100–200 m high and a retreating wave that occurred 10 hours later.
- A huge cloud of steam, gas, dust, and other material rose up, forming a dense layer of soot in the stratosphere with sulfate aerosols that blocked sunlight and caused temperatures on Earth to plunge as low as -10–19° C. The biggest drop occurred in tropical zones, which experienced temperatures of just 5° C for three years. This led to an extreme drought, during which photosynthesis ceased in vascular plants and plankton, collapsing the global ecosystem.
- Oxygen levels dropped drastically, and intense winds, torrential acid rains, hurricanes, and earthquakes occurred in different parts of the world.
- Sauropods, ornithischians, and non-avian theropods disappeared completely at this time, as did 50% of all other dinosaur species. Even that other group of endothermal animals—mammals—suffered the extinction of 93% of all species.
- In the geological record, 90% of planktonic foraminifera species disappeared "instantaneously," indicating the catastrophic nature of this event.
- Plants did not change significantly, although for some time the environment was dominated by ferns, which even today are often the first plants to recolonize areas after a disaster.
- The layers of iridium that define the end of the Mesozoic era and the beginning of the Cenozoic were deposited over a period of 10,000–100,000 years.
- Although no sauropods remained alive, life on Earth returned over the 300,000 years following the end of the Cretaceous, while the ocean required some 3 million years to recover. See more: *Orth et al. 1981; Pollack et al. 1983; Officer & Drake 1985; Wolbach et al. 1985; Sigurdsson et al. 1991; Canudo & Molina 1992; Coccioni & Galeotti 1994; D'Hondt et al. 1994, 1998; Matsui et al. 2002; Molina et al. 2006; Schulte et al. 2010; Longrich et al. 2016; Brugger et al. 2017; Kaiho & Oshima 2017*

Most enigmatic mass extinction of the Mesozoic

The Triassic-Jurassic mass extinction (approx. 201.3 Ma) was one of the worst catastrophes of all time and is the fifth-largest such event in the entire history of the planet. This event is one of the least-known ever in terms of its causes, although evidence has slowly accumulated over time to explain it.

Sauropodomorphs suffered major losses at the time, although ultimately they thrived widely, taking advantage of new ecological niches abandoned by large herbivorous species, including a diverse array of archosaurs and, to a lesser extent, therapsids.

The worst mass extinction of the Mesozoic

The Mesozoic era was ushered in by the greatest mass extinction on Earth and ended with the second worst we know of. That phenomenon led to the disappearance of 95% of life on land and sea, and thus was the event that came closest to leaving the planet uninhabited, at least for multicellular life-forms. It ended at the beginning of the Mesozoic era (approx. 252.17 Ma).

The best-known mass extinction of the Mesozoic

This catastrophic event has been the most widely studied and, through direct and indirect research, has yielded the most evidence of its causes. It is believed that 75% of all species on Earth disappeared, with certain groups, such as non-avian dinosaurs, including the giant sauropods, completely decimated some 66 Ma ago.

1650—Ireland
The first theory of the extinction of the dinosaurs

Archbishop James Ussher estimated that Earth was created in 4004 B.C. at a time when the prevailing belief was "fixism," which held that species remained exactly the same after appearing on Earth. Catastrophism emerged to explain the extinction of beings, and one of its proponents was Georges Cuvier, who collaborated in studies leading to the creation of stratigraphy, a scientific discipline that studies the correlation of geological units and thus can help estimate the age of fossils. This provided evidence that fauna had changed over time and that certain periods of change had led to a renewal of life-forms on Earth.

It is important to note that this theory is still employed today to explain the extinction of the dinosaurs, as it is consistent with the mass extinctions that occurred. While the theory emerged long before the first dinosaurs were discovered, these creatures became part of the hypothesis, with the understanding that their disappearance was the result of a sudden, violent change. Another theory that contradicts the catastrophe theory should also be mentioned—gradualism, which holds that dinosaurs disappeared slowly over time.

THEORIES OF THE EXTINCTION OF NON-AVIAN DINOSAURS

The disappearance of dinosaurs has given rise to the greatest number of theories in history, many of them based on scientific evidence, while others propose events without any proof to support them or offer ideas verging on the impossible. We have grouped these theories into six different categories and briefly review several of them below:

1—Theories of dinosaur extinction caused by the dinosaurs themselves

Ideas that emerged to explain the disappearance of the dinosaurs include a lack of insulating hair or feathers that made them poorly adapted to atmospheric conditions; diseases like infections, arthritis, broken bones, or dental cavities; stunted embryos; racial aging; excessive speciation or sterility among all species; excessive intestinal gas; self-destructive evolution; sexually transmitted diseases; and the lack of a survival instinct. Others include extreme size, hyperactive glands, starvation, eating their young, lack of intelligence, genetic mutation, abnormalities, loss of interest in sex, spinal problems, rickets, overpopulation of predators, collective suicide, and mental or metabolic disorders. None of these, however, explains the disappearance of 75% of other life-forms, including microscopic ones.

The least likely

The least defensible theory is perhaps collective suicide provoked by psychosis from overpopulation. It would be unlikely that something like this would affect all species on all continents, including those living on islands.

The most likely

Death by starvation is the most likely theory; from what is known about the extinction of life at the time, ecological problems prevented Earth's animals from obtaining enough food, as even the number of cadavers would eventually be exhausted.

2—Theories of dinosaur extinction caused by climate change

This category encompasses hypotheses that mention environmental anomalies as the cause of such problems as eggshells becoming too fragile, too thick, or double-walled; the absence of breeding males or females; blindness due to global warming; an overly dry climate; carbon dioxide pollution; decalcification; and the loss of freshwater due to excessive runoff into the oceans. Others include the greenhouse effect, global glaciation, the elimination of major habitats, a lack of oxygen in the ocean, excessive humidity, male infertility, flooding, low carbon-dioxide levels, and intense volcanism, among others. Several of these causes could also have affected non-dinosaur species, as they would have impacted the global environment itself.

The least likely

A change in temperature that would cause the birth of male or female dinosaurs alone does not explain the present-day presence of birds or the extinction of other life-forms.

The most likely

Unusually severe volcanic activity has been well studied and firmly demonstrated; volcanoes in the Hindustan zone, for instance, decimated life some 500,000 years before an enormous meteorite fell from the sky. Today researchers believe that the two occurrences combined, along with their secondary effects, could have led to mass extinction.

3—Theories of dinosaur extinction caused by other species

Some proposed theories refer to an abundance of egg-eating mammals, pollen allergies, digestive alterations, less nutritious food, the disappearance of plants the dinosaurs consumed, ecological disorders, global disease epidemics, a lack or excess of oxygen, toxic fungi or venomous plants, inability to compete with other species, lower intelligence than other animals, parasitic vegetation, a caterpillar plague, and the spread of very virulent or pathogenic viruses across the entire globe. None of the theories mentioned, however, adequately explains the extinction of non-dinosaur species.

The least likely

The appearance of armies of dinosaur-egg-eating mammals is certainly a famous theory, but it is not supported by any evidence. It would not have taken place suddenly across the globe and would also have eliminated oviparous animals, including birds and reptiles.

The most likely

Disease epidemics is the most likely theory, as having a large number of dead animals on both land and sea could have allowed plagues to spread, decimating different species.

4—Theories of dinosaur extinction from geological causes

These theories include changes in Earth's gravity or atmospheric pressure, a damaged ozone layer that allowed ultraviolet rays to reach Earth, the concentration of toxic elements, the rejoining of continents, uranium contamination, planetary evolution, sea-level rise or fall, a shift in the planet's rotational axis, and a lack of livable habitat. Also in this category are oceanic stagnation, inversion of the magnetic poles, enormous mountains causing drought, the birth of the moon, continental separation, and intense volcanism.

The least likely

One theory that emerged held that the moon may have originated directly from Earth at the end of the Cretaceous, wreaking havoc with life on Earth; however, the moon is known to have existed for almost as long as Earth itself.

The most likely

Again, large-scale volcanic activity emerges as a possible cause, and is the most likely among those proposed here. Even so, it is also worth mentioning the sea-level drop at the end of the Cretaceous period that left 29 million km² of new land exposed. Although the effects of this phenomenon would not have been intense enough to have led to such wide-scale extinction, if it was simultaneously accompanied by one or more meteorites striking Earth, then it could have contributed, thus leading to the theory of multiple causes.

5—Theories of dinosaur extinction from astronomical causes

This group of theories includes intense solar activity; the expansion of sunspots; instability of the galactic plane; 26-million-year cyclical effects leading to global disasters; the impact of a comet or meteorite; a cloud of interstellar gas and dust; cosmic, electromagnetic, or ionizing radiation; a supernova whose effects reached the planet; and lunar volcanism.

The least likely

We know that active volcanoes existed on the moon 100 and 50 million years ago, and it has been estimated that they could have had a harmful effect on Earth's ecosystem. However, these dates do not coincide with the extinction of the dinosaurs.

The most likely

The meteorite impact hypothesis has accumulated quite a lot of evidence in its favor, including the layer of iridium that is found between the Cretaceous-Paleogene boundary layers in different parts of the world, as well as in several contemporary craters; the overwhelming evidence of tsunamis at that time; and the presence of microtektites, grains of quartz and other minerals that display evidence of having been subjected to enormous pressure. Although some investigators suspect that the massive volcanoes in Hindustan limited life on the planet for some time, hardly any would deny that the meteor strike would have been the determining factor, as it occurred in the worst place possible, a site with abundant sulfur and hydrocarbons.

6—Theories of dinosaur extinction from improbable causes

We cannot fail to mention some of the most extravagant theories that have been put forward, with some seriousness. These include a lack of interest in living, divine punishment, immoral behavior leading to an existential crisis, other nonexistent dinosaurs, extreme stupidity, extraterrestrial kidnapping, and overhunting by humans or extraterrestrials. Other unlikely theories hold that dinosaurs still exist in remote places, that dinosaurs were not saved from the great flood, that beings from other planets created a supernova to enable intelligent life on Earth to evolve, and that dinosaurs' time on Earth had simply come to an end.

The least likely
All of them.

The most likely
None of them.

MYTH: Sauropods still exist somewhere on the planet.
Impossible. Supposed sightings are figments of the imagination, fraud, or jokes that have no real evidence to sustain them.

MYTH: Mammals, birds, and insects survived the K/T extinction easily.

The event that caused the mass extinction at the end of the Mesozoic era annihilated virtually all (93%) mammalian species as well. However, thanks to their attributes and ways of life, they recovered quickly, doubling in diversity over the following 300,000 years. In regard to insects, pollinating and other specialized species suffered major losses; bees, for example, were on the verge of extinction, with just 8% of species surviving that period. *See more: Rehan et al. 2013; Longrich, Scriberas & Will 2016*

The world of dinosaurs
The geography of the past

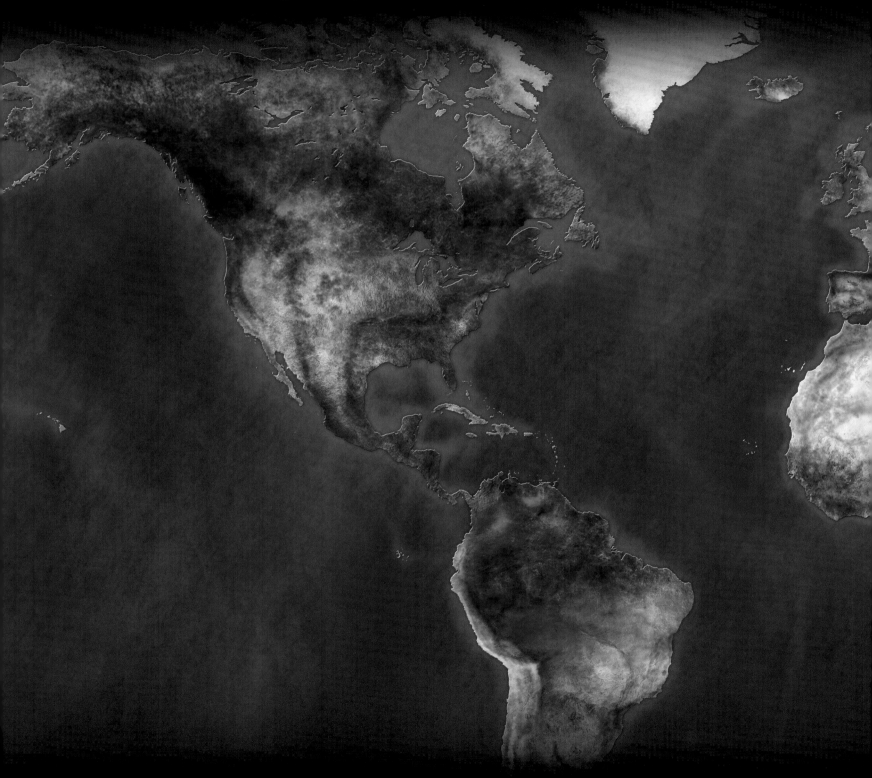

Records: The largest and smallest by geographic location

In 1858, Sclater defined six zoological realms, as follows: Australasian, Ethiopian, Indomalaya-India, Nearctic, Neotropical, and Palaeoarctic. These zoological realms are still in use today, although some authors consider island or subcontinental regions as independent zones (Antilles, Arabian zone, Australia, Central America, Greenland, Madagascar, Southeast Asia, and New Zealand, among others).

Dinosaurs are present on all continents as fossil remains and/or living species.

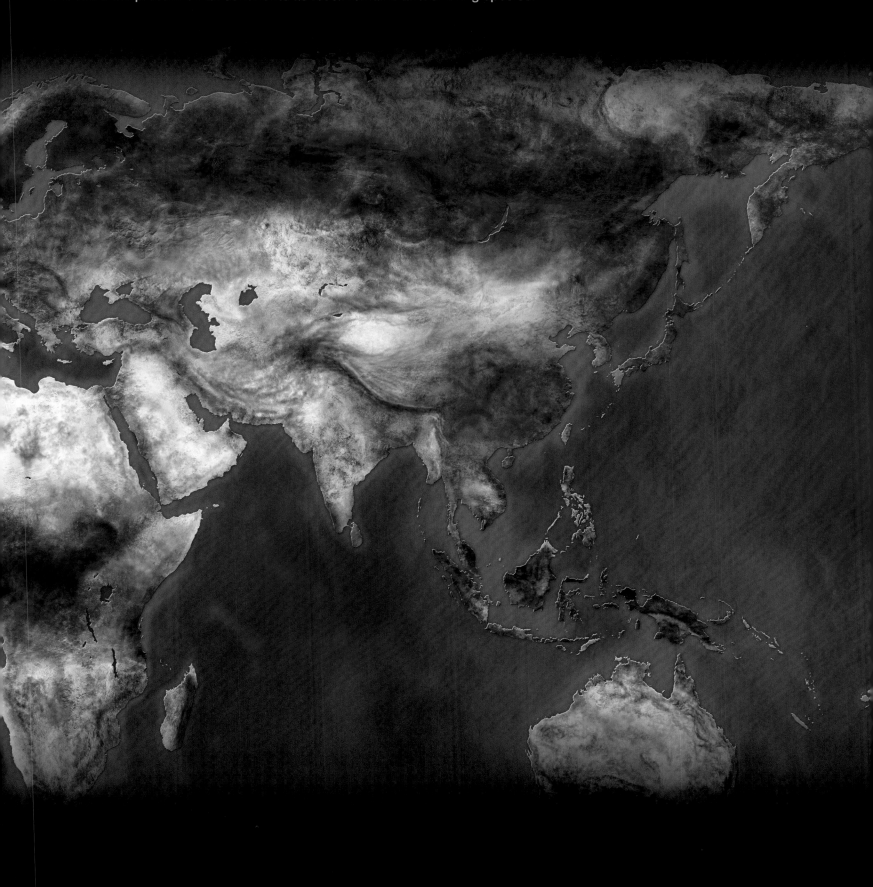

Maraapunisaurus fragillimus
Cope 1877

Specimen: AMNH 5777
(Cope 1877)

Length: 35 m
Hip height: 7.7 m
Body mass: 70 t
Material: incomplete thoracic vertebrae and femur
ESR: ◐○○○

The largest of western North America

Sauropod: *Maraapunisaurus fragillimus,* from the Upper Jurassic (present-day Colorado, western USA) was the largest sauropod of its time. However, cf. *Barosaurus lentus* BYU 9024, 45 m in length, was longer. See more: *Cope 1877; Jensen 1985, 1987; Carpenter 2006; Lovelace et al. 2007; Woodruff & Forster 2014; Carpenter 2018; Taylor & Wedel**

Primitive sauropodomorph: The largest biped in the western zone was *Sarahsaurus aurifontanalis* ("Sarah Butler's gold spring lizard") from the Lower Jurassic (present-day Arizona, USA), 4.3 m long and weighing 193 kg. See more: *Rowe, Sues & Reisz 2011*

The largest of eastern North America

Sauropod: *Astrodon johnsoni* ("dentist Christopher Johnson's star-toothed lizard") of the late Lower Cretaceous (present-day Maryland, USA). The species name was created six years after the genus. Most known specimens are juveniles or small individuals, and most were as long as five buses end to end and weighed about as much as four African elephants. See more: *Johnston 1859; Leidy 1865; Kranz 2004*

Primitive sauropodomorphs: *Plateosaurus* cf. *longiceps* from the Upper Triassic (present-day Greenland), 6.6 m long and weighing 775 kg. Even larger was the owner of the footprints of *Otozoum moodii* from the Lower Jurassic (present-day Massachusetts, USA), with a probable length of 7.55 m and weight of 895 kg. See more: *Hitchcock 1847; Jenkins et al. 1995; Clemmensen et al. 2015*

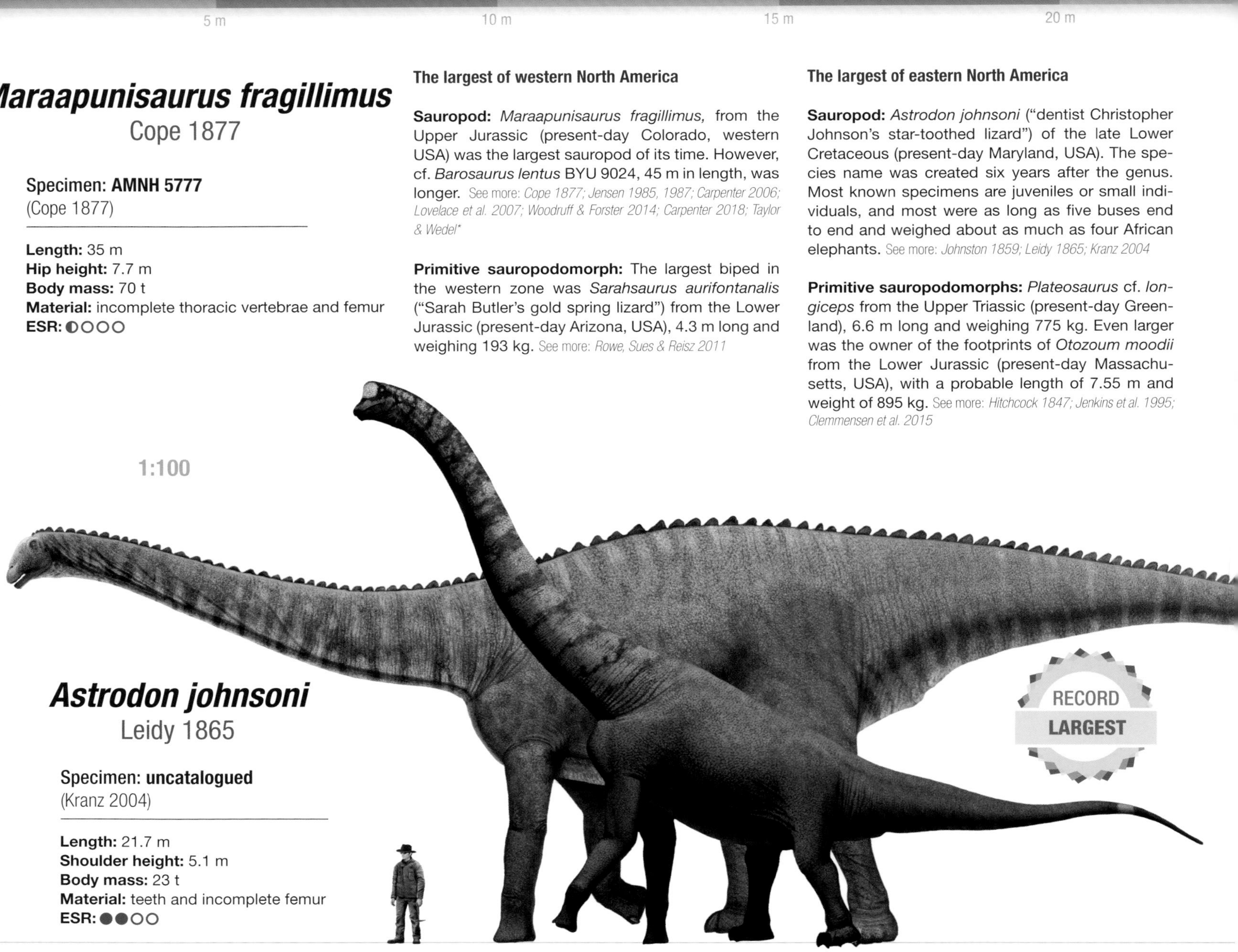
5 m
10 m
15 m
20 m
15 m
10 m
5 m
1:100
RECORD
LARGEST

Astrodon johnsoni
Leidy 1865

Specimen: uncatalogued
(Kranz 2004)

Length: 21.7 m
Shoulder height: 5.1 m
Body mass: 23 t
Material: teeth and incomplete femur
ESR: ●●○○

Footprints

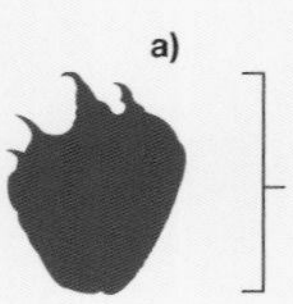
a)
67 cm

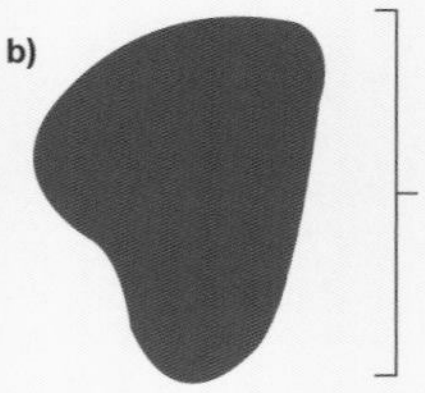
b)
1.1 m

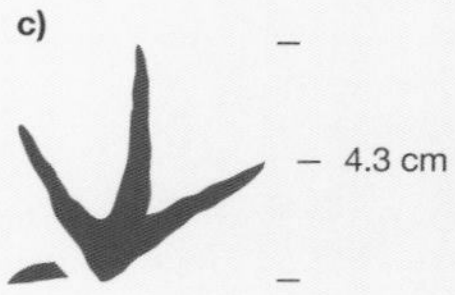
c)
4.3 cm

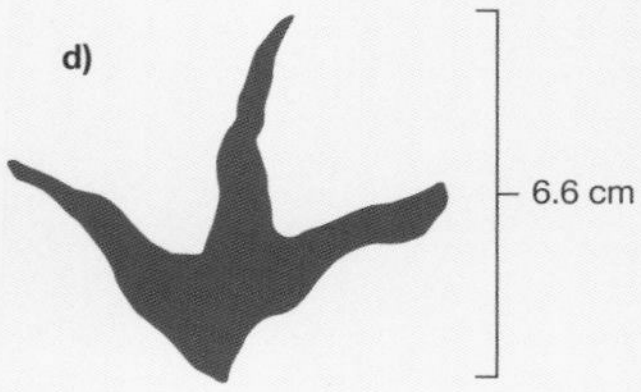
d)
6.6 cm

The largest

a) Unnamed: This is the largest sauropod print ever found in eastern North America (present-day Maryland, USA). It was a titanosauriform, as toe II was more pronounced than toe I, unlike a somphospondylid footprint. See more: *Standford et al. 2011*

b) *Brontopodus birdi*: The largest sauropod ever known, estimated from a footprint found in western North America (Texas, USA). Its reported 1.37 m length includes surrounding mud marks; another record 1.47 m long contains two overlapping prints. See more: *Brown 1940; Farlow 1987*

The smallest

c) *Sillimanius gracilior*: From eastern North America (present-day Connecticut and Massachusetts, USA), this print was similar to a bird print. It would have been produced by a primitive sauropod calf. See more: *Hitchcock 1841* **d) *Trisauropodiscus moabensis*:** This has been considered a footprint of an ornithischian (*Anomoepus*). It was found in eastern North America (present-day Utah, USA). See more: *Lockley et al. 1992; Lockley & Gierlinski 1993*

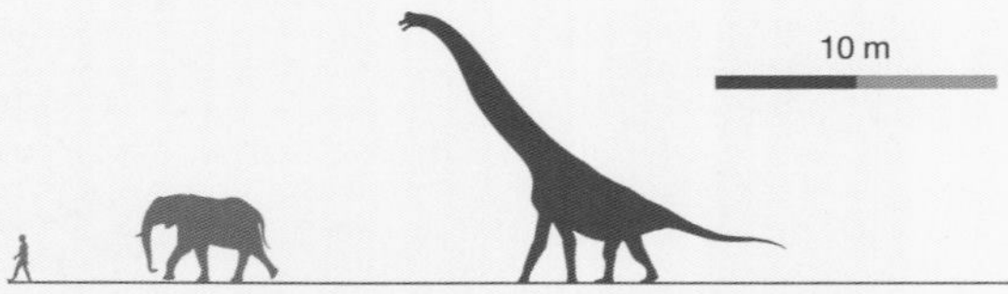
10 m

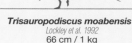

Unnamed footprint
Standford et al. 2011
17.5 m / 17 t

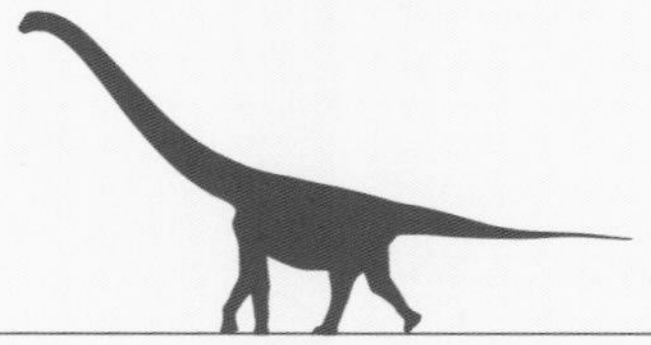

Brontopodus birdi
S5
23.7 m / 32 t

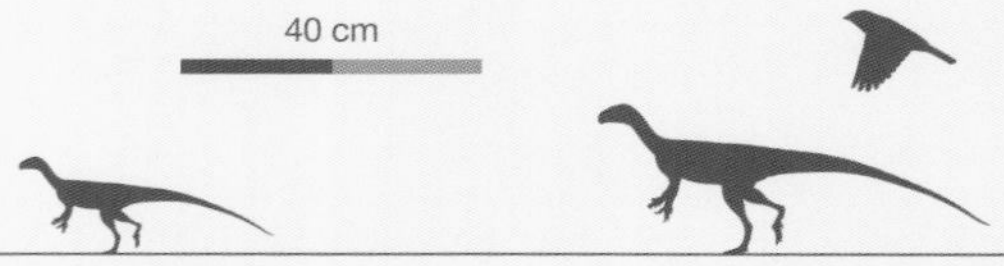
40 cm

Sillimanius gracilior
Hitchcock 1841
43 cm / 440 g

Trisauropodiscus moabensis
Lockley et al. 1992
66 cm / 1 kg

Sauropodomorph registry in North America

The imaginary division between the eastern and western zones did not hinder the movement of organisms except in the late Upper Cretaceous. In that era, the continent was divided by the "western inland sea." The western zone was known as Laramidia and the eastern as Appalachia.

Direct remains of sauropodomorphs have been located in the western zone in the western USA (South Dakota, Montana, and Washington), while mixed remains (bones and footprints) have been found in western Canada, Mexico, and the United States (Arizona, Colorado, New Mexico, Oklahoma, Texas, Utah, and Wyoming).

In the eastern part, direct remains of sauropodomorphs have been discovered in the eastern United States (District of Columbia, Pennsylvania, and Virginia) and mixed remains in Greenland, eastern Canada (Nova Scotia), and the eastern USA (Arkansas, Connecticut, Maryland, and Massachusetts).

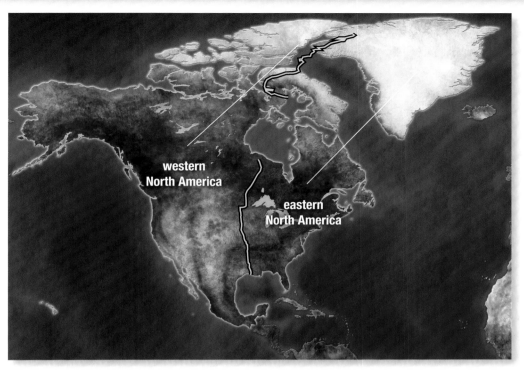

western North America

eastern North America

The smallest of western North America

Primitive sauropodomorph: *Seitaad ruessi* ("artist Everett Ruess's sand monster") of the Lower Jurassic (present-day Utah, USA) was a little larger than an adult human. See more: *Sertich & Loewen 2010*

Sauropods: *Kaatedocus siberi* ("Hans-Jakob Siber's little beam")

of the Upper Jurassic (present-day Wyoming, USA) had a length of 14 m and weight of 1.9 t. An embryo of *Camarasaurus* sp. BYUVP 8967 (present-day Colorado, USA) had a length of 76 cm and weight of 1.7 kg. See more: *Britt & Naylor 1994; Tschopp & Mateus 2013*

The smallest of eastern North America

Primitive sauropodomorphs: *Anchisaurus polyzelus* ("much-coveted near-lizard") of the Lower Jurassic (present-day Connecticut and Massachusetts, USA). *Ammosaurus major*, 2.9 m long and 55 kg in weight, is suspected to be an adult of the same species, with anatomical differences perhaps due to the difference in age. The smallest young *Anchisaurus polyzelus* were 1 m in length and 2.7 kg in weight. See more: *Hitchcock 1865; Marsh 1889; Huene 1932; Yates 2004*

Sauropods: *Pleurocoelus nanus* ("hollow-sided dwarf"), from the late Lower Cretaceous (present-day Maryland, USA), could reach a length of 10 m and a weight of up to 3.3 t. Some authors suggest that *P. altus* as well as *P. nanus* are, in fact, remains of young *Astrodon johnsoni*, but that cannot be confirmed at present. See more: *Marsh 1888*

The oldest in North America

The sauropodomorphs NMMNH P- 18405 and NMMNH P 26400 (present-day New Mexico and Texas, USA) date to the Upper Triassic (Upper Carnian, approx. 232–227 Ma). See more: *Heckert 2001, 2004*

The most recent in North America

Alamosaurus sanjuanensis (present-day New Mexico, Texas, and Utah, USA) dates to the late Upper Cretaceous (Upper Maastrichtian, approx. 69–66 Ma). See more: *Gilmore 1921, 1922; Ratkevich & Duffek 1996; McCord 1997; Rivera-Sylva et al. 2009*

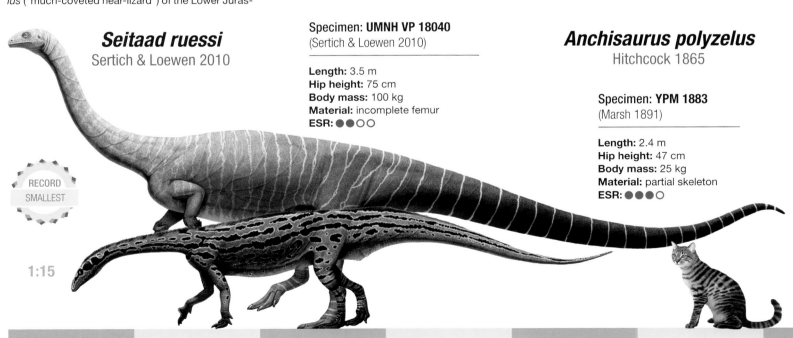

Seitaad ruessi
Sertich & Loewen 2010

RECORD SMALLEST

1:15

Specimen: UMNH VP 18040
(Sertich & Loewen 2010)

Length: 3.5 m
Hip height: 75 cm
Body mass: 100 kg
Material: incomplete femur
ESR: ●●○○

Anchisaurus polyzelus
Hitchcock 1865

Specimen: YPM 1883
(Marsh 1891)

Length: 2.4 m
Hip height: 47 cm
Body mass: 25 kg
Material: partial skeleton
ESR: ●●●○

50 cm   100 cm   150 cm   200 cm   250 cm   300 cm

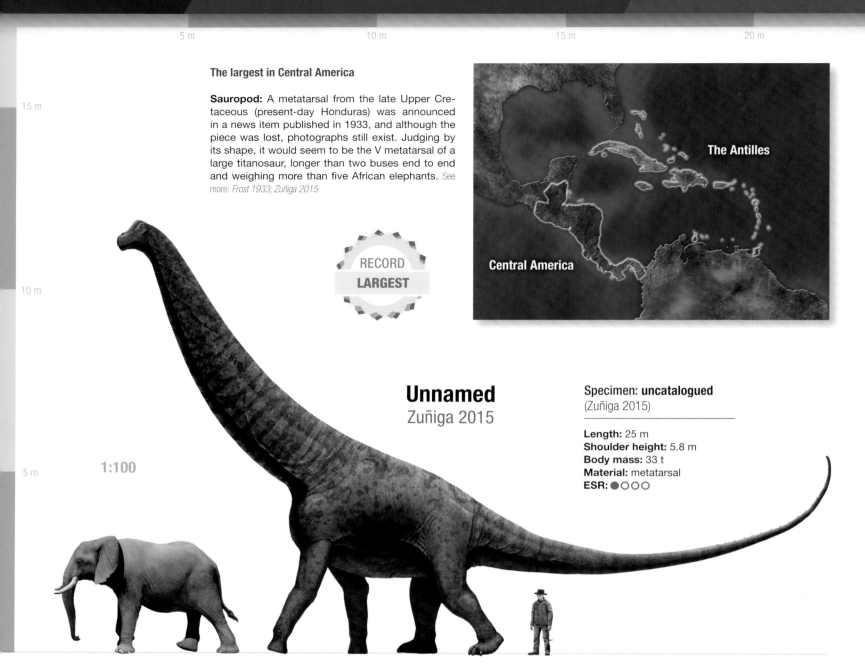

5 m   10 m   15 m   20 m

15 m

The largest in Central America

Sauropod: A metatarsal from the late Upper Cretaceous (present-day Honduras) was announced in a news item published in 1933, and although the piece was lost, photographs still exist. Judging by its shape, it would seem to be the V metatarsal of a large titanosaur, longer than two buses end to end and weighing more than five African elephants. *See more: Frost 1933; Zuñiga 2015*

10 m

The Antilles

Central America

RECORD
LARGEST

Unnamed
Zuñiga 2015

Specimen: uncatalogued
(Zuñiga 2015)

Length: 25 m
Shoulder height: 5.8 m
Body mass: 33 t
Material: metatarsal
ESR: ●○○○

5 m   1:100

Sauropodomorph registry in Central America

There are no reports of other sauropods in Central America, except for the previously mentioned metatarsal from Honduras.

Sauropodomorph registry in the Antilles

Only two reports are known, one metacarpal and one caudal vertebra in Cuba. The latter is of doubtful identification, as several remains of marine vertebrae came to be represented as those of "dinosaurs." Some footprints were reported in the Dominican Republic and assigned to the early Lower Cretaceous (Berriasian-Hauterivian, approx. 145–129.4 Ma); however, the kind of animal they belonged to has not been identified.

The smallest in the Antilles

Sauropod: A 15-cm-long vertebra found in Sierra de los Órganos, Pinar el Río Province, was identified as a possible sauropod from the Upper Jurassic (present-day Cuba). It may have belonged to a marine animal and not a dinosaur, and thus more detailed analysis is required to clarify the matter. *See more: Gasparini & Iturralde-Vinent 2006*

The oldest in Central America

The only sauropod in Honduras may be from the late Upper Cretaceous (Campanian-Maastrichtian, approx. 83.6–66 Ma). *See more: de la Torre & Callejas 1949; Gasparini & Iturralde-Vinent 2006; Iturralde-Vinent & Ceballos-Izquierdo 2015*

The oldest in the Antilles

The sauropods of Cuba date to the Upper Jurassic (Tithonian, approx. 152.1–145 Ma) . *See more: Zuñiga 2015*

30 m 35 m 40 m 45 m

Unnamed
de la Torre & Callejas 1949

RECORD
LARGEST

Specimen: uncatalogued
(de la Torre & Callejas 1949)

Length: 19 m
Shoulder height: 4.5 m
Body mass: 15.5 t
Material: metacarpal
ESR: ●○○○

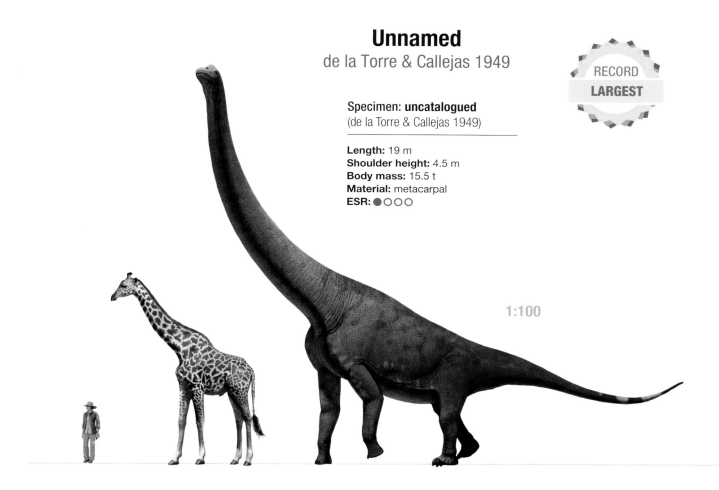

1:100

The largest in the Antilles

Sauropod: An incomplete bone from the Upper Jurassic (present-day Cuba) was presented in a thesis in 1949. At the time, it was identified as the humerus of a "Brontosaurus" or "Diplodocus." Sometime later, it was identified as a meta-carpal of a primitive Macronarian sauropod; however, at the end of this book, has been identified as the oldest somphospondylan. See more: *de la Torre & Callejas 1949; Gasparini & Iturralde-Vinent 2006; Iturralde-Vinent & Ceballos-Izquierdo 2015; Apesteguia et al. 2019*

The paleo-Caribbean may have begun to take shape in the Middle Jurassic (Bathonian, approx. 168.3–166.1 Ma), although no reliable stratigraphic data has been found up to the Upper Jurassic (Oxfordian, approx. 163.5–157.3 Ma).

During the Triassic and Lower Jurassic, the Antilles were part of the inland zone of the supercontinent Pangea. It began fracturing in the Middle Jurassic until separating completely in the Upper Jurassic, giving rise to a Caribbean oceanic passage between the northern (Laurasia) and southern (Gondwana) zones. This zone, known as the paleo-Caribbean, remained in place throughout the entire Cretaceous, as evidenced by an abundance of marine fossils and much-less-prevalent terrestrial fossils (present-day Bahamas, Cuba, and the Dominican Republic).

Part of Central America belonged to Neopangea, and another part had a differ-ent origin, as it apparently emerged from the collision of the Caribbean, Cocos, and North American tectonic plates. This collision caused the appearance of temporary islands, as well as some drops in sea level that allowed terrestrial plants and animals to survive. Apparently, all of this allowed some brief migra-tions of the fauna of Laramidia (western North America) and western Gondwana (northern South America). See more: *Iturralde-Vinent 2005; Kielan-Jaworoska et al. 2007; Mann et al. 2007; Juárez Valieri et al. 2010; Prieto-Márquez 2014; Jiménez-Lara**

Unnamed

Specimen: uncatalogued (-)

Length: 9 m
Shoulder height: 2.5 m
Body mass: 3.3 t
Material: caudal vertebra
ESR: ●○○○

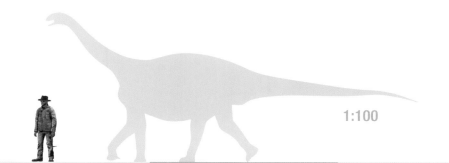

RECORD
SMALLEST

1:100

5 m 10 m 15 m 20 m

5 m   10 m   15 m   20 m

cf. *Argentinosaurus*
Bonaparte & Coria 1993

Specimen: MLP-DP 46-VIII-21-3
(Mazzetta et al. 2004)

Length: 36 m
Shoulder height: 7 m
Body mass: 80 t
Material: incomplete femur
ESR: ●◑○○○

15 m

10 m

aff. *Malawisaurus* sp.
Jacobs et al. 1993

Specimen: UFMA 1.20.473
(Medeiros & Schultz 2002)

Length: 22.5 m
Hip height: 4.5 m
Body mass: 24 t
Material: tooth
ESR: ●○○○

5 m

RECORD
LARGEST

1:100

The largest of southern South America

Sauropod: cf. *Argentinosaurus* from the early Upper Cretaceous (present-day Argentina). Without taking into account other doubtful remains, this was the heaviest sauropod. See more: *Bonaparte & Coria 1993; Mazzetta et al. 2004*

Primitive sauropodomorph: A sauropodomorph similar to *Riojasaurus*, from the Upper Triassic (present-day Argentina), reached up to 14.5 m in length and 7.8 t in weight. It was never formally described, but the measurements of the bones of this large specimen are known. See more: *Martinez et al. 2004*

The largest of northern South America

Sauropod: aff. *Malawisaurus* sp. (lizard of the Malawi Republic) are teeth identical to *Malawisaurus* but 50% larger. It was larger than *Austroposeidon magnificus* ("magnificent god of the southern earthquakes"), which is nicknamed "Brazil's largest sauropod." It lived in the early Upper Cretaceous. See more: *Medeiros & Schultz 2002; Carvalho-Freire et al. 2007*

Primitive sauropodomorph: *Lessemsaurus sauropoides* CRILAR-PV 302 specimen, from the Upper Triassic (present-day Argentina), was up to 10.3 m in length and 2.9 t in weight. Because it was described in the same article as *Ingentia prima*, the two have been confused with each other in the press. See more: *Martinez et al. 2004; Apaldetti et al. 2018*

Footprints

a) ⸺ 90 cm

b) ⸺ 86 cm

c) ⸺ 28 cm

d) ⸺ 58 cm

The largest

The smallest

a) Unnamed: The largest sauropod, estimated from a footprint in northern South America (present-day Brazil) that probably belonged to a lithostrotian titanosaur, dates to the early Lower Cretaceous. See more: *Leonardi & Dos Santos 2006*

b) "cf. Brontopodus birdi": From southern South America (present-day Argentina), it may have been similar to *Futalognkosaurus*. It is not the longest but is the largest footprint. See more: *Krapovickas 2010; Mesa & Perea 2015*

c) Unnamed: This is the smallest print that may have belonged to a South American sauropodomorph (present-day Argentina) and dates to the Upper Triassic. **d) Unnamed:** A track from northern South America (present-day Peru) that belongs to a diplodocoid from the late Lower Cretaceous. See more: *Marsicano et al. 2007; Vildoso et al. 2011*

12 m

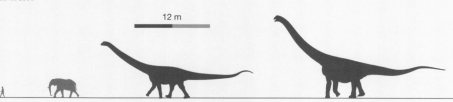

Unnamed footprint
Leonardi & Dos Santos 2006
25 m / 37 t

"cf. Brontopodus birdi"
Krapovickas 2010
28 m / 57 t

4 m

Unnamed footprint
Type 1
2.4 m / 17 kg

Unnamed footprint
Vildoso et al. 2011
16.8 m / 3.9 t

Sauropodomorph registry in South America

The sauropodomorphs of northern South America were rarely as enormous as those in the south. This may be because of the climate, which would have led to different ecological conditions in the southern region (also known as the "Southern Cone").

Direct remains have been located in the northern zone in places like Maranhão, Matto Grosso, Minas Gerais, and Paraná in northern Brazil; mixed remains have been found in Bolivia, northern Brazil (Goiás, Rio Grande do Sul, and São Paulo), Colombia, and Peru; and indirect remains (footprints) in northern Brazil (Paraíba). In the southern zone, direct remains have been found in southern Brazil (Paraná); and mixed remains in southern Brazil (Río Grande do Sul and São Paulo) and in Argentina, Chile, and Uruguay.

The smallest of southern South America

Primitive sauropodomorph: *Pampadromaeus barberenai*, from the Upper Triassic (present-day Brazil), might be the smallest of all, although a fossil known as cf. *Pampadromaeus barberenai* also exists and may be another larger individual, with a length of 1.65 m and a weight of 4.8 kg. See more: *Cabreira et al. 2011; Muller et al. 2016*

Sauropod: *Bonatitan reigi* ("titan of paleontologists José Bonaparte and Osvaldo Reig"), from the late Upper Cretaceous (present-day Argentina), with a length of 6 m and weight of 600 kg. The smallest calf is *Laplatasaurus* sp. MCF-PVPH-272, from the late Upper Cretaceous (present-day Argentina), with a length of 39 cm and weight of around 230 g. See more: *Bonaparte 1999; Chiappe et al. 2001; García 2007*

The smallest of northern South America

"Primitive sauropodomorph": The presence of *Thecodontosaurus* sp. was identified in Cretaceous deposits (present-day northern Brazil) and was first assigned to the Triassic period, but may actually be the remains of a sauropod or theropod. No dinosaurs this old have been found to date in northern South America. Triassic fossils found in Brazil are all from the southern zone. See more: *Woodward 1910; Ihering 1911; Kellner & Campos 2000*

Sauropod: *Gondwanatitan faustoi,* from the early Upper Cretaceous (present-day Brazil) presents fusions on the sacrum and on the pelvis. *Amazonsaurus maranhensis* was the longest but lightest, measuring 10.5 m in length and weighing just 1.2 t; however, it displays no features that might indicate the probable age of the animal, and no histological study was performed. See more: *Carvalho et al. 2003*

The oldest of South America

Buriolestes schultzi (present-day Brazil), *Chromogisaurus novasi*, *Eoraptor lunensis*, and *Panphagia protos* (present-day Argentina) date to the Upper Trias-

sic (Lower Carnian, approx. 237–232 Ma). The oldest sauropod recorded for this continent corresponds to footprints from the southwestern zone of Pangea (present-day Argentina) that date to the Upper Triassic (Upper Carnian, approx. 232–227 Ma). See more: *Sereno et al. 1993; Marsicano & Barredo 2004; Wilson 2005; Martínez & Alcober 2009; Cabreira et al. 2016*

The most recent of South America

The most recent record from the continent (present-day Peru) is from *Fusioolithus baghensis* (formerly *Megaloolithus pseudomamillare*) eggshells dating to the late Upper Cretaceous (Upper Maastrichtian, approx. 66 Ma). See more: *Sigé 1968; Vianey-Liaud et al. 1997*

Gondwanatitan faustoi
Kellner & Azevedo 1999

Specimen: MN 4111-V
(Kellner & Azevedo 1999)

Length: 10 m
Shoulder height: 2.15 m
Body mass: 2.5 t
Material: partial skeleton
ESR: ●○○○

1:50

Pampadromaeus barberenai
Broom 1915

RECORD
SMALLEST

Specimen: ULBRA-PVT016
(Cabreira et al. 2011)

Length: 1.4 m
Hip height: 28 cm
Body mass: 1.4 kg
Material: partial skeleton
ESR: ●●●○

2.5 m   5 m   7.5 m   10 m

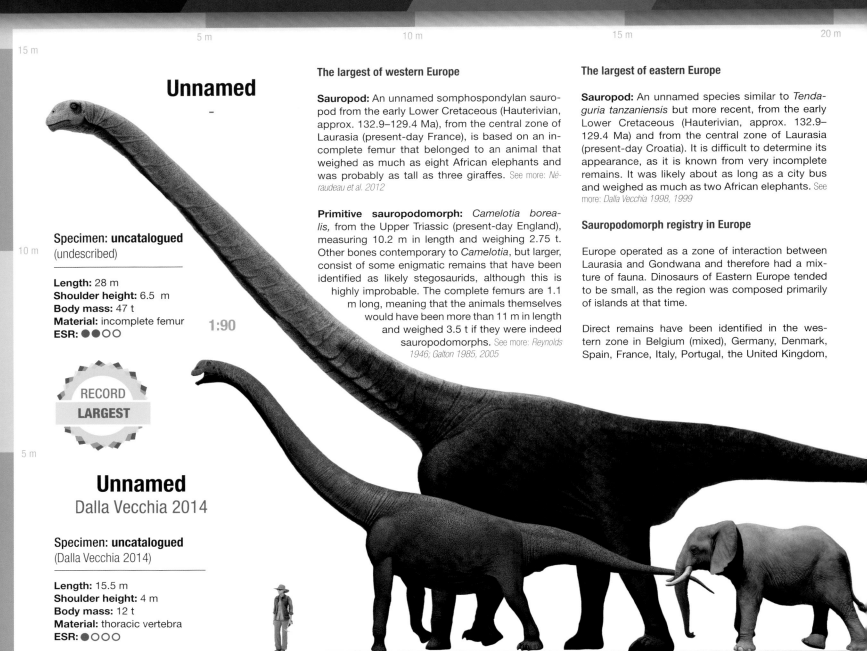

Unnamed

–

Specimen: uncatalogued
(undescribed)

Length: 28 m
Shoulder height: 6.5 m
Body mass: 47 t
Material: incomplete femur
ESR: ●●○○

1:90

RECORD
LARGEST

Unnamed
Dalla Vecchia 2014

Specimen: uncatalogued
(Dalla Vecchia 2014)

Length: 15.5 m
Shoulder height: 4 m
Body mass: 12 t
Material: thoracic vertebra
ESR: ●○○○

The largest of western Europe

Sauropod: An unnamed somphospondylan sauropod from the early Lower Cretaceous (Hauterivian, approx. 132.9–129.4 Ma), from the central zone of Laurasia (present-day France), is based on an incomplete femur that belonged to an animal that weighed as much as eight African elephants and was probably as tall as three giraffes. See more: *Néraudeau et al. 2012*

Primitive sauropodomorph: *Camelotia borealis,* from the Upper Triassic (present-day England), measuring 10.2 m in length and weighing 2.75 t. Other bones contemporary to *Camelotia,* but larger, consist of some enigmatic remains that have been identified as likely stegosaurids, although this is highly improbable. The complete femurs are 1.1 m long, meaning that the animals themselves would have been more than 11 m in length and weighed 3.5 t if they were indeed sauropodomorphs. See more: *Reynolds 1946; Galton 1985, 2005*

The largest of eastern Europe

Sauropod: An unnamed species similar to *Tendaguria tanzaniensis* but more recent, from the early Lower Cretaceous (Hauterivian, approx. 132.9–129.4 Ma) and from the central zone of Laurasia (present-day Croatia). It is difficult to determine its appearance, as it is known from very incomplete remains. It was likely about as long as a city bus and weighed as much as two African elephants. See more: *Dalla Vecchia 1998, 1999*

Sauropodomorph registry in Europe

Europe operated as a zone of interaction between Laurasia and Gondwana and therefore had a mixture of fauna. Dinosaurs of Eastern Europe tended to be small, as the region was composed primarily of islands at that time.

Direct remains have been identified in the western zone in Belgium (mixed), Germany, Denmark, Spain, France, Italy, Portugal, the United Kingdom,

---

Footprints

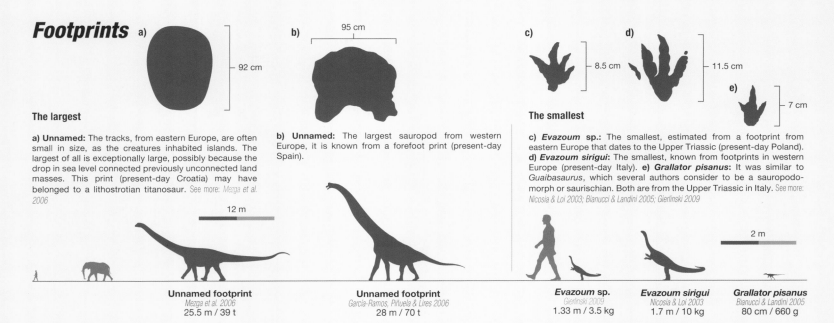

a) 92 cm

The largest

a) Unnamed: The tracks, from eastern Europe, are often small in size, as the creatures inhabited islands. The largest of all is exceptionally large, possibly because the drop in sea level connected previously unconnected land masses. This print (present-day Croatia) may have belonged to a lithostrotian titanosaur. See more: *Mezga et al. 2006*

b) 95 cm

b) Unnamed: The largest sauropod from western Europe, it is known from a forefoot print (present-day Spain).

c) 8.5 cm   d) 11.5 cm   e) 7 cm

The smallest

c) *Evazoum* **sp.:** The smallest, estimated from a footprint from eastern Europe that dates to the Upper Triassic (present-day Poland). **d)** *Evazoum sirigui:* The smallest, known from footprints in western Europe (present-day Italy). **e)** *Grallator pisanus:* It was similar to *Guaibasaurus,* which several authors consider to be a sauropodomorph or saurischian. Both are from the Upper Triassic in Italy. See more: *Nicosia & Loi 2003; Bianucci & Landini 2005; Gierlinski 2009*

12 m

2 m

Unnamed footprint
Mezga et al. 2006
25.5 m / 39 t

Unnamed footprint
García-Ramos, Piñuela & Lires 2006
28 m / 70 t

Evazoum **sp.**
Gierlinski 2009
1.33 m / 3.5 kg

Evazoum sirigui
Nicosia & Loi 2003
1.7 m / 10 kg

Grallator pisanus
Bianucci & Landini 2005
80 cm / 660 g

and Switzerland; indirect remains have been found in Norway.

In the eastern zone, direct remains have been found in Georgia and European Russia; indirect remains in Slovakia and Poland; and mixed remains in Croatia and Romania.

The smallest of western Europe

Primitive sauropodomorphs: *Asylosaurus yalensis* ("sanctuary lizard of Yale [University]") of the Upper Triassic (present-day England) is based on partial remains previously identified as those of *Thecodontosaurus antiquus*. The specimen was assigned to a separate species based on differences in the fossils. The specimen escaped destruction in World War II as it was on loan to Yale University at the time. It was a small animal the size of an Iberian lynx. The smallest calf is *Pantydraco caducus* from the Upper Triassic (present-day Wales, UK), with a length of 85 cm and a weight of 760 g. See more: *Riley & Stutchbury 1836; Kermack 1984; Yates 2003; Galton 2007; Galton et al. 2007*

Sauropods: *Europasaurus* from the Upper Jurassic (present-day Germany) looked like a miniature Brachiosaurus. It was barely twice the height of an adult human and weighed the same as two panda bears. The smallest juvenile sauropods are the specimens MPZ 96/111 and MPZ 96/112, from the late Lower Cretaceous (present-day Spain), with lengths of 1.35 and 1.7 m and weighing 11.8 and 24 kg, respectively. See more: *Ruiz-Omeñaca, Canudo & Cuenca-Bescós 1995; Windolf 1998; Sander et al. 2004, 2006; D'Emic 2012; Mannion et al. 2013*

western Europe

eastern Europe

The smallest in eastern Europe

Sauropod: *Magyarosaurus dacus,* from the Upper Cretaceous (present-day Romania), with a length of 4.9 m and weight of 520 kg. The smallest calf found in the zone is from that species. Specimen FGGUB 1007 would have been 72 cm in length and 1.5 kg in weight. See more: *Nopcsa 1915; Huene 1932; Weishampel, Grigorescu & Norman 1991; Stein et al. 2010; Curry-Rogers et al. 2011*

The oldest of Europe

Efraasia minor and *Plateosaurus gracilis* ((present-day Germany) date to the Upper Triassic (Middle Norian, approx. 217.7 Ma). *Pseudotetrasauropus* sp. (pre-

sent-day Italy) are even older footprints (Carnian, approx. 237–227 Ma). It was previously believed that the *Prosauropodichnus bernburgensis* footprints from the Middle Triassic (present-day Germany) were the oldest, although they actually belong to archosaurus. The sauropod ISRNB R211 (present-day Belgium), dated to the end of the Upper Triassic (Rhaetian, approx. 208.5–201.3 Ma), is known from teeth similar to those of a eusauropod. See more: *Huene 1905, 1908; Heckert 2001, 2004; Dal Sasso 2003; Godefroit & Knoll 2003; Diedrich 2009, 2012*

The most recent of Europe

Hypselosaurus sp. (present-day Spain), cf. *Magyarosaurus* sp., and *Paludititan nalatzensis* from central Laurasia (present-day Romania) date to the late Upper Cretaceous (Upper Maastrichtian, approx. 69–66 Ma). See more: *Casanovas et al. 1987; Codrea et al. 2010; Csiki et al. 2010*

Asylosaurus yalensis
Galton 2007

Specimen: YPM 2195
(Riley & Stutchbury 1836)

Length: 2.25 m
Shoulder height: 57 cm
Body mass: 14 kg
Material: tooth
ESR: ●○○○○

Magyarosaurus dacus
Nopcsa 1915

1:40

Specimen: FGGUB R.1992
(Nopcsa 1915)

Length: 5.4 m
Shoulder height: 1.2 m
Body mass: 520 kg
Material: femur
ESR: ●●○○○

RECORD
SMALLEST

2 m   4 m   6 m   8 m

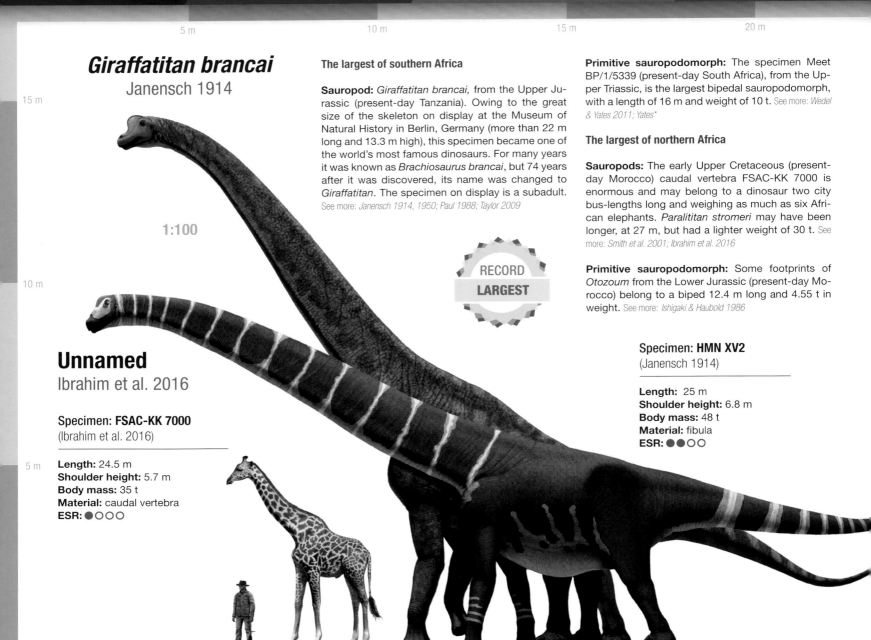

Giraffatitan brancai
Janensch 1914

1:100

Unnamed
Ibrahim et al. 2016

Specimen: **FSAC-KK 7000**
(Ibrahim et al. 2016)

Length: 24.5 m
Shoulder height: 5.7 m
Body mass: 35 t
Material: caudal vertebra
ESR: ●○○○

The largest of southern Africa

Sauropod: *Giraffatitan brancai,* from the Upper Jurassic (present-day Tanzania). Owing to the great size of the skeleton on display at the Museum of Natural History in Berlin, Germany (more than 22 m long and 13.3 m high), this specimen became one of the world's most famous dinosaurs. For many years it was known as *Brachiosaurus brancai*, but 74 years after it was discovered, its name was changed to *Giraffatitan*. The specimen on display is a subadult. See more: *Janensch 1914, 1950; Paul 1988; Taylor 2009*

Primitive sauropodomorph: The specimen Meet BP/1/5339 (present-day South Africa), from the Upper Triassic, is the largest bipedal sauropodomorph, with a length of 16 m and weight of 10 t. See more: *Wedel & Yates 2011; Yates*

The largest of northern Africa

Sauropods: The early Upper Cretaceous (present-day Morocco) caudal vertebra FSAC-KK 7000 is enormous and may belong to a dinosaur two city bus-lengths long and weighing as much as six African elephants. *Paralititan stromeri* may have been longer, at 27 m, but had a lighter weight of 30 t. See more: *Smith et al. 2001; Ibrahim et al. 2016*

Primitive sauropodomorph: Some footprints of *Otozoum* from the Lower Jurassic (present-day Morocco) belong to a biped 12.4 m long and 4.55 t in weight. See more: *Ishigaki & Haubold 1986*

RECORD
LARGEST

Specimen: **HMN XV2**
(Janensch 1914)

Length: 25 m
Shoulder height: 6.8 m
Body mass: 48 t
Material: fibula
ESR: ●●○○

Footprints

a) — 94 cm

b) — 1.15 m

c) ↓ ⊐ 1.8 cm

d) — 24 cm

The largest

a) Unnamed: The largest sauropod, estimated from footprints in southern Africa (present-day Zimbabwe), may belong to a brachiosaurid from the Upper Jurassic. See more: *Ahmed et al. 2004*

b) Breviparopus taghbaloutensis: This was a diplodocoid from south-central Neopangea (present-day Morocco). Some contemporary prints are longer but narrower. See more: *Dutuit & Ouazzou 1980; Ishigaki 1985; Thulborn 1990*

The smallest

c) Trisauropodiscus aviforma passer: This is the smallest sauropodomorph footprint from southern Africa (present-day Lesotho), belonging to a calf. **d) Unnamed:** The smallest print from northern Africa (present-day Morocco), it could have been left by a young rebbachisaurid. See more: *Ellenberger 1972; Masrour et al. 2014*

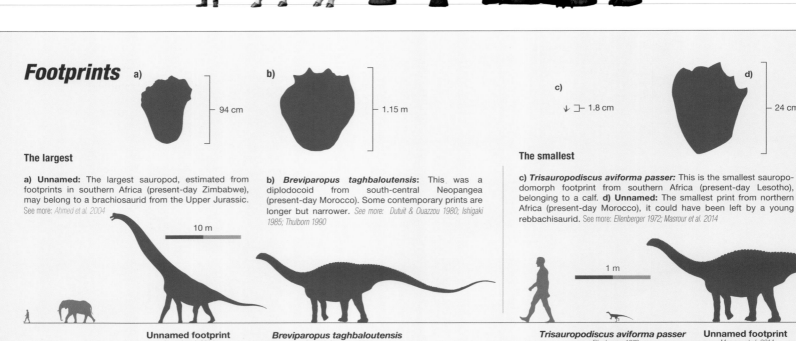

10 m

Unnamed footprint
Ahmed et al. 2004
25 m / 50 t

Breviparopus taghbaloutensis
Dutuit & Ouazzou 1980
33 m / 62 t

1 m

Trisauropodiscus aviforma passer
Ellenberger 1972
29 cm / 30 g

Unnamed footprint
Masrour et al. 2014
7.8 m / 1 t

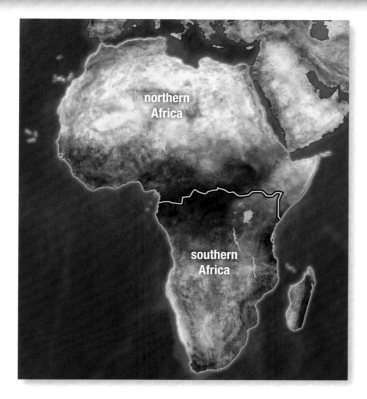

Sauropodomorph registry in Africa

No direct sauropodomorph remains have been identified in northern Africa, only footprints. In the southern zone, however, large numbers of both sauropodomorph bones and footprints have been found.

Direct remains have been found in the northern zone, in Angola, Chad, Egypt, Libya, Sudan, and Tunisia, while mixed remains have been found in Algeria, Cameroon, Morocco, and Niger. In the southern zone, direct remains have been found in Congo, Kenya, Malawi, Mozambique, Namibia, South Africa, Tanzania, and Zambia, and mixed remains in Lesotho and Zimbabwe.

The smallest of northern Africa

Primitive sauropodomorph: The footprints of *Otozoum* from the Lower Jurassic (present-day Morocco) belong to a four-legged animal 6.5 m long and 580 kg in weight. See more: *Masrour & Pérez-Lorente 2014*

Sauropod: *Nigersaurus taqueti* ("paleontologist Philippe Taquet's Niger lizard") from the late Lower Cretaceous (present-day Niger). This dinosaur had a snout proportionately wider than any other, even wider than that of a hadrosaurid (the so-called "duck-billed" dinosaur), and weighed half as much as an Asian elephant. The smallest calf from that geographic zone is specimen Vb 719, from the early Upper Cretaceous (present-day Sudan), 1.35 m long and 7 kg in weight. See more: *Werner 1994; Sereno et al. 1999*

The smallest of southern Africa

Primitive sauropodomorphs: *Thecodontosaurus minor,* from the Lower Jurassic (present-day South Africa), may not have been a juvenile *Massospondylus carinatus*, as suspected, but instead a small sauropodomorph that weighed about as much as a house cat. The smallest calf is BP/1/5347a, an embryo of *Massopondylus carinatus*, 13 cm long and 7 g in weight. See more: *Haughton 1918; Kitching 1979; Reisz et al. 2005, 2010; Yates*

Sauropods: *Pulanesaura eocollum,* from the Lower Jurassic (present-day South Africa), was an adult 7.5 m long and weighing 1.1 t. *Blikanasaurus cromptoni*, from the Upper Triassic (present-day South Africa), was previously considered a primitive sauropod but is now known to be an advanced sauropodomorph. It was 5.4 m in length and weighed 420 kg, although its age is unknown. The smallest calf was *Algoasaurus bauri*, 4.8 m long and weighing 285 kg. See more: *Broom 1904; Galton & van Heerden 1985; McPhee et al. 2015*

The oldest of Africa

cf. *Saturnalia* sp.(present-day Zimbabwe) dates to the Upper Triassic (Carnian, approx. 237–227 Ma). It is 2.5 m long and weighed 16 kg. It may have been an indeterminate saurischian. The oldest sauropod on this continent was *Vulcanodon karibaensis*, from the Lower Jurassic (Hettangian, approx. 201.3–199.3 Ma). See more: *Bond, Wilson & Raath 1970; Raath 1972; Raath 1996; Ezcurra 2012*

The most recent of Africa

Surprisingly, the most recent sauropods of this continent were not titanosaurs, but primitive titanosauriforms. Specimens Vb-646 (present-day Egypt) and OCP-DEK/GE 31 (present-day Morocco) date to the late Upper Cretaceous (Upper Maastrichtian, approx. 69–66 Ma). See more: *Rauhut & Werner 1997; Pereda-Suberbiola et al. 2004*

Nigersaurus taqueti
Sereno et al. 1999

Specimen: MNN GAD517
(Sereno et al. 1999)

Length: 10 m
Hip height: 2.15 cm
Body mass: 1.9 t
Material: cranium and partial skeleton
ESR: ●●●●

Thecodontosaurus minor
Haughton 1918

Specimen: uncatalogued
(Haughton 1918)

Length: 1.45 m
Hip height: 26 cm
Body mass: 3.8 kg
Material: partial skeleton
ESR: ●●●○

RECORD
SMALLEST

1:50

2.5m · 5 m · 7.5 m · 10 m

4 m   8 m   12 m   16 m

12 m

8 m

4 m

Bothriospondylus madagascariensis
Lydekker 1895

Specimen: uncatalogued
(Thevenin 1907)

Length: 14 m
Shoulder height: 5.1 m
Body mass: 16 t
Material: tooth
ESR: ●○○○

Jainosaurus septentrionalis
Huene & Matley 1933

Specimen: GSI K27
(Huene & Matley 1933)

Length: 20 m
Shoulder height: 4.2 m
Body mass: 18 t
Material: incomplete humerus
ESR: ●●○○

The largest of Hindustan

Sauropod: Ruling out the doubtful *Bruhathkayosaurus matleyi*, the largest dinosaur known from its bones in Hindustan was *Jainosaurus septentrionalis* ("paleontologist Sohan Lal Jain's northern lizard"), from the late Upper Cretaceous (present-day India). It was longer than a sperm whale and weighed more than three African elephants. It shared more features with the specimen known as "Malagasy Taxon B," *Muyelensaurus* and *Pitekunsaurus*, than with *Antarctosaurus*, with which it is sometimes associated. See more: *Huene & Matley 1933; Yadagiri & Ayyasami 1989; Hunt et al. 1995; Calvo, González-Riga & Porfiri 2007; Curry-Roger & Imker 2007; Wilson et al. 2009, 2011*

Primitive sauropodomorph: *Massospondylus hislopi* ("Stephen Hislop's long-vertebra"), from the Lower Triassic (present-day India), is a bipedal dinosaur 4.8 m in length and 280 kg in weight. The species is doubtful, however, as it is known from a single caudal vertebra. It is possibly a large specimen of *Jaklapallisaurus asymmetrica*. See more: *Lydekker 1890; Novas et al. 2011*

The largest of Madagascar

Sauropod: *Bothriospondylus madagascariensis*, from the Middle Jurassic (present-day Madagascar), may be a relative of or synonymous with the neosauropod *Lapparentosaurus madagascariensis*, while specimens of the same name from northern Neopangea (present-day France) may have been titanosauriforms. It weighed almost as much as four Asian elephants. See more: *Lydekker 1895; Thevenin 1907; Mannion 2010*

Sauropodomorph registry in Hindustan and Madagascar

The zone that currently consists of Bangladesh, India, the Maldives, Nepal, Pakistan, Sri Lanka, and Madagascar was formerly joined to South Africa and north Antarctica (from before the Mesozoic until the Cretaceous). It comprised one great island that ultimately broke into two parts—Hindustan and Madagascar. In the Cenozoic era, the first part fused with South Asia, while Madagascar was left on its own. See more: *Fang et al. 2006*

Sauropodomorph registry in Hindustan

Mixed remains have been found in India and Pakistan.

RECORD LARGEST

1:80

Fooprints

a) — 50 cm

b) — 1.3 m

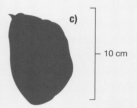

c) — 10 cm

The largest

a) Unnamed: The only track of a sauropod in Madagascar includes five hindfoot prints and four forefoot prints; it has an irregular width that ranges from narrow to broad. It dates to the Middle Jurassic and is possibly a neosauropod. See more: *Wagensommer et al. 2011*

b) *Malakhelisaurus mianwali*: This is an enormous print that accidentally crossed a *Samandrina* theropod print. This does not mean that the dinosaurs encountered each other; the prints may have been left at different times. It was found in southern Neopangea (present-day Pakistan). See more: *Malkani 2007, 2008*

The smallest

c) Unnamed: This is the smallest track from the late Upper Cretaceous in Hindustan (present-day India). It may belong to a eutitanosaur, a group that was abundant in that locality. See more: *Ghevariya & Srikami 1991*

2 m

12 m

Unnamed footprint
Wagensommer et al. 2011
9.8 m / 2.5 t

Malakhelisaurus mianwali
Malkani 2007, 2008
21.5 m / 55 t

Unnamed footprint
Ghevariya & Srikami 1991
2.5 m / 50 kg

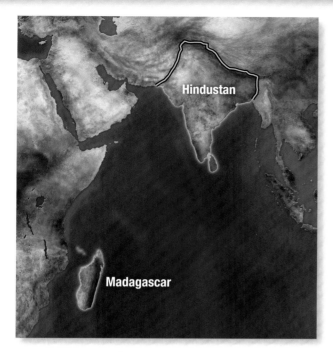

Sauropodomorph registry in Madagascar

Direct remains have been found on the island of Madagascar, although there are also some unofficial reports of sauropod footprints.

The smallest of Hindustan

Primitive sauropodomorph: *Alwalkeria maleriensis,* from the Upper Triassic (present-day India), may be a basal saurischian or a sauropodomorph, as it was similar to *Eoraptor lunensis.* If it does not belong to this group, then the smallest may be *"Massospondylus"* sp., 1.85 m in length and 7.3 kg in weight, although that identification is problematic. As the previous two identifications are doubtful, the smallest conclusively identified species is therefore *Nambalia roychowdhurtii,* which reached 3.7 m in length and 100 kg in weight. See more: *Chatterjee 1987; Kutty et al. 1987; Sereno et al. 2013; Novas et al. 2011*

Sauropods: *Brohisaurus kirthari* ("lizard of the Brohi tribe and the Kirthar mountains"), from the Upper Jurassic (present-day Pakistan), could be a titanosauriform or a primitive titanosaur, 8 m in length and 1.5 t in weight. See more: *Malkani 2003; Wilson & Upchurch 2003*

The smallest juvenile is the specimen GSI/GC/2901–2904, from the late Upper Cretaceous (Upper Maastrichtian, approx. 69–66 Ma), from the central zone of Hindustan (present-day India). It was 1.3 m in length and weighed approximately 9.4 kg. A snake, *Sanajeh indicus,* was found along with this calf, suggesting that the snake may have eaten the newly hatched calves, as the enormous *Megaloo-lithus dhoridungriensis* eggs, 22 cm in diameter, would have been too large to eat. See more: *Mohabey 1987; Lockley 1989, 1994; Wilson et al. 2010*

The smallest of Madagascar

"Primitive sauropodomorph": Reports of Triassic sauropodomorphs refer to the archosauromorph *Azendohsaurus madagaskarensis,* which has some convergences with phytophagous dinosaurs. See more: *Flynn et al. 2010*

Sauropods: *Vahiny depereti* ("paleontologist Charles Depéret's traveler"), from the late Upper Cretaceous (present-day Madagascar). It has some similarities to *Muyelensaurus, Pitekunsaurus,* and *Jainosaurus,* as well as notable differences from *Antarctosaurus* and *Rapetosaurus,* making it difficult to classify. See more: *Huene 1929; Nowinski 1971; Calvo, González-Riga & Porfiri 2007; Wilson et al. 2009, 2011; Curry-Rogers et al. 2011; Curry-Rogers & Wilson 2014; Poropat et al. 2016*

The smallest calf is the *Rapetosaurus krausei* specimen UA 9998 ("paleontologist David W. Krause's giant lizard"), from the late Upper Cretaceous (present-day Madagascar). It is 1.95 m in length and weighed 23 kg. Newborns had an estimated length of 80–85 cm, weighed 2–3 kg, and were precocious like all sauropods, able to fend for themselves shortly after birth. See more: *Curry-Rogers et al. 2011; Curry-Rogers et al. 2016*

The oldest of Hindustan

Alwalkeria maleriensis (present-day India) dates to the Upper Triassic (Lower Carnian, approx. 237–234.5 Ma). The oldest sauropod is *Kotasaurus yamanpallienis,* from the Lower Jurassic (Sinemurian, approx. 199.3–190.8 Ma). See more: *Yadagiri 1986; Chatterjee 1987; Remes & Rauhut 2005*

The most recent of Hindustan

Isisaurus colberti, Jainosaurus septentrionalis, Titanosaurus blandfordi, T. indicus and *T. rahioliensis* (present-day India) date to the late Upper Cretaceous (Upper Maastrichtian, approx. 69–66 Ma). See more: *Lydekker 1877, 1879; Huene 1932; Huene & Matley 1933; Lapparent 1947; Mathur & Srivastava 1987; Jain & Bandyopadhyay 1997; Wilson & Upchurch 2003*

The oldest of Madagascar

Archaeodontosaurus descouensi ("Dr. Didier Descouens' old-toothed lizard"), from the Middle Jurassic (Bathonian, approx. 237–227 Ma), had some teeth similar to those of primitive sauropodomorphs and a mandible similar to that of a sauropod. Some potential sauropodomorphs were also reported on the island, but those remains were ultimately identified as belonging to the archosauromorph *Azhendosaurus madagaskariensis.* See more: *Buffetaut 2006; Flynn et al. 2008, 2010*

The most recent of Madagascar

cf. *Laplatasaurus madagascariensis, Rapetosaurus kausei* and *"Titanosaurus" madagascariensis* (present-day Madagascar) date to the late Upper Cretaceous (Maastrichtian, approx. 72.1–66 Ma). See more: *Depéret 1896; Huene & Matley 1933; Wilson & Upchurch 2003*

Vahiny depereti
Rogers & Wilson 2014

RECORD SMALLEST

Alwalkeria maleriensis
Chatterjee 1987

Specimen: ISI R 306
(Chatterjee 1987)

Length: 1.3 m
Shoulder height: 38 cm
Body mass: 2 kg
Material: femur and vertebrae
ESR: ●●○○

Specimen: UA 9940
(Rogers & Wilson 2014)

Length: 13.7 m
Shoulder height: 3.15 m
Body mass: 5.8 t
Material: incomplete cranium
ESR: ●○○○

1:60

3 m   6 m   9 m   12 m

8 m · 16 m · 24 m · 32 m

24 m

16 m

8 m

RECORD LARGEST

The largest of eastern Asia (Paleoasia)

Sauropod: *Mamenchisaurus jingyanensis* ("lizard of Mamenchi train station and Jingyan county), from the Upper Jurassic (present-day China). These sauropods had very long necks that accounted for about half their total body length. See more: *Zhang et al. 1998*

Primitive sauropodomorph: cf. *Yunnanosaurus* sp. ZLJ 0035, from the Lower Jurassic (present-day China), was a bipedal dinosaur as long as a bus and almost as heavy as an Asian elephant. Its remains were colonized by social insects such as termites, leaving numerous galleries in the skeleton. See more: *Xing et al. 2013*

The largest of western Asia (Paleoasia)

Sauropod: A titanosaur from Uzbekistan dating from the early Upper Cretaceous (Middle Turonian, approx. 91.8 Ma). It could be similar to *Nemegtosaurus*. See more: *Nesov 1995*

Sauropodomorph registry in Asia (Paleoasia)

In the Mesozoic Era, the land that would become the Asian continent was fragmented into geographically separate zones in Laurasia (Paleoasia), Gondwana (Hindustan and the Middle East), and the paleocontinent Cimmeria. This section presents records from eastern and central Asia only.

Specimen: **uncatalogued**
(Nesov 1995)

Length: 13.5 m
Shoulder height: 3.5 m
Body mass: 16 t
Material: thoracic vertebra
ESR: ●●○○

Mamenchisaurus jingyanensis
Zhang et al. 1998

Specimen: **JV002**
(Zhang et al. 1998)

Length: 31 m
Shoulder height: 5.6 m
Body mass: 45 t
Material: femur
ESR: ●●○○

Unnamed
Nesov 1995

1:150

Footprints

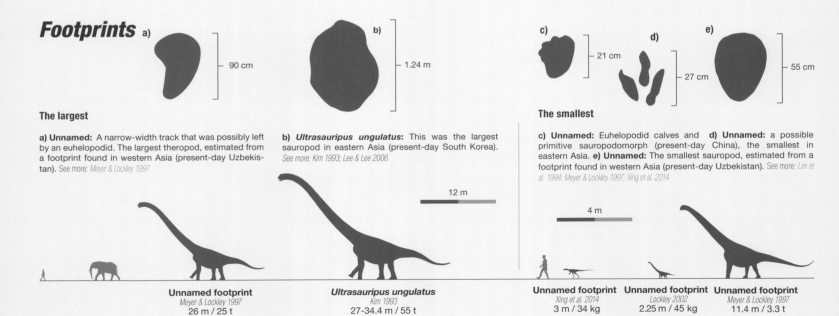

a) — 90 cm

b) — 1.24 m

c) — 21 cm

d) — 27 cm

e) — 55 cm

The largest

The smallest

a) Unnamed: A narrow-width track that was possibly left by an euhelopodid. The largest theropod, estimated from a footprint found in western Asia (present-day Uzbekistan). See more: *Meyer & Lockley 1997*

b) *Ultrasauripus ungulatus*: This was the largest sauropod in eastern Asia (present-day South Korea). See more: *Kim 1993; Lee & Lee 2006*

c) Unnamed: Euhelopodid calves and **d) Unnamed:** a possible primitive sauropodomorph (present-day China), the smallest in eastern Asia. **e) Unnamed:** The smallest sauropod, estimated from a footprint found in western Asia (present-day Uzbekistan). See more: *Lim et al. 1994; Meyer & Lockley 1997; Xing et al. 2014*

12 m

4 m

Unnamed footprint
Meyer & Lockley 1997
26 m / 25 t

Ultrasauripus ungulatus
Kim 1993
27-34.4 m / 55 t

Unnamed footprint
Xing et al. 2014
3 m / 34 kg

Unnamed footprint
Lockley 2002
2.25 m / 45 kg

Unnamed footprint
Meyer & Lockley 1997
11.4 m / 3.3 t

Direct remains have been found in the western zone, in Kazakhstan, Kyrgyzstan, and western Russia, and mixed remains in Tajikistan and Uzbekistan. In the eastern zone, direct sauropod fossils have been found in eastern Russia and mixed fossils in China, South Korea, Japan, and Mongolia.

The smallest of eastern Asia (Paleoasia)

Primitive sauropodomorphs: This Lower Jurassic (present-day China) creature was known for 66 years as *Gyposaurus* until the new name *"Gripposaurus" sinensis* was proposed. However, the proposed name is considered invalid as it has not been made official. The juvenile *Lufengosaurus* sp. of the Lower Jurassic (present-day China) was 13.5–25 cm in length and weighed 8–50 g. See more: *Young 1941; Barrett et al. 2007; Reisz et al. 2013*

Sauropod: *Sanpasaurus yaoi* ("lizard of Sanpa and Yao") of the Lower Jurassic (present-day China) measured 6.4 m in length and weighed 1.1 t, or even more, as it was a subadult. Some bones attributed to this species belong to a bipedal ornithischian. Even smaller was the titanosaurus embryo NSM60104403–20554450, from the late Lower Cretaceous (present-day Mongolia). It was 31 cm long and weighed 125 g. See more: *Young 1944; Upchurch 1995; Grellet-Tinner et al. 2011; Kim et al. 2012; McPhee et al. 2016*

The smallest of western Asia (Paleoasia)

Sauropod: *Ferganasaurus verzilini* ("lizard of the Fergana Valley and of Nikita N. Verzilin") from the Middle Jurassic (present-day Kyrgyzstan). This fossil was unofficially named 34 years before its scientific publication. Additionally, hundreds of cylindrical teeth have been found in Uzbekistan, from the Central Asian Upper Cretaceous. The smallest may be a young saltasaurid weighing some 65 kg. See more: *Rozhdestvensky 1969; Alifanov & Averianov 2003; Sues et al. 2015; Averianov & Sues 2016*

The oldest of Asia (Paleoasia)

Pengxianpus cifengensis (present-day China), from the Upper Triassic (Rhaetian, approx. 208.5–201.3 Ma), are footprints of a bipedal sauropodomorph that was up to 4.3 m long and 200 kg in weight. The oldest sauropod from this paleocontinent is also represented by some footprints dating to the Lower Jurassic (Toarcian, approx. 182.7–174.1 Ma). See more: *Young & Young 1987; Xing et al. 2013, 2014*

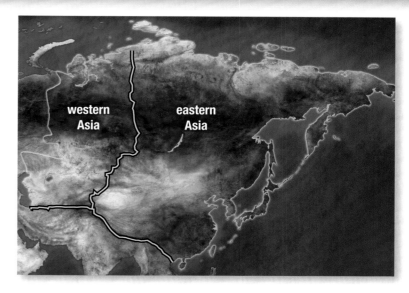

The most recent of Asia (Paleoasia)

Gannansaurus sinensis and *Qinlingosaurus luonanensis* (present-day China) date to the late Upper Cretaceous (Maastrichtian, approx. 72.1–66 Ma). See more: *Xue et al. 1996; Lu et al. 2013*

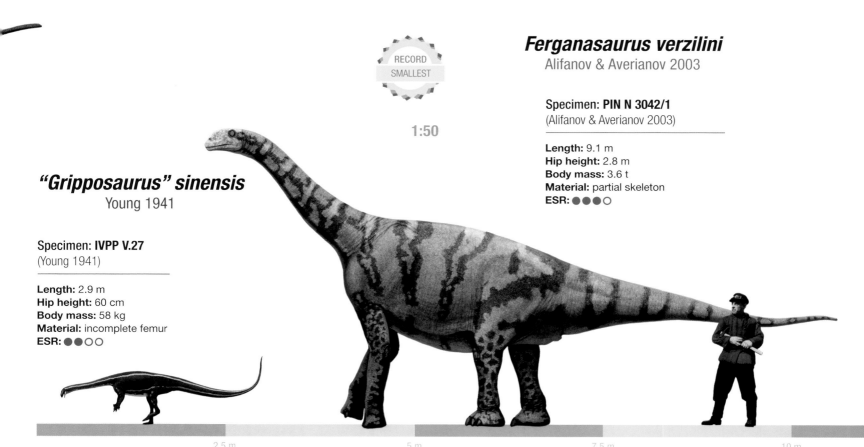

RECORD SMALLEST

1:50

Ferganasaurus verzilini
Alifanov & Averianov 2003

Specimen: PIN N 3042/1
(Alifanov & Averianov 2003)

Length: 9.1 m
Hip height: 2.8 m
Body mass: 3.6 t
Material: partial skeleton
ESR: ●●●○

"Gripposaurus" sinensis
Young 1941

Specimen: IVPP V.27
(Young 1941)

Length: 2.9 m
Hip height: 60 cm
Body mass: 58 kg
Material: incomplete femur
ESR: ●●○○

2.5 m   5 m   7.5 m   10 m

5 m   10 m   15 m   20 m   25 m

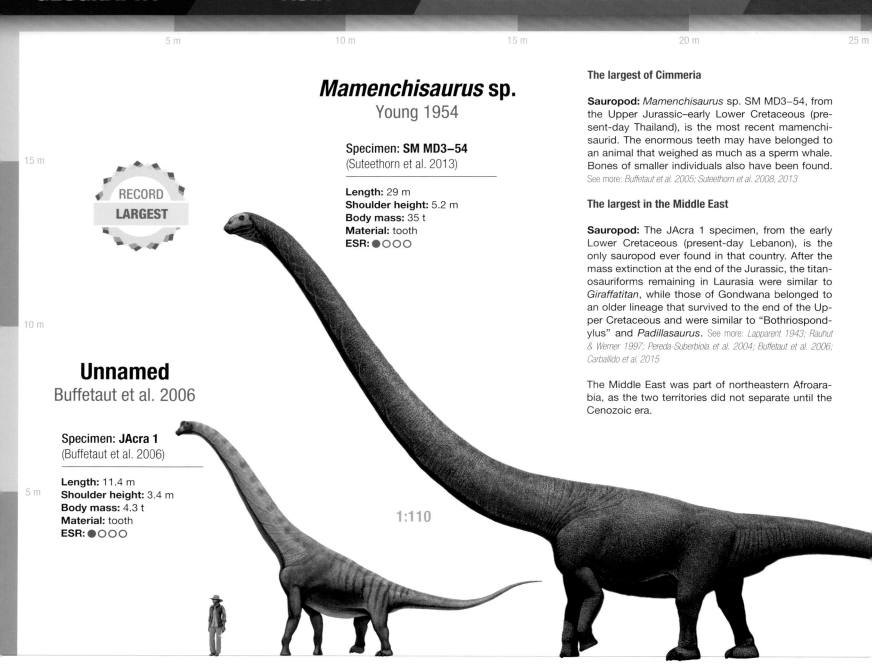

15 m

10 m

5 m

RECORD
LARGEST

Mamenchisaurus sp.
Young 1954

Specimen: SM MD3–54
(Suteethorn et al. 2013)

Length: 29 m
Shoulder height: 5.2 m
Body mass: 35 t
Material: tooth
ESR: ●○○○

Unnamed
Buffetaut et al. 2006

Specimen: JAcra 1
(Buffetaut et al. 2006)

Length: 11.4 m
Shoulder height: 3.4 m
Body mass: 4.3 t
Material: tooth
ESR: ●○○○

1:110

The largest of Cimmeria

Sauropod: *Mamenchisaurus* sp. SM MD3–54, from the Upper Jurassic–early Lower Cretaceous (present-day Thailand), is the most recent mamenchisaurid. The enormous teeth may have belonged to an animal that weighed as much as a sperm whale. Bones of smaller individuals also have been found. See more: *Buffetaut et al. 2005; Suteethorn et al. 2008, 2013*

The largest in the Middle East

Sauropod: The JAcra 1 specimen, from the early Lower Cretaceous (present-day Lebanon), is the only sauropod ever found in that country. After the mass extinction at the end of the Jurassic, the titanosauriforms remaining in Laurasia were similar to *Giraffatitan*, while those of Gondwana belonged to an older lineage that survived to the end of the Upper Cretaceous and were similar to "Bothriospondylus" and *Padillasaurus*. See more: *Lapparent 1943; Rauhut & Werner 1997; Pereda-Suberbiola et al. 2004; Buffetaut et al. 2006; Carballido et al. 2015*

The Middle East was part of northeastern Afroarabia, as the two territories did not separate until the Cenozoic era.

Fooprints

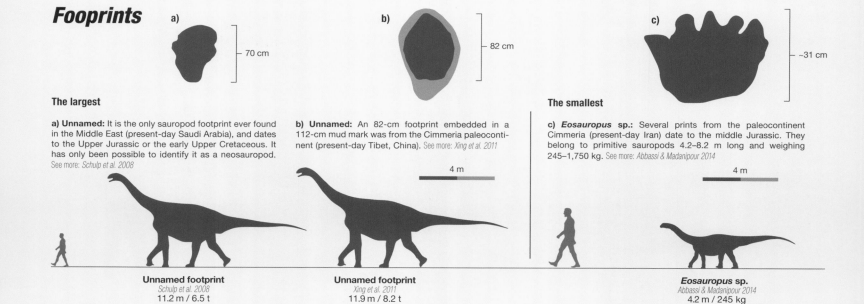

a) ― 70 cm

b) ― 82 cm

c) ~31 cm

The largest

a) Unnamed: It is the only sauropod footprint ever found in the Middle East (present-day Saudi Arabia), and dates to the Upper Jurassic or the early Upper Cretaceous. It has only been possible to identify it as a neosauropod. See more: *Schulp et al. 2008*

b) Unnamed: An 82-cm footprint embedded in a 112-cm mud mark was from the Cimmeria paleocontinent (present-day Tibet, China). See more: *Xing et al. 2011*

4 m

The smallest

c) *Eosauropus* sp.: Several prints from the paleocontinent Cimmeria (present-day Iran) date to the middle Jurassic. They belong to primitive sauropods 4.2–8.2 m long and weighing 245–1,750 kg. See more: *Abbassi & Madanipour 2014*

4 m

Unnamed footprint
Schulp et al. 2008
11.2 m / 6.5 t

Unnamed footprint
Xing et al. 2011
11.9 m / 8.2 t

Eosauropus sp.
Abbassi & Madanipour 2014
4.2 m / 245 kg

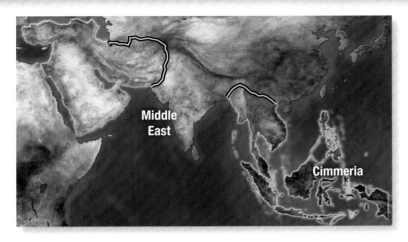

Sauropods: *Isanosaurus attavipachi* ("lizard of Sanpa and Yao") from the Upper Triassic (present-day Thailand) reached 8.3 m in length and weighed 1.3 t. Another sauropod known as *Isanosaurus* sp. (MH 350) may be an adult of this same species or another species altogether. It would have been 13.8 m long and weighed up to 6 t. The smallest calves from the zone are of *Phuwiangosaurus sirinhornae* from the late Lower Cretaceous (present-day Thailand); they were 1.9 m in length and weighed 23 kg. See more: *Martin 1994; Martin et al. 1994; Buffetaut et al. 2000, 2002*

The smallest of the Middle East

Sauropod: Specimen SGS 0366, dated to the late Upper Cretaceous (present-day Saudi Arabia), was the first sauropod found in that country. It was longer than a killer whale and heavier than a giraffe and a saltwater crocodile combined. See more: *Kear et al. 2013*

The oldest of Cimmeria

Isanosaurus attavipachi and *Isanosaurus* sp. (present-day Thailand) date to the Upper Triassic (Norian, approx. 227–208.5 Ma). The latter may be an adult specimen of *I. attavipachi*. See more: *Buffetaut et al. 2000, 2002; Paul 2010*

The most recent of Cimmeria

"Megacervixosaurus tibetensis" (present-day Tibet, China) was a titanosaur from the late Upper Cretaceous that has only been described in a thesis. See more: *Zhao 1983, 1985; Weishampel et al. 2004*

The oldest of the Middle East

The age of some footprints up to 70 cm in length (present-day Saudi Arabia) is uncertain. They may date to the Middle Jurassic or to the late Lower Cretaceous. In contrast, the oldest fossilized bones (present-day Yemen) date to the Upper Jurassic (Kimmeridgian, approx. 157.3–152.1 Ma). See more: *Jacobs et al. 1999; Schulp et al. 2008*

The most recent of the Middle East

A lithostrotian titanosaurus (present-day Jordan) is known solely from a thoracic vertebra dated to the late Upper Cretaceous (Maastrichtian, approx. 72.1–66 Ma). See more: *Wilson et al. 2006*

Sauropodomorph registry in the Middle East

This geographic zone has the lowest number of sauropod fossils, except for Antarctica. Direct remains have been identified in Jordan, Lebanon, Oman, and Yemen, and mixed remains in Saudi Arabia. The fauna in this zone was a mixture of that found in Gondwana and in Laurasia, suggesting that it may have been a natural land bridge between those two zones.

Sauropodomorph registry in Cimmeria

Direct remains have been found in Turkey, mixed remains in Thailand and China, and indirect remains (footprints) in Afghanistan, Iran, and Laos.

The smallest of Cimmeria

Primitive sauropodomorph: A bipedal species from the Upper Triassic (present-day Thailand) was reported but has not yet been formally described. It would have been as large as a fighting bull. See more: *Buffetaut et al. 2008*

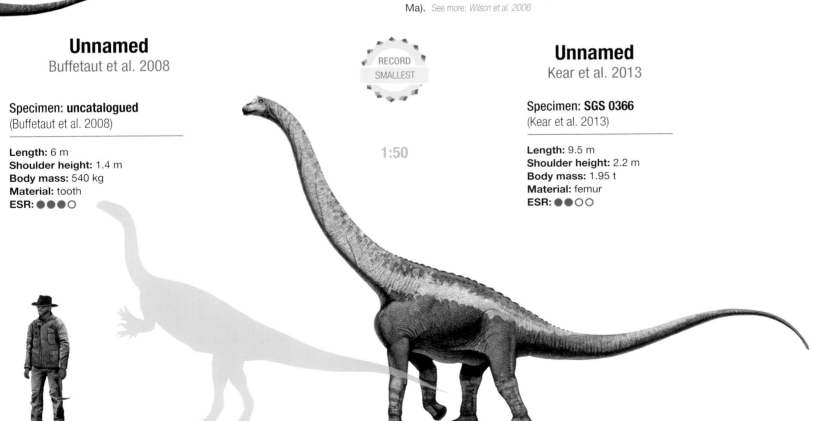

Unnamed
Buffetaut et al. 2008

Specimen: uncatalogued
(Buffetaut et al. 2008)

Length: 6 m
Shoulder height: 1.4 m
Body mass: 540 kg
Material: tooth
ESR: ●●●○

RECORD
SMALLEST

1:50

Unnamed
Kear et al. 2013

Specimen: SGS 0366
(Kear et al. 2013)

Length: 9.5 m
Shoulder height: 2.2 m
Body mass: 1.95 t
Material: femur
ESR: ●●○○

2.5 m   5 m   7.5 m   10 m

3 m   6 m   9 m   12 m   15 m

9 m
6 m
3 m

"Bananabendersaurus"

—

Specimen: uncatalogued
(undescribed)

Length: 21.5 m
Shoulder height: 4.7 m
Body mass: 24 t
Material: Humerus
ESR: ●●○○

The largest of Oceania

Sauropod: A specimen known as "Bananabendersaurus" from the late Lower Cretaceous (present-day Australia), may have been similar to *Diamantinasaurus matildae* (a primitive Titanosauria), so its body might have been very robust. The fossils were described when this edition went to press. See more: *Anonymous 2005*

The largest in Antarctica

Sauropod: Specimen MLP 11-II-20–1 from the late Upper Cretaceous (present-day Antarctica) was a titanosaur as long as a city bus and weighing about as much as an Asian elephant and a hippopotamus combined. See more: *Cerda et al. 2011*

Antarctica and Oceania were connected to Pangea in the Triassic-late Lower Cretaceous and to Gondwana during the early Upper Cretaceous, until they began to separate and move away from the other continents in the late Upper Cretaceous. About 110 Ma, the Kerleguen Plateau was formed, serving as a bridge between Hindustan and Antarctica. Recently, Zealandia, or Tasmania, has been recognized as a continent in its own right that separated from Oceania in the late Cretaceous (85 Ma). It was approximately half the size of Australia, although the bulk of its land mass is now submerged. See more: *Luyendyk 1995; Hay et al. 1999; Mortimer et al. 2017*

Unnamed

Cerda et al. 2011

Specimen: MLP I 1-II-20-1
(Cerda et al. 2011)

Length: 13.5 m
Shoulder height: 2.7 m
Body mass: 5.4 t
Material: incomplete caudal vertebra
ESR: ●○○○

1:70

RECORD
LARGEST

Footprints

a)

├ 1.75 m

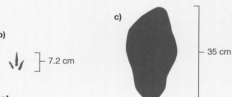

b)

c)

├ 7.2 cm

├ 35 cm

The largest

a) Unnamed: Dating to the early Lower Cretaceous and imprinted in eastern Gondwana (present-day Australia), this print, produced by a sauropod similar to *Wintonotitan*, is almost always underwater, except at exceptionally low tides. See more: *Thulborn 2012; Salisbury et al. 2017*

No sauropod prints have been found in Antarctica.

12 m

The smallest

b) cf. *Grallator*: Some prints from Oceania (present-day Australia) display similar aspects to the feet of *Guaibasaurus*, a dinosaur that some authors believe to be a sauropodomorph. **c) Unnamed:** The only sauropod known from a print in Zealandia (present-day New Zealand), it may have been left by a titanosaur from the late Upper Cretaceous. The print is shaped like a shoe print, which does not mean it is from a human, as some in the tabloid press have interpreted it. See more: *Thulborn 1998; Browne 2010*

4 m

Unnamed footprint
BSM ?A
31 m / 72 t

cf. *Grallator*
Thulborn 1998
98 cm / 1.2 kg

Unnamed footprint
Browne 2010
7.7 m / 1 t

Sauropodomorph registry in Antarctica, Oceania, and Zealandia

Direct remains have been found in Antarctica and mixed remains in Australia and New Zealand.

The smallest of Antarctica

Primitive sauropodomorph: *Glacialisaurus hammeri* ("paleontologist William Hammer's frozen lizard"), from the Lower Jurassic (present-day Antarctica), was comparable in length and weight to a saltwater crocodile. Specimen FMNH PR1823 was a calf 2.7 m in length and 54 kg in weight. See more: *Hammer & Hickerson 1994, 1996; Smith & Pol 2007*

Sauropod: A Lower Jurassic fossil (present-day Antarctica), which has not yet been formally described, may have been 8 m in length and weighed 2.4 t. See more: *Hammer & Hickerson 1996*

The smallest of Oceania

Sauropods: *Wintonotitan wattsi* ("Keith Watts's titan of the Winton Formation"), from the early Upper Cretaceous (present-day Australia), was longer than a city bus and weighed more than an African elephant. The smallest calf is specimen UWA 82468 from the Middle Jurassic (present-day Oceania), with a probable length of 5.8 m and weight of 890 kg. See more: *Coombs & Molnar 1981; Long 1992, 1998; Hocknull et al. 2009*

The oldest of Oceania

Rhoetosaurus brownei and the sauropod UWA 82468 (present-day Australia) date to the Middle Jurassic (Lower Bajocian, approx. 170.3–168.3 Ma). The former is a primitive sauropod 14.2 m in length and 9 t in weight, while the latter is a macronarian 5.8 m in length and 890 kg in weight. See more: *Longman 1926; Long 1992, 1998*

The most recent of Oceania

A caudal vertebra of a potential primitive lithostrotian or saltasaurid (present-day New Zealand), dating to the late Upper Cretaceous (Campanian, 83.6–72.1 Ma). See more: *Molnar & Wiffen 2007*

The oldest in Antarctica

Glacialisaurus hammeri and an as yet undescribed sauropod (present-day Antarctica) date to the Lower Jurassic (Sinemurian, approx. 199.3–190.8 Ma). See more: *Hammer & Hickerson 1996*

The most recent of Antarctica

The lithostrotian sauropod MLP 11-II-20–1 (present-day James Ross Island, Antarctica) dates to the late Upper Cretaceous (Campanian, 83.6–72.1 Ma). See more: *Cerda et al. 2011a, 2011b*

The only known sauropod in Zealandia

Specimen CD.586 from New Zealand's North Island dates to the late Upper Cretaceous (Campanian, 83.6–72.1 Ma). It consists of an incomplete caudal vertebra that could belong to a saltasaurid or a primitive lithostrotian measuring more than 13 m in length and weighing almost 7 t. See more: *Molnar & Wiffen 2007*

Wintonotitan wattsi
Hocknull et al. 2009

Specimen: QMF 7292
(Coombs & Molnar 1981)

Length: 14.3 m
Hip height: 3.45 m
Body mass: 7 t
Material: partial skeleton
ESR: ●●●●○

RECORD
SMALLEST

1:70

Glacialisaurus hammeri
Smith & Pol 2007

Specimen: FMNH PR1822
(Hammer & Hickerson 1994)

Length: 6.25 m
Hip height: 1.3 m
Body mass: 590 kg
Material: partial skeleton
ESR: ●●●○

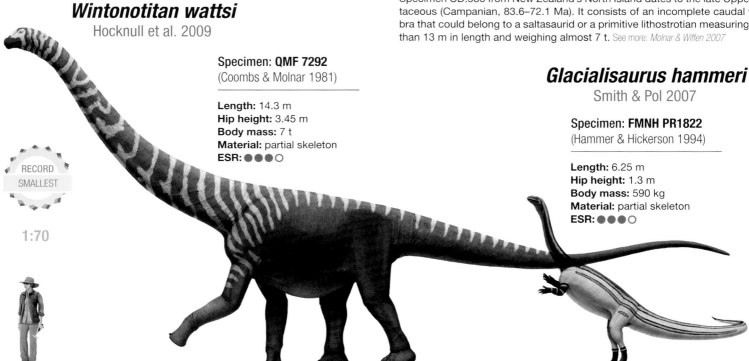

3 m   6 m   9 m   12 m   15 m

RECORD PRIMITIVE SAUROPODOMORPH AND SAUROPOD DISCOVERIES AROUND THE GLOBE

1699—England—First report of a Cretaceous sauropod tooth in western Europe

Even before reports of a giant bone surfaced, a sauropod tooth was published as part of a fossil collection and named as "Rutellum implicatum." See more: *Lhuyd 1699; Gunther 1945; Delair & Sarjeant 2002*

1809—England—First report of fossilized Jurassic sauropod bones in western Europe

A caudal vertebra put into storage by paleontologist Harry Govier Seeley was identified as belonging to a sauropod 60 years later. However, some publications have reported that one vertebra, along with rib and forelimb bones of a *Cetiosaurus* reported in 1875 by John Kingdon, were the first ever discovered. See more: *Owen 1841; Seeley 1869; Phillips 1871; Delair & Sarjeant 1975; Upchurch & Martin 2002, 2003; Upchurch et al. 2009*

1818—Massachusetts, USA—First report of fossilized bones of a Jurassic sauropodomorph in eastern North America

Discovered by Solomon Ellsworth and considered a human skeleton at the time. Today we know the bones belong to *Anchisaurus polyzelus*. See more: *Smith 1818; Hitchcock 1865*

1834—England—First report of fossilized bones and teeth of a Triassic sauropodomorph in western Europe

A report from 1835 mentions a mandible with teeth discovered a year earlier. It was named *Thecodontosaurus*; then a year later *T. antiquus* species was named. See more: *Riley & Stutchbury 1836; Morris 1843*

1834—Germany—First report of a sauropodomorph in a second country

Plateosaurus engelhardti was described three years after being discovered. See more: *Meyer 1837*

1842—England—First reports of fossil bones of a Cretaceous sauropod in western Europe

Cetiosaurus brevis was a chimera of the sauropod *Pelorosaurus conybearei* (named seven years later) and of *Iguanodon anglicus*. *C. brachyurus* is synonymous with *Iguanodon anglicus*. See more: *Owen 1842; Melville 1849; Mantell 1850*

1844—Australia—First mistaken report of a sauropodomorph in Oceania

The fossils of *Agrosaurus macgillivrayi* were mistakenly thought to have been found in Australia, as the material acquired in 1879 and studied in 1891 was mistakenly labeled as from that country when it had actually been found in England. See more: *Seeley 1891; Huene 1906; Molnar 1991; Galton & Cluver 1976; Vickers-Rich et al. 1999*

1852—England—First report of a Cretaceous sauropod tooth in western Europe

Oplosaurus armatus is the largest Cretaceous sauropod tooth ever found to date. See more: *Gervais 1852*

1852—France—First report of a sauropodomorph in a second country

Aepisaurus elephantinus is sometimes mistakenly cited as *Aepysaurus*. Before Gervais's publication, all known sauropods had been found in England. See more: *Gervais 1852*

1854—South Africa—First report of fossil bones of a Jurassic sauropodomorph in southern Africa

Different vertebrae identified as *Leptospondylus capensis*, *Massospondylus carinatus*, and *Pachyspondylus orpenii* belong to a single species. The name *Massospondylus* takes priority, because it is mentioned first in the index. See more: *Owen 1854*

1858—Maryland, USA—First report of fossil teeth of a Cretaceous sauropod in eastern North America

Astrodon was discovered by Philip Tyson, and its remains were published a year later by a dentist. See more: *Johnston 1859*

1859—India—First fossil bones of a Cretaceous sauropod in Asia (Hindustan)

The first report of a sauropod in India was by Hislop in 1859, from the Lameta Formation in Pisdura. The species *Titanosaurus indicus* was named in 1877, like *T. montanus* in North America, and thus takes priority. See more: *Lydekker 1877; Marsh 1877*

1861—England—First report of fossilized bones of a Jurassic sauropodomorph in western Europe

An ungual phalange identified as GSM 109561 is similar to *Jingshanosaurus xiwanensis*. See more: *Owen 1861; Mortimer**

1866—South Africa—First report of fossil bones of a Triassic sauropodomorph in southern Africa

Euskelosaurus browni is based on material that cannot be identified with certainty and so has become potentially synonymous with *Plateosauravus stormbergensis*. See more: *Huxley 1866; Broom 1915; Yates & Kitching 2003; Yates 2004, 2006*

1869—England—First sauropod specimen found in two different places

A partial tail of *Macrurosaurus* with 25 vertebrae was discovered by William Farren, while another 15 vertebrae were discovered by Reverend W. Stokes-Shaw. Both parts are thought to belong to the same individual. See more: *Seeley 1869*

1877—England—First reports of fossil bones of a Jurassic sauropod in western North America

Amphicoelias altus, *Apatosaurus ajax*, *Apatosaurus grandis* (now *Camarasaurus*), *Atlantosaurus montanus*, *Camarasaurus supremus* and *Dystrophaeus viaemalae* were described in the "Bone Wars," the magnitude of which eclipsed the work of other actors, such as geologist Arthur Lakes, who discovered the first remains of *Apatosaurus*. See more: *Cope 1877; Marsh 1877*

1877—USA—First fossil teeth of a Jurassic sauropod in western North America

The teeth identified as *Caulodon diversidens* are actually *Camarasaurus supremus*, which was described in the same year. See more: *Cope 1877*

1888—Maryland, USA—First fossil bones of Cretaceous sauropods in eastern North America

Pleurocoelus altus and *P. nanus* were young individuals of the same species. See more: *Marsh 1888*

1889—England—Second species of a genus created in another country

Astrodon valdensis are teeth similar to *A. johnstoni*, from Maryland, USA. See more: *Lydekker 1889*

1890—India—First fossil bones of a Triassic sauropodomorph in Asia (Hindustan)

Massospondylus hislopi is a questionable name that was reported the same year as *M. rawesi*, but the latter is a theropod from the late Upper Cretaceous. See more: *Lydekker 1890*

1893—Argentina—First fossil bones of a Cretaceous sauropod in southern South America

Argyrosaurus superbus, *Titanosaurus australis* (currently *Neuquensaurus*) and *T. nanus* (synonymous with *N. australis*). The first of these was formerly believed to be one of the largest sauropods. See more: *Lydekker 1893; Huene 1929; Mannion & Otero 2012*

1895—Madagascar—First Jurassic sauropod discovered in Madagascar

Bothriospondylus madagascariensis was a sauropod that may have been similar to *Atlasaurus*, judging by the teeth attributed to it. See more: *Lydekker 1895*

1896—Madagascar—First Cretaceous sauropod discovered in Madagascar

Titanosaurus madagascariensis are very incomplete remains and could be a synonym of *Rapetosaurus krausei*. See more: *Depéret 1896; Curry-Rogers 2001; Curry-Rogers et al. 2011*

1898—Argentina—First fossil teeth of a Cretaceous sauropod in southern South America

Clasmodosaurus spatula is known solely from some incomplete teeth. See more: *Ameghino 1898*

1903—South Africa—First fossil bones of a Cretaceous sauropod in southern Africa

Algoasaurus bauri was recovered from a quarry a year before it was described. Several of the fossils went unidentified and were used as building material by laborers. See more: *Broom 1904*

1908—Tanzania—First fossil bones of a Jurassic sauropod in southern Africa

Gigantosaurus africanus is currently a synonym of *Tornieria africana* and *G. robustus* is *Janenschia robusta*. See more: *Fraas 1908*

1910—Brazil—First mistaken report of a sauropodomorph in northern South America

Some remains of *Thecodontosaurus* are mentioned; however, the zone is dated to the Lower Cretaceous, and so they're likely theropod bones See more: *Woodward 1910; Ihering 1911; Pacheco 1913; Kellner & Campos 2000*

1915—Romania—First report of fossil bones of a Cretaceous sauropod in eastern Europe

Titanosaurus dacus (currently *Magyarosaurus*) was published just 90 days after the first reports of bones in western Europe. See more: *Nopcsa 1915*

1918—South Africa—First fossil teeth of a Jurassic sauropodomorph in southern Africa

Thecodontosaurus minor is a small species known from an incomplete cranium, teeth, and a partial skeleton. See more: *Haughton 1918*

1920—China—First report of fossil teeth and bones of a Cretaceous sauropod in eastern Asia

Helopus zdanskyi (currently *Euhelopus*) was discovered nine years before it was described. It has been dated to the Upper Jurassic as well as the early Lower Cretaceous. See more: *Wiman 1929; Romer 1956*

1922—Texas, USA—First fossil bones of a Cretaceous sauropod in western North America

Alamosaurus sanjuanensis was one of the last sauropods on that continent. See more: *Gilmore 1922*

1924—Mongolia—First report of fossil teeth of a Cretaceous sauropod in eastern Asia

Asiatosaurus mongoliensis resembles the teeth of *Brachiosaurus* more than those of *Euhelopus*. It was found after *Euhelopus* but described five years before the latter. See more: *Osborn 1924; Calvo 1994*

1932—Egypt—First fossil bones of a sauropod in northern Africa

The remains of *Aegyptosaurus baharijensis* were destroyed in World War II, 12 years after being described. See more: *Stromer 1932*

1932—Australia—First report of fossil bones of a Cretaceous sauropod in Oceania

Austrosaurus mckillopi was found a year before being described, and although several more specimens have been reported, some were from different genera or were material from different eras.

See more: *Longman 1933*

1937—China—First report of fossil bones of a Jurassic sauropod in eastern Asia
Tienshanosaurus chitaiensis has been classified within different families, such as "Astrodontidae," Brachiosauridae, "Camarasauridae," Euhelopodidae, or Mamenchisauridae. See more: *Young 1937*

1938—Kazakhstan—First report of fossil bones of a Cretaceous sauropod in western Asia
Antarctosaurus jaxarticus was mentioned as *A. jaxarctensis* a year later by the same author who coined the name. See more: *Riabinin 1938, 1939*

1939—China—First report of fossil teeth of a Jurassic sauropod in eastern Asia
The teeth of *Omeisaurus junghsiensis* were assigned to the skeleton of the same name. See more: *Young 1939*

1941—China—First reports of fossil teeth and bones of a Jurassic sauropodomorph in eastern Asia
Some authors consider *Gyposaurus sinensis* (currently *Gripposaurus*) and *Lufengosaurus huenei* different species; others suspect that the former were juvenile individuals of the latter. See more: *Young 1941a, 1941b; Galton 1976*

1942—Laos—First fossil bones of a Cretaceous sauropod on the paleocontinent Cimmeria
"*Titanosaurus*" *falloti* is also known as "*Tangvayosaurus*" *falloti*. However, its assignment to these genera is doubtful. See more: *Hoffett 1942; Pang & Cheng 2000; Upchurch, Barrett & Dodson 2004*

1947—Argentina—First fossil teeth and bones of a Jurassic sauropod in southern South America
Amygdalodon patagonicus ("almond-toothed from Patagonia"). See more: *Cabrera 1947*

1956—Lesotho—First Triassic sauropod in Africa
"Thotobolosaurus mabeatae" or "Kholumolumosaurus ellenbergerorum" was reported in 1956 with six individuals and over time was given two names, both unofficial and hence invalid. The former is simply mentioned, and the second appeared in a thesis. See more: *Ellenberger & Ellenberger 1956; Charig et al. 1965; Ellenberger & Ginsburg 1966; Ellenberger 1970, 1972*

1959—India—First fossil bones of a Jurassic sauropod in Asia (Hindustan)
Barapasaurus tagorei was described 16 years after being discovered. See more: *Jain et al. 1975, 1977*

1960—Algeria—First report of fossil bones of a Jurassic sauropod in Africa
"*Brachiosaurus*" *nougaredi* is thought to be from the Middle Jurassic or early Upper Cretaceous; however, in the latest reviews it has been assigned to the Upper Jurassic. See more: *Lapparent 1960; Upchurch et al. 2004; Buffetaut et al. 2006; Mannion et al. 2013*

1961—Brazil—First report of fossil bones of a Cretaceous sauropod in northern South America
An illustration of a partially complete femur appears in an unpublished monograph. See more: *Price 1961; Kellner & Campos 2000*

1966—Brazil—First report of fossil teeth of a Cretaceous sauropod in northern South America
Dr. Sérgio Mezzalira reported the find in a geology newsletter. See more: *Mezzalira 1966; Kellner & Campos 2000*

1969—Kyrgyzstan—First report of fossil bones of a Jurassic sauropod in western Asia
Ferganasaurus verzilini remained an unofficial name for 34 years before it was formalized. See more: *Rozhdestvensky 1969; Alifanov & Averianov 2003*

1974—Texas, USA—First report of fossil teeth of a Cretaceous sauropod in western North America
Some teeth assigned to *Pleurocoelus* sp. are similar to *Astrodon johnsoni*. See more: *Langston 1974*

1975—India—First fossil teeth of a sauropod in southern Asia (Hindustan)
The teeth of *Barapasaurus tagorei* were mentioned without illustrations. See more: *Jain et al. 1975*

1980—Zimbabwe—First sauropodomorph to change nationality
Some *Massospondylus carinatus* specimens were discovered in what was then Southern Rhodesia, but in 1980 the site became part of the Republic of Zimbabwe. See more: *Cooper 1980*

1985—Arizona, USA—Firsts report of fossil bones of a Jurassic sauropodomorph in western North America
Massospondylus sp. was a specimen of *Sarahsaurus aurifontanalis*. See more: *Attridge et al. 1985; Rowe et al. 2011*

1986—Argentina—First fossil bones of a Triassic sauropod in southern South America
Lessemsaurus sauropoides was described eight years before it received an official name. See more: *Bonaparte 1986, 1999; Pol & Powell 2007*

1988—Kazakhstan—First report of fossil sauropod teeth in eastern Asia
Hundreds of teeth have been found in Kazakhstan, Tajikistan, and Uzbekistan. See more: *Nesov 1988, 1995; Sues et al. 2015; Averianov & Sues 2016*

1990–1991—Antarctica—First fossil bones of a Jurassic sauropodomorph in Antarctica
Glacialisaurus hammeri was described 16 or 17 years after it was first discovered. See more: *Hammer & Hickerson 1994, 1996; Smith & Pol 2007*

1990–1991—Antarctica—First fossil bones of a Jurassic sauropod in Antarctica
Some bones contemporary to *Glacialisaurus hammeri* have yet to be described. See more: *Hammer & Hickerson 1996; Smith & Pol 2007*

1995—Thailand—First fossil bones of a Triassic sauropod from the paleocontinent Cimmeria
This incomplete ischium was described five years before *Isanosaurus*. See more: *Buffetaut et al 1995; 2000*

1997—The sauropod reported in the most countries
The genus *Titanosaurus* has been reported in Argentina, France, Hungary, India, England, Kenya, Laos, Madagascar, Niger, Romania, and Uruguay, and may have been present in Brazil, Spain, Kenya, and Niger. Its chronological range extends from the late Lower Cretaceous to the late Upper Cretaceous. Although all the species are uncertain, the holotype is from the late Cretaceous in India.

1999—Madagascar—First mistaken report of a sauropodomorph in Madagascar
The teeth and bones were identified as *Azendohsaurus madagaskarensis*, a strange phytophagous animal similar to *Trilophosaurus*. See more: *Flynn et al. 1999, 2008, 2010*

2001—Texas, USA—First report of fossil bones of a Triassic sauropodomorph in western North America
The tooth NMMNH P- 18405 may have been that of a primitive sauropodomorph. See more: *Heckert 2001*

2003—Belgium—First report of a Triassic sauropod tooth in western Europe
It is the oldest in Europe. See more: *Godefroit & Knoll 2003*

2003—Thailand—First fossil bones of a Jurassic sauropod in the paleocontinent Cimmeria
Eight years after a sauropod was identified as *Mamenchisaurus* sp., it was reported to have lived between the end of the Upper Jurassic and the early Lower Cretaceous. See more: *Buffetaut et al. 2003; 2005*

2006—Lebanon—First fossil teeth of a Cretaceous sauropod in the Middle East
The teeth are similar to *Giraffatitan*. See more: *Buffetaut et al. 2006*

2006—Jordan—First fossil bones of a Cretaceous sauropodomorph in the Middle East
The bones consist of thoracic vertebrae similar to those of *Malawisaurus* but have not been described to date. See more: *Wilson et al. 2006*

2007—South Africa—First fossil teeth of a Triassic sauropodomorph in southern Africa
The cranium of *Melanorosaurus readi*, including teeth, was not widely known until 83 years after its discovery. See more: *Haughton 1924; Yates 2007*

2007—India—First fossil bones of a Jurassic sauropodomorph in southern Asia (Hindustan)
Pradhania gracilis is the most recent primitive sauropodomorph in Hindustan. See more: *Kutty et al. 2007*

2008—Thailand—First fossil bones of a Triassic sauropodomorph on the paleocontinent Cimmeria
The material consists of an as-yet-unidentified, possibly bipedal animal. See more: *Buffetaut et al. 2008*

2009—Ecological niche where the most sauropods have been found
Coastal paleoenvironments account for more sauropod fossils than any other niche. See more: *Mannion & Upchurch 2009*

2009—Ecological niche where the most titanosaurs have been found
Unlike fossils of other sauropods, titanosaur fossils have been found in inland environments, including fluvial-lacustrine systems. See more: *Mannion & Upchurch 2009*

2011—Antarctica—First fossil bone of a Cretaceous sauropod in Antarctica
An incomplete caudal vertebra of a titanosaur represents the largest sauropod on the continent. See more: *Cerda et al. 2011*

HIGHEST-LATITUDE DISCOVERIES OF SAUROPODOMORPHS AND SAUROPODS AROUND THE GLOBE

NORTHERN AND SOUTHERN RECORDS
(Based on information from the Paleobiology Database)

Northernmost Triassic sauropodomorph
Plateosaurus cf. *longiceps* (present-day Greenland), at a latitude of 71.8° N (Upper Triassic paleolatitude of 46° S), is presently the northernmost discovery. *Plateosaurus* sp. (present-day Norway) is currently located farther south, at 61.5° N, but at the time, it was located in a more northerly zone, at the Upper Triassic paleolatitude of 46.9° S. See more: *Jenkins et al. 1995; Hurum et al.2006; Clemmensen et al. 2015*

Southernmost Triassic sauropodomorph
cf. *Plateosaurus* sp. (present-day Argentina), at 50.1° S, Upper Triassic paleolatitude of 58.2° N, is possibly an adult specimen of *Mussaurus patagonicus*. See more: *Casamiquela 1964*

Northernmost Triassic sauropodomorph footprints
Footprints of *Otozoum* sp. (present-day England) were reported at a latitude of 51.5° N, Upper Triassic paleolatitude of 30.8° N. Footprints of *Pseudotetrasauropus* sp. (present-day England) are presently located farther south, at 51.4° N, but at the time, they were at the more northerly Upper Triassic paleolatitude of 31.1° S. See more: *Lockley, Lucas & Hunt 2006; Fichter & Kunz 2013*

Southernmost Triassic sauropodomorph footprints
Lavinipes jaquesi, Pseudotetrasauropus acutunguis and *Pseudotetrasauropus bipedoida* (present-day Lesotho) were found at a latitude of 29.4° S, Upper Triassic paleolatitude of 29.4° S. See more: *Ellenberger et al. 1963; Ellenberger 1970*

Southernmost Triassic sauropodomorph fossil egg
Those attributed to *Mussaurus patagonicus* were found at a latitude of 48.1° S, Upper Triassic paleolatitude of 55.5° S. See more: *Bonaparte & Vince 1979*

Northernmost Jurassic sauropodomorph
cf. *Ammosaurus* sp. was found at the present-day latitude of 45.4° N, Lower Jurassic paleolatitude of 64.2° N (present-day eastern Canada). See more: *Olsen et al. 1982*

Southernmost Jurassic sauropodomorph
Glacialisaurus hammeri, at a latitude of 84.3° S, Lower Jurassic paleolatitude of 57.7° S (present-day Antarctica). See more: *Hammer & Hickerson 1994, 1996; Smith & Pol 2007*

Northernmost Jurassic sauropodomorph footprints
Otozoum sp. was found at 45.4° N latitude, Lower Jurassic paleolatitude of 27.4° N (present-day eastern Canada).

Southernmost Jurassic sauropodomorph footprints
Kalosauropus masitisii and *T. pollex* (present-day Lesotho) were discovered at a latitude of 28.9° S, Lower Jurassic paleolatitude of 43° S. See more: *Ellenberger et al. 1963; Ellenberger 1970*

Northernmost Jurassic sauropodomorph fossil egg
Eggshells of *Lufengosaurus* sp. (present-day China) were found at a latitude of 25.2° N, Lower Jurassic paleolatitude of 34.1° N. See more: *Reisz et al. 2013*

Southernmost Jurassic sauropodomorph fossil egg
Seven oolites were found at a latitude of 29.5° N, Lower Jurassic paleolatitude of 43.2° N (South Africa). See more: *Kitching 1979*

Northernmost Triassic sauropod
The sauropod tooth ISRNB R211 (present-day Belgium) was located at a latitude of 49.7° N, Upper Triassic paleolatitude of 36.3° S. It is also the northernmost discovery to date. See more: *Godefroit & Knoll 2003*

Southernmost Triassic sauropod
The specimen PULR 136 (present-day Argentina) was found at a latitude of 29.7° S, Upper Triassic paleolatitude of 38.9° S. See more: *Ezcurra & Apaldetti 2011*

Northernmost Triassic sauropod footprints
Eosauropus sp. (present-day Greenland) are footprints of primitive sauropods that were found at 71.4° N, Upper Triassic paleolatitude of 45.8° S. See more: *Jenkins et al. 1994*

Southernmost Triassic sauropod footprints
The most southerly were reported for a latitude of 29.1° S, Upper Triassic paleolatitude of 45.8° S (present-day Argentina). See more: *Marsicano & Barredo 2004; Wilson 2005*

Northernmost Jurassic sauropod
The teeth of euhelopodid PIN 4874/7 were found at a latitude of 62.7° N, Middle-Upper Jurassic paleolatitude of 67.2° N (present-day eastern Russia). See more: *Kurzanov et al. 2003*

Southernmost Jurassic sauropod
Some remains contemporary to *Glacialisaurus* were found at a latitude of 84.3° S, Lower Jurassic paleolatitude of 57.7° S (present-day Antarctica). See more: *Hammer & Hickerson 1994, 1996; Smith & Pol 2007*

Northernmost Jurassic sauropod footprints
Some unnamed footprints (present-day Denmark) were found at 55.2° N latitude, Middle Jurassic paleolatitude of 45.2° N. See more: *Milan & Bonde 2001*

Southernmost Jurassic sauropod footprints
Parabrontopodus frenkii (formerly *Iguanodonichnus*) were previously thought to be prints of an ornithopod. They were found at a latitude of 34.8° S, Upper Jurassic paleolatitude of 33.4° S (present-day Chile). Some dates suggest that they belong to the early Lower Cretaceous. See more: *Casamiquela & Fasola 1968*

Northernmost Jurassic sauropod fossil egg
The oldest *Megaloolithus* sp. was found at a latitude of 44.8° N, Upper Jurassic paleolatitude of 34.4° N (present-day France). See more: *Garcia & Vianey-Liaud 2001*

Northernmost Cretaceous sauropod
A sauropod mentioned as cf. *Camarasaurus* sp. PM TGU 16/0—80/88 was located at a latitude of 62° N, late Lower Cretaceous paleolatitude of 65.7° N (present-day Russia). See more: *Averianov et al. 2002; Paleobiology database**

Southernmost Cretaceous sauropod
The sauropod MLP 11-II-20—1 is from a locality with a current latitude of 63.9° S, late Upper Cretaceous paleolatitude of 61.8° S (present-day Antarctica). See more: *Cerda et al. 2011*

Northernmost Cretaceous sauropod footprints
Footprints attributed to sauropods (present-day England) were discovered at a latitude of 50.6° N, early Lower Cretaceous paleolatitude of 41.5° N. Other footprints (present-day Canada) are less northerly today (49.6° N), but when imprinted they were farther north, at the early Lower Cretaceous paleolatitude of 50° N. See more: *Wright et al. 1998; McCrea et al .2014*

Southernmost Cretaceous sauropod footprints
Some footprints identified as sauropods were found at a latitude of 41.1° S, late Upper Cretaceous paleolatitude of 65° S (present-day New Zealand). See more: *Browne 2010*

Northernmost Cretaceous sauropod fossil egg
The eggs of *Megaloolithus aureliensis* were discovered at a latitude of 43.7° N, late Upper Cretaceous paleolatitude of 36.4° N (present-day France). See more: *Vianey-Liaud & López-Martinez 1997*

Southernmost Cretaceous sauropod fossil egg
Megaloolithus patagonicus (currently *M. jabalpurensis*) was found at a latitude of 37.9° N, Lower Jurassic paleolatitude of 40.8° N (present-day Argentina). See more: *Garcia & Vianey-Liaud 2001*

MOST OR FEWEST
DISCOVERIES AND DESCRIPTIONS
BY COUNTRY OR CONTINENT

South Africa—Country where the most named sauropodomorphs have been discovered
Twenty species have been named, although several are doubtful. China and Argentina are tied for second place, each with 11.

Wales and Antarctica—Countries where the fewest named sauropodomorphs have been discovered
Pantydraco caducus and *Glacialisaurus hammeri*, respectively.

Lesotho—Country where the most named sauropodomorph footprints have been discovered
A total of 20, although some are doubtful, as they are very similar to those of primitive saurischians.

France, Namibia—Countries where the fewest named sauropodomorph footprints have been discovered
Pseudotetrasauropus grandcombensis from the Upper Triassic in France. *Saurichnium anserinum*, from Namibia, may belong to a sauropodomorph, although the assignment is doubtful.

China—Country where the most named sauropods have been discovered
73 species of sauropods.

Angola, Argelia, Croatia, Kazakhstan, Kyrgyzstan, Switzerland, Tunisia, Zimbabwe—Country where the fewest named sauropods have been discovered
Only a single species has been described.

Spain—Country where the most named sauropod footprints have been discovered
Brontopodus oncalensis, Gigantosauropus asturiensis and *Parabrontopodus distercii*.

Germany, Chile, Croatia, Morocco, Pakistan, Portugal, and Tajikistan—Countries where the fewest sauropod footprints have been found
With a single species described in each.

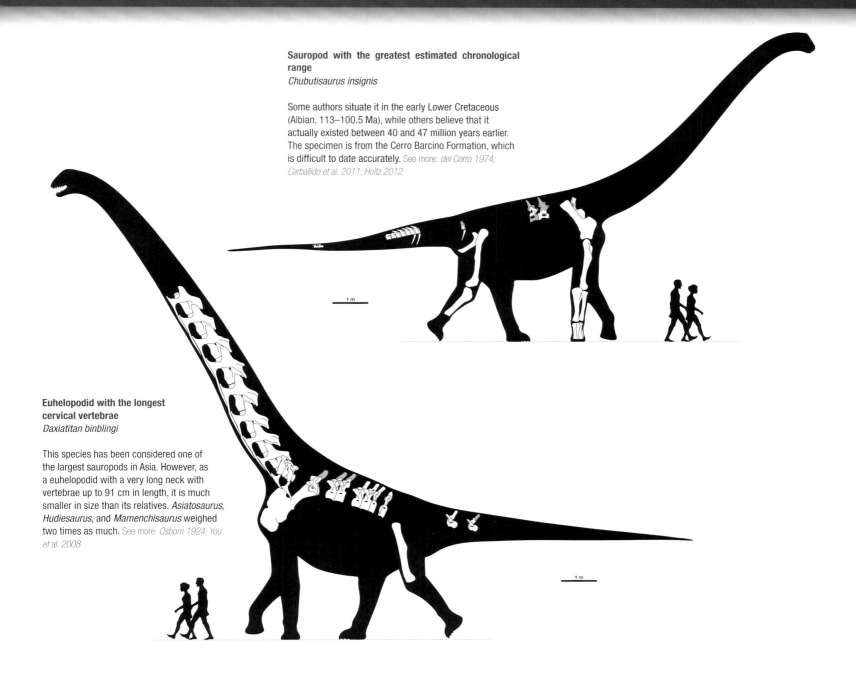

Sauropod with the greatest estimated chronological range
Chubutisaurus insignis

Some authors situate it in the early Lower Cretaceous (Albian, 113–100.5 Ma), while others believe that it actually existed between 40 and 47 million years earlier. The specimen is from the Cerro Barcino Formation, which is difficult to date accurately. See more: *del Corro 1974; Carballido et al. 2011; Holtz 2012*

Euhelopodid with the longest cervical vertebrae
Daxiatitan binblingi

This species has been considered one of the largest sauropods in Asia. However, as a euhelopodid with a very long neck with vertebrae up to 91 cm in length, it is much smaller in size than its relatives. *Asiatosaurus*, *Hudiesaurus*, and *Mamenchisaurus* weighed two times as much. See more: *Osborn 1924; You et al. 2008*

The sauropod reported in the most countries
Demandasaurus darwini

The species name *Demandasaurus darwini* refers to one of the world's most influential scientists and the "father" of modern biology, Charles Darwin. The name was published in 2011 in the paginated issue of the descriptive study, but as the online publication came out a year before, several studies cite the date as 2010. See more: *Fernández-Baldor et al. 2011*

Prehistoric puzzle
The anatomy of sauropodomorphs

Almost all sauropodomorphs had small heads and long necks and tails. The majority of the most primitive ones were bipedal or electively bipedal, with large claws on their forefeet, while sauropods had robust bodies and a quadrupedal posture, making them slow-moving creatures. Some of them were larger than any other terrestrial animal species that has ever existed, up to four times as large.

Sauropod bones are especially fascinating because of their enormous size, with some being the largest among all terrestrial animals. Leg bones could be much larger than an adult human's, while the longest bones, such as cervical ribs, could reach up to 4.1 m in length.

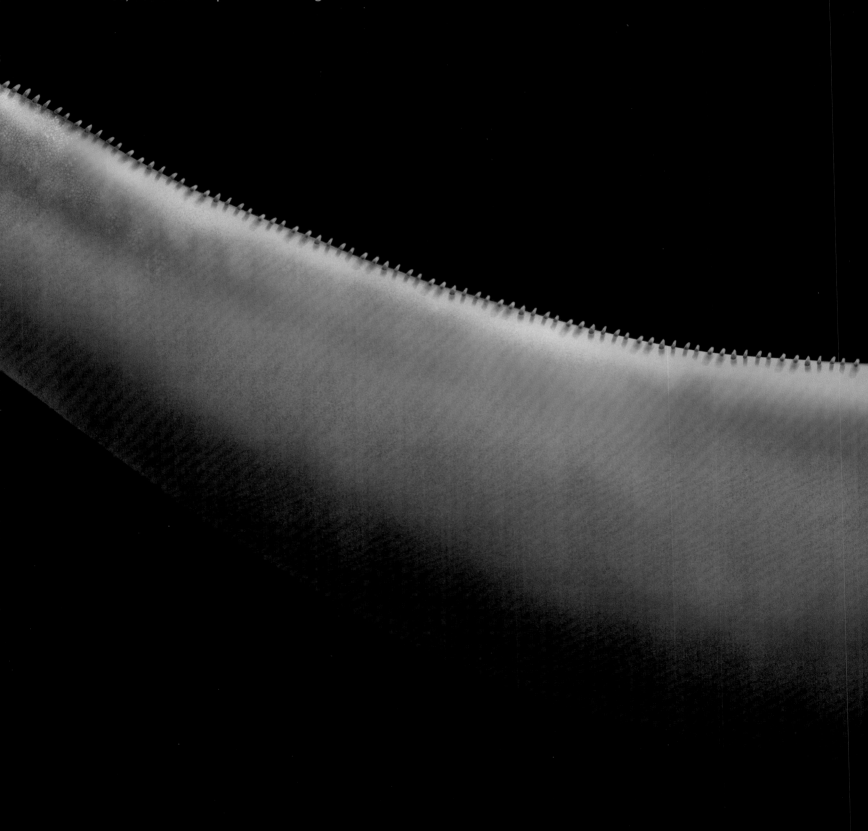

BONES

COMPARATIVELY SMALL HEADS

Sauropodomorph heads consisted of the skull and lower jaws, each consisting of a set of closely linked bones that were very similar to those of reptiles and, in some cases, modern birds.

Measures applied to skulls:

- **OL**: Length from the snout to the occipital condyle
- **ML**: Length of the mandible

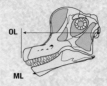

Side view

| **Largest heads** | 1:9 |

Plateosaurus longiceps
AMNH FARB 6810
OL: 36.6 cm
ML: 32.6 cm
RECORD:
The longest skull and jaw of the Triassic.
The best-preserved piece.
See more: *Galton 1985; Prieto-Márquez & Norell 2011*

Giraffatitan brancai
HMN S116
OL: 88 cm
ML: ~69 cm
RECORD:
Longest skull and jaw of Africa. Sub-adult, reconstructed from specimen T1.
See more: *Janensch 1914, 1935*

Turiasaurus riodevensis
CPT-1195 & 1210
OL: 78 cm
ML: 71 cm
RECORD:
Longest skull and jaw of Europe.
See more: *Royo-Torres et al. 2006*

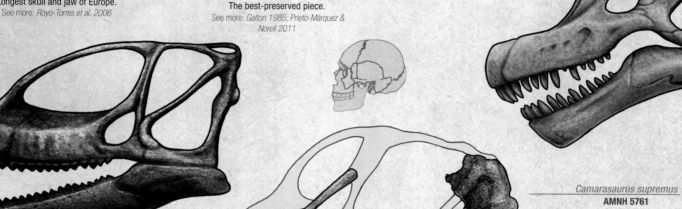

50 cm

Camarasaurus supremus
AMNH 5761
OL: ~85 cm
ML: ~73 cm
RECORD:
Longest and most voluminous skull and jaw of the Mesozoic.
See more: *Osborn & Mook 1921*

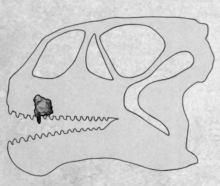

Dreadnoughtus schrani
MPM-PV 1156
OL: ~60 cm
RECORD:
Longest skull of the Cretaceous and of South America.
See more: *Lacovara et al. 2014*

Nemegtosaurus mongoliensis
Z. Pal. MgD-I/9
OL: 57 cm
ML: 45 cm
RECORD:
Longest skull of Asia.
See more: *Nowinski 1971*

Mamenchisaurus sinocanadorum
IVPP V10603
ML: 60.3 cm
RECORD:
Longest jaw of Asia
The skull may have been 65.5 cm in length.
See more: *Russell & Zheng 1994*

Smallest heads 1:2

2 cm

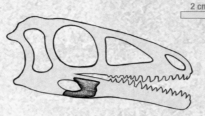

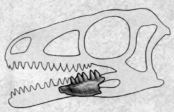

1:1

1 cm

Buriolestes schultzi
ULBRA-PVT280
OL: ~9 cm
ML: 9 cm
RECORD:
Shortest skull and jaw of the Triassic.
See more: *Cabreira et al. 2016*

Saturnalia tupiniquin
MCP 3844-PV
OL: ~10 cm
RECORD:
Shortest omnivore jaw of the Triassic.
See more: *Langer et al. 1999*

Thecodontosaurus minor
uncatalogued
SL: ~8.8 cm
ML: ~8.8 cm
RECORD:
Shortest skull and jaw of the Jurassic.
See more: *Haughton 1918*

Mussaurus patagonicus
PVL 4068
OL: 3.5 cm
ML: 2.8 cm
RECORD:
Smallest skull and jaw of the Triassic
(juvenile).
See more: *Bonaparte & Vince 1979*

1:5

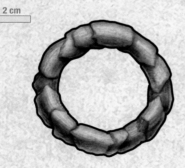

Demandasaurus darwini
MPS-RV II
OL: ~34 cm
ML: ~21 cm
RECORD:
Shortest skull of the Cretaceous.
See more: *Fernández-Baldor et al. 2011*

Unnamed
MCF-PVPH 263
OL: 3.45 cm
ML: ~2.75 cm
RECORD:
Smallest skull and jaw of the Creta-
ceous. Found with an "egg tooth" for
breaking the shell. Newborn.
Not illustrated.
See more: *Chiappe et al. 2001; García 2007;
García et al. 2010*

Massospondylus carinatus
BP/1/5347A
OL: 1.95 cm
ML: ~1.8 cm
RECORD:
Smallest skull and jaw of the Jurassic. From an
embryo discovered in 1974.
See more: *Reisz et al. 2005*

10 cm

SCLEROTIC RING

A ring formed of small bones found inside the eyes of some "reptiles" and birds
that supports the muscles of the iris.

Measures applied to sclerotic rings:

Side view

Diameter

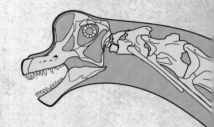

Largest sclerotic rings 1:2

2 cm

Smallest sclerotic rings 1:1

1 cm

Massospondylus carinatus
BP/1/5347A
D: ~0.5 cm
RECORD:
Smallest sclerotic ring of an embryo.
See more: *Reisz et al. 2005*

Plateosaurus longiceps
SMNS 13200
D: ~4.8 cm
RECORD:
Largest sclerotic ring of the Triassic.
It was known as *Plateosaurus integer* or *P.
fraasianus*.
See more: *Huene 1932; Nowinski 1971*

Nemegtosaurus mongoliensis
Z. Pal. MgD-I/9
D: 7.6 cm
RECORD:
Largest sclerotic ring of the Cretaceous.
See more: *Nowinski 1971*

Giraffatitan brancai
HMN SII
D: ~8.3 cm
RECORD:
Largest sclerotic ring of the Jurassic.
Not illustrated.
See more: *Janensch 1914; Nowinski 1971*

HYOID

The tongue is supported by several bones that form the hyoid apparatus. These bones have rarely been found in dinosaur discoveries, as they tend to be cartilaginous structures that do not necessarily ossify.

Side view

Length

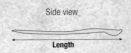

Largest hyoid bones   1:4

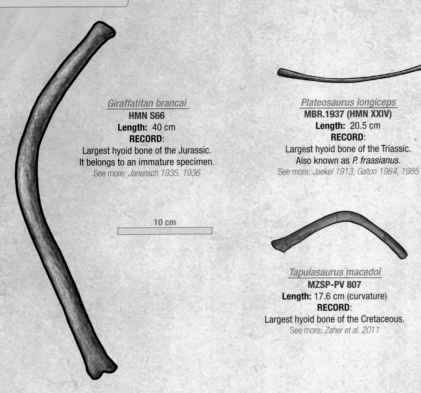

Giraffatitan brancai
HMN S66
Length: 40 cm
RECORD:
Largest hyoid bone of the Jurassic.
It belongs to an immature specimen.
See more: *Janensch 1935, 1936*

10 cm

Plateosaurus longiceps
MBR.1937 (HMN XXIV)
Length: 20.5 cm
RECORD:
Largest hyoid bone of the Triassic.
Also known as *P. fraasianus*.
See more: *Jaekel 1913; Galton 1984, 1985*

Tapuiasaurus macedoi
MZSP-PV 807
Length: 17.6 cm (curvature)
RECORD:
Largest hyoid bone of the Cretaceous.
See more: *Zaher et al. 2011*

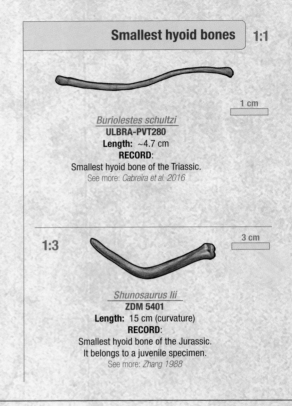

Smallest hyoid bones   1:1

1 cm

Buriolestes schultzi
ULBRA-PVT280
Length: ~4.7 cm
RECORD:
Smallest hyoid bone of the Triassic.
See more: *Cabreira et al. 2016*

1:3

3 cm

Shunosaurus lii
ZDM 5401
Length: 15 cm (curvature)
RECORD:
Smallest hyoid bone of the Jurassic.
It belongs to a juvenile specimen.
See more: *Zhang 1988*

COLUMELLA (Stirrup)

Sauropodomorphs, modern birds, reptiles, and amphibians have a single bone in the middle ear known as the *Columella auris* or stirrup.

Measures applied to the columella:

Side view

Length

Largest columellas   1:1

2 cm

Plateosaurus longiceps
MBR.1937 (HMN XXIV)
Length: 4 cm
RECORD:
Largest sauropodomorph columella.
Also known as *P. fraasianus*.
See more: *Jaekel 1913; Huene 1926; Galton
1984, 1985; Upchurch et al. 2004*

Spinophorosaurus nigerensis
GCP-CV-4229
Length: 6.93 cm
RECORD:
Largest sauropod columella.
See more: *Knoll et al. 2012*

Smallest columellas   1:1

1 cm

Anchisaurus polyzelus
YPM 1883
Length: 0.95 cm
RECORD:
Smallest columella.
See more: *Galton 1976*

VERTEBRAE

A few sauropod species have the largest vertebrae of any vertebrate. The necks of some have up to 17 cervical vertebrae; in general, these animals have 10 thoracic vertebrae and tails with 80 or more caudal vertebrae. Some sauropods even have a small club at the tip of the tail.

Measures applied to the vertebrae:

- **VL**: Anterior-posterior length of the vertebral body
- **ML**: Maximum length of the vertebra
- **VH**: Maximum height of the vertebra
- **MW**: Maximum width of the vertebra

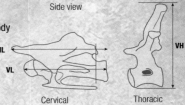

Side view

ML

VL

VH

Cervical

Thoracic

Largest cervical vertebrae 1:15

50 cm

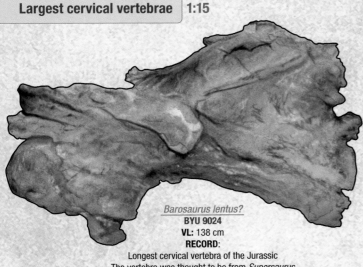

Barosaurus lentus?
BYU 9024
VL: 138 cm
RECORD:
Longest cervical vertebra of the Jurassic
The vertebra was thought to be from *Supersaurus*
but is apparently the C9-C11 cervical vertebra of
an enormous *Barosaurus lentus*.
See more: *Jensen 1985, 1987; Lovelace et al. 2007;
Taylor & Wedel 2016; Taylor & Wedel**

Giraffatitan brancai
HMN SII
VL: 100 cm
ML: 115.5 cm
One of the longest cervical vertebrae ever found,
and the longest of Gondwana.
See more: *Janensch 1914*

Camelotia borealis
BMNH R2870-R2874
VL: 25.5 cm
RECORD:
Longest cervical vertebra of the Triassic.
See more: *Galton 1985*

Median cervical of a giraffe

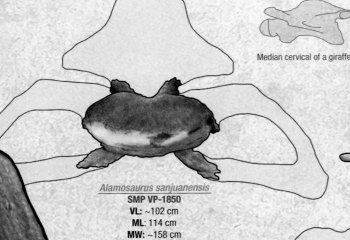

Alamosaurus sanjuanensis
SMP VP-1850
VL: ~102 cm
ML: 114 cm
MW: ~158 cm
RECORD:
Widest cervical vertebra (incomplete).
See more: *Fowler & Sullivan 2011*

Sauroposeidon proteles
OMNH 53062
LCV: 125 cm
LM: 140 cm
RECORD:
Longest cervical vertebra of the Cretaceous.
Piece C8.
See more: *Wedel et al. 2000*

Futalognkosaurus dukei
MUCPv-323
VL: 82 cm
VH: 102 cm
MW: 113 cm
RECORD:
Second highest cervical vertebra. The absolute
record belongs to *Alamosaurus sanjuanensis* with
a cervical 117.5 cm high. Not illustrated.
See more: *Calvo 2000; Calvo et al. 2007;
Fowler & Sullivan 2011; Tykoski & Fiorillo 2016*

Puertasaurus reuili
MPM 10002
ML: ~118 cm
MW: ~140 cm
RECORD:
Widest cervical vertebra (complete).
See more: *Fowler & Sullivan 2011*

Amargasaurus cazaui
MACN-N 15
VL: ~22.7 cm
VH: ~96 cm
RECORD:
Highest cervical vertebra of the Lower Creta-
ceous. The spines would have had a keratin
covering, like ceratopsian horns.
See more: *Salgado & Bonaparte 1991; Schwarz et al.
2007*

Smallest cervical vertebrae   1:15

Nigersaurus taqueti
MNN GAD513
VL: ~ 25 cm
RECORD:
Shortest cervical vertebra of the Cretaceous.
See more: *Sereno et al. 1999*

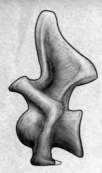

Isisaurus colberti
ISI R335/8
VL: 26 cm
RECORD:
Shortest cervical vertebra of the Cretaceous.
The shortest is 22 cm long.
See more: *Jain & Bandyopadhyay 1997; Wilson & Upchurch 2003*

4 cm

1:1

Eoraptor lunensis
PVSJ 512
VL: 2.4 cm
RECORD:
Shortest cervical vertebra of the Triassic.
The shortest of all measures 1.7 cm. Pieces from
the *Mussaurus patagonicus* calf PVL 4068 are
just 7 mm.
See more: *Bonaparte & Vince 1979; Sereno et al. 1993, 2013*

Leonerasaurus taquetrensis
MPEF-PV 1663
VL: 5 cm
RECORD:
Shortest cervical vertebra of the Jurassic.
The smallest measures 4.1 cm, with an axis of
3.2 cm. The vertebrae of *Massospondylus carinatus* embryo BP/1/5347A measure 2.3 mm.
See more: *Reisz et al. 2005; Pol, Garrido & Cerda 2011*

Largest thoracic vertebrae   1:20

Hudiesaurus sinojapanorum
IVPP V. 11120
VL: 55 cm
VH: 76 cm
RECORD:
Longest thoracic vertebra of the Jurassic. It has been speculated that it is a
posterior cervical vertebra.
See more: *Dong 1997; Taylor & Wedel**

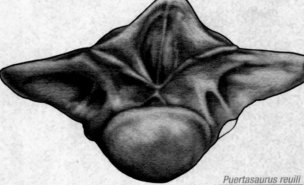

Puertasaurus reuili
MPM 10002
VL: 45 cm
AnV: 168 cm
RECORD:
The widest thoracic vertebra
See more: *Novas et al. 2005*

50 cm

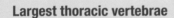

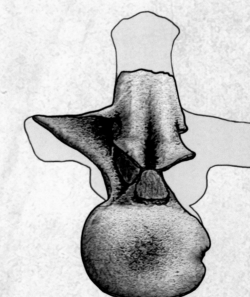

Vertebra T10 of an African elephant.

Maraapunisaurus fragillimus
AMNH 5777
VH: ~ 240 cm
RECORD:
Highest thoracic vertebra of the Jurassic.
There is significant doubt about its actual
size, as the fossil was lost.
See more: *Cope 1878; Carpenter 2006; Woodruff & Forster 2014*

Argentinosaurus huinculensis
PVPH-1
VL: ~50 cm
VH: ~159 cm
RECORD:
Longest thoracic vertebra of the Creta-
ceous. Another complete piece also has
a vertebral body 50 cm long.
See more: *Bonaparte & Coria 1993*

Camelotia borealis
BMNH R2870-R2874
VL: 15.7 cm
RECORD:
Longest thoracic vertebra of the
Triassic.
See more: *Galton 1985*

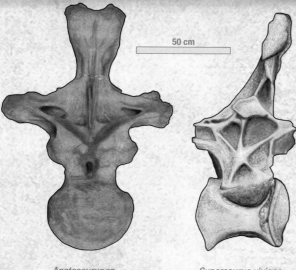

50 cm

Apatosaurus sp.
OMNH 1670
VH: 135 cm
Highest thoracic vertebra of the Jurassic based on solid evidence.
See more: *Taylor & Wedel**

Supersaurus viviane
BYU 9044
VL: 40 cm
VH: 131 cm
One of the largest thoracic vertebrae. It was assigned to the famous but invalid genus *Ultrasauros*.
See more: *Jensen 1985; Curtice 1996*

Smallest thoracic vertebrae 1:2

2 cm

Magyarosaurus dacus
BMNH R.3853
VL: 7 cm
RECORD:
Shortest thoracic vertebra of the Cretaceous. That of juvenile specimen cf. *Rebbachisaurus* sp. NMC 50809 measures just 2.8 cm.
See more: *Nopcsa 1915; Russell 1996*

Alwalkeria maleriensis
ISI R 306
VL: 2 cm
RECORD:
Second shortest thoracic vertebra of the Triassic.
See more: *Chatterjee 1987*

"Gripposaurus" sinensis
IVPP V.27
VL: 3.9 cm
RECORD:
Shortest thoracic vertebra of the Jurassic. The shortest is 3.1 cm long. The one belonging to *Gyposaurus* cf. *sinensis* IVPP V43 measures 4.1 cm. The vertebrae of *Massospondylus carinatus* embryo BP/1/5347A are 2.4 mm long.
See more: *Young 1941, 1948; Reisz et al. 2005*

Largest sacral vertebrae 1:10

Argentinosaurus huinculensis
PVPH-1
VL: 45 cm
RECORD:
Longest sacral vertebra of the Cretaceous.
See more: *Bonaparte & Coria 1993*

20 cm

Plateosaurus longiceps
SMNS 80664
VL: 17 cm
RECORD:
Longest sacral vertebra of the Jurassic. It was known as *Gresslyosaurus plieningeri*.
See more: *Fraas 1896; Huene 1905*

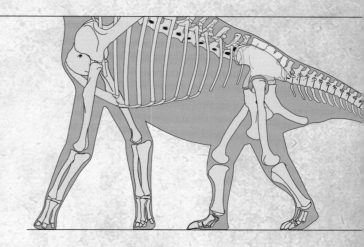

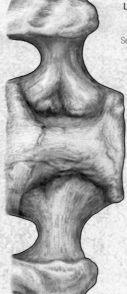

"Titanosaurus" montanus
YPM 1835
VL: 30 cm
RECORD:
Longest sacral vertebra of the Jurassic. It probably belonged to *Apatosaurus ajax*.
See more: *Marsh 1877*

Smallest sacral vertebrae 1:5

5 cm

"Gripposaurus" sinensis
IVPP V.27
VL: 3.9 cm
RECORD:
Shortest sacral vertebra of the Jurassic. The shortest measures 3.8 cm. The vertebrae of *Massospondylus carinatus* embryo BP/1/5347A measure 2.5 mm.
See more: *Young 1941; Reisz et al. 2005*

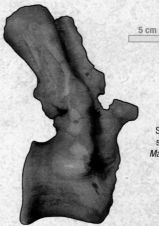

Baurutitan britoi
MCT 1490-R
VL: ~12.8 cm
RECORD:
Second shortest sacral vertebra of the Cretaceous. The unnamed species MLP 46-VIII-21−2 had vertebrae 5.27−8.25 cm long.
See more: *Kellner et al. 2005; Filippini et al. 2016*

Panphagia protos
PSVJ-874
VL: ~1.7 cm
RECORD:
Shortest sacral vertebra of the Triassic.
See more: *Martinez & Alcober 2009*

Largest sacra 1:20

Side view

SVL: Length along the sacral bodies

SVL

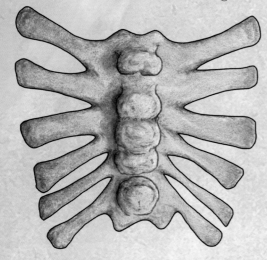

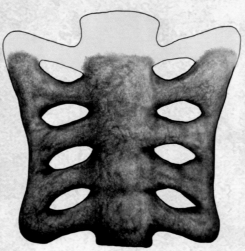

50 cm

Diplodocus hallorum (Seismosaurus)
NMMNH-P3690
SVL: 110 cm
RECORD:
Longest sacrum of the Jurassic.
See more: *Gillette 1991*

cf. *"Brachiosaurus" nougaredi*
uncatalogued
SVL: ~130 cm
RECORD:
The length of the four sacral vertebrae
were mistakenly reported as 130 cm
when first published, but it was likely
about 105 cm.
See more: *Fraas 1896; Huene 1905*

Plateosaurus longiceps
SMNS 80664
SVL: ~47 cm
RECORD:
Longest sacrum of the Triassic.
It was known as *Gresslyosaurus
plieningeri.*
See more: *Fraas 1896; Huene 1905*

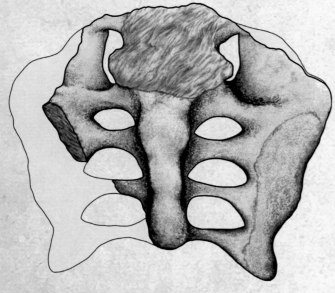

Smallest sacra 1:1

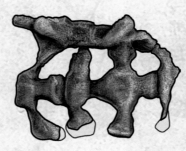

1 cm

Leonerasaurus taquetrensis
MPEF-PV 1663
SVL: 4.3 cm
RECORD:
Shortest sacrum of the Jurassic.
See more: *Pol et al. 2011*

Pampadromaeus barberenai
ULBRA-PVT016
SVL: ~4.7 cm
RECORD:
Shortest sacrum of the Triassic.
Not illustrated.
See more: *Cabreira et al. 2011*

Argentinosaurus huinculensis
PVPH-1
SVL: ~135 cm
RECORD:
Second longest sacrum of the Creta-
ceous. The incomplete piece is 120 cm
long. The absolute record belongs to
Ruyangosaurus giganteus with a
sacrum 147 cm in length.
Not illustrated.
See more: *Bonaparte & Coria 1993;
Lü et al. 2014*

1:20

25 cm

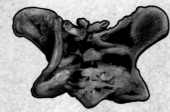

Unnamed
MLP 46-VIII-21-2
SVL: ~50.5 cm
RECORD:
Shortest sacrum of the Cretaceous.
Adult specimen.
See more: *Filipinni et al. 2016*

Largest caudal vertebrae 1:15

25 cm

Unnamed
Meet BP/1/5339
SVL: 23.2 cm
RECORD:
Longest caudal vertebra of the Triassic.
See more: *Yates 2008*; *Wedel & Yates 2011*

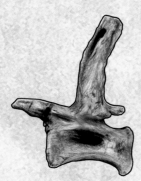

Futalognkosaurus dukei
MUCPv-323
SVL: 30 cm
AM: 70 cm
RECORD:
The vertebra of the *Alamosaurus sanjuanensis* specimen SMP-2104 was a similar size.
See more: *Calvo 2000; Calvo et al. 2007; Fowler & Sullivan 2011*

Diplodocus hallorum (Seismosaurus)
NMMNH-P3690
SVL: 35 cm
RECORD:
Longest caudal vertebra of the Jurassic.
See more: *Gillette 1991*

Smallest caudal vertebrae 1:3

Buriolestes schultzi
ULBRA-PVT280
SVL: ~2.1 cm
RECORD:
Shortest caudal vertebra of the Triassic.
The shortest measures 1.2 cm.
See more: *Cabreira et al. 2016*

Eoraptor lunensis
PVSJ 512
SVL: 2.2 cm
RECORD:
Second-shortest cervical vertebra of the Triassic. The shortest measures 1.7 cm.
See more: *Cabreira et al. 2016*

3 cm

"Gripposaurus" sinensis
IVPP V.2
SVL: 3.3 cm
RECORD:
Shortest caudal vertebra of the Jurassic. The shortest is 2.8 cm long. The vertebrae of *Gyposaurus capensis* SAFM 990 (a juvenile *Massospondylus carinatus*) measures 1.8 cm.
See more: *Young 1941*

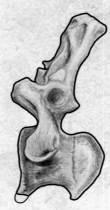

Magyarosaurus dacus
ULBRA-PVT280
SVL: ~2.1 cm
RECORD:
Shortest caudal vertebra of the Cretaceous. The vertebrae from a juvenile of indeterminate species GSI/GC/2901–2904 measure ~1.8 cm.
See more: *Nopcsa 1915; Mohabey 1987*

RIBS

The ribs form the rib cage, protecting the internal organs, and their flexibility facilitates breathing. Cervicals are another kind of rib that are found in the neck; in some cases, cervicals are fused with the vertebrae.

Largest cervical ribs 1:5

Side view

Length

10 cm

Mamenchisaurus sinocanadorum
IVPP V10603
Length: 4.1 m
RECORD:
Longest cervical rib of the Jurassic.
Not illustrated.
See more: *Russell & Zheng 1994*

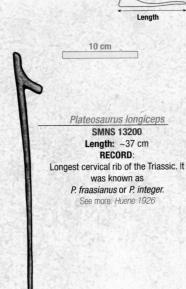

Plateosaurus longiceps
SMNS 13200
Length: ~37 cm
RECORD:
Longest cervical rib of the Triassic. It was known as *P. fraasianus* or *P. integer*.
See more: *Huene 1926*

Sauroposeidon proteles
OMNH 53062
Length: 3.42 m
RECORD:
Longest cervical rib of the Cretaceous.
Not illustrated.
See more: *Wedel et al. 2000*

Smallest cervical ribs 1:2

Pampadromaeus barberenai
ULBRA-PVT016
Length: 6.65 cm
RECORD:
Shortest cervical rib of the Triassic.
See more: *Cabreira et al. 2011*

2 cm

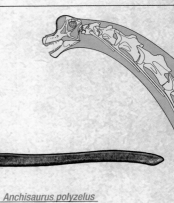

Anchisaurus polyzelus
YPM 1883
Length: ~11.8 cm
RECORD:
Shortest cervical rib of the Jurassic.
See more: *Marsh 1891*

1:5

10 cm

Amargasaurus cazaui
MACN-N 15
Length: ~23 cm
RECORD:
Shortest cervical rib of the Cretaceous.
See more: *Salgado & Bonaparte 1991*

Largest ribs   1:20

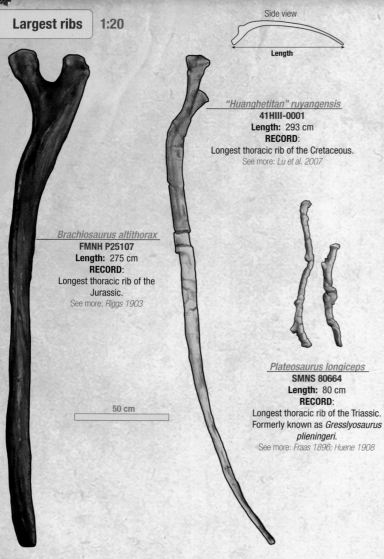

Side view

Length

"Huanghetitan" ruyangensis
41HIII-0001
Length: 293 cm
RECORD:
Longest thoracic rib of the Cretaceous.
See more: *Lu et al. 2007*

Brachiosaurus altithorax
FMNH P25107
Length: 275 cm
RECORD:
Longest thoracic rib of the
Jurassic.
See more: *Riggs 1903*

50 cm

Plateosaurus longiceps
SMNS 80664
Length: 80 cm
RECORD:
Longest thoracic rib of the Triassic.
Formerly known as *Gresslyosaurus
plieningeri.*
See more: *Fraas 1896; Huene 1908*

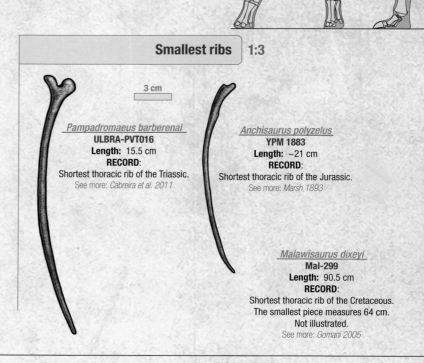

Smallest ribs   1:3

3 cm

Pampadromaeus barberenai
ULBRA-PVT016
Length: 15.5 cm
RECORD:
Shortest thoracic rib of the Triassic.
See more: *Cabreira et al. 2011*

Anchisaurus polyzelus
YPM 1883
Length: ~21 cm
RECORD:
Shortest thoracic rib of the Jurassic.
See more: *Marsh 1893*

Malawisaurus dixeyi
Mal-299
Length: 90.5 cm
RECORD:
Shortest thoracic rib of the Cretaceous.
The smallest piece measures 64 cm.
Not illustrated.
See more: *Gomani 2005*

CHEVRONS

Sauropods have numerous bones known as chevrons or hemal arches, situated
at the end of the tail. These bones protect the blood vessels and caudal nerves
and support the tail muscles.

Side view

Length

Largest chevrons   1:10

Antetonitrus ingenipes
BP/1/4952
Length: 24 cm
RECORD:
Highest chevron of the Triassic.
See more: *Yates & Kitching 2003*

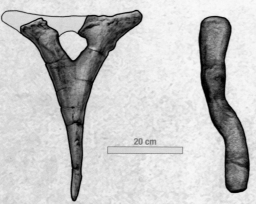

20 cm

Diplodocus hallorum (Seismosaurus)
NMMNH-P3690
Length: ~52.5 cm
RECORD:
Highest chevron of the Jurassic.
See more: *Gillette 1991*

Dreadnoughtus schrani
MPM-PV 1156
Length: 49 cm
RECORD:
Highest chevron of the Triassic.
See more: *Yates & Kitching 2003*

Smallest chevrons   1:1

Buriolestes schultzi
ULBRA-PVT280
Length: ~3.1 cm
RECORD:
Shortest chevron of the
Triassic.
See more: *Cabreira et al. 2016*

"Gripposaurus" sinensis
IVPP V43
Length: ? cm
RECORD:
Shortest chevron of the Jurassic.
The sizes of the pieces are not men-
tioned; however, they would have been
very small. Not illustrated.
See more: *Young 1948*

1:5

Malawisaurus dixeyi
Mal- 277-3
Length: 22.1 cm
RECORD:
Shortest chevron of the Cre-
taceous. The smallest piece is
over 2 cm.
See more: *Gomani 2005*

GASTRALIA

Gastralia, a series of "floating" ribs, are small bones that support the viscera and facilitate breathing. They were present in some sauropodomorphs but are absent in sauropods.

Largest gastralium 1:15

Plateosaurus engelhardti
Nr. XXIV
Length: ~50 cm
RECORD:
Longest gastralium of the Triassic.
It was assigned to _Zanclodon quenstedti_.
See more: _Huene 1932; Fechner & Gobling 2014_

20 cm

Jobaria tiguidensis
MNN TIG3
Length: 40 cm
RECORD:
Longest gastralia of the Jurassic?
They may have been costal cartilage.
Not illustrated.
See more: _Sereno et al. 1999; Tschopp & Mateus 2012_

Diamantinasaurus matildae
MNN TIG3
Length: 64 cm
RECORD:
Longest gastralia of the Cretaceous?
They may have been costal cartilage.
Not illustrated.
See more: _Hocknull et al. 2009; Tschopp & Mateus 2012_

Largest scapulas and coracoids 1:22

SCAPULAS AND CORACOIDS

These bones connect the humerus and the clavicle or sternum with the back, supporting the muscles and tendons of the front limbs of sauropods.

Measures applied to the vertebrae:

- **CL**: Coracoid length
- **CW**: Coracoid width
- **SL**: Length of the scapula
- **SCL**: Length of the scapula and the coracoid

Side view

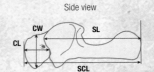

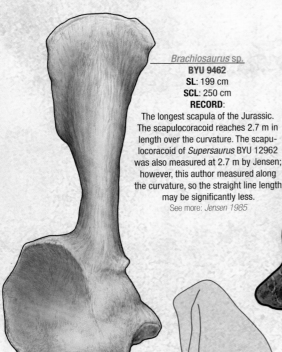

Scapula of an African elephant

Brachiosaurus sp.
BYU 9462
SL: 199 cm
SCL: 250 cm
RECORD:
The longest scapula of the Jurassic. The scapulocoracoid reaches 2.7 m in length over the curvature. The scapu-locoracoid of _Supersaurus_ BYU 12962 was also measured at 2.7 m by Jensen; however, this author measured along the curvature, so the straight line length may be significantly less.
See more: _Jensen 1985_

Dreadnoughtus schrani
MPM-PV 1156
SL: 174 cm
RECORD:
Second longest scapula of the Cretaceous.
See more: _Lacovara et al. 2014_

Patagotitan mayorum
ZPAL MgD-I/6
SL: 196.5 cm
RECORD:
Longest scapula of the Cretaceous.
See more: _Carballido et al. 2017_

Patagotitan mayorum
ZPAL MgD-I/6
CL: 61.5 cm
CW: 114.5 cm
RECORD:
Largest coracoid of the Cretaceous.
See more: _Carballido et al. 2017_

50 cm

Lessemsaurus sauropoides
CRILAR-PV 303
SL: 80 cm
RECORD:
Longest scapula of the Triassic.
It was published after this book went to press.
See more: _Martinez et al. 2004; Apaldetti et al. 2018_

Isanosaurus attavipachi
CH4-1
CL: 30 cm
RECORD:
Longest coracoid of the Triassic.
See more: _Buffetaut et al. 2000_

Brachiosaurus altithorax
FMNH P25107
CL: 54 cm
CW: 84 cm
RECORD:
Largest coracoid of the Jurassic. It may have belonged to _Camarasaurus supremus_.
See more: _Riggs 1903; Paul 2012_

Camarasaurus supremus
AMNH 5761
CL: 56 cm
CW: 69 cm
RECORD:
Second largest coracoid of the Jurassic. Specimen AMNH 222 has a coracoid 73.6 cm wide.
See more: _Cope 1877; Osborn 1921_

Paralititan stromeri
CGM 81119
CL: >45 cm
RECORD:
Second largest coracoid of the Cretaceous.
See more: _Smith et al. 2001_

Smallest scapulas and coracoids   1:5

1:10

5 cm

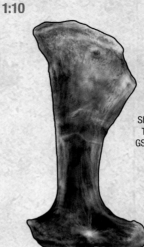

Buriolestes schultzi
ULBRA-PVT280
SL: ~7.4 cm
RECORD:
Shortest scapula of the Triassic.
See more: *Cabreira et al. 2016*

Leonerasaurus taquetrensis
MPEF-PV 1663
SL: ~17.4 cm
RECORD:
Shortest scapula of the Jurassic
(tie).
The *Anchisaurus polyzelus* calf YPM
209 has a ~6.7 cm scapula.
See more: *Pol et al. 2011*

"Gripposaurus" sinensis
IVPP V.27
SL: ~17.5 cm
RECORD:
Shortest coracoid of the Jurassic.
It is probably deformed and could
measure only 15.5 cm.
See more: *Pol et al. 2011*

Saltasaurus loricatus
PVL 4017-106
SL: 64 cm
RECORD:
Shortest scapula of the Cretaceous.
The scapula of juvenile specimen
GSI/GC/2901-2904, of indeterminate
species, measures some 7 cm.
See more: *Bonaparte & Powell 1980;
Mohabey 1987*

"Gripposaurus" sinensis
IVPP V.26
SL: ~6.9 cm
RECORD:
Shortest coracoid of the Jurassic.
Specimen IVPP V.27 was similar
in size.
See more: *Young 1941*

Saturnalia tupiniquin
MCP 3845-PV
CL: 5.5 cm
RECORD:
Shortest coracoid of the Triassic.
The coracoid of the juvenile *Pantydraco cadu-
cus* specimen BMNHP 24 measures 2.5 cm.
See more: *Langer et al. 2007; Yates 2003*

Uberabatitan riberoi
CPP-UrHo
SL: 24 cm
RECORD:
Shortest coracoid of the Cretaceous.
See more: *Salgado & Carvalho 2008*

STERNAL PLATES AND CLAVICLES

The sternal plates protect the heart and lungs.

Measures applied to sternal plates, clavicles, and
interclavicles:

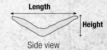

Length

Height

Side view

Sternal plates and clavicles   1:15

Plateosaurus longiceps
GPIT 1
Length: 14 cm
RECORD:
Longest clavicle of the Triassic.
Not illustrated.
See more: *Huene 1926; Galton 2001*

Omeisaurus tianfuensis
T5704
Length: ~90 cm
RECORD:
Longest clavicle of the Jurassic.
The incomplete piece is 85 cm long.
See more: *He et al. 1988*

Giraffatitan brancai
HMN SII
Length: 110 cm
RECORD:
Longest sternal plate of the
Jurassic.
See more: *Janensch 1914*

Isanosaurus attavipachi
CH4-1
Altura: ~18 cm
Length: ~16.5 cm
RECORD:
Longest sternal plate of the Triassic.
Not illustrated.
See more: *Buffetaut et al. 2000*

Dreadnoughtus schrani
MPM-PV 1156
Length: 114 cm
RECORD:
Longest sternal plate of the Cretaceous.
Not illustrated.
See more: *Lacovara et al. 2014*

Unnamed
SMA M 25-3
Length: 65 cm
RECORD:
The only known interclavicle.
See more: *Tschopp et al. 2012*

Smallest sterna and furculae   1:1

Lufengosaurus magnus
IVPP V.82
Length: 18.5 cm
RECORD:
Shortest sternal plate of the
Jurassic.
See more: *Young 1947*

Uberabatitan riberoi
1027-UrHo
Length: 38 cm
RECORD:
Shortest sternal plate of the Cretaceous.
Not illustrated.
See more: *Salgado & Carvalho 2008*

HUMERUS

This bone connects the shoulder and forelimb.

Measures applied to the humerus::

Side view

Length

Largest humeri 1:20

Humerus of an African elephant

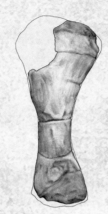

50 cm

Isanosaurus sp.
MH 350
Length: >100 cm
RECORD:
Longest humerus of the Triassic.
See more: *Buffetaut et al. 2002*

Plateosaurus engelhardti
GPTI V
Length: ~55 cm
RECORD:
Longest bipedal sauropodomorph
humerus of the Triassic.
It was known as *Pachysaurus
wetzelianus*. The humerus of
Mussaurus patagonicus MLP 68- II-27
may have been larger, measuring ~57
cm in length.
See more: *Huene 1932; Casamiquela 1980;
Carrano 1998; Otero & Pol 2013*

cf. *Sinosaurus triassicus*
uncatalogued
Length: 48 cm
RECORD:
Longest bipedal sauropodomorph
humerus of the Jurassic.
The remains represent a mixed
theropod-sauropodomorph species.
See more: *Young 1948*

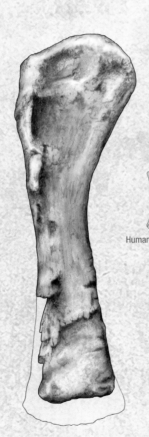

Human humerus

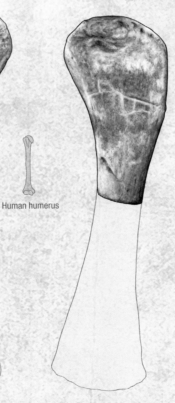

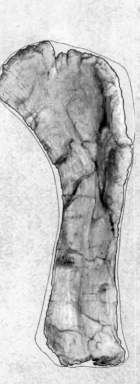

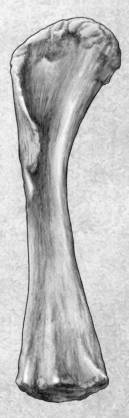

Brachiosaurus altithorax
USNM 21903
Length: 213 cm
RECORD:
Second longest humerus of the
Jurassic.
See more: *Jensen 1985*

Brachiosaurus altithorax
FMNH P25107
Length: ~216 cm
RECORD:
Longest humerus of the Jurassic.
See more: *Riggs 1903; Taylor 2009*

Lusotitan atalaiensis
MIGM Col.
Length: ~205 cm
RECORD:
Longest humerus of Europe.
See more: *Lapparent & Zbyszewski
1957; Antunes & Mateus 2003*

Turiasaurus riodevensis
CPT-1195 & 1210
Length: 179 cm
RECORD:
Longest complete humerus of
Europe.
See more: *Royo-Torres et al. 2006*

Giraffatitan brancai
HMN SII
Length: 213 cm
RECORD:
Longest humerus of Africa.
See more: *Janensch 1914*

Largest humeri 1:20

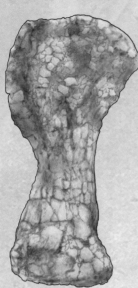

"Bananabendersaurus"
uncatalogued
Length: 150 cm
RECORD:
Longest humerus of Oceania.
Known as Cooper. It has not been
published.

Notocolossus gonzalezparejasi
CUNCUYO-LD 301
Length: 176 cm
RECORD:
Longest humerus of South
America.
See more: *Gónzalez-Riga et al. 2016*

Humerus of an African
elephant

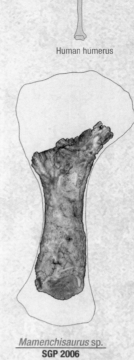

Atlasaurus imelakei
uncatalogued
Length: 195 cm
RECORD:
Longest humerus of the Middle
Jurassic.
See more: *Monbaron & Taquet 1981;
Monbaron 1983; Monbaron et al. 1999*

Human humerus

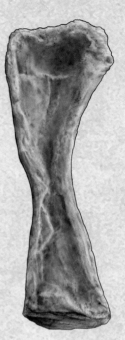

Mamenchisaurus sp.
SGP 2006
Length: ~142 cm
RECORD:
Longest humerus of Asia. The incom-
plete 99-cm piece was erroneously
estimated to be 180 cm long.
See more: *Wing et al 2011*

Paralititan stromeri
SGP 2006
Length: 169 cm
RECORD:
Second-longest humerus of the
Cretaceous.
See more: *Smith et al. 2001*

Smallest humeri 1:3

Buriolestes schultzi
ULBRA-PVT280
Length: ~7 cm
RECORD:
Shortest humerus of the Triassic.
The humerus of the *Mussaurus
patagonicus* calf PVL 4068 is
2.54 cm.
See more: *Bonaparte & Vince 1979;
Cabreira et al. 2016*

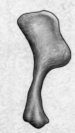

Saturnalia tupiniquin
MCP 3845-PV
Length: 9.8 cm
RECORD:
Second shortest humerus of the
Triassic.
See more: *Langer et al. 2007*

3 cm

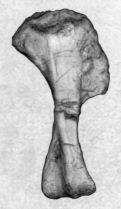

Unaysaurus tolentinoi
UFSM11069
Length: 15.8 cm
See more: *Leal et al. 2004*

1:10

Melanorosaurus readi
NM QR1551
Length: 45 cm
RECORD:
Shortest quadrupedal sauropodo-
morph humerus of the Jurassic.
See more: *Kitching & Raath 1984;
Bonnan & Yates 2007*

Tonganosaurus hei
MCDUT 14454
Length: 62.8 cm
RECORD:
Shortest quadrupedal sauropodo-
morph humerus of the Jurassic.
See more: *Li et al. 2010*

"Gripposaurus" sinensis
IVPP V.27
Length: 15 cm
RECORD:
Shortest humerus of the Jurassic.
The humerus of the *Massospondylus
carinatus* embryo BP/1/5347A mea-
sures 9.5 mm.
See more: *Young 1941; Reisz et al. 2005*

10 cm

Bonatitan reigi
MACN RN 821
Length: 36.3 cm
RECORD:
Shortest humerus of the
Cretaceous.
It belongs to an embryo of
the unidentified species
NSM60104403–20554450 and
measures 1.89 cm.
See more: *Martinelli & Forasiepi 2004;
Grellet-Tinner et al. 2011*

THORACIC LIMB

These two bones form the lower forelimb and tend to be long and thin.

Measures applied to ulnae and radii:

Side view

Length

Side view

Length

Largest ulnae 1:20

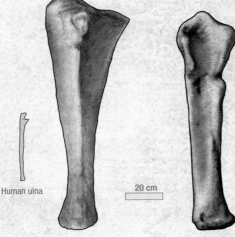

Human ulna

20 cm

Ulna of an African elephant

Antetronitrus ingenipes
BP/1/4952
Length: 42 cm
RECORD:
Longest ulna of the Triassic.
See more: _Yates & Kitching 2003_

Giraffatitan brancai
HMN SII
Length: 130 cm
RECORD:
Longest ulna of the Jurassic.
See more: _Janensch 1914, 1935_

Paralititan stromeri
CGM 81119
Length: 116 cm
RECORD:
Second longest ulna of the Creta-
ceous. The largest is 118 cm long,
from an unnamed sauropod, but it
was not illustrated.
See more: _Martinez et al. 1989; Smith
et al. 2001_

Smallest ulnae 1:5

5 cm

Eoraptor lunensis
PVSJ 512
Length: 5.3 cm
RECORD:
Shortest ulna of the Triassic. The
ulna of _Buriolestes schultzi_ may
have been the same length.
See more: _Sereno et al. 1993, 2013;
Cabreira et al. 2016_

Unaysaurus tolentinoi
UFSM11069
Length: ~11 cm
RECORD:
Second shortest ulna of the
Triassic.
See more: _Leal et al. 2004_

"Gripposaurus" sinensis
IVPP V.27
Length: 9.6 cm
RECORD:
The ulna of the _Massospondylus
carinatus_ embryo BP/1/5347A is
6.5 mm long.
See more: _Young 1941; Reisz et al. 2005_

1:10

10 cm

Magyarosaurus dacus
BMNH R.3853
Length: 35 cm
RECORD:
Shortest ulna of the Cretaceous.
See more: _Nopcsa 1915_

Largest radii 1:20

Human radius

Antetronitrus ingenipes
BP/1/4952
Length: 37.6 cm
RECORD:
Longest radius of the Triassic.
See more: _Yates & Kitching 2003_

Giraffatitan brancai
HMN SII
Length: 124 cm
RECORD:
Longest radius of the Jurassic.
At the end of this book, an even
larger _Brachiosaurus_ radius (BYU
4744) was published, with a
length of 134 cm.
See more: _Janensch 1914, 1935;
D'Emic, & Carrano 2019_

Patagotitan mayorum
MPEF PV 3400
Length: 107.5 cm
RECORD:
Longest radius of the Cretaceous.
See more: _Carballido et al. 2017_

Smallest radii 1:2

Buriolestes schultzi
ULBRA-PVT280
Length: ~4.6 cm
RECORD:
Shortest radius of the Triassic.
See more: _Cabreira et al. 2016_

Eoraptor lunensis
PVSJ 512
Length: 6.3 cm
RECORD:
Second shortest radius of the
Triassic.
See more: _Sereno et al. 1993, 2013_

"Gripposaurus" sinensis
IVPP V.27
Length: 8.5 cm
RECORD:
Shortest radius of the Jurassic.
See more: _Young 1941_

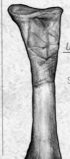

Unaysaurus tolentinoi
UFSM11069
Length: ~10.3 cm
See more: _Leal et al. 2004_

1:10

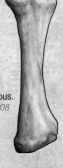

Uberabatitan riberoi
CPP-UrHo
Length: 45 cm
RECORD:
Shortest radius of the Cretaceous.
See more: _Salgado & Carvalho 2008_

METACARPAL BONES

Metacarpals are the bones of the hands or forefeet.

Measures applied to metacarpals:

Side view

Length

Largest metacarpals — 1:10

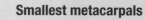

20 cm

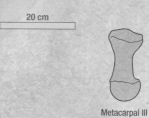

Metacarpal III
of an African elephant

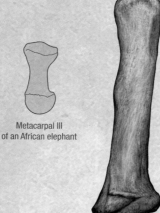

Metacarpal III
of a human

Smallest metacarpals — 1:1

1 cm

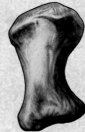

Eoraptor lunensis
PVSJ 512
Length: 2 cm
RECORD:
Shortest metacarpal of the Triassic.
The shortest measures 0.8 cm.
See more: *Sereno et al. 1993, 2013*

"Gripposaurus" sinensis
IVPP V.27
Length: 3.5 cm
RECORD:
Shortest metacarpal of the Jurassic.
The smallest is 1.7 cm.
See more: *Young 1941*

1:10

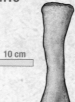

10 cm

Epachthosaurus sciuttoi
UNPSJB-PV 920
Length: 30.3 cm
RECORD:
Shortest metacarpal of the
Cretaceous.
See more: *Martínez et al. 2004*

Riojasaurus incertus
PVL 3808
Length: 15 cm
RECORD:
Longest metacarpal of the
Triassic.
See more: *Bonaparte 1969*

Giraffatitan brancai
HMN SII
Length: 63.5 cm
RECORD:
Longest metacarpal of the Jurassic. Other measurements indicate
a length of 64.8 cm.
See more: *Janensch 1914, 1935*

Sonorasaurus thompsoni
ASDM 500
Length: 56 cm
RECORD:
Longest metacarpal of the
Cretaceous.
See more: *Ratkevich 1998; D'Emic et
al. 2016*

HAND PHALANGES

The bones of the fingers are known as phalanges. Claws are formed from specialized phalanges known as ungual phalanges.

Measures applied to phalanges and claws:

Side view

Length

Largest forefoot phalanges — 1:8

Plateosaurus engelhardti
GPTI B
Length: ~15 cm
RECORD:
Largest forefoot phalange of the
Triassic. Known as
Gresslyosaurus robustus.
See more: *Huene 1907,1908;
Galton 2001*

Shunosaurus lii
ZDM 5402
Length: 23 cm
RECORD:
Longest forefoot phalange of Asia.
See more: *Zhang 1988*

Hudiesaurus sinojapanorum
CM 3018
Length: 21 cm
RECORD:
Longest forefoot phalange of
the Jurassic. From a juvenile
specimen.
See more: *Dong 1997*

Smallest forefoot phalanges — 1:2

Diamantinasaurus matildae
AODF 603
Length: 17.1 cm
RECORD:
Longest forefoot phalange of the
Cretaceous. Also the longest of
Oceania.
See more: *Hocknull et al. 2009*

Apatosaurus louisae
CM 3018
Length: 21.5 cm
RECORD:
Longest forefoot phalange of
North America.
See more: *Gilmore 1936*

Eoraptor lunensis
PVSJ 512
Length: 1.4 cm
RECORD:
Shortest forefoot phalange of the
Triassic. The shortest measures
~1.2 cm.
See more: *Sereno et al. 1993, 2013*

"Gripposaurus" sinensis
IVPP V.27
Length: 3.3 cm
RECORD:
Shortest forefoot phalange of the
Jurassic. The shortest phalange is
0.8 cm long.
See more: *Young 1941*

Curiously, in *Opisthocoelicaudia
skarzynskii*, the phalanges of
the forefoot have completely
disappeared.

PELVIC GIRDLE

The ilium, pubis, and ischium form the pelvis, or pelvic girdle, and are the hip bones that connect to the sacrum and hind legs. The pubis and ischium help provide room for the viscera and the reproductive system.

Side view

Length

Largest ilia   1:20

50 cm

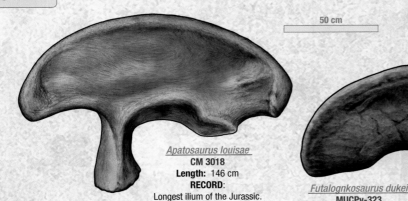

Apatosaurus louisae
CM 3018
Length: 146 cm
RECORD:
Longest ilium of the Jurassic.
See more: *Gilmore 1936*

Futalognkosaurus dukei
MUCPv-323
Length: ~137 cm
RECORD:
Widest pelvis of all the dinosaurs, at 255 cm. The incomplete ilium of *Argentinosaurus huinculensis* PVPH-1 was likely larger, but it was never illustrated or described.
See more: *Bonaparte & Coria 1993; Calvo 2000; Calvo et al. 2007*

Lessemsaurus sauropoides
CRILAR-PV 302
Length: 75 cm
RECORD:
Longest ilium of the Triassic. Published after this book went to press. The length initially mentioned was 95 cm.
See more: *Martinez et al. 2004; Apaldetti et al. 2018*

Smallest ilia   1:5

5 cm

Buriolestes schultzi
ULBRA-PVT280
Length: ~6,1 cm
RECORD:
Shortest ilium of the Triassic. The ilium of the juvenile *Pantydraco caducus* specimen BMNHP24 measures 5.5 cm.
See more: *Yates 2003; Cabreira et al. 2016*

Panphagia protos
PSVJ-874
Length: ~10.8 cm
RECORD:
Second shortest ilium of the Triassic.
See more: *Martinez & Alcober 2009*

"Gripposaurus" sinensis
IVPP V.27
Length: 14.1 cm
RECORD:
Shortest ilium of the Jurassic. The ilium of *Massospondylus carinatus* embryo BP/1/5347A is 6.5 mm long.
See more: *Young 1941; Reisz et al. 2005*

20 cm

1:20

Saltasaurus loricatus
PVL 4017-92
Length: 66 cm
RECORD:
Second-shortest ilium of the Cretaceous.
See more: *Bonaparte & Powell 1980*

Unnamed
MLP 46-VIII-21-2
SVL: ~50.5 cm
RECORD:
Shortest sacrum of the Cretaceous. Adult specimen.
See more: *Filipinni et al. 2016*

Largest pubes   1:20

50 cm

Plateosaurus engelhardti
GPTI V
Length: 72 cm
RECORD:
Longest pubis of the Triassic. Known as *Pachysaurus wetzelianus*. Not illustrated.
See more: *Huene 1932*

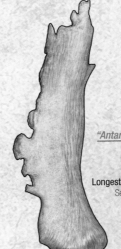

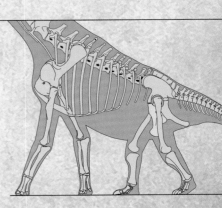

Giraffatitan brancai
HMN SII
Length: 121 cm
RECORD:
Longest pubis of the Jurassic (tie).
See more: *Janensch 1914, 1935*

Brontosaurus excelsus
FMNH 7163
Length: 121 cm
RECORD:
Longest pubis of the Jurassic (tie).
See more: *Riggs 1903*

"Antarctosaurus" giganteus
MLP 26-316
Length: 145 cm
RECORD:
Longest pubis of the Cretaceous.
See more: *Huene 1929*

Side view

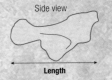

Length

Smallest pubes   1:5

Buriolestes schultzi
ULBRA-PVT280
Length: ~8.8 cm
RECORD:
Shortest pubis of the Triassic.
See more: *Cabreira et al. 2016*

Panphagia protos
PSVJ-874
Length: ~11.3 cm
RECORD:
Second shortest pubis of the Triassic.
See more: *Martinez & Alcober 2009*

5 cm

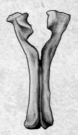

"Gripposaurus" sinensis
IVPP V.27
Length: 16.3 cm
RECORD:
Shortest pubis of the Jurassic.
See more: *Young 1941*

1:10   20 cm

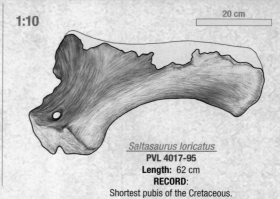

Saltasaurus loricatus
PVL 4017-95
Length: 62 cm
RECORD:
Shortest pubis of the Cretaceous.
See more: *Bonaparte & Powell 1980*

Largest ischia   1:20

Camelotia borealis
BMNH R2870-R2874
Length: ~66.5 cm
RECORD:
Longest ischium of the Triassic.
The broken piece measures 22.5 cm.
See more: *Galton 1985*

50 cm

Plateosauravus stormbergensis
SAM 3608
Length: 57 cm
RECORD:
Second longest ischium of the Triassic.
It was known as
Euskelosaurus africanus.
See more: *Haughton 1924*

Side view

Length

Apatosaurus louisae
CM 3018
Length: 128 cm
RECORD:
Longest ischium of the Jurassic.
See more: *Gilmore 1936*

Patagotitan mayorum
MPEF PV 3399
Length: 107.5 cm
RECORD:
Longest ischium of the Cretaceous.
See more: *Carballido et al. 2017*

Smallest ischia   1:5

5 cm

20 cm

Buriolestes schultzi
ULBRA-PVT280
Length: ~8.6 cm
RECORD:
Shortest ischium of the Triassic.
The ilium of juvenile *Pantydraco caducus*
specimen BMNHP24 measures 4 cm.
See more: *Yates 2003; Cabreira et al. 2016*

Panphagia protos
PSVJ-874
Length: ~11.3 cm
RECORD:
Second shortest ischium of the Triassic.
See more: *Martinez & Alcober 2009*

Leonerasaurus taquetrensis
MPEF-PV 1663
Length: 14.6 cm
RECORD:
Shortest ischium of the Jurassic.
See more: *Pol et al. 2011*

Rinconsaurus caudamirus
MRS-Pv 94, 101
Length: 36 cm
RECORD:
Shortest ischium of the Cretaceous.
See more: *Calvo & Riga 2003*

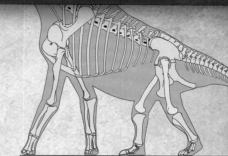

Largest femurs 1:22

FEMURS

The femur is the bone that forms the thigh. Among sauropods in general, it is the bone that supports the most weight.

Measures applied to femurs:

Side view

Length

<u>*Camelotia borealis*</u>
BMNH R2870-R2874
Length: ~108 cm
RECORD:
Longest femur of the Triassic.
See more: *Galton 1985*

<u>*Maraapunisaurus fragillimus*</u>
AMNH 5777
Length: ~300 cm
RECORD:
Longest femur of the Jurassic.
A large distal fragment was not
illustrated or described.
See more: *Cope 1878*

<u>Unnamed</u>
uncatalogued
Length: 236 cm
RECORD:
Longest femur of Africa. Also the
longest of the Middle Jurassic.
Not illustrated.
See more: *Charroud & Fedan 1992*

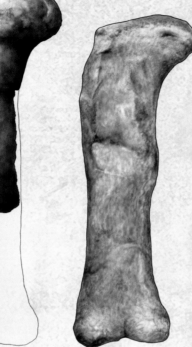
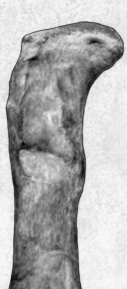

<u>*Brachiosaurus* sp.</u>
uncatalogued
Length: ~220 cm
RECORD:
Longest femur of North America
based on solid evidence.
See more: *Jensen 1985*

<u>*Brachiosaurus altithorax*</u>
uncatalogued
Length: 203 cm
RECORD:
Longest complete femur of North
America.
See more: *Riggs 1903*

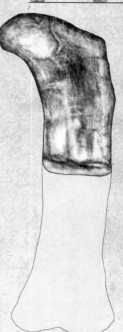

<u>*Diplodocus hallorum (Seismosaurus)*</u>
NMMNH-P3690
Length: ~182 cm
See more: *Gillette 1991*

<u>*Lusotitan atalaiensis*</u>
MIGM Col.
Length: ~195 cm
See more: *Lapparent & Zbyszewski 1957*

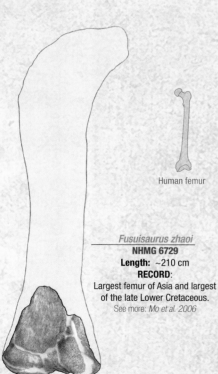

Human femur

<u>*Fusuisaurus zhaoi*</u>
NHMG 6729
Length: ~210 cm
RECORD:
Largest femur of Asia and largest
of the late Lower Cretaceous.
See more: *Mo et al. 2006*

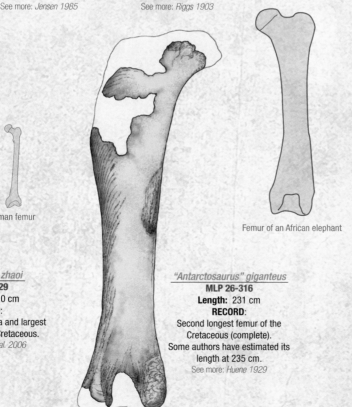

<u>*"Antarctosaurus" giganteus*</u>
MLP 26-316
Length: 231 cm
RECORD:
Second longest femur of the
Cretaceous (complete).
Some authors have estimated its
length at 235 cm.
See more: *Huene 1929*

Femur of an African elephant

50 cm

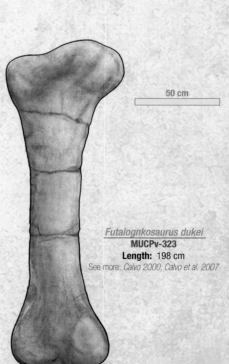

<u>*Futalognkosaurus dukei*</u>
MUCPv-323
Length: 198 cm
See more: *Calvo 2000; Calvo et al. 2007*

Largest femurs   1:22

50 cm

Human femur

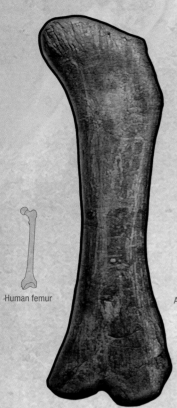

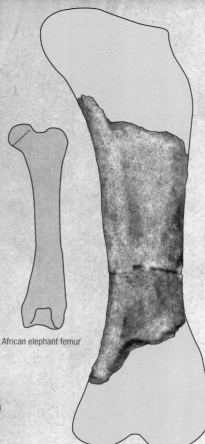

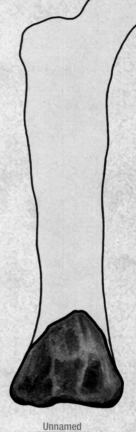

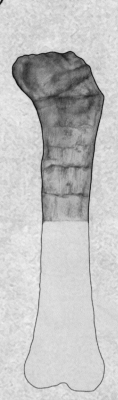

African elephant femur

Patagotitan mayorum
MPEF-3399/44
Length: 238 cm
RECORD:
Longest femur (complete).
See more: *Carballido et al. 2017*

cf. *Argentinosaurus*
MLP-DP 46-VIII-21-3
Length: ~270 cm
RECORD:
Longest femur (incomplete).
See more: *Mazzetta et al. 2004*

Unnamed
ANG 10-400
Length: 220 cm
RECORD:
Longest complete femur of
Europe.
See more: *Néraudeau et al. 2012*

Unnamed
uncatalogued
Length: ~255 cm
RECORD:
Largest incomplete femur of
Europe and of the early Lower
Cretaceous.

Ruyangosaurus giganteus
41HIII-0002
Length: ~207 cm
Its length has been estimated at
235 cm.
See more: *Zhao 1985*

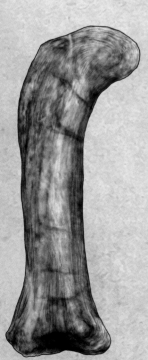

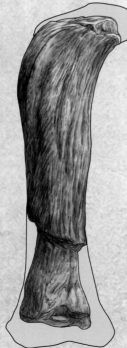

Smallest femurs   1:3

"*Dachungosaurus yunnanensis*"
uncatalogued
Length: ~99.5 cm
RECORD:
Longest bipedal sauropodomorph
femur of the Lower Jurassic
Jingshanosaurus xiwanensis?
See more: *Zhao 1985*

Plateosaurus engelhardti
IFG uncatalogued
Length: 99 cm
RECORD:
Longest bipedal sauropodomorph fe-
mur of the Triassic. From a specimen
on display. Not illustrated.
See more: *Moser 2003; Sander & Klein
2005*

Pampadromaeus barberenai
ULBRA-PVT016
Length: ~12.1 cm
RECORD:
Shortest femur of the Triassic (tie).
See more: *Cabreira et al. 2011*

Alwalkeria maleriensis
ISI R 306
Length: ~12.2 cm
RECORD:
Shortest femur of the Triassic (tie).
See more: *Chatterjee 1987*

Undetermined
FMNH-P 13018
Length: 200 cm
Considered an *Argyrosaurus*.
See more: *Huene 1929; Mannion & Otero
2012*

"*Argyrosaurus*" sp.
uncatalogued
Length: ~207 cm
One of the largest femurs of South
America. The diaphysis is 188 cm
long.
See more: *Huene 1929*

"*Damalasaurus*"
uncatalogued
Length: ~150 cm
RECORD:
Longest femur of the Lower Jurassic.
Not illustrated.
See more: *Zhao 1985*

Smallest femurs   1:3

`3 cm`

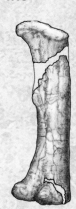

Saturnalia tupiniquin
MCP 3844-PV
Length: 15.7 cm
RECORD:
Third shortest femur of the Triassic.
See more: *Langer et al. 1999; Langer 2003*

Thecodontosaurus minor
uncatalogued
Length: 13.5 cm
RECORD:
Shortest femur of the Jurassic.
See more: *Haughton 1918*

Pantydraco caducus
BMNHP24 (P65/24)
Length: 7.9 cm
RECORD:
Second smallest femur of the Triassic.
It belongs to a juvenile individual.
See more: *Yates 2003*

1:15

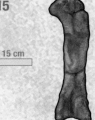

`15 cm`

Meroktenos thabanensis
MNHN LES-16
Length: 51.6 cm
RECORD:
Shortest quadrupedal sauropodomorph
femur of the Triassic.
See more: *Gauffre 1993; Peyre de Fabrègues
& Allain 2016*

1:1

`1 cm`

Massospondylus carinatus
BP/1/5347a
Length: 1.15 cm
RECORD:
Smallest femur of the Jurassic.
It belongs to an embryo.
See more: *Reisz et al. 2005*

Mussaurus patagonicus
PVL 4068
Length: 3 cm
RECORD:
Smallest femur of the Triassic.
From a juvenile.
See more: *Bonaparte & Vince 1979*

1:10

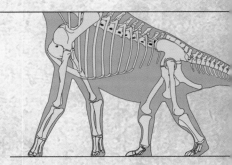

`10 cm`

Europasaurus holgeri
DFMMh/FV415
Length: 51 cm
RECORD:
Shortest sauropod femur of the
Jurassic.
See more: *Sander et al. 2006*

Magyarosaurus dacus
FGGUB R.1992
Length: ~54 cm
RECORD:
Shortest femur of the Cretaceous.
See more: *Nopcsa 1915*

TIBIAS AND FIBULAS

In sauropods, these two leg bones are always shorter than the femur.

Measures applied to tibias and fibulas:

Side view   Side view
Length   Length

Largest tibias   1:20

`20 cm`

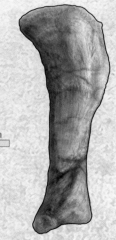

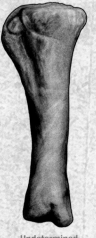

Plateosaurus engelhardti
GPTI V
Length: 80 cm
RECORD:
Longest tibia of the Triassic.
Known as *Pachysaurus wetzelianus*.
See more: *Huene 1932*

Apatosaurus sp.
OMNH 01668
Length: 134 cm
RECORD:
Longest tibia of the Jurassic.
Not illustrated.
See more: *Wilhite 2003*

Ruyangosaurus giganteus
41HIII-0002
Length: 127 cm
RECORD:
Longest tibia of the Cretaceous.
Another incomplete tibia from Argenti-
na has an estimated length of 128 cm.
See more: *Calvo et al. 2002; Lu et al. 2009*

Undetermined
FMNH-P 13020
Length: 124 cm
RECORD:
Third longest tibia of the Cretaceous.
It has been referred to *Antarctosaurus
wichmannianus* and *Argyrosaurus
superbus*.
See more: *Huene 1929; Powell 2003; Mannion
& Otero 2012*

1:5

Buriolestes schultzi
ULBRA-PVT280
Length: ~12.3 cm
RECORD:
Shortest tibia of the Triassic.
The tibia of the *Mussaurus patagoni-
cus* calf PVL 4068 measures 2.69 cm.
See more: *Bonaparte & Vince 1979; Cabreira
et al. 2016*

`5 cm`

Thecodontosaurus minor
uncatalogued
Length: ~11.7 cm
RECORD:
Shortest tibia of the Jurassic. Not
illustrated. The tibia of the *Massopondylus carinatus* embryo BP/1/5347a is
1.1 cm long.
See more: *Haughton 1918; Reisz et al. 2005*

1:10

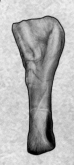

`10 cm`

Bonatitan reigi
MACN RN 821
Length: 38.3 cm
RECORD:
From the embryo of unidenti-
fied species NSM60104403–
20554450. It is 1.82 cm long.
See more: *Martinelli & Forasiepi 2004;
Grellet-Tinner et al. 2011*

ANATOMY   BONES

Largest fibulas 1:20

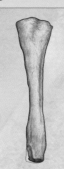

Argentinosaurus huinculensis
PVPH-1
Length: 155 cm
RECORD:
Longest fibula of the Cretaceous.
It was originally thought to be a tibia.
See more: *Janensch 1914*

Plateosaurus engelhardti
GPTI V
Length: 80 cm
RECORD:
Longest fibula of the Triassic.
Known as *Pachysaurus wetzelianus*.
See more: *Huene 1932*

20 cm

Giraffatitan brancai
HMN XV2
Length: 134 cm
RECORD:
Longest fibula of the Jurassic.
Not illustrated.
See more: *Janensch 1914*

Bruhathkayosaurus matleyi
uncatalogued
Length: 200 cm
RECORD:
Longest fibula of the Cretaceous?
Very doubtful; it may be fossilized
wood. Not illustrated.
See more: *Yadagiri & Ayyasami 1989; Krause et al. 2006*

Smallest fibulas 1:10

10 cm

Bonatitan reigi
MACN RN 821
Length: 38.5 cm
RECORD:
Shortest fibula of the Cretaceous.
See more: *Martinelli & Forasiepi 2004*

Buriolestes schultzi
ULBRA-PVT280
Length: ~13.5 cm
RECORD:
Shortest fibula of the Triassic.
The fibula of the juvenile *Pantydraco caducus* specimen BMNHP24 is 6.5 cm long.
See more: *Yates 2003; Cabreira et al. 2016*

Saturnalia tupiniquin
MCP 3844-PV / MCP 3845-PV
Length: 15.4 cm
RECORD:
Second shortest fibula of the Triassic.
The two specimens are equal in length.
See more: *Langer et al. 1999; Langer 2003*

"Gripposaurus" sinensis
IVPP V.27
Length: 20 cm
RECORD:
Shortest fibula of the Jurassic.
The fibula of *Massospondylus carinatus* embryo BP/1/5347A is 1.14 cm long.
See more: *Young 1941; Reisz et al. 2005*

Fact: The fibulas of *Pachysaurus giganteus* were mistakenly identified as metatarsals that would have belonged to a gigantic sauropodomorph, as they are 41–52 cm long. See more: *Huene 1932; Galton 2001*

TARSALS

Tarsals are the bones usually found between the tibia and the metatarsals; they form the ankle.

Measures applied to tarsals:

Side view

10 cm

Length

Largest tarsals 1:10

Plateosaurus engelhardti
GPTI V
Length: 19 cm
RECORD:
Longest calcaneus of the Triassic.
It was known as *Pachysaurus wetzelianus*. Not illustrated.
See more: *Huene 1932*

Diplodocus sp.
CM 30707
Length: 10.9 cm
RECORD:
Longest calcaneus of the Jurassic.
Sauropod calcaneus bones are rarely conserved.
See more: *Bonnan 2000*

Turiasaurus riodevensis
CPT-1195 & 1210
Length: 37 cm
RECORD:
Longest talus of the Jurassic.
See more: *Royo-Torres et al. 2006*

Dreadnoughtus schrani
MPM-PV 1156
Length: 23 cm
RECORD:
Longest talus of the Cretaceous.
See more: *Lacovara et al. 2014*

Elaltitan lilloi
PVL 4628 & MACN-CH 217
Length: 7.1 cm
RECORD:
Longest calcaneus of the Cretaceous.
See more: *Mannion & Otero 2012*

Smallest tarsals 1:1

1 cm

Eoraptor lunensis
PVSJ 512
Length: 1.1 cm
RECORD:
Shortest calcaneus of the Triassic.
See more: *Sereno et al. 1993, 2003*

Saturnalia tupiniquin
MCP 3844-PV
Length: 2.4 cm
RECORD:
Shortest talus of the Triassic.
See more: *Langer 2003*

1:3

3 cm

Ammosaurus major
YPM 208
Length: ~3.3 cm
RECORD:
Shortest calcaneus of the Jurassic.
See more: *Marsh 1889*

Ammosaurus major
YPM 208
Length: ~6.5 cm
RECORD:
Shortest talus of the Jurassic.
See more: *Marsh 1889*

1:10

10 cm

Euhelopus zdanskyi
YPMU.R233a
Length: 14.7 cm
RECORD:
Shortest talus of the Cretaceous.
It may be from the Upper Jurassic.
See more: *Wiman 1929*

METATARSALS

These long bones form the upper part of the foot. Sauropods usually have five of them. In cursorial animals they are often very long and narrow, while in gravi-portal animals they are short and broad.

Measurements applied to metatarsals:

Side view

Length

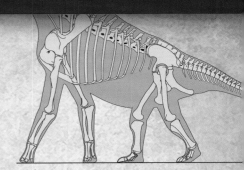

Largest metatarsals 1:10

20 cm

Plateosaurus engelhardti
GPTI V
Length: 38 cm
RECORD:
Longest metatarsal of the Triassic.
It was known as *Pachysaurus wetzelianus*
See more: *Huene 1932*

Jingshanosaurus xiwanensis
LV003
Length: 39.5 cm
RECORD:
Longest metatarsal of the Jurassic.
Sauropods in this period had shorter, more robust metatarsals. The longest belonged to "Cetiosaurus epioolithicus" (sometimes considered "*Cetiosauriscus*" longus), at 32 cm.
See more: *Owen 1842; Zhang & Yang 1994; Upchurch & Martin 2003*

Alamosaurus sanjuanensis
NMMNH P-49967
Length: 29 cm
RECORD:
Longest metatarsal of the Cretaceous.
See more: *D'Emic et al. 2011*

Smallest metatarsals 1:2

Panphagia protos
PSVJ-87
Length: 7.7 cm
RECORD:
Shortest metatarsal of the Triassic.
It belonged to *Pampadromaeus barberenai*. ULBRA-PVT016 may have been ~6 cm, but the piece was never illustrated. The metatarsal of the *Mussaurus patagonicus* calf PVL 4068 is 1.29 cm long.
See more: *Bonaparte & Vince 1979; Martínez & Alcober 2009; Cabreira et al. 2011*

Thecodontosaurus minor
uncatalogued
Length: 6.4 cm
RECORD:
Shortest metatarsal of the Jurassic.
That of *Massopondylus carinatus* embryo BP/1/5347A is 5.1 mm.
See more: *Haughton 1918; Reisz et al. 2005*

2 cm

1:5

Rinconsaurus caudamirus
MRS-Pv 111
Length: 16 cm
RECORD:
Shortest metatarsal of the Cretaceous
Not illustrated in detail.
See more: *Calvo & Riga 2003*

5 cm

PEDAL PHALANGES

The bones found on the digits of the feet are known as phalanges. Claws are a special type known as ungual phalanges.

Measures applied to phalanges and claws:

Side view

Length

Side view

Curvature length

Straight length

Largest pedal phalanges 1:5

10 cm

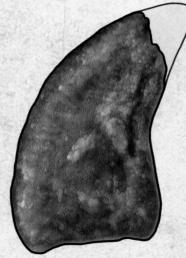

Plateosaurus engelhardti
GPTI V
Straight length: ~14 cm
RECORD:
Longest pedal phalange of the Triassic.
Known as *Gresslyosaurus robustus*, the incomplete piece is 11.5 cm long.
See more: *Huene 1932*

Turiasaurus riodevensis
CPT-1195 & 1210
Straight length: 30 cm
RECORD:
Longest pedal phalange of the Jurassic.
See more: *Royo-Torres et al. 2006*

Unnamed
uncatalogued
Straight length: 34 cm
RECORD:
Longest pedal phalange of the Cretaceous. It is also the longest of Europe (unpublished).
See more: *Tournepiche 2015*

Alamosaurus sanjuanensis
NMMNH P-49967
Straight length ~23.7 cm
RECORD:
Longest pedal phalange of North America.
See more: *D'Émic et al. 2011*

Largest pedal phalanges 1:1

Eoraptor lunensis
PVSJ 512
Straight length: 2.7 cm
RECORD:
Shortest pedal phalange of the Triassic. The shortest measures 1.1 cm.
See more: *Sereno et al. 1993; 2003*

Thecodontosaurus minor
uncatalogued
Straight length: 3.6 cm
RECORD:
Shortest pedal phalange of the Jurassic.
See more: *Haughton 1918*

`1 cm`

Bonatitan reigi
MACN 821 RN 1061
Straight length: ~4.3 cm
RECORD:
Shortest pedal phalange of the Cretaceous. It belonged to an individual 20% smaller than the largest known specimen.
See more: *Salgado et al. 2014*

CLUBS

A few sauropods developed clubs, bony masses at the tip of their tails, to defend themselves against predators.

Largest clubs 1:7

`10 cm`

Shunosaurus lii
ZDM 5045
Length: 25 cm
RECORD:
Largest sauropod club.
See more: *Zhang 1988*

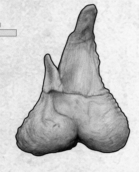

Spinophorosaurus nigeriensis
GCP-CV-4229 (HB 62)
Length: 29 cm
MYTH:
Longest sauropod club?
These were sternal bones that were mistaken for osteoderms.
See more: *Remes et al. 2009; Mocho et al. 2015*

Smallest clubs 1:7

`10 cm`

"Mamenchisaurus" hochuanensis
ZDM 0126
Length: 15.6 cm
RECORD:
Smallest sauropod club.
This apparently belonged to a genus and species different from *M. hochuanensis*.
See more: *Zhang 1988; Sekiya 2011*

INTEGUMENT (skin and its specialized forms)

The integumentary system covers an animal completely and includes skin, dermal plates, osteoderms, beaks, horns, and nails.

Dermal plates and osteoderms

Some sauropods developed ossified skin structures (osteoderms), while others had non-ossified ones (dermal plates).

Saltasaurus loricatus?
uncatalogued
Length: 39 cm
RECORD:
Longest osteoderm of South America. Not yet formally described.
See more: *Powell 1986, 2003; D'Emic et al. 2009*

Largest osteoderms 1:7

Diplodocus sp.
Uncatalogued
Length: ~18 cm
RECORD:
Largest dermal plate of the Jurassic. Subadult specimen.
See more: *Czerkas 1992*

`10 cm`

Rapetosaurus krausei
FMNH PR 2342
Length: 57 cm
RECORD:
Largest osteoderm of Africa.
In contrast, the largest morphotype 1 (elipsoid) osteoderm has a volume of 9.63 liters.
See more: *Curry Rogers 2001; D'Emic et al. 2009; Curry-Rogers et al. 2011*

Lohuecotitan pandafilandi
HUE 00950 (HUE-EC-11)
Length: 52 cm
RECORD:
Largest osteoderm of Europe.
See more: *Vidal et al. 2014; Díez-Díaz et al. 2016*

Unnamed
AMNH 1959
Length: 31.4 cm
RECORD:
Largest osteoderm of Asia.
See more: *D'Emic et al. 2009*

Ampelosaurus atacis
MDE-C3-192
Length: 28 cm
See more: *Le Loeuff et al. 1994*

Alamosaurus sanjuanensis
USNM 15660
Length: 24 cm
RECORD:
Largest osteoderm of North America.
See more: *Carrano & D'Emic 2015*

Laplatasaurus madagascariensis
UCB 92827 (FSL 92827)
Length: 25 cm
RECORD:
Largest morphotype 3 (cylindrical) osteoderm. The first sauropod osteoderm ever discovered.
See more: *Deperet 1896; D'Emic et al. 2009*

Nequensaurus australis
MPCA-Pv 45
Length: 20 cm
RECORD:
Largest morphotype 2 (keeled) osteoderm.
See more: *Salgado et al. 2003, 2005*

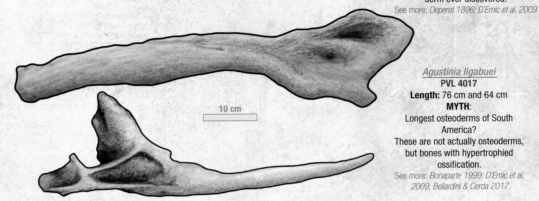

10 cm

Agustinia ligabuei
PVL 4017
Length: 76 cm and 64 cm
MYTH:
Longest osteoderms of South America?
These are not actually osteoderms, but bones with hypertrophied ossification.
See more: *Bonaparte 1999; D'Emic et al. 2009; Bellardini & Cerda 2017*

Smallest osteoderms 1:3

5 cm

1:1

1 cm

Unnamed
CPP-674
Length: 7.5 cm
RECORD:
Largest morphotype 4 (mosaic) osteoderm.
See more: *Marinho & Candeiro 2005*

Unnamed
uncatalogued
Length: 3.7 cm
RECORD:
Smallest morphotype 1 (elipsoid) osteoderm.
See more: *Powell 1980*

Unnamed
C.S.1200
Length: 7.2 cm
RECORD:
Smallest morphotype 2 (keeled) osteoderm.
See more: *Huene 1929*

Saltasaurus loricatus
PVL 4017
Length: 0.7 cm
RECORD:
Smallest morphotype 4 (mosaic) osteoderm. These were found together in a large group.
See more: *Powell 2003*

First armored sauropod
Saltasaurus loricatus

The first sauropod osteoderms discovered (*Lametasaurus*, *Neuquensaurus*) were thought to be ankylosaurs, until proven to belong to *Saltasaurus*.
See more: *Matley 1923; Huene 1929; Bonaparte & Powell 1980*

TEETH

The teeth are organs that are housed in the premaxillary and maxillary (bones of the upper jaw) and in the dentary (bones of the lower jaw).

Measures applied to teeth:

- **CH**: Crown height
- **APW**: Anteroposterior width
- **LMT**: Lateromedial thickness

CH

crown

root

Side view

LMT

APW

Side view

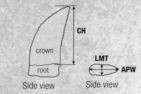

Largest teeth 1:1

<u>*Buriolestes schultzi*</u>
ULBRA-PVT280
CH: ~6 mm
APW: 3 mm
RECORD:
Largest ziphodont tooth of the Triassic.
The smallest measures CH: ~1.4 mm
and APW: ~1.4 mm.
See more: *Cabreira et al. 2016*

<u>*"Fendusaurus eldoni"*</u>
FGM998GF 13-II
CH: 9.7 mm
APW: 5.9 mm
RECORD:
Largest lanceolate-foliodont tooth of
the Jurassic.
Described in a doctoral thesis but not
yet formally published.
See more: *Fedak 2007*

<u>*Plateosaurus longiceps*</u>
uncatalogued
CH: 17 mm
APW: 8 mm
RECORD:
Largest lanceolate-foliodont tooth of the
Triassic. Originally known as *Gresslyosaurus
plieningeri*. The tooth "*Thecodontosaurus*"
elisae measures CH: ~20 mm and APW: 13
mm, but it was not from a dinosaur.
See more: *Sauvage 1907; Huene 1914; Galton
1985*

<u>*Archaeodontosaurus descouensis*</u>
HNDPal 2003-396
CH: ~18.8 mm
APW: ~13.7 mm
RECORD:
Largest lanceolate-foliodont tooth of
the Jurassic.
See more: *Buffetaut 2005*

1:2

<u>*Neosodon praecursor*</u>
BHN2R 113
CH: 60 mm
APW: 35 mm
RECORD:
Largest triangular-crowned spatulate-
foliodont tooth of the Jurassic.
Largest tooth of Europe
See more: *Moussaye 1885*

<u>*Oplosaurus armatus*</u>
GSI 20005
CH: 51 mm
APW: ~24.5 mm
RECORD:
Largest triangular-crowned spatulate-
foliodont tooth of the Cretaceous. It is
85 mm high, including the root.
See more: *Gervais 1852; Lydekker 1893*

<u>*Omeisaurus tianfuensis*</u>
T5705
CH: 42 mm
APW: 26 mm
RECORD:
Largest broad triangular-crowned,
spatulate-foliodont tooth of the
Jurassic.
See more: *He et al. 1984, 1988*

<u>*Barapasaurus tagorei*</u>
ISIR 717
CH: 24 mm
APW: 15 mm
RECORD:
The complete piece is 58 mm long.
Specimens ISIR 721 & ISIR 720 were
wider and shorter, measuring CH:
~20–20.5 / APW: ~16.5–16 mm.
See more: *Bandyopadhyay et al. 2010*

<u>Unnamed</u>
UT-TENi5
CH: 74 mm (incomplete)
APW: 33.4 mm
RECORD:
Largest circular-crowned, spatulate-
foliodont tooth of the Cretaceous.
Largest tooth of Africa.
See more: *Le Loeuff et al. 2010*

5 cm

<u>*Camarasaurus supremus*</u>
AMNH 5761
CH: 50 mm
APW: 35 mm
RECORD:
Largest broad circular-crowned spatu-
late-foliodont tooth of the Jurassic.
Largest tooth of North America.
See more: *Cope 1877; Osborn 1921*

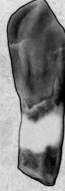

<u>*Brachiosaurus* sp.</u>
NA USVM 5737
CH: ~57 mm
APW: ~33 mm
RECORD:
Highest circular-crowned spatulate-
foliodont tooth of the Jurassic.
It is ~102 mm high, including the root.
See more: *Carpenter & Tidwell 1997*

<u>*Yongjinglong datangi*</u>
GSI 20005
CH: 81 mm
APW: 27 mm
RECORD:
Longest spatulate-foliodont tooth of
the Cretaceous. It is 124 mm high,
including the root. Largest tooth of
Asia (tie).
See more: *Saegusa & Ikeda 2014*

<u>*Asiatosaurus mongoliensis*</u>
AMNH 6296
CH: 74 mm (incomplete)
APW: 27 mm
RECORD:
Largest tooth of Asia (tie).
See more: *Osborn 1924*

Unnamed
MML-Pv 1030
CH: 75 mm
APW: 15 mm
LMT: 11 mm
RECORD:
Largest type-D cylindrodont tooth.
See more: *Garcia 2012*

Rebbachisaurus garasbae
MUCPv-205
CH: 48 mm
APW: 14 mm
RECORD:
Largest type-O cylindrodont tooth of
the Cretaceous.
Not illustrated.
See more: *Russell 1996*

Morinosaurus typus
MPEF-PV 1716
CH: 50 mm
APW: 16 mm
GML: 16 mm
RECORD:
Largest type-O cylindrodont tooth of
the Jurassic.
Widest morphotype 5 tooth.
See more: *Sauvage 1874*

Mongolosaurus haplodon
AMNH 6717
CH: 27 mm
APW: 9 mm
LMT: 7 mm
RECORD:
Cylindrodont tooth with the largest
serrated edges.
See more: *Gilmore 1933*

1:1

Ampelosaurus atacis
MDE C3-52
CH: 21 mm
APW: 6 mm
LMT: 3.3 mm
RECORD:
Largest mixed tooth. Specimen C3–396
displays alveoli up to 9 mm in diameter.
See more: *Le Loeuff 1995, 2005*

Riojasaurus insertus
MPEF-PV 1716
CH: ~10.5 mm
APW: ~5 mm
RECORD:
Largest cylindrodont tooth of the
Triassic.
It belonged to a calf.
See more: *Bonaparte & Pumares 1995*

Nigersaurus taqueti
MNN GDF512
CH: 25 mm
APW: 4 mm
RECORD:
Smallest type-O cylindrodont tooth of
the Jurassic.
See more: *Sereno et al. 1999*

1:2

Unnamed
MPZ 97/557
CH: 22 mm
APW: 4.8 mm (4 mm on the distal part)
Intermediate tooth.
While most sauropod teeth are clas-
sified as phylodonts (leaf-shaped) or
cylindrodonts, this piece is unusual in
having a cylindrical base and a broad,
leaf-shaped tip.
See more: *Bonaparte & Pumares 1995*

Smallest teeth **X2** 🔍

Eoraptor lunensis
PVSJ 512
CH: 2 mm
APW: 1 mm
RECORD:
Largest palatal tooth of the Triassic.
The smallest are 0.5 mm in
diameter.
See more: *Sereno et al. 2013*

Unnamed
ISRNB R211
CH: ~14.6 mm
APW: ~9.3 mm
RECORD:
Smallest spatulate tooth of the
Triassic.
See more: *Godefroit & Knoll 2003*

Saturnalia tupiniquin
MCP 3844-PV
CH: ~4.2 mm
APW: ~2 mm
RECORD:
Smallest lanceolate-foliodont
tooth of the Triassic.
See more: *Langer et al. 1999*

Pitekunsaurus macayai
BHN2R 113
CH: ~27.5 mm
APW: 4.8 mm
GML: 3.8 mm
RECORD:
Smallest type-D cylindrodont tooth of
the Cretaceous.
See more: *Filippi & Garrido 2008*

Atsinganosaurus velauciensis
MHN-Aix-PV.1999.48
CH: 24.5 mm
APW: 5.5 mm
GML: 4.5 mm
RECORD:
Smallest foliodont tooth of the Creta-
ceous. Specimen MHN-AixPV.1999.21
measures CH:16 mm and APW:4 mm
LMT: 3 mm
See more: *Diez-Diaz et al. 2013*

They belonged to juvenile individuals

Thecodontosaurus minor
uncatalogued
CH: 7 mm
APW: ~3 mm
RECORD:
Smallest lanceolate-foliodont tooth
of the Jurassic.
See more: *Haughton 1918*

Mussaurus patagonicus
PVL 4068
CH: ~3.8 mm
APW: ~0.8 mm
RECORD:
Smallest sauropodomorph tooth
of the Triassic. The smallest teeth
measure approximately CH: ~5.5
mm and APW: ~0.5 mm.
See more: *Reisz et al. 2013*

cf. *Lufengosaurus* sp.
C2019 2A233
CH: ~1 mm
APW: ~1 mm
RECORD:
Smallest sauropodomorph tooth
of the Jurassic.
It belongs to a newborn calf.
See more: *Reisz et al. 2013*

Pleurocoelus cf. valdensis
BMNH R1626
CH: 29 mm
APW: 5.8 mm
RECORD:
Smallest foliodont tooth of the
Cretaceous.
Incomplete piece.
See more: *Ruiz-Omeñaca & Canudo 2005*

Titanosaurus rahioliensis
GSI 20005
CH: 39 mm (incomplete)
APW: 8.5 mm
GML: 7.5 mm
RECORD:
Smallest cylindrodont tooth of Hindustan.
Specimen GSI 20000 measures CH:3.2
mm / APW: 4mm / LMT: 4.5 mm.
See more: *Diez-Diaz et al. 2013*

Unnamed
MCF-PVPH Col.
CH: 1 mm
APW: 0,26 mm
LMT: 0,14 mm
RECORD:
Smallest cylindrodont tooth.
It belongs to an embryo or newborn
calf. The largest measure CH: 3mm /
APW: 0.29 mm / LMT: 0.16 mm.
See more: *Chiappe et al. 2001; Garcia & Cerda 2010*

Unnamed
CHVm03.Col.
CH: 2.9 mm
APW: 1 mm
RECORD:
Smallest foliodont tooth of the
Cretaceous.
See more: *Barrett et al. 2016*

Camarasaurus sp.
BYUVP 8967
CH: 9 mm
APW: 3 mm
RECORD:
Smallest sauropod tooth of the
Jurassic.
See more: *Britt & Naylor 1994*

Yunnanosaurus huangi
IVPP V94
CH: 12 mm
APW: 9 mm
RECORD:
Smallest spatulate-foliodont tooth of
the Jurassic.
See more: *Young 1951*

Europasaurus holgeri
DFMMh/FV 427
CH: 23.7 mm
APW: 8.5 mm
RECORD:
Smallest spatulate-foliodont
tooth of the Jurassic.
Another piece also exists,
measuring 5.8 mm high.
See more: *Laven 2011*

ANATOMICAL RECORDS OF PRIMITIVE SAUROPODOMORPHS AND SAUROPODS

1836—England—First sauropodomorph lanceolate-foliodont tooth

Based on the shape of the teeth, it was thought to belong to the lizard species *Thecodontosaurus antiquus*, then was later included in the Dinosauria clade. See more: *Riley & Stutchbury 1836; Morris 1843*

1841—England—First sauropod species based on a single tooth

Although it was suspected that *Cardiodon* ("heart-shaped tooth") was a *Cetiosaurus* tooth piece, it was classified separately and even given its own family, "Cardiodontidae." See more: *Owen 1841; Lydekker 1895*

1852—Spain, England—Smallest Cretaceous sauropod with triangular-crowned foliodont-spatulate teeth

Oplosaurus armatus was considered a brachiosaurid for a long time, but the shape of the teeth reveals that it was a more primitive sauropod. It may have been 15.6 m long and weighed 12.4 t. See more: *Gervais 1852; Royo-Torres & Cobos 2007; Mocho et al. 2013*

1856—Germany—First sauropodomorph pelvic bone

It belongs to *Gresslyosaurus ingens* specimen NMB NB10. It was reported as *Dinosaurus gresslyi* a year before receiving its current name. See more: *Rutimeyer 1857*

1858—Maryland, USA—First sauropod oval-crowned spatulate-foliodont tooth

Astrodon was described a year after being discovered. It was named "star-toothed" because dentist Christopher Johnston discovered a star-shaped pattern when he sliced the piece into cross sections. See more: *Johnston 1859*

1865—Connecticut, USA—First sauropodomorph claws

The holotype of *Anchisaurus polyzelus* (formerly *Megadactylus*) includes four claws, but only two are complete. See more: *Hitchcock 1865; Marsh 1896*

1869—England—First sauropod claw

The large claw of piece BMNH 32498–99 gave it the name *Gigantosaurus megalonyx* ("giant large-clawed lizard"). See more: *Seeley 1869a*

1871—England—First sauropod leg bones

The femur BMNH R1095 and tibia BMNH R1096, belonging to *Cetiosaurus oxoniensis*, revealed that it was a terrestrial animal, not an aquatic one as previously believed. See more: *Phillips 1871*

1871—England—First sauropod breast bones

Cetiosaurus oxoniensis specimens BMNH R1092 and OUMNH J13614 had sternal plates. See more: *Phillips 1871*

1871—England—First sauropod chevrons

The *Cetiosaurus oxoniensis* lectotype specimen OUMNH J13605 conserved some chevrons. See more: *Phillips 1871*

1874—France—First sauropod type-O cylindrodont tooth

This *Morinosaurus typus* tooth is now lost. See more: *Sauvage 1874*

1874—France—Holotype specimen of a Jurassic sauropod known from the tiniest material

Morinosaurus typus is based on a tooth 5 cm high, with an anterioposterior length of 1.6 cm and a longitudinal length of 1.2 cm. The piece is now lost. See more: *Sauvage 1874*

1877—USA—First sauropod to be identified with the presence of articular cartilage

The surface of the articular limb joints of *Dystrophaeus viaemalae* were rough, indicating that they had more articular cartilage than modern mammals. We now know that this was common in all sauropods. See more: *Cope 1877; Huene 1922; Scharz, Wings & Meyer 2007; Holliday et al. 2010*

1877—Colorado, USA—First sauropod cervical vertebrae

Camarasaurus supremus comprises several specimens that were found together, and several individuals were classified with the same catalogue number (AMNH 5760). See more: *Cope 1877*

1877—Colorado, USA—First sauropod skull and jaw

It belongs to *Camarasaurus supremus* and was the only cranium known at that time. Some people believed that the head of *Brontosaurus* was very similar. See more: *Cope 1877*

1877—Colorado, USA—First almost complete sauropod

The *Camarasaurus supremus* specimen AMNH 5761 contained enough bones to enable a reliable reconstruction, assisted by numerous other specimens found nearby. John A. Ryder directed the creative effort. See more: *Cope 1877*

1877—USA—First sauropod sacral vertebrae

The holotype of *Atlantosaurus immanis* YPM 1835 is an incomplete sacrum. See more: *Marsh 1877*

1878—USA—Jurassic sauropod with the fewest cylindrodont teeth

Diplodocus longus had 8 premaxillary and 18–22 maxillary teeth, as well as 20 in the dentary, for a total of 46–50. See more: *Marsh 1878; McIntosh & Berman 1975*

1883—USA—First sauropod skull and jaw placed on the wrong skeleton

The skull YPM 1911 was used for the first illustration of the *Brontosaurus excelsus* skeleton, as well as for the skeleton assembled in 1905. Some investigators believe that it was actually the skull of a sauropod similar to *Camarasaurus* or *Brachiosaurus*. See more: *Marsh 1883, 1891; Carpenter & Tidwell 1997; Taylor 2010; Tschopp et al. 2015; Taylor**

1883—USA—First sauropod body mass estimation

For the first time, the probable weight of *Brontosaurus excelsus* was formally estimated at 20 t, which is very close to some current estimations, as the weight of the holotype specimen was around 14.9–15.5 t, while larger specimens were estimated to be 16.5 t. See more: *Marsh 1877, 1878; Marsh 1883; Paul 2010*

1890—South Dakota, USA—Sauropod with the shortest legs in proportion to its size

Barosaurus lentus had very short hind legs, equal to 9% of its total length, largely because its neck and tail were extremely long. See more: *Marsh 1890; Paul**

1890—South Dakota, USA—Sauropod with the smallest head in proportion to its size

It is estimated that the skull of *Barosaurus lentus* was just 2% of its total length. See more: *Marsh 1890; Paul**

1890—England—Least elongated Cretaceous sauropod tooth

Some *Pleurocoelus valdensis* teeth were just 1.02 times as high as they were wide. See more: *Lydekker 1890; D'Emic et al. 2013*

1891—USA—First sauropodomorph cervical vertebrae

Some conserved vertebrae showed that the neck of *Yaleosaurus colurus* (now *Anchisaurus polyzelus*) was disproportionately long for the animal's size. See more: *Marsh 1893*

1891—USA—First sauropodomorph skull

Yaleosaurus colurus (now *Anchisaurus polyzelus*) is the first skull known completely enough for a reliable reconstruction. See more: *Marsh 1891*

1891—USA—First almost complete sauropodomorph

The large amount of preserved material from *Anchisaurus polyzelus* YPM 1883 enabled the first reconstruction of this species. See more: *Huxley 1865; Marsh 1891*

1891—USA—First case in which the sex of a sauropodomorph was identified

It has been proposed that *Anchisaurus colurus* represents a female *A. polyzelus*. The dimorphism of dinosaur bones is currently in doubt. See more: *Marsh 1891*

1899—USA—Sauropod with the largest head in proportion to its size

Among sauropods, *Camarasaurus lentus* had the proprtionately largest skull, approximately 5% of its total length. See more: *Marsh 1899*

1899—USA—Most pneumatized sauropod

Diplodocus presents more pneumatized vertebrae than any other dinosaur, extending as far as vertebra 19 in the tail. See more: *Osborn 1899; Gilmore 1932; Wedel 2007, 2009*

1901—Wyoming, USA—First sauropod clavicle discovered

Diplodocus carnegii specimen CM 84 is mentioned as having a clavicle; however, the interpretation is doubtful. See more: *Hatcher 1901; Tschopp & Mateus 2012*

1903—Colorado, USA—First sauropod with forelimbs longer than its hind limbs

The name *Brachiosaurus altithorax* means "high-chested arm lizard" as it was the first quadrupedal dinosaur found to have an anterior trunk that was higher than the posterior. See more: *Riggs 1903*

1905—Germany—First sauropodomorph gastralia

The *Plateosaurus longiceps* specimen SMNS 80664 was found with fragmented or loose gastralia. Ten years later, a complete articulated gastrial series was discovered in *Plateosaurus gracilis* (formerly *Sellosaurus*). See more: *Huene 1905, 1915; Fechner & Gößling 2014*

1911—Germany—Sauropodomorph with the most teeth

Plateosaurus longiceps had 5 or 6 teeth in each premaxillary, 48–62 maxillary teeth, and 44–56 in the dentaries, for a total of 98–124 teeth. See more: *Jaekel 1911, 1913; Huene 1926; Galton 1984*

1913—Germany—Sauropodomorph with the most premaxillary teeth

Plateosaurus longiceps had 5 or 6 teeth in each premaxillary, for a total of 10–12 premaxillary teeth. See more: *Jaekel 1913*

1914—Tanzania—Sauropod with the longest forelegs in relation to its hind legs

Giraffatitan brancai had forelimbs that were 107% longer than the total length of its hind legs. See more: *Janensch 1914*

1914—Tanzania—Greatest difference between foreleg and hind leg length

Dicraeosaurus hansemanni was a very upright dinosaur, with forelegs just 60% the length of its hind legs. The average among the Flagellicaudata (dicraeosaurids and diplodocids) is 70%. See more: *Janensch 1914; Schwarz-Wings & Bohm 2014*

1914—Tanzania—Oldest sauropods with high thoracic vertebrae

Dicraeosaurus hansemanni and *D. sattleri* date to the Upper Jurassic (upper Kimmeridgian, approx. 154.6–152.1 Ma). See more: *Janensch 1914; Bailey 1997*

1915—Romania—Smallest sauropod with type-D cylindrodont teeth

Magyarosaurus dacus was a titanosaur that lived on islands; therefore it was a dwarf. Its size was barely 4.9 m long, and it weighed 520 kg. See more: *Nopcsa 1915*

1915—Romania—First small sauropod
Magyarosaurus dacus was the first sauropod to be recognized as a small-size adult. Previously, the young *Pleurocoelus nanus* came to be considered a dwarf species. See more: *Nopcsa 1915; Marsh 1888; Stein et al. 2010*

1915—USA—Sauropod with the most caudal vertebrae
Apatosaurus louisae had a very long tail consisting of 82 vertebrae in all. See more: *Holland 1915*

1915—Hungary, Romania—Smallest sauropod of the Mesozoic
The titanosaur *Magyarosaurus dacus* is the smallest adult sauropod known to date, measuring 5.4 m in length and weighing 520 kg. *Blikanasaurus cromptoni*, 5.4 m long and weighing 420 kg, is considered a sauropod or a derived sauropodiform, by different authors. See more: *Nopcsa 1915; Galton & van Heerden 1985; Stein et al. 2010; McPhee et al. 2015*

1916—South Africa—The Triassic sauropodomorph holotype specimen known from the tiniest material
It was very difficult to correctly identify this record, as several pieces assigned to sauropodomorphs were very fragmented or are isolated pieces that could belong to another type of dinosaur. The most incomplete type material that undoubtedly belongs to a sauropodomorph is the incomplete femur of *Gigantoscelus molengraaffi*, which is the only piece of this species known. The doubtful pieces include "*Plateosaurus*" *ornatus*, a tooth 7.5 mm high and 6 mm in anteroposterior length, very similar in appearance to those of ornithischians. "*Plateosaurus*" *elizae* are teeth measuring 17 mm x 8 mm; this is a doubtful species that could be a theropod or a primitive Archosaurus. The species "*Palaeosaurus*" *fraserianus* consists of a tooth measuring 20 x 6.5 mm but is suspected to be a phytosaur. On the other hand, it is not known whether the tooth known as "*Plateosaurus*" *obtusus*, measuring 26 mm x 8 mm, was a sauropodomorph, theropod, or another indeterminate archosaur. See more: *Henry 1876; Cope 1878; Huene 1905; Sauvage 1907; Hoepen 1916*

1916—South Africa—Sauropodomorph species known from the most incomplete material
Gigantoscelus molengraaffi is based solely on the distal part of a femur. See more: *Hoepen 1916*

1922—Switzerland—Smallest Jurassic sauropod with triangular-crowned, spatulate-foliodont teeth
"*Ornithopsis*" *greppini* of the Upper Jurassic, weighing 1 t. See more: *Huene 1922*

1924—South Africa—Sauropodomorph with the smallest head in proportion to its size
Massospondylus carinatus had a skull that was just 4.4% of its total length. See more: *Haughton 1924*

1924—South Africa—Most elongated Jurassic sauropod tooth
Diplodocus carnegii teeth were 5.32 times higher than they were wide. See more: *Holland 1924; D'Emic, Mannion et al. 2013*

1925—USA—Jurassic sauropod with the fewest foliodont teeth
Camarasaurus lentus had 8 premaxillary teeth, 18–20 maxillary teeth, and 26 in the dentary, for a total of 52–54 teeth. Juveniles had 50 teeth, as specimen CM 11338 shows. See more: *Gilmore 1925; Madsen, McIntosh & Berman 1995*

1926—Germany and South Africa—First sauropodomorph clavicle discovered

Massospondylus carinatus and *Plateosaurus engelhardti* were reported in the same publication. See more: *Huene 1926*

1929—China—Cretaceous sauropod with the most cervical vertebrae
Euhelopus zdanskyi had 17 vertebrae in its neck, so it would have been similar in appearance to a mamenchisaurid, although the two were not closely related. See more: *Wiman 1929*

1929—Argentina—First sauropod with type-D cylindrodont teeth
The teeth of *Antarctosaurus wichmannianus* and "*Titanosaurus*" sp. were considered similar to those of *Diplodocus*. See more: *Huene 1929; Calvo & Gónzalez-Riga 2018*

1929—Argentina—Sauropod with the most cylindrodont teeth
"*Titanosaurus*" sp. had teeth that were 6.45 times taller than they were wide. See more: *Huene 1929; D'Emic et al. 2013*

1936—Tanzania—Sauropod with the most prominent forehead
The nasal and frontal bones of *Giraffatitan brancai* were extremely elevated, forming a very prominent arch. See more: *Janensch 1936*

1942—China—Most robust Jurassic sauropodomorph femur
The femur of *Lufengosaurus magnus* IVPP V.98 had a minimum circumference of 29.5 cm (37.8% the total length of the femur). Other larger specimens exist that may have had thicker femurs. See more: *Young 1942*

1951—China—The most incomplete skull of a sauropodomorph species
The only specimen of *Pachysuchus imperfectus* (IVPP V 40) is based on a fragment of premaxillary, maxillary, and possibly nasal bone. It was considered a phytosaur. See more: *Young 1951; Barrett & Xing 2012*

1951—USA—First study of the barometric consequences of submersion on sauropod lungs
For decades, most sauropods were considered semi-aquatic animals, as they had their noses on top like aquatic animals and had "floaters" between their vertebrae, like air sacs. In 1957 it was demonstrated that water pressure would collapse these creatures' respiratory system. Today there is some doubt as to how sauropods managed to pump blood from the heart to the head. See more: *Kermack 1951; Choy & Altman 1992; Badeer & Hicks 1996; Seymour & Lillywhite 2000; Henderson 2004; Alexander 2006*

1954—Morocco—First sauropod with very high vertebrae
Rebbachisaurus garasbae had a very high back, as the spines of its thoracic vertebrae are extremely elongated. It was thought to have had a "sail" to regulate its temperature, but new studies have identified these structures as humps for storing water and fat. See more: *Lavocat 1954; Bailey 1997*

1954—Morocco—Sauropod with the highest thoracic vertebrae
Rebbachisaurus garasbae had vertebral spines 4.4 times as high as the vertebral body. See more: *Lavocat 1954; Allain 2015*

1957—Portugal—Most robust sauropod femur of the Jurassic
Lusotitan atalaiensis MG 4986 is the thickest, with a minimum circumference of 99.8 cm (49.9% of the estimated length of the femur). See more: *Lapparent & Zbyszewski 1957*

1962–1980—Tanzania—Most extreme weight estimation for a sauropod specimen
The weight of *Giraffatitan brancai* has been estimated with differing results that range from 13,618 t (14,900 US t) to 78,258 t (85,630 US t), a factor of 5.75. Weights vary according to the type

of model, estimated density, and method used, which could include allometric methods based on equations from bone dimensions, volumetric methods based on water or sand displaced, 3-D computer modeling, and graphic double integration, among others. See more: *Janensch 1940; Colbert 1962; Russell, Beland & McIntosh 1980; Anderson et al. 1985; Paul 1988; Alexander 1989; Gunga et al 1995, 2008; Christiansen 1997; Henderson 2004, 2006; Taylor 2010*

1969—Argentina—Sauropodomorph with the longest forelegs in proportion to its hind legs
Riojasaurus incertus had forelegs that were 60% as long as its hind legs. It has been represented as a quadrupedal or bipedal animal. See more: *Bonaparte 1969; Paul 2010; Hartmann**

1972—Zimbabwe—Sauropods with the fewest sacral vertebrae
Basal sauropods display only four vertebrae in the sacrum, *Antetonitrus* and *Shunosaurus* being two examples. See more: *Raath 1972*

1972—China—Jurassic sauropod with the most cervical vertebrae
Mamenchisaurus hochuanensis had 19 vertebrae in its neck. See more: *Young & Zhao 1972*

1977—Mongolia—Sauropod with the fewest phalanges in the feet
Opisthocoelicaudia skarzynskii had seven phalanges in each hind foot. See more: *Borsuk-Białynicka 1977*

1977—Mongolia—Sauropod with the fewest phalanges in its forefeet
Opisthocoelicaudia skarzynskii lacked phalanges completely in its forefeet. See more: *Borsuk-Białynicka 1977*

1977—Mongolia—Sauropod with the fewest caudal vertebrae
Opisthocoelicaudia skarzynskii's tail comprised 34 or 35 vertebrae. See more: *Borsuk-Bialynikca 1977*

1978—Argentina—Least elongated Triassic sauropod tooth
Some teeth of *Coloradisaurus brevis* were just 1.19 times as high as they were wide. See more: *Bonaparte 1978; Mocho et al. 2013*

1981—South Africa—First mistaken report of a sauropodomorph interclavicle
A clavicle of *Massospondylus carinatus* was mistaken for an interclavicle. See more: *Cooper 1981; Yates & Vasconcelos 2005*

1981—Morocco—Sauropod with the longest legs in proportion to its size
Atlasaurus imelakei had hind legs that were 23% of its total length, as it had a very short neck and tail. See more: *Monbaron & Taquet 1981; Monbaron et al. 1999; Paul**

1982–2014—Highest calculated sauropod weights
The highest weight estimated in a scientific publication is 180 t, for *Ultrasaurus mcintoshi*. The estimate is excessive, as specimen BYU 9462 was actually no larger than *Giraffatitan brancai* HMN XV2, which weighed about 48 t. The highest calculation in an official document is 122.4–150 t for *Maraapunisaurus fragillimus*; however, the fossil has been called into doubt, and some authors believe the measurements presented were incorrect. An even greater estimate, this time performed by a reliable investigator, albeit informally, is for the doubtful remains of *Bruhathkayosaurus matleyi*, with a possible range of 175–220 t. In other publications of records, an unnamed titanosaur was estimated as weighing 90–110 t, but this last was smaller than *Argentinosaurus huinculensis*, which apparently has not been surpassed to date, even though its estimated weight has been reduced to 60–100 t. See more: *Cope 1878; Wood 1982; Jensen 1985; Bonaparte & Coria, 1993; Paul 1994; Yadagiri & Ayyasami*

1989; Curtice, Stadtman & Curtice 1996; Mazzetta et al. 2004; Carpenter 2006; Benson et al. 2014; Woodruff & Forster 2014; Mortimer*

1984—China—Sauropod with the shortest tail in proportion to its size

The tail of *Omeisaurus tianfuensis* was 32% of its total length, as it had an exceptionally long neck and a very short tail. See more: *He et al. 1984*

1984—South Africa—Sauropodomorphs with the most sacral vertebrae

Advanced sauropodomorphs, and some primitive ones, are known to have had four vertebrae in the sacrum. The first time this characteristic was discovered, it was identified as "Roccosaurus tetrasacralis," a specimen of *Melanorosaurus readi*. See more: *Heerden in Kitching & Raath 1984; Pol, Garrido & Cerda 2011; García et al. 2016*

1985—Colorado, USA—Largest Jurassic sauropod with type-O cylindrodont teeth

cf. *Barosaurus lentus* BYU 9024 was the longest of all the sauropods, measuring 45 m in length and weighing 60 t. See more: *Jensen 1985, 1987; Taylor & Wedel 2016*

1985—Utah, USA—Largest Jurassic sauropod with oval-crowned spatulate-foliodont teeth

Brachiosaurus sp. may have been a large specimen of *B. altithorax*, 26 m in length and 50 t in weight. See more: *Jensen 1985*

1987—India—Cretaceous sauropod species known from the tiniest material

The *"Titanosaurus" rahioliensis* tooth GSI 20005 is 26 mm high (incomplete), with a 5.5-mm anteroposterior length and a 4-mm labiolingual length. Although there are 35 more teeth associated with this species, it is not known if they belong to the same individual. See more: *Mathur & Srivastava 1987*

1991—Argentina—Sauropod with the fewest cervical vertebrae

Calculations report that *Amargasaurus cazaui* had 11 or 12 neck vertebrae. See more: *Salgado & Bonaparte 1991*

1993—Argentina—Largest Cretaceous sauropod with oval-crowned, spatulate-foliodont teeth

The teeth of *Argentinosaurus huinculensis* are not known, but the creature's likely phylogenetic position means its teeth could have been that shape. It was the largest sauropod, reaching a length of 36 m and a weight of 75 t. See more: *Bonaparte & Coria 1993; Mazzetta et al. 2004*

1993—China—Largest Jurassic sauropod with triangular-crowned, spatulate-foliodont teeth

Mamenchisaurus sinocanadorum was a giant mamenchisaurid 25 m long and weighing 24 t. Specimen IVPP V10603 included one preserved tooth. See more: *Russell & Zheng 1993*

1994—China—Sauropodomorph with the shortest tail in proportion to its size

The tail of *Jingshanosaurus xiwanensis* was 47% of its total length. See more: *Zhang & Yang 1994*

1994—Niger—Least elongated sauropod tooth of the Jurassic

Some teeth of *Jobaria tiguidensis* were as wide as they were high. See more: *Sereno et al. 1994, 1999; D'Emic et al. 2013*

1994—USA—First mistaken report of gastralia in a sauropod

The presence of gastralia were reported for *Apatosaurus yahnahpin* (formerly *Eobrontosaurus*); however, it is now known that these structures were not present in sauropods and were another kind of bone. See more: *Filla & Redman 1994; Claessens*

2004; Tschopp & Mateus 2012

1994—China—Sauropodomorph with the fewest caudal vertebrae

Jingshanosaurus xinwaensis had a tail comprised of 44 vertebrae. See more: *Zhang & Yang 1994*

1995—Argentina—First cylindrical sauropodomorph tooth

The skull of *Riojasaurus incertus* displays type-O cylindrical teeth, which were thought to be unique to diplodocoids. See more: *Bonaparte & Pumares 1995*

1996—Morocco—Largest Cretaceous sauropod with type-O cylindrodont teeth

The largest *Rebbachisaurus garasbae* specimens are known solely from very large cylindrical teeth. This animal was up to 22 m in length and weighed 24 t. See more: *Russell 1996*

1997—South Korea—Sauropod species known from the most incomplete material

Several sauropods are known from their teeth alone, and some such as *Chiayusaurus asianensis* are only known from a single piece. See more: *Lee, Yang & Park 1997*

1997—USA—First primitive sauropodomorph body mass estimations

First formal estimations of the probable weights of *Massospondylus carinatus*, *Plateosaurus engelhardti*, and *Riojasaurus insertus* yielded measurements of 93 kg, 440 kg, and 500 kg, respectively. See more: *Paul 1997*

1997—Spain—Strangest sauropod tooth

This piece, with a very long cylindrical root and spatulate point, seems to be an intermediate form between foliodont and cylindrodont morphotypes. See more: *Cuenca Bescós et al. 1997*

1998—China—Sauropod with the most foot phalanges

Gongxianosaurus shibeiensis had 15 phalanges on each foot. See more: *He et al. 1998*

1998—Argentina—Most robust Triassic sauropodomorph femur

The *Mussaurus patagonicus* femur PVL uncat 4 (1971) is the thickest, with a minimum circumference of 36.5 cm (49.7% of the total femur length). See more: *Carrano 1998*

1998—USA—First study of the supersonic speed of sauropod tails

Computer modeling has estimated that some sauropods such as *Apatosaurus louisae* could flick their tails faster than the speed of sound (more than 1200 km/h) to make noise and defend themselves. However, some researchers doubt that they achieved such extreme speeds. See more: *Alexander 1989, 2006; Myhrvold & Currie 1997; Naish 2011*

1998—Argentina—Sauropodomorph with the shortest neck in proportion to its size

The *Lessemsaurus sauropoides* piece PVL 4822–1 is a sacral vertebra 10.8 cm long. See more: *Bonaparte & Pumares 1995; Paul 2010*

1999—Argentina—Triassic sauropod holotype specimen known from the tiniest material.

The *Lessemsaurus sauropoides* piece PVL 4822–1 is a sacral vertebra 10.8 cm long. See more: *Bonaparte 1999*

1999—Argentina—Cretaceous sauropod with the fewest cylindrodont teeth

An unnamed titanosaur presents 8 premaxillary, 14–16 maxillary, and 22 dentary pieces, for a total of 44–46 teeth. The calves of this species may have had only 20 teeth in the dentary. See more: *Coria & Salgado 1999; García & Cerda 2010*

1999—Niger—Cretaceous sauropod with the most teeth

Nigersaurus taqueti possessed a total of more than 500 active and replacement teeth divided into dental batteries, with 68 columns in the upper jaws and 60 columns in the lower jaws. See more: *Sereno et al. 1999*

1999—Germany—Sauropodomorph with the most caudal vertebrae

The tail of *Plateosaurus* had at least 50 vertebrae in all. See more: *Bonaparte 1999*

2000—France—Sauropodomorph with the longest tail in proportion to its size

The tail of *Thecodontosaurus antiquus* may have been approximately 60% of its total length. See more: *Benton et al. 2000; Headden**

2001—Germany—Sauropodomorph with the fewest thoracic vertebrae

Ruehleia dedheimensis had 13 or 14 vertebrae in the thorax. See more: *Galton 2001*

2002—China—Sauropod with the most foliodont teeth

Shunosaurus lii had 8–10 pieces in the premaxillaries, 34–40 in the maxillaries, and 50–52 in the dentaries, for a total of 184–204 teeth. See more: *Chatterjee & Zheng 2002*

2003—Wales, UK—Sauropodomorph with the fewest foot phalanges

Pantydraco caducus had just 13 phalanges in each foot, fewer than the usual 15. See more: *Yates 2003*

2003—South Africa—Most robust Triassic sauropod femur

Antetonitrus ingenipes BP/1/4952 is a femur with a minimum circumference of 41 cm (52.9% of the femur length). Another incomplete bone, BRSMG Cb3869 (present-day England), which was identified as a giant ornithischian but was likely a large sauropodomorph or sauropod, had a diameter of 43 cm. See more: *Yates & Kitching 2003; Galton 2005*

2003—Wales, UK—Most elongated Triassic sauropodomorph tooth

Pantydraco caducus had teeth that were 2.18 times higher than they were wide. See more: *Yates 2003; Mocho et al. 2013*

2003—Wales, UK— Primitive sauropodomorph with the fewest teeth

Pantydraco caducus had 8 premaxillary, 20 maxillary, and 28 dentary teeth; however, the specimen was a juvenile, and juveniles often had fewer teeth than adults, although this cannot be confirmed here. These specimens were considered *Thecodontosaurus antiquus* calves. On the other hand, *Massospondylus carinatus* calves were believed to have been born toothless, while adults had 96–104 teeth. See more: *Yates 2003; Galton, Yates & Kermack 2007; Reisz et al. 2005, 2010*

2004—South Africa—Most elongated Jurassic sauropodomorph tooth

Massospondylus carinatus had fang-like teeth that were 3.29 times as high as they were wide. See more: *Sues et al. 2004; Mocho et al. 2013*

2004—Argentina—Most robust Cretaceous sauropod femur

Argentinosaurus huinculensis specimen MLP-DP 46-VIII-21–3 is the thickest, with a minimum circumference of 119 cm (44% of the estimated femur length). See more: *Lamanna 2004; Mazzetta, Christiansen & Fariña 2004*

2004—South Africa—Fanged sauropodomorph

Some *Massospondylus carinatus* teeth are so long and cylindrical that they look like fangs. See more: *Sues et al. 2004*

2004—South Africa—First conical sauropodomorph tooth
Some *Massospondylus carinatus* teeth had a conical shape, like fangs. See more: *Sues, Reisz, Hinic & Raath 2004*

2005—Argentina—Smallest Cretaceous sauropod with oval-crowned, spatulate-foliodont teeth
"*Pleurocoelus*" cf. *valdensis* is considered a possibly valid species owing to the shape of its teeth. It may have been 10 m long and weighed 2.4 t. *Campylodoniscus ameghinoi*, *Chondrosteosaurus gigas*, and *Clasmodosaurus spatula* belong to smaller individuals but are considered doubtful. See more: *Owen 1876; Ameghino 1898; Huene 1929; Ruiz-Omeñaca & Canudo 2005*

2005—Argentina—Sauropod with the most sacral vertebrae
Most sauropods had 5 or 6 sacral vertebrae; in contrast, *Neuquensaurus australis* had 7 in all. See more: *Salgado, Apesteguia & Heredia 2005*

2005—Argentina—Sauropod with the longest tail in proportion to its size
The tail of *Brachytrachelopan mesaorum* may have been 64% of the animal's total length. See more: *Rauhut et al. 2005*

2005—Argentina—Largest sauropod with type-D cylindrodont teeth
The shape of lognkosaurian titanosaur teeth is not known, but their similarity to *Malawisaurus* means they were likely cylindrical. This makes *Puertasaurus reuili* the largest in this category, with a length of 28 m and a weight of 50 t. See more: *Novas et al. 2005*

2005—Argentina—Sauropod with the shortest neck in proportion to its size
Unlike virtually all sauropods, *Brachytrachelopan mesai* had a comparatively short neck that was approximately 12.8% of its total length. See more: *Rauhut et al. 2005*

2005—Niger—Fastest tooth replacement for a sauropod
When a *Nigersaurus taqueti*'s tooth was worn out, another took its place almost immediately, in 14–30 days. See more: *Sereno et al. 1999; Sereno & Wilson 2005; D'Emic et al. 2013*

2005—France—Sauropod with the fewest teeth
A specimen of *Ampelosaurus atacis* had just 18 teeth in the dentary. See more: *Le Loeuf 2005; Calvo & Gónzalez-Riga 2018*

2006—Germany—Smallest Jurassic sauropod with oval-crowned, spatulate-foliodont teeth
With a length of 6 m and weighing 760 kg, *Europasaurus holgeri* looked like a small version of *Brachiosaurus*. See more: *Sander et al. 2006*

2007—South Africa—Sauropodomorph with the fewest forefoot phalanges
Melanorosaurus readi presents just nine phalanges on each forefoot. See more: *Bonnan & Yates 2007*

2007—India—The Jurassic sauropodomorph holotype specimen known from the tiniest material
Pradhania gracilis includes an incomplete maxillary, a fragment of neurocranium, a portion of dentary, some teeth, two cervical vertebrae, one sacrum, and parts of digits 1 and 2 of the left forefoot. Its length has been calculated at 4 m. See more: *Kutty et al. 2007*

2007—Switzerland—First sauropod fossil articular cartilage
A large quantity of fossilized articular cartilage at least 3- to 5-cm thick was identified on one end of humerus MH 260, belonging to *Cetiosauriscus greppini*. It is unusual for this type of soft tissue to fossilize. Before this find, the presence and size of this material had only been speculated upon. See more: *Huene 1922; Scharz, Wings & Meyer 2007*

2007—Niger—Sauropod with the most inclined head
The head of *Nigersaurus taqueti* may have been habitually inclined downward, like a vacuum cleaner. However, it is also possible that its natural posture was similar to that of other sauropods. See more: *Sereno et al. 2007; Taylor et al. 2009; Marugán-Lobón et al. 2013*

2007—Argentina—First sauropod egg tooth
In the Anacleto Formation of Auca Mahuevo, a group of titanosaur embryo skulls were found to have a structure known as an "egg tooth," which the animals used to break their shells at birth. Unlike other animals, such as birds, crocodiles, and turtles, this "tooth" was made not of keratin, but of the premaxillary bone itself. Its possible presence was suggested five years before it was confirmed. See more: *Chiappe et al. 2001, Mueller-Towe et al. 2002; Garcia 2007a, 2007b; Garcia et al. 2010*

2008—USA—First case of sex identification of a sauropod?
A histological assessment of the long bones of *Camarasaurus* showed the presence of two distinct morphotypes, one small and one large, which could indicate sexual dimorphism, although it is also possible that they were two different species. See more: *Klein & Sander 2008*

2008—China—Sauropod with the most forefoot phalanges
Tazoudasaurus naimi had 11 phalanges on each forefoot. See more: *Allain & Aquesbi 2008*

2009—South Africa—Sauropodomorph with the most prominent nose
The skull of *Aardonyx celestae* had a very prominent anterior face, a trait that has not been found in any other sauropodomorph. See more: *Yates et al. 2009*

2009—China—First detailed study of a sauropod club
Specimen ZDM 0126 is sometimes referred to as *Mamenchisaurus hochuanensis*, but it was more recent than that. See more: *Ye et al. 2001; Xing et al. 2009*

2010—China—Least elongated Jurassic sauropodomorph tooth
Some teeth of *Lufengosaurus huenei* were just 1.19 times higher than they were wide. See more: *Chure et al. 2010; Mocho et al. 2013*

2010—Thailand—Most elongated Asian sauropod tooth
The teeth of *Phuwiangosaurus* were 6.31 times as high as they were wide. See more: *Chure et al. 2010; Mocho et al. 2013*

2010—China—Strangest sauropodomorph feet
Xixiposaurus suni is the only sauropodomorph with a longer toe IV than toe III (toe III is usually longer). The footprints of *Navahopus coyoteensis* seem to have been made by a similar sauropodomorph. See more: *Milàn et al. 2008; Sekiya 2010*

2011—Brazil—Sauropodomorph with the largest head in proportion to its size
The skull of *Pampadromaeus barberenai* was approximately 8.3% of its total length. See more: *Cabreira et al. 2011*

2011—Brazil—Smallest sauropodomorph of the Mesozoic
This category is difficult to establish as it is not known whether *Pampadromaeus barberenai*, 1.4 m in length and 1.8 kg in weight, was a juvenile or an adult. Specimen CAPPA/UFSM 0027, 15% larger, has also been assigned to this species. In this case, the smallest would be *Alwalkeria maleriensis*, approximately 1.1 m long and 2 kg in weight. See more: *Chatterjee 1987; Cabreira et al. 2011, 2016; Muller et al. 2016*

2011—Utah, USA—Sauropod with the strongest hind legs
It is speculated that the strange shape and unusually large size of *Brontomerus mcintoshi*'s ilium indicate that its hind legs were extra strong. See more: *Taylor et al. 2011*

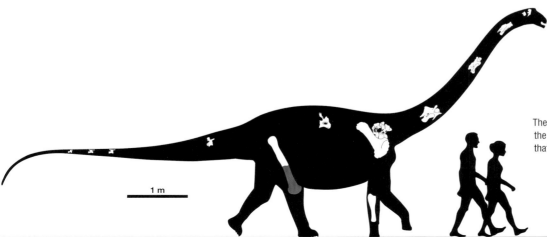

Titanosaur with the smallest head in proportion to its body
Pitekunsaurus macayai

The ratio of the occipital bone to the femur of this sauropod is the most disproportionate among the titanosaurs. This means that its head was relatively small, comparable to the heads of some diplodocoidea. See more: *Filippi & Garrido 2008*

1 m

2012—France—Largest Cretaceous sauropod with triangular-crowned, spatulate-foliodont teeth
The unnamed species ANG 10–10 is based on teeth very similar to those of *Turiasaurus riodevensis*, so it may have been around 19 m long and 22 t in weight. See more: *Néraudeau et al. 2012*

2012—Wyoming, USA—First sauropod interclavicles discovered
Five interclavicles from possible diplodocids have been reported. See more: *Tschopp & Mateus 2012*

2013—China—Cretaceous sauropod with the fewest foliodont teeth
The skull of *Euhelopus zdanskyi* was reconstructed with 8 premaxillary, 20 maxillary, and 26 dentary teeth, for a total of 54. See more: *Wiman 1929; Poropat & Kear 2013*

2013—China—The sauropod with the proportionally longest neck
The neck of *Xinjiangtitan shanshanesis* was equivalent to approximately 55% of its total length. See more: *Wu et al. 2013*

2013—Argentina—Sauropodomorph with the fewest cervical vertebrae
Like primitive theropods, *Eoraptor lunensis* had just nine vertebrae in the neck. See more: *Sereno 2013*

2013—China—Cretaceous sauropod with the longest neck in proportion to its total length
Erketu ellisoni had a neck that was approximately 47% of its total length. See more: *Ksepka & Norell 2006*

2013—Niger—Sauropod with the strangest tooth enamel
The teeth of *Nigersaurus taqueti* were notably asymmetrical, ten times thicker on the exterior side than the interior. See more: *D'Emic et al. 2013*

2013—South Africa—Sauropodomorph tooth replacement
The teeth of *Massospondylus carinatus* were in use for just 17–30 days, on average. No information is available about its relatives. See more: *D'Emic et al. 2013*

2013—USA—Sauropod with the most rigid neck
The complex structure of the cervical vertebrae of *Barosaurus lentus* allowed tremendous lateral flexibility but very limited vertical movement, indicating that the animal may have obtained its food from the ground, or sat down to raise its neck, as some researchers suggest. See more: *Siegwarth et al. 2011*

2013—Tunisia—Only pneumatized ischium in a sauropod
Tataouinea hannibalis was so pneumatized that even the ischium presents that condition, a unique characteristic among dinosaurs. See more: *Fanti et al. 2013*

2013—Wyoming, USA—Smallest Jurassic sauropods with type-0 cylindrodont teeth
Kaatedocus siberi was 14 m long and weighed 1.9 t, while *Brachytrachelopan mesai* was shorter, just 9 m long, but weighed 2.4 t. See more: *Rauhut et al. 2005; Tschopp & Mateus 2013*

2014—USA—The lowest estimated body temperature in a sauropod
An analysis deduced that *Apatosaurus* had a body temperature of 16° C, a controversial finding, as body temperatures were usually calculated as 36° to 38° C. See more: *Grady et al. 2014; Eagle et al. 2015*

2014—Tanzania—Slowest sauropod tooth replacement
Estimates show that the premaxillary teeth of *Tornieria africana* remained in use for 96–162 days on average. See more: *Sattler 2014*

2014—Japan—Sauropod with the largest chevrons relative to its size
The chevrons of *Tambatitanis amicitiae* are 41 cm high, making them proportionately large for the animal's sizes. See more: *Saegusa & Ikeda 2014*

2014—Argentina—Most incomplete skull of a sauropod species
The head of *Dreadnoughtus schrani* (MPM-PV 1156) is known solely from a fragment of maxillary. Although it has been reconstructed in elongated form, it seems to be similar to the reconstructed skull of *Malawisaurus dixeyi* or *Antarctosaurus wichmannianus*, its closest relatives, which had short faces. See more: *Lacovara et al. 2014*

2015—Argentina—First ossified ligaments in sauropods
Thick ossified ligaments were found on the sacral vertebrae spines of *Epachthosaurus sciuttoi* UNPSJB-PV 920 and the unnamed species MDT-Pv 4. These ossified ligaments only occur in titanosauriforms, and their function is a mystery. See more: *Cerda et al. 2015*

2016—Brazil—Sauropodomorph with the longest hind legs in proportion to its size
The legs of *Buriolestes schultzi* were 26% of the length of its body. See more: *Cabreira et al. 2016*

2016—Argentina—Strangest sauropod feet
Notocolossus Gónzalezparejasi had truncated ungual phalanges, a trait unknown in any other sauropod. It may have been an adaptation to support its enormous size. See more: *González-Riga, Lammanna et al. 2016*

2016—Brazil—Sauropodomorph with the shortest foreleg in relation to its hind legs.
Buriolestes schultzi's forelegs may have been just 40% of the length of its hind legs. See more: *Cabreira et al. 2016*

2016—Brazil—Sauropod with the largest teeth in proportion to its size
Buriolestes schultzi had large, knife-shaped (zyphodont) dental pieces. The largest ones of the maxillary were 5.5% of the length of its skull. See more: *Cabreira et al. 2016*

2016—Brazil—First sauropodomorph with zyphodont teeth
Buriolestes schultzi is the only one that presents knife-shaped teeth. It was a very primitive species. See more: *Cabreira et al. 2016*

2016–2017—Argentina, China—Bipedal sauropodomorphs with the most sacral vertebrae
Xingxiulong chengi and another unnamed species from Argentina present four vertebrae in the sacrum. Before it was discovered, that number of vertebrae had been exclusive to quadrupedal sauropodomorphs and primitive sauropods. See more: *García et al. 2016; Wang, You & Wang 2017*

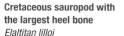

Cretaceous sauropod with the largest heel bone
Elaltitan lilloi

The heel bone was in a cartilaginous state in many sauropods, so it is almost never preserved. However, it calcified in some species, including *Camarasaurus, Diplodocus, Gobititan,* and *Neuquensaurus*. See more: *Huene 1929; Bonnan 1999, 2000; You et al. 2003; Mannion & Otero 2012*

1 m

2017—New Mexico, USA—Largest preserved sauropod tendon
An ossified tendon 1.8 m long came from the neck of specimen LACM 7948, an intermediate titanosaur of the late Upper Cretaceous. See more: *Bansal 2017*

2018—India—Oldest sauropod with a club tail
Caudal clubs were identified on the bones of different individuals of *Kotasaurus yamanpalliensis*. The largest is 30.8 cm long and 21.1 cm wide. See more: *Kareem & Wilson 2018*

RECORDS OF FOSSIL SKIN IMPRESSIONS, BEAKS, AND OSTEODERMS IN PRIMITIVE SAUROPODOMORPHS AND SAUROPODS

An outstanding feature of some species in this group is the presence of osteoderms. Recent interpretations suggest that a titanosaur's osteoderms served as a source of calcium, but this hypothesis about titanosaur osteoderms is still open to debate. See more: *Gomes-Da Costa Pereira et al. 2018*

1852—England—First sauropod skin impression of Europe
The skin of *Haestasaurus becklesii* (formerly *Pelorosaurus*) had several hexagonal marks, the largest being 21 x 20 cm, and the smallest from 95 x 68 to 26 x 9 mm in diameter. See more: *Mantell 1852; Upchurch et al. 2015*

1888—USA—First sauropod skin impression of North America
It was mistaken for a bone structure instead of a skin impression. See more: *Marsh 1888*

1896—Madagascar—First osteoderm discovered in Southern Africa
"*Titanosaurus*" *madagascariensis* (also known as "*Laplatasaurus*") was the first sauropod found with osteoderms (specimen FSL 92827). The osteoderms were cylindrical, the least common of all known morphotypes. See more: *Déperet 1896; D'Emic et al. 2009*

1877—India—First osteoderm discovered in eastern Asia
Material assigned to *Lametasaurus indicus* (a chimera with sauropod and theropod characteristics) includes some large plates that were related to armored ornithischians (stegosaurians). See more: *Lydekker 1877*

1923—India—Greatest concentration of osteoderms
Some 5000 *Lametasaurus indicus* shields were found in the same zone. See more: *Matley 1923*

1929—Argentina—First osteoderm discovered in southern South America
Mosaic-type osteoderms were described 51 years before being linked to *Saltasaurus*. See more: *Huene 1929*

1929—Argentina—First keeled osteoderm
The first osteoderms with one or more keels on their internal surface. See more: *Huene 1929*

1933—India—First elipsoid osteoderm
Specimen AMNH 1959 is one of the most recent, dating to the end of the late Upper Cretaceous (upper Maastrichtian, approx. 66 Ma). See more: *Huene & Matley 1933; Courtillot et al. 1986, 1996; Allégre et al. 1999; D'Emic et al. 2012*

1937—Utah, USA—First osteoderm found in North America
Specimen USNM 15660 has been assigned to *Alamosaurus sanjuanensis*, 75 years after being discovered. See more: *Gilmore 1938, 1946; Carrano & D'Emic 2015*

1970—Zimbabwe—Largest armored sauropod of the early Lower Cretaceous
Sauropods 9 m long and weighing 2.4 t have been found associated with osteoderms. Thanks to these and their procelic vertebrae, we know they are the oldest lithostrotians. See more: *Bond & Bromley 1970; Munyikwa et al. 1998*

1980—Argentina—First armored sauropod identified
The first osteoderm unquestionably related to a sauropod was *Saltasaurus loricatus*, which made this a very popular dinosaur. See more: *Bonaparte & Powell 1980*

1986—Canada—Most recent skin impression in a sauropodomorph footprint
Skin impressions have been found in a footprint of *Otozoum* sp. that dates to the beginning of the Lower Jurassic (lower Hettangian, approx. 201.3–200 Ma). See more: *Grantham 1986, 1989*

1987—China—Oldest skin impression on a sauropodomorph footprint
Skin impressions of *Pengxianpus cifengensis* dating to the end of the Upper Triassic (Rhaetian, approx. 208.5–201.3 Ma) have been found. See more: *Young & Young 1987*

1989—China—Oldest sauropod with osteoderms
Shunosaurus lii, from the Middle or Upper Jurassic (Bathonian-Oxfordian, approx. 168.3–157.3 Ma), had osteoderms at the tip of its tail, which thickened into a club used to defend against predators. See more: *Dong et al. 1989*

1992—Russia—Oldest armored sauropod of Asia
Some sauropod osteoderms date to the late Lower Cretaceous (Barremian, approx. 129.4–125 Ma). See more: *Nesov & Starkov 1992; Averianov, Starkov & Stutschas 2003*

1992—USA—First sauropod dermal plate
Triangular structures found along the back of *Diplodocus* sp. are interpreted as dermal spines (with no bone inside) that would have been similar to the spines of modern green iguanas. See more: *Czerkas 1992*

1993—Spain—First osteoderm discovered in western Europe
The dermal shields AR/86–102 and Ar.86–103 have been identified as those of an ankylosaur. See more: *Sanz & Buscalioni 1987*

1996—China—First sauropod skin impression of Asia
The skin of *Mamenchisaurus youngi* had some very fine scales 6–15 mm in diameter that differ from other known sauropod

impressions. See more: *Pi et al.1996; Ye 2008*

1996—Brazil—First conserved *Titanosaurus carinas*
In the Marília Formation (Bauru Group) of the Peirópolis Region, some teeth were found with anterior and posterior carinas. This material has only been preserved on rare occasions, other cases being *Rinconsaurus caudamirus* (Argentina) and *Rapetosaurus krausei* (Madagascar). See more: *Kellner 1996; Calvo & González-Riga 2003; Curry-Rogers & Forster 2004*

1996—China—Oldest sauropod skin impression
Skin impressions have been found in the *Mamenchisaurus youngi* holotype specimen ZDM 0083, dating to the end of the Upper Jurassic (Oxfordian, approx. 163.5–157.3 Ma). See more: *Pi, Quyang & Ye 1996; Ye 2006*

1998—Zimbabwe—Oldest sauropod osteoderm
A massive 31-cm-long osteoderm was found associated with the teeth and caudal vertebrae of a lithostrotian titanosaur, dated to between the Upper Jurassic and the early Lower Cretaceous (Berriasian, approx. 145 Ma). The osteoderm CAMSM J.29481 that was attributed to *Gigantosaurus megalonyx* was even older, as it dates to the Upper Jurassic (Kimmeridgian, approx. 157.3–152.1 Ma); however, it is doubtful that it was a sauropod. See more: *Upchurch 1993; Munyikwa et al. 1998; Martill et al. 2006*

1998—Argentina—First fossilized sauropod skin of South America
Among the shell and bone remains of titanosaurus calves, the remains of permineralized skin were also found. They were dated to the late Upper Cretaceous (Campanian, approx. 83.6–72.1 Ma). See more: *Chiappe et al. 1998*

1998—Brazil—First osteoderm discovered in northern South America
The shield CPPLIP 297 belonged to an indeterminate titanosaur. See more: *Azevedo & Kellner 1998*

1998—England, UK—Oldest armored sauropod
One of the oldest lithostrotian titanosauruses found with elongated osteoderms, it has been dated to between the Upper Jurassic and early Lower Cretaceous (approx. 145 Ma). See more: *Munyikwa et al. 1998*

1999—Romania—First osteoderm discovered in eastern Europe
The osteoderm FGGUB R.1410 has been assigned to the small sauropod *Magyarosaurus dacus*. See more: *Csiki 1999*

1999—Romania—Smallest armored sauropod of the late Upper Cretaceous
Magyarosaurus dacus up to 5.4 m in length and weighing 520 kg, had osteoderms 8 x 6.8 cm in diameter and 4.2 cm high on the back. See more: *Nopcsa 1915; Csiki 1999*

2002—Spain—First skin impression in a sauropod footprint
Skin impressions in ichnites of cf. *Brontopodus birdi* that date to the Upper Jurassic (Kimmeridgian, approx. 157.3–152.1 Ma). A previous report from Utah is currently questioned. See more: *Lockley et al. 1992; García-Ramos, Lires & Piñueña 2002; Platt & Hasiotis 2003*

2003—Mongolia—Most recent sauropod skin impression
Skin impressions have been found in titanosaur prints dated to the end of the late Upper Cretaceous (lower Maastrichtian, approx. 72.1–69 Ma). See more: *Currie et al. 2003*

2003—Argentina—Sauropod with the most flexible tail
Rinconsaurus caudamirus had a variety of vertebral forms on its tail, including forms that were amphicoelous (with two concave surfaces), biconvex (with two opposing convex surfaces), opisthocoelous (convex on the anterior and concave on the pos-

terior side), and procoelous (concave on the anterior and convex on the posterior side). These would have made its tail the most flexible of all sauropods. See more: *Calvo & González-Rig2003*

2003—Argentina—Largest armored sauropod of the early Upper Cretaceous

The paratype of *Mendozasaurus neguyelap* consists of the four osteoderms IANIGLA-PV 080/1–2, 081/1–2. The largest specimens of this species measured almost 23 m in length and weighed 32 t. See more: *Gónzalez-Riga 2003*

2004—Mali—First osteoderm discovered in northern Africa

Specimen CNRST-SUNY-1 has been identified as belonging to a sauropod. Other osteoderms found in northern Africa are deemed to belong to ornithschian ankylosaurs. See more: *Lapparent 1960; O'Leary et al. 2004*

2004—Argentina—First evidence of keratin in a sauropod

The jaw of *Bonitasaura salgadoi* had a distinctive crest that could have supported a sharp, beak-like keratin sheath to cut through the plants it consumed. See more: *Apesteguía 2004*

2005—Malawi—Largest armored sauropod of the late Lower Cretaceous

The shield MAL 204 is associated with *Malawisaurus dixeyi*. The largest specimens of this species were 9.5 m long and weighed 2.8 t. See more: *Haughton 1928; Gomani 2005*

2009—Argentina—First evidence of keratin in a primitive sauropodomorph

Adeopapposaurus mognai had some marks on its jaws that could indicate that a keratin beak was attached to it. It is possible that this characteristic was present in other sauropodomorphs like Plateosauria. See more: *Martínez 2009*

2012—Romania—First fossil sauropod embryonic tissue

Among the titanosaur eggs found at Hateg was an embryo skin and part of the organic membrane (testacean membrane) found inside the shells of the amniote eggs. See more: *Grellet-Tinner et al. 2012*

2013—Brazil—Only sauropod with inward-pointing front teeth

Brasilotitan nemophagus had square jaws like *Antarctosaurus* and *Bonitasaura*, but unlike them, its front teeth point inward, not outward, a trait never before seen in a titanosaur. See more: *Machado et al. 2013*

2014—Argentina—Smallest Cretaceous sauropod with type-O cylindrodont teeth

Leinkupal laticauda was a small diplodocid 13 m long and weighing 1.8 t. There is no histological study confirming whether it was an adult or a juvenile. See more: *Tschopp & Mateus 2012; Gallina et al. 2014*

2015—USA—Largest armored sauropod of the late Upper Cretaceous

Alamosaurus sanjuanensis is the largest sauropod that has been found with osteoderms. The largest specimens reached 26 m in length and weighed 38 t. See more: *Gilmore 1938, 1946; Brett-Surman et al. 2015*

2017—South Korea—Largest skin impression in a sauropod footprint

Measuring approximately 63 cm long and 43 cm wide, a broken print from the late Lower Cretaceous (Aptian, approx. 125–113 Ma) presents a polygonal texture on the skin. See more: *Paik et al. 2017*

NECKS

Apart from their large size, the most outstanding feature of sauropods was their long necks; some were extraordinarily long. The precise function of those long necks is still under discussion, and several theories exist to explain them; what is undeniable, however, is that their long necks allowed these creatures to access food more efficiently than other extremely large herbivorous animals, providing them with more energy for less effort. This was only possible, however, because of their small heads and high degree of pneumatization, which offset the weight of those enormous necks.

One of the most commonly asked questions about sauropods' actual appearance is how their necks were positioned—horizontally, vertically, curved, or in an S-shape. This doubt has arisen despite the discovery of individual specimens with all cervical vertebrae, because the cartilage between the vertebral pieces was not preserved, leading to a long-standing debate among investigators that is still going on.

It is also not known how sauropods managed to raise their heads so high without a drop in their blood pressure, but we can compare this to the extraordinary ability of mammals to dive very deep in water, a similarly impressive evolutionary achievement. See more: *Martin 1987; Christian & Heinrich 1998; Seymour & Lillywhite 2000; Christian 2002, 2010; Christian & Dzemski 2007, 2011; Dzemski & Christian 2007; Stevens & Parrish 2005; Sander et al. 2011; Taylor et al. 2009, 2011; Taylor 2014; Paul 2017*

Osteoderms in sauropods

Osteoderms have been found in:

Lower Cretaceous
Malawisaurus.

Upper Cretaceous
Aeolosaurus, Alamosaurus, Ampelosaurus, Balochisaurus, Lirainosaurus, Lohuecotitan, Magyarosaurus, Maxakalisaurus, Mendozasaurus, Neuquensaurus, Pakisaurus, Rapetosaurus, Saltasaurus, Sulaimanisaurus and *"Titanosaurus."*

Sauropod with the shortest neck in relation to its size
Brachytrachelopan mesai

Dicraeosaurids have some of the shortest necks among the sauropods. *Brachytrachelopan* is one outstanding example; its neck was 40% shorter than those of its relatives. Its 12-vertebrae neck is estimated to have been 1.1 m long.
See more: *Rauhut et al. 2005*

NECK AND TAILS

In a book of sauropodomorph records, the most spectacular characteristics that define them, that is their necks and tails, cannot be overlooked. These could reach incredible dimensions, longer than four cars placed end-to-end. But not all were gigantic; some were also quite small, especially in baseline sauropodomorphs. Others, on the other hand, stood out for being disproportionately long or short in relation to the total length of the animal, resulting in very peculiar-looking animals as far as proportions are concerned.

The following tables show only the necks and tails in which at least one of the vertebrae is preserved. Therefore, there could have been animals with even longer or shorter necks and tails.

Most extreme necks				
Species	Specimen	Length	Records and facts	Specimen reference
Macrocollum itaquii	CAPPA/UFSM 0001b	70 cm	The longest neck in proportion to its body from the Triassic (represents ~20.5% of the total length).	Temp-Muller et al. 2018
Brachytrachelopan mesai	MPEF-PV 1716	1 m	The shortest sauropod neck in proportion to its body (represents ~12% of the total length).	Rauhut et al. 2005
Bonatitan reigi	MACN RN 821	1.3 m	The shortest neck from the Cretaceous. *Magyarosaurus* could have been shorter, but no cervical vertebrae of this genus has been preserved.	Martinelli & Forasiepi 2004; Gallina & Carabajal 2015
Camelotia borealis	BMNH R2870-R2874	1.8 m	The longest neck from the Triassic.	Galton 1985
Shunosaurus lii	ZG65430	1.9 m	The shortest neck from the Middle Jurassic. It is proportionally very short (represents ~20% of the total length).	Zhang et al.1984
Isisaurus colberti	ISI R335/1-65	2.5 m	The shortest neck from the Cretaceous. It is proportionally very short (represents ~23% of the total length).	Jain & Bandyopadhyay 1997
Atlasaurus imelakei	uncatalogued	4 m	The shortest neck from the Jurassic and Gondwana. It is proportionally very short (represents ~26% of the total length).	Monbaron et al. 1999
"Hughenden sauropod"	QM F6142	4.5 m	The shortest neck of Oceania.	Coombs & Molnar 1981
Erketu ellisoni	IGM 100/1803	7.5 m	The longest neck in proportion to its body from the Cretaceous (represents ~47% of the total length).	Ksepka & Norell 2006
Giraffatitan brancai	HMN SII	9 m	The longest neck of Africa.	Janensch 1914, 1950
Mamenchisaurus hochuanensis	IVPP 3	9.5 m	Historically considered as the longest neck.	Young & Zhao 1972
Daxiatitan binblingi	GSLTZP03-001	11 m	One of the longest preserved necks.	You et al. 2008
"Francoposeidon"	uncatalogued	11–13 m	The longest neck of Europe.	Pending publication
Superasurus vivianae	WDC DMJ-021	11.2 m	One of the longest preserved necks.	Jensen 1985
Patagotitan mayorum	MPEF PV 3399	11.7 m	The longest neck of South America.	Carballido et al. 2017
Ruyangosaurus giganteus	KLR1508	12 m	The longest neck from the Upper Cretaceous. *Argentinosaurus* may have had a longer neck.	Lu et al. 2009
Sauroposeidon proteles	OMNH 53062	12 m	The longest neck from the Early Cretaceous	Wedel et al. 2000
Xinjiangtitan shanshaensis	SSV12001	15 m	The longest neck in proportion to its body from the Jurassic and of Asia.It is also the longest complete preserved neck (represents ~55% of the total length).	Wu et al. 2013; Zhang et al. 2018
cf. *Barosaurus lentus*	BYU 9024	16 m	The longest neck from the Jurassic and Mesozoic.	Jensen 1985, 1987

1:100

The widest neck
Puertasaurus reuilli

Some sauropods had a very wide necks, so it is believed that they used them for intraspecies combat in order to gain territories or resources. *Puertasaurus* stands out among the other species for having cervicals up to 1.4 m wide, although some remains of *Alamosaurus* suggest cervicals up to 1.6 m wide. Other sauropods with particularly wide necks are the apatosaurines (*Apatosaurus* or *Brontosaurus*) and some titanosaurs, such as *Austroposeidon*.
See more: *Novas et al. 2005; Fowler & Sullivan 2011; Taylor et al. 2015; Bandeira et al. 2016*

The longest neck in proportion to its body
Xinjiangtitan shanshaensis

Because of its short tail, its neck represents the ~55% of its total length. This surpasses *Erketu ellison* which had a neck length of ~ 47% of its body length. See more: *Wu et al. 2013; Zhang et al. 2018*

Most extreme tails

Species	Specimen	Length	Records and facts	Specimen reference
Pampadromaeus barberenai	ULBRA-PVT016	70 cm	The shortest tail from the Triassic and South America? There is a 17% larger specimen that could belong to this species.	Cabreira et al. 2011; Muller et al. 2016
Alwalkeria maleriensis	ISI R 306	75 cm	The shortest tail from the Triassic and Hindustan? It is possible that it was a chimera.	Chatterjee 1986; Remes & Rauhut 2005
Unnamed	BP/1/4559	1.05 m	The shortest tail from Africa.	Choiniere & Barrett 2015
"*Gripposaurus*" *sinensis*	IVPP V.27	1.2 m	The shortest tail of Asia (Paleosasia).	Young 1941
Anchisaurus polyzelus	Uncatalogued	1.4 m	The shortest tail from the Lower Jurassic and North America. It is possible that the adult YPM 1883 specimen had a tail 1.6 m long.	Huene 1932
Europasaurus holgeri	DFMMh/FV 553.1	2.1 m	The shortest tail from the Upper Jurassic and Europe.	Sander et al. 2006; Carballido & Sander 2013
Ferganasaurus verzilini	PIN N 3042/1	4 m	The shortest tail from the Middle Jurassic.	Alifanov & Averianov 2003
Magyarosaurus dacus	BMNH R.3861a	2.9 m	The shortest tail from the Upper Cretaceous.	Huene 1932
Venenosaurus dicrocei	DMNH 40932	4.2 m	The shortest tail from the Lower Jurassic.	Tidwell et al. 2001
Wintonotitan wattsi	QMF 7292	6.5 m	The longest tail of Oceania.	Coombs & Molnar 1981
Unnamed	MLP 11-II-20	7 m	The longest tail of Antarctica.	Cerda et al. 2011a, 2011b
Unnamed	Meet BP/1/5339	8 m	The longest tail from the Triassic.	Wedel & Yates 2011
Yunmenglong ruyangensis	KLR-07-50	8.5 m	The longest tail of Asia.	Lu et al.2013
Dreadnoughtus schrani	MPM-PV 1156	10 m	The longest complete preserved tail from the Cretaceous.	Lacovara et al. 2014
Alamosaurus sanjuanensis	SMP-2104	10.7 m	The longest tail among the saltasaurids.	Fowler & Sullivan 2011
Futalognkosaurus dunkei	MUCPv-323	11 m	-	Calvo et al. 2007
Tornieria africana	SMNS 12141a	12.8 m	The longest tail of Africa.	Remes 2006
Apatosaurus louisae	CM 3018	13 m	The longest complete tail from the Jurassic.	Holland 1916; Gilmore 1936
Barosaurus lentus	AMNH 6341	13 m	-	Lull 1919
Puertasaurus reuili	MPM 10002	13 m	The longest tail from the Upper Cretaceous.	Novas et al. 2005
Patagotitan mayorum	MPEF PV 3399	13.5 m	The longest tail from the Lower Cretaceous and South America.	Carballido et al. 2017
Unnamed	DGO-3500	14.5 m	The longest tail of Europe.	Ruiz-Omeñaca et al. 2008
Supersaurus vivianae	WDC DMJ-021	15 m	-	Lovelace et al. 2008
Diplodocus carnegii	CM 84	15.5 m	The second longest tail from the Mesozoic.	Hatcher 1901
Diplodocus hallorum	NMMNH-P3690	18 m	The longest tail from the Jurassic, Mesozoic, and North America.	Gillette 1991

1:100

The longest tail
Diplodocus hallorum

The diplodocids had the longest tails among all the vertebrates that have existed. The famous dinosaur known as "*Seismosaurus*" (= *Diplodocus hallorum*) had a tail longer than a bus and a car lined up. The tails of other species of the family such as *Diplodocus canegii, Supersaurus vivianae,* and *Barosaurus lentus* were very long, measuring 15.5, 15, and 13 m respectively.
See more: *Hatcher 1901; Lull 1919; Gillette 1991; Novas et al. 2005; Taylor et al. 2015; Bandeira et al. 2016*

Sauropod life
Sauropodomorph biology

Records: The fastest, the largest and smallest eggs, diet, and other facts

Sauropodomorphs were very large animals that moved slowly, devoured large quantities of food, and, among other traits, had much lower cognitive abilities than most other terrestrial vertebrates.

To defend themselves, some species increased their size considerably, others had whip-like or club tails, and some also had osteoderms. These creatures may have suffered heavily from predation and may have compensated by laying large numbers of eggs.

Unlike other dinosaurs, sauropods had few forms of locomotion; they could move only on two or four feet. Some species may have occasionally moved through water, but they were not specially adapted for it.

Sauropodomorphs were among the slowest dinosaurs. The most derived ones, sauropods, were graviportal animals with columnar legs. As bipeds with flexible feet, primitive sauropodomorphs were the fastest movers of the group, although the maximum speeds they could attain were not very high compared to theropods and ornithischians.

Indeed, the maximum speeds of the fastest sauropodomorphs were comparable to that of humans. Sauropods, for their part, moved like present-day elephants: rather than running with a suspended phase (all feet leaving the ground at once), at least one of their feet would have always been in contact with the ground when they moved quickly. This limited their speed to a range comparable to that of modern-day elephants, never exceeding 25 km/h.

MYTH *Diplodocus* could run at 52 km/h

This is the highest speed ever calculated for a sauropod. According to some estimations for giant sauropods, these creatures could reach speeds over 40 km/h, up to 52 km/h in the case of *Diplodocus*. But the biomechanics of graviportal animals show that this would not have been possible, as they would have to have been able to trot, and trotting would have broken their bones owing to their tremendous weight. Accidental falls would also almost certainly have been fatal. See more: *Bakker 1975*

1 meter

1:10

Galapagos turtle
0.37 km/h
Chelonoidis nigra
is now extinct.

Leopard turtle
1.01 km/h
"Bertie" *Stigmochelys
pardalis* holds the 2016
Guinness World Record.

Massospondylus carinatus
2.8 km/h
Sauropodomorphs were quadrupedal as
newborns and adopted a bipedal posture as
they grew.

Apalone sp.
>10 km/h
Some soft-shelled turtles
(Trionychidae) can run very
fast to escape their enemies,
reaching speeds similar to that
of a human jogging.

0–10 km/h

Whales on land

Large sauropods led a relatively inactive life, spending most of their time eating. They could not move quickly, as the inertia associated with their enormous body mass meant that even minor accidents could lead to serious injury. Scientists have estimated that *Argentinosaurus* walked at an average speed of just 7 km/h to avoid expending too much energy. In order to survive on land, this giant sauropod would have required a heart eight times as large as the heart of a whale of the same weight. See more: *Schmidt-Nielsen 1984; Sellers et al. 2013*

1:100

Ligabuesaurus leanzai
32 km/h
Fastest sauropod of the Upper
Cretaceous.

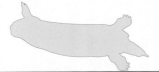

Asian elephant
25 km/h
The speed of present-
day elephants has been
calculated erroneously as
reaching up to 40 km/h.

Gresslyosaurus ingens
26.4 km/h
Slowest sauropodomorph
of the Triassic.

Kenichi Ito
23 km/h
The fastest human
running on four limbs.

25–30 km/h

Some sauropodomorphs were able to move on two or four feet. The first few species known to have this ability include *Antetonitrus*, *Melanorosaurus*, and *Riojasaurus*, among others. As strictly quadrupedal animals, they could barely have exceeded 15 km/h (despite being relatively small), because their front feet were disproportionately short, preventing them from moving quickly. Like most of their close relatives, however, these animals could have moved bipedally at more than 30 km/h.

By studying sauropod footprints, investigators have discovered that their locomotion was similar to that of elephants, in which both legs on a side move at the same time (ambling gait). This form of locomotion ensures the animal's body is always in contact with the ground while dramatically reducing vertical oscillation of the center of mass, which helped, in turn, to reduce stress on the legs of these huge animals as they carried their enormous weight around.

The fastest sauropods (*Atlasaurus*, *Euhelopus*, *Vouivria* …) were those with longer legs that enabled a longer stride. A few may have even moved at more than 30 km/h. In contrast, the slowest (*Amargasaurus*, *Apatosaurus*, *Malawisaurus* …) had shorter front legs and very short lower forelegs, which would have limited the stride of the hind legs. Most of these animals would probably not have reached 20 km/h.

MYTH Sauropods were awkward animals

Years ago, scientists believed that sauropods were very slow and clumsy animals that dragged their tails along the ground and lived in swamps, where the water helped them stay upright.

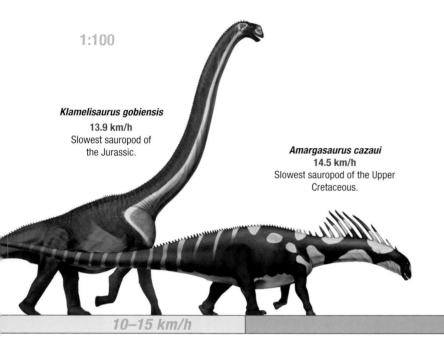

1:100

Klamelisaurus gobiensis
13.9 km/h
Slowest sauropod of the Jurassic.

Amargasaurus cazaui
14.5 km/h
Slowest sauropod of the Upper Cretaceous.

2 meters

Anchisaurus polyzelus
23.3 km/h
Slowest sauropodomorph of the Jurassic.

10–15 km/h

15–25 km/h

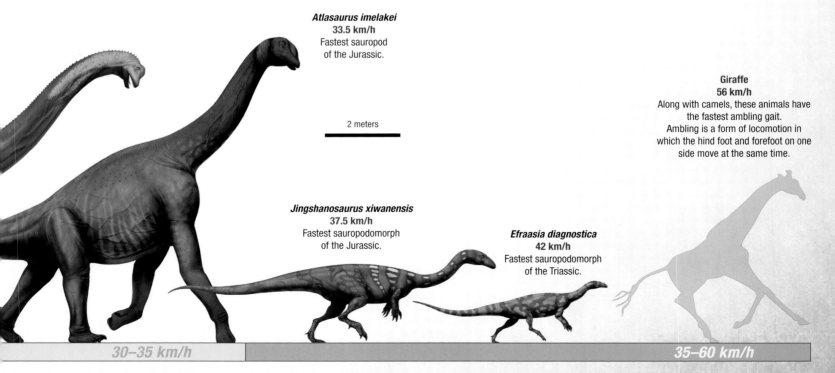

Atlasaurus imelakei
33.5 km/h
Fastest sauropod of the Jurassic.

2 meters

Giraffe
56 km/h
Along with camels, these animals have the fastest ambling gait.
Ambling is a form of locomotion in which the hind foot and forefoot on one side move at the same time.

Jingshanosaurus xiwanensis
37.5 km/h
Fastest sauropodomorph of the Jurassic.

Efraasia diagnostica
42 km/h
Fastest sauropodomorph of the Triassic.

30–35 km/h

35–60 km/h

CALCULATING SAUROPOD SPEEDS

In the previous volume, *Dinosaur Facts and Figures: The Theropods and Other Dinosauriformes*, a methodology was presented for estimating the approximate maximum speeds of those bipedal creatures. In this book, that formula is applied to primitive sauropods only, as only they walked on their hind feet. The situation is quite different for sauropods that walked on all four feet.

The only modern-day animals that are biomechanically analogous to sauropods are elephants. The maximum verified speed of an elephant, obtained for an Asian elephant (*Elephas maximus*) weighing 2.8 tons and in optimal physical condition, is 25 km/h (6.8 m/s). Previously cited speeds around 40 km/h are erroneous.

Graviportal animals have lower maximum speeds because they cannot have all feet in the air at once while moving quickly; at least one foot must always be in contact with the ground. Curiously, when moving quickly, juvenile elephants move at a speed very similar to that of adults, even though the former have much shorter strides. This is because younger animals take more strides per second (5) than adults (3), given that angular velocity decreases as size increases.

This book presents a new methodology for speed estimation developed from observation and video analysis of elephants "running," limb proportion studies, and the application of Newtonian principles. Full details of the methodology will be published in a scientific journal. It is important to note that calculations of sauropod leg length must take into account the enormous cartilages that wrapped around the ends of these creatures' long bones, which, when combined with the soft tissue and the skin on the soles, would have added an extra 10% to that length.

Speeds estimated here should be taken as approximate. See more: *Coombs 1978; Thulborn 1982, 1990; McGowan 1992; Hutchinson et al. 2003; Hutchinson 2005; Hutchinson & Gatesy 2006 Schmitt et al. 2006; Schwarz et al. 2007; Holliday et al. 2010; Larramendi 2016; Molina-Pérez & Larramendi 2016*

Tables applicable to animals with shorter **front** legs

CURSORIALITY (optimal)		
Body mass (kg)	Optimal cadence	Optimal stride ratio
0–250	5.5	1.5
+250–500	4.9	1.5
+500–1000	4.4	1.5
+1000–2000	3.9	1.5
+2000–4000	3.5	1.5
+4000–8000	3.1	1.5
+8000–16000	2.8	1.35
+16000–32000	2.5	1.2
+32000–64000	2.2	1.05
+64000	1.95	0.95

Ulna-radius + MCS/humerus	x Optimal cadence and optimal stride
<0.8	0.68
0.8–0.85	0.72
0.85–0.9	0.76
0.9–0.95	0.8
0.95–1	0.84
1–1.05	0.88
1.05–1.1	0.92
1.1–1.15	0.96
1.15–1.2	0.98
1.2	1

Tables applicable to animals with shorter **hind** legs

CURSORIALITY (optimal)		
Body mass (kg)	Optimal cadence	Optimal stride ratio
0–250	5.5	1.5
+250–500	4.9	1.5
+500–1000	4.4	1.5
+1000–2000	3.9	1.5
+2000–4000	3.5	1.5
+4000–8000	3.1	1.5
+8000–16000	2.8	1.35
+16000–32000	2.5	1.2
+32000–64000	2.2	1.05
+64000	1.95	0.95

Tibia + MTS/femur	x Optimal cadence and optimal stride
0.5–0.55	0.68
0.55–0.6	0.72
0.6–0.65	0.76
0.65–0.7	0.8
0.7–0.75	0.84
0.75–0.8	0.88
0.8–0.85	0.92
0.85–0.9	0.96
0.9–0.95	0.98
0.95–1	1

Calculating the speed of quadrupedal graviportal animals. The two series of tables above can be used to calculate the speed of any columnar quadrupedal animal. The tables on the left show optimal cursorial values estimated for animals with the specified body mass. The table on the right presents values that can be multiplied with the optimal parameters in the left-hand table, based on the proportion obtained from the sum of the tibia + third metatarsal length (multiplied by 1.1) divided by the femur length, where the hind legs of the specimen used for the calculation are shorter. Where the specimen in question has shorter front legs, the calculation should be based on the sum of (ulna or radius length) + (third metacarpal length) (multiplied by 1.1), divided by the length of the humerus, always taking body mass into account. Once the cadence or steps per second (C) and the stride ratio (SR, ratio of stride length to leg height) are obtained, they are multiplied by the length of the shortest leg (LL) in millimeters. To obtain the speed in km/h, the spatiotemporal variable (ST) must have an assigned value equal to: 0.0036. To obtain the speed in m/s, SV = 0.001.

$$V= (LL \times C \times SR) \times ST$$

E.g.: *Brontosaurus excelsus* CM 563. Because its front legs were shorter than its hind legs, the front leg length is used. This specimen included a humerus measuring 1100 mm, a radius 775 mm long, and a metacarpal III of 285 mm. Applying a factor of 1.1 yields the sum of 2354 mm, with a radius length + MCS III/humerus proportion of 0.95. The estimated body mass of this animal is 15,500 kg. Optimal cadence for an animal of this size would be 2.8, with a stride ratio of 1.35. Nevertheless, the result obtained from the proportion of radius to + MCS III/humerus indicates that cadence (C) and stride ratio (SR) should be multiplied by 0.8 (table on the right), which yields 2.24 and 1.08, respectively, giving a final speed of 20.5 km/h or 5.7 m/s: $V_{(km/h)}= (2354 \times 2.24 \times 1.08) \times 0.0036$ | $V_{(m/s)}= (2354 \times 2.24 \times 1.08) \times 0.001$

Table of the speed of bipedal sauropodomorphs. The speeds estimated here were calculated using the formula published in the previous volume of this series, *Dinosaur Facts and Figures: The Theropods and Other Dinosauriformes.*

SPEED OF BIPEDAL SAUROPODOMORPHS

Genus and species	Specimen	Leg length (mm)	Tibia + Met/femur	Mass (kg)	Cadence	Stride ratio	Speed km/h	Speed m/s	Record
Primitive sauropodomorphs									
Pantydraco caducus (juvenile-estimated)	BMNHP24	193	1.44	0.76	9.4	2.7	17.6	4.9	
Thecodontosaurus minor	uncatalogued	316	1.34	3.8	8.37	2.67	25.4	7.1	
Panphagia protos (juvenile-estimated)	PSVJ-874	386	1.54	7.8	7.6	2.73	28.9	8	
Eoraptor lunensis	PVSJ 512	390	1.57	5	7.6	2.73	29.1	8.1	
Buriolestes schultzi	ULBRA-PVT280	363	1.54	3	8.55	2.73	30.5	8.5	
Saturnalia tupiniquin	MCP 3844-PV	399	1.54	6	7.6	2.73	29.8	8.1	
Pampadromaeus barberenai (estimated)	ULBRA-PVT016	326	1.69	1.8	9.6	2.79	31.4	8.7	
Thecodontosaurus antiquus (estimated)	uncatalogued	614	1.41	34	5.64	2.7	33.7	9.4	
Xixiposaurus suni	ZLJ0108	945	1.2	160	4.1	2.44	34	9.5	
Efraasia diagnostica (juvenile)	uncatalogued	650	1.32	45	5.58	2.67	34.9	9.7	
Efraasia diagnostica	SMNS 11838	1110	1.36	213	4.19	2.49	41.7	11.6	Fastest sauropodomorph of the Triassic and of Europe
Primitive Plateosauria									
"Gripposaurus" sinensis	IVPP V.27	556	1.28	58	4.6	2.64	24.3	6.8	
Gresslyosaurus ingens (estimated)	uncatalogued	1893	1.05	2010	2.25	1.72	26.4	7.3	Slowest sauropodomorph of the Triassic
Adeopapposaurus mognai	PVSJ610	515	1.34	27	5.58	2.67	27.6	7.7	
Massospondylus carinatus (M. harriesi)	BMNH R.8171	790	1.21	126	4.14	2.46	29	8.1	
Lufengosaurus huenei (L. magnus)	IVPP V.82	1590	1.15	1115	2.73	1.91	29.8	8.3	
Plateosaurus longiceps (Dimodosaurus poligniensis)	POL	1610	1.12	1160	2.73	1.91	30.2	8.4	
Massospondylus carinatus (M. browni)	MT 124	810	1.31	120	4.19	2.49	30.4	8.4	
Gresslyosaurus ingens (subadult)	uncatalogued	1620	1.16	1110	2.73	1.91	30.4	8.4	
Plateosaurus engelhardti (Pachysaurus wetzelianus)	GPTI V	2160	1.2	2480	2.28	1.74	30.8	8.6	
Lufengosaurus huenei	Young 1941	1098	0.98	470	3.56	2.21	31.1	8.6	
Plateosaurus longiceps (Gresslyosaurus torgeri)	HMN III	1300	1.13	600	3.19	2.09	31.2	8.7	
Lufengosaurus huenei	IVPP V 15	1137	1.03	480	3.6	2.24	33	9.2	
Plateosaurus engelhardti	uncatalogued	1404	1.24	650	3.19	2.09	33.7	9.4	
Plateosaurus gracilis	SMNS 17928	1138	1.30	330	3.68	2.26	34.1	9.5	
Plateosaurus engelhardti (Zanclodon quenstedti)	uncatalogued	1400	1.5	720	3.22	2.11	34.2	9.5	
Gryponyx africanus	SAM 3357	1193	1.21	435	3.68	2.29	36.2	10.1	Fastest sauropodomorph of Africa
Gresslyosaurus ingens (subadult)	uncatalogued	1515	1.16	900	3.19	2.09	36.4	10.1	
Plateosauravus cullingworthi	SAM 3602	1266	1.11	435	3.64	2.26	37.5	10.4	
Plateosaurus gracilis	SMNS 11838	1196	1.43	325	3.76	2.34	37.9	10.5	
Plateosaurus longiceps (Plateosaurus sp.)	SMNS F.10	1583	1.20	975	3.19	2.09	38	10.6	
Primitive Sauropodiformes									
Mussaurus patagonicus (neonate)	PVL 4068	70	1.33	0.04	11.2	2.67	7.5	2.1	Slowest bipedal sauropodomorph
Anchisaurus polyzelus	YPM 1883	454	1.15	25	5.46	2.61	23.3	6.5	Slowest sauropodomorph of the Jurassic
Yunnanosaurus robustus (juvenile)	ZMNH-M8739	580	1.33	21	5.58	2.67	31.1	8.6	
Riojasaurus insertus	PVL 3808	1353	1.23	800	3.22	2.11	33.1	9.2	
Melanorosaurus readi (estimated)	NM QR1551	1347	1.16	650	3.19	2.26	35	9.7	
Yunnanosaurus robustus	IVPP V94	1185	1.15	430	3.64	2.26	35.1	9.8	
Ammosaurus major	uncatalogued	620	1.75	28	5.82	2.85	37	10.3	Fastest sauropodomorph of North America
Mussaurus patagonicus (juvenile)	PVL uncat (1) (6/73)	1176	1.27	380	3.68	2.29	35.7	9.9	Fastest sauropodomorph of South America
Jingshanosaurus xiwanensis	LV003	1945	1.29	1600	2.76	1.94	37.5	10.4	Fastest sauropodomorph of the Jurassic and of Asia

Tables showing the speed of quadrupedal sauropodomorphs. The speeds estimated in the tables below were calculated using the formula presented on page 166 of this book, always based on the length of the shortest leg. Following the tables, two present-day elephant specimens are presented for comparison. It is worth noting that elephant leg length was calculated by adding 4.5% for soft tissue, which is considerably less than the 10% used for sauropods, as present-day mammals have much finer cartilage than dinosaurs had. Some specimens lack the metacarpal or metatarsal III (or another long bone), and so these were estimated from very phytogentically similar specimens.

Abbreviations: Lfl, length of foreleg; Lhl, length of hind leg; R1, ulna-radius + MCs/humerus; R2, tibia + MTs/femur; C, cadence; SR, stride ratio

SPEED OF QUADRUPEDAL SAUROPODOMORPHS

Genus and species	Specimen	Lfl	Lhl	R1	R2	Mass kg	C	SR	Speed km/h	Speed m/s	Record
Primitive Plateosauria											
Massospondylus carinatus (calf)	BP/1/5347A	20	30	0.91	1.4	0.007	4.4	1.2	0.4	0.1	
Primitive Sauropodiformes	(Note that the first three below were likely bipedal for running. See the results of the previous table on page 167.)										
Melanorosaurus readi (estimated)	NM QR1551	802	1482	0.62	1.16	650	2.99	1.02	8.8	2.4	
Antetonitrus ingenipes	BP/1/4952	1422	1731	0.71	0.91	1250	2.65	1.02	13.8	3.8	
Riojasaurus insertus (estimated)	PVL 3808	926	1488	0.75	1.23	800	3.7	1.26	15.5	4.3	
"*Thotobolosaurus mabeatae*"	MNHN.F.LES394	1532	1706	1.03	0.94	3600	3.08	1.32	22.4	6.2	Fastest quadrupedal sauropodomorph of the Triassic
Primitive sauropods											
Gongxianosaurus shibeiensis (estimated)	uncatalogued	1977	2610	0.95	1.04	4000	2.8	1.2	23.9	6.6	Slowest sauropod of the Lower Jurassic
Vulcanodon karibaensis (estimated)	QG 24	1775	2167	1.31	0.79	4300	3.1	1.5	29.7	8.3	Fastest sauropod of the Lower Jurassic
Gravisauria											
Shunosaurus lii	ZDM 5402	1509	2304	0.91	0.75	7000	2.48	1.2	16.2	4.5	Slowest sauropod of the Middle Jurassic
Cetiosaurus oxoniensis	OUMNH J13605–13613	2640	3025	0.9	0.7	11100	2.13	1.03	20.9	5.8	Slowest sauropod of Europe
Mamenchisauridae											
Omeisaurus maoianus	ZNM N8510	1661	2241	0.92	0.82	5900	2.48	1.2	17.8	4.9	
Mamenchisaurus youngi (estimated)	ZDM 003	1766	2247	0.92	0.76	7000	2.48	1.2	18.9	5.3	
Omeisaurus tianfuensis	ZDM T5701	2282	2607	0.92	0.81	7500	2.48	1.2	24.5	6.8	
Cetiosauriscus stewarti (estimated)	BMNH R.3078	2152	2596	1.08	0.74	10800	2.58	1.24	24.8	6.9	
Turiasauria											
Turiasaurus riodevensis (estimated)	CPT-1195-1210	3745.5	3997	0.9	0.73	30000	1.9	0.912	23.4	6.5	
Mierasaurus bobyoungi (estimated)	UMNH.VP.26004	1621.4	2123	0.9	0.69	4800	3.1	1.5	27.1	7.5	
Neosauropoda											
Bellusaurus sui (juvenile)	IVPP V17768	721	925	0.87	0.75	315	3.72	1.14	11	3.1	
Klamelisaurus gobiensis	IVPP V.9492	1793	2431	0.77	0.84	6000	2.11	1.02	13.9	3.9	Slowest sauropod of the Upper Jurassic and of Asia (Paleoasia)
Jobaria tiguidensis (estimated)	MNN TIG3	3069	3498	1.05	0.77	17000	2.2	1.06	25.7	7.1	
Atlasaurus imelakei	uncatalogued	3993	3916	0.86	0.78	21000	2.2	1.06	33.5	9.3	Fastest sauropod of the Middle Jurassic and of Africa
Diplodocoidea											
Limaysaurus tessonei (estimated)	MUCPv-205	2006	2677	1.03	0.69	7500	2.73	1.32	26	7.2	
Dicraeosauridae											
Amargasaurus cazaui (estimated)	MACN-N 15	1471	2000	0.84	0.73	4000	2.52	1.08	14.4	4.0	Slowest sauropod of the Lower Cretaceous and of South America
Diplodocidae											
Apatosaurus louisae	CM 3018	2467	3461	0.95	0.76	20000	2	0.96	17.1	4.8	Slowest sauropod of North America
Galeamopus hayi (estimated)	HMNS 175	2032	2837	0.97	0.78	10000	2.35	1.13	19.5	5.4	
Unnamed	NSMT-PV 20375	2108	2885	0.85	0.78	7900	2.36	1.14	20.4	5.7	
Brontosaurus excelsus	CM 563	2354	3298	0.95	0.75	15500	2.24	1.08	20.5	5.7	
Diplodocus carnegii (estimated)	CM 94	2211	2960	1.05	0.83	10000	2.46	1.19	23.3	6.5	
Diplodocus longus (estimated)	YPM 1920	2328	3113	1.05	0.75	13000	2.46	1.19	24.5	6.8	
"*Amphicoelias brontodiplodocus*" (estimated)	DQ-EN	2090	3008	1.09	0.93	8000	2.85	1.38	29.6	8.2	

Genus and species	Specimen	Lfl	Lhl	R1	R2	Mass kg	C	SR	Speed km/h	Speed m/s	Record
Macronaria											
Camarasaurus lentus (juvenile)	CM 11238	971.3	1120	0.96	0.76	700	3.7	1.26	16.3	4.5	
Camarasaurus grandis	GMNH 101	2424	2902	0.95	0.78	11700	2	1.08	18.9	5.3	
Janenschia robusta (estimated)	HMN IX	2002	2578	1.04	0.76	8540	2.46	1.19	21.1	5.9	Fastest sauropod of the Upper Jurassic
Camarasaurus lentus (estimated)	CM11393	2589	2964	0.97	0.72	12800	2.35	1.134	24.8	6.9	
Titanosauriformes											
Brachiosaurus sp. (juvenile)	SMA 0009	399.3	504	0.99	1.04	45	4.62	1.26	8.4	2.3	
Giraffatitan brancai (estimated)	HMN SII	4278	3868	0.93	0.71	33000	1.85	0.882	25.1	7.0	
Vouivria damparisensis (subadult)	NHM R2598	2860	2816	0.95	0.75	9200	2.35	1.134	27.4	7.6	Fastest sauropod of Europe
"Rebbachisaurus" tamensnensis	uncatalogued	2728	2805	1.02	0.7	9700	2.46	1.19	28.7	8.0	
Cedarosaurus weiskopfae (estimated)	DMNH 39045	2882	2728	0.9	0.78	10500	2.46	1.19	30.4	8.4	Fastest sauropod of North America
Somphospondyli											
Pleurocoelus nanus (juvenile; estimated)	USNM 2263	850	886	1.13	1.04	170	5	1.44	23.3	6.5	
Chubutisaurus insignis (estimated)	MACN 18222 S	3074	3263	0.9	0.74	14000	2.13	1.03	24.3	6.8	
Ligabuesaurus leanzai (estimated)	MCF-PVPH-233	3355	3278	1.05	0.73	14500	2.35	1.13	32.1	8.9	Fastest sauropod of the Lower Cretaceous and of South America
Euhelopodidae											
Phuwiangosaurus sirinhornae (estimated)	P.W. 1-1 to 1-21	2318	2475	1.13	0.8	8000	2.69	1.3	29.2	8.1	Fastest sauropod of Cimmeria
Euhelopus zdanskyi (estimated)	PMU R234	2045	1862	1.04	0.77	3400	3.08	1.32	29.9	8.3	Fastest sauropod of Asia (Paleoasia)
Lithostrotia											
Malawisaurus dixeyi (estimated)	MAI-201	1474	1815	0.84	0.74	2800	2.52	1.08	14.4	4.0	Slowest sauropod of Africa
Rapetosaurus krausei (juvenile)	FMNH PR 2209	1180	1371	1.05	0.9	940	3.87	1.32	21.7	6.0	
Laplatasaurus araukanicus	MLP CS 1127-1128	1732	2013	1	0.74	3800	2.94	1	23.1	6.4	
Antarctosaurus wichmannianus (estimated)	MACN 6804	2409	2846	1.09	0.81	9500	2.58	1.24	27.7	7.7	Fastest sauropod of the Upper Cretaceous
Saltasauroidea											
Futalognkosaurus dukei (estimated)	MUCPv-323	3250	3685	0.94	0.69	30000	1.76	0.84	17.3	4.8	
Epachthosaurus sciuttoi	UNPSJB-PV 920	1974	2178	0.92	0.81	4300	2.48	1.2	21.2	5.9	
Saltasauridae											
Dreadnoughtus schrani (estimated)	MPM-PV 1156	3245	3696	1	0.76	35000	1.58	1	15.9	4.4	Slowest sauropod of the Upper Cretaceous
Opisthocoelicaudia skarzynskii	ZPAL MgD-I/48	2103	2645	0.91	0.72	8600	2.08	1.08	17	4.7	
Saltasaurus loricatus (estimated)	PVL 4017	1300	1694	1	0.76	2500	2.94	1.26	17.3	4.8	
Bonatitan reigi (estimated)	MACN 821 RN 821	864	1130	1.17	0.76	600	4.31	1.47	19.7	5.5	
Magyarosaurus dacus (estimated)	BMNH R.3853	991	1185	1.25	0.99	520	4.4	1.5	23.5	6.5	
Other animals - elephants											
Asian elephant (Elephas maximus)	A 1225	1860	1916	0.96	0.74	3100	1.26	2.94	24.8	6.9	
African elephant (Loxodonta africana)	AMNH 3283	2239	2416	0.91	0.75	6150	1.2	2.48	25.1	7.0	

The first quadrupedal sauropodomorph
"Thotobolosaurus mabeatae"

Its large forefeet, the four vertebrae in its sacrum, and the characteristics of its thoracic vertebrae suggest that this animal may have usually walked on four legs. It is also known as "Kholumolumosaurus ellenbergerorum."

See more: *Ellenberger & Ellenberger 1956; Charig et al. 1965; Ellenberger 1970; Gauffre 1996*

RECORDS: POSTURE AND LOCOMOTION OF SAUROPODOMORPHS AND SAUROPODS

1818—USA—First bipedal sauropodomorph
The first remains of *Anchisaurus polyzelus* were mistaken for a human skeleton, perhaps because of their size and long trunk. See more: *Smith 1820; Hitchcock 1865; Marsh 1882, 1885; Baur 1883*

1857—USA—Least cursorial bipedal sauropodomorph of the Triassic
Gresslyosaurus ingens had a very long femur in comparison to the sum of the tibia and metatarsal, with a ratio of 1.04. See more: *Rutimeyer 1857*

1871—England—Least cursorial sauropod of the Jurassic
Cetiosaurus oxoniensis had a very long femur compared to the sum of its tibia and metatarsal, with a ratio of 0.7. See more: *Phillips 1871*

1889—USA—Most cursorial bipedal sauropodomorph of the Jurassic
Ammosaurus major had a very short femur in comparison to the length of its tibia and metatarsal combined, with a ratio of 1.7 to 1.75. See more: *Marsh 1889*

1924—South Africa—First quadrupedal sauropodomorph
Melanorosaurus readi (black mountain lizard), sometimes mistakenly referred to as "Melanosaurus," was named after the place it was discovered—Thaba 'Nyama (Black Mountain). See more: *Haughton 1924*

1924—South Africa—Least cursorial quadrupedal sauropodomorph
Melanorosaurus readi had a very long femur compared to the length of its tibia and metatarsal, with a ratio of 1.16. See more: *Haughton 1924*

1941—China—Least cursorial bipedal sauropodomorph of the Triassic
Some *Lufengosaurus huenei* individuals had femurs that were longer than the sum of their tibias and metatarsals compared to others, with a ratio of 0.98. Those differences may have been due to the age of the specimens. See more: *Young 1941, 1942*

1969—Argentina—Oldest quadrupedal sauropodomorph
Riojasaurus insertus was described at the same time as *Strenusaurus procerus*, but the latter was actually a juvenile of the same species. Some authors believe it would not have been able to stand with a bipedal posture, while others have reconstructed it as bipedal. It dates to the Upper Triassic (Norian, approx. 227–208.5 Ma). Specimen MFR 1–4 (present-day France) may have been from the same epoch. See more: *Bonaparte 1969; Gauffre 1995; Van Heerden & Galton 1997; Hartmann**

1969—Argentina—Most cursorial quadrupedal sauropodomorph
Riojasaurus incertus had the shortest femur relative to the sum of its tibia and metatarsal of all the other quadrupedal sauropodomorphs, with a ratio of 1.23. See more: *Bonaparte 1969*

1972—Lesotho—Most cursorial sauropod of the Triassic
"Thotobolosaurus mabeatae" had a relatively shorter femur in comparison to the sum of its tibia and metatarsal than its relatives, with a ratio of 0.94. See more: *Ellenberger 1972; Gauffre 1996*

1975–1979—India—Earliest gregarious sauropods
Groups of at least twelve *Kotasaurus yamanpalliensis* and groups of six *Barapasaurus tagorei* from the Lower Jurassic (Sinnemurian, approx. 199.3–190.8 Ma) were discovered. See more: *Jain et al. 1975; Yadagiri et al. 1979; Jain 1980; Yadagiri 1988, 2001; Bandyopadhyay et al. 2010; Day et al. 2004; Myers & Fiorillo 2009*

1977—Mongolia—First tripedal sauropod
Although sauropods have been illustrated moving with a bipedal posture through water or occasionally while feeding or defending themselves, no sauropod has been found with the anatomical features that would have made this possible. The hips of *Opisthocoelicaudia skarzynskii* were shaped differently than those of other sauropods. They were wider, similar to those of today's giant sloths, capable of supporting the large muscles used for bipedal movement. This would have enabled them, especially titanosaur sauropods, to use a three-footed stance to reach the treetops to obtain food. See more: *Gregory 1951; Borsuk-Białynicka1977; Tanimoto 1991*

1985—England—Most recent quadrupedal sauropodomorph
Some authors consider *Camelotia borealis* a basal sauropod, while others maintain it is a very advanced sauropodomorph. It dates to the Upper Triassic (Rhaetian 208.5–201.3 Ma). See more: *Galton 1985*

1988—Texas, USA—Most recent gregarious sauropods
Three juvenile specimens of *Alamosaurus sanjuanensis* were preserved together and dated to the Upper Cretaceous (Maastrichtian, approx. 72.1–66 Ma). See more: *Fiorillo 1988; Myers & Fiorillo 2009*

1998—China—Most cursorial sauropod of the Jurassic
Gongxianosaurus shibeiensis had a very short femur in comparison to the sum of its tibia and metatarsal, with a ratio of 1.04. The calf SMA 0009 known as *Brachiosaurus* sp. also had the same ratio. See more: *He et al. 1998; Carballido et al.2012*

1990—China—Largest group of Jurassic sauropods discovered together
A group of 17 young *Bellusaurus sui* dating to the Middle Jurassic (Callovian, approx. 166.1–163.5 Ma) was reported. See more: *Dong 1990, 1992*

1994—Argentina—Earliest group of sauropods to include adults and juveniles
Some five adult and juvenile *Patagosaurus fariasi* individuals from the Middle Jurassic (Callovian, approx. 166.1–163.5 Ma) were reported. See more: *Coria 1994; Myers & Fiorillo 2009*

1996—Lesotho—Largest quadrupedal primitive sauropodomorph
The remains known as "Thotobolosaurus mabeatae" are larger than *Lessemsaurus* and *Ledumahadi*, which have been estimated as weighing 10–12 t on the basis of femur circumference, although that method is quite unreliable. "Thotobolosaurus" weighed 3.6 t and was 11 m long. See more: *Ellenberger & Ellenberger 1956; Charig et al. 1965; Gauffre 1996*

1999—Niger—Sauropod that could stand on its hind legs
Based on its center of gravity, researchers speculate that, like modern-day elephants, *Jobaria tiguidensis* could perform this action. It would not have been easy, of course, as it weighed some 17 t, and so it is unlikely to have done so. See more: *Sereno**

2000—Texas, USA—Largest group of Cretaceous sauropods found together
A group of four *Paluxysaurus jonesi* from the late Lower Cretaceous (upper Aptian, approx. 119–113 Ma) was discovered. They were probably juvenile *Sauroposeidon proteles*. See more: *Winkler et al. 2000; Rose 2007; Myers & Fiorillo 2009; D'Emic 2012*

2003—South Africa—Least cursorial sauropod of the Triassic
Antetronitrus ingenipes had a longer femur divided by the sum of its tibia and metatarsal than its near relatives, with a ratio of 0.91. From the time this animal first appears in the fossil record onward, sauropods were ill-adapted to attaining high speeds. See more: *Yates & Kitching 2003*

2007—Argentina—Least cursorial sauropod of the Cretaceous
Futalognkosaurus dukei had a very long femur in comparison to the tibia, with a ratio of 0.55. See more: *Calvo et al. 2007*

2008—Argentina—Most cursorial sauropod of the Cretaceous
The unnamed titanosaur MUCPv-1533 had a very short femur in comparison to the sum of its tibia and metatarsal, with a ratio of 1.1. See more: *Riga et al. 2008*

2011—Brazil—Most cursorial bipedal sauropodomorph of the Triassic
Pampadromaeus barberenai (ULBRA-PVT016) had a short femur in comparison to the sum of its tibia and metatarsal, with a ratio of 1.69. It may have been a juvenile specimen and, in any case, would have been fast enough to catch prey and to flee from predators. See more: *Cabreira et al. 2011*

2011—Argentina—Smallest quadrupedal sauropodomorph
Leonerasaurus taquetrensis was 2.8 m in length and weighed 60 kg. See more: *Pol, Garrido & Cerda 2011; McPhee et al. 2015*

2013—China—Largest bipedal sauropodomorph
The skeleton cf. *Yunnanosaurus* (ZLJ 0035), which housed a colony of insects, possibly termites, represents an animal 12 m long and weighing up to 3.6 t. The supposedly giant *Plateosaurus giganteus* GPIT E 3, is based on three fibulas that were mistaken for metatarsals. See more: *Xing et al. 2013*

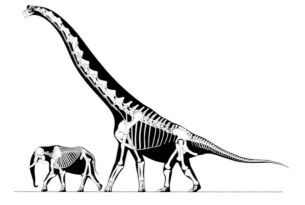

More than similar

Sauropods are known to have walked like elephants, with the same-side forelimbs and hind limbs moving at the same time. Camels and giraffes walk the same way, although the latter trot when they run, like most quadrupedal animals. The illustration on the left shows an African elephant and a *Giraffatitan* in motion.

PLANT PULLERS

Sauropodomorph jaws were designed to rip out or pull off branches, not to grind them. These giants did not chew their food; they merely bit off and swallowed it. Because of this, they did not develop large muscles for chewing, and so despite the large size of some of their skulls, their bite force was relatively weak. Comparatively, however, the different types of food consumed by different species led to notable differences among their bite forces. Some authors believe that these animals ingested stones and kept them in giant gizzards to help break up the food they consumed and allow it to ferment to better extract the nutrients.

This proposal is currently open to debate, however. Few studies to date have focused on estimating the bite force of sauropodomorphs, but fortunately that has been changing in recent years.

4050 N / 413 Kg
Measure: Bilateral

Sauropod with the most powerful bite force

Extrapolating the estimated bite force for the skull of a juvenile *Camarasaurus lentus* and the skull of an adult *C. supremus* shows that these sauropods could have had a bite force comparable to that of an adult lion, greater than that of any sauropod, so they may have taken advantage of foods that other sauropods could not consume. The juvenile specimen had an estimated bite force of 610 N. See more: *Button et al. 2014, 2016*

107 N / 11 Kg
Measure: Bilateral

The weakest sauropod bite force

Diplodocus carnegii had an extremely weak bite force for its enormous size. Although *Diplodocus* is the only estimated diplodocid with a bite force of just 324 N, the bite force of *Kaatedocus* may have been only 1/3 of that, similar to the bite force of a monitor lizard, or 1/40 the force of a *Camarasaurus supremus*. See more: *Degrange et al. 2010; Button et al. 2016*

188 N / 19 Kg
Measure: Bilateral

The only estimated bite force for a primitive sauropodomorph

According to a recent study (2016), *Plateosaurus longiceps* had a very weak bite force despite having a skull larger than that of a Labrador retriever. Even so, *Plateosaurus*'s bite force was greater than that of *Erlikosaurus*, the herbivorous theropod with the weakest bite force ever estimated. See more: *Strom & Holm 1992; Button et al. 2016; Molina-Pérez & Larramendi 2016*

SAUROPODOMORPH INTELLIGENCE

As we explained in the previous volume on theropods, the encephalization quotient (EQ, a measure of cognitive abilities) of an extinct animal can be estimated from its endocranium. In the case of sauropodomorphs, the type of EQ that should be used is the REQ, which is used for reptiles and less-derived non-avian dinosaurs.

Contrary to popular opinion, sauropods were not inept, as their encephalization quotients are in many cases comparable to those of present-day reptiles and some giant theropods. The idea that large sauropods were quite "stupid" is based on their very large, long size and comparatively small heads. Errors in calculation led to the mistaken belief that some sauropods had an EQ of 0.01, a result so low the creatures would have been completely lacking in intelligence. Today, however, it is generally accepted that sauropod EQs ranged from 0.18 to 0.8, a cognitive capacity similar to some iguanas and even of some giant theropods.

Recent studies suggest that some sauropods had highly developed hearing and balance, although their sight and sense of smell were weak, comparable to those of *Nigersaurus*, *Quaesitosaurus*, and *Spinophorosaurus*. Others, like *Ampelosaurus* sp., however, were not very capable of detecting rapid movements. See more: *Jerison 1973; Kurzanov & Bannikov 1983; Hurlburt 1996; Franzosa, 2004; Witmer et al. 2008; Knoll & Schwarz-Wings 2009; Knoll, Witmer, Ortega, Ridgely & Schwarz-Wings 2012; Knoll, Ridgely, Ortega, Sanz & Witmer 2013; Kundrat, Poropat & Elliot 2015*

Animal Intelligence

Sauropods

Species	Specimen	Endocranial volume (ml)	*Brain mass (g)	Body mass (kg)	REQ	Endocranial volume reference
Galeamopus hayi (=*Diplodocus*)	CM 662	88	32.6	9500	0.29	Franzosa 2004
Giraffatitan brancai	MB.R.2223.1	309	114.3	21000	0.66	Janensch 1935
Nigersaurus taqueti	MNN GAD512	73	27	800	0.95	Sereno et al. 2007
Amargasaurus cazaui	MACN-N 15	98	36.3	4000	0.52	Paulina-Carabajal 2014
Antarctosaurus wichmannianus	MACN 6904	75	27.8	9500	0.25	Paulina-Carabajal 2012
Unnamed Rio Negro Titanosaur	MGPIFD-GR 118	64	23.7	13000	0.18	Paulina-Carabajal 2012
Bonatitan reigi	MACN-RN 821	25	9.3	600	0.38	Paulina-Carabajal 2012
Apatosaurus sp.	BYU 17096	125	46.3	17000	0.30	Balanoff et al. 2010
Ampelosaurus sp.	MCCM-HUE-1667	41.6	15.4	5000	0.20	Knoll et al. 2015
Plateosaurus longiceps	AMNH FARB 6810	45	16.7	450	0.80	This book
Shunosaurus lii	ZG65430	47	17.4	7000	0.18	This book
Camarasaurus lentus	DNM28	130	48.1	4500	0.65	This book
Diamantinasaurus matildae	AODF 836	225	83.3	10000	0.72	Kundrát et al. 2015

Present-day reptiles

Species	Specimen	Endocranial volume (ml)	*Brain mass (g)	Body mass (kg)	REQ	Endocranial volume reference
American alligator	ROM 8328	27	10	238	0.69	Hurlburt et al. 2013
American alligator	ROM 8333	33	12.2	277	0.77	Hurlburt et al. 2013
American alligator	uncatalogued	-	14.4	205	1.05	Crile & Quiring 1940
Common boa	uncatalogued	-	0.44	1.83	0.45	Crile & Quiring 1940
American crocodile	uncatalogued	-	15.6	134	1.47	Crile & Quiring 1940
Iguana	uncatalogued	-	1.44	4.2	0.92	Crile & Quiring 1940
Python	uncatalogued	-	1.13	6.1	0.59	Crile & Quiring 1940
Green sea turtle	uncatalogued	-	8.6	114	0.89	Crile & Quiring 1940

* To obtain the brain mass of the sauropodomorphs the volume of the endocranium should be multiplied by 0.37. See more: *Hurlbut 2013*

Sauropod with the highest cognitive ability
Nigersaurus taqueti

This apparently defenseless sauropod was small, lacked armor, and was not capable of running fast. We don't know whether it had other defenses such as crypsis, repulsiveness, or some other quality, but we do know it had a greater brain capacity than other sauropods, close to that of the least capable theropod species, so it may have developed more complex behavior that allowed it to evade predators. See more: *Sereno et al. 2007*

THE BRAIN AND SENSES OF SAUROPODOMORPHS AND SAUROPODS

1926—Germany—The only primitive sauropodomorph with a calculated REQ

Plateosaurus longiceps AMNH 6810 had an REQ of 0.8, greater than that of most sauropods. See more: *Huene 1926; Prieto-Marquez & Norell 2011*

1935—Tanzania—Jurassic sauropod with the highest cognitive ability

Giraffatitan brancai MB.R.2223.1 had an REQ of 0.66. Previous errors in calculation had given this animal the lowest EQ of any sauropod. See more: *Janensch 1935; Jerison 1973*

1935—Tanzania—Largest-brained sauropod of the Jurassic

The endocranium of *Giraffatitan brancai* MB.R.223.1 had a volume of 309 ml and belonged to a specimen weighing about 21 t. Its REQ is similar to that of an American alligator (*Alligator mississippiensis*). See more: *Janensch 1935*

1983—Mongolia—Sauropod with the most well-developed hearing

Quaesitosaurus orientalis had a very large "resonator" that, combined with the opening of the middle ear, gave it very acute hearing. See more: *Kurzanov & Bannikov 1983; Lessem & Glut 1993*

1996—China—Jurassic sauropod with the lowest cognitive ability

Shunosaurus lii ZG65430 had an REQ of just 0.18. This figure is very low, even less than that of several reptiles. See more: *Zheng 1996; Chatterjee & Zheng 2002*

1997—USA—Noisiest land animal

Computer analysis has estimated that the sound of *Apatosaurus's* tail would have reached up to 200 decibels when snapped like a whip. The animal likely would not have been able to withstand hard blows so may have used its tail to threaten predators or even communicate with other members of its species. In comparison, a lion's roar reaches 114 decibels, an elephant's trumpet 117 decibels, the howling monkeys' howl 128 decibels, and the kakapo's scream 137 decibels. See more: *Myhrvold & Currie 1997; Zimmer 1997*

2007—Niger—Sauropod with the highest cognitive ability

Nigersaurus taqueti MNN GAD512 had a brain mass of approximately 27 g and a body mass of 800 kg, placing it above those of all other sauropods, with an REQ of 0.95. See more: *Sereno et al. 2007*

2007—Argentina—Cretaceous sauropod with the lowest cognitive ability

Titanosaur MGPIFD-GR 118 had an REQ of just 0.18. See more: *Paulina-Carabajal & Salgado 2007; Paulina-Carabajal 2012*

2011—First study on sauropodomorph sense of sight

An analysis of the sclerotic rings of *Lufengosaurus*, *Plateosaurus*, and *Riojasaurus* in comparison to those of modern-day birds found that the former was cathemeral (able to see both diurnally and nocturnally). See more: *Schmitz & Motani 2011*

2011—First study on sauropod sense of sight

Diplodocus and *Nemegtosaurus mongoliensis* had cathemeral sight, which enabled them to be active in both daytime and nighttime. See more: *Schmitz & Motani 2011*

2015—Spain—Sauropod with the least developed hearing

Ampelosaurus sp. MCCM-HUE-1667 had a very undeveloped middle ear, which also indicates that it did not have very good balance and may have moved slowly. See more: *Knoll et al. 2015*

MYTH Giraffatitan was as unintelligent as a "zombie"

Throughout history, this creature was believed to be extremely lacking in intelligence, because the weight of the holotype specimen HMN SII, a relatively complete skeleton of a very large animal that was missing a skull, was used to estimate the EQ of other individuals such as MB.R.2223.1 (formerly known as HMN t 1), which belonged to a much smaller animal, leading to very low EQ results.

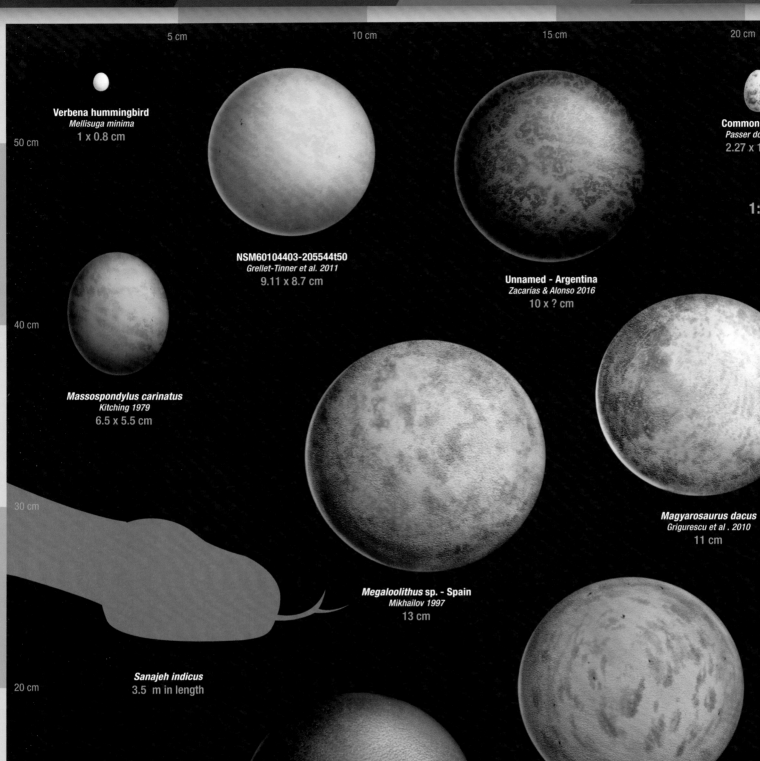

5 cm   10 cm   15 cm   20 cm

50 cm

40 cm

30 cm

20 cm

10 cm

Verbena hummingbird
Mellisuga minima
1 x 0.8 cm

Common sparrow
Passer domesticus
2.27 x 1.55 cm

1:2

NSM60104403-205544t50
Grellet-Tinner et al. 2011
9.11 x 8.7 cm

Unnamed - Argentina
Zacarías & Alonso 2016
10 x ? cm

Massospondylus carinatus
Kitching 1979
6.5 x 5.5 cm

Magyarosaurus dacus
Grigurescu et al . 2010
11 cm

Megaloolithus sp. - Spain
Mikhailov 1997
13 cm

Sanajeh indicus
3.5 m in length

Megaloolithus cylindricus
Kholsa & Sahni 1995
12 cm

Rock dove
Columbia livia
4 x 2.9 cm

Unnamed
Magalhaes-Ribeiro 2000
12.5 cm

Chicken
Gallus domesticus
5.9 x 4.4 cm

THE SMALLEST

LJ South Africa—Smallest sauropodomorph egg
This *Massospondylus* sp. egg measures 6.5 x 5.5 cm. See more: *Kitching 1979; Grine & Kitching 1987; Reisz et al. 2005*

C Mongolia—Smallest sauropod egg of Asia (Paleoasia)
Specimen NSM60104403–20554450 had a diameter of just 9.11 x 8.7 cm and included a lithostrotian titanosaur embryo. See more: *Grellet-Tinner et al. 2011*

IUC Argentina—Smallest sauropod egg of southern South America
Some subspherical eggs 10–16 cm long were presented at a paleontological conference.
See more: *Zacarías & Alonso 2016*

IUC Romania—Smallest sauropod egg of eastern Europe?
Megaloolithus sp., attributed to *Magyarosaurus dacus*, were 11–13 cm in diameter. One surprising case involves some eggs 14–16 cm in diameter that were practically identical both externally and in microstructure to the ornithischian *Telmatosaurus transsylvanicus*, presenting a difficult enigma. See more: *Weishampel & Jianu 2011; Sellés 2012; Sellés et al. 2014; Grigorescu et al. 2010; Botfalvai, Csiki-Sava, Grigorescu & Vasile 2016*

IUC Spain—Smallest sauropod egg of western Europe
These *Megaloolithus* sp. eggs were 13–20 cm in diameter. See more: *Mikhailov 1997a,1997b*

IUC India—Smallest sauropod egg of southern Asia (Hindustan)
These *Megaloolithus cylindricus* eggs were 12–20 cm in diameter. See more: *Kholsa & Sahni 1995*

IUC Brazil—Smallest sauropod egg of northern South America
An egg with a diameter of 15 x 10 cm was deformed and found to have an actual diameter of approximately 12.5 cm. See more: *Magalhaes-Ribeiro 2000, 2002; Grellet-Tinner & Zaher 2007*

1:1

The largest insect pupa found inside a sauropodomorph nest and the oldest found in a dinosaur nest

These pupae were mistaken for *Mussaurus patagonicus* eggs. There have been other supposed fossil eggs, including strange ones, that turned out not to be eggs at all but actually stones or wasp or beetle pupae.
See more: *Bonaparte & Vince 1979; Carpenter 1999*

OTHER RECORDS

1966—IUC France—First sauropod eggs laid in a line
This line of 15–20 eggs was laid by a titanosaur. See more: *Dughi & Sirugue 1966*

1966—IUC France—Most numerous line of sauropod eggs
These lines have 6–20 eggs. The fact that the sauropod moved forward as she laid them indicates that the species did not care for their young. See more: *Dughi & Sirugue 1966*

1976—First family of oospecies created
The family Faveoloolithidae includes the oogenera *Faveoloolithus, Hemifaveoloolithus, Parafaveoloolithus*, "Paquiloolithus," and *Sphaerovum*. See more: *Zhao & Dong 1976*

1979—LJ China and South Africa—Oldest sauropodomorph nests
Mussaurus patagonicus, from the Upper Triassic, was found in a nest with five hatchlings and broken eggshells. The calves may have been raised by their parents, as they seem to have been born without the ability to survive on their own. See more: *Bonaparte & Vince 1979; Moratalla & Powell 1994*

1979–2013—LJ China and South Africa—Oldest sauropodomorph nesting colonies
These nests of *Massospondylus carinatus* and *Lufengosaurus* sp. date to the Lower Jurassic (Hettangian, approx. 201.3–199.3 Ma). See more: *Kitching 1979; Reisz et al. 2005; Reisz et al. 2013*

1979—South Africa—Thinnest sauropodomorph eggshell
The shells of *Massospondylus* sp. eggs were 0.75–1.2 mm thick. See more: *Kitching 1979; Grine & Kitching 1987*

1981—IUC France—Sauropod nest with the most nesting layers
Sauropods reused their nests, leading to multiple nesting layers. One such nest contained eight eggs in three or four different layers. See more: *Kérourio 1981; Vila et al. 2010*

1981—IUC France—First sauropod mixed nest
One nest contained eight eggs, some laid in a line, others in a clutch. See more: *Kérourio 1981; Vila et al. 2010*

1984—IUC India—First nesting site found in Asia
These large concentrations of *Megaloolithus*, found in the Lameta Formation, yielded several different species. See more: *Mohabey 1984, 1987, 1998; Srivastava et al. 1986; Mohabey & Masthur 1989; Mohabey 2005*

1987—LJ South Africa—First sauropodomorph embryo of Africa
Massospondylus carinatus is the first evidence of an unhatched sauropodomorph. See more: *Grine & Kitching 1987; Reisz et al. 2005*

1990—IUC India—First sauropod group nest
Several lines of eggs were found before sauropod nests were discovered. This group nest contained 13 eggs. See more: *Mohabey 1990*

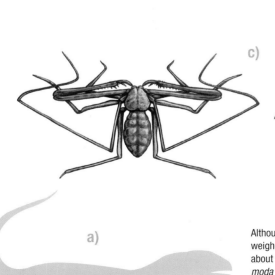

a)

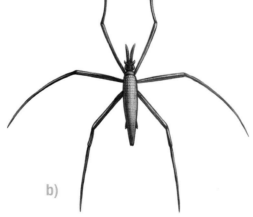

c)

b)

d)

1:2

Although the adult **(a)** *Massospondylus* was 5.7 m long and weighed 450 kg, the newborn calf was just 13 cm in length, about the same as the longest insect of the Jurassic **(b)** *Chresmoda oscura*, which reached 14–17 cm overall (with a 4-cm body length). In contrast, **(c)** *Britopygus weygoldti* and **(d)** *Mongoloarachne jurassica*, the largest arachnids of the Mesozoic, measured 2 and 2.5 cm in length, respectively, but with their legs the total span was 15 cm.

20 cm

40 cm

60 cm

80 cm

1 m

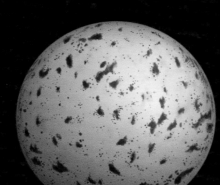

cf. *Sphaerovum erbeni*
Tauber 2007
21 cm

80 cm

Megaloolithus siruguei
*Vianey-Liaud, Mallan,
Buscail & Montgelard 1994*
25 cm

Unnamed - Argentina
Simón 2006
21 cm

1:4

Unnamed - Argentina
Argañaraz et al. 2013
15 cm

60 cm

Unnamed - Brazil
Price 1951
15 cm

Magyarosaurus dacus
Grigurescu et al. 2010
13 cm

Fusioolithus baghensis
Khosla & Sahni 1995
20 cm

40 cm

**Faveoloolithus sp.
South Korea**
Huh & Zelenitsky 2002
20 cm

Megaloolithus cylindricus
Kholsa & Sahni 1995
20 cm

20 cm

Chicken
Gallus domesticus
5.9 x 4.4 cm

Ostrich
Struthio camelus
Khanna 2005
17 x 13.6 cm

Megaloolithus walpurensis
Khosla & Sahni 1995
20 cm

THE LARGEST

IUC France—Largest sauropod egg of Europe

Megaloolithus siruguei eggs were 18–25 cm in diameter. The well-known case of *Hypselosaurus*, with eggs 30 cm in diameter, is erroneous. The specimen was actually a crushed egg, and it is uncertain whether it belonged to this sauropod species.

See more: *Vianey-Liaud, Mallan, Buscail & Montgelard 1994*

IUC Argentina, Uruguay—Largest sauropod eggs of southern South America

cf. *Sphaerovum erbeni*, found in Uruguay, included an egg 21 cm in diameter, as did other faveoolithids found in Argentina. See more: *Mones 1980; Simón 2006; Tauber 2007; Grellet-Tinner & Fiorelli 2010*

IUC India—Largest theropod egg of southern Asia (Hindustan)

Fusioolithus baghensis, Megaloolithus cylindricus and *M. walpurensis* (formerly *M. khempurensis*) had diameters of 20 cm. An abnormal diameter measuring 28 x 22 cm appeared, along with a group of eggshells with an oval shape, perhaps due to expansion after the shells were broken and rearranged. See more: *Sahni et al 1994; Mohabey 1998; Kholsa & Sahni 1995; Fernández & Khosla 2015*

IUC South Korea—Largest sauropod egg of Asia (Paleoasia)

These *Faveoloolithus* sp. eggs ranged from 15 to 20 cm in diameter. See more: *Huh & Zelenitsky 2002*

IUC Brazil—Largest sauropod eggs of northern South America

An egg 15 cm in diameter was reported in the Bauru Formation. See more: *Price 1951*

eLC Argentina—Largest sauropod eggs of the Lower Cretaceous

These crushed eggs were 14–16 cm in diameter. See more: *Argañaraz et al. 2013*

OTHER RECORDS

1992–2002—IUC Argentina, Brazil—Thinnest sauropod eggshell of South America

The minimum shell thickness is 0.5 mm for shells found in the province of Salitral Moreno, Argentina, and in Bauru municipality, Brazil. See more: *Powell 1992; Magalhaes-Ribeiro 2002*

1995—IUC India—Thinnest sauropod shell of Asia (Hindustan)

Fusioolithus baguensis had shells 1–1.7 mm thick. See more: *Khosla & Sahni 1995; Fernández & Khosla 2014*

1997—IUC Argentina—First nesting site of South America

Several eggs of *Sphaerovum* were found 2–3 meters apart in the Auca Mahuevo zone. See more: *Chiappe et al. 1998; Coria & Chiappe 2007; Chiappe et al. 2004; Sander et al. 2008*

1997—IUC Argentina—Sauropod nesting colony with the most nests

Some 180 nests of *Sphaerovum* were found in the Auca Mahuevo zone. See more: *Chiappe et al. 1998; Coria & Chiappe 2007; Chiappe et al. 2003*

1997—IUC Spain—First nesting site of Europe

Among several concentrations of *Megaloolithus* nests reported on the continent, the one in Basturs locality was the first to be discovered. See more: *Sanz et al.1995; Sanz & Moratalla 1997; Sander et al. 1998, 2008*

Egg/sauropod ratio

Weights are estimated using Dickinson 2007 method

Oogenus and species	Largest egg	Largest egg Weight - egg/ adult theropod	Bibliography
Massospondylus carinatus	65 x 55 mm 111 g	0.025 % or 4000 times as large	Kitching 1979; Gottfried et al. 2004
Magyarosaurus dacus	150 x 150 mm 2000 g	0.38 % or 260 times as large	Grigorescu et al. 1990
Laplatasaurus sp.	122 x 122 mm 1090 g	0.02 % or 4500 times as large	Calvo et al. 1997

1998—IUC China—The most ovaloid sauropod egg

Parafaveoloolithus xipingensis (formerly *Youngoolithus*) ranged from 10.94 to 17.34 cm in anteroposterior diameter and 9.1–15.6 cm around the equator. It is uncertain whether or not *Youngoolithus xiaguanensis* belonged to a sauropod, as it is even more ovaloid: 16–17.5 cm in length and 9.1–10.9 cm around. See more: *Zhao 1979; Xiaosi et al. 1998; Zou et al. 2013*

2003—IUC China—Thinnest sauropod shell of Asia (Paleoasia)

This shell of *Similifaveoloolithus shuangtangensis* was 1.05–1.27 mm thick. See more: *Fang, Lu, Jiang & Yang, 2003; Wang, Zhao, Wang & Jiang 2011*

2003—IUC China—Thinnest sauropod eggshell of the early Upper Cretaceous

These *Similifaveoloolithus shuangtangensis* eggs had a minimum thickness of 1.05 mm. See more: *Fang, Lu et al. 2003; Wang et al. 2011*

2006—IUC France—Most porous sauropod egg

These *Megaloolithus siruguei* eggs, measuring 18.5 x 18.5 cm, had 475,434 pores. See more: *Deeming 2006*

2006—IUC France—Least-porous sauropod egg

An egg known as *Hypsylosaurus priscus*, measuring 15.4 x 15.4 cm, had approximately 24,000 pores. See more: *Deeming 2006*

2008—IUC Argentina—Sauropod nest with the most eggs

This nest of *Sphaerovum erbeni* contained an estimated 25–35 eggs. See more: *Jackson et al. 2008*

2009—eLC Spain—Thinnest sauropod eggshell of Europe

Some of these *Megaloolithus* sp. eggshells were just 0.5 mm thick, the thinnest of the Lower Cretaceous. See more: *Moreno-Aranza et al. 2009*

2010—IUC France—Largest sauropod nest

This irregularly shaped *Megaloolithus sirugei* nest measured 2.3 meters long, 89 cm wide, and 35 cm deep and contained 28 eggs. See more: *Vila et al. 2010*

2010—Argentina—First hydrothermal nests

Paleontological, sedimentological, and geochemical studies demonstrated the presence of paleogeysers that sauropods apparently took advantage of to incubate their eggs. See more: *Grellet-Tinner & Fiorelli 2010*

2010—USA—First comparison of excavated sauropod nests

The comparison showed that sauropod nest marks are morphologically similar to the scratches that some turtles make when laying their eggs. See more: *Fowler & Hall 2010*

2010—India—First sauropod nest found with a predator

Sanajeh indicus, a constrictor species about 3 m long, was found curled up near the eggs of *Megaloolithus dhoridungriensis* and a sauropod hatchling. As the constrictor would not have been able to eat the eggs, it is believed to have been preying upon the titanosaur hatchlings. See more: *Wilson et al. 2010*

2011—IUC Argentina—First pupae found in a sauropod egg

Eight wasp cocoons were found inside a titanosaur egg. A complex invertebrate community may have developed inside, attracted by the decomposing organic matter. See more: *Genise & Sarzetti 2011*

2013—IUC Morocco—Thinnest sauropod egg

Some shells identified as *Pseudomegaloolithus atlasi* had a minimum thickness of 0.443 mm, unlike the holotype specimen, whose shells range from 0.6 to 1.14 mm thick. See more: *Vianey-Liaud & García 2003; Chassagne-Manoukian et al. 2013*

2013—LJ China—The first sauropodomorph embryos of Asia

Embryos and calves of *Lufengosaurus* sp. were discovered with femurs 12–22 mm in length, indicating that these animals were likely 13.5–25 cm long and weighed 8–50 g. See more: *Reisz et al. 2013*

2013—eLC Argentina—Oldest sauropod eggs of South America

Some eggs 14–16 cm in diameter lengthwise were discovered in the Cerro Barcino Formation, which dates to the early Lower Cretaceous (Hauterivian, approx. 132.9–129.4 Ma). See more: *Argañaraz et al. 2013*

2013—First calculated incubation time for sauropod eggs

When compared to the incubation times and number of eggs in bird and reptile nests, this study estimated that sauropod eggs would have hatched after 65–82 days of incubation. It would have taken a long time for viable hatchlings to develop and come out of the shell. As the large eggs of an ostrich need 42 days of incubation, researchers believe that sauropods laid relatively small eggs that would not take too long to develop, to prevent them from falling prey to oviphagous theropods. See more: *Ruxton et al. 2014*

2015—Most recent oospecies family created

Fusioolithidae includes a single oogenus, *Fusioolithus*, with two species—*F. baghensis* (formerly *Megaloolithus*) and *F. berthei*. See more: *Fernández & Khosla 2015*

2015—Oolite species with the widest global distribution

Fusioolithus baguensis includes *Megaloolithus balasinorensis* (India), *Megaloolithus pseudomamilare* (France), *Megaloolithus trempii* (Spain), and *Patagoolithus salitralensis* (Argentina) and is also present in Peru. See more: *Sigé 1968; Khosla & Sahni 1995; Vianey-Liaud, Herisch, Sahni & Sigé 1997; Moratalla 1998; Simón 2006; Fernández & Khosla 2015*

FOSSIL EGGS (OOLITES) OF SAUROPODOMORPHS AND SAUROPODS

1859—IUC France—First sauropod eggs of western Europe
The shells discovered would have been from an egg 18 cm in diameter, and indeed later discoveries came very close to this estimate. The shells were interpreted as belonging to giant birds or the broken carapaces of late Upper Cretaceous animals (Maastrichtian, approx. 72.1–66 Ma). See more: *Pouech 1859; D'Archiac 1859*

1869—IUC France—First sauropod eggs of western Europe
The first dinosaur eggs discovered were identified as those of a giant crocodile (the sauropod *Hypselosaurus priscus*) eight years later and not recognized as dinosaur eggs until the early 20th century. See more: *Matheron 1869; Gervais 1877; Buffetaut & Le Loeuff 1994*

1950—ILC Tanzania—Oldest sauropod eggs of Africa?
Some eggs measuring 14–22 cm in diameter that were reported may be ovoid concretions, as they do not display the typical characteristics of eggshells. The find dates to the late Lower Cretaceous. See more: *Swinton 1950; Gottfried et al. 2004*

1951—IUC Brazil—First sauropod eggs in northern South America
The eggs, known as "*Hypselosaurus* sp.," were not described in detail, but they are known to have been 15 cm in diameter. They date to the late Upper Cretaceous (Campanian, approx. 83.6–72.1 Ma). See more: *Price 1951*

1957—IUC India—First sauropod eggs in southern Asia (Hindustan)
Eggs similar to *Megaloolithus* were dated to the early Upper Cretaceous (Cenomanian, approx. 100.5–93.9 Ma). See more: *Sahni 1957; Sahni & Gupta 1982; Buffetaut & Le Loeuff 1994*

1957—eUC India—Oldest eggs of southern Asia (Hindustan)
All sauropod eggs found in India date to the end of the late Upper Cretaceous, except for these, reportedly from the early Upper Cretaceous (Cenomanian, approx. 100.5–93.9 Ma). See more: *Sahni 1957*

1968—IUC Peru—Most recent sauropod shells
Shells of *Fusioolithus baghensis* (formerly *Megaloolithus pseudomamillare*), 0.81–1.44 mm thick, were dated to the end of the late Upper Cretaceous (upper Maastrichtian, approx. 66 Ma). They were associated with Paleocene fauna, which may indicate that they are eggs of more recent sauropods. See more: *Sigé 1968; Vianey-Liaud et al. 1997*

1976—IUC China—First sauropod eggs of eastern Asia
Faveoloolithus ningxiangensis is the species that represents the Faveoloolithidae family, which is known only in eastern Asia (China, South Korea, and Mongolia) and South America (Argentina and Uruguay). See more: *Zhao & Dong 1976*

1976—IUC China—First named sauropod eggs of Asia
Faveoloolithus ningxiangensis may be Saltasauroides eggs. See more: *Zhao & Dong 1976*

1976—IUC China—Thickest sauropod eggshell of Asia (Paleoasia)
The shell of *Faveoloolithus ningxiaensis* was 1.2–2.6 mm thick. The shells of *Protodictyoolithus hongpoensis* were even thicker (2.5–2.8 mm), but it is uncertain if they belonged to sauropods or not. See more: *Zhao & Dong 1976; Zhao 1994; Wang, Zhao et al. 2013*

1979—LJ South Africa—Shells and eggs of the oldest sauropodomorphs of Africa
These *Massospondylus* sp. eggs were 65 x 55 mm in diameter, with shells 0.75–1.2 mm thick. Based on the egg's structure, researchers suspected that they were actually crocodile eggs, but a new analysis indicates that they belonged to a sauropodomorph. See more: *Kitching 1979; Grine & Kitching 1987; Zelenitsky & Modesto 2002; Reisz et al. 2005*

1979—UT Argentina—Oldest sauropodomorph eggs of South America
Two 2.5-cm subspherical pieces that accompanied the remains of *Mussaurus patagonicus* calves were not confirmed under a microscope as authentic dinosaur eggs, so their true nature is still a mystery. See more: *Bonaparte & Vince 1979; Carpenter 1999*

1980—IUC Uruguay—First sauropod eggs of southern South America
Sphaerovum erbeni consists of some intermediate eggs, between *Megaloolithus* and *Faveoloolithus*, that date to the late Upper Cretaceous (upper Campanian-lower Maastrichtian, approx. 77.85–66 Ma). See more: *Mones 1980*

1980—IUC Uruguay—First named sauropod egg of South America
There was an unsuccessful attempt to change the name of *Sphae-*

rovum erbeni to *Sphaeroolithus*. See more: *Mones 1980; Carpenter & Alf 1994*

1988—IUC Romania—First sauropod eggs of eastern Europe
These eggs, 17 cm in diameter, may belong to the ornithischian *Telmatosaurus* or to sauropods similar to *Magyarosaurus*. The latter is more likely based on the shell structure. They date to the late Upper Cretaceous (upper Maastrichtian, approx. 69–66 Ma). See more: *Grigorescu 1993; Grigorescu et al. 1994; Carpenter 1999*

1994—IUC France—First named sauropod eggs of Europe
Megaloolithus aureliensis, M. mammilare, M. petralta, and *M. siruguei* have also been reported in Spain. See more: *Vianey-Liaud, Mallan, Buscail & Montgelard 1994; Vianey-Liaud & López-Martínez 1997; López-Martínez 2000; Sellés & Vila 2015*

1994—IUC India—First sauropod egg mistaken for an ornithischian egg
Cairanoolithus dughii were believed to belong to a sauropod, but the current proposal is that they belonged to armored ornithischians. See more: *Vianey-Liaud, Mallan, Buscail & Montgelard 1994; Sellés & Galobart 2017*

1994—IUC Spain and France—Thickest sauropod shell of Europe
These shells of *Megaloolithus sirugei* are 1.7–3.2 mm thick. See more: *Vianey-Liaud, Mallan, Buscali & Montgelard 1994*

1995—IUC India—Thickest sauropod shell of Asia (Hindustan)
This *Megaloolithus walpurensis* shell is 3.5–3.6 mm thick. See more: *Khosla & Sahni 1995*

1995—IUC India—First named sauropod eggs in southern Asia (Hindustan)
Megaloolithus cylindricus, M. jabalpurensis, M. mohabeyi, M. baghensis, M. dholiyaensis, M. padiyalensis, and *M. walpurensis* are all based on eggs or shells. *M. baghensis* is now considered part of the genus *Fusioolithus*. See more: *Kholsa & Sahni 1995; Fernández & Khosla 2015*

1997—IUC Argentina—First named sauropod egg of South America
Megaloolithus patagonicus is now considered a synonym of the species *Megaloolithus jabalpurensis*, found in India, which suggests that they belonged to the same group of sauropods. See more: *Kholsa & Sahni 1995; Calvo, Engelland, Heredia & Salgado 1997*

1997—Peru—Most recent sauropod egg?
Shells of *Megaloolithus pseudomamillare* have been reported in Paleocene or Eocene rocks; however, they may be older remains that were displaced by geological activity. See more: *Vianey-Liaud, Hirsch, Sahni-Sahni & Sigé 1997*

1998—IUC India—First sauropod egg mistaken for a theropod egg
Researchers suspected that these shells of *Megaloolithus rahioliensis* belonged to the genus Macroolithus until some complete eggs were found later. See more: *Mohabey 1998*

1999—IUC Argentina—First sauropod egg named in a thesis
"Paquiloolithus rionegrinus" is currently an informal name. See more: *Simón 1999*

2003—IUC Morocco—Oldest sauropod shells of northern Africa
Pseudomegaloolithus atlasi dates to the late Upper Cretaceous (upper Maastrichtian, approx. 69–66 Ma). See more: *Vianey-Liaud & García 2003; Chassagne-Manoukian et al. 2013*

2003—IUC Morocco—First named sauropod egg of Africa
Pseudomegaloolithus atlasi are shells 0.44–1.14 mm thick. See more: *Vianey-Liaud & García 2003; Chassagne-Manoukian et al. 2013*

Sauropod oolites (Their silhouettes are illustrated on the previous page)
(Masses estimated as per Dickison 2007)

N.°	Oogenus and species	Size (mm)	Mass (g)	Bibliography
	Sauropodomorph oolites without an oofamily			
1	*Massospondylus carinatus - LJ, South Africa*	65 x 55	111	Kitching 1979; Gottfried et al. 2004
	Megaloolithidae			
2	*Megaloolithus aureliensis - IUC, Spain, France*	220 x 220	6389	Vianey-Liaud et al. 1994
3	*Megaloolithus cylindricus (M. rahioliensis) - IUC, India*	200 x 200	4800	Khosla & Sahni 1995
4	*Megaloolithus dhoridungriensis - IUC, India*	180 x 180	3499	Mohabey 1998
5	*Megaloolithus jabalpurensis (Megaloolithus matleyi) - IUC, India*	180 x 180	3499	Khosla & Sahni 1995; Mohabey 1996
6	*Megaloolithus mamillare - IUC, Spain, France*	230 x 230	7300	Vianey-Liaud, Mallan, Buscail & Montgelard 1994
7	*Megaloolithus megadermus - IUC, India*	180 x 180	3499	Mohabey 1998
8	*Megaloolithus microtuberculata - IUC, France*	160 x 160	2458	García & Vianey-Liaud 2001
9	*Megaloolithus mohabeyi (M. phensaniensis) - IUC, India*	190 x 190	4115	Khosla & Sahni 1995; Mohabey 1998
10	*Megaloolithus jabalpurensis (Megaloolithus patagonicus) - IUC, Argentina*	122 x 122	1090	Khosla & Sahni 1995; Calvo et al.1997
11	*Megaloolithus petralta - IUC, France*	200 x 200	4800	Vianey-Liaud et al. 1994
12	*Megaloolithus sirugei - IUC, France*	250 x 250	9375	Vianey-Liaud et al. 1994
13	*Megaloolithus walpuriensis (M. khempurensis) - IUC, India*	200 x 200	4800	Khosla & Sahni 1995; Mohabey 1998
	Fusioolithidae			
14	*Fusioolithus baghensis (Megaloolithus balasinorensis, Megaloolithus pseudomamilare, Megaloolthus trempii, and Patagoolithus salitralensis) - IUC, Argentina, Spain, France, India, Peru*	210 x 210	5557	Sigé 1968; Khosla & Sahni 1995; Vianey-Liaud et al. 1997; Moratalla 1998; Simón 2006; Fernández & Khosla 2015
	Faveoloolithidae			
15	*Faveoloolithus ningxiaensis - IUC, China*	165 x 138	1885	Zhao & Dong 1976
16	*Hemifaveoloolithus muyhusanensis - eUC, China*	137 x 121	1203	Wang, Zhao, Wang & Jiang 2011
17	*Parafaveoloolithus macroporus - IUC, China*	137 x 13	1389	Zhang 2010
18	*Parafaveoloolithus microporus - IUC, China*	149 x 129.4	1497	Zhang 2010
19	*Parafaveoloolithus guoqingsiensis - eUC, China*	187 x 177	3515	Fang et al. 2000; Zhang 2010
20	*Parafaveoloolithus pingxiangensis - IUC, China*	138 x 120	1193	Zou et al. 2013
21	*Parafaveoloolithus xipingensis - IUC, China*	173 x 109	1245	Xiaosi et al. 1998
22	*Sphaerovum erbeni (Sphaeroolithus erbeni) - IUC, Argentina, Uruguay*	206 x 206	5245	Mones 1980; Casadío et al. 2002
	Similifaveoloolithidae			
23	*Similifaveoloolithus gongzhulingensis - eUC, China*	119 x 116	905	Wang et al. 2006; Wang et al. 2013
24	*Similifaveoloolithus shuangtangensis - eUC, China*	135 x 130	1369	Fang et al. 2003; Wang et al. 2013
	Dictyoolithidae (Sauropod or ornithischian eggs?)			
25	*Paradictyoolithus xiaxishanensis - IUC, China*	150 x 127	1449	Wang et al. 2013
26	*Paradictyoolithus zhuangqianensis - IUC, China*	135 x 13	1369	Wang et al. 2013
27	*Protodictyoolithus hongpoensis - eUC, China*	158 x 14	1858	Zhao 1994
28	*Protodictyoolithus jiangi - IUC, China*	144 x 124	1328	Liu & Zhao 2004
29	*Protodictyoolithus neixiangensis - eUC, China*	120 x 120	976	Zhao 1994
	Youngoolithidae (Sauropod or ornithischian eggs?)			
30	*Youngoolithus xiaguanensis - IUC, China*	175 x 109	1248	Liu & Zhao 2004
	Umbellaoolithidae (Sauropod or ornithischian eggs?)			
31	*Umbellaoolithus xiuningensis - IUC, China*	139 x 104	905	Huang et al. 2017

1:10 The eggs of sauropods and of hadrosauromorphs, such as *Telmatosaurus* (left), are very similar in both shape and shell structure. See more: *Grigorescu et al.1990; Grigorescu 2016*

2003—ILC Tanzania—Oldest sauropod shells of southern Africa

Some shells of *Megaloolithus* sp. 1.1–1.7 mm thick were discovered and dated to the late Lower Cretaceous (Aptian, approx. 125–113 Ma). See more: *O'Connor et al. 2003; Gottfried et al. 2004*

2003—IUC Morocco—Thickest sauropod shell of Africa

This shell of *Megaloolithus maghrebiensis* was up to 2.59 mm thick. See more: *García et al. 2003*

2006—MJ France—Oldest sauropod shells of western Europe

These shells 0.15–0.25 mm thick, belonging to *Megaloolithus* sp., date to the Middle Jurassic (upper Bajocian, approx. 169.3–168.3 Ma). See more: *García et al. 2006*

2010—ILC Mongolia—Oldest sauropod shells of eastern Asia

Some reported shells of *Parafaveoloolithus* sp. were dated to the late Lower Cretaceous (Aptian, approx. 125–113 Ma). See more: *Zhang 2010*

2010—IUC Argentina—Thickest sauropod shell

The thickest shell reported is from the Sanastaga Formation and measures 7.94 mm. That is 3.6 times the thickness of an ostrich (*Struthio camelus*) shell, which measures 1.6–2.2 mm. A shell of cf. *Sphaerovum erbeni* was reported as 8 mm thick, but it was a pathological specimen produced when stressful environmental conditions affecting the mother caused her to develop an egg with several layers of shell. See more: *Senut 2000; Jackson et al. 2004; Grellet-Tinner & Fiorelli 2010*

2011—ILC Mongolia—Oldest sauropod egg of Asia

The egg NSM60104403–20554450, 8.7 x 9.1 cm in diameter and including an embryo, was discovered and dated to the late Lower Cretaceous (Aptian, approx. 125–113 Ma). See more: *Grellet-Tinner et al. 2011*

2011—IUC China—Thickest sauropod shell of the early Upper Cretaceous

This *Hemifaveoloolithus muyushanensis* egg was 1.6 mm thick. Even thicker were the shells of *Protodictyoolithus hongpoensis*, at 2.5–2.8 mm, but it is not certain if they belonged to sauropods. See more: *Wang et al. 2011; Wang et al. 2013*

2012—ILC Uruguay—Thickest sauropod shells of the late Lower Cretaceous

Shells of *Sphaerovum* sp. up to 5 mm thick were discovered. They date to the late Lower Cretaceous (Aptian, approx. 125–113 Ma). See more: *Soto, Perea & Cambiaso 2012*

2013—IUC China—Oldest sauropodomorph shells of Asia

Shell fragments of *Lufengosaurus* sp. were found, along with hatchlings and embryos of the same species. See more: *Reisz et al. 2013*

2013—eLC Argentina—Thickest sauropod shells of the early Lower Cretaceous

Shells up to 1.5 mm thick were reported. See more: *Argañaraz et al. 2013*

2013—LJ China—Thickest sauropodomorph shell

The eggshells of *Lufengosaurus* sp. were 1.1–1.4 mm thick. See more: *Reisz et al. 2013*

2013—ILC Argentina—Thickest sauropod shells of the late Lower Cretaceous

Shells up to 1.5 mm thick were reported. See more: *Argañaraz et al. 2013*

2015—Spain—Oolites that suffered the worst act of vandalism

One or more unidentified people destroyed fossil nests containing 20+ eggs that were on display at the Coll de Nargó town hall. The eggs belonged to the species *Megaloolithus aureliensis*, *M. sirugei*, and *M.* cf. *baghensis* and represent the largest deposit discovered in that country. The display was intended to share this paleontological heritage with the public. See more: *Sellés et al. 2014; Visa 2015*

2014—IUC China—Most recently named sauropod egg

A new species of *Fusioolithus berthei* was discovered, and *Megaloolithus baghensis* was reassigned to this new genus. See more: *Fernández & Khosla 2015*

2015—Covered-nesting of sauropods confirmed

Certain aspects of some shells discovered in 2015 confirmed that the eggs had developed underground. See more: *Tanaka et al. 2005*

2017—Sauropods stressed by competition with hadrosaurids?

A series of anomalies were documented in shells discovered in eastern Europe. One theory is that this was caused by competition between titanosaurs and the contemporary hadrosaurids around 72.1–69 Ma. See more: *Sellés et al. 2017*

2018—Oldest hard-shelled sauropod eggs

Dinosaur shells increased in thickness as atmospheric oxygen increased in the Middle Jurassic. This occurred convergently among theropods, sauropodomorphs, and ornithischians. See more: *Stein et al. 2019*

2018—The color of sauropod eggs is identified

One study on the nature of sauropod eggshells found that they were completely white. See more: *Wiemann et al. 2018*

The following abbreviations were used for the epochs:

UJ = Upper Jurassic
eLC = early Lower Cretaceous
ILC = late Lower Cretaceous
eUC = early Upper Cretaceous
IUC = late Upper Cretaceous

Eggshells

Oogenus and species	Shell thickness (mm)	Period and location	Bibliography
Oolites of indeterminate sauropodomorphs			
Mussaurus patagonicus	?	UT, Argentina	Bonaparte & Vince 1979
Lufengosaurus sp.	1.1-1.4	LJ, China	Reisz et al. 2013
Megaloolithidae			
Megaloolithus dholiyaensis	2.26-2.36	IUC, India	Khosla & Sahni 1995
Megaloolithus maghrebiensis	1.86-2.59	IUC, Morocco	García et al. 2003
Megaloolithus padiyalensis	1.12-1.68	IUC, India	Khosla & Sahni 1995
Pseudomegaloolithus atlasi	1.12-1.68	IUC, Morocco	Vianey-Liaud & García 2003; Chassagne-Manoukian et al. 2013
Fusioolithidae			
Fusioolithus berthei	2.45-2.9	IUC, Argentina	Fernández & Khosla 2015
Faveoloolithidae			
Faveoloolithus zhangi	1.2-2.6	IUC, China	Jin 2008
Parafaveoloolithus tiansicunensis	1.37 x 1.45	eUC, China	Zhang 2010
"Paquiloolithus rionegrinus"	6.7	IUC, Argentina	Simón 1999, 2000
Dictyoolithidae (Sauropod or ornithischian eggs?)			
"Dictyoolithus lishuiensis"	?	eUC, China	Jin 2008
Stromatoolithus pinglingensis	?	IUC, China	Zhao et al. 1991; Mikhailov 1997

Smallest juvenile sauropodomorph of the Triassic
Mussaurus patagonicus
Specimen: PVL 4068

Material: Skull and partial skeleton
Southwestern Pangea (present-day Argentina).
Considered a tiny species and named as such ("mouse lizard"),
it actually was a calf approximately 30 cm long and weighing 60
g. It was linked to large individuals up to 8 m long and weighing
1350 kg, so it would grow to 20,000 times that size. See more:
*Bonaparte & Vince 1979; Casamiquela 1980; Montague 2006; Otero & Pol
2013; Cuff et al. 2019*

Smallest juvenile sauropodomorph of the Jurassic
Massospondylus carinatus
Specimen: BP/1/5347A

Material: Skull and partial skeleton
The 13-cm-long calves weighing 7 g were believed to have
been born with teeth, but the only skull known seems to have
no teeth. See more: *Kitching 1979; Reisz et al. 2005, 2010, 2013*

The smallest juvenile sauropod of the Cretaceous
Unnamed
Specimen: NSM60104403-20554450

Material: Partial skeleton
Eastern Laurasia (Mongolia)
This embryo was 30 cm long and weighed 125 g; it was
found inside an egg 9.1 x 8.7 cm in diameter. See more:
Grellet-Tinner et al. 2011; Kim et al. 2012

GROWTH

Some very large sauropods reached adulthood at 20–30 years of age, so they grew more quickly than researchers had believed when these animals were thought to be cold-blooded (heterothermic). Preliminary calculations indicated that *Hypselosaurus* lived for 82–188 years, although some time later the figure was reduced to 40 years. Regardless, these life-spans are not very realistic when compared to present-day animals.

Thanks to histological studies conducted on fossil eggs, we know that these animals had a very fast growth rate up to the subadult stage, then grew more slowly during adulthood. See more: *Currey 1962, 1999; Case 1978; de Ricqle 1983; Rimblot-Baly et al. 1995; Sanz 2007; Klein & Sanger 2007; Griebeler, Klein & Sander 2013; Woodruff et al. 2017; Cerda et al. 2017*

Size as a sauropod defensive strategy

One of the most notable characteristics of sauropods is their great size. The average weight of all species combined is 11.5 t (in a range of 500 kg to 80 t). The fact that 40% of potential species weighed more than 10 t leads us to question what advantage that giant size gave them over other dinosaurs—whether it protected them from predators or allowed them to take advantage of food sources out of reach to the competition, to defend a territory, preserve body heat, or consume large quantities of food of low nutritional quality. The problem is that, to maintain such an enormous weight, their bodies would have had to change in ways that ultimately made them slow, clumsy creatures that were forced to spend much of their time eating. They would also have had more difficulty adapting to sudden changes in the environment. Young sauropods seem to have been relatively defenseless, given their lack of armor and speed, so they may have been very vulnerable to predators until reaching a certain age. Because of this, females may have laid large clutches of eggs to maintain the population. However, the situation is not quite so simple, as many small species lived alongside large carnivorous dinosaurs, suggesting that they may have had defensive strategies we are unaware of today.

Adult and subadult sauropodomorphs

Species	Record
Triassic sauropodomorphs	
Plateosaurus engelhardt (12-year-old adutl)	Oldest Triassic primitive sauropodomorph. It lived for 27 years.
Ledumahadi mafube (14-year-old adult)	
Jurassic sauropodomorphs	
Massospondylus carinatus (15-year-old adult)	Oldest Jurassic primitive sauropodomorph.
Sauropods	
Janenschia robusta (11-year-old adult)	Formerly calculated to be 20–26 years old. Youngest adult sauropod.
Mamechisaurus sp. SGP 2006 (20-year-old adult)	
Camarasaurus sp. CM 36664 (20-year-old adult)	
Camarasaurus lentus (25-year-old adult)	
Apatosaurus louisae (15- to 30-year-old adult)	Subadults 8 to 10 years old.
Diplodocus carnegii (24- to 34-year-old adult)	Oldest sauropod?

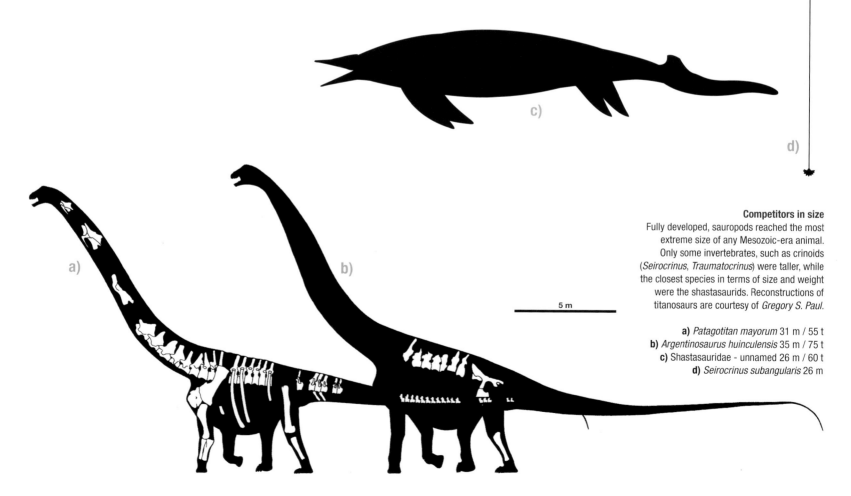

Competitors in size
Fully developed, sauropods reached the most extreme size of any Mesozoic-era animal. Only some invertebrates, such as crinoids (*Seirocrinus*, *Traumatocrinus*) were taller, while the closest species in terms of size and weight were the shastasaurids. Reconstructions of titanosaurs are courtesy of *Gregory S. Paul.*

a) *Patagotitan mayorum* 31 m / 55 t
b) *Argentinosaurus huinculensis* 35 m / 75 t
c) Shastasauridae - unnamed 26 m / 60 t
d) *Seirocrinus subangularis* 26 m

5 m

SAUROPODOMORPH TEETH

Most sauropodomorphs were phytophagous animals, although it is believed that the most primitive forms were omnivores or carnivores. Sauropods often had more homogeneous teeth than sauropodomorphs, although individual teeth often differ according to position, with front ones being longer. In this section we offer a classification that includes 11 tooth groups developed by Ramírez-Velasco and Molina-Pérez based on the work of Calvo 1994; Bonaparte & Pumares 1995; Zheng 1996; Carpenter & Tidwell 1998; Barrett 2000; Pang & Cheng 2000; You et al. 2004; Buffetaut 2005; Le Loeuff 2005; D'Emic et al. 2013; Mocho et al. 2013, 2015; Hendrickx, Mateus & Araujo 2015; and Cabreira et al. 2016.

ZIPHODONT TEETH
Type 1—Ziphodont teeth

Ziphodonts are knife-shaped, laterally to medially flat, and slightly curved. These kinds of teeth are common in carnivorous animals such as the primitive dinosaurs that preceded sauropodomorphs. *Buriolestes* would have been a predator sauropodomorph, as all its teeth were ziphodonts. Surprisingly, however, these same kinds of teeth were found in the lower jaw of *Shunosaurus*, though their function is unknown, as the animal's maxillary teeth are the spatulate kind suitable for eating plants.

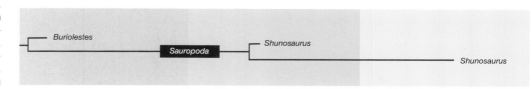

FOLIODONT TEETH

Foliodont (leaf-shaped) teeth were very common from the Triassic to the Lower Cretaceous, then declined, perhaps as angiosperm plants were replaced by gymnosperms. They also diversified among ornithischian dinosaurs that, over time, competed for the same ecological niches. They are believed to have been useful for consuming pine needles and similar foods, whether selectively by narrow-jawed species or in large quantities by broad-jawed species.

Type 2—Lanceolate-foliodont teeth

These teeth, both with and without serrated edges, are the most common type found in primitive sauropodomorphs. Given their similarities to the teeth of some present-day iguanas and other lizards, they are associated with an omnivorous diet and were very abundant during the Upper Triassic and the Lower Jurassic. The only sauropod that had these teeth was *Archaeodontosaurus*, a primitive species from the Middle Jurassic.

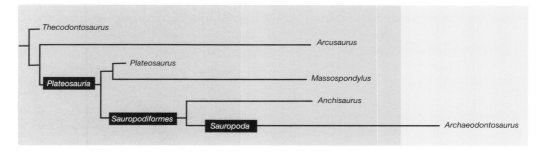

Type 3A—Triangular-crowned spatulate-foliodont (with convex mesial and distal edges)

These kinds of teeth proliferated widely in the Triassic and Jurassic but virtually disappeared in the Cretaceous, only surviving in the last remaining species in North America, which were isolated during the late Lower Cretaceous. This form appeared among sauropodiforms and their direct descendants, sauropods.

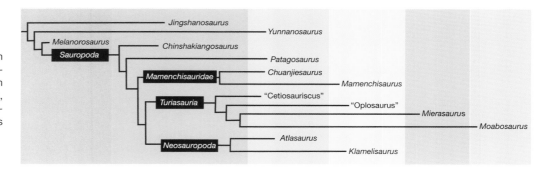

Panphagia protos
PSVJ-874

CH: 5.1 mm
APW: 2 mm

Some primitive sauropodomorphs present pointed teeth like those of carnivores and leaf-shaped teeth like those found in herbivores.

See more: *Martinez & Alcober 2009*

Unnamed
MPZ 97/557

CH: 22 mm
APW: 4.8 mm (4 mm in the distal part)
Intermediate tooth

Most sauropod teeth are classified as foliodonts (leaf-shaped) or cylindrodonts. This piece is unusual, as it has a cylindrical base and a broad, leaf-shaped tip.

See more: *Bonaparte & Pumares 1995*

Type 3B—Broad, triangular-crowned spatulate-foliodont (with convex mesial and distal edges)

In Asia, which was almost completely isolated from the rest of the world during the Middle and Upper Jurassic, a type of dinosaur tooth emerged that resembled the teeth of other species of Neopangea (which encompassed all continents except Asia). The tooth was present in species of the *Omeisaurus* genus, which had more robust jaws than their relatives that were undoubtedly useful for eating tougher plants that other animals avoided. It is not known whether this form of tooth was present in the Lower Jurassic as well, as no teeth have been found for *Tonganosaurus*, which was similar to *Omeisaurus* but from the earlier period. The similarity between these teeth and those of Cretaceous euhelopodids leads us to suspect that both forms consumed the same kind of plants.

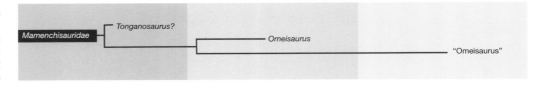

Type 3C—Triangular-crowned, heart-shaped spatulate-foliodont (with convex mesial and distal edges)

A very distinctive type of tooth, exclusive to some *Turiasauria*, had the shape of a human heart. It may have been specialized for consuming a certain type of plant that has not yet been identified.

Type 4A—Oval-crowned spatulate-foliodont (with straight mesial and distal edges)

These teeth are similar to Type 3A and replaced the latter gradually, as they are present in the most derived forms. The type arose all at once, was inherited by different sauropod groups, and became widespread from the Upper Jurassic to the early Upper Cretaceous. It remained present until the end of the Mesozoic era in a few species.

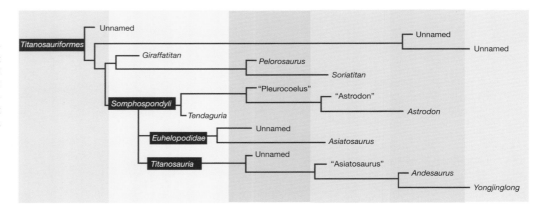

Type 4B—Broad, oval-crowned spatulate-foliodont (with straight mesial and distal edges)

This specialization has appeared on at least three occasions among macronarians similar to *Camarasaurus* in the Neopangean zone and in euhelopodids in eastern Laurasia (present-day Asia). It also arose independently in *Brachiosaurus*, during the Jurassic, then declined in the late Lower Cretaceous. This kind of dentition did not emerge again.

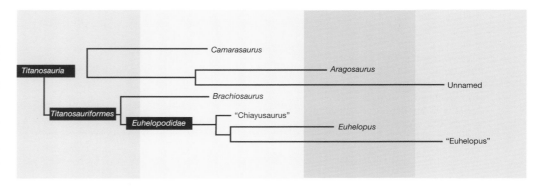

CYLINDRODONT TEETH

Cylindrical teeth are very distinctive, appearing independently in at least six clades. They are associated with the consumption of ferns and bushes, as they were not useful for grinding but were simply instruments for removing the leaves from soft branches. Two distinctive forms are known, both with one typical and one broad morphotype.

Type 5A—Type-O cylindrodont (circular cross section)

This form is unique to *Riojasaurus* from the Triassic and Diplodocoidea that appear in the Middle Jurassic. It was common from the Upper Jurassic to the early Upper Cretaceous, then became very rare toward the end of the Cretaceous. Sauropodomorphs with these teeth may have consumed ferns, as many species had downward-facing heads and lived alongside titanosaurs for millions of years, perhaps suggesting that they did not eat the same kinds of plants.

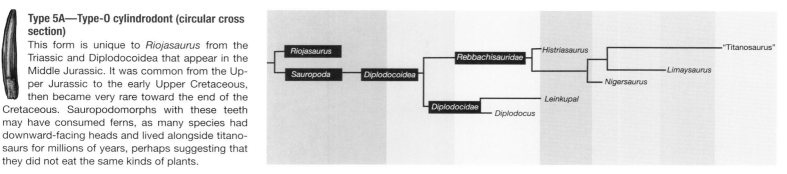

Type 5B—Type-O broad cylindrodont (circular cross section)

Dicraeosaurids were a group of Diplodocoidea with more robust jaws and teeth than their relatives, with whom they coexisted for millions of years. This indicates that they shared food sources in some way, perhaps by consuming tougher plants or those that diplodocids or rebbachisaurids found difficult to digest.

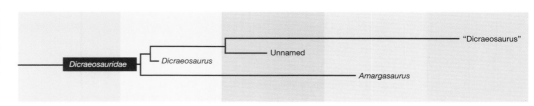

Type 6A—Type-D cylindrodonts (D-shaped cross section)

This is the most common tooth shape, present in the greatest number of species. The type appeared independently four times in the titanosauriform lineage, in brachiosaurids, somphospondylids, euhelopidids, and lithostrotians. Its presence in the two former groups owed to the fact that North America was isolated in the late Lower Cretaceous. The situation was similar with a group of euhelopodids in eastern Laurasia known as "huabeisaurids," a family that has not yet been defined properly but notably had the same kind of teeth. It also emerged among lithostrotians with forms similar to *Malawisaurus*, then became almost the norm among its relatives, which were distributed around the world with great success, perhaps because of the increase in shrub-type plants as angiosperms proliferated.

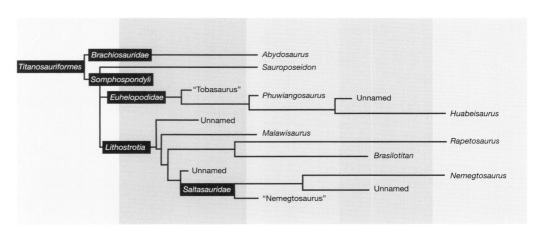

Type 6B—Type-D broad cylindrodonts (D-shaped cross section)

Few cases of this kind of robust tooth have been identified. Two of them are *Borealosaurus* and *Ampelosaurus*. They may have enabled the consumption of other plants apart from bushes.

WHAT DID SAUROPODS EAT?

Sauropods ate all kinds of terrestrial plants, although only on rare occasions do they appear to have consumed cycadophytes and angiosperms (flowering plants). This section presents the plants that were most commonly consumed by these dinosaurs, in the following categories: lycophytes, sphenophytes, pteridophytes, pteridospermophytes, ginkgoopsids, and coniferophytes. We have left marchentiophytes, briophytes, cicadophytes, and angiosperms for another occasion, as they comprised a very limited part of the sauropod diet. See more: *Barrett & Willis 2001; Ambwani et al. 2003; Ghost et al. 2003; Mohabey & Samant 2003; Prasad et al. 2005; Samant & Mohabey 2005; Sharma et al. 2005; Singh et al. 2006; McLoughlin et al. 2008; Sander et al. 2010; Gee 2011; Prasad et al. 2011; Mukherjee 2014; Samant & Mohabey 2014; Khosla et al. 2015; Sonkusare et al. 2017*

Lycophytes (isoetales, lycopodiales, pleuromeiales, selaginellales)

These ancient aquatic and terrestrial plants emerged in the upper Silurian. Pleuromeiales grew very large during the Mesozoic Era, although they ultimately became extinct.

Oldest Lycopodiopsida

Selaginella (from the Carboniferous, approx. 318.1–314.6 Ma) was already a "living fossil" during the age of dinosaurs. This aquatic plant is found in warm, humid environments and includes 700 extant species. See more: *Schlanker & Leisman 1969; Galtier 1997*

Sphenophytes or horsetails (equisetales and sphenophyllales)

Present since the Devonian, these were the most nutritious non-angiosperm plants, but they contained large quantities of abrasive silica, which wore down the teeth of the animals that consumed them. They were considered more primitive but may have been derived ferns.

Oldest existing sphenophyte

Equisetum was believed to be from the Carboniferous (lower Pliensbachian, approx. 318.1–314.6 Ma), although all confirmed fossils date to the Lower Jurassic. The genus includes 15 extant species. See more: *Pryer et al. 2001; Elorriaga et al. 2015, 2018*

Marattiaceae pteridophytes (primitive ferns)

These primitive ferns first appeared in the lower Carboniferous. Sauropods likely did not consume those that grew in the forest.

Oldest extant Marattiaceae
Angiopteris and *Marattia* emerged during the Upper Triassic (Norian, approx. 268.0–252.3 Ma). There are 160 extant species in all. See more: *Anonymous 1976; Gee 2011*

Pteridophytes (chain ferns)

Ophioglossaceae and Psilotaceae are living clades that have virtually no associated fossil remains, despite being very primitive.

Polypodiopsida pteridophytes (ferns)

Present since the Carboniferous, there are both aquatic and terrestrial species in herbaceous and arborescent forms. They were of intermediate caloric value, compared to other Mesozoic plants. The group is divided into cyatheales, gleicheniales, polypodiales, salviniales, schizaceas, and osmundales. Fern pollen and tissues (*Azolla* sp., *Biretisporites* sp., *Cyathidites* sp., *Equisetitriletes* sp., *Gabonisporis* sp., *Trilobosporites* sp.) have been discovered in coprolites.

Oldest existing Polypodiopsida
Dicksonia, from the Middle Permian (approx. 268.0–252.3 Ma), predates the Mesozoic era and was an arboresccent fern. The genus includes 21 extant species. See more: *Maheshwari 1991*

Oldest existing Gleicheniales
Dicranopteris, from the Upper Triassic (Carnian, approx. 237–227 Ma). There are 73 extant species. See more: *Cornet & Olsen 1990*

Oldest existing Polypodiales
Pteris, from the Lower Jurassic (Hettangian, approx. 201.3–199.3 Ma). There are 280 extant species. See more: *Popa 2000*

Oldest existing Salviniales
Marsilea, from the Lower Jurassic (Hettangian, approx. 201.3 - 199.3 Ma). This aquatic plant looks like a four-leafed clover. There are currently 26 extant species. See more: *Maheshwari 1991*

Oldest existing Schizaeaceae
Anemia from the early Lower Cretaceous (upper Valanginian, approx. 136.3–132.9 Ma). There are 100 extant species. See more: *Hernandez-Castillo et al. 2006*

Oldest extant Osmundaceae
Todea and *Osmunda*, from the early Lower Cretaceous (Valanginian, approx. 139.8–132.9 Ma). Between the two there are 12 extant species. See more: *Hernandez-Castillo et al. 2006*

Pteridospermophytes or seed ferns (caytoniales, corytospermales, glossopteridales, medulosales, peltaspermales)

This now-extinct group dates back to the upper Devonian. They may have declined as a result of competition from angiosperms. Their caloric value was low compared to other plants. See more: *Galtier 1997*

Ginkgoopsids (caytoniales, Czekanowskiales, ginkgoales, pentoxylaceae)

This group emerged in the lower Permian. Despite having only moderate caloric value, it was a favorite among sauropods.

Oldest extant Ginkgoopsida
Ginkgos date to the Lower Triassic (Induan, approx. 252.17–251.2 Ma). There is only one extant species, which is endangered. See more: *Anonymous 1989*

Coniferophytes (coniferales, cordaitales, gnetales, voltziales)

These herbaceous plants and trees date to the lower Carboniferous. Araucarias provided the most caloric value among the conifers, while podocarpaceae provided the least. The group includes pines or conifers and gnetales. Leaves and pollen of araucarias (*Araucaria*, *Araucariacites* sp.), cheirolepidiaceae (*Classopollis* sp.), and podocarpaceas (*Podocarpidites* sp.) have been found in coprolites.

Oldest extant coniferophyte
Abies (firs) emerged in the Middle Triassic (Ladinian, approx. 242–237 Ma). There are 55 extant species. See more: *Dobruskina 1994*

Oldest extant gnetal
The genus *Ephedra*, from the late Lower Cretaceous (Barremian, approx. 129.4–125 Ma), shares some characteristics with angiosperms. Its prolonged consumption provoked a heightened state of alertness and increased physical performance, but it was toxic and could be addictive. There are 68 extant species. See more: *Yang et al. 2005*

Accidental or occasional foods?

Small freshwater plants and animals
Sauropods accidentally consumed small plants and animals while drinking water. Bacteria, amoebas (*Centropyxis*, *Difflugia*), charophyte algae (*Gyrogonite* sp.), chlorophytes (*Botrycoccus*, *Lacaniella*, *Oedogonium*), chrysophytes (*Aulacoseira* sp.), sponge spicules, snails (*Physa* sp.), and insect ostracods have been found in coprolites.

Fungi
Some sauropods may have deliberately eaten leaves with phytopathogenic fungi such as *Colletotrichum* (Glomerellales), *Erysiphe*, *Uncinula* (Erysiphales), *Frasnacritetrus* (Pleosporales), *Meliola* sp., and *Meliolinites* sp. (Meliolales) to take advantage of the nutrients, although they may also have been consumed accidentally. Other fungi discovered in coprolites colonized the feces externally, including *Alternaria* sp., *Archaeoglomus* sp., *Aspergillus* sp., *Dicellaesporites*, *Helminthosporum* sp., *Monocellaete* sp., *Multicellaesporites* sp., *Quilonia* sp.

Cicadophytes
Bennettitales and cycads were among the plants that sauropods consumed least of all, as they had very tough tissues and the animals preferred soft-tissue plants. Cycadophyta pollen (*Cycadopites* sp.) has been found in coprolites.

Angiosperms
These plants were scarce in the era of sauropods, so they could not have been a major part of their diet. Different analyses have found flowers, fruit, pollen, seeds, and tissues of different angiosperms (*Capper* sp. *Multiareolites* sp., *Phoenix* sp.), legumes (*Cretacaeiporites*, *Compositoipollenites*, *Graminidites*, *Longapertites*) and palms (*Palmaepollenites*).

The strangest object found among sauropod stomach contents is a 2.5-cm-long *Allosaurus* tooth. It may have been eaten by accident or been broken off from the predator while it was consuming the sauropod. See more: *Stokes 1963*

Mesozoic vegetarian menu

What kinds of plants existed and were consumed by phytophagous dinosaurs? What were those plants like in the different eras in which these dinosaurs lived? The plants of the Mesozoic era included some of the same ones that exist today (cycads, equisets, ginkgos, gnetales, lycopodia, ferns, pines, and flowering plants), as well as others that are now extinct (Bennettitales, seed ferns, pleuromeia, among others), although their proportions and relative abundance varied.

LOWER TRIASSIC MENU

After the mass extinction that occurred in the Permian and gave rise to the Triassic, both plants and phytophagous vertebrates were very scarce. The former were entirely absent in near-equatorial latitudes, which were virtually devoid of life. Very large lycopodia known as pleuromeia appeared in this era. See more: *Retallack, Veevers & Morante 1996; Scott 2000; Grauvogel-Stamm & Ash 2005*

Lycophytes (isoetales, lycopodiales, pleuromeiales, selaginellales)

1908—South Africa—Largest pleuromeial *Pleuromeia dubia*, 2 m high (Induan, approx. 251.2–242 Ma), were found in a marginal marine zone. See more: *Seward 1908; Retallack 1995*

1997—Russia—Oldest Isoetaceae *Tomiostrobus radiatus* (Induan, approx. 252.17–251.2 Ma). Today 150 species exist. See more: *Retallack 1997; Naugolnykh 2012*

Sphenophytes (equisetales and sphenophyllales)

1828—Germany, Spain, France, England, Italy, Serbia, Montenegro—Largest equiset of the Lower Triassic *Equisetites mougeotii* (Olenekian-Ladinian, approx. 251.2–242 Ma) was considered a species of *Calamites* based on its height of up to 4 m. See more: *Brongniart 1828; Alvarez-Ramis 1982; Wachtler 2011*

1982—South Africa—Most recent Sphenophyllales *Trizygia* sp. (Induan, approx. 252.17–251.2 Ma) is a now-extinct family that thrived in the Paleozoica era. See more: *Dobruskina 1982*

Pteridophytes (ferns)

1828—Germany, France, Italy—The largest fern leaf of the Mesozoic *Anomopteris mougeotii*, 1.5 m in length. See more: *Brongniart 1828; Grauvogel-Stamm 1978; Kandutsch 2011*

1979—Australia—Oldest Gleicheniaceae fern *Microphyllopteris* sp. (Olenekian, approx. 251.2–247.2 Ma). See more: *Holmes & Ash 1979*

1994—Norway—Oldest Ophioglossaceae fern *Licopodiacidites* sp. (Induan, approx. 252.17–251.2 Ma). See more: *Mangerud 1994*

1:20

Anomopteris mougeotti

Pteridospermophytes or seed ferns (caytoniales, corytospermales, glossopteridales, medulosales, peltaspermales)

1990—Antarctica—Largest corytospermal of the Middle Triassic *Dicroidium fremouwensis* was estimated to have grown up to 30 m high, based on the trunks of *Jeffersonioxylon gordoniense*, 60 cm in diameter (Anisian, approx. 252.1 Ma). See more: *Pigg 1990; Meyer-Berthaud, Taylor & Taylor 1992; Del Fueyo et al. 1995; Cúneo et al. 2003*

2003—Chile, Wales, and New Zealand—Oldest Petriellales pteridosperm *Kannaskoppifolia* sp. (Olenekian, approx. 251.2–247.2 Ma). See more: *Anderson & Anderson 2003*

2007—Canada—Oldest creeping pteridosperm of the Triassic *Lepidopteris ottonis* was a plant that climbed up other plants (lower Olenekian, approx. 251.2–249.2 Ma). See more: *Vavrek, Larsson & Rybczynski 2007*

2011—Australia—Oldest gall on a Triassic pteridosperm A structure in a *Dicroidium* leaf was formed in response to a parasite attack from another organism (Olenekian-Anisian, approx. 247.2 Ma). See more: *McLoughlin 2011; Wappler et al. 2015*

2013—Russia—Largest concentration of carbon dioxide in a Mesozoic plant The peltaspermacea *Lepidopteris callipteroides* presented a concentration of 7832 ± 1676 ppm of CO_2. It was an immediate survivor of the Permian-Triassic extinction (lower Induan, approx. 252.1 Ma). See more: *Retallack 2013*

Ginkgoopsids (caytoniales, Czekanowskiales, ginkgoales, pentoxylaceae, petriellales)

1994—Germany—Oldest Palissyaceae *Palissya* sp. (Induan, approx. 252.17–251.2 Ma). See more: *Dobruskina 1994*

Coniferophytes (coniferales, cordaitales, gnetales, voltziales)

1986—Antarctica—Oldest Mesozoic conifer with pathology Some fungi caused rot in an *Araucarioxylon* trunk (Induan-Olenekian, approx. 251.2 Ma). See more: *Stubblefield & Taylor 1986*

Miscellaneous facts

1990—Antarctica—Southernmost plants of the Triassic *Dicroidium* sp., *Glossopteris* sp., and *Taeniopteris* sp. were found at paleolatitude 74.5° S. See more: *Bose et al. 1990*

Pleuromeia dubia

1:30

MIDDLE TRIASSIC MENU

The world's flora gradually recovered, taking hold in equatorial zones that had been completely uninhabited by plants and animals of any type. Very few angiosperm plant species remained, and the few that did exist had leaves and stalks so different that they would not be recognizable as such. The flora was dominated by plants that modern animals would have found very difficult to eat and digest—equisets were very abrasive; conifer leaves were very hard, had a waxy cuticle, and were also full of resin that was indigestible by many animals; araucarias, while abundant, were unappetizing, as each mouthful would have included wood as well as tannins and phenols; lastly, cycads had very hard, fibrous leaves. Cheirolepidiaceae, ferns, and pteridosperms may have been the best option for plant eaters in those days.

Lycophytes (isoetales, lycopodiales, pleuromeiales, selaginellales)

1980—Rusia—Largest Isoetal *Takhtajanodoxa mirabilis* was 4 m high and 20 cm in diameter (Anisian, approx. 247.2–242 Ma). See more: *Snigirevskaya 1980*

1995—China—Smallest pleuromeial *Pleuromeia sanxiaensis* was 5 cm high and had a 2.5-cm cone (strobilus) (Anisian, approx. 247.2–242 Ma). See more: *Meng 1995, 1996*

Sphenophytes (equisetales, sphenophyllales)

1827—Germany—Largest equiset of the Middle Triassic *Equisetites arenaceus* (Ladinian, approx. 242–237 Ma) had stems up to 20 cm in diameter and so could reach a height of 5 m. Their shape was very similar to that of present-day equisets. See more: *Jaeger 1827; Husby 2009; Taylor et al. 2009; Wachtler 2016*

1877—Switzerland—Oldest oviposited equiset Some possible tiny insect eggs were found in an *Equisetites* (Ladinian, approx. 242–237 Ma). See more: *Heer 1887; Wappler et al. 2015*

2008—Antarctica—Most recent sphenophylial (Sphenophyllales) *Spaciinodum collinsonii* (Anisian, approx. 247.2–242 Ma). See more: *Ryberg, Hermsen, Taylor et al. 2008*

Pteridophytes (ferns)

1835—Germany, Italy—Largest sphenopterid fern leaf (Sphenopteridae) The leaves of *Sphenopteris schoenleiniana* grew up to a length of 80 cm (Anisian-Carnian, approx. 242–237 Ma). See more: *Brongniart 1835; Kandutsch 2011*

1960—Arizona, USA—Most recent Itopsidemoideae (Itopsidemoinea) *Itopsidema vancleaveii* and *Donwelliacaulis chlouberii* were arborescent ferns (Anisian, approx. 247.2–242 Ma). See more: *Daugherty 1960; Miller 1971; Ash 1994*

1982—Tajikistan—Oldest Aspleniaceae fern *Asplenium* sp. (Ladinian, approx. 242–237 Ma). See more: *Dobruskina 1982*

1989—Germany—Oldest plant-insect interaction Continuous edge damage was reported on leaves of the pentoxylales cycad *Danaeopsis angustifolia* (Ladinian, approx. 242–237 Ma). See more: *Kelber & Geyer 1989; Scott et al. 1992*

1989—China—Oldest Dipteridaceae fern *Hausmannia* sp. (Ladinian, approx. 242–237 Ma). See more: *Anonymous 1989*

Pteridospermophytes or seed ferns (caytoniales, corytospermales, glossopteridales, medulosales, peltaspermales)

1837—Argentina—Tallest corytosperma of the Middle Triassic "Darwin's forest" is a zone containing the trunks of different types of conifers, as well as corytosperms in anatomical position, some of the latter up to 30 m in height. It was discovered in 1835 by Charles Darwin (Ladinian, approx. 242–237 Ma). See more: *Darwin 1837, 1846; Brea, Artabe & Spalletti 2009*

1856—Germany, Italy—Largest leaves on a peltaspermal *Scytophyllum bergeri* had leaves up to 1 m in length (Ladinian, approx. 242–237 Ma). See more: *Bornemann 1856; Kustatscher & Van Konijnenburg-van Cittert 2010*

1917—New Zealand, Tasmania—Oldest Matatielliaceae *Linguifolium lillieanum* (Ladinian, approx. 242–237 Ma). See more: *Arber 1917; Townrow 1965; Pattemore, Rigby & Playford 2015*

1990—Antarctica—Thickest corytospermal trunk of the Middle Triassic *Dicroidium fremouwensis* was estimated to have been up to 30 m in height, based on the trunks of *Jeffersonioxylon gordonense*, which were 60 cm in diameter (Anisian, approx. 247.2–242 Ma). See more: *Pick 1990; Meyer-Berthaud, Taylor & Taylor 1992; Del Fueyo et al. 1995; Cúneo et al. 2003*

1995—Antarctica—Largest seed fern Trunks of *Jeffersonioxylon gordonense* reached 60 cm in diameter, which suggests they were at least 30 m tall (Anisian, approx. 247.2–242 Ma). See more: *de Fueyo et al. 1995; Cúneo et al. 2003*

Ginkgoopsids (caytoniales, Czekanowskiales, ginkgoales, pentoxylaceas, petriellales)

1980—Antarctica, Australia, New Zealand—Oldest Petriellacea *Rochipteris lacerata, Rudixylon serbetianum* (Ladinian, approx. 242–237 Ma). See more: *Retallack 1980; Taylor et al. 1994; Herbst et al. 2001; Barone-Nugent et al. 2003; Bomfleur et al. 2014*

1:50

Equisetites arenaceus

Coniferophytes (coniferales, cordaitales, gnetales, voltziales)

1865—Germany—Oldest Cordaitaceae conifer *Cordaites keuperianus* (Ladinian, approx. 242–237 Ma). The family was abundant in the Paleozoic era. See more: *Heer 1865*

1982—Kyrgyzstan—Oldest Palissyaceae conifer *Stachyotaxus* sp. (Ladinian, approx. 242–237 Ma). See more: *Dobruskina 1982*

1994—Brazil—Oldest conifer trunks with insect tunneling Coprolites and tunnels were found on a trunk of *Araucarioxylon* (Ladinian, approx. 242–237 Ma). See more: *Minello 1994*

1994—Hungary—Oldest fir (Abietoideae) *Abies* sp. dates from the Ladinian (approx. 242–237 Ma). See more: *Dobruskina 1994*

1996—Spain—Most recent Ullmanniaceae *Ullmannia* sp. (Anisian-Ladinian, approx. 247.2–242 Ma). This family was abundant in the Permian era. See more: *Diez et al. 1996*

1997—Antarctica—Oldest cypress (Cupressaceae) *Parasciadopitys aequata* (Anisian-Ladinian, approx. 247.2–237 Ma). Only a single species exists today. See more: *Yao et al. 1997*

1997—Argentina—Tallest conifer of the Middle Triassic Some *Araucaria* trunks from this era measure 1.52 m in diameter, so were probably 30–40 m tall (Ladinian, approx. 242–237 Ma). See more: *Brea 1997; Brea et al. 2008; 2009*

1997—Antarctica—Oldest cone infected by a fungus *Parasciadopitys aequata* is a cone 3.4x1.4 cm that was found to have been attacked by *Combresomyces cornifer* and *Mycocarpon asterineum* (Ladinian, approx. 242–237 Ma). See more: *Yao et al. 1997*

2000—Italy—Oldest Alpiacea (Alpiaceae) *Alpia anisica* (*Alpianthus anisicus, Dolomitostrobus anisicus*) had trunks up to 15 cm in diameter (Anisian, approx. 247.2–242 Ma). See more: *WWachtler & Van Konijnen-Burg-Van Cittert 2000; Wachtler 2011; Michael 2016*

2011—Italy—Oldest Schizolepisacea (Schizolepisaceae) *Schizolepis ungeri, Alpianthus ungeri*, and *Dolomitostrobus bellunensis* belong to the same species (Anisian, approx. 247.2–242 Ma). See more: *Wachtler 2011*

2017—Italy—Oldest amber of the Mesozoic Amber was found in association with *Voltzia recubariensis* (Anisian, approx. 247.2–242 Ma). See more: *Roghi et al. 2017*

UPPER TRIASSIC MENU

In this era, the first phytophagous dinosaurs appeared, including sauropodomorphs and the first sauropods, which competed with the various archosaurs that were also equipped to eat plants. Perhaps for this reason, plant species with spines, fibers, or filaments that made them harder to digest increased, although it is impossible to know if some plants also had chemical defenses that caused a bad taste, inflammation, or illness. Because of this, it is likely that sauropodomorphs hardly chewed their food, as it was easier to rip it off and let their internal bacteria digest it, helped along by the stones the animals ingested to crush the plants in their gizzards. These kinds of plants were so successful that the ones that have survived to the present day are still very effective at preventing phytophagous mammals from eating them. See more: *Tiffney 1989, 2012*

Lycophytes (isoetales, lycopodiales, pleuromeiales)

1994—Argentina—Most recent Pleuromeiaceae *Pleuromeia* sp. (Carnian, approx. 237–227 Ma). See more: *Morel 1994*

1996—North Carolina, USA—Most recent Lepidodendraceae *Lepidodendron* sp. (Norian, approx. 227–208.5 Ma). See more: *Fraser et al. 1996*

1997—Mexico—Most recent Sigillariaceae *Sigillaria* cf. *icthyolepis* (Norian, approx. 227–208.5 Ma). See more: *Weber 1997*

2012—Switzerland—Oldest oviposited Isoetales Marks of dragonfly eggs were found on *Isoetites* (Carnian, approx. 237–227 Ma). See more: *Moisan et al. 2012; Wappler et al. 2015*

Sphenophytes or horsetails (equisetales, sphenophyllales)

1962—Argentina—Largest Asterotecacea (Asterothecaceae) *Asterotheca falcata* had pinnas 4 cm wide, so its fronds could have been up to 154 cm long. See more: *de la Sota & Archangelsky 1962*

2005—Mexico—Largest equiset of the Middle Triassic *Equisetites* cf. *arenaceus* (Carnian or Norian, approx. 227 Ma) reached diameters of 15 cm, so could have been up to 3.8 m tall. This specimen is difficult to date, as some fossil evidence suggests it is more recent, while other evidence is often older. See more: *Silva-Pineda 1961; Zambrano-García & Amozurrutia-Silva 1980; Ash 1992; Weber 1985, 1997, 2005*

Pteridophytes (ferns)

1984—Russia—Oldest pteridophyte fern (Pteridaceae) *Adiantopteris* sp. (Carnian, approx. 237–227 Ma). See more: *Dagis & Kazakov 1984; Mogucheva 1984*

1987—Russia—Oldest Cyatheaceae fern *Cyathea* sp. (Carnian, approx. 237–227 Ma). See more: *Mogucheva & Batyaeva 1987*

2001—North Carolina, USA—Oldest Hymenophyllaceae fern *Hopetedia praetermissa* (Carnian, approx. 237–227 Ma). Some 650 species of these drought-resistant ferns exist today. See more: *Axsmith et al. 2001*

Pteridospermophytes or seed ferns (glossopteridales, medulosales, peltaspermales)

1932—Greenland—Strangest seed fern leaf of the Triassic? The identity of *Furcula granulifer* is unknown, although some suggest it is related to the seed fern *Dicroidium*, while the leaf is similar to that of an angiosperm. It has two points on the distal end. See more: *Harris 1932*

1998—Argentina—Tallest seed fern of the Triassic A trunk of *Rexoxylon brunoi* attributed to *Dicroidium* measured 71 cm in diameter, so the plant would have been an estimated 34 m tall (Carnian, approx. 237–227 Ma). See more: *Archangelsky 1968; Artabe, Brea & Zamuner 1998*

Ginkgoopsids (caytoniales, Czekanowskiales, ginkgoales, pentoxylaceas, petriellales)

1838—Virginia, USA—Oldest caytonial *Sagenopteris rhoifolia* (Carnian, approx. 237–227 Ma). See more: *Prels in Sternberg 1838*

1876—Alaska (USA), Afghanistan, Australia, Canada, China, South Korea, Georgia, Japan, Kazakhstan, Kyrgystan, Mongolia, Romania, Russia, South Africa, Tajikistan, Ukraine, Uzbekistan—The most abundant Czekanowskial of the Triassic and Jurassic *Phoenicopsis* became so proliferate in some zones it accounts for up to 90% of fossil plants in Africa and Asia dated to the Upper Triassic and Jurassic. See more: *Heer 1876; Vakhrameev, Dobruskina & Zaklinskaya 1970; Flint & Gould 1975; Krassilov & Shorokhova 1975; Vakhrameev et al. 1978; Anderson & Anderson 1983*

1977—Iran—Oldest *Irania* *Irania hermaphroditica* has a reproductive structure similar to that of angiosperm flowers (Rhaetian, approx. 208.5–201.3 Ma). See more: *Harris 1935; Schweitzer 1977*

1989—China—Oldest Arctobaieracea (Arctobaieraceae) *Arctobaiera* sp. (Norian, approx. 227–208.5 Ma). See more: *Anonymous 1989*

1994—Antarctica—Smallest Petriellacea (Petriellaceae) ovules Ovules 1 mm in diameter were discovered. See more: *Taylor et al. 1994; Bomfleur et al. 2014*

1994—Argentina—Largest Petriellacea (Petriellaceae) leaves The leaves of *Scleropteris grandis* were up to 15 cm long and 8 cm wide (upper Carnian, approx. 217.7–208.5 Ma). See more: *Artabe, Morel & Zamuner 1994*

1:40

Equisetites cf. *arenaceus*

1:400

Rhexoxylon brunoi

1:4

Glyptolepis keuperiana

Coniferophytes (coniferales, cordaitales, gnetales, voltziales)

1870—Germany—Largest pinecones of the Triassic The cones of *Glyptolepis keuperiana* measured 18 x 2 cm, while those of *G. richteri* measured 14 x 3.5 cm (Carnian, approx. 237–227 Ma). See more: *Schimper 1870; Axsmith & Taylor 1997*

1870—Arizona, New Mexico, and Utah, USA—Tallest conifer of the Triassic The largest trunks of *Pullisilvaxylon* (*Araucarioxylon*) *arizonicum* were 3 m in diameter, so they were an estimated 60 m in height (Norian, approx. 227–208.5 Ma). See more: *Kraus 1870; Knowlton 1889; Ash & Creber 2000; Savidge 2007*

1906—Arizona, USA—Longest petrified trunk of the Triassic
This 34-meter-long trunk is part of the Agate Bridge, a tourist attraction in the Petrified Forest National Park (Norian, approx. 227–208.5 Ma). See more: *Parker 2005*

1934—Arizona, USA—Tallest indeterminate "cheirolepidiaceae" gymnosperm of the Triassic
The largest in this family of extinct conifers may have been *Schilderia adamanica*, approximately 36 m tall (Norian, approx. 227–208.5 Ma). See more: *Daugherty 1934; Creber & Ash 2004*

1935—Greenland—Largest *Araucaria* cone of the Triassic A cone of *Araucarites charcottii* measures 6 x 2.5 cm (Rhaetian, approx. 208.5–201.3 Ma). See more: *Harris 1935*

1970—Arizona, New Mexico, and Texas, USA—Oldest spiny gnetal *Dinophyton spinosus* had extremely sharp leaves (Rhaetian, approx. 208.5–201.3 Ma). See more: *Ash 1970*

1972—Arizona, USA—Oldest Ephedraceae gneptopsid *Dechellyia gormanii, Ephedra chinleana,* and *Masculostrobus clathratus* (Norian, approx. 227–208.5 Ma). See more: *Ash 1972*

1973—North Carolina, USA—Oldest pinecones (Pinaceae) The cones of *Compsostrobus neoreticus* and *Millerostrobus pekinensis* are ancient pine remains (Carnian, approx. 237–227 Ma). Today 220 species exist. See more: *Delevoryas & Hope 1973; Taylor et al. 1987*

1973—Connecticut, Massachusetts, USA—Largest Cheirolepidiacea pollen The pollen grains of *Classopollis meyeriana* or *C. meyerianus* were 52–75 microns in diameter. These plants lived during the Triassic-Jurassic boundary, from the upper Rhaetian to the lower Hettangian (approx. 201.3 Ma). See more: *Klaus 1960; Raine, Mildenhall & Kennedy 2011; Kurschner, Batenburg & Mander 2013*

1976—Sweden—Oldest Taxaceae conifer *Palaeotaxus rediviva* from the Rhaetian (approx. 208.5–201.3 Ma). Today 12 species exist. See more: *Nathorst 1908*

1978—South Africa—Most recent "Dordrechtitaceous" gymnosperm *Dordrechtites elongatus* (Carnian, approx. 237–227 Ma). See more: *Anderson 1978*

1:400

Pullisilvaxylon (Araucarioxylon) arizonicum

1981—Iran—Most recent Voltziaceae conifer *Voltzia* sp. from the Norian (approx. 227–208.5 Ma). Other plants such as Podozamites were formerly considered part of the family, so the record of this family extends to the Cretaceous. See more: *Bragin, Golubev & Polyanskii 1981*

1982—Russia—Oldest Pinoideida (Pinoideideae) *Pinus* sp. (Carnian, approx. 237–227 Ma). See more: *Dobruskina 1982*

1991—Arizona, USA—Oldest Mesozoic amber of North America
It was produced by *Agathoxylon arizonicum* (upper Carnian, approx. 217.7–208.5 Ma) See more: *Litwin & Ash 1991; Savidge 2007*

1994—Argentina—Largest seed of the Triassic *Cordaicarpus* sp. belonged to a Cordaitales and was similar to modern-day conifers (lower Norian, approx. 227–221 Ma). The seed is 1.8 cm long and 1.4 cm wide. See more: *Artabe et al. 1994*

1996—Arizona, USA—Oldest gall on a gnetal The leaves of *Dechellyia gormanii* display swelling similar to that caused today by some kinds of mites (Norian-Rhaetian, approx. 208.5 Ma). See more: *Ash 1996; Diéguez-Jiménez 2003*

2004—Brazil—Oldest Taxaceae conifer (Taxaceae) *Sommerxylon spiralosus* from the Carnian (approx. 237–227 Ma). Twelve species exist today. See more: *Pires & Guerra-Sommer 2004*

2006 – Arizona, USA–Longest Triassic conifer cone A cone of *Araucarites rudicula* is 6.35 x 1.94 cm (Carnian, approx. 237–227 Ma). See more: *Axsmith & Ash 2006*

2012—Italy—Oldest Triassic amber with arthropods The specimen contains phytophagous mites and a mosquito and is the oldest resin found to date that was produced by a cheirolepidiacea (Carnian, approx. 227–208.5 Ma). See more: *Roghi, Ragazzi & Gianolla 2006; Schmidt et al. 2012*

2017—China—Oldest Taxodiaceae conifer The fossilized wood of *Medulloprotaxodioxylon triassumum* is similar to *Sequoiadendron giganteum* (Norian-Carnian, approx. 227 Ma). See more: *Mingli et al. 2017; Wan et al. 2017*

2018—Lesotho—Southernmost amber of the Mesozoic Found in the Molteno Formation at a latitude of ~40° S. See more: *Seyfullah et al. 2018*

2018—Lesotho—Oldest amber from Africa The amber is related to the Pluvial Episode in the upper Carnian, approx. 217.7–208.5 Ma. See more: *Seyfullah et al. 2018*

LOWER JURASSIC MENU

In the Lower Jurassic, phytophagous dinosaurs were the main plant eaters, including most sauropodomorphs, sauropods, and ornithischians. The only group of animals that competed with them for plants were insects, which undoubtedly surpassed all vertebrates combined in terms of their biomass.
See more: *Doria 2007; Wang et al 2007a, 2007b*

Pteridophytes (ferns)

1958—Poland, Serbia, and Montenegro—Oldest Schizaeaceae ferns *Klukia acutifolia, K. exilis, K. phillipsii, Kuklisporites neovariegatus,* and *K. variegatus* (Toarcian, approx. 182.7–174.1 Ma). See more: *Couper 1958; Filatoff 1975; Pantic 1981*

1964—Russia—Oldest clover fern (Marsileaceae) *Marsilea* sp. (Hettangian, approx. 201.3–199.3 Ma). This family contains aquatic ferns. Today 75 species exist. See more: *Teslenko 1964*

1971—Argentina—Oldest Osmundales fern *Rugulatisporites* sp. (upper Sinnemurian, approx. 195–190.8 Ma). See more: *Volkheimer 1971*

1991—Tasmania, Australia—Most recent Guireoideae (Guireanea) *Lunea jonesii* fern (Pliensbachian, approx. 190.8–182.7 Ma). See more: *Tidwell 1991; Tidwell & Ash 1994*

2013—Sri Lanka—Mesozoic ferns with the strangest damage Some leaves of *Cladophlebis* sp. display circular and semicircular cuts made by insects. See more: *Edirisooriya & Dharmagunawardhane 2013*

2014—Sweden—Oldest fern nuclei and chromosomes Fossil chromosomes and nuclei of the aquatic fern *Osmundastrum cinnamomea* date to the early Jurassic (Toarcian, approx. 182.7–174.1 Ma). See more: *Bomfleur, McLoughlin & Vajda 2014*

Pteridospermophytes or seed ferns (glossopteridales, medulosales, peltaspermales)

1950—Sweden—Most recent Peltaspermales seed fern *Lepidopteris ottonis* was reported for the Upper Triassic in Germany, China, Greenland, and Poland, along with Vietnam in the Lower Jurassic. See more: *Schimper 1869; Lundblad 1950*

Ginkgoopsids (caytoniales, Czekanowskiales, ginkgoales, pentoxylaceas, petriellales)

1833—Germany and Poland—Oldest Schmeissneriaceae gnetal *Schmeissneria microstachys* (Hettangian, approx. 201.3–199.3 Ma) displays some female organs 77 mm long and 12 mm wide. Some scientists consider it a primitive angiosperm. See more: *Presl 1833; Kirchne & Van Konijnenburg 1994; Wang et al 2007a, 2007b*

1984—Hong Kong—Most recent Leuthardtiaceae? *Arberophyllum* (Lower Sinnemurian, approx. 199.3–195 Ma) may be a ginkgoal or a seed fern. See more: *Lee 1984*

1992—Germany—Oldest Yimaiaceae ginkgoal *"Baiera" muensteriana* (Hettangian, approx. 201.3–199.3 Ma). See more: *Kirchner 1992*

1994—Germany—Oldest Karkeniaceae ginkgoal *Karkenia hauptmanii,* from the Lower Jurassic (Hettangian, approx. 201.3–199.3 Ma). See more: *Kirchner & van Konijnenburg-van Cittert 1994*

2017—Argentina—Most recent Petriellaceae *Rochipteris copiapensis* has been reported from the Norian to the Hettangian (approx. 227–199.3 Ma). The family is also known as Kannaskoppiaceae. See more: *Herbst et al. 2001; Gnaedinger & Zavattieri 2017*

Coniferophytes (coniferales, cordaitales, gnetales, voltziales)

1833—Germany and Poland—Oldest Schmeissneriaceae gnetal *Schmeissneria microstachys* (Hettangian, approx. 201.3–199.3 Ma) has two female organs 77 mm long and 12 mm wide. Some consider it a primitive angiosperm. See more: *Presl 1833; Kirchner & Van Konijnenburg 1994; Wang et al 2007a, 2007b*

1906—England—Oldest miroviacea (Miroviaceae) *Xenoxylon phyllocladoides* (Pliensbachian, approx. 190.8–182.7 Ma). See more: *Gothan 1906*

1968—Germany—Largest floating fossil trunk of the Mesozoic A conifer trunk 13 m long contained a colony of 5000 bivalves (*Pseudomytiloides dubius*) and 280 crinoids (*Seirocrinus subangularis*), some of them up to 19 cm long. A trunk of this kind would have remained floating in the sea for about two years. See more: *Seilacher, Drozdzewski & Haude 1968, Hess 1999*

1999—England—Oldest Cupressoidea (Cupressoideae) *Cupressinoxylon* sp. (Pliensbachian, approx. 190.8–182.7 Ma). See more: *Morgans 1999*

2008—Argentina—Smallest pinecone of the Jurassic The cones of *Austrohamia minuta* are 2 mm in diameter (Toarcian, approx. 182.7–174.1 Ma). See more: *Escapa et al. 2008*

x2

Austrohamia minuta

1:1

Schmeissneria microstachys

MIDDLE JURASSIC MENU

Dinosaur fauna changed dramatically, along with plants, which were damaged considerably by animal consumption, even in the upper canopy, because of both the size of some phytophagous dinosaurs and the large volumes they consumed.

1:4

Araucaria sphaerocarpa

Pteridophytes (ferns)

1998—China—Largest arborescent fern (Cyatheales) *Coniopteris nikaensis* had leaves up to 15 cm wide and fronds 9 m in diameter; it reached a height of 27 m (upper Callovian, approx. 164.8–163.5 Ma). See more: *Zhang & Sun 1998; Xin et al. 2018*

2006—Russia—Oldest creeping fern of the Mesozoic *Stachypteris psammitica* is the only creeping plant known to have existed in the Jurassic. It dates to the middle of that period (Bajocian, approx. 170.3–168.3 Ma) and belonged to the same family as present-day schizaeaceous ferns. See more: *Gordenko & Krassilov 2006; Burnham 2009*

Pteridospermophytes (caytoniales, corytospermales, glossopteridales, medulosales, peltaspermales)

1945—England—Oldest coprolite found with pollen A coprolite of an unidentified dinosaur was found to contain the pollen of *Caytonia* (Aalenian, approx. 174.1–170.3 Ma). See more: *Harris 1945*

Coniferophytes (coniferales, cordaitales, gnetales, voltziales)

1851—Italy—Oldest Geinitzacea (Geinitziaceae) *Geinitzia divaricata* (upper Bajocian, approx. 169.3–168.3 Ma). There is an insect with the same genus name. See more: *Bunbury 1851; Handlirsch 1906*

1866—England—Largest conifer cone of the Jurassic A cone of *Araucaria sphaerocarpa* measured 13 x 15 cm (Bajocian, approx. 170.3–168.3 Ma). See more: *Carruthers 1866*

1:400

Araucaria mirabilis

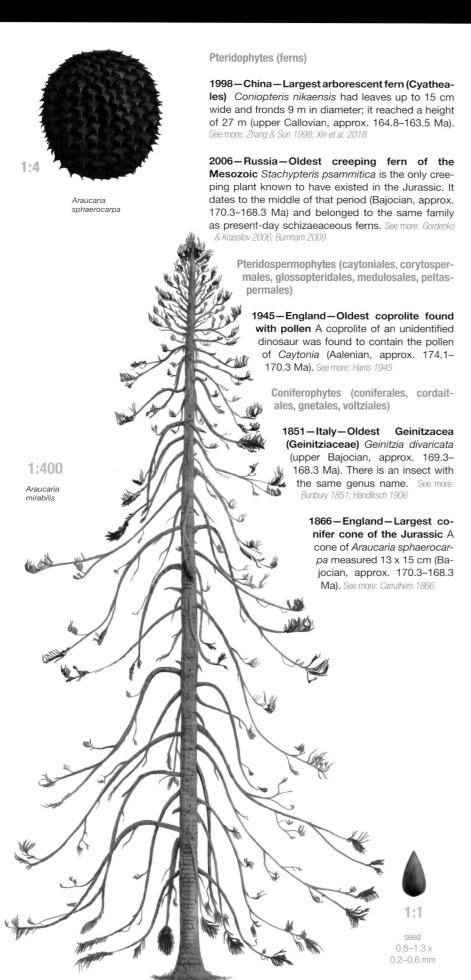

Coniopteris nikaensis

1:200

1982—Argentina—Tallest conifer of the Jurassic The largest trunks of *Araucaria mirabilis* were 3–3.5 m in diameter and lived for more than 1000 years; they could have been more than 75 m tall (Bathonian, approx. 168.3–166.1 Ma). See more: *Anonymous 1982*

1985—Mongolia—Most recent Cordaitales conifer The seed *Samaropsis* sp. (Bathonian, approx. 168.3–166.1 Ma). See more: *Sinitsa 1985*

2001—Russia—Oldest Piceioidea (Piceioideae) *Picea* sp. (Bathonian, approx. 168.3–166.1 Ma). See more: *Alifanov & Sennikov 2001*

2005—Argentina—Longest petrified trunk This 35-meter-long trunk was found in the Petrified Forest of Jaramillo Natural Monument. It belongs to the conifer *Araucaria mirabilis* (Bathonian, approx. 168.3–166.1 Ma). See more: *Bocanera 2005*

2007—China—Most recent Schmeissneriaceae *Schmeissneria sinensis* (Callovian, approx. 166.1–163.5 Ma). See more: *Wang et al 2007a, 2007b*

2010—Argentina—Longest conifer cone of the Mesozoic The cone is 18 x 8 cm (Bajocian, approx. 170.3–168.3 Ma). See more: *Escapa & Cúneo in Gee & Tidwell 2010*

2012—China—Oldest umbrella pine (Sciadopityaceae) *Protosciadopityoxylon* sp. is the first fossil in this family and shows the structure in great detail. Only a single species remains today, endemic to Japan. See more: *Jiang et al. 2012*

2016—Niger—Oldest Taxodioidea (Taxodioideae) *Taxodium* sp. (Bathonian, approx. 168.3–166.1 Ma). See more: *Witzmann et al. 2016*

1:1

seed
0.8–1.3 x
0.2–0.6 mm

UPPER JURASSIC MENU

At this time, sauropods were the first among the diplodocoids to develop cylindrodont teeth. These teeth were so successful that they proliferated in areas where shrubby plants predominated, while sauropods with foliodont teeth tended to inhabit areas with more coniferous trees. See more: *Hummel et al. 2008; Whitlock 2011; Young et al. 2012*

Pteridophytes (ferns)

1939—South Korea—Most recent asterotecacea (Asterothecaceae) *Asterotheca naktongensis* had 10 cm pinnas and its fronds were an estimated 77 cm long. They were relatives of the Marattiaceas (Marattiaceae). See more: *Oishi 1939*

1965—Cuba—First Mesozoic plant of the Antilles *Piazopteris branneri* (formerly thought to be *Phlebopteris cubensis*) dates to the Upper Jurassic (Oxfordian, approx. 163.5–157.3 Ma). See more: *Jongmans & Gothan 1951; Vakhrameev 1965; Ceballos 2016*

1979—China—Oldest Dryopteridaceae fern *Dryopteris* sp. (Kimmeridgian, approx. 157.3–152.1 Ma). See more: *Anonymous 1979*

1981—France—Most recent Trichopitys (Trichopityaceae) *Trichopitys laciniata* (middle Oxfordian, approx. 160 Ma). See more: *Barale 1981*

1986—India, Wyoming, Utah, USA—Oldest Loxsomataceae ferns *Solenostelopteris jurassica* from southern Neopangea, along with *S. leithii* and *S. medlynii* from northern Neopangea (Kimmeridgian, approx. 157.3–152.1 Ma). Only two species exist today. See more: *Bohra & Sharma 1986; Tidwell & Skog 1999*

2009—Russia—Oldest Blechnaceae fern The presence of this family is mentioned among ferns from the Upper Jurassic (Tithonian, approx. 152.1–145 Ma). See more: *Markevich & Bugdaeva 2009*

Pteridospermophytes or seed ferns (glossopteridales, medulosales, peltaspermales)

1972—India—Most recent Glossopteridaceae The most recent *Glossopteris* sp. were found in late-Jurassic deposits. See more: *Shah 1972*

Ginkgoopsids (caytoniales, Czekanowiskiales, ginkgoales, pentoxylaceas, petriellales)

1981—France—Most recent Yimaiaceae ginkgoal *Baiera verrucosa* (upper Kimmeridgian, approx. 154.6–152.1 Ma). See more: *Barale 1981*

Coniferophytes (coniferales, cordaitales, gnetales, voltziales)

1905—China, France, and California, USA—The genus *Sequoia* appears The species *S. jeholensis*, *S. portlandica*, and *S. fairbanksi* (Tithonian, approx. 152.1–145 Ma) are similar to the only extant species, *Sequoia sempervirens*, the world's largest plant. See more: *Fliche & Zeiller 1904; Fontaine 1905; Davis 1913; Chaney 1951; Barale 1981; Anonymous 1982; Ahuja & Neale 2002*

1962—Colorado, Utah, USA—Oldest Hermanophytales (Hermanophytales) *Hermanophyton glismanii*, *H. owensii*, *H. kirkbyorum* and *H. taylorii* are enigmatic gymnosperms, with a liana-like shape (Kimmeridgian, approx. 157.3–152.1 Ma). See more: *Arnold 1962; Tidwell & Ash 1990; Tidwell 2002*

1981—France—Oldest Callitroidea (Callitroideae) *Callitris* sp. (Tithonian, approx. 152.1–145 Ma). Its wood is highly flammable. See more: *Barale 1981*

1983—England—Tallest Cheirolepidiaceae conifer of the Jurassic The trunk of *Cupressinocladus* (*Protocupressinoxylon*) *purbeckensis* was a meter in diameter, and so was probably up to 20 m in height. See more: *Francis 1983; Coram, Jepson & Penney 2012*

1987—Norway—Oldest Sciadopityaceae conifers *Sciadopitys lagerheimii* and *S. macrophylla* sp. (Oxfordian, approx. 163.5–157.3 Ma). See more: *Manum 1987*

1990—Utah, USA—Largest liana of the Mesozoic *Hermanophyton taylorii* presents diameters of 3.0–22.5 cm, which suggests they were up to 18 m in length (Kimmeridgian, approx. 157.3–152.1 Ma). See more: *Tidwell & Ash 1990*

2000—China—Longest petrified trunk of the Jurassic This world-record-holding trunk is 38 meters long and was found in Qitai District, (Oxfordian, approx. 163.5–157.3 Ma). See more: *Wang, Zhang & Saiki 2000; Guiness World Records*

2005—Thailand—Oldest amber of Cimmeria Produced by the Araucariacea *Agathoxylon* (Tithonian, approx. 152.1–145 Ma). See more: *Le Loeuff 2005*

2010—Argentina—Largest conifer cone of the Upper Jurassic This cone of *Araucaria delevoryasii* was 8.5 x 8.5 cm in size (upper Kimmeridgian, approx. 154.6–152.1 Ma). See more: *Gee & Tidwell 2010*

2010—Lebanon—Oldest amber of the Middle East It was produced by the Araucariacea *Agaucarioxylon* (Tithonian, approx. 152.1–145 Ma). See more: *Azar et al. 2010; Nohra et al. 2013*

2010—China—Highest tree of the Upper Jurassic *Araucaria* presents trunks up to 2.9 m in diameter; in comparison to its present-day relative *A. bidwillidi*, this suggests it could have reached 70 m in height (Oxfordian (approx. 163.5–157.3 Ma). See more: *Hinz et al. 2010*

1:5

Sauropod with the largest gastroliths?
Diplodocus hallorum

A specimen of this diplodocid (formerly known as *Seismosaurus halli*) was associated with extremely large gastroliths measuring 107 x 58 x 35 mm, 77 x 75 x 28 mm, and 57 x 51 x 45 mm in length, width, and height, respectively. Some authors have called them "gastromyths" as they suspect the specimens were merely rocks found with the fossil. Researchers assume that sauropods ingested stones to help grind the plants they consumed, as they were not equipped to chew. See more: *Gillette et al.1990; Johnston et al. 1990; Lucas 2000*

2014—Utah, USA—Smallest conifer cone of the Upper Jurassic This conifer had cones just 1.7 x 1.8 cm in diameter (Kimmeridgian, approx. 157.3–152.1 Ma). See more: *Gee et al. 2014*

Various

1998—New Zealand—Southernmost plants of the Jurassic *Cladophlebis* sp., *Taeniopteris* sp., some conifers, and a hepatica were found at paleolatitude 85.9° S. Present-day gymnosperms do not live at latitudes greater than 55° S (Tithonian, approx. 152.1–145 Ma). See more: *Molnar, Wiffen & Hayes 1998*

Gymnosperm pollinators

1904—Germany—Largest pollinating insect of the Upper Jurassic *Kalligramma haeckeli* had a 24-cm wingspan (lower Tithonian, approx. 152.1–149.5 Ma). See more: *Walther 1904*

1:2

Kalligramma haeckeli

Dinosaur that was mistaken for a plant

Praeornis is based on an incomplete feather discovered in 1971 and identified as a cycad leaf in 1986. Analysis under an electron microscope demonstrated that it was actually a fossil bird feather. See more: *Rautian 1978; Bock 1986; Glazunova et al. 1991; Nesov 1992; Agnolin et al. 2017*

EARLY LOWER CRETACEOUS MENU

Plant types remained virtually unchanged during the transition from the Jurassic to the Cretaceous. It is evident, however, that angiosperm pollen increased and thick-trunked tempskyaceous ferns appeared, along with the first modern families of angiosperms. See more: *Martinez-Delclós et al. 2004; Labandeira 2014*

Sphenophytes (equisetales and sphenophyllales)

2001—Egypt—Most recent equiset similar to ***Calamites*** *Neocalamites* sp. (Berriasian, approx. 145–139.8 Ma) was similar to *Calamites*, a genus of ancient Paleozoic plants. It is a relative of modern-day equisets. See more: *Konijenburg-van Cittert & Bandei 2001*

Pteridophytes (ferns)

2003—Argentina—Oldest Tempskyaceae fern *Tempskya dernbachii* (Valanginian, approx. 139.8–132.9 Ma) belonged to a family that existed exclusively in the Cretaceous. See more: *Tidwell & Wright 2003; Martinez & Olivo 2015*

2006—Canada—Oldest Anemiaceae *Anemia* sp. (upper Valanginian, approx. 136.3–132.9 Ma). There are currently 100 extant species. See more: *Hernandez-Castillo et al. 2006*

Coniferophytes (coniferales, cordaitales, gnetales, voltziales)

1861—Ukraine—Oldest Cunninghamioideae *Cunninghamites priscus* dates to the Valanginian (approx. 139.8–132.9 Ma). *C. dubius* was dated to the Upper Triassic and has been re-identified as *Palyssia braunii*. Only two species currently exist. See more: *Eichwald 1861; Sternberg 1820–1838; Bosma et al. 2012*

1975—India—Araucaria with branch dehiscence *Araucaria* displays a loss of branches in the lower trunk, like *A. araucana* in its adult stage. Both belong to the group Columbea. This may have been an adaptation to protect the plant from damage from sauropods (Berriasian, approx. 145–139.8 Ma). See more: *Sukh-Dev & Zeba-Bano 1975; Apesteguia 1998*

1982—Japan—Oldest amber of Paleoasia First believed to be from the lower Barremian, it is now dated to the Hauterivian (approx. 132.9–129.4 Ma). See more: *Obata et al. 1982; Martinez-Delclós et al. 2004*

1983—England—Thickest trunk *Protocupressinoxylon* sp. These trunks were up to 2 m in diameter, so their height was estimated to be 40 m (Berriasian, approx. 145–139.8 Ma). See more: *Francis 1983; Schnyder et al. 2005; Philippe et al. 2009*

1990—England—Oldest bark burrowed into by an insect A bark beetle caused damage to this conifer (Berriasian-Valanginian, approx. 145–132 Ma. See more: *Jarzembowski 1990; Chaloner et al. 1991; Scott et al 1992*

2002—Germany—Oldest amber from a Miroviacea (Miroviaceae) It was produced by *Tritaenia linkii* (Berriasian, approx. 145–139.8 Ma). See more: *Otto et al. 2002*

2002—South Africa—Oldest amber from Africa (Valanginian, approx. 139.8–132.9 Ma). See more: *Gomez, Bamford & Martinez-Delclós 2002*

2009—Thailand—Tallest Cheirolepidiacea (Cheirolepidiaceae) conifer *Brachyoxylon* sp. alcanzaba grew up to 45 m tall, according to estimates based on its 1.5-m trunk diameter (Berriasian, approx. 145–139.8 Ma). See more: *Philippe et al. 2004; Philippe et al. 2009*

LATE LOWER CRETACEOUS MENU

Bennettitales plants begin to decline (they are now extinct), while at the same time, new types of sauropods with cylindrical teeth begin to emerge and spread, along with the diplodocoids, such as lithostrotians and some euhelopodids, somphospondylids, and titanosauriforms. All of these species may have preferred to eat bushy plants. See more: *Bakker 1986; Cao et al. 1998*

1:50

Tempskya knowltoni

Pteridophytes (ferns)

1924—Idaho, USA—Largest fern of the Mesozoic This *Tempskya knowltoni* trunk is 50 cm in diameter, so the tree was an estimated 6 m tall (Albian, approx. 113–100.5 Ma). See more: *Seward 1924; Andrew & Kern 1947*

1955—Tanzania—Largest fern spore of the Cretaceous *Concavissimisporites verrucosus-crassatus* may have belonged to a Cyatheaceae or Dicksoniaceae fern and measures 97 microns in diameter (Albian, approx. 113–100.5 Ma). See more: *Delcourt & Sprumont 1955; Delcourt et al. 1963; Schrank 2010*

1967—China—Largest arborescent fern (Cyatheales) of the Cretaceous *Coniopteris saportana* was 16 m tall (Albian, approx. 113–100.5 Ma). See more: *Vakhrameev 1958*

1978—Egypt—Oldest Salviniales water fern *Ariadnaesporites* sp. (Aptian, approx. 125–113 Ma). See more: *Saad 1978*

1982—Germany—Oldest Polypodiaceae fern An indeterminate species (Aptian, approx. 125–113 Ma). See more: *Huckriede 1982*

2001—Wyoming, USA—Oldest Lindsaeacea (Lindsaeaceae) This epiphytic fern grew on a *Tempskya* trunk (Albian, approx. 113–100.5 Ma). See more: *Schneider & Kenrick 2001*

2010—Antarctica—Oldest Thyropteridaceae fern This fern was reported and dated to the Aptian period (approx. 125–113 Ma). See more: *Vera 2010*

1:40

Weichselia reticulata

2014—Saudi Arabia and Spain—Largest Matoniaceae fern *Weichselia reticulata* inhabited mangrove swamps and had leaves up to 1 m long that formed fronds up to 1.5 m in diameter (middle Albian-lower Cenomanian, approx. 106–97 Ma). See more: *Stokes & Webb 1824; El-Khayal 1985; Sender et al. 2014*

Pteridospermophytes or seed ferns (glossopteridales, medulosales, peltaspermales)

1969—Belgium—Most recent Alethopteridae *Alethopteris* sp. (Barremian, approx. 129.4–125 Ma) is a genus that emerged in the lower Carboniferous and survived for 234 Ma. See more: *Quinet 1969*

2007—Argentina—Most recent corytosperm (Corytospermales) *Pachypteris crassa* (upper Albian, approx. 106–100.5 Ma). See more: *Passalia 2007*

Ginkgoopsids (caytoniales, Czekanowskiales, ginkgoales, pentoxylaceas, petriellales)

1965—Argentina—Most recent Karkeniaceae ginkgoal *Karkenia incurva* (Aptian, approx. 125–113 Ma). See more: *Archangelsky 1965*

2007—Argentina—Most recent corytosperm (Corytospermales) *Pachypteris crassa* (upper Albian, approx. 106–100.5 Ma). See more: *Passalia 2007*

Coniferophytes (coniferales, cordaitales, gnetales, voltziales)

1973—Lebanon—Oldest amber containing a feather Feathers have been found in amber in different parts of the world. The first case ever reported is still the oldest (upper Barremian, approx. 127.2–125 Ma). Birds make up 0.04% of animal inclusions preserved. See more: *Schlee 1973; Schlee & Glockner 1978; Azar et al. 2010*

1986—China—Largest Miroviacea conifer (Miroviaceae) The trunk of *Xenoxylon latiporosum* reached diameters of up to 2.5 m, indicating that the tree could have been 40 m tall (upper Aptian, approx. 119–113 Ma). See more: *Duan 1986*

1977—Ecuador—Thickest trunk of the late Lower Cretaceous The fossilized wood of *Araucarioxylon* was up to 2.2 m in diameter, and the tree may have been 45 m tall (Lower Aptian, approx. 125–119 Ma). See more: *Shoemaker 1977, 1982; Jimenez et al. 2001*

1991—Argentina—Smallest Araucariaceae cone of the Mesozoic *Notopehuen brevis* Aptian, approx. 125–113 Ma) had cones just 2 x 1.8 mm in diameter. See more: *del Fueyo 1991; Archangelsky & del Fueyo 2010*

1993—Texas, USA—Highest carbon isotope levels in non-angiosperm plants Found in *Frenelopsis oligostomata* (Cheirolepidiaceae) (upper Aptian, approx. 119–113 Ma). See more: *Bocherens, Friis, Mariotti & Pedersen 1993*

1:3

Makarkinia adamsi

x4

Notopehuen brevis

1996—Spain—Strangest amber of the Mesozoic The El Soplao deposit contains amber that is an extremely rare bright purplish-blue; most amber is reddish-yellow. It is from Cheirolepidiaceas that were exposed to very high temperatures during a fire (lower Albian, 113–106.7 Ma). See more: *Menor-Salván et al. 2009*

2004—Brazil—Largest conifer cone of the Lower Cretaceous This *Araucaria* sp. cone measures 8.3 x 4.7 cm (Aptian, approx. 125–113 Ma). See more: *Kunzmann et al. 2004*

2005—Colombia and Texas, USA—Tallest Cheirolepidiacea conifer This 34-cm-diameter trunk of *Pseudofrenelopsis ramosissima* is from a tree that could reach up to 22.4 m tall. *Pseudofrenelopsis* cf. *ramosissima* has also been reported in South America (upper Albian, approx. 106–100.5 Ma). See more: *Watson 1977; Axsmith & Jacobs 2005; Sanchez, Cruz & González 2007*

2006—England—Oldest conifer trunk with termites Termite coprolites were found in this conifer trunk. See more: *Francis & Harland 2006*

2007—Argentina—Thickest Ephedracea (Ephedraceae) stalk of the Mesozoic The stalk of *Ephedra verticillata* was 2 mm in diameter, but the plant still could have been up to 2 m tall (lower Aptian, approx. 125–119 Ma). See more: *Cladera, Del Fueyo, Seoane & Archangelsky 2007*

2010—Spain—Strangest amber The piece of amber from the El Soplao deposit is a deep purplish-blue color from impurities (Barremian, approx. 129.4–125 Ma). See more: *Menor-Salván et al. 2009; Penney 2010*

2012—Rusia—Largest tree in the lower Cretaceous *Sequoia lebedevii*, compared to the living *S. sempevirens*, would have reached 75 m in height and 5.9 m in diameter (upper Albian-lower Cenomanian, approx. 100.5 Ma). See more: *Golovneva & Nosova 2012*

2014—China—Oldest Athrotaxoidea (Athrotaxoideae) *Athrotaxites yumenensis* (Barremian, approx. 129.4–125 Ma). See more: *Dong et al. 2014*

2014—Maryland, USA—Oldest Welwitschiaceae *Bicatia costata* and *B. juncalensis* are seeds (lower Albian, approx. 113–106 Ma). Only a single species exists today. See more: *Friis et al. 2014*

2018—Spain—Oldest amber from a cupressacea Some of the amber found was identified as belonging to this family (lower Albian, approx. 113–106.7 Ma). See more: *Seyfullah et al. 2018*

2019—Russia—Oldest Schizolepisacea (Schizolepisaceae) *Schizolepidopsis borealis* (upper Albian, approx. 106.7–100.5 Ma). See more: *Domogatskaya & Herman 2019*

Miscellaneous facts

2005—Antarctica—Southernmost plants of the Cretaceous *Coniopteris* cf. *frutiformis*, *Microphyllopteris unisora*, *Phyllopteroides antarctica* and *Sphenopteris sanjuliensis* were found at paleolatitude 77.9° S. See more: *Cantrill & Nagalingum 2005*

2005—Alaska, USA—Northernmost plants of the Cretaceous *Equisetites ex gr. burejensis*, *Pityophyllum* sp. and *Podozamites* spp. were found at paleolatitude 80.2° N, which is now a polar desert. See more: *Spicer & Herman 2001*

Gymnosperm eaters and pollinators

1992—Brazil—Largest pollinator insect of the Cretaceous *Makarkinia adamsi* was 34 cm in width, wider than the largest butterflies, *Ornithoptera alexandrae* and *Thysania agrippina*, both measuring 33 cm. This insect pollinated the now-extinct cheirolepidiaceous pines; today conifers are all wind-pollinated (upper Aptian, approx. 119–113 Ma). See more: *Martins-Neto 1992; Bechly & Makarkin 2016; Labandeira et al.2016*

2002—China—Oldest pollinating dinosaur? Seeds of *Beania* (*Carpolithus*), 8–10 mm in size, were found inside a *Jeholornis prima* (*Shenzhouraptor*). They were thought to be from a *Nilssonia* cycad but were actually ginkgos. See more: *Zhou & Zhang 2002; Pott et al. 2012*

2012—Spain—Smallest insect gymnosperm pollinator of the Lower Cretaceous *Gymnopollisthrips minor*, just 973 microns long, had 137 grains of pollen stuck to its body (lower Albian, approx. 113–106.7 Ma). See more: *Peñalver et al. 2012*

EARLY UPPER CRETACEOUS MENU

Flowering plants became more diverse in this period, competing effectively against ferns, pines, and other gymnosperms. That may have impacted Earth's atmosphere, as angiosperm leaves absorb CO_2 more effectively. This era also witnessed the appearance of very large flowers and the proliferation of cylindrical teeth among most sauropods, although foliodont teeth remained in a limited number of species until the end of the Cretaceous. See more: *Poinar & Brown 2003; Brodribb & Field 2010*

Chrysophytes algae (diatoms)

2004—Mexico—Oldest freshwater diatoms *Amphora* (Catenulaceae), *Fragilaria* (Fragilariaceae), *Melosira* (Melosiraceae) and *Tabellaria* (Tabellariaceae) belong to genera that are still extant (upper Turonian, approx. 91.8– 89.8 Ma). They may be in fact much older, as thaumaleid mosquitos (Thaumaleidae), which were specialized in grazing on diatoms, existed from the Upper Jurassic. See more: *Kovalev 1989; Beraldi-Campesi, Ceballos-Ferris & Chakon-Bacae 2004*

Pteridophytes (ferns)

1957—Canada—Most recent Sphenopteridae fern *Sphenopteris hollicki* (Coniacian, approx. 100.5–93.9 Ma). See more: *Bell 1957*

Pteridospermophytes (glossopteridales, medulosales, peltaspermales)

1996—Japan—Oldest cone with a larva inside A pentoxylal cone was found to contain the larva of a sap beetle (Nitidulidae) 8 mm long (upper Turonian, approx. 91.8–89.8 Ma). See more: *Nishida & Hayashi 1996*

Ginkgoopsids (caytoniales, Czekanowskiales, ginkgoales, pentoxylaceas, petriellales)

1988—Russia—Most recent Umaltolepidiaceae ginkoal *Pseudotorellia postuma* (Cenomanian, approx. 100.5–93.9 Ma). See more:*Samylina 1988*

Coniferophytes (coniferales, cordaitales, gnetales, voltziales)

1889—Czech Rep.—Most complex Cheirolepidiacea cone *Alvinia bohemica,* a cone corresponding to *Frenelopsis alata*, has a deep, funnel-shaped opening surrounded by several appendages that may have served to attract small insects, or large ones with long proboscises, to aid in pollination (Cenomanian, approx. 100.5–93.9 Ma). See more: *Velenovsky 1889; Kvacek 2000*

1939—Syria—Fossil wood with the longest genus name *Protophyllocladoxylon*, with 21 letters, is the name of a Podocarpacea. See more: *Krausel 1939*

1951—North Dakota, New Mexico, USA, Canada, China, Japan, Norway, Russia—Longest surviving conifer species *Metasequoia occidentalis* dates from the Cenomanian to the Pliocene (approx. 100–5.3 Ma), so it was on Earth for 95 Ma. It was very similar to the present-day species *M. glyptostroboides*, a tree that has remained virtually unchanged for at least 53 Ma, according to one biomolecular study. See more: *Chaney 1951; Ozaki 1991; Juvik et al. 2016*

1955—Canada, Alaska, Montana, USA—Most abundant conifer of the Cretaceous *Parataxodium wigginsii* was a small conifer 20–50 cm in trunk diameter (calculated height of 3–7.5 m) that predominated in vast zones of North America (Cenomanian, approx. 100.5–93.9 Ma). See more: *Arnold & Lowther 1955; Krassilov 1981*

1958—Australia, Canada, USA, New Zealand—Largest conifer spore of the Cretaceous *Balmeisporites glenelgensis* (middle Cenomanian, approx. 97.2 Ma) is an Araucaracea spore 150 to 190 microns in diameter. See more: *Cookson & Dettmann 1958; Hu et al. 2008*

1974—Germany, Czech Rep., Russia—Smallest Sequioidea (Sequioideae) of the early Upper Cretaceous *Sequoia minuta* grew up to 29 m tall (upper Coniacian, approx. 89.8–88 Ma). See more: *Svesnikova 1974*

1987—Antarctica—Oldest Phyllocladea (Phyllocladaseae) *Phyllocladidites mawsoniidata* (upper Turonian, approx. 91.8–89.8 Ma). See more: *Dettmann & Thomson 1987*

1992—Japan—Oldest narrow-leafed Araucaria (Eutacta) *Araucaria nihongii* (Turonian, approx. 93.9–89.8 Ma). See more: *Stockey, Nishida & Nishida 1992*

1993—Japan—Oldest Taiwanioide (Taiwanioideae) *Mikasastrobus hokkaidoensis* (Coniacian, approx. 89.8–86.3 Ma). See more: *Saiki & Kimura 1993*

1997—Russia—Oldest Cephalotaxacea (Cephalotaxaceae) *Cephalotaxus* sp. (Coniacian, approx. 89.8–86.3 Ma). See more: *Lukashevich & Shcherbakov 1997*

2002—Myanmar—Oldest Taxodiacea amber It was produced by a *Metasequoia* sp. (lower Cenomanian, approx. 100.5–97.2 Ma). See more: *Grimaldi, Engel & Nascimbene 2002*

2016—Myanmar—Amber with the most complete bird inside A newborn specimen of the bird *Enantiornite*, including feathers and soft tissue, was preserved in amber from a metasequoia (Taxodiaceae). See more: *Xing et al. 2016*

Spain—World's largest amber specimen Found in Utrillas, it weighs approximately 1 kg and dates to the Turonian (approx. 93.9–89.8 Ma). See more: *https://puroambar.es/*

Gymnosperm pollinators

2005—Lebanon—Smallest insect gymnosperm pollinator of the Upper Cretaceous *Parapolycentropus paraburmiticus* was 2.88 mm long and 7.3 mm wide (lower Cenomanian, approx. 100.5–97.2 Ma). See more: *Grimaldi & Rasnitsyn 2005; Ollerton & Coulthard 2009*

LATE UPPER CRETACEOUS MENU

Gymnosperms account for 22% of all fossil wood, much less than that of angiosperms, with 78%. This disproportion must have had a profound effect on sauropods; although a limited number of species retained foliodont teeth, including some in Asia (euhelopodids), Europe, and South America (Titanosauria), the majority had developed cylindrodont teeth. The lithostrotian *Ampelosaurus* presents an interesting case, as its cylindrical teeth had a broader part that recalls foliodonts, perhaps as an adaptation to enable the consumption of gymnosperms. See more: *Ameghino 1898; Huene 1929; Jardiné & Magloire 1965; Bertini et al. 1993; Le Loeuff 1995; Pereda-Suberbiola & Ruiz-Omeñaca 2001; Prasad et al. 2005, 2010; Falcon-Lang & Peralta-Medina 2012; Martínez 2012*

Chrysophyte algae (diatoms)

India—Smallest plant consumed by a sauropod Various types of unicellular algae have been found in titanosaur coprolites, consumed accidentally while the animals were drinking water. *Aulacoseira* sp. measured 5 x 3 microns and often formed chains of several individuals (upper Maastrichtian, approx. 69–66 Ma). See more: *Ambwani et al. 2003; Singh et al. 2006; Mukherjee 2014; Sonkusare et al. 2017*

Aulacoseira

1000:1

Pteridophytes (ferns)

1911—Japan—Most recent Tempskyaceae fern *Tempskya iwatensis* and *T. uemurae* (Santonian, approx. 86.3–83.6 Ma). Other species such as *T. cretacea* in Germany and *T. rossica* from Russia have not yet been assigned an exact age. See more: *Hosius & Marck 1880; Kidston & Gwynne-Vaughan 1911; Nishida 1986, 2001; Martinez & Olivo 2015; Puente-Arauzo et al. 2014*

1998—Wyoming, USA—Most recent Cladophlebis fern *Cladophlebis* sp. (lower Campanian, approx. 100.5–93.9 Ma) is a genus that has existed since the Permian. See more: *Van Boskirk 1998*

Pteridospermophytes or seed ferns (corytospermales, glossopteridales, medulosales, peltaspermales)

2015—Spain—Most recent Sphenopteridacea (Sphenopteridae) *Sphenopteris* sp. (upper Maastrichtian, approx. 69–66 Ma). See more: *Marmi, Martin-Closas, Fernández-Marrón et al. 2015*

Ginkgoopsids (caytoniales, Czekanowskiales, ginkgoales, pentoxylaceas, petriellales)

1966—Russia—Most recent caytonial (Caytoniales) *Sagenopteris variabilis* (Campanian, approx. 83.6–72.1 Ma). See more: *Vakhrameev 1966*

1997—Russia—Most recent Czekanoswskial *Phoenicopsis* sp. (lower Campanian, approx. 100.5–93.9 Ma) had deciduous leaves. It belonged to an extinct group of enigmatic plants that appeared shortly before the Mesozoic era. See more: *Lukashevich & Shcherbakov 1997*

Coniferophytes (coniferales, cordaitales, gnetales, voltziales)

1988—Russia—Smallest Sequioidea (Sequioideae) of the Mosozoic *Sequoia parvifolia* grew up to 18 m tall. See more: *Samylina 1988*

1:600

Araucaria sp.

1994—South Dakota, USA—Tallest trunk and tree of the Mesozoic? An *Araucaria* trunk 116 m long was reportedly discovered by paleobotanist Kirk Johnson. It may have been up to 140 m tall when alive, but given its similarity to *A. bidwilli*, it could have been 120 m tall (160 m, including the roots). It would have been taller than "Hyperion" (*Sequoia sempervirens*), the tallest known tree on Earth, at 115.92 m, and would have been lower than *Eucalyptus regnans*, measuring a record 143 m. Unfortunately, it was not published formally, and the measurements could have been mistaken. See more: *Horner & Lessem 1994*

2000—Antarctica—Oldest Phyllocladacea (Phyllocladaceae) *Phyllocladus* aff. *aspleniifolius* (upper Campanian, approx. 77.8–72.1 Ma). See more: *Dutra & Batten 2000*

2002—Argentina—The most recent Cheirolepidiaceae conifers *Classopollis classoides*, *Classopollis intrareticulatus* pollens and *Frenelopsis* sp. leave (Maastrichtian, approx. 72.1–66 Ma). See more: *Papú 2002*

2004—Russia—Most recent amber of the Mesozoic This amber was dated to the boundary between the upper Maastrichtian and the lower Paleocene (approx. 69–61.6 Ma). See more: *Martínez-Delclòs et al. 2004*

2004—Argentina—Most recent Yezonia type Araucariacea *Brachyphyllum* sp. (upper Campanian-Maastrichtian, approx. 72.1 Ma). See more: *Álvarez-Ramis et al. 2004*

2004—Russia—Northernmost amber of the Mesozoic Found in the Taimyr Peninsula, at latitude 75° N. See more: *Martínez-Delclòs et al. 2004*

2008—Alaska, USA, Russia—Most recent Miroviacea (Miroviaceae) *Xenoxylon latiporosum* (Maastrichtian). See more: *Philippe & Cantrill 2007; Afonin 2008*

2010—Belgium—Most recent Hermanophytal (Hermanophytales) *Hermanophyton* sp. is a liana 6 cm in diameter, so it may have reached a length of 4.8 m (Santonian, approx. 86.3–83.6 Ma). See more: *Knoll 2010*

1:5

Araucaria bladenensis

2012—Alabama, USA—The largest coniferous pineapple in the Upper Cretaceous A cone of *Araucaria bladenensis* (Santonian, approx. 86.3–83.6 Ma) has an estimated diameter of 18 x 18 cm, which suggests a weight of 2.4 kg. See more: *Stults et al. 2012*

2016—Russia—Largest tree of the Mesozoic *Sequoiadendron tchucoticum* may have been 80 m tall (105 m, including the root mass), 9.35 m in diameter, and weighed some 800 t, or up to 1,000 t with the rootmass included (lower Campanian, approx. 83.6–77.8 Ma). See more: *Sokolovaa & Moiseeva 2016*

2018—Argentina—Tallest tree of Gondwana *Araucaria lefipanensis* is a close relative of the present-day *A. hunsteinni*. Both belong to the Intermedia section. The largest trunk is 30 m long and 3 m in diameter, which suggests it reached a height of 89 m (119 m in total, including the root mass) (upper Maastrichtian, approx. 69–66 Ma). See more: *Laubenfels 1988; Carder 1995; Andruchow-Colombo et al. 2018*

Miscellaneous facts

2002—North Dakota, USA—Most recent plant-insect interaction of the Mesozoic One fossilized area presents a total of 49 bite marks, tunnels, holes, or suction marks on moss, ferns, conifers, cycads, ginkgos, and angiosperms. The find dates to the late Upper Cretaceous (Maastrichtian, approx. 68.2–64.6 Ma).

Sequoiadendron tchucoticum

x400

cf. Argentinosaurus for comparison

Araucaria lefipanensis

x400

Sauropodomorphs consumed as food

Undoubtedly, these dinosaurs were sometimes attacked by predators. Adults could have been preyed upon by primitive saurischians or theropods, as well as different archosaurs such as crocodiles, phytosaurs, and rauisuchids, among others. In contrast, juvenile sauropodomorphs could have fallen prey to a wider variety of predators, as they were small, defenseless creatures at birth. We do know that in some species the adults protected their young, while in others the females gave birth to a large number of hatchlings that were left to fend for themselves.

These animals would have had a variety of defensive strategies, as primitive forms had strong claws, moderate speed, and in some cases were very large in size; others lived in herds, and some may even have had cryptic capacities to disguise themselves. Sauropods, in contrast, had one very effective defense—their large size—although some also had strong tails armed with clubs or whips, thick necks or necks armored with spines, incredibly strong feet, good hearing, excellent balance, and/or osteoderms. These creatures, especially the smaller species, also must have had many ways of defending themselves that we do not yet know of.

In the Upper Triassic, herrerasaurids and coelophysoids could reach speeds of more than 40 km/h, while gracile sauropodomorphs were not as fast, which suggests that the latter could not use their speed as a defense against the former kinds of predators. Perhaps they saw them from far off and ran away to hide or waited for their least capable companions to fall victim to the attackers. Larger forms were very well armed and reached 5 to 27 times the size of their carnivorous contemporaries (a predator cannot usually hunt prey that is more than 5 to 8 times its own size).

In the Upper Jurassic, theropods reached impressive sizes, weighing up to 6.5 t and able to run slightly faster than 30 km/h; but several sauropod species were 5 to 11 times as large, although smaller non-island-dwelling forms also existed, such as *Haplocanthosaurus* sp. FHPR 1106, which only weighed 3 t as an adult. It is clear that sauropods could not outrun their predators, unless some relatively fast species had more stamina, which is very unlikely, or identified the predator early enough to have time to flee.

During the Cretaceous, carnivorous dinosaurs grew as large as 8.5 t and could reach speeds of more than 30 km/h; some smaller forms were able to run even faster, up to 35 km/h, and could also have hunted sauropods. In contrast, sauropods could achieve speeds of 14 km/h to more than 30 km/h. In terms of size, several were 5 to 9 times heavier than the largest theropods, which suggests that certain forms were invulnerable to attack. The smallest non-insular sauropod was *Bonatitan*, which weighed just 600 kg. Several other small forms like *Bonatitan* would have had to use strategies other than speed to avoid being killed.

MYTH Sauropods submerged themselves in water to escape from predators

This antiquated idea came from the belief that these animals were too heavy to walk on dry land.

Most severe traumatic pathology in a sauropodomorph
Massospondylus sp.
This sauropodomorph survived having its tail amputated at vertebra 25, but the damage may have shifted its center of mass. See more: *Butler et al. 2013*

RECORDS OF THE SAUROPODOMORPH AND SAUROPOD DIET

1836—England—First omnivorous sauropodomorph
Thecodontosaurus antiquus was a bipedal creature 2.5 m long and weighing about as much as a German shepherd (34 kg). See more: *Riley & Stutchbury 1836; Morris 1843*

1837—Germany—Largest omnivorous sauropodomorph
Unlike larger sauropodomorphs, *Plateosaurus engelhardti* had lanceolate foliodont teeth, a trait associated with a mixed diet. The largest specimen known was 9.3 m long and weighed 2.6 t. See more: *Meyer 1837; Moser 2003*

1870—Switzerland—Oldest sauropod showing teeth marks
"Ornithopsis" *greppini* (also known as "Cetiosauriscus") displayed marks that match the teeth of the crocodile *Machimosaurus*. It may have fallen prey to this animal or been eaten as carrion. See more: *Seeley 1870; Meyer & Thuring 2003*

1904—First sauropod bone showing theropod teeth marks
A caudal vertebra of *Brontosaurus* had marks from a theropod bite, and so it was used in a display that included an *Allosaurus* skeleton. See more: *Osborn 1904*

1906—Montana, USA—First Jurassic sauropod with gastroliths
The presence of gastroliths was reported in *Atlantosaurus immanis*, a sauropod that has sometimes been considered a synonym of *Apatosaurus ajax*, although it now appears not to be. The same year another report was issued of sauropod gastroliths, but they were actually from a *Plesiosaurus*. See more: *Cannon 1906; Wieland 1906; Tschopp et al. 2015*

1920—South Africa—First obligate phytophagous sauropodomorph
No teeth of *Eucnemesaurus fortis* have been identified, but given its proximity to *Riojasaurus*, we can infer that it was also an obligate phytophage. However, that kinship has recently been placed in doubt, and if it is ruled out, then *Melanorosaurus readi*, described four years later from a skull and teeth known since 2007, would have been the first. See more: *Hoepen 1920; Haughton 1924; McPhee et al. 2015*

1924—USA—First sauropod mistaken for a carnivore
It was proposed that *Diplodocus* consumed clams, as its teeth were not suitable for grinding plants yet did display prominent wear on their tips. We now know that those teeth were useful for raking and pulling out ferns, pines, and other similar plants. See more: *Holland 1924*

1929—Tanzania—First sauropods with gastroliths in Africa
These structures were found in *Dicraeosaurus hansemanni* and possibly in *Tornieria africana*. See more: *Janensch 1929*

1932—Germany—First sauropodomorph with gastroliths
Some stones associated with a *Plateosaurus gracilis* (formerly *Sellosaurus*) were identified as gastroliths. See more: *Huene 1932*

1934—Australia—First mistaken report of a sauropod "coprolite"
A spiral-shaped structure 2 m long and 22 cm wide was interpreted as an enormous coprolite produced by *Austrosaurus*. It is now believed to be a mold of the interior of a cave or rock gallery that may have been dug out by an ornithischian or burrowing mammiferoid. See more: *Whitehouse 1934; Thulborn 1991*

1941—India—First sauropod coprolite of the Cretaceous
Some large phytophagous coprolites 17 cm long and 10 cm wide have been interpreted as feces of titanosaurs. See more: *Matley 1941*

1955—South Africa—Sauropodomorph having the most specimens with gastroliths

The presence of gastroliths was reported in *Gyposaurus capensis* and in *Massospondylus harriesi*, which are juvenile specimens of *M. carinatus*. See more: *Bond 1955; Raath 1974; Cooper 1981; Galton 1990*

1964—Utah, USA—Most unexpected sauropod stomach contents?
Stomach contents reported for an Upper Jurassic sauropod include a large volume of wood, indeterminate bones, and a theropod tooth. The tooth may have been ingested by accident. See more: *Stokes 1964*

1987—Portugal—First sauropod with gastroliths in Europe
A partial skeleton with gastroliths was found in 1987 by Carlos Anunciação and identified as a specimen of *Lourinhanosaurus alenquerensis*. However, it ultimately was identified as the holotype specimen of *Supersaurus lourinhanensis* (formerly *Dinheirosaurus*) ML 414. See more: *Dantas et al. 1993, 1998; Bonaparte & Mateus 1999*

1987–1993—Argentina, India—Oldest omnivorous sauropodomorphs
Alwalkeria maleriensis and *Eoraptor lunensis* date to the Upper Triassic (Lower Carnian, approx. 237–232 Ma). See more: *Chatterjee 1987; Sereno et al. 1993*

1989—India—Largest sauropod coprolite
This coprolite is 20 cm long and 10 cm in diameter and would have weighed 2 kg when excreted. In comparison, an African elephant excretes feces 10–20 cm long and 12–15 cm in diameter in groups of four to six some 15 times a day. See more: *Matley 1939; Jain 1989*

1989—USA—First Cretaceous sauropod with gastroliths
In a personal communication, Frank DeCourten reported the presence of gastroliths in a sauropod that was possibly of the *Astrodon* genus. See more: *Whittle & Everhart 2000*

1989—India—Oldest sauropod coprolite
These large coprolites associated with *Barapasaurus tagorei* were dated to the Lower Jurassic (Sinemurian, approx. 199.3–190.8 Ma). See more: *Jain 1989*

1991—New Mexico, USA—Jurassic sauropod with the most gastroliths
Between 230 and 240 gastroliths were found in specimen NMMN-HP3690, *Diplodocus hallorum* (formerly *Seismosaurus halli*). Some investigators suspect that they were only dispersed stones ("gastromyths"), while others believe they are authentic. See more: *Gillette et al. 1991; Johnston et al. 1990; Gillette 1994; Lucas 2000; Lucas et al. 2004; Carpenter 2006; Wings 2015*

1991—New Mexico, USA—Largest sauropod gastrolith
The largest gastroliths of *Diplodocus hallorum* (formerly *Seismosaurus*) NMMNH-P3690 reached 107 x 58 x 35, 77 x 75 x 28, and 57 x 51 x 45 mm in length, width, and height, respectively. See more: *Gillette et al. 1991; Johnston et al. 1990; Lucas 2000*

1990—New Mexico, USA—Largest sauropod with gastroliths
Specimen NMMNH-P3690 of *Diplodocus hallorum* (formerly *Seismosaurus halli*) was 31 m long and weighed 21 t. Due to an erroneous arrangement of the vertebrae, it was believed to be 54 m long and to have weighed more than 100 t. See more: *Gillette et al. 1990; Gillette 1994; Carpenter 2006*

1991—Argentina—First South American sauropod with gastroliths
This indeterminate species was known as "*Rebbachisaurus*". See more: *Calvo & Salgado 1991; Ford**

1993—Argentina—Highest-feeding sauropod
Argentinosaurus huinculensis could reach up to 17 m in height,

although the length of its neck is unknown. *Asiatosaurus mongoliensis* could have been taller, but it is only known by several gigantic teeth. Even taller was cf. *Barosaurus*, which could reach 22 m when standing on its hind legs. See more: *Osborn 1924; Bonaparte & Coria 1993; Taylor**

1993—India—First coprolite assigned to a sauropod genus
Fossil coprolites were assigned to *Antarctosaurus* sp. or *Titanosaurus* sp. See more: *Mohabey et al.1993*

1993–1994—China—Sauropod that starved to death?
The teeth of *Mamenchisaurus sinocanadorum* were found completely erupted but without any wear, leading some researchers to suggest that it may have died of hunger. See more: *Russell & Zheng 1993-1994; Tanke & Rothschild 2002*

1994—Canada—Sauropodomorph with the most gastroliths
A large quantity of gastroliths 1–3 cm in diameter were found in a circle 25 cm in diameter in Nova Scotia and assigned to cf. *Ammosaurus* sp. See more: *Shubin et al. 1994; Grantham in Whittle & Everhart 2000*

1994—Canada—Sauropodomorph with another animal inside?
A mandible of *Clevosaurus bairdi* was found close to gastroliths of cf. *Ammosaurus* sp.; the idea emerged that it had been part of the stomach contents, indicating that the sauropodomorph had eaten the other creature. See more: *Shubin et al. 1994; Ramírez-Velasco com. pers.*

1995—Argentina—Oldest obligate phytophagous sauropodomorph
A specimen attributed to *Riojasaurus incertus* had cylindrical, slightly cone-shaped teeth and was quadrupedal; thus it was adapted to eating ferns and other soft-tissue plants. It dates to the Upper Triassic (Norian, approx. 227–208.5 Ma). See more: *Bonaparte & Pumares 1995; McPhee & Choiniere 2017*

1995—Argentina—Most recent sauropod with gastroliths
Gastroliths weighing 350–850 g were found in *Limaysaurus tessonei* (formerly *Rebbachisaurus*) and dated to the early Upper Cretaceous (upper Cenomanian, approx. 97.2–93.9 Ma). See more: *Calvo & Salgado 1995*

1995—Spain—Oldest colonized coprolite
A group of Scarabeidae (beetles) built their nest in a coprolite of a phytophagous dinosaur that was dated to the late Lower Cretaceous (Upper Barremian, approx. 129.4–127.2 Ma). See more: *Martinez et al. 1995*

1997—Tanzania—First calculation of sauropod dietary needs
The calculation found that *Giraffatitan brancai* would have needed to eat 182 kg of food daily if it was endothermic (warm-blooded) and much less if it was ectothermic (cold-blooded). See more: *Bakker 1972; Weaver 1983; Bailey 1997; Grady et al. 2014*

1997—Zimbabwe—Oldest sauropod with gastroliths
Some gastrolith-like stones were identified in *Vulcanodon karibaensis*, dating to the Lower Jurassic (Hettangian 201.3–199.3 Ma). See more: *Raath 1972; Dodson 1997*

1998—USA—First sauropod coprolite of the Jurassic?
Some coprolites 15.5 cm long, 14 cm wide, and 7.8 cm high found with fossil cycad and conifer wood remains were suspected of belonging to a young sauropod or an ornithischian similar to *Mymoorapelta*. See more: *Chin & Kirkland 1998*

1999—Utah, USA—Cretaceous sauropod with the most gastroliths
Up to 115 gastroliths weighing 7 kg in total were found in a specimen of *Cedarosaurus weiskopfae*. See more: *Tidwell et al. 1999*

2001—South Korea—First Asian sauropod with gastroliths
An indeterminate sauropod specimen consisting of cervical and dorsal vertebrae and ribs also included gastroliths. See more: *Paik et al. 2001*

2002—Colorado, USA—First sauropod fossil urine
Wavy marks 3 m long, 1.5 m wide, and 25–30 cm deep were interpreted as marks left by a sauropod urinating. See more: *McCarville & Bishop 2002*

2004—China—Most recent omnivorous sauropodomorphs
cf. *Lufengosaurus huenei* was believed to be from the Middle Jurassic, but it is now known to be older, from the Lower Jurassic (Toarcian, approx. 182.7–174.1 Ma). See more: *Dong et al. 1983; Wang & Sun 1983; Dong et al. 1983; Weishampel et al. 2004*

2005—India—Oldest grass consumed by a sauropod
Fragments of grasses (*Anomochloa*, *Graminidites*, *Pharus*, and *Streptochaeta*) were found in titanosaur coprolites that date to the late Upper Cretaceous (upper Maastrichtian, approx. 69–66 Ma). See more: *Prasad et al. 2005*

2005—India—Sauropod coprolite with the largest variety of fungi
The coprolites attributed to *Isisaurus colberti* contained a wide variety of fungi, including *Protocolletotrichum deccanensis*, which causes red streak disease on leaves; *Archaeoglomus globatus*; *Lithouncinula lametaensis*; *Notothyrites* sp.; *Phragmothyrites eocaenica*; and *Protoerysiphe indicus*. All of them invaded the feces after they were deposited. See more: *Kar et al. 2004; Sharma et al. 2005*

2007—Virginia, USA—Oldest sauropodomorph with gastroliths
A group of gastroliths have been interpreted as belonging to a sauropodomorph whose skeleton was not preserved. They date to the Upper Triassic (middle Norian, approx. 217.75 Ma). See more: *Weems, Culp & Wings 2007*

2007—Virginia, USA—Largest sauropodomorph gastrolith
Specimen HE-4–152 is 103.4 x 79 x 51.5 mm in size and weighs 660 g. It dates to the Upper Triassic (middle Norian, approx. 217.8 Ma). See more: *Weems et al. 2007*

2007—Niger—Lowest-feeding sauropod
The mouth of *Nigersaurus taqueti* was very wide, and its teeth were angled straight forward, a unique feature among sauropods and a specialization that would have enabled it to eat small plants growing close to the ground. See more: *Sereno et al. 2007*

2008—South Africa—Largest phytophagous sauropodomorph
Specimen Meet BP/1/5339 was similar to *Aardonyx celestae*, but older and more enormous, measuring 16 m long and weighing 10 t. It was mentioned in a blog three years before being formally published. See more: *Wedel & Yates 2011*

2008—First simulated sauropod digestion
Researchers built an artificial sauropod gut and added ground-up horsetails, sheep gastric juice, minerals, carbonate, and water to analyze the possible digestive process of these enormous animals. See more: *Hummel et al. 2008*

2011—Brazil, India—Smallest omnivorous sauropodomorphs
Pampadromaeus barberenai was more like a carnivore than a herbivore, but its teeth were suitable for eating both kinds of food. It appears to have been 1.4 m long and weighed 1.8 kg. In contrast, *Alwalkeria malerienesis* was less long but heavier, at 1.1 m in length and 2 kg in weight. See more: *Chatterjee 1987; Cabreira et al. 2011*

2011—Argentina—Smallest phytophagous sauropodomorph
Leonerasaurus taquetrensis had teeth similar to those of sauropods but also angled frontward, as in advanced sauropods, which suggests that it had an exclusively plant-based diet. This animal was 3.2 m long and weighed 73 kg. See more: *Pol et al. 2011*

2012—France, England—First study of sauropod digestive gas
Based on the large number of sauropods living on Earth during the Upper Jurassic, it is believed that a greenhouse effect was created from the methane gas they emitted (some 520 million t per year) while consuming and digesting plants. See more: *Wilkinson et al. 2012*

2012—India—Sauropod coprolite with the most varied plants
The presence of araucarias (cones, spores, wood, and pollen), Capparidaceae, Arecaceae (palms), and ferns were confirmed in titanosaur coprolites dated to the late Upper Cretaceous (upper Maastrichtian, approx. 69–66 Ma). See more: *Mukherjee et al. 2012*

2012—Most common taphonomic marks (fossil damage) on sauropod remains
Bite marks (scratches and holes) have been documented for *Apatosaurus*, *Brontosaurus*, *Camarasaurus*, *Cathetosaurus*, "*Cetiosauriscus*" *greppini*, *Dongbeititan*, *Opisthocoelicaudia*, *Pukyongosaurus*, and *Rapetosaurus*. The animals that consumed the dead sauropod bodies may not have usually crushed the bones, but simply tore the meat from the bones, leaving these marks. See more: *Borsuk-Bialynicka 1977; Hunt et al. 1994; Dong et al. 2001; Rogers et al. 2003; Paik et al. 2011; Xing et al. 2012*

2014—USA—First calculation of urination duration in sauropods
It was estimated that some very large sauropods would have taken 50 seconds to urinate; however, elephants eliminate 160 liters in an average of 22 seconds, and all mammals take a similar time to urinate, regardless of their size. See more: *Gillingham et al. 2014*

2016—Brazil—First carnivorous sauropodomorph
Buriolestes schultzi was the only exclusively carnivorous sauropodomorph, as is evident from its knife-shaped teeth (ziphodonts). It was 1.5 m long and weighed 2.5 kg. See more: *Jensen 1985; Cabreira et al. 2016*

2018—Myanmar—Oldest aromatic flowers preserved in amber
Cascolaurus burmensis and *Tropidogyne pentaptera* display tissues that secrete floral scents. These aromas would have attracted pollinating insects and maybe even some dinosaurs. The first scented flowers may have appeared in the Lower Cretaceous. See more: *Poinar 2017; Poinar et al. 2017; Poinar & Poinar 2018*

The sauropod with the largest stomach relative to its torso
Futalognkosaurus dukei

It did not chew its food, but simply bit off and swallowed the plants it ate, leaving the food to ferment in its enormous stomach. Estimates show that the less ground-up the food was, the longer it would need to have remained in the stomach to most effectively extract the nutrients. It is still unclear how this may have occurred, although digestion must have been quite efficient, as these dinosaurs apparently had no problem reaching spectacular sizes. See more: *Farlow 1987; Clauss et al. 2009; Franz et al. 2009; Sander et al. 2011*

When we speak about pathology in dinosaurs, we are referring to evidence of illness or injury they suffered that affected their bones. In some cases, pathologies can be identified in footprints, teeth, skin, and/or eggs as well. We divide the paleopathologies described in this book into two categories: 1) physical-traumatic disorders or traumas incurred by accidental damage or aggression from another organism (fractures, bites, scratches, blows, etc.) and 2) non-traumatic osteopathies (or simply osteopathies), which include diseases that did not involve physical impact damage (such as deformations, bone fusion, malformations, tumors, and infections).

RECORD OF PATHOLOGIES IN SAUROPODOMORPHS AND SAUROPODS

1899—USA—First pathology recorded for a sauropod in North America
Some fused vertebrae are mentioned for a specimen of *Diplodocus*. See more: *Osborn 1899*

1901—Colorado, USA—First mating injury reported for sauropods
It was first believed that the fused caudal vertebrae observed in *Diplodocus longus* FMNH 7163 were caused when the animal sat on its tail, but that is now known to be impossible. The current suggestion is that they were caused by the use of the tail as a weapon or when it was stepped upon during mating. See more: *Hatcher 1901; Gilmore 1932; Rothschild & Berman 1991; Rothschild 1994*

1903—Colorado, USA—First traumatic pathology in a North American sauropod
Brontosaurus excelsus FMNH 7163 suffered fractured ribs that later healed imperfectly. See more: *Riggs 1903*

1905—England—First traumatic pathology in a European sauropod
Some vertebrae near the end of the tail of *Cetiosaurus leedsi* had been broken. See more: *Woodward 1905*

1905—England—Most northerly sauropod showing signs of trauma
A specimen of *Cetiosaurus leedsi* presented some fractured caudal vertebrae. It was found at the present-day latitude of 52.6° N, but its latitude in the Middle Jurassic was 42.7° N. See more: *Woodward 1905*

1916—Wyoming, USA—First non-traumatic pathology in a sauropod
Two caudal vertebrae of an unidentified species were found joined together by a large nodule. This has been interpreted as a chronic infection or bone tumor (hemangioma), although some time later it was interpreted as abnormal bone growth (hyperostosis). See more: *Moodie 1916; Rothschild & Berman 1991*

1918—New Mexico, USA—First sauropod with a benign tumor The presence of a benign tumor (hemangioma) was reported in an unidentified sauropod. See more: *Moodie 1918*

1954—Tanzania—First traumatic pathology in an African sauropod
Fractured bones were reported in a specimen of *Giraffatitan brancai*. See more: *Kaiser 1954; Blasius & Kaiser 1980*

1954—Tanzania—Southernmost sauropod with trauma
Some specimens of *Giraffatitan brancai* (formerly *Brachiosaurus*) presented fractured ribs. They were found at a present-day latitude of 39.2° N, Upper Jurassic paleolatitude of 29.4° N. See more: *Kaiser 1954; Blasius & Kaiser 1980*

1963—First sauropodomorph displaying pathology
A bone from the Upper Triassic showed indications of decalcification when analyzed under a microscope. See more: *Isaacs et al. 1963; Tanke & Rothschild 2002*

1965—China—First pathology in an Asian sauropod
Pathologies on the cervical and caudal vertebrae, femur, and tibia of *Mamenchisaurus hochuanensis* were mentioned but were not illustrated. See more: *Anonymous 1965; Tanke & Rothschild 2002*

1969—France—First sauropod egg in Europe showing pathology
Some eggs formerly assigned to "Hypselosaurus priscus" have up to seven shell layers. See more: *Anonymous 1969; Erben 1969; Hoefs & Wedepohl 1979; Tanke & Rothschild 2002*

1971—Texas, USA—First footprints interpreted as evidence of a dinosaur fight
Some prints of a large theropod parallel to a sauropod track have been interpreted as evidence of an attack. However, researchers currently believe there is insufficient evidence to confirm this and that the sauropod may have walked by first and the theropod later. See more: *Bird 1939; Lockley et al. 2007; Farlow et al. 2012*

1972—Zimbabwe—Oldest sauropod with pathology
Vulcanodon karibaensis presents a chevron fused with some caudal vertebrae. It dates to the early Lower Jurassic (Hettangian, approx. 201.3–199.3 Ma). See more: *Raath 1972*

1972—France—First extremely thin sauropod eggshell
Megaloolithus (formerly "*Hypselosaurus priscus*") eggs with very thin walls were reported. See more: *Anonymous 1972: Erben et al. 1979*

1972—Zimbabwe—First non-traumatic pathology in an African sauropod
A chevron fused with some caudal vertebrae were observed in *Vulcanodon karibaensis*. It may have been caused by a form of degenerative arthritis. See more: *Raath 1972*

1972—Zimbabwe—Southernmost sauropod showing pathology
Vulcanodon karibaensis QG 24 had a chevron fused with some caudal vertebrae. It was found at the present-day latitude 48.1°N, Lower Jurassic paleolatitude of 57°N. See more: *Raath 1972*

1984—India—First sauropod egg with pathology in Asia
A specimen of *Megaloolithus walpurensis* (formerly *M. khempurensis*) has two layers of shell, the usual one 2.3 mm thick, and another overlayer 1.8 mm thick, for a total thickness of 4.1 mm. See more: *Vianey-Liaud et al. 1994*

1985—England—Northernmost sauropodomorph showing pathology
An abnormally thick *Camelotia borealis* fibula was found at the present-day latitude of 51.2° N, but its position in the Upper Triassic was 35.7° N. See more: *Galton 1985*

1989—Morocco—Oldest sauropod footprints showing pathology
Based on the irregular pattern of the treads, one short and one long, the track is believed to have been made by an injured animal. It dates to the Upper Jurassic (Oxfordian, approx. 163.5–157.3 Ma). See more: *Ishigaki 1989; Lockley & Rice 1990; Lockley et al. 1994*

1991—New Mexico, USA—First calcified tendon in a sauropod
The ischium of *Diplodocus hallorum* (formerly *Seismosaurus halli*) was an abnormal shape, which some researchers suggest resulted from an illness. See more: *Gillette 1991*

1991—New Mexico, USA—First case of exostosis in a sauropod
The presence of a benign tumor (exostosis) was reported in *Di-*

plodocus hallorum (formerly *Seismosaurus halli*). See more: *Gillette 1991*

1992—Switzerland—Oldest traumatic pathology in a sauropodomorph
Plateosaurus sp. MSF 22 presents some healed fractures in its gastralia. It dates to the Upper Triassic (middle Norian, approx. 204.9 Ma). See more: *Sander 1992*

1992—Germany—The oldest mass death in sauropodomorphs
Plateosaurus longiceps is one of the best known species because more than 100 specimens have been preserved. Many of them died due to major disasters that ended up with several individuals at the same time (a pack). Their abundance caused them to be nicknamed "Schwäbischer Lindwurm" (Swabian dragon). It is important to highlight that several individuals were found with fractures. They date from the upper Triassic (upper Norian, approx. 204.9–208.5 Ma) See more: *Quenstedt 1856; Sander 1992; Norell et al. 1995*

1994—New Mexico, USA—An asphyxiated sauropod?
It has been suggested that specimen NMMNH-P3690 of *Diplodocus hallorum* (formerly *Seismosaurus halli*) may have died by asphyxiation from the giant gastroliths it ingested, although the idea is purely speculation and some investigators find it doubtful. See more: *Gillette 1994; Lucas 2000*

1994—USA—First mating injuries interpreted for sauropods
Certain injuries to the spinal columns of *Apatosaurus*, *Camarasaurus*, and *Diplodocus* have been interpreted as accidents that occurred during mating. See more: *Rothschild 1994*

1995—Portugal—Most recent sauropod footprints with pathologies
This sauropod track showed signs that the animal walked with a limp from an injured right foot. The find dates to the Upper Jurassic (Tithonian, approx. 152.1–145 Ma). See more: *Dantas et al. 1995*

1996—USA—First sauropod with spina bifida
A specimen of *Camarasaurus* presents a pathology that affected 13 vertebrae in the tail, an abnormality known as spina bifida. See more: *McIntosh et al. 1996*

1997—USA—Sauropod genus with the most numerous pathologies
Diverse specimens of *Camarasaurus* have been reported to have suffered accidents, arthritis, spondylitis, fusion of vertebrae, hyperostosis, trauma, and rare diseases of unknown origin. See more: *Moodie 1919; Sokoloff 1960; Hagood 1971; Fiorillo 1998; McWhinney et al. 2001; Rothschild 1994, 1997*

1998—England—Oldest bone callus in a sauropodomorph
A fibula of *Camelotia borealis* BMNH R2878a was enlarged from an unknown cause. The find dates to the Upper Triassic (Rhaetian, approx. 208.5–201.3 Ma). See more: *Galton 1998*

1998—Wyoming, USA—Marks mistaken for a strange pathology
Certain circular bone lesions found only on a fossil turtle and a *Camarasaurus* specimen were believed to be signs of pathology but were actually produced by very alkaline soil. See more: *Fiorillo 1998; Tanke & Rothschild 2000*

2001—Colorado, USA—First avulsion (separation) reported

in a sauropod

The lesion caused by a torn ligament (periostitis) on the humerus of *Camarasaurus grandis* DMNH 2908 would have caused the animal to walk with a limp, as prints of other sauropod species can attest to. See more: *Ishigaki 1989; Dantas et al. 1995; McWhinney et al. 2001*

2001—Mongolia—Northernmost sauropod with pathology

This unidentified sauropod (possibly eutitanosaur or saltasauroid) presents fused caudal vertebrae. It was found at a present-day latitude of 43.5° N, but its original late Upper Cretaceous position was 40.8° N. See more: *Currie 2001*

2002—Most common pathology found in sauropods

Thickening of the caudal vertebrae is the most frequently reported damage in sauropod species and has been reported for specimens of *Alamosaurus, Apatosaurus, Astrodon, Barosaurus, Camarasaurus, Diplodocus, Haplocanthosaurus* and *Titanosaurus*. See more: *Tanke & Rothschild 2002*

2002—Most common traumas in sauropods

Broken bones or fractures are the most widely reported injuries among some sauropod species, including specimens of *Apatosaurus, Camarasaurus,* "*Cetiosaurus*" *leedsi, Diplodocus, Giraffatitan,* and *Nurosaurus,* most often in the metatarsals and pedal phalanges. See more: *Tanke & Rothschild 2002*

2003—Most common traumas in sauropodomorphs

Among 27 individuals of *Plateosaurus,* 50 broken bones were reported, including scapulae, femurs, fibulas, gastralia, ischia, pubes, and tibias. See more: *Moser 2003; Bonn 2004*

2003—Germany—Northernmost sauropods with traumas

Several fractures have been reported among several specimens of *Plateosaurus* sp. (*Plateosaurus engelhardti* or *P. longiceps*?). The present-day latitude of these finds is 49.2° N, but the Upper Triassic paleolatitude was 32.8° N. See more: *Moser 2003; Bonn 2004*

2004—Argentina—First sauropod egg with pathology in South America

Some specimens of cf. *Sphaerovum* sp. have a double shell, resulting in the thickest shells ever reported, at 8 mm (4.5 mm + 3.5 mm), and some even have three shell layers. See more: *Jackson et al. 2004*

2005—Colorado, USA—Oldest sauropodomorph with pathology?

Specimen CU-MWC 153.3, 6, 8 of *Evazoum gatewayensis* (formerly *Pseudotetrasauropus* sp.) was extremely short, but it is not known whether this was caused by disease or was a natural adaptation. The animal dates to the Upper Triassic (middle Norian, approx. 227–208.5 Ma). See more: *Gaston et al. 2003; Lockley & Lucas 2013*

2005—USA—First traumatic pathologies found on sauropod feet

A review of several specimens of *Apatosaurus* sp., *Brachiosaurus* sp., *Diplodocus* sp., and *Camarasaurus grandis* found metatarsals or phalanges with signs of fracturing. See more: *Rothschild & Molnar 2005*

2005—China—First traumatic pathology in an Asian sauropod

A fractured phalange of the invalid species "Nurosaurus qaganensis" was reported. See more: *Rothschild & Molnar 2005*

2006—Argentina—Oldest pathology in a sauropodomorph

Coloradisaurus brevis PVL 5094 has some fused caudal vertebrae. The find dates to the Upper Triassic (middle Norian, approx. 227–208.5 Ma). See more: *Pol & Powell 2006; Apaldetti et al. 2013*

2012—Argentina—First traumatic pathology in a South American sauropod

A histological study of a tail vertebra of *Bonitasaura salgadoi* yielded a possible pathology—an amorphous protuberance. The presence of two fused thoracic vertebrae has also been reported for *Argentinosaurus,* but the study has not been formally published. See more: *Gallina 2012; Coria in Ford**

2013—Argentina—Oldest pathology in a sauropodomorph

Coloradisaurus brevis PVL 5094 has some fused caudal vertebrae. The find dates to the Upper Triassic (middle Norian, approx. 227–208.5 Ma). See more: *Apaldetti et al. 2013*

2013—South Africa—Most severe traumatic pathology in a sauropodomorph

This specimen of *Massospondylus* sp. BP/1/6771 had its tail amputated, leaving caudal vertebrae 23 and 25 severely damaged. It dates to the Lower Jurassic (Hettangian, approx. 201.3–199.3 Ma). See more: *Butler et al. 2013*

2013—South Africa—Southernmost sauropodomorph showing trauma

The posterior tail of a *Massospondylus* sp. specimen was wrenched off by a large predator. The specimen was found at present-day latitude 30.8° N, Lower Jurassic paleolatitude of 44.5° N. See more: *Butler et al. 2013*

2014—Argentina—Southernmost sauropodomorph with pathology

Abnormal bone tissue found in the femur of *Mussaurus patagonicus* specimen MLP 61-III-20–22 could have been caused by a retrovirus, based on similar responses in present-day birds. The present-day latitude of these finds is 48.1° N, but the Upper Triassic paleolatitude was 57° N. See more: *Cerda et al. 2014*

2014—Argentina—Largest sauropod eaten by theropods

A titanosaur 24 m long and weighing 28 t was found along with 5 skeletons and 57 teeth of *Tyrannotitan chubutensis,* abelisaurids, and other dinosaurs, but it is not known whether it had been hunted or eaten as carrion. See more: *Canale et al. 2014*

2015—China—Most common non-traumatic pathology in sauropodomorphs

Fusion of vertebrae has been reported in *Coloradisaurus brevis* and *Lufengosaurus huenei.* See more: *Xing et al. 2015; Apaldetti et al. 2013*

2016—Wyoming, USA—First enthesitis reported in a sauropod

Calcifications were found on the phalanges and claws of this specimen of *Cathetosaurus,* SMA 0002. See more: *Tschopp et al. 2016*

2017—France—Highest frequency of sauropod egg pathologies

Some 450 shells of *Megaloolithus siruguei* and *M. mamillare* found in what was central Laurasia present a malformation associated with dystocia, which leads to abnormal retention of eggs in the oviduct of females. It is suspected that one of the factors that caused it was competition with the hadrosaurs. See more: *Sellès et al. 2017*

2018—Wyoming, USA—Sauropod with the most serious injury

Diplocodus specimen WDC FS-325 presents evidence of healed fractures on the pubis and a swollen femur, which would have made it unable to raise itself on its hind legs or to move backward. See more: *Clayton 2018*

Dinosaurs most at risk of being hit by lightning
Like giraffes, sauropods were likely at greater risk of lightning strikes than other animals, as their great height left them more exposed. Additionally, the voltage differential affects the hearts of quadrupeds more, as all four legs on the ground receive current. Fortunately, such accidents seem to have been quite rare among these animals.

SWARMS OF MESOZOIC BLOODSUCKERS

The previous book in this series, on theropods, mentions *Burmaculex antiquus* as the oldest bloodsucking mosquito; Culicidae is the only family of blood-sucking insects today. However, the oldest Chironomidae were also bloodsuckers, although none of them are today. Indeed, some species still display the atrophied remnants of their sucking organs. This means that the first hematophagous insects were the "snipe flies" (Rhagionidae) of the Middle Triassic, followed by mosquitoes (Chironomidae) from the Upper Triassic, and "black flies" (Simuliidae) in the Upper Jurassic. "Horseflies" (Tabanidae) and Ceratopogonidae came later, in the early Lower Cretaceous, then culicid mosquitos (Culicidae) in the early Upper Cretaceous. All of these insects belong to the Diptera group, and only the females bite. See more: *Labandeira 2002; Borkent & Grimaldi 2004; Littlewood & De Baets 2015*

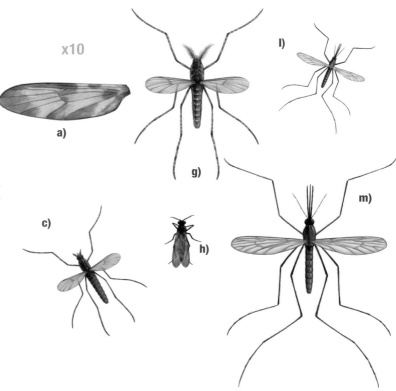

a)

a) Smallest hematophagous insect of the Triassic and oldest chironomid mosquito

 Aenne triassica
Wingspan 3.5 mm
Body 3.8 mm
North-central Pangea (present-day England)
The oldest chironomids were hematophagous. No modern-day species are, but some display the atrophied remnants of the sucking organs. These insects date to the Upper Triassic (Rhaetian, approx. 205.6–201.6 Ma). See more: *Krzeminski & Krzeminska 1999; Lukashevich & Mostovski 2003; Lukashevich & Przhiboro 2011; Azar & Nel 2012*

b) Largest hematophagous insect of the Triassic? and oldest "snipe fly" (Rhagionidae)

 Gallia alsatica
Wingspan 6 mm
Body 5 mm
North-central Pangea (present-day France)
These insects date to the Middle Triassic (Anisian, approx. 205.6–201.6 Ma) and may have sucked blood. See more: *Labandeira 2002; Krzeminski & Krzeminska 2003; Littlewood & De Baets 2015*

c) Smallest hematophagous insect of the Jurassic

 Podonomius minimus
Wingspan 2 mm
Body 1.6 mm
Northeastern Pangea (present-day Russia). See more: *Kalugina 1985*

d) Largest hematophagous insect of the Jurassic

 Podonomius robustus
Wingspan 8.2 mm
Body 3.7 mm
Eastern Paleoasia (present-day Mongolia). See more: *Lukashevich & Przhiboro 2011*

e) The largest larva of a Mesozoic hematophagous insect and the oldest "black fly" (Simuliidae)

Simulimima grandis
Body 12 mm
Eastern Paleoasia (present-day Russia)
The larva belonged to a "black fly" (Simuliidae). The 6-mm-long adult may have been the largest insect in this family. It dates to the Upper Jurassic (Oxfordian, approx. 163.5–157.3 Ma). See more: *Kalugina 1985; Crosskey 1991*

f1) and f2) Largest hematophagous insect of the Jurassic?

  Palaeoarthroteles mesozoicus
Wingspan 10.2 mm
Body 8.1 mm
Eastern Paleoasia (present-day Russia)
It used its massive proboscis to suck blood. The species *P. pallidus* (present-day China) was larger, with a wingspan of 20 mm and length of 11.2 mm, but it is not known whether it was hematophagous. See more: *Kovalev & Mostovski 1997; Stuckenberg 2003; Zhang 2011*

g) Smallest hematophagous insect of the Lower Cretaceous

Libanochlites neocomicus
Wingspan 1.9 mm
Body 0.95 mm
South-central Gondwana (present-day Lebanon)
The specimen, preserved in amber, contains mammal blood cells. See more: *Brundin 1976*

h) Oldest Ceratopogonidae

Archiaustroconops besti
Wingspan 1.9 mm
Body 1.15 mm
Central Laurasia (present-day England)
It dates to the early Lower Cretaceous (upper Berriasian, approx. 142.85–140.2 Ma). See more: *Borkent et al. 2013*

Blood cells have been found inside *Cretaenne kobeyssii*, *Haematotanypus libanicus*, *Libanochlites neocomicus*, and *Wadelius libanicus*. There is evidence of acytoplasmic polyhedrosis virus (*Cypovirus*) and trypanosomes in *Protoculicoides* sp. *Archicnephia ornithoraptor* was preserved in amber with some feathers. See more: *Brundin 1976; Grimmaldi & Engel 2005; Poinar & Poinar 2005; Veltz, Azar & Nel 2007; Azar et al. 2008; Grimaldi 2009*

The Mesozoic hematophagous insects with the most similar names are *Baisomyia* (Simuliidae) and *Baissomyia*, a horsefly (Tabanidae), both blood-sucking Dipteras. See more: *Kalugina 1991; Mostovski et al. 2003*

i) Smallest horsefly of the Lower Cretaceous

Cratotabanus stenomyomorphus
Wingspan 17 mm
Body 10.2 mm
Western Gondwana (present-day Brazil)
See more: *Martins-Neto & Kucera-Santos 1994*

j) Oldest horsefly

Eotabanoid lordi
Wingspan 17.2 mm
Central Laurasia (present-day England)
It existed some 145.5–140.2 Ma ago and was the largest of
Mesozoic Europe. See more: *Mostovski et al. 2003*

k) Largest hematophagous insect of the Mesozoic

Laiyangitabanus formosus
Wingspan 17.6 mm
Body 16.5 mm
Eastern Laurasia (present-day China)
Horseflies bite warm-blooded animals, and their bites are
painful. Comparable to *Tabanus nigrovittatus*, this insect would
have weighed some 115 mg, five times the weight of a large common housefly
(*Musca domestica*). See more: *Haupt & Busvine 1968; Magnarelli & Stoffolano 1980; Sofield et al
1984; Zhang 2012*

l) Smallest hematophagous mosquito of the Upper Cretaceous

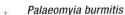

Palaeomyia burmitis
Wingspan 1.89 mm
Body 0.887 mm
Central Laurasia (present-day Germany)
A culicid mosquito as old as *Burmaculex antiquus*, it dates to the early Upper
Cretaceous (lower Cenomanian, approx. 100.5–97.2 Ma). The insect weighed
a mere 0.05 mg, based on the comparable *Aedes aegypti*, but could consume
double its own weight in blood. See more: *Poinar 2004, 2016*

m) Largest hematophagous mosquito of the Mesozoic

Paleoculicis minutus
Wingspan 4.2 mm
Body 3 mm
Western Laurasia (present-day western Canada)
It is one of the smallest culicids known but was one of the largest of
that era. See more: *Poinar et al. 2000*

n) Smallest horsefly of the Upper Cretaceous

Cratotabanus newjerseyensis
Wingspan 16.5 mm
Body 10 mm
Western Laurasia (present-day New Jersey, USA).
See more: *Grimaldi 2011*

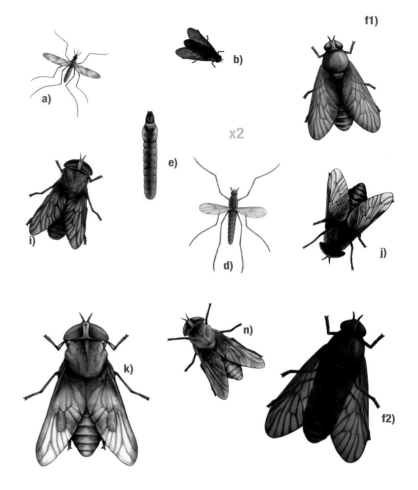

Pathologies in Sauropodomorpha

Non-traumatic osteopathies

Triassic
Coloradisaurus brevis, Mussaurus patagonicus, Plateosaurus engelhardti

Jurassic
Apatosaurus louisae, Barosaurus sp., Brontosaurus sp., Camarasaurus grandis, C. lentus, C. supremus, Cathetosaurus lewisi, Cetiosauriscus leedsi, Diplodocus longus, Diplodocus hallorum, Europasaurus holgeri, Haplocanthosaurus sp., Lufengosaurus huenei, Mamenchisaurus sinocanadorum, Massospondylus sp., Qijianglong guokr, Vulcanodon karibaensisis

Cretaceous
Alamosaurus sanjuanensis, Argentinosaurus huinculensis, Astrodon johnsoni, Bonitasaura salgadoi, Nurosaurus qaganensis, Titanosaurus sp., Uberabatitan riberoi

Traumatic osteopathies

Triassic
Camelotia borealis, Isanosaurus attavipachi, Plateosaurus sp.

Jurassic
Apatosaurus, Brachiosaurus sp., Brontosaurus sp., Camarasaurus grandis, Cathetosaurus lewisi, Cetiosaurus oxoniensis, Giraffatitan brancai, Haplocanthosaurus sp., Massospondylus carinatus, Morosaurus sp., Spinophorosaurus nigerensis

Cretaceous
Baurutitan, Bonitasaura salgadoi, Diamantinasaurus, Nurosaurus qaganensis

Sauropod oolites displaying pathologies

Megaloolithus khempurensis, M. mammilare, M. sirugei, cf. Sphaerovum sp.

Records: The largest and smallest, the oldest and most recent, the strangest, and others

The largest sauropod footprints are stunning for their enormous size, both length and width. Amazingly, they can make an elephant's print look tiny, as sauropods had proportionately longer toes and claws, as well as a huge fleshy heel that made the print seem even bigger.

Triassic

Upper

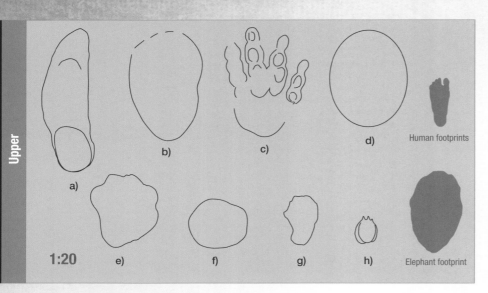

b)   c)   d)   Human footprints

a)

1:20   e)   f)   g)   h)   Elephant footprint

The largest footprint of the Upper Triassic (Class: Very large)

The largest footprint of the Triassic was 78.7 cm long **(a)**, although apparently the animal slipped in the mud, leaving an unnatural print. Its foot would actually have been 25 cm long. The largest sauropodomorph footprints are from *Tetrasauropus* sp. **(b)** and *Pseudotetrasauropus mekalingensis* **(c)**, both 60 cm long. There was a report of some enormous, possibly deformed sauropodomorph footprints up to 1 m long; however, they belonged not to dinosaurs, but rather to *Pentasauropus* sp., a type of dicynodont. See more: *Ellenberger 1972; Furrer 1993; Manera de Bianco & Calvo 1999; Lockley & Meyer 2000; Tomassini et al. 2005; Domnanovich et al. 2008; Xing et al. 2013*

The strangest sauropodomorph footprints of the Triassic

Several impressions left by *Evazoum* sp. (previously *Pseudotetrasauropus* sp.) were didactyl prints, although the tip of the third toe can be seen in some of them, indicating that toe II was slightly raised. This characteristic has been reported for the Upper Triassic in North America (in Canada as well as Colorado and Utah, USA). See more: *Olsen 1988, 1989; Gaston et al. 2003; Lockley & Lucas 2013*

1:10

Oldest sauropodomorph footprints

Several impressions are from the early Upper Triassic (Carnian, approx. 237–227 Ma), including *Pseudotetrasauropus* sp. (Italy), as well as several species from Lesotho, which, however, have been dated to the Carnian-Norian boundary (approx. 232–208.5 Ma) and so may be more recent. The footprints known as *Prosauropodichnus bernburgensis* (Germany) and *Tetrasauropus* sp. (Argentina), from the Middle Triassic, were not left by sauropodomorphs, as the former has more similarities to impressions left by *Chirotherium*, a group of terrestrial archosaurs, while the latter are doubtful, as it is unlikely that such a derivative form would have existed at that time. They are from the Cerro de las Cabras Formation (Anisian, approx. 247.2–242 Ma). See more: *Dal Sasso 2003; Melchor & de Valais 2006; Diedrich 2009*

Oldest sauropod footprints

The quadrupedal impressions (Argentina) of the Portezuelo Formation (upper Carnian, 232–227 Ma) have been interpreted as those of primitive sauropods based on the shape of their forefeet. See more: *Marsicano & Barredo 2004; Wilson 2005*

Highest-altitude sauropodomorph footprints of the Triassic

In the Swiss Alps, *Tetrapodosaurus* sp. impressions were found at 2450 m above sea level. See more: *Furrer 1993*

Triassic sauropodomorph footprint with the greatest toe spread

Cridotrisauropus cruentus, discovered in Lesotho, had a 60° spread between toes II and IV, for a total of 120° on the foot, similar to the prints of some birds, although based on the widely separated toes and prominent claws, it has been identified as the print of a probable theropod. As there were no theropods with feet that shape in the Upper Triassic, it likely belonged to a sauropodomorph. See more: *Ellenberger 1970*

Notable large Triassic footprints

Species, size (length)	Record, group	Country, reference
Upper Triassic		
a) Unnamed 78.7 cm (34.3 cm)	**Largest Asian Upper Triassic** (primitive sauropodomorph)	China *Xing et al. 2013*
b) *Tetrasauropus* sp. 60 cm	**Largest European Upper Triassic** (primitive sauropodomorph)	Switzerland *Lockley & Meyer 2000*
c) *Pseudotetrasauropus mekalingensis* - 60 cm	**Largest African Upper Triassic** (primitive sauropodomorph)	Lesotho *Ellenberger 1972*
d) Unnamed 53 cm	**Largest North American Upper Triassic** (sauropod?)	Greenland *Jenkins et al .1994*
e) Unnamed 40 cm	**Largest European Upper Triassic** (sauropod?)	Slovakia *Niedzwiedzki 2011*
f) Unnamed 27 cm	**Largest South American Upper Triassic** (sauropod?)	Brazil *Da Silva 2007*
g) Unnamed 27 cm	**Largest South American Upper Triassic** (sauropod)	Argentina *Marsicano & Barredo 2004*
h) cf. *Tetrasauropus unguiferus* - 27 cm	**Largest North American Upper Triassic** (sauropod)	Colorado, USA *Gaston et al. 2003*

i)

1:20

j)

The largest sauropodomorph forefoot print of the Triassic

(i) The front foot of *Lavinipes jaquesi* (formerly *Pseudotetrasauropus*) was 20 cm long and 45 cm wide. It dates to the Upper Triassic (Lesotho). See more: *Ellenberger 1972; Avanzini et al. 2003*

The largest sauropod forefoot print of the Triassic

(j) The largest front footprint of the only Triassic sauropod track measures 10 cm in length and 15 cm in width. It dates to the Upper Triassic (Argentina). See more: *Marsicano & Barredo 2004; Wilson 2005*

The longest quadrupedal sauropodomorph stride of the Triassic

Tetrasauropus sp., in the Upper Triassic (Switzerland), has a stride up to 2 m long. *Deuterosauropodopus major* (Lesotho) footprints displayed a stride 2.34 m long; however, they are now considered not to be dinosaur prints. See more: *Ellenberger 1972; Furrer 1993; Lockley & Meyer 2000*

The longest bipedal sauropodomorph stride of the Triassic

Lavinipes jaquesi (formerly *Pseudotetrasauropus*) of the Upper Triassic (Lesotho) had a stride up to 2.26 m long. See more: *Ellenberger 1972*

Fastest speed for any sauropodomorph footprints of the Triassic?

A speed of 3.5 km/h was estimated for some prints of *Agrestipus hottoni* (Virginia, USA). The impressions are 15 cm long, and the largest stride is 78 cm long. They may belong to quadrupedal sauropodomorphs or to the archosaur *Brachychirotherium parvum*. See more: *Weems 1987; Weems et al. 2007*

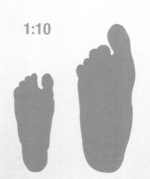

1:10

Average measurements vs. records

The foot used for comparison is an average length for humans, 27 cm long. Venezuelan Jeison Orlando Rodríguez holds the record for the longest human foot on the planet, at 40.55 centimeters. See more: *Guinness World Records*

The smallest of the Upper Triassic (Class: Tiny)

Owing to the small size of *Trisauropodiscus aviforma* **(a)**, it probably belonged to a juvenile individual. The smallest sauropod footprint **(f)** (Argentina) is 23 cm long. Another impression from the same track measures 19 cm but is incomplete. See more: *Ellenberger 1970; Marsicano & Barredo 2004; Wilson 2005*

The proportionately narrowest sauropodomorph footprints of the Triassic

A footprint that is excessively long, as the foot was dragged through the mud (China), is approximately 35% as wide the total foot length. The narrowest undeformed prints are *Evazoum* sp. (Colorado, USA) and *Tetrapodosaurus* sp. (Switzerland), which are 60% as wide as they are long. See more: *Furrer 1993; Gaston et al. 2003, Xing et al. 2013*

The proportionately narrowest sauropod footprints of the Triassic

The tracks of the only sauropods found from the Triassic (Argentina) are 50% as wide, on average, as they are long. See more: *Marsicano & Barredo 2004; Wilson 2005*

The proportionately widest sauropodomorph footprint of the Triassic

A specimen of *Trisauropodiscus aviforma* (Lesotho) has a footprint approximately 23% wider than its length. See more: *Ellenberger 1972*

The proportionately widest sauropod footprint of the Triassic

A footprint from the Upper Triassic (Argentina) measures 24 cm long and 13 cm wide, or 54% as wide as it is long. See more: *Marsicano & Barredo 2004; Wilson 2005*

The proportionately narrowest sauropodomorph forefoot print of the Triassic

The forefoot of *Tetrasauropus unguiferus* (Lesotho) is approximately 1.85 times as long as it is wide. See more: *Ellenberger 1972*

The proportionately widest sauropodomorph forefoot print of the Triassic

The forefeet of *Lavinipes jaquesi* (formerly *Pseudotetrasauropus*) are approximately 17% wider than they are long (Lesotho). An impression left by a quadruped animal (Brazil) is 10% wider than it is long but is deformed. See more: *Ellenberger 1972; Da Silva et al. 2007; Porchetti & Nicosia 2007*

The proportionately narrowest sauropod forefoot print of the Triassic

An Upper Triassic (Argentina) footprint is 59% as wide as its total length. See more: *Marsicano & Barredo 2004; Wilson 2005*

The proportionately widest sauropodomorph forefoot print of the Triassic

Because it is deformed, the forefoot print (Brazil) was approximately 3.7 times as wide as it is long; the front foot may have slid horizontally. See more: *Da Silva 2007*

The proportionately widest sauropod forefoot print of the Triassic

The width of an Upper Triassic impression (Argentina) is 71% of its total length. See more: *Marsicano & Barredo 2004; Wilson 2005*

Theropod, bird, ornithishcian, or sauropodomorph?

Trisauropodiscus and similar creatures have been thought to belong to very ancient birds, as they date to the Upper Triassic and Lower Jurassic; however, this is not possible as they appeared several million years later. Given the spread of the toes, they have been considered juvenile ornithischians related to *Anomoepus*, although to date they have not been compared to those of basal sauropodomorphs like *Saturnalia*. The feet of these dinosaurs present several morphological similarities and are contemporary. This ichnogenus has become synonymous with *Gruipes* of the Cenozoic, owing to confusion regarding the age of some bird prints in Argentina.
See more: *Ellenberger 1970; Olsen & Galton 1984; Lockley et al. 1992; Garton 1996; Gierlinski 1996; Vizan et al. 2005; De Valais & Melchor 2008; Wagensommer et al. 2016; Abrahams et al. 2017; Gierlinski et al 2017*

1:5

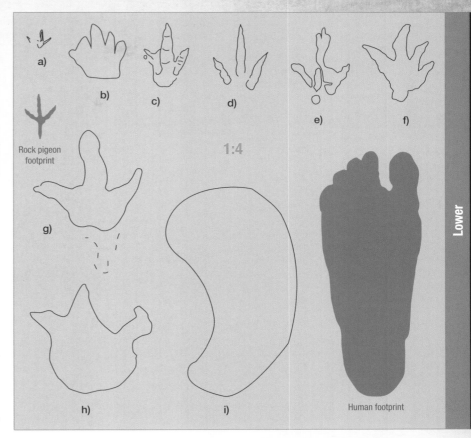

a)

Rock pigeon footprint

b) c) d) e) f)

1:4

g)

h) i)

Human footprint

Notable small Triassic footprints

Species, size (length)	Record, group	Country, reference
Upper Triassic		
a) *Trisauropodiscus aviforma* - 2 cm	**Smallest African Upper Triassic** (primitive sauropodomorph)	Lesotho *Ellenberger 1978*
b) *Barrancapus cresapi* 6 cm	**Smallest North American Upper Triassic** (primitive sauropodomorph)	New Mexico, USA *Hunt et al. 1993*
c) *Grallator pisanus* 7 cm	**Smallest European Upper Triassic** (primitive sauropodomorph?)	Italy *Bianucci & Landini 2005*
d) cf. *Grallator* 7.2 cm	**Smallest Oceanian Upper Triassic** (primitive sauropodomorph?)	Australia *Thulborn 1998*
e) *Saurichnium anserinum* 8.4 cm	**Smallest African Upper Triassic** (primitive sauropodomorph?)	Namibia *Gurich 1926*
f) *Evazoum* sp. 8.5 cm	**Smallest African Upper Triassic** (primitive sauropodomorph)	Poland *Gierlisnki 2009*
g) Unnamed 11 cm	**Smallest Asian Upper Triassic** (primitive sauropodomorph)	China *Xing et al. 2013*
h) Unnamed 12 cm	**Smallest South American Upper Triassic** (primitive sauropodomorph)	Brazil *Da Silva 2007*
i) Unnamed 23 cm	**Smallest South American Upper Triassic** (sauropod)	Argentina *Marsicano & Barredo 2004*

The smallest sauropodomorph forefoot print of the Triassic

(j) The front footprint of *Barrancapus cresapi* measures 4 cm in length and 5 cm in width. It was recognized as being from a sauropodomorph 8 years after being described (New Mexico, USA). See more: *Hunt et al. 1993; Hunt et al. 2001; Hunt & Lucas 2007*

The smallest sauropod forefoot print of the Triassic

(k) The largest front footprint presented in a sauropod track of the Triassic measures 4.5 cm long and 6.8 cm wide. It dates to the Upper Triassic (Argentina). See more: *Marsicano & Barredo 2004; Wilson 2005*

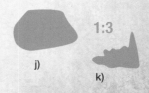

1:3

j)

k)

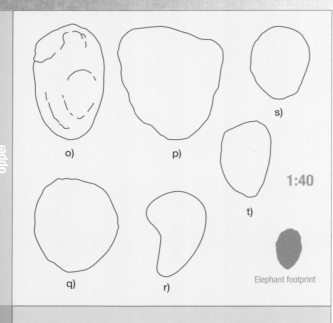

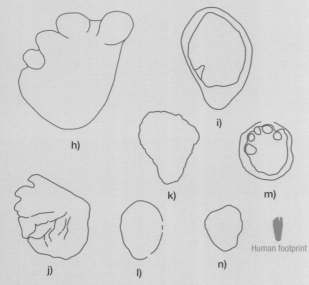

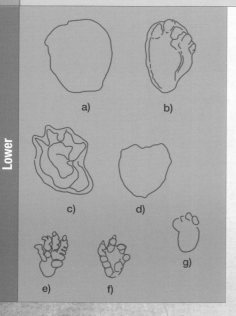

Elephant footprint

Human footprint

The largest of the Middle Jurassic (Class: Giant)
(h) *Malakhelisaurus mianwali* (formerly *Malasaurus*) is a gigantic print 1.3 m long and 1.3 m wide. Its enormous size is due to the fact that primitive sauropods had more elongated toes than their derivatives. It was not adequately described, and so is a doubtful name at present (Pakistan). See more: *Malkani 2007, 2008*

The largest of the Upper Jurassic (Class: Giant)
(p) *Gigantosauropus asturiensis* (Spain) had footprints measuring 1.25 m long, although previous estimates presented a length of 1.36 m; they were also considered to be theropod impressions. Giant footprints *Parabrontopodus* sp. (France) have also been mentioned in print, with a diameter of 1.5 m; however, the maximum size is 91 cm, although the mark of the undertrack brings it to 122 cm. Another footprint **(o)** (Morocco) tentatively estimated at 1.4 m, was actually approximately 1.26 m long. See more: *Mensink & Mertmann 1984; Ishigaki 1985; Thulborn 1990; Le Loeuff et al. 2005*

The largest of the Lower Jurassic (Class: Very large)
Parabrontopodus sp. **(a)** from Italy and another unnamed print from Morocco **(b)** measure 80 cm in length. The largest sauropodomorph footprint of the Lower Jurassic is 75 cm long (Morocco). See more: *Ishigaki & Haubold 1986; Ishigaki 1988; Avanzini et al. 2006*

The longest sauropod tracks of the Upper Jurassic of North America
A track of *Parabrontopodus* sp. (Colorado, USA) is 215 m long. It was left by a diplodocid sauropod of the Upper Jurassic whose footprints were 65 cm long. See more: *Lockley et al. 1986; McFarlan 1991; Lockley & Hunt 1995*

The strangest sauropodomorph footprint of the Jurassic (left)

(left) These impressions from the Lower Jurassic (Italy) have a strange shape and have been interpreted, with great difficulty, as belonging to sauropodomorphs. The hind foot measures 30 cm long and the forefoot 14.2 cm long. See more: *Avanzini et al. 2012*

The strangest sauropod footprint of the Jurassic (right)
(right) *Parabrontopodus frenki* (formerly *Iguanodonichnus*) of the Upper Jurassic (Chile), is very long and appears to have very prominent claws. At first, the prints were interpreted as being from ornithischians similar to *Iguanodon*. See more: *Casamiquela & Fasola 1968; Dos Santos et al. 1992; Farlow 1992; Sarjeant et al. 1998; Moreno & Pino 2002; Rubilar-Rogers 2003; Moreno & Benton 2005*

The longest sauropod tracks of the Upper Jurassic in Europe
A track from a *Brontopodus plagnensis* is 155 m long (upper Jurassic in France) and includes 115 steps. See more: *Mazin et al. 2017*

The longest sauropod tracks of the Middle Jurassic
The track of footprints similar to *Polyonyx*, but with a narrower gauge, is up to 200 m long. It was found in England (Bathonian, approx. 168.3–166.1 Ma). Another reported track from the Middle Jurassic is up to 147 m in length (Portugal) and includes 97 steps of *Polyonyx* sp. See more: *Day et al. 2004; Santos et al. 2009*

Fastest Jurassic sauropod, estimated from footprints
Some *Parabrontopodus* sp. footprints measure 52 cm in length, with a 2.2-m-long stride, for an estimated speed of 6.8 m/s (24.5 km/h) (Colorado, USA). One extraordinary case is that of a medium-gauge sauropod track (Switzerland) that could represent a speed of up to 18 km/h. See more: *Lockley et al. 1986; Meyer 1993*

The oldest sauropodomorph tail impression
Otozoum caudatum of the Lower Jurassic (Hettangian, approx. 201.3–199.3 Ma) is a specimen of *Otozoum moodii* that left a sinuous tail mark as it walked (Massachusetts, USA). See more: *Hitchcock 1858, 1871; Lull 1915; Kim & Lockley 2013*

The largest dinoturbation
When a herd of very heavy dinosaurs walked through a place with somewhat soft soil, they caused damage so significant it could destroy more than half a meter of soil, down to the substrate. In the Castellar Formation, dating from the Upper Jurassic to the early Lower Cretaceous (present-day Spain), there is an immense dinoturbation caused by more than 800 footprints of very large sauropods and stegosauruses. See more: *Alcalá et al. 2003; Cobos et al. 2008*

The longest bipedal sauropodomorph stride of the Jurassic
Some 75-cm-long footprints similar to *Otozoum* present a stride up to 2.35 m long (Morocco). See more: *Ishigaki 1988*

The longest narrow-gauged sauropod tracks of the Jurassic
One track has strides 1.57–5.71 m in length. The longest stride must have been made when the animal changed direction, and so it is believed to have been moving at 2–8 km/h and pivoting at 18 km/h. The longest stride of a sauropod moving in a straight line was made by a diplodocoid (Morocco) and measures 3.4 m. See more: *Dutuit & Ouazzou 1980; Meyer 1993; Ishigaki & Matsumoto 2009*

The longest semi-wide-gauge sauropod stride of the Jurassic
Brontopodus sp. (Portugal) of the Upper Jurassic had a stride 2.65 m long. The track is not very wide, falling in the intermediate range, which means it could have belonged to a macronarian or primitive neosauropod. See more: *Lockley et al. 1994*

The largest sauropodomorph forefoot print of the Jurassic
The front foot of an impression similar to *Otozoum* measures 25 cm long and 44 cm wide and dates to the Lower Jurassic (Morocco). See more: *Ishigaki 1988*

The largest sauropod forefoot prints of the Jurassic
An enormous natural cast (Spain), 95 cm wide, is similar to forefoot impressions left by *Brontopodus*, which belong to either titanosauriforms or somphospond-ylids. Owing to its age, it most likely belongs to the former group, as it dates to the Upper Jurassic (below, compared to the forefoot print of an African elephant). See more: *García-Ramos et al. 2006*

1:30

The oldest record of animals trodden upon by a sauropod
In the Morrison Formation (Colorado, USA) a sauropod trod upon two dozen bivalves as it strode along. This event dates to the Upper Jurassic (Kimmeridgian, approx. 157.3–152.1 Ma). See more: *Lockley et al. 1986*

The longest sauropodomorph tail impression
cf. *Brontopodus* (Utah, USA), as it walked forward slowly at 1 km/h, left a tail mark 4.2 m long and 20 cm wide. It dates to the Middle Jurassic (Bathonian, approx. 168.3–166.1 Ma). See more: *Foster et al. 2000*

Deepest sauropod footprint
Some enormous mamenchisaurids of the Upper Jurassic (China) left 2-m-deep impressions in the mud. This kind of dinoturbation would have left fatal traps for some small dinosaur species (*Guanlong* or *Limusaurus*). See more: *Lockley et al. 1986; Lockley 1991; Li 2011*

Sauropod footprint in 4-D
A forefoot mold of a sauropod of the Upper Jurassic (Portugal) up to 32 cm deep, shows both the shape and the marks of movement the creature left behind as it walked. This discovery revealed that the forefoot had a helmet shape, that the skin on the foot was rough, and that the movement as it walked was vertical and not parasagittal. See more: *Milan et al. 2005*

The Jurassic sauropod footprints found at the highest altitude
In Tibet, China, a series of prints were found at an altitude of 4900 m above sea level. They are from the Lower or Middle Jurassic. See more: *Xing et al. 2011*

Notable large Jurassic footprints

Species, size (length)	Record, group	Country, reference
Lower Jurassic		
a) *Parabrontopodus* sp. 80 cm	Largest European Lower Jurassic (sauropod)	Italy *Avanzini et al. 2006*
b) Unnamed 80 cm	Largest African Lower Jurassic (sauropod)	Morocco *Ishigaki 1988*
c) Unnamed 76 cm	Largest European Lower Jurassic (primitive sauropodomorph)	Morocco *Ishigaki & Haubold 1986*
d) Unnamed 58 cm	Largest Asian (Paleoasia) Lower Jurassic (sauropod)	China *Zhang et al. 2016*
e) *Otozoum moodii* 49 cm	Largest North American Lower Jurassic (primitive sauropod)	Massachusetts, USA *Hitchcock 1847*
f) *Lavinipes cheminii* 46 cm	Largest European Lower Jurassic (primitive sauropodomorph)	Italy *Avanzini et al. 2003*
g) *Liujianpus shunan* ~42.5 cm	Largest Asian (Paleoasia) Lower Jurassic (primitive sauropodomorph)	China *Xing et al. 2015*
Middle Jurassic		
h) *Malakhelisaurus mianwali* 1.3 m	Largest Asian (Hindustan) Middle Jurassic (sauropod)	Pakistan *Malkani 2007, 2008*
i) Unnamed 1.12 m (82 cm)	Largest Asian (Paleoasia) Middle Jurassic (sauropod)	Tibet, China *Xing et al. 2011*
j) *Brontopodus* sp. 1 m (94 cm)	Largest European Middle Jurassic (sauropod)	England, UK *Long 1998*
k) *Parabrontopodus* sp. 80 cm	Largest African Middle Jurassic (sauropod)	Morocco *Gierlinski et al. 2009*
l) cf. *Brontopodus* 65 cm	Largest North American Middle Jurassic (sauropod)	Utah, USA *Foster et al. 2000*
m) *Eosauropus* isp. ~56 cm	Largest Middle East and Middle Jurassic (sauropod)	Iran *Abbassi & Madanipour 2014*
n) Unnamed 50.5 cm	Largest Madagascarian Middle Jurassic (sauropod)	Madagascar *Wagensommer et al. 2011*
Upper Jurassic		
o) Unnamed ~1.26 m	Largest African Upper Jurassic (sauropod)	Morocco *Ishigaki 1985*
p) *Gigantosauropus asturiensis* - 1.25 m	Largest European Upper Jurassic (sauropod)	Spain *Mensink & Mertmann 1984*
q) Unnamed 1.097 m	Largest South American Upper Jurassic (sauropod)	Uruguay *Mesa 2012*
r) Unnamed 1 m	Largest Asian (Paleoasia) Upper Jurassic (sauropod)	Uzbekistan *Meyer & Lockley 1997*
s) Unnamed 83 cm	Largest North American Upper Jurassic (sauropod)	Colorado, USA *Lockley et al. 1986*
t) Unnamed 17 cm	Smallest South American Upper Jurassic (sauropod)	Chile *Moreno et al. 2004*

1:20

The oldest record of plants trodden upon by a sauropod
(left) The specimen of *Eosauropus* isp. 1Rp (Iran) had some fragments of wood under its footprint. It dates to the Middle Jurassic (Bathonian, approx. 170.3–168.3 Ma). See more: *Abbassi & Madanipour 2014*

1:30

MYTH The great brachiosaurid that never was
Breviparopus taghbaloutensis (on the left) is one of the most famous sauropod footprints ever, owing to its great length (1.15 m). It was tentatively estimated as that of a sauropod similar to *Brachiosaurus*, 48 m long and weighing more than 55 t. However, based on its narrow gauge, its age (Upper Jurassic), locality (present-day Morocco), and the presence of four claws, it probably belonged to a very large primitive diplodocoid. See more: *Dutuit & Ouazzou 1980*

The smallest footprint of the Lower Jurassic (Very small)
(b) *Otozoum pollex* (formerly *Kalosauropus*) measures 6 cm in length (Lesotho). It is possible that **(a)** *Sillimanius gracilior* (formerly *Ornithoidichnites*), even smaller at 4.3 cm long, belonged to a sauropodomorph (Massachusetts, USA). The **(e)** smallest sauropod footprints of the Lower Jurassic (China) are less than 25 cm in length. See more: *Hitchcock 1841; Ellenberger 1970; Xing et al. 2015*

Notable small Jurassic footprints

Species, size (length)	Record, group	Country, reference
Lower Jurassic		
a) *Sillimanius gracilior* 4.3 cm	Smallest North American Lower Jurassic (primitive sauropodomorph)	Massachusetts, USA *Hitchcock 1841*
b) *Otozoum pollex var minusculus* - 6 cm	Smallest African Lower Jurassic (primitive sauropodomorph)	Lesotho *Ellenberger 1970*
c) *Otozoum* cf. *pollex* 17 cm	Smallest European Lower Jurassic (primitive sauropodomorph)	Poland, *Gierlinski & Niedzwiedzki 2005*
d) *Pengxianpus yulinensis* 24 cm	Smallest Asian Lower Jurassic (primitive sauropodomorph)	China *Wang et al. 2016*
e) Unnamed 24.5 cm	Smallest Asian Lower Jurassic (sauropod)	China *Xing et al. 2011*
f) Unnamed ~28 cm	Smallest European Lower Jurassic (sauropod)	France *Gand et al. 2007*
Middle Jurassic		
g) *Trisauropodiscus* sp. 7 cm	Smallest African Middle Jurassic (primitive sauropodomorph)	Morocco *Gierlinski et al. 2015*
h) Unnamed 16 cm	Smallest North American Middle Jurassic (sauropod)	Mexico *Ferrusquia et al. 2007*
i) Unnamed 21.2 cm	Smallest Asian Jurassic (sauropod)	China *Xing et al. 2015*
j) Unnamed ~31 cm	Smallest European Jurassic (sauropod)	Denmark *Milàn 2011*
k) *Eosauropus* isp. ~31 cm	Smallest Middle Eastern and Middle Jurassic (sauropod)	Iran *Abbassi & Madanipour 2014*
l) *Parabrontopodus* sp. 40 cm	Smallest African Middle Jurassic (sauropod)	Morocco *Gierlinski et al. 2009*
Upper Jurassic		
m) Unnamed ~8.3 cm	Smallest North American Upper Jurassic (sauropod)	Colorado, USA *Mossbruckertk 2010*
n) Unnamed 12 cm	Smallest European Upper Jurassic (sauropod)	Spain *García-Ramos et al. 2005; 2006*
o) Unnamed 22.7 cm	Smallest Asian Upper Jurassic (sauropod)	China *Xing et al. 2015*
p) Unnamed ~38 cm	Smallest African Upper Jurassic (sauropod)	Morocco *Martí et al. 2011*
q) Unnamed 50 cm	Smallest South American Upper Jurassic (sauropod)	Brazil *Dentzien-Dias et al. 2008*

The smallest footprint of the Upper Jurassic (Class: Small)
A track attributed to *Apatosaurus* **(m)** is notable for its very small footprints, which measured a mere 8.3–8.5 cm in length (Colorado, USA). It has not yet been formally described; however, the report mentions that its stride was twice as long as its footprint See more: *Mossbruckertk 2010*

The smallest footprint of the Middle Jurassic (Class: Small)
The most recent **(g)** *Trisauropodiscus*, measuring 7–9.1 cm, were found in Morocco and may belong to young sauropodomorphs. **(h)** The smallest sauropod footprints are identified as "Morphotype A"; they measure 16–19 cm in length and belong to small primitive sauropods (present-day Mexico). See more: *Ferrusquia-Villafranca et al. 2007; Gierlinski et al. 2015*

Oldest sauropod footprint displaying pathology
A track from the Middle Jurassic (Morocco) displays a short stride on the right side and a longer stride on the left, with a difference ranging from 108 to 147 cm. This anomaly is interpreted as that of an animal with a possible physical injury. See more: *Ishigaki 1989; Lockley et al. 1994*

The smallest sauropod forefoot print of the Jurassic
Some unnamed footprints of the Upper Jurassic (Spain) are very small, ranging in size from 6 to 9 cm in length and 9 to 12 cm in width. They are associated with feet 12–16 cm long and 8–11 cm wide. They were not illustrated. See more: *García-Ramos et al. 2005*

The proportionately narrowest sauropodomorph footprint of the Jurassic
The footprint width of a specimen of *Otozoum masitisii* (now *Kalosauropus*) is approximately 50% of its total footprint length (Lesotho). See more: *Ellenberger 1970*

The proportionately narrowest sauropod footprint of the Jurassic
The width of a specimen of *Parabrontopodus frenkii* (formerly *Iguanodonichnus*) is approximately 50% of its total length, owing to the very elongated claw on toe I (Chile). See more: *Casamiquela & Fasola 1968*

The proportionately widest sauropodomorph footprint of the Jurassic
A specimen of *Cridotrisauropus cruentus* is approximately 18% wider than it is long (Lesotho). See more: *Ellenberger 1970*

The proportionately widest sauropod footprint of the Jurassic
A quadruped footprint from the Lower Jurassic (Morocco) is almost as wide as it is long. See more: *Ishigaki 1988*

The proportionately narrowest sauropodomorph forefoot print of the Jurassic
A forefoot impression of *Otozoum* sp. from the Lower Jurassic (Morocco) is approximately 87% as wide as its total length. See more: *Masrour & Pérez-Lorente 2014*

The proportionately widest sauropodomorph forefoot print of the Jurassic
The forefoot of *Navahopus falcipollex* (Arizona, USA) is approximately 1.6 times as wide as its total length and has a very prominent claw. See more: *Baird 1980*

The proportionately narrowest sauropod forefoot print of the Jurassic
The forefoot of *Brontopodus* sp. from the Upper Jurassic (Wyoming, USA) is approximately 84% as wide as it is long. It is strange because most forefeet are wider than they are long. See more: *Platt & Hasiotis 2006*

The proportionately widest sauropod forefoot print of the Jurassic
The forefoot impression from the Upper Jurassic (Spain) is approximately 195% of its total length. See more: *Da Silva 2007*

Sauropodomorph footprint with the greatest toe spread of the Triassic
Trisaurodactylus superavipes, from Lesotho, has a spread of 60–70° between toes II and IV, for a total of 130°, similar to the footprints of some birds. "Trisauropodiscidae" has been considered synonymous with *Gruipeda* (footprints of birds similar to cranes); however, the age makes this very debatable. They are synonyms because some footprints of *Gruipeda* were found in Eocene rocks (approx. 37.2–33.9 Ma), which initially were considered from the Upper Triassic or the Lower Jurassic. Some authors suggest that *Trisauropodiscus* and its close relatives belong to the ornithischians, although the length of toe I (hallux), the large toe spread, and gracile forms coincide with the feet of the most primitive sauropodomorphs. See more: *Ellenberger 1972, 1974; Lockley & Gierlisnski 2006; de Valais & Melchor 2008; Genise et al. 2009*

The oldest gregarious sauropod footprints
Some 40 individuals (England) date to the Middle Jurassic (Bathonian, approx. 168.3–166.1 Ma). We know that sauropods formed groups at least from the Lower Jurassic onward (Sinnemurian, approx. 199.3–190.8 Ma). See more: *Jain et al. 1975; Yadagiri et al. 1979; Day et al. 2004; Myers & Fiorillo 2009*

The most numerous gregarious sauropod footprints of the Jurassic
Several footprints similar to *Polyonyx* (England) date to the Middle Jurassic (Bathonian, approx. 168.3–166.1 Ma). They may belong to 40 individuals in the Turiasauria clade See more: *Day et al. 2004; Myers & Fiorillo 2009*

The oldest gregarious footprints of young sauropods
Groups of young sauropods have been reported in Colorado and Utah, USA, and in Switzerland, from the Upper Jurassic (Kimmeridgian, approx. 83.6–72.1 Ma). See more: *Lockley 1986; Barnes & Lockley 1984; Myers & Fiorillo 2009; Belvedere et al. 2016*

The most numerous gregarious footprints of young sauropods
Eight impressions from Switzerland, 11.6 cm long and 7.8 cm wide, show a parallel gait and are assigned to the Upper Jurassic (Kimmeridgian, approx. 83.6–72.1 Ma). Their small size and the presence of another impression almost 1 m long means that these were young animals. See more: *Belvedere et al. 2016*

Most mysterious sauropod footprint of the Jurassic

"Ophysthonyx portucalensis" from the Middle Jurassic in Portugal was mentioned in a summary where the name *Polyonyx gomesi* is also cited for the first time. It was not described and may be ruled out completely as the two were synonyms. See more: *Santos et al. 2004*

The oldest sauropod that changed direction while moving

A sauropod with a narrow-gauge gait from the Lower Jurassic (middle Pliensbachian, approx. 186 Ma) in Morocco changed its original direction in a gradual curve. See more: *Ishigaki & Matsumoto 2009*

Most recent sauropodomorph footprint

Trisauropodiscus sp. (Morocco) of the Middle Jurassic date to the upper Bajocian or lower Bathonian, approx. 169.3–167.2 Ma. Others considered more recent have turned out to be older. See more: *Gierlinski et al. 2017*

The proportionately widest sauropod track of the Jurassic

An indeterminate sauropod (England) had the most widely separated right and left feet of any known sauropod. See more: *Day et al. 2004; Romano et al. 2007*

Proportion of claws or quantity of sharp claws as an identifying feature

Primitive sauropods had four sharp claws on their hind feet, derived forms had three, and those in the Diplococinae subfamily had just two.

This is interesting because the footprints of *Parabrontopodus mcintoshi* coincide with those of *Apatosaurus* in having three claws on each foot. In other types of *Parabrontopodus*, the feet are narrower, with a marked slope where the sharp claws and round nails would have been present, which coincides with diplodocine diplococids such as *Diplodocus* and *Tornieria*.

In some cases, the proportional length of the claws is a very useful tool for identifying the type of sauropod. For example, in the titanosauriform feet discovered to date, toe I is shorter than toe II (*Cedarosaurus*), and those feet appear much more frequently during the Jurassic, then become much rarer in the Cretaceous. Meanwhile, somphospondylids had a more developed claw I (*Pleurocoelus*) and are almost exclusively from the Cretaceous.

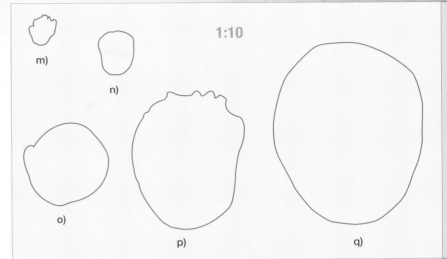

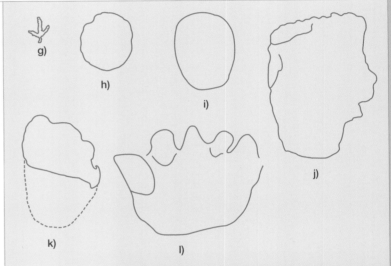

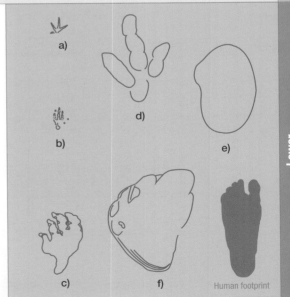

1:10

Jurassic — Upper / Middle / Lower

Polyonyx gomesi
See more: *Santos et al. 2009*

Breviparopus taghbaloutensis
See more: *Dutuit & Oazz ou 1980; Ishigaki 1989*

Brontopodus plagnensis
See more: *Mazin et al. 2017*

Parabrontopodus mcintoshi
See more: *Lockey et al. 1994*

Sin nombre
See more: *Lockey et al. 1986*

Brontopodus birdi
See more: *Brwon 1940; Farlow 1987*

Human footprint

Upper Cretaceous

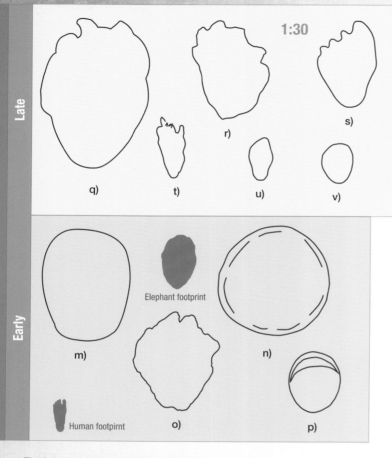

Late

Early

1:30

r)

s)

q)

t)

u)

v)

Elephant footprint

m)

n)

Human footpirnt

o)

p)

The longest sauropod stride of the early Lower Cretaceous
Parabrontopodus distercii (Spain) left tracks with a stride 3.1 m long for the rear feet and 3.2 m long for the front. See more: *Meijide-Fuentes et al. 2001*

The longest stride of a sauropod from the late Lower Cretaceous
Footprints S5 (Texas, USA) of *Brontopodus birdi* had a stride up to 4.2 m long. Specimen S2U-S2W presents a stride up to 3.36 m for the rear feet, while the front had a stride 3.29 m long. See more: *Bird 1939; Farlow 1987*

The longest sauropod stride of the early Upper Cretaceous
Sauropodichnus giganteus (Argentina) presents a stride up to 2.2 m long on the rear feet and 2.34 m on the front. The speed estimated from these titanosaur prints was 4.1 km/h. See more: *Calvo & Mazetta 2004*

The longest sauropod stride of the late Upper Cretaceous
Some titanosaur footprints of the late Upper Cretaceous (Spain) present a stride 2.5 m long. See more: *Le Loeuff & Martínez-Rius 1997a, 1997b*

The Cretaceous sauropod footprints found at the highest altitude
In Huanzalá-Antamina, Ancash (Peru), a deposit containing footprints at 4840 m above sea level. Among them were some diplodocoid footprints dating to the late Lower Cretaceous. See more: *Moreno et al. 2004; Obata et al. 2006; Vildoso et al. 2011*

The longest sauropod track of the Cretaceous
The locality of Toro Toro (Bolivia) has a series of footprints that extend for up to 200 m. See more: *Lockley et al. 2002*

Highest speed estimated from sauropod prints in the Lower Cretaceous
The estimated velocity of *Rotundichnus muenchenhagensis* (Germany) was 3.1–4.5 km/h. The footprints belong to a primitive macronarian of the early Lower Cretaceous (Berriasian, approx. 145–139.8 Ma). See more: *Lockley et al. 2004*

The largest of the early Lower Cretaceous (Class: Giant)
UQL-DP8–1 **(a)** is an enormous footprint 1.75 m long and 1.25 m wide that was found in the city of Broome, Australia. It also had surrounding marks up to 1.4 m in width. The longest footprint from Laurasia is **(b)** *Parabrontopodus distercii* (Spain), a sauropod with a narrow gauge that slid or glided in the mud. Its footprints measure up to 165 cm in length and 85 cm in width. The largest undeformed one measures 140 cm long and 75 cm wide. See more: *Meijide-Fuentes et al. 2001; Castañeda et al. 2010; Thulborn 2012; Salisbury et al. 2017*

The largest of the late Lower Cretaceous (Class: Giant)
Ultrasauripus ungulatus **(g)** specimen RP2 reached 124 cm long and 90 cm wide. See more: *Lee & Lee 2006*

The largest of the late Upper Cretaceous (Class: Giant)
An unnamed natural cast track **(q)** measures 1.2 m in length and belonged to an extremely large titanosaur. See more: *Ishigaki 2016*

The largest of the early Upper Cretaceous (Class: Very large)
Sauropods found in Croatia are generally very small in size, except the most recent, which date to the upper Turonian (approx. 91.8–89.8 Ma). The largest footprint found is 92 cm long and 77 cm wide **(m)**. Even wider are those of the holotype specimen of *Sauropodichnus giganteus* **(n)**, which are circular and 90 cm in diameter. They are poorly preserved, but another smaller one has been found, 70 cm long and with a shape that reveals it was the print of a primitive titanosaur. See more: *Calvo 1991; Calvo & Mazzeta 2004; Mezga et al. 2006*

Notable large Cretaceous footprints

Species, size (length)	Record, group	Country, reference
Early Upper Cretaceous		
m) Unnamed 92 cm	**Largest European early Upper Cretaceous** (sauropod)	Croatia *Mezga et al. 2006*
n) *Sauropodichnus giganteus* 90 cm	**Largest South American early Upper Cretaceous** (sauropod)	Argentina *Calvo 1991*
o) Unnamed 81 cm	**Largest African early Upper Cretaceous** (sauropod)	Morocco *Ibrahim et al. 2014*
p) *Chuxiongpus zheni* 50 cm	**Largest Asian early Upper Cretaceous** (sauropod)	China *Cheng & Huang 1993*
Late Upper Cretaceous		
q) Unnamed 1.20 m	**Largest Asian late Upper Cretaceous** (sauropod)	Mongolia *Stettner et al. 2017*
r) Unnamed 81 cm	**Largest South American late Upper Cretaceous** (sauropod)	Bolivia *Rios 2005*
s) Unnamed 71 cm	**Largest European late Upper Cretaceous** (sauropod)	Spain *Viladrich 1986; Vila et al. 2008; Castanera et al. 2016*
t) Unnamed 50 cm	**Largest Asian (Hindustan) late Upper Cretaceous** (sauropod)	India *Ghevariya & Srikarni 1990*
u) Unnamed 35 cm	**Largest Oceanian late Upper Cretaceous** (sauropod)	New Zealand *Browne 2010*
v) Unnamed 32.6 cm	**Largest North American late Upper Cretaceous** (sauropod)	Mexico *Servín-Pichardo 2013*

The highest speed estimated from sauropod footprints of the Upper Cretaceous
It has been calculated that *Titanopodus mendozensis* (Argentina) moved at 4.7–4.9 km/h. The footprints belonged to a derived titanosaur of the late Upper Cretaceous (upper Campanian, approx. 78–72.1 Ma). See more: *Gónzalez Riga & Calvo 2009*

MYTH : Sauropods left prints while swimming

Because sauropod forefoot prints have been found without accompanying hind footprints, it was suggested that they were made while the animals were swimming. Nevertheless, what actually occurred is that some sauropods exerted greater pressure on the front feet than the back, or vice versa, which caused some impressions to be deeper. For example, it has been estimated that a *Diplodocus* weighing 11.5 t stepped with a force of 99.4 N per cm^2 on the hind foot and 12.9 N per cm^2 on the front, while a *Giraffatitan* weighing 26 t stepped with a force of 159.2 N per cm^2 and 95.1 N per cm^2, respectively. Weathering and/or erosion of the substrate could erase shallower impressions, making quadrupedal animal prints appear like those of bipedal ones. See more: *Bird 1944; Ishigaki 1989; Pittman 1990; Dutuit & Ouazzou 1980; Falkingham et al. 2011; Xing et al. 2016*

The strangest footprints of the Cretaceous

(below) Some late Lower Cretaceous footprints have an extraordinary shape, with radial crests inside the footprint. This anomaly was caused by the raising and trampling of the elastic sediment as the animal trod upon it. The largest of these prints were 77–112.3 cm long and 95 cm wide, with an intermediate-gauge gait. They are from the Uhangri Formation (South Korea). See more: *Lee & Huh 2002; Thulborn 2004; Lee & Lee 2006; Hwang et al. 2008*

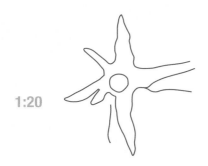

1:20

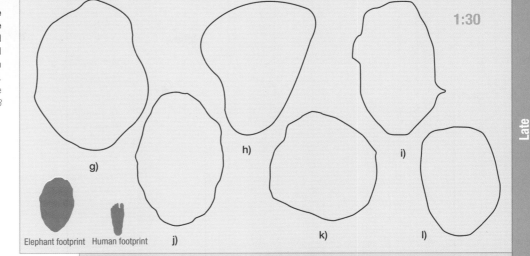

1:30

Elephant footprint   Human footprint

g)   h)   i)

j)   k)   l)

Late

Early

The largest sauropod forefoot print of the Cretaceous

The forefoot of specimen LM3, an *Ultrasauripus ungulatus* **(2)** (South Korea), was 67 cm long and 69 cm wide, while specimen RM3 **(3)** was 58 cm long and 72 cm wide. A gigantic forefoot print of *Brontopodus birdi* **(4)** (Texas, USA) was reported as 1.11 m long and 1.29 m wide; however, it is an impression of two superimposed back feet (below, compared to the manual print of an African elephant **[1]**). See more: *Farlow 1987; Lee & Lee 2006*

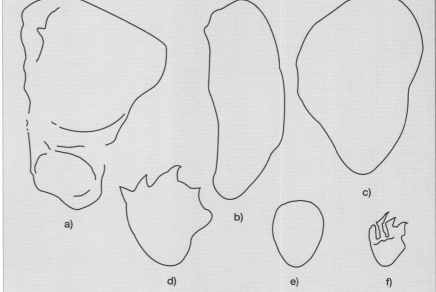

a)   b)   c)

d)   e)   f)

1:40

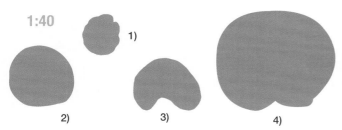

1)   2)   3)   4)

Notable large Cretaceous footprints

Species, size (length)	Record, group	Country, reference
Early Lower Cretaceous		
a) Unnamed 1.75 m	Largest Oceanian early Lower Cretaceous (sauropod)	Australia *Salisbury et al. 2017*
b-c) *Parabrontopodus distercii* - 1.49-1.65 m	Largest European early Lower Cretaceous (sauropod)	Spain *Meijide-Fuentes et al. 1999, 2001*
d) Unnamed ~83 cm	Largest North American early Lower Cretaceous (sauropod)	Canada *McCrea et al. 2014*
e) Unnamed 55 cm	Largest Asian early Lower Cretaceous (sauropod)	Uzbekistan *Meyer & Lockley 1997*
f) Unnamed 45 cm	Largest African early Lower Cretaceous (sauropod)	Niger *Ginsburg 1966*
Late Lower Cretaceous		
g) *Ultrasauripus ungulatus* 1.24 m	Largest Asian late Lower Cretaceous (sauropod)	South Korea *Kim 1993*
h) Unnamed 1.1 m	Largest European late Lower Cretaceous (sauropod)	Spain *Fuentes Vidarte 1996*
i) Unnamed 1.1 m	Largest African late Lower Cretaceous (sauropod)	Algeria *Mahboubi et al. 2007*
j) *Brontopodus birdi* 1.1 m	Largest North American late Lower Cretaceous (sauropod)	Texas, USA *Bird 1985*
k) Unnamed 90 cm	Largest South American late Lower Cretaceous (sauropod)	Brazil *Leonardi & Dos Santos 2006*
l) Unnamed 90 cm	Largest Asian (Cimmeria) late Lower Cretaceous (sauropod)	Laos *Allain et al. 1997*

The longest sauropod track of the Cretaceous

The track of footprints is 200 m long and was found in the locality of Toro Toro (Bolivia). See more: *Lockley et al. 2002*

The highest speed estimated from sauropod footprints of the Lower Cretaceous

The estimated speed of *Rotundichnus muenchenhagensis* (Germany) is 3.1–4.5 km/h. The footprints belong to a primitive macronarian of the early Lower Cretaceous (Berriasian, approx. 145–139.8 Ma). See more: *Lockley et al. 2004*

The highest speed estimated from sauropod footprints of the Upper Cretaceous

It has been calculated that *Titanopodus mendozensis* (Argentina) moved at 4.7–4.9 km/h. The footprints belong to a titanosaur derivative of the late Upper Cretaceous (upper Campanian, approx. 78–72.1 Ma). See more: *Gónzalez Riga & Calvo 2009*

1994—Period with the greatest percentage of broad tracks

Some 96% of sauropod tracks from the Cretaceous are broad, and just 4% are narrow. See more: *Lockley et al. 1994*

Most recent sauropod natural cast

Natural casts of a titanosaur were found in the Nemegt Formation of Mongolia (Maastrichtian). See more: *Currie et al. 2003; Ishigaki et al. 2009; Nakajima et al. 2017; Stettner et al. 2017*

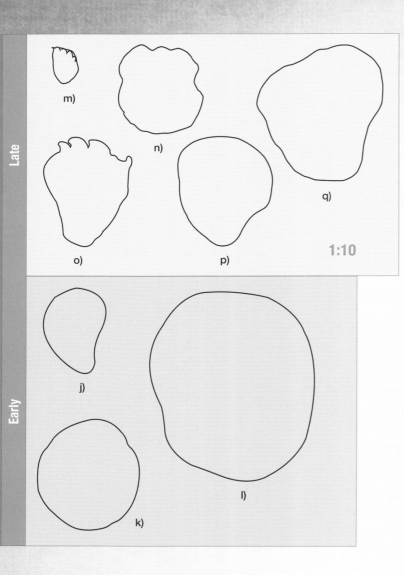

1:10

Upper Cretaceous

Late

Early

The smallest of the late Lower Cretaceous (Class: Very small)
(d) The smallest footprints of *Brontopodus birdi* (Texas, USA) measure 5.8 cm in length. It is important to consider that the largest are 1.11 m in length, or 19 times as long. See more: *Stanford & Stanford 1998; Standford et al. 2011*

The smallest of the early Lower Cretaceous (Class: Medium)
A single footprint in Spain **(a)** measures 17.5 cm in length. It is the smallest of all those found in Europe. See more: *Casanovas et al. 1995*

The smallest of the early Upper Cretaceous (Class: Medium)
Prints from Eastern Europe are often small, and the smallest of the time was similar to *Brontopodus*. It was found in Croatia and measures 23.5 cm long and 19.3 cm wide. See more: *Tisljar et al. 1983; Mezga & Bajraktarevic 1999*

The smallest of the late Upper Cretaceous (Class: Medium)
In India, sauropod footprints have been found that are 10–50 cm long **(m)**. See more: *Ghevariya & Srikarni 1990*

Notable small Cretaceous footprints		
Species, size (length)	**Record, group**	**Country, reference**
Early Upper Cretaceous		
j) Unnamed 23.5 cm	Smallest European early Upper Cretaceous (sauropod)	Croatia *Tisljar et al. 1999*
k) Unnamed 30.5 cm	Smallest Asian early Upper Cretaceous (sauropod)	China *Xing et al. 2015*
l) Unnamed ~52 cm	Smallest South American early Upper Cretaceous (sauropod)	Brazil *Carvalho 1991*
Late Upper Cretaceous		
m) Unnamed 10 cm	Smallest Asian (Hindustan) late Upper Cretaceous (sauropod)	India *Ghevariya & Srikarni 1990*
n) Unnamed 24.5 cm	Smallest North American late Upper Cretaceous? (sauropod or ankylosaur?)	Mexico *Bravo-Cuevas & Jiménez-Hidalgo 1996*
o) Unnamed ~30 cm	Smallest European late Upper Cretaceous (sauropod)	Spain *Vila et al. 2013*
p) Unnamed 30 cm	Smallest South American late Upper Cretaceous (sauropod)	Bolivia *Lockley et al. 2002*
q) Unnamed 37.3 cm	Smallest Asian late Upper Cretaceous (sauropod)	China *Xing et al. 2015*

1:20

Footprints in 4-D
The only footprints that present movement marks are some natural casts (internal molds) that were imprinted on dense mud. They have a visible imprint of the skin, with different forms of scales including pentagons and hexagons, as well as grooves caused by movement. They are known as "four-dimensional prints" because they show movement.

Footprint of a floating sauropod
(above) A footprint from the late Lower Cretaceous in China may have been left by a sauropod that was treading in an aquatic environment. See more: *Li et al. 2006*

1:20

The smallest sauropod forefoot of the Cretaceous
(below) A front footprint of *Brontopodus birdi* from the late Lower Cretaceous (Maryland, USA) measures 3 cm in length and 3.9 cm in width. See more: *Stanford & Stanford 1998; Standford et al. 2011*

Sauropod forefoot print or ornithischian footprint?
(right) Some forefoot prints of *Brontopodus pentadactylus* (South Korea) are identical to those of certain ornithischian prints, so much so that when they are not found associated with a foot, it is very difficult to determine their true identity. See more: *Kim & Lockley 2012*

The deepest footprint of the Cretaceous
Some *Brontopodus birdi* (Texas, USA) have a volume capable of holding 80 liters of water. See more: *Farlow et al. 1989*

1:1

The footprint with "truncate" claws
Notocolossus gonzalezparejasi is the first sauropod to present short, rounded claws on its feet. However, this characteristic is suggestive of a titanosaur footprint described 14 years previously (present-day Bolivia). See more: *Lockley et al. 2002; González Riga et al. 2016*

Lower Cretaceous

The proportionately narrowest sauropod footprint of the Cretaceous

The width of a footprint of *Parabrontopodus distercii* from the early Lower Cretaceous is approximately 43% of its total length, suggesting that the animal slipped or dragged its foot in the mud (Spain). See more: *Casamiquela & Fasola 1968*

The proportionately widest sauropod footprint of the Cretaceous

cf. *Brontopodus birdi*, from the early Upper Cretaceous (Argentina), has an oval-shaped footprint 17% wider than it is long. See more: *Krapovickas 2010*

The proportionately narrowest sauropod forefoot print of the Cretaceous

This sauropod forefoot print from the late Lower Cretaceous (China) is approximately 97.5% as wide as it is long. See more: *Xing et al. 2010*

The proportionately widest sauropod forefoot print of the Cretaceous

The forefoot print (Canada) is approximately twice as wide as it is long, although it may be deformed or incomplete. See more: *McCrea et al. 2014*

The oldest gregarious footprints of young and adult sauropods

A group of young and adult individuals lived together in the early Lower Cretaceous (Berriasian, approx. 145–139.8 Ma) in Brazil. See more: *Leonardi 1989; Myers & Fiorillo 2009*

The most recent gregarious sauropod footprints

Groups of subadult or adult and young titanosaur specimens have been found in Bolivia. Both date to the late Upper Cretaceous (Campanian, approx. 83.6–72.1 Ma). See more: *Leonardi 1989; Lockley et al. 2002; Myers & Fiorillo 2009*

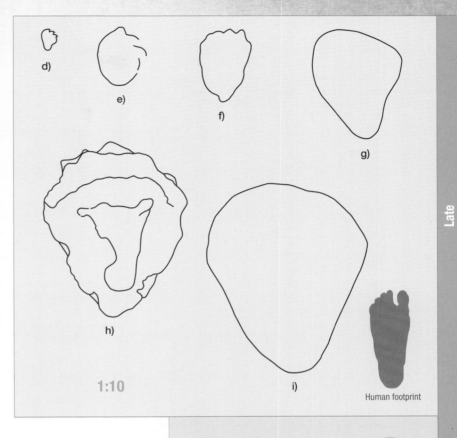

1:10

Human footprint

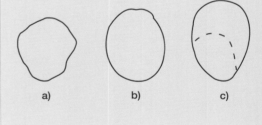

Notable small Cretaceous footprints

Species, size (length)	Record, group	Country, reference
Early Lower Cretaceous		
a) Unnamed 17.5 m	**Smallest European early Lower Cretaceous** (sauropod)	Spain, *Casanovas et al. 1995*
b) Unnamed 17.5 m	**Smallest Oceanian early Lower Cretaceous** (sauropod)	Australia, *Thulborn 2012*
c) Unnamed 22.3 cm	**Smallest Asian early Lower Cretaceous** (sauropod)	China, *Xing et al. 2015*
Late Lower Cretaceous		
d) *Brontopodus birdi* 5.8 cm	**Smallest North American early Lower Cretaceous** (sauropod)	Texas, USA, *Stanford & Stanford 1998*
e) Unnamed 16 cm	**Smallest Asian early Lower Cretaceous** (sauropod)	South Korea, *Lim et al. 1994*
f) Unnamed 30 cm	**Smallest African early Lower Cretaceous** (sauropod)	Morocco, *Masrour et al. 2013*
g) *Titanosaurimanus nana* 48 cm	**Smallest European early Lower Cretaceous** (sauropod)	Croatia, *Dalla Vecchia & Tarlao 2000*
h) Unnamed 52 cm	**Smallest Asian (Cimmerian) early Lower Cretaceous** (sauropod)	Thailand, *Le Loeuff et al. 2002*
i) Unnamed 20 cm	**Smallest South American early Lower Cretaceous** (sauropod)	Argentina, *Canudo et al. 2017*

Strangest sauropod track

Specimen QQ-S1 of cf. *Parabrontopodus* walked with an uneven gait in which the front feet did not move in unison with the back, leading to an estimated speed of 1.1 km/h. With an extremely narrow gauge, the track traces a gentle curve to the northwest. Based on this, the animal is suspected to have suffered from a traumatic pathology or may have been poisoned. See more: *Xing et al. 2016*

The largest sauropod forefoot print of the Cretaceous

The forefoot print of specimen LM3, an *Ultrasauripus ungulatus* (South Korea), is 67 cm long and 69 cm wide, while that of specimen RM3 is 58 cm long and 72 cm wide. A gigantic forefoot print of *Brontopodus birdi* (Texas, USA) has been reported, measuring 111 cm long and 129 cm wide; however, it is an impression of two superimposed back feet. See more: *Farlow 1987; Lee & Lee 2006*

The most mysterious sauropod footprint of the Cretaceous

"*Elephantosauripus metacarpus*" is the informal name given to a footprint from South Korea of unknown origin.

The sauropod that turned 180°

Most sauropod tracks moved in a straight line or changed direction gradually; however, in one case—that of *Parabrontopodus* sp. (China)—the animal retreated in the precise direction it came from for an unknown reason. See more: *Xing et al. 2015*

The most recent sauropod track showing a change in direction

A titanosaur (Spain) moved forward as though it was circling some object. See more: *Vila et al. 2008; Castañera et al. 2014*

The most recent sauropod footprints

In the locality of Arén (Spain) and in Quebrada de Humahuaca (Argentina), some titanosaur prints have been found that date to the end of the late Upper Cretaceous (upper Maastrichtian, approx. 66 Ma). See more: *Riera et al. 2009; Cónsole-Gonella et al. 2017; Díaz-Martínez et al. 2017*

The proportionately widest sauropod track of the Cretaceous

Footprints of a titanosaur of the late Upper Cretaceous (Bolivia) have the greatest separation between impressions of any Cretaceous sauropod. See more: *Lockley et al. 2002; Romano et al. 2007*

HISTORIC RECORDS OF FOOTPRINTS OF PRIMITIVE SAUROPODOMOPRHS AND SAUROPODS

1410—Portugal—First sauropod footprints of the Jurassic in western Europe
These footprints from the Upper Jurassic gave rise to the legend of Nossa Senhora da Pedra Mua (Our Lady of the Mule Stone), as they were assumed to be impressions left by the mule that Mary, the mother of Christ, rode upon. See more: *Antunes 1976; Sanz 2000, 2003; Santos & Rodrigues 2008; Pérez-Lorente 2015*

1836—USA—First sauropodomorph footprints of the Jurassic in western North America
The footprints of *Otozoum moodii* were interpreted alternately as belonging to bipedal amphibians, ancient marsupials, gigantic birds, and ornithischian dinosaurs, until it was discovered that they belonged to sauropodomorphs able to walk on four legs or two. See more: *Hitchcock 1836, 1847; Owen 1861; Quenstedt 1867; Lull 1904; Rainforth 2003*

1836—USA—First tetradactyl sauropodomorph footprints
Otozoum moodii were sauropodomorph prints exclusive to the Lower Jurassic. See more: *Hitchcock 1836, 1847; Rainforth 2003*

1858—Massachusetts, USA—First impression of a sauropodomorph tail
The species *Otozoum caudatum* shows a tail being dragged in a sinuous line. Some authors believe it belongs to an ornithischian dinosaur. See more: *Hitchcock 1858, 1871; Lull 1915; Kim & Lockley 2013*

1871—USA—First species created in an existing sauropodomorph ichnogenus
Edward Hitchcock created the ichnospecies *Otozoum moodii*, and 30 years later it includes *O. caudatum*. Today they are considered synonyms. See more: *Hitchcock 1871; Rainforth 2003*

1934—Texas, USA—First sauropod footprints of the Cretaceous in western North America
The footprints found by Charlie and Moss were considered elephant prints until, 10 years later, Roland T. Bird identified them as sauropod prints, so they chose to call them *Brontopodus birdi*. See more: *Wilson 1975; Bird 1944; Farlow et al. 1989*

1934—Texas, USA—First wide sauropod footprints
Brontopodus birdi is the species that presents, for the first time, tracks with a considerable distance between the back feet. This characteristic can be confirmed in the skeletons of mamenchisaurids, turiasaurs, and in most macronarians, a group that includes *Camarasaurus, Giraffatitan, Euhelopus* and Titanosauria. See more: *Wilson 1975; Bird 1985; Farlow et al. 1989, Lockley et al. 1994*

1939—Texas, USA—First gregarious sauropod footprints of the Cretaceous in North America
They consist of 10 *Brontopodus birdi* specimens. There is some doubt as to whether they were walking at the same time. They are dated to the late Lower Cretaceous (Albian, approx. 113–100.5 Ma). See more: *Bird 1939; Lockley & Matsukawa 1999; Myers & Fiorillo 2009*

1943—China—Smallest footprint mistaken for that of a sauropod
Kuangyuanpus szechuanensis are some quadrupedal impressions with a hind foot 5.4 cm long and a forefoot 3.7 cm long. They were interpreted as belonging to small young sauropods but today are thought to belong to crocodiles. See more: *Young 1943; Lockley et al. 2000*

1951—Colorado, USA—First quadruped sauropodomorph footprints of the Triassic in western North America
Some round footprints with claw marks were identified originally as belonging to synapsids (mammal precursors), then later identified as belonging to sauropodomorphs. Specimen USNM 18408 has been tentatively assigned to *Tetrasauropus unguiferus*, although they are actually very different. They are similar in certain ways to the footprints of *Eosauropus cimarroensis*, Upper Triassic impressions found in New Mexico. See more: *Faul & Robert 1951; Ellenberer 1972; Lockley 1991; Lockley & Hunt 1995; Lockley et al. 2006*

1958—Lesotho—First sauropodomorph footprints of the Triassic in southern Africa
Pseudotetrasauropus bipedoida was named 14 years after being discovered. See more: *Ellenberger & Ellenberger 1958; Ellenberger 1965; Porchetti & Nicosia 2007*

1958—Georgia—First sauropod footprints of the Cretaceous in western Asia
Illustrations of some round footprints with a narrow-gauge track are from a zone that has been situated in both eastern Europe and western Asia. See more: *Gabunia 1958*

1965—France—First tridactyl sauropodomorph footprint
Cridotrisauropus unguiferus may belong to a primitive sauropodomorph similar to *Efraasia*. See more: *Ellenberger 1965, 1970*

1966—Niger—First sauropod footprints of the Cretaceous in northern Africa
Some narrow-gauge footprints with four prominent claws were reported and illustrated. See more: *Ginsburg 1966*

1968—Chile—First narrow-gauge sauropod tracks
Parabrontopodus frenkii (formerly *Iguanodonichnus*) had been identified as an ornithopod because it appeared to be a bipedal animal; however, some of the shallower prints have not been preserved as they were left in a different substrate layer. The distance between the two feet is very small, and so we know the animal was not a sauropod in the Mamenchisauria, Turiasauria, or Macronaria clades. See more: *Casamiquela & Fasola 1968; Dos Santos et al. 1992; Farlow 1992; Sarjeant et al. 1998; Moreno & Pino 2002; Rubilar-Rogers 2003; Moreno & Benton 2005*

1968—Chile—First sauropod footprints of the Jurassic in southern South America
Parabrontopodus frenkii (formerly *Iguanodonichnus*) measures 55 cm in length and is considered an ornithopod. See more: *Casamiquela & Fasola 1968; Dos Santos et al. 1992; Farlow 1992; Sarjeant et al. 1998; Moreno & Pino 2002; Rubilar-Rogers 2003; Moreno & Benton 2005*

1970—Lesotho—First sauropodomorph footprints of the Jurassic in southern Africa
Kalosauropus masitisii and *K. pollex* (with three varieties—minor, minusculus, and victor) are now considered part of *Otozoum*. See more: *Ellenberger 1970, 1972, 1974*

1971—Lesotho—Largest footprint mistaken for a sauropodomorph print
Deuterotetrapous sp. 50 cm long, were thought to belong to *Euskelosaurus*. Today some investigators believe them to be therapsids (ancient relatives of mammals) as they are present from the Middle Triassic (Anisian-Ladinian, approx. 247.2–237 Ma) and walked with a wider gait than sauropodomorphs. See more: *Charig et al. 1965; Haubold 1971, 1984; Ellenberger 1972*

1972—USA—First sauropod footprints to change name
Tetrasauropus jaquesi was changed to the ichnogenus *Pseudotetrasauropus* two years later by the same author who created it. It is currently assigned to the *Lavinipes*. See more: *Ellenberger 1970, 1972; Porchetti & Nicosia 2007*

1972—Germany—First sauropod footprints of the Jurassic in western Europe
Elephantopoides barkhausensis was found on a bluff in an almost vertical position. See more: *Friese 1972, 1979; Kaever & Lapparent 1974; Lockley & Meyer 2000*

1972—Afghanistan—First sauropod footprints of the Jurassic from the paleocontinent Cimmeria
Some prints that were not illustrated are mentioned as belonging to sauropods. See more: *Lapparent & Stocklin 1972; Weishampel et al. 2004*

1972—Lesotho—Largest footprint mistaken for a sauropod print
Pentasauropus gigas (formerly *Tetrasauropus*), 60 cm in length, were thought to belong to primitive sauropods, but are now believed to be from large dicynodonts. See more: *Ellenberger 1972*

1975—Croatia—First sauropod footprints of the Cretaceous in eastern Europe
Sauropod footprints dating to the late Lower and early Upper Cretaceous have been reported. See more: *Dalla Vecchia & Tarlao 2000*

1976—Germany—First sauropod footprints of the Cretaceous in western Europe
Neosauropus lagosteirensis has been assigned to Sauropoda or possibly Ornithopoda, though the circular shape makes the former interpretation more likely. See more: *Antunes 1976*

1980—Brazil—First sauropod footprints of the Jurassic in northern South America
This wide track has prints 80 cm in diameter. See more: *Leonardi 1980*

1980—Morocco—First sauropod footprints of the Jurassic in northern Africa
For many years, the prints belonging to *Breviparopus taghbaloutensis* were thought to be impressions of enormous brachiosaurids 48 m long; however, the narrow-gauge track and four well-preserved nails show they more likely belonged to a type of primitive diplodocoid. As the bones were compared to the bones of ichnites without considering the fleshy heel, the authors' size estimate was very exaggerated. See more: *Dutuit & Ouazzou 1980*

1980—Arizona, USA—First sauropodomorph footprints of the Jurassic in western North America
Navahopus falcipollex are footprints of a quadruped sauropodomorph with forefeet very similar to those of *Massospondylus*. See more: *Baird 1980*

1986—India—First footprint mistakenly identified as a Cretaceous sauropod of Hindustan
A theropod impression with a long talon and short toes was identified as that of a sauropod. See more: *Mohabey 1986*

1986—Colorado, USA—First gregarious sauropod footprints of the Jurassic
A group of subault or young diplodocoids of the ichnogenus *Parabrontopodus* sp. from the Upper Jurassic (Kimmeridgian, approx. 157.3–152.1 Ma). See more: *Lockley et al. 1986*

1987—China—First sauropodomorph footprints of the Triassic in eastern Asia
It has been suggested that the impressions of *Pengxianpus cifengensis* identified as a sauropodomorph are actually those of a theropod. The two dinosaurs left very similar impressions, so it is difficult to confirm the identity of these prints. See more: *Young & Young 1987; Xing et al. 2013*

1987—South Korea—First sauropod footprints of the Cretaceous in eastern Asia
Hamanosauripus ungulatus and *Koreanosauripus cheongi* were insufficiently described and thus are doubtful names; the situation

became more complicated when, six years later, the species *Hamanosauripus ovalis* and *Ultrasauripus ungulatus* were presented. See more: *Kim 1986, 1993*

1987—Virginia, USA—First quadruped sauropodomorph footprints of the Triassic in eastern North America
There is some doubt as to whether *Agrestipus hottoni* is a sauropod or a specimen of *Brachychirotherium parvum*, an archosaur. However, assuming the print did belong to a dinosaur, given its age, it would have been left by a quadrupedal sauropodomorph. See more: *Weems 1987; Weems et al. 2007*

1988—Utah, USA—First bipedal sauropodomorph footprints of the Triassic in western North America
Evazoum sp. are tetradactyl footprints in which the impression of toe II is often shallower, or the toe is raised, in the substrate. See more: *Olsen 1988*

1988—Italy, Morocco—Oldest traces of a wide-gauge track
The tracks of *Otozoum* sp. and of a possible sauropodomorph or sauropod of the Lower Jurassic (Pliensbachian, 190.8–182.7 Ma) represent the oldest evidence in which the feet are separated beyond the imaginary central line, indicating that these animals had wide bodies or splayed their feet while walking See more: *Ishigaki 1988; Lockley et al. 2006*

1988—Morocco—First wide-gauge sauropodomorph footprints
Otozoum sp., of the Lower Jurassic, are quadrupedal footprints with the greatest distance between the right and left feet of any sauropodomorph. Other impressions from the Upper Triassic (Utah, USA), with an even wider separation, were attributed to a sauropodomorph, but the shape of the feet suggests they likely do not belong to a dinosaur. See more: *Ishigaki 1988; Lockley & Hunt 1995; Romano et al. 2007*

1988—Utah, USA—First didactyl sauropodomorph footprints
The impressions left by some specimens of *Evazoum* sp. include only two toes and the claw of the second phalange; amputations have been ruled out as a cause. Most likely the animal raised its toes as it walked, for unknown reasons. See more: *Olsen 1988; Olsen et al 1989; Gaston et al. 2003; Lockley et al. 2006*

1989—South Korea—First gregarious sauropod footprints of Asia
Impressions left by groups of sauropods were reported in the Jindong Formation and assigned to the late Lower Cretaceous (Albian, approx. 113–100.5 Ma). See more: *Lim et al. 1989*

1989—Morocco—First gregarious sauropod footprints in Africa
Groups of *Breviparopus taghbaloutensis* were believed to be from the Middle Jurassic but are now assigned to the Upper Jurassic (Oxfordian, approx. 163.5–157.3 Ma). See more: *Ishigaki 1989*

1989—Bolivia and Brazil—First gregarious sauropod footprints in South America
In a review of dinosaur prints found in South America, impressions left by groups of sauropods were reported for the late Lower Cretaceous of Brazil (Barremian, approx. 129.4–125 Ma) and for the late Upper Cretaceous of Bolivia (Maastrichtian, approx. 72.1–66 Ma). See more: *Leonardi 1989*

1989—Argentina—First sauropod footprints of the Cretaceous in southern South America
Sauropodichnus giganteus were difficult to identify because of their completely round form; however, more well-defined prints also exist. See more: *Calvo 1989, 1991;Calvo & Mazzetta 2004*

1990—Utah, USA—First report of a wide-gauge track that

shows a change in direction during movement
An Upper Jurassic sauropod (Utah, USA) changed course at an angle of almost 66°. See more: *Lockley 1990, 1991*

1990—Switzerland—First report of a narrow-gauge track that shows a change in direction during movement
A sauropod similar to *Breviparopus* from the Upper Jurassic (Switzerland) turned at an angle of nearly 61°. See more: *Meyer 1990, 1993; Lockley & Meyer 2000*

1993—New Mexico, USA—First quadrupedal sauropodomorph footprints of the Triassic in western North America
Barrancapus cresapi are some enigmatic impressions that probably belong to very ancient sauropodomorphs. See more: *Hunt et al. 1993*

1993—Portugal—First gregarious sauropod footprints of Europe
Impressions left by a group of diplodocids *Parabrontopodus* sp. date to the Upper Jurassic (upper Kimmeridgian, approx. 154.7–152.1 Ma). See more: *Lockley & Santos 1993*

1993—Tajikistan—First sauropod footprints of the Jurassic in western Asia
As the position of the claws of *Mirsosauropus tursunzadei* show, the prints belong to a primitive sauropod, not within the neosauropod group, but possibly a mamenchisaurid. See more: *Djalilov & Novikov 1993*

1994—USA—First sauropod footprints of the Jurassic in eastern North America
Sauropod footprints have been divided according to the distance between the feet, which leads to a narrow or wide gauge, although some tracks have an intermediate separation and others are extremely wide. *Parabrontopodus mcintoshi* has a narrow-gauge gait, like *Breviparopus*, but the claws on its feet are fewer and inclined outward. See more: *Farlow 1992; Lockley, Farlow & Meyer 1994*

1994—Australia—First sauropod footprints of the Cretaceous in Oceania
In the touristy, pearl-producing city of Broome, several sauropod footprints were found that were at times submerged in the sea, making them difficult to study and liable to be erased over time by tidal forces. See more: *Thulborn et al. 1994; Thulborn 2012*

1995—Bolivia—First sauropod footprints of the Cretaceous in northern South America
Some titanosaur impressions that formed a track of intermediate width were found in the Humaca locality. See more: *Lockley et al 2002*

1996—Switzerland—First quadrupedal sauropodomorph footprints of the Triassic in western Europe
Tetrasauropus sp. was pre-dated by *Deuterosauropodopus minor*, *Parasauropodopus corbesiensis*, *Pseudotetrasauropus andusiensis*, and *P. lehmani* (present-day France) 63–65 years earlier, but those reports actually belong to footprints of large archosaurs or therapsids. See more: *Ellenberger 1965, 1970; Lockley et al. 1996; Lockley & Meyer 2000; Porchetti & Nicosia 2007; Gand et al. 2007*

1996—Wales, United Kingdom—First quadrupedal sauropodomorph footprints of the Triassic in eastern Europe
They were identified as belonging to the ichnogenus *Eosauropus* 10 years after being described. See more: *Lockley et al. 1996; Lockley et al. 2006*

1997—Spain—Footprints of a frightened sauropod?
A track containing 36 sauropod prints reflect a change in direction and speed for reasons unknown, but some have suggested it

may have been frightened. It's a mystery that's difficult to solve. See more: *Casanovas, Fernández, Pérez-Lorente & Santafé 1997; Pérez-Lorente 2017*

1997—Polonia—First sauropod footprints of the Jurassic in eastern Europe
Parabrontopodus sp. is one of the oldest reports for that ichnogenus, as it dates to the Lower Jurassic (Hettangian, approx. 201.3–199.3 Ma). See more: *Gierlinski 1997*

1997—Laos—First sauropod footprints of the Cretaceous from the paleocontinent Cimmeria
These 80-cm impressions display a medium-width gait. See more: *Allain 1997*

1999—Spain—Deposit with the largest number of sauropod prints
The Fumanya deposit covers 64,560 m² and contains 3,500 titanosaur ichnites. See more: *Schulp & Brokx 1999; Alcalá et al. 2016*

2000—USA—First sauropod tail mark of the Jurassic
Sinuous tail marks can be seen in cf. *Brontopodus* of the Middle Jurassic. See more: *Foster et al. 2000; Breithaupt et al. 2004; Kim & Lockley 2013*

2000—USA—Oldest sauropod tail impression
cf. *Brontopodus* includes a tail track with one well-defined segment. It dates to the Middle Jurassic (Callovian, approx. 166.1–163.5 Ma). See more: *Foster et al. 2000; Breithaupt et al. 2004; Kim & Lockley 2013*

2000—Croatia—Most recent sauropod tail impression
Some probable sauropod prints include a 2-cm-wide line produced by its tail. The impressions are dated to the late Lower Cretaceous (Albian, approx. 113–100.5 Ma). See more: *Dalla Vecchia et al. 2000; Kim & Lockley 2013*

2000—Croatia—First sauropod tail impression of the Cretaceous
Some tail marks can be seen in a set of possible sauropod footprints; unfortunately, they were not illustrated. See more: *Dalla Vecchia et al. 2000; Kim & Lockley 2013*

2000—Croatia—First sauropod footprints named in eastern Europe
Based on the shape of the forefeet, *Titanosaurimanus nana* is clearly a Titanosauria print. See more: *Dalla Vecchia & Tarlao 2000*

2004—Argentina—First sauropodomorph footprints of the Triassic in southern South America
Several 27-cm-long impressions date to the upper Triassic (Carnian, approx. 237–227 Ma). See more: *Marsicano & Barredo 2004*

2004—Argentina—First sauropod footprints of the Triassic in southern South America
A study of footprints from the Portezuelo Formation (not to be confused with the identically named formation of the Upper Cretaceous) suggest that the ichnites found were very similar to those produced by primitive sauropods. This is because they were more derivative than the impressions left by the quadrupedal sauropodomorphs *Blikanasaurus* and *Antetonitrus*. See more: *Marsicano & Barredo 2004; Wilson 2005*

2004—Zimbabwe—First sauropod footprints of the Jurassic in southern Africa
Some large impressions up to 94 cm long and 56 cm wide could belong to a sauropod similar to *Giraffatitan*, although they are older. See more: *Ahmed et al. 2004*

2004—Portugal—Tracks with the largest mixed footprints

Most sauropods walked with a narrow, semi-wide, or wide gait, and only in exceptional cases did an animal change its posture, for reasons unknown. Specimen T90 of the Middle Jurassic includes impressions 108 cm in length, with forefeet similar to those of the ichnogenus *Polyonyx*. See more: *Day et al. 2004*

2005—Portugal—First sauropodomorph footprints of the Jurassic in eastern Europe

Otozoum cf. *pollex* is similar to *Kalosauropus pollex* (sometimes referred to as *Otozoum*). See more: *Rainforth 2003; Gierlinsky & Niedzwiedzki 2005*

2005—India—Deepest sauropod nest

Depths of up to 50 cm have been reported. See more: *Mohabey 2005*

2006—Wyoming, USA—First sauropod footprint associated with a fossil?

The sizes of a forefoot print and skeleton of a young *Camarasaurus* sp. correspond to an individual approximately 11 m long and weighing 5.6 t. A taphonomic study suggests that the fossils found are related to each other. The individual died from unknown causes and was later devoured by a group of *Allosaurus*. See more: *Jennings & Hasiotis 2006*

2007—Pakistan—First sauropod footprints of the Jurassic in Hindustan

Malasaurus mianwali had its name changed to *Malakhelisaurus* the year after being described. These enormous footprints are 1.3 m long. See more: *Malkani 2007, 2008*

2008—Saudi Arabia—First sauropod footprints of the Middle East

It is not yet known whether these prints up to 70 cm long date to the Middle or Upper Jurassic or to the Lower Cretaceous. See more: *Schulp et al. 2008*

2009—Poland—First sauropodomorph footprint of the Triassic in eastern Europe

Evazoum sp. is a small tetradactyl print. See more: *Gierlinski 2009*

2009—United States—First estimate of per-day distance traveled

Based on the sauropod's tracks, it could travel 20–40 km per day on average and could reach a maximum speed of 20–30 km/h. See more: *Fastovsky & Weishampel 2009*

Bipedal sauropodomorph footprints

N.º	Ichnospecies	Country	Epoch	Bibliography
1	*Anatrisauropus camisardi*	Lesotho	LJ	Ellenberger 1970
2	*Anatrisauropus ginsburgi*	Lesotho	LJ	Ellenberger 1972
3	*Anatrisauropus hereroensis*	Lesotho	LJ	Ellenberger 1972
4	*Cridotrisauropus cruentus*	Lesotho	LJ	Ellenberger 1970
5	*Cridotrisauropus unguiferus*	France	UT	Ellenberger 1965
6	*Evazoum sirigui*	Italy	UT	Nicosia & Loi 2003
7	*Kalosauropus masitisii*	Lesotho	LJ	Ellenberger 1970
8	*Kalosauropus pollex var minor*	Lesotho	LJ	Ellenberger 1970
9	*Kalosauropus pollex var minusculus*	Lesotho	LJ	Ellenberger 1970
10	*Kalosauropus pollex var victor*	Lesotho	LJ	Ellenberger 1970
11	*Ornithopus loripes*	Massachusetts, USA	LJ	Hitchcock 1848
12	*Otozoum minus*	Massachusetts, USA	LJ	Lull 1915
13	*Parasauropodopus corbesiensis*	France	LJ	Ellenberger 1970
14	*Pengxianpus cifengensis*	China	UT	Young & Young 1987
15	*Pengxianpus yulinensis*	China	LJ	Wang et al. 2016
16	*Pseudotetrasauropus acutunguis*	Lesotho	UT	Ellenberger 1972
17	*Pseudotetrasauropus andusiensis*	Lesotho	UT	Ellenberger 1972
18	*Pseudotetrasauropus bidepoidea*	Lesotho	UT	Ellenberger 1972
19	*"Pseudotetrasauropus lehmani"*	Lesotho	UT	Ellenberger 1970
20	*Pseudotetrasauropus mekalingensis*	Lesotho	UT	Ellenberger 1972
21	*Saurichnium tetractis*	Namibia	LJ	Gurich 1926
22	*Senqutrisauropus priscus*	Lesotho	UT	Ellenberger 1972
23	*Sillimanius gracilior*	Connecticut & Massachusetts, USA	LJ	Hitchcock 1841
24	*Sillimanius tetradactylus*	Connecticut & Massachusetts, USA	LJ	Hitchcock 1836
25	*Trichristolophus dubius*	Lesotho	UT	Ellenberger 1970
26	*Trisaurodactylus superavipes*	Lesotho	LJ	Ellenberger 1970, 1974
27	*Trisauropodiscus aviforma var columba*	Lesotho	UT	Ellenberger 1972
28	*Trisauropodiscus aviforma var merula*	Lesotho	UT	Ellenberger 1972
29	*Trisauropodiscus aviforma var passer*	Lesotho	UT	Ellenberger 1972
30	*Trisauropodiscus aviforma var turtur*	Lesotho	UT	Ellenberger 1972
31	*Trisauropodiscus aviforma vanellus*	Lesotho	UT	Ellenberger 1972
32	*Trisauropodiscus galliforma*	Lesotho	UT	Ellenberger 1972
33	*Trisauropodiscus levis*	Lesotho	UT	Ellenberger 1972
34	*Trisauropodiscus moabensis*	Utah, USA	LJ	Lockley et al. 1992
35	*Trisauropodiscus phasianiforma*	Lesotho	UT	Ellenberger 1972
36	*Trisauropodiscus popompoi*	Lesotho	UT	Ellenberger 1972
37	*Trisauropodiscus superaviforma*	Lesotho	LJ	Ellenberger 1972

Bipedal sauropodomorph footprints | Non-sauropodomorph footprints

Bipedal sauropodomorph footprints (numbered 1–37)

Non-sauropodomorph footprints:

Anchisauripus — Lull 1904

Eubrontes — Hitchcock 1845

Deuterosauropodopus sedunensis — UT, Switzerland — Demathieu & Weidmann 1982

Deuterosauropodopus sedunensis — UT, Switzerland — Demathieu & Weidmann 1982

Pentasauropus erectus — UT Lesotho Ellenberger 1972

Tetrapodium elmenhorsti — LJ Namibia Gürich 1926

Synonyms

Kalosauropus = Otozoum
Ellenberger 1970; Rainforth 2003

Quadrupedal sauropodomorph foorprints

1

2
3

4
5

6
7

8
9

10
11

Sauropod footprints

1
10
2
11
3
12
4
13
5
14
6
15
7
16
8
17
9
18
19

Non-sauropodomorph footprints

Deuterosauropodopus major
UT Lesotho *Ellenberger 1970*

Deuterosauropodopus minor
UT Lesotho *Ellenberger 1972*

Deuterotetrapous plancus
MT England *Sarjeant 1967*

Kuangyuanpus szechuanensis
MJ China *Young 1943*

Neosauropus lagosteirensis
ILC Germany *Antunes 1976*

Paratetrasauropus swinnertoni
UT England *Sarjeant 1970*

Paratetrasauropus seakensis
LJ Lesotho *Ellenberger 1972*

Pashtosaurus zhobi
IUC Pakistan *Malkani 2014*

Pentasauropus erectus
UT Lesotho *Ellenberger 1972*

Pentasauropus incredibilis
UT Lesotho *Ellenberger 1972*

Pentasauropus morobongensis
UT Lesotho *Ellenberger 1970*

Pseudotetrasauropus dulcis
LJ Lesotho *Ellenberger 1972*

Pseudotetrasauropus elegans
UT Lesotho *Ellenberger 1972*

Pseudotetrasauropus francisci
UT Lesotho *Ellenberger 1972*

Pentasauropus maphutsengi
UT Lesotho *Ellenberger 1972*

Pentasauropus motlejoi
LJ Lesotho *Ellenberger 1972*

Prosauropodichnus bernburgensis
MT Diedrich *2009*

Sauropodopus antiquus
UT Lesotho *Ellenberger 1972*

Tetrasauropus gigas
UT Lesotho *Ellenberger 1972*

Quadrupedal sauropodomorph footprints

N.º	Ichnospecies	Country	Epoch	Bibliography
1	Agrestipus hottoni	Virginia, USA	UT	Weems 1987
2	Barrancapus cresapi	New Mexico, USA	UT	Hunt et al. 1993
3	Eosauropus cimarroensis	New Mexico, USA	UT	Lockley et al. 2006
4	Lavinipes cheminii	Italy	LJ	Avanzini et al. 2003
5	Lavinipes jaquesi	Lesotho	UT	Ellenberger 1972
6	Liujianpus shunan	China	LJ	Xing et al. 2015
7	Navahopus coyoteensis	Arizona, USA	LJ	Milan et al. 2008
8	Navahopus falcipollex	Arizona, USA	LJ	Baird 1980
9	Otozoum moodii	Connecticut & Massachusetts, USA	LJ	Hitchcock 1847
10	Pseudotetrasauropus grandcombensis	France	UT	Gand et al. 2000
11	Tetrasauropus unguiferus	Lesotho	UT	Ellenberger 1972

Sauropod footprints

N.º	Ichnospecies	Country	Epoch	Bibliography
1	Breviparopus taghbaloutensis	Morocco	UJ	Dutuit & Ouazzou 1980
2	Brontopodus birdi	Texas, USA	ILC	Farlow, Pittman & Hawthorne 1989
3	Brontopodus changlingensis	China	eUC	Cheng & Huang 1993
4	Brontopodus oncalensis	Spain	eLC	Meijide-Fuentes et al. 2004
5	Brontopodus pentadactylus	China	ILC	Kim & Lockley 2012
6	Calorckosauripus lazari	Bolivia	IUC	Meyer, Marty & Belvedere 2018
7	Dgkhansaurus maarri	Pakistan	IUC	Malkani 2018
8	Elephantophoides barkhausensis	Germany	UJ	Kaever & Lapparent 1974
9	Gigantosauropus asturiensis	Spain	UJ	Mensink & Mertmann 1984
10	Malakhelisaurus mianwali	Pakistan	MJ	Malkani 2007, 2008
11	Mirsosauropus tursunzadei	Tajikistan	UJ	Djalilov & Novikov 1993
12	Polyonix gomesi	Portugal	MJ	Santos, Moratalla & Royo-Torres 2009
13	Parabrontopodus distercii	Spain	eLC	Meijide-Fuentes et al. 2001
14	Parabrontopodus mcintoshi	Colorado, USA	UJ	Lockley, Farlow & Meyer 1994
15	Rotundichnus munchehagensis	Germany	eLC	Hendriks 1981
16	Sauropodichnus giganteus	Argentina	eUC	Calvo 1991
17	Titanopodus mendozensis	Argentina	IUC	Gónzalez-Riga & Calvo 2009
18	Titanosaurimanus nana	Croatia	ILC	Dalla Vecchia & Tarlao 2000
19	Ultrasauripus ungulatus	South Korea	ILC	Kim 1993

2009—Portugal—First footprint with a previously used name

Polyonyx refers to some Turiasauria prints and was formalized 151 years after being named after the porcelain crab *Polyonyx*. See more: *Stimpson 1858; Santos 2002; Santos et al. 2004, 2009*

2010—China—First sauropod footprints of the Jurassic in eastern Asia

Some narrow-gauge tracks are reported for the Lower Jurassic (Toarcian, approx. 182.7–174.1 Ma). See more: *Xing 2010*

2010—Portugal—First Jurassic skin impression

A 58 cm-long print displays scales 2–3 cm in diameter. See more: *Mateus & Milàn 2010*

2011—Maryland, USA—First sauropod prints of the Cretaceous in eastern North America

These prints form a 50.5 m-long, intermediate-gauge track. See more: *Wagensommer et al. 2011*

2011—Madagascar—First sauropod footprints of the Jurassic in Madagascar

Some very small or medium-sized prints of a sauropod with a wide-gauge gait were reported. See more: *Standford et al. 2011*

2012—Australia—Most complex layering of sauropod impressions

Multiple layers reaching to a depth of 96 cm were found in northwestern Australia. The ground shows constant deformation from the treading, so some of the prints are fragmented. See more: *Thulborn et al. 1994; Thulborn 2012*

2013—China—First quadrupedal sauropodomorph impressions of the Triassic in eastern Asia

Some strangely elongated ichnites that seem as though the dinosaur made them when sliding, doubling the print length from 34 cm to 79 cm. See more: *Xing et al. 2014*

2014—Spain—Evidence of several sauropod impressions being conserved by a tsunami

A study revealed that gigantic waves produced by an undersea earthquake 129 Ma ago preserved a large number of prints, including those of several sauropods. Teruel Province contains the largest deposit of prints in Europe. See more: *Navarrete et al. 2014*

2016—Angola—First Cretaceous skin print

Impression MGUAN-PA602 preserved skin marks and are the first prints reported for that country. See more: *Mateus et al. 2016*

2016—China—Most recently named sauropodomorph print

Pengxianpus yulinensis may be prints of a sauropodomorph (they are considered so here) or of a theropod. See more: *Xing et al. 2013; Wang et al. 2016*

2016—China—Oldest broad tracks

These footprints, which may belong to mamenchisaurids, date to the Hettangian-Sinemurian (approx. 199.3 Ma). See more: *Xing et al. 2016*

2018—Argentina—Most recent narrow track

This track dates to the lower Cenomanian (approx. 93.9–97.2 Ma) and may have belonged to a large rebbachisaurid. See more: *Heredia et al. 2018*

2018—Brazil—Largest sauropod impressions

Some prints dating to the late Lower Cretaceous (Barremian, approx. 129.4–125 Ma) are accompanied by some enormous resting impressions, the longest of which is 2.4 x 2.1 m and the widest 1.9 m x 2.22 m. See more: *Lopes et al. 2018*

2018—Bolivia—The most recently named

Calorckosauripus lazari was created as this book was being finalized. See more: *Meyer et al. 2018*

Synonyms	
Chuxiongpus = Brontopodus *Cheng & Huang 1993*	***Malasaurus = Malakhelisaurus*** *Malkani 2007*
Name from academic thesis or abstracts	
"*Digitichnus zambujalensis*" *Santos 2002*	**"*Brontopus youngjingensis*"** *Peng 2004*
"*Brontopus gansuensis*" *Peng 2004*	**"*Ophysthonyx portucalensis*"** *Santos, Moratalla, Rodrigues & Sanz, 2004*
"*Brontopus megaensis*" *Peng 2004*	**"*Transonymanus portucalensis*"** *Santos 2002*
Indeterminate dinosaur ichnospecies	
"*Elephantosauripus*" ILC South Korea Anonymous	**"*Koreanosauripus cheongi*"** ILC South Korea Kim 1986, 1987

False sauropodomorph footprints

"*Saurischichnus primitivus*" are supposed footprints found in Germany but have numerous anomalies. For example, the digits are deeper than the soles of the feet, each individual has different proportions, and the size of the prints in the track do not match each other, neither in size nor in form. It is possible that they were manufactured for later sale. See more: *Huene 1941; Seilacher 2007*

Narrow, intermediate, broad, and very broad tracks

An important aspect in the study of sauropod prints is the distance between the right and left impressions in the same track. Based on this separation, tracks have been divided into four groups: narrow, intermediate, broad, and very broad, which reflect the body shape and posture while in motion. Some experts suspect that these differences may be the result of different behaviors, although the distance between right and left tracks is primarily related to anatomy, as they tend to vary little within each sauropod group. Proof of this is that broad tracks have yielded dates that are contemporary to taxonomic groups that produce them, and account for 56% of all sauropod tracks dated to the Jurassic and 96% of those from the Cretaceous. See more: *Lockley et al.1994; Wilson & Carrano 1999; Calvo et al. 2007; Romano et al. 2007; Scharz et al. 2007; Otero & Vizcaíno 2008; Castañera et al. 2012; Stevens et al. 2016*

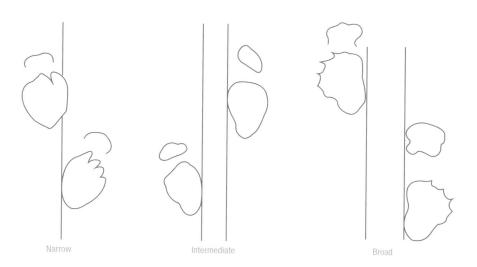

Narrow   Intermediate   Broad

Narrow vs. wide tracks

Narrow: In a characteristic of primitive sauropods, diplodocoides, and some euhelopodids, the heels seem to touch a central imaginary line. Found from the Lower Jurassic to the late Upper Cretaceous, they are more abundant throughout the Jurassic and rare in the Cretaceous, with just one report from the late Upper Cretaceous.

Intermediate: Some turiasaurs, macronarians, and titanosaurs had narrower footprints but wider hips than the ones described above. From the Lower Jurassic to the late Upper Cretaceous.

Broad: Produced by broad bodies, including the mamenchisaurids, derived turiasaurs, titanosauriforms, and robust titanosaurs. Found from the Lower Jurassic to the late Upper Cretaceous, they are more abundant in the Cretaceous.

Very broad: Though very rare, these have been associated with the prints of titanosauriforms and the Lognkosauria titanosaurs. All such finds date to the Upper Jurassic or Upper Cretaceous. See more: *Lockley et al. 1994; Wilson & Carrano 1999; Calvo et al. 2007; Romano et al. 2007; Scharz et al. 2007; Otero & Vizcaíno 2008*

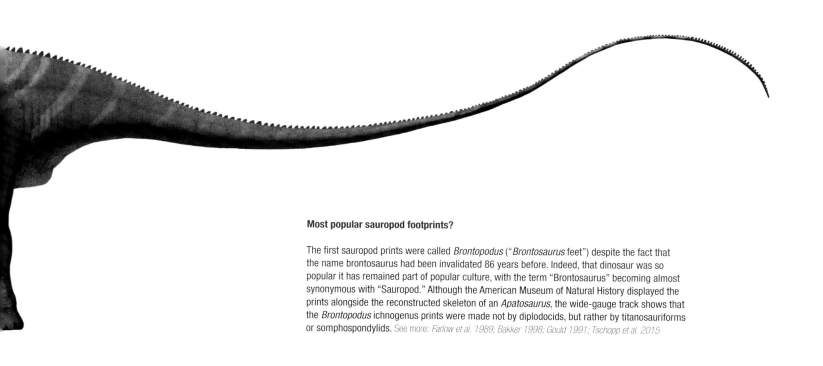

Most popular sauropod footprints?

The first sauropod prints were called *Brontopodus* ("*Brontosaurus* feet") despite the fact that the name brontosaurus had been invalidated 86 years before. Indeed, that dinosaur was so popular it has remained part of popular culture, with the term "Brontosaurus" becoming almost synonymous with "Sauropod." Although the American Museum of Natural History displayed the prints alongside the reconstructed skeleton of an *Apatosaurus*, the wide-gauge track shows that the *Brontopodus* ichnogenus prints were made not by diplodocids, but rather by titanosauriforms or somphospondylids. See more: *Farlow et al. 1989; Bakker 1998; Gould 1991; Tschopp et al. 2015*

Records: Historic and cultural

Brontosaurus is the most famous sauropod, and although it was considered a synonym of *Apatosaurus* for 112 years, it remained present in popular culture. Like many other species, it is often represented in the media and in popular figures known as "dinomorphs" with anatomical details that are realistic, deformed (dinosauroids), mixed (paradinosauroids), or monstrous (dracodinosauroids).

CHRONOLOGY OF SAUROPODOMORPH AND SAUROPOD RECORDS

This section presents record discoveries and major investigations into sauropods and sauropodomorphs throughout history, divided into the Archaic, Heroic, Classic, Mythological, Modern, and Renaissance historic periods proposed by Michael K. Brett-Surman (1997), José Luis Sanz (1999), and Molina-Pérez & Larramendi (2016).
See more: *Glut & Brett-Surman 1997; Sanz 1999, 2007; Pereda-Suberbiola et al. 2010; Spalding & Sarjeant 2012*

Mythological period	Early Mythological (~130,000—3300 B.C.)
	Late Mythological (~3300 B.C.–~1670 A.D.)
Archaic period	Early Archaic (1671–1762)
	Late Archaic (1763–1823)
Heroic period	Early Heroic (1824–1857)*
	Late Heroic (1858–1896)*
Classic period**	Early Classic (1897–1928)
	Late Classic (1929–1938)
Modern period ***	Early Modern (1939–1946)
	Late Modern (1947–1968)
Renaissance period	Early Renaissance (1969–1995)
	Late Renaissance (1996–present)

* Ancient Period according to Sanz 2007
** First Modern Period according to Sanz 2007
*** Second Modern Period according to Sanz 2007

Early Mythological Subperiod (~130,000–~3300 B.C.) ~126,700 years

NO KNOWN REFERENCES TO SAUROPODS IN THAT PERIOD

Mythological Subperiod (~3300 B.C.–~1670 A.D.) ~4970 years

FIRST DINOSAUR FOSSIL CATALOGUED!

Some old texts mention the existence of giant animal fossils that at the time were interpreted as belonging to mythological beings, and they are still fascinating today.

~300 B.C.—China—First fossil bones of very large land animals
Some "dragon" bones reported by Chinese historian Cheng Qu may have belonged to very large mammals or sauropod dinosaurs, but nothing more is known about them. See more: *Dong & Milner 1988; Needham 1959*

1410—Portugal—First legend caused by sauropod footprints
At Lagosteiros Beach, in Cabo Espichel, some Upper Jurassic sauropod tracks were found that gave rise to the legend of Nossa Senhora da Pedra da Mua (Our Lady of Pedra da Mua) that claims the tracks were left on the cliff side by a huge mule that the Virgin Mary rode upon. The Nossa Senhora do Cabo Espichel shrine was built at the site in the 15th century, and a mural was painted commemorating the event in the 18th century, the same century in which the true nature of the tracks became evident. See more: *Antunes 1976; Sanz 2000, 2003; Santos & Rodrígues 2008; Pérez-Lorente 2015*

Early Archaic Subperiod (1671–1762) 91 years

THE FIRST SAUROPOD COLLECTORS!

Some enormous bones were discovered between 1669 and 1671. Unfortunately, we do not know what kind of animals they might have belonged to. See more: *Mares 1681; Pereda-Suberbiola et al. 2010*

1671—Spain—First sauropod bones?
Giant animal bones were reported between 1669 and 1671 but cannot be identified as they were neither illustrated nor described. See more: *Mares 1681; Pereda-Suberbiola et al. 2010*

1755—England—First sauropod vertebra?
Joshua Platt found three vertebrae 74 cm high and 20 cm long. Some time later, they were identified as belonging to a rhinoceros or hippopotamus. It has recently been suggested that they belong to *Megalosaurus*, but they are too large for that. See more: *Anonymous 1759; Delair & Sarjeant 1975*

1776—Congo—Oldest record of Mokèlé-mbèmbé, the legend of the "surviving sauropod"
Some very large tracks became part of Pygmy tribal legends, and investigators later learned they were made by a sauropod. See more: *Bonaventure-Poyart 1776; Gratz 1909*

Late Archaic Subperiod (1763–1823) 60 years

FIRST DECISIVELY IDENTIFIED SAUROPOD BONES!

The study of dinosaurs had become more formalized, although they were still considered enormous reptiles similar to present-day lizards.

1809—England—First unmistakable sauropod bone
A caudal vertebra was identified 60 years later as that of an animal similar to *Cetiosaurus*. Unlike previous discoveries, this piece is currently accessible in the collections of the Sedgwick Museum under catalogue number J230 05. See more: *Seeley 1869; Delair & Sarjeant 1975, 2002*

1809—England—Oldest conserved sauropod fossil
Caudal vertebra J230 05 in the Sedgwick Museum collection. See more: *Seeley 1869; Delair & Sarjeant 1975*

1818—USA—First remains of a prosauropod
Solomon Ellsworth discovered the remains of *Anchisaurus polyzelus*, originally identified as human remains. See more: *Smith 1818*

Early Heroic Subperiod (1824–1857) 33 years

DINOSAURS RECEIVE THEIR FIRST FORMAL NAMES!

Dinosaurs are recognized as a group separate from present-day reptiles that has some similarities to birds and mammals. The first scientific documents formally describing dinosaurs are published. Giant species are identified as marine animals similar to whales.

1836—England—First scientific description of a sauropodomorph
Henry Riley and Samuel Stutchbury's publication of *Thecodontosaurus* in 1836 established the official nomenclature for sauropodomorphs. The remains were assigned only a genus; the species name was not given until seven years later. See more: *Riley & Stutchbury 1836; Morris 1843*

1836—England—First group of sauropodomorphs discovered
Several *Thecodontosaurus antiquus* were preserved in fissures or caves, leading investigators to believe a herd of the creatures had fallen into rock crevasses. See more: *Riley & Stutchbury 1836*

1837—Germany—First named sauropodomorph discovered in a second country
Plateosaurus engelhardti was described a year after *Thecodontosaurus*, but both were discovered the same year, in 1834. See more: *Meyer 1837*

1841—England—First scientific description of a sauropod
Henry Richard Owen's publication of *Cardiodon* and *Cetiosaurus* in 1841 established the official nomenclature for sauropods, although species names were not assigned until three years later. See more: *Owen 1841, 1844*

1852—France—First sauropod discovered in a second country
All sauropods had been reported from England until *Aepisaurus elephantinus* was described. Unfortunately, the fossil was lost. See more: *Gervais 1852; Taylor 2010*

1856—Germany—Most abundant sauropodomorph of the Triassic
More than 100 specimens of *Plateosaurus longiceps* (species described by Rütimeyer 1856) have been discovered over time, including juveniles and adults. See more: *Quenstedt 1856*

Late Heroic Subperiod (1858–1896) 38 years

THE FIRST RIVALRY AMONG PALEONTOLOGISTS BEGINS!

Scientists make the first-ever reconstructions of (bipedal) sauropodomorphs and (quadrupedal) sauropods, representing the latter as slow, heavy, semi-aquatic creatures. The intense rivalry that erupted between fossil hunters came to be known as the "Bone Wars." The dispute greatly expanded the number of species described. The first discoveries were in Europe and North America.

1859—Maryland, USA—First internal analysis of a sauropod tooth
A tooth of Astrodon was cut into cross sections, revealing a star-shaped pattern and giving rise to the creature's name, "star-toothed." See more: *Johnston 1859*

1865—India, Russia—Oldest mistaken report of a sauropodomorph
Some protorosaurs or proterosuchids were mistaken for sauropodomorphs such as *Ankistrodon indicus* (considered *T. indicus* by some authors) and possibly *Thecodontosaurus* sp. from Russia. Both are from the Lower Triassic (Induan, approx. 252.17–251.2 Ma). Other reports of Middle Triassic creatures were also found not to be sauropodomorphs. Current thinking affirms that the group lived exclusively from the Upper Triassic to the late Upper Cretaceous. See more: *Huxley 1865; Yakovlev 1923*

1877—USA—The "Bone Wars" begin
The "Bone Wars" refers to the ruthless rivalry between Edward Drinker Cope and Othniel Marsh, each vying to be the preeminent paleontologist. Their competition dramatically increased the discovery and description of several species of dinosaurs in North America. See more: *Wallace 1999; Preston 1993*

1877—USA—First sauropods found in a group
Several specimens of *Camarasaurus supremus* were found with the bones so mixed up that they were all catalogued under the same number, AMNH 5761. See more: *Cope 1877*

1877—Connecticut, USA—First sauropodomorph skeleton reconstructed
Camarasaurus supremus was reconstructed as a quadrupedal animal with a straight trunk and relatively short neck. Its correct appearance was established 44 years later. See more: *Cope 1877; Osborn & Mook 1921*

1883—present—The longest-lasting scientific debate involving sauropods
Sauropod weights are very difficult to estimate, as the many different criteria, considerations, methods, and models used yield very different results. *Brontosaurus excelsus* was the first sauropod to have its weight estimated, at 18.4 t (20 US t, Marsh 1883). Later estimates include 40 t (Gregory 1905); 27.9–32.4 t (Colbert 1962); 27.9–32.3 t (Anderson et al. 1984), and 14.9 t (Paul 2010, 2016). Some of these do not specify which specimen was used in the calculation. After the discovery of an extremely complete skeleton of *Apatosaurus louisae* CMNH 3018 (Holland 1915), many authors chose to base their estimates on this specimen to ensure the results were comparable, with the following results: 34 t (Alexander 1989); 19.5 t (Christiansen 1997); 17.5 t (Paul 1997); 22.4 t (Seebacher 2001); 17.3 t (Henderson 2004); 16.4 t (Henderson 2006); 27.4 t (Bates et al. 2015); and 20 t (in this book). It should

be noted that with no living animal to measure from, all estimations involve some margin of error. A volumetric method must also be applied to all, so the results are calculated using the same criteria. See more: *Marsh 1883; Gregory 1905; Holland 1915; Colbert 1962; Anderson et al. 1984; Alexander 1989; Christiansen 1997; Paul 1997, 2010*; Seebacher 2001; Henderson 2004, 2006; Paul 2010; Bates et al. 2015*

1891—USA—First correction of a sauropod skeleton
Othniel Marsh changed his first reconstruction of *Brontosaurus excelsus* eight years later, improving the relative bone proportions and lengthening the neck and thorax by adding more vertebrae. The skull was also modified to appear more elongated. It was based on material discovered in 1879. See more: *Marsh 1883; 1891*

1892—USA—The "Bone Wars" come to a close
The sauropods described during this long-standing dispute included *Maraapunisaurus fragillimus, A. altus, A. latus* (synonym of *Camarasaurus supremus*), *Apatosaurus ajax, A. grandis* (now *Camarasaurus*), *Apatosaurus laticollis* (synonym of *Apatosaurus louisae*), *Atlantosaurus immanis, A. montanus* (formerly *Titanosaurus*), *Barosaurus lentus, Brontosaurus amplus* (synonym of *Brontosaurus excelsus*), *Brontosaurus excelsus, Camarasaurus leptodirus* (synonym of *C. supremus*), *Camarasaurus supremus, Caulodon diversidens* (synonym of *Camarasaurus supremus*), *C. leptoganus* (synonym of *Camarasaurus supremus*), *Diplodocus lacustris, Diplodocus longus, Dystrophaeus viaemalae, Morosaurus impar* (synonym of *Camarasaurus grandis*), *Morosaurus agilis, M. lentus* (now *Camarasaurus*), *M. robustus* (synonym of *Camarasaurus grandis*), *Pleurocoelus altus* (synonym of *P. nanus*) and *Pleurocoelus nanus. Epanterias amplexus* was thought to be a sauropod but was actually the remains of a very large theropod. In all, 23 species were identified, including 12 valid and 3 doubtful names and 9 synonyms. See more: *Wallace 1999; Preston 1993*

1893—Massachusetts, USA—First reconstruction of a sauropodomorph skeleton
Anchisaurus colurus (now *A. polyzelus*) was restored so accurately that the model is still considered valid. Only the skull has changed, as it was initially based on a deformed piece, then was corrected 117 years later. See more: *Marsh 1893; Yates 2010*

1899—Wyoming, USA—First to-scale comparison of human and sauropod skeletons
A skeleton discovered by Barnum Brown in 1877 was illustrated along with a human skeleton. See more: *Osborn 1899*

Early Classic Subperiod (1897–1928) 41 years

FIRST SAUROPOD SKELETONS REASSEMBLED!

The first small sauropod species is discovered. Dinosaurs begin to capture public attention beyond the academic sphere and play a leading role in the "prehistoric film" genre. The first skeletons are reassembled from actual bones.

1903—USA—Most famous sauropod name invalidated
Brontosaurus excelsus was believed to be a species of *Apatosaurus*, so the name that had long captivated the public through the media was deemed invalid. However, the skeleton mounted at the American Museum of Natural History was named *Brontosaurus*, so the public adopted the name widely, equating "*Brontosaurus*" with "Sauropod." However, 112 years later, the validity of the genus proposed 95 years earlier was reconfirmed. See more: *Riggs 1903; Bakker 1998; Tschopp et al. 2015*

1903—South Africa—First sauropod fossil destroyed
Some fossils that laborers were using to make bricks were recovered in 1903. See more: *Broom 1904*

1905—USA—First mounted sauropod skeleton
The American Museum of Natural History unveiled the first mounted exhibit of a sauropod, the *Brontosaurus excelsus* specimen AMNH 460. Exactly 100 years later, the first replica of *Diplodocus carnegii* was unveiled at the same museum. See more: *Osborn 1905*

1905—England—Oldest sauropod discovered in marine deposits
"*Cetiosaurus*" *leedsi* (sometimes considered a synonym of *Cetiosauriscus stewarti*) dates to the Middle Jurassic (middle Callovian, approx. 164.8 Ma). See more: *Woodward 1905; Ford**

1909—Germany—Strangest sauropod skeletal reconstruction
Because people assumed that dinosaurs were lizards, these animals were thought to have walked with their bellies close to the ground. This model was applied to a *Diplodocus*, taking for granted that it suffered greatly from dislocated limbs. This reconstruction is curious, as the same specimen had been rebuilt previously with the limbs below the trunk, like a mammal, which we now know is the correct posture. See more: *Cope 1877; Tornier 1909*

1915—Romania—First island-dwelling sauropod discovered
"*Titanosaurus*" *dacus* (now *Magyarosaurus*) was identified as an island-dwelling species based on its small size. Some specimens known as *M. hungaricus* are larger, so it is possible that, depending on the zone, there were different populations of the species with larger and smaller adults. See more: *Nopcsa 1915; Huene 1932; Stein et al. 2010*

1920—USA—First organic material from a sauropod
Possible blood cells were reportedly found in an *Apatosaurus*. See more: *Moodie 1920; Reid 1993; Tanke & Rothschild 2002*

Late Classic Subperiod (1929–1938) 9 years

SAUROPODS RECOGNIZED AS LAND ANIMALS AND NOT AMPHIBIANS!

In 1938, Roland Bird discovered some footprints that had been made on dry land, without marks of tail dragging.

1932—Germany—Strangest reconstruction of a sauropodomorph
The skeleton of *Sellosaurus gracilis* SMNS 12667 was mounted with a reptilian posture—the belly touching the ground and the legs splayed to the side—at the Naturaliensammlung in Stuttgart. See more: *Huene 1932; Hungerbuhler 1998*

1934—France—First sauropod species to be reported on two continents
New remains of *Bothriospondylus madagascariensis* (a species originally reported for the Middle Jurassic in Madagascar) were reported for the Upper Jurassic in France. It is now known that the

specimen discovered in France represents the new species *Vouivria damparisensis*. See more: *Dorlodot 1934; Mannion 2010, 2017*

1937—Germany, Tanzania—World's largest mounted non-replicated skeleton
This relatively complete skeleton of *Giraffatitan brancai* measures some 22 m in length and more than 13.27 m in height. It was mounted at the Museum für Naturkunde de Berlin (Natural History Museum of Berlin) and is based primarily on the holotype specimen HMN SII. This specimen was saved from destruction in World War II and is still on display today, after a slight modification in 2005 to correct its posture. See more: *Janensch 1938; Gunga et al. 2008*

Early Modern Subperiod (1939–1946) 8 years

FOSSILS DESTROYED OR LOST FOREVER!

The outbreak of World War II interrupted research on dinosaurs, and some entire collections were destroyed in the shelling. Some people were even murdered for attempting to save them.

1940—England—First sauropodomorph remains destroyed in World War II
The holotype specimen of *Thecodontosaurus antiquus*, the first European sauropodomorph, was destroyed along with *Palaeosaurus cylindricum*, a tooth believed to be a close relative of *Thecodontosaurus*. It is now known that the latter did not belong to a dinosaur. See more: *Riley & Stutchbury 1836; Anonymous 1961*

1940—England, USA—Sauropodomorph fossil saved from destruction in World War II
The holotype specimen of *Asylosaurus yalensis* was loaned to Yale University sometime between 1888 and 1890 and so was saved from being destroyed by air raids on England, prompting its name "Yale asylum lizard." See more: *Riley & Stutchbury 1836; Galton 2008*

1940—Germany, South Africa—First sauropodomoroh replica destroyed
Although the holotype material of *Massospondylus carinatus* was destroyed along with the holotypes of its synonyms *Aristosaurus erectus*, *Leptospondylus capensis*, and *Pachyspondylus orpenii*, a replica exists in South Africa. A neotype specimen was later designated to represent the species. Specimen BP/1/4934 consists of a skull and partial skeleton of a juvenile individual. See more: *Owen 1854; Anonymous 1961; Yates & Barrett 2010*

1944—Germany—Most skeletons destroyed of a sauropodomorph species
Many skeletons of *Plateosaurus longiceps* were destroyed by the fires caused by air raids on the Naturaliensammlung (Natural History Museum) in Stuttgart and the Museum für Naturkunde (Natural History

Museum) of Berlin. An estimated 40 pieces assigned to *P. trossingensis*, a junior synonym of *P. longiceps*, were destroyed. See more: *Schoch 2011; Ford**

1944—Germany—First sauropod remains destroyed in World War II
Aegyptosaurus baharijensis 1912VIII61 was a very complete specimen that included several front and hind leg bones, an incomplete scapula, and some tail vertebrae. It was destroyed in a Royal Air Force bombing that affected the Bavarian State Museum in Munich. See more: *Stromer 1932; Ford**

1944—Germany, Egypt—Fastest destruction of a described sauropod
The holotype of *Aegyptosaurus baharijensis* was bombed 12 years after having been described. Fortunately, it was well illustrated and measured. However, it was destroyed because Karl Beurlen, the curator in charge, refused to remove the fossils to a safer place despite the urging of Ernst Stromer (who had discovered and described the fossils). See more: *Stromer 1932; Sanz 2007*

1944—Germany, Tanzania—Sauropod species with the most skeletons destroyed
Some 442 pieces of 630 *Janenschia africana* fossils were destroyed in World War II. See more: *Remes 2006*

Late Modern Subperiod (1947–1968) 21 years

DINOSAUR RESEARCH RECOMMENCES!

Scientific publications on dinosaur paleontology begin to increase. The first books focused on fossil records of dinosaur families are published. For the first time, sauropods are depicted not dragging their tails.

1953—China—First sauropod with dieresis in the name
Chiayüsaurus lacustris was changed to *Chiayusaurus,* as no diacritics are allowed in scientific names. See more: *Bohlin 1953*

1967—First book of fossil records to include the oldest and most recent sauropodomorphs
Eucnemesaurus fortis, Euskelosaurus africanus, E. browni, Melanorosaurus readi, Plateosauravus cullinworthi and *P. stombergensis* were considered the oldest at the time, while *Avalonianus sanfordi, Gresslyosaurus ingens, Gyposaurus capensis, G. erectus, G. skirtopodus, G. sinensis, Lufengosaurus huenei, L. magnus, Plateosaurus poligniensis, Plateosaurus* spp., "Sinosaurus triassicus," *Thecodontosaurus dubius, Yunnanosaurus huangi,* and *Y. robustus* were considered the most recent. See more: *Appleby et al. 1967*

1967—First book of fossil records to include the oldest and most recent sauropods
Rhoetosaurus browni was considered the oldest, except for some unnamed species discovered in Lesotho (footprints that were not made by sauropods) and in India (*Barapasaurus tagorei*), while *Alamosaurus sanjuanensis, Hypselosaurus priscus, H. sp.* nov., *Magyarosaurus* spp., *Titanosaurus indicus,* and *Titanosaurus* cf. *indicus* were considered the most recent at the time. See more: *Jain et al. 1962, Charig et al. 1965; Appleby et al. 1967*

1968—USA—First evidence of protein in a sauropod
Found in a specimen of *Diplodocus.* See more: *Miller & Wyckoff 1968*

Early Renaissance Subperiod (1969–1995) 26 years

DINOSAURS NO LONGER CONSIDERED SLOW, CLUMSY CREATURES!

Although researchers now accept that some dinosaurs were warm-blooded, sauropods were not as easily included among them because of the dispute about how they were able to obtain enough food to sustain their enormous size.

1969—USA—Sauropodomorph fossil recovered from under a bridge
Part of a specimen of *Ammosaurus major* was lost when the South Manchester Bridge was constructed but was recovered when the bridge was demolished in 1969. See more: *Marsh 1891; Weishampel & Young 1996*

1969—USA—First encephalization quotient study on sauropods
Diplodocus and *Giraffatitan* (fomerly *Brachiosaurus*) were included in the study, although the weights assigned were higher than current estimates. See more: *Jerison 1969; Buchholtz 2012*

1972—Most sauropodomorph ichnospecies named in a single year
Six species of *Trisauropodiscus* were created. See more: *Ellenberger 1972*

1975—USA—Some scientists argue that sauropods had trunks
The positioning of nasal fossae in the upper part of the sauropod skull led to the hypothesis that these animals had trunks, and some creative reconstructions show the animal with that appendage. This is very unlikely, however, as sauropods lacked deep facial nerve roots. See more: *Coobs 1975; Bakker 1986; Witmer 2001*

1983—USA—Sauropod forefoot claws are reinterpreted
Claws on sauropod forefeet were previously thought to have been used for defense against predators or even for fighting members of their own species. One novel proposal suggests that they were useful for grabbing tree trunks in order to reach food in the high canopy. This was supported by the fact that sauropods could not otherwise do so; *Giraffatitan,* for example, had much smaller claws. A later interpretation was that they were used to hold mates during copulation. See more: *McLoughlin 1979; Fritz 1988; Tanimoto 1991; Upchurch 1994; Isles 2009*

1983—China—Cretaceous sauropod discovered at the highest altitude
"Megacervixosaurus tibetensis" was found at 4900 m above sea level but has not been formally published to date. See more: *Zhao 1985; Xing et al. 2011*

1985—England—Oldest sauropodomorph discovered in marine deposits
Remains of *Camelotia borealis* were previously identified as belonging to *Avalonianus* and *Gresslyosaurus.* They date to the Upper Triassic (Rhaetian, approx. 208.5–201.3 Ma). See more: *Galton 1985; Ford**

1987—Japan—A "microscopic sauropod from the Silurian period" is reported
A tiny silhouette on a piece of Paleozoic limestone was identified as "*Brontosaurus excelus minilorientalus*" but was not taken seriously by the scientific community. See more: *Okamura 1987*

1989—USA—The term dinoturbation is coined
This term describes the process in which dinosaur treading or other activities disturbs the primary structure of sedimentary rock. Sauropods produced this effect more frequently than other animals due to their enormous size. See more: *Lockley & Conrad 1989*

1989—USA—The term "sauropod hiatus" is coined
This term refers to a gap in the sauropod fossil record in North America that spans some 22.5 million years (Cenomanian to upper Campanian). These animals may have become extinct on that continent at the time for unknown causes, or it may just be that the fossils are yet to be found. It is important to note, however, that North America was isolated at the time, allowing *Alamosaurus sanjuanensis* to repopulate an ecosystem devoid of sauropods. See more: *Lucas & Hunt 1989; D'Emic et al. 2012*

1989—India—Largest plant fossil mistaken for dinosaur bones?
These remains were identified as *Bruhathkayosaurus matleyi* but unfortunately were lost in a flood. As the photos and illustrations were not very clear or detailed, there was speculation that they were actually fossilized palm trunks (*Palmoxylon*). The largest piece, 2 m long, was thought to be a theropod tibia, although it also appeared similar to a titanosaur fibula. See more: *Yadagiri & Ayyasami 1989; Krause et al. 2006*

1990—USA—The term "gigantothermy" is coined
The term is based on Latin words—gigant ("giant") and thermia ("temperature")—and describes an energy production mechanism commonly found in the leatherback sea turtle (*Dermochelys coriacea*) and other animals. See more: *Spotila 1980; Paladino et al. 1990; Spotila et al. 1991*

1990—USA—First association of gigantothermy with dinosaur metabolism
Animals with a gigantothermal or inertial homothermal metabolism, in which their very large bodies lose heat very slowly (thermal inertia), often possess an insulating integument making it unnecessary for them to eat excessive amounts of food, unlike ectothermal animals. Sauropods may also have had this kind of system to enable them to maintain a constant body temperature. See more: *Paladino et al. 1990; Lucas 2007; Sander et al. 2011*

1990–1991—Antarctica—Highest-altitude discovery of a sauropodomorph fossil
Glacialisaurus hammeri was found in Antarctica at an altitude of 4,000 m. See more: *Hammer & Hickerson 1994*

1991—Tanzania—A famous sauropod changes its name
Brachiosaurus brancai was switched to the genus *Giraffatitan.* This species most frequently represents the genus, as the type species *B. altithorax* is much less well known. The name *Giraffatitan* was originally coined as a subgenus. See more: *Riggs 1903; Janensch 1914; Paul 1987, 1988; Olshevsky 1991; Taylor 2009*

1991—New Mexico, USA—First evidence of collagen in a sauropod
This specimen of *Diplodocus hallorum* (formerly *Seismosaurus halli*) included preserved protein fractions. See more: *Gurley et al. 1991*

1993—USA—Highest price ever paid for sauropod eggs
A nest with 10 eggs estimated to be 100 Ma old was auctioned off by the Bonham Gallery and sold for US$76,000 to an anonymous buyer who phoned in their bid. That same day, the same collector paid US$18,750 for another nest with five eggs. The previous record was held by a specimen of *Megaloolithus*

(at the time considered "Hypselosaurus priscus"), which was auctioned off for 1 million pesetas (equal to US$6,500). See more: *http://articles.baltimoresun.com/*

1993—Most sauropod ichnospecies named in a year
Based on footprints, the species *Barrancapus cresapi, Chuxiongpus changlinensis, C. zheni, Hamanosauripus ovalis,* and *Ultrasauripus ungulatus* were created in that year. The first has been considered a sauropodomorph, the second and third are synonyms, and the last two are doubtful names. See more: *Chen & Huang 1993; Hunt et al. 1993; Kim 1993; Lockley et al. 2002*

1994—Argentina—First sauropod tooth classification
This proposed system divided sauropod teeth into four morphotypes: "spoon-like," which includes some mamenchisaurids, primitive macronarians, and euhelopodids; "peg-like," including only diplodocoides; "spatulate," encompassing primitive sauropods, titanosauromorphs, some somphospondylids, euhelopodids, and the most basal titanosaurs; and "chisel-like," for lithostrotian titanosaurs. See more: *Calvo 1994*

1995—France—Oldest sauropodomorph discovered in marine deposits
A quadrupedal sauropodomorph known only from a femur, a humerus, a scapula, and an ischium was dated to the Upper Triassic (Norian, approx. 227–208.5 Ma). See more: *Gauffre 1995; Ford**

1995—USA—First skeleton mounted without a dragging tail
The American Museum of Natural History changed the mounted skeleton of "Brontosaurus excelsus" to reflect a tail that was held up, not dragged along the ground, and with the skull more suited to its genus, based on *Apatosaurus louisae*. See more: *Norell et al. 1995*

1995 and 1998—Most sauropod species named in a single year
Seven species of *Megaloolithus* were created in 1995, although *M. baghensis* is now considered to belong to the genus *Fusioolithus*. In 1998, eight species were named, although three are synonyms of other species (*M. khempurensis, M. phesaniensis,* and *M. rahioliensis)* and one is doubtful (*M. problematica).*

1996—Antarctica—Sauropodomorph discovered at the highest altitude
Glacialisaurus hammeri was found at 4000 m above sea level, along with the remains of a sauropod. See more: *Hammer & Hickerson 1996*

Late Renaissance subperiod (1996–present)

PRIMITIVE SAUROPODOMORPHS FOUND TO BE OBLIGATE BIPEDS!

Filaments have been confirmed in all dinosaur groups, except sauropodomorphs, for which only impressions of scales have been found. However, some researchers suggest that, like their theropod relatives, these structures would have been present at least in the most primitive sauropodomorph species.

1997—Norway—Sauropodomorph fossil discovered deep under the sea
While drilling through sandstone during North Sea petroleum explorations, a bone identified as belonging to *Plateosaurus* was found at 2256 m under the seabed. The material consists of a cylinder that was initially thought to be a plant fossil, until nine years after its discovery, when it was identified as a sauropodomorph tibia. See more: *Hurum et al. 2006*

1999—Spain—The term "dinomorph" is coined
Paleontologist and science commentator José Luis Sanz García proposed the term *dinomorfo* ("dinomorph") for objects shaped like dinosaurs. See more: *Sanz 1999*

1999—Argentina—Most abundant sauropod of the Triassic
Several *Lessemsaurus sauropoides* individuals were found mixed together. Other sauropods from the same era have usually been found singly. See more: *Bonaparte 1999*

2001—Egypt—First sauropod found preserved in a mangrove swamp
Paralititan stromeri was preserved on what was once the southern shore of the now-extinct Tethys Ocean. Fossil plants found at the site indicate the animal lived in a mangrove swamp. See more: *Smith et al. 2001*

2004—South Africa—Most abundant sauropodomorph of the Jurassic
Some 80 partial skeletons and numerous fragments of *Massospondylus carinatus* representing individuals of different ages were found. See more: *Galton & Upchurch 2004*

2004—China—Most abundant sauropod of the Jurassic
Some 20 skeletons of *Shunosaurus lii* were found, 10 of which died together in a natural disaster. See more: *Xia et al. 1983; Upchurch et al. 2004*

2007—Antarctica—Last country in which a sauropodomorph was named
Glacialisaurus hammeri was similar to *Lufengosaurus huenei,* from Asia, although the two were found thousands of kilometers apart. See more: *Smith & Pol 2007*

2007—Switzerland—Largest sauropodomorph deposit
After finding 300 bones of *Plateosaurus longiceps* in a streambed, scientists discovered that the deposit extended for 1.5 km. See more: *Sander 2007*

2007—Argentina—First sauropod found underwater
Remains of *Andesaurus delgadoi* were found by Alejandro Delgado while scuba diving at the Ezequiel Ramos Mejía Reservoir. They were extracted when the water level dropped. See more: *Sander 2007*

2007—New York, USA—First sauropod skeleton mounted on two legs
The 24-m-long skeleton of "Gordo," a *Barosaurus lentus* (AMNH 6341), was unveiled in the lobby of the American Museum of Natural History in New York. The fossils had been forgotten in storage for 40 years at the Royal Ontario Museum in Toronto. Its posture caused quite a stir, including much controversy. The reconstruction was accompanied by a calf (actually *Kaatedocus siberi*) and an *Allosaurus.*

See more: *McInstosh 2005; Tschop et al. 2015*

2007—Some sauropodomorphs identified as obligate bipeds
Several bipedal sauropodomorphs were mistakenly believed to be quadrupeds, or at least able to walk on four legs, but an anatomical study demonstrated that the palms of their forefeet pointed inward, making this form of locomotion impossible for the animal. Thus, it showed that *Lufengosaurus, Massospondylus, Plateosaurus, Yunnanosaurus,* and their close relatives could only have walked on two legs. See more: *Bonnan & Senter 2007; Paul 2010*

2008—Thailand—Country with the most recent sauropodomorph find
Before this discovery, only sauropods had been discovered in Thailand. This animal, similar *to Plateosaurus,* was reported but has not yet been formally described. See more: *Buffetaut et al. 2008*

2009—First morphotype classification of osteoderms
After analyzing the shape of osteoderms, the cylindrical, ellipsoid, mosaic, and keeled morphotypes were created. See more: *D'Emic et al. 2009*

2010—Tanzania—Highest temperature estimated for a sauropod
Isotopic analysis determined that *Giraffatitan brancai* had a body temperature of 100.8° Fahrenheit (38°C), suggesting it was warm-blooded. However, other authors estimate that dinosaurs had a lower body temperature. See more: *Eagle et al. 2010; Grady et al. 2014*

2013—England—Highest price paid for a sauropod at auction
"Misty," a *Diplodocus* fossil 17 m long, was found in Wyoming and sold for US$639,000 at Summers Place Auctions, although it had been expected to go for US$966,000. It was found by Benjamin and Jacob, the sons of paleontologist Raimund Albersdoerfer

2015—China, Spain—Highest estimated temperature of sauropod eggs
Isotope analysis of titanosaur oolites from Argentina, China, Spain, France, and Mongolia determined that the average sauropod egg temperature was 36–38°C. Some anomalous cases recorded for Coll de Nargó (Spain) and Nanxiong Basin (China) had estimated temperatures of 55–65°C, owing to diagenesis (chemical and physical alteration of sediments). See more: *Eagle et al. 2015*

2015—Colombia—Country with the most recently named sauropod
Padillasaurus leivaensis was named in honor of Carlos Bernardo Padilla, who founded the Paleontology Research Center at Villa de Leyva. See more: *Carballido et al. 2015*

2018—Bulgaria—Country with the most recent sauropod discovery
Specimen K21586 consists of a broken titanosaur bone. See more: *Nikolov et al. 2018*

POPULAR AND FORMAL

Because *Apatosaurus* and *Brontosaurus* were apparently synonymous, in films and cartoons from 1903 to 2015 sauropods were often portrayed as one or the other of these two genera, although the animal referred to is usually *B. excelsus*, so readers are urged to exercise caution with records presented as *Apatosaurus.*

SCULPTURES OF PRIMITIVE SAUROPODOMORPHS AND SAUROPODS

1905—USA—First replica donated to other museums
Diplodocus carnegii became one of the most famous dinosaur replicas, thanks to donations from Andrew Carnegie that enabled plaster copies of the original model in the Pittsburgh Museum to be given to museums in Germany, Argentina, Austria, Chicago (USA), Spain, England, Italy, Mexico, and Russia between 1905 and 1932. See more: *Bakker 1986*

1907—Germany—First sauropod sculpture to be exhibited
A statue of *Brontosaurus* was created at the Carl Hagenbeck Zoo in Hamburg. See more: *Lambert 1990*

1933—Illinois, USA—First popular sauropod figure
A hollow *Brontosaurus* figure made of painted metal was created by the Messemore & Damon company for a display at the Chicago (1933) and New York (1939) world's fairs. See more: *www.dinosaurcollectorsitea.com/messermoreDamon.html (Accessed December 31, 2018)*

1949—USA—First plastic sauropod toy
The Ajax Plastic company produced two models of *Brontosaurus*, one with the head looking backward, the other with the neck lowered. See more: *Cain & Fredericks 1999*

Museum skeletons do not always reflect the precise dimensions of the animal when it was alive.

Most dinosaurs are known only from a few broken bones or incomplete skeletons, so complete reconstructions require a degree of speculation about the possible size and sometimes may distort the true appearance of these animals when they were alive. Fortunately, new discoveries help museums to show us increasingly authentic skeletons.

1945—Mexico—First fraudulent sauropod sculptures
The Acámbaro figures of Guanajuato state are fraudulent pieces that were claimed to be from the preclassical Chupícuaro culture (800 B.C.–A.D. 200). In 1972 it was discovered they were of recent manufacture. A similar and more famous hoax was perpetrated with the Inca stones of Peru. See more: *Pezatti 2005*

1955—USA—First plastic scale model of a sauropod
A 1:30 replica of *Brontosaurus* was manufactured by toymaker Louis Marx and Company. See more: *Cain & Fredericks 1999*

1958—Germany, Austria—Oldest cereal-box sauropod figure
A *Brontosaurus* figurine was included inside boxes of Shreddies, manufactured by the Nabisco company. See more: *www.dinosaurcollectorsitea.com/Schredies.htm*

1966—Peru—First falsified recordings of sauropods
Copies of some classic dinosaur illustrations with anatomical errors widely credited at the time were engraved on stones to be sold to unsuspecting tourists as supposedly authentic relics. See more: *Paris 1998*

1981—California, USA—Largest steel and concrete sauropod sculpture
The steel and concrete sculpture of "Dinny," an *Apatosaurus* 46 m long, 14 m tall, and more than 100 t in weight, was built in the town of Cabazon. The sculpture has a hollow segment that allows visitors to explore inside, and the attraction includes a souvenir shop.

1987—Hong Kong—First articulated sauropod toy
Diplodocus was introduced to Tyco's Dino-Riders collection. See more: *Cain & Fredericks 1999*

2000—Argentina—Largest replica of a described sauropod skeleton
The municipal museum of Carmen Funes exhibited a skeleton of *Argentinosaurus huinculensis* 39.7 m long and 7.3 m tall. An exact copy has existed in Germany since 2009. The original skeleton was rather incomplete, so the sculpture was based on estimations from other sauropods. See more: *Haines & Chambers 2006; Sellers et al. 2013*

2012—Spain—Largest sauropod model
In order to attract tourists, the town of Fuentes de Magaña built a plastic sculpture of *Apatosaurus* 32 m long, 8 m high, and some 3 t in weight. It was created by sculptor Logroño Ricardo González and six assistants with a budget of €59,000 and took five months to complete. See more: *http://www.abc.es*

2015—New York, USA—Largest replica of an undescribed sauropod skeleton
The American Museum of Natural History unveiled a sauropod skeleton 37.2 m long. The species, *Patagotitan mayorum*, had not yet been described at the time

2017—Argentina—Largest sauropod resin sculpture
A metal and resin sculpture of a dinosaur 40 m long, 12 m tall, and weighing 15 t was created in Trelew, Chubut province, representing the giant titanosaur *Patagotitan mayorum*.

Countries with reconstructed primitive sauropodomorph skeletons:
Argentina, Australia, China, France, Germany, South Africa, Switzerland, USA, and Zimbabwe

Countries with museums housing reconstructed sauropod skeletons:
Argentina, Australia, Brazil, Canada, China, England, France, Germany, Italy, Morocco, Mexico, Poland, Russia, Spain, Sweden, USA, and Zimbabwe

SAUROPODOMORPHS AND SAUROPODS IN LITERATURE

~1776—Cameroon, Congo, Gabon, Central African Republic—Most popular myth of a living sauropod
Mokèle-mbèmbé ("the one who stops the river"), Amali, Badigui, and Nyamala are some names given to supposedly living dinosaurs reported in Africa. Of all the fabricated reports about living dinosaurs, *Mokèle-mbèmbé* has been the most widespread, perhaps because it has been linked to ancient legends of the Pygmy tribes and mistaken interpretations of markings left by crocodiles, hippopotamuses, and rhinoceroses. The creature supposedly eats plants but does not spurn human or hippopotamus flesh. It is described as an enormous animal that drags its tail on the ground, although those who claim to have seen it have offered different descriptions. See more: *Bonaventure-Poyart 1776; Andersson 1934; Sjogren 1980; Mackal 1987*

1884—USA—First sauropod named but never illustrated
Diplodocus lacustris is a doubtful species. Its small size suggests that it was a juvenile of some other known species. See more: *Marsh 1884*

1912—USA—First poem dedicated to a sauropod
The verse was composed by *Chicago Tribune* columnist Bert Leston Taylor (See more: *Wilford 1975*):

> Behold the mighty dinosaur,
> Famous in prehistoric lore,
> Not only for his weight and length,
> But for his intellectual strength.
> You will observe by these remains,
> The creature had two sets of brains,
> The one in his head, the usual place,
> The other at his spinal base.
> Thus he could reason a priori
> As well as a posteriori.
> No problem bothered him a bit,
> He made both head and tail of it.
> So wise he was
> So wise and solemn
> Each thought filled just a spinal column,
> If one brain found the pressure strong,
> It passed a few ideas along.
> If something slipped the forward mind,
> 'Twas rescued by the one behind.
> And if in error he was caught
> He had a saving afterthought.
> As he thought twice before he spoke.
> He had no judgment to revoke.
> For he could think without congestion.
> Upon both sides of every question.
> O gaze upon this noble beast,
> Defunct ten million years at least.

1939—New Guinea—First crytpozoological fraud involving a sauropod
The so-called "Rau" (or "Row") was an animal thought up by Charles Miller and his wife that allegedly had the head of *Protoceratops*, osteoderms of *Stegosaurus*, and a *Diplodocus* body. It was also apparently aquatic. The fraud was uncovered by one of the founders of cryptozoology, Bernard Heuvelmans. See more: *Miller 1939, 1941; Heuvelmans 1995, 2003*

1954—USA—First heroic sauropod
The Genial Dinosaur by John Russell Fearn—also known by his pseudonym Volsted Gridban—featured a sauropod with *Stegosaurus* osteoderms (armored plates and thagomizer) that saves humankind when aliens from Venus attack. See more: *Fearn 2012*

Most famous living sauropod myth

Mokèle-mbèmbé is one of several dinosaurs that have supposedly been seen alive in some parts of the world. Of course, many of these sightings have been proven false. In all cases involving a sighting of a living non-avian dinosaur, the evidence has turned out to be extremely weak, falsified, or indirect enough that it could have been produced by other animals, and the witnesses were non-scientists

1959—USA—First novel featuring sauropod parasites
The novel *Poor Little Warrior* is about a hunter who kills a sauropod, then is killed in turn by its enormous lice. See more: *Aldiss 1959; Sanz 1999*

1984—USA—First sauropod "Transformer"
Issue 4 of the comic *Transformers: The Last Stand* introduces dinobots, one of which is a *Brontosaurus* called Sludge. See more: *Furman 2008*

1991—USA—A sauropod recovers its name
In *Bully for Brontosaurus: Reflections in Natural History*, written by paleontologist and writer Stephen Jay Gould, the author declares himself a "Brontophile," admitting his preference for the name *Brontosaurus* over *Apatosaurus*. He died 13 years before the two were separated into distinct genera. See more: *Gould 1991; Tschopp et al. 2015*

1993—USA—First novel involving a sauropod in a three-legged posture
In the novel *Tyrannosaur*, by David Drake, a titanosaur adopts a tripedal posture. See more: *Drake 1993; Sanz 1999*

ILLUSTRATIONS AND PHOTOS OF SAUROPODOMORPHS AND SAUROPODS

1699—England—First illustration of a sauropod tooth
Naturalist Edward Lhuyd illustrated a tooth that was named "Rutellum implicatum." See more: *Lhuyd 1699; Delair & Sarjeant 2002*

18th century—Portugal—First illustration of sauropod footprints
A painted mural featured the footprints that gave rise to the legend of Our Lady of Pedra da Mua, which says that these tracks were left by an enormous mule that the Virgin Mary rode along the cliff at the shrine of Nossa Senhora do Cabo Espichel. See more: *Antunes 1976; Sanz 2000, 2003; Santos & Rodrigues 2008; Pérez-Lorente 2015*

1877—Colorado, USA—First illustration of a sauropod skeleton
Several bones of *Camarasaurus supremus* found by Oramel W. Lucas were used by paleontologist Edward Drinker Cope to create a preliminary reconstruction. It wasn't until 1925 that a complete skeleton, of a juvenile individual, was found. See more: *Cope 1877; Gilmore 1925*

1878—USA—First illustration of a living sauropod
Paleontologist Edward Drinker Cope's early illustrations include one of *Amphicoelias* as an animal with short forelimbs and long hind limbs that looked more like a bipedal sauropodomorph than a sauropod. See more: *Cope 1878*

1883—USA—First illustration of the most famous sauropod skeleton
Brontosaurus excelsus was represented with plantigrade feet and a shorter neck, torso, and tail, as the total number of its vertebrae was not known at the time. Eight years later, it was updated with more precise details, including a skull that was found to be that of a possible *Brachiosaurus* sp. YPM 1911. See more: *Marsh 1883, 1891; Taylor 2010; Taylor**

1884—Colorado, USA—"Largest" bone illustrated
The incomplete femur of *Amphicoelias fragillimus* (now *Maraapunisaurus fragillimus*) was reconstructed in two versions: one assuming it was comparable to *Amphicoelias altus*, with the bone approxi-

mately 3 m long, and one comparable to a caiman, at around 2 m. Today the femur is estimated to have been close to 3 m in length. See more: *Gould 1884; Woodruff & Foster 2014; Carpenter 2018*

1886—France—First scale drawing of a sauropod
An *Atlantosaurus immanis* was illustrated to scale by Camille Flammarion and compared to an African elephant in the book Earth Before Man. It looks somewhat like an iguana. See more: *Flammarion 1886*

1892—USA—First sauropods illustrated in a best-selling book
Brontosaurus was reconstructed as it appeared in life by Joseph Smit, while its skeleton, a femur of *Atlantosaurus*, and a skull of *Diplodocus* also appeared in the book, based on illustrations by paleontologist Othniel Charles Marsh. See more: *Neville 1892*

1892—Germany—First cards featuring sauropods
The company Liebig Continental Trading Cards created Prehistoric Animals in Different Ages cigarette cards, including one of *Brontosaurus*. See more: *Moore 2014*

1893—USA—First illustration of a sauropodomorph skeleton
This illustration of an *Anchisaurus colurus* (now *A. polyzelus*) skeleton is similar to current ones. See more: *Marsh 1893; Paul 2010*

1894—England—First illustration portraying a living sauropodomorph
Dutch illustrator Joseph Smit reconstructed an *Anchisaurus* in the book *Creatures of Other Days*, based on the skeleton reconstructed by Marsh. See more: *Hutchinson 1894*

1897—USA—First painting depicting living sauropods
Brontosaurus and *Diplodocus* were reconstructed by Charles R. Knight. The posture the artist proposed for *Brontosaurus* has become classic since then and has been used in other illustrations and even sculptures. See more: *Paul 1996*

1899—Spain—Sauropod illustrated as an ornithopod
The newspaper *Alrededores del Mundo* featured a reconstruction of *Diplodocus* that resembled a hadrosaurid. It was an estimated 20 t in weight and 6 m tall. See more: *Anonymous 1899*

1905—USA—First illustration of a sauropod gastrolith
The cartoon strip *Dreams of the Rarebit Fiend* by Winsor McCay features a sauropod ingesting stones. See more: *Dover 1973*

1907—USA—First illustration of a sauropod being eaten by a theropod
An illustration showing the remains of a *Brontosaurus* tail being devoured by an *Allosaurus* was created by Charles R. Knight for *Scientific American* magazine. See more: *Paul 1996*

1910—USA—First illustration of a sauropod in sprawling posture
Mary Mason illustrated two *Diplodocus* individuals dragging their bellies on the ground with legs dislocated like a lizard's for the journal *Proceedings of the Washington Academy of Sciences*. See more: *Hay 1910*

1927—Russia—First illustration of a sauropod to include a human for scale
The skeleton of *Brontosaurus excelsus* AMNH 460 was compared to that of a human in the first edition of the Soviet encyclopedia *Bolshaya soviétskaya entsiklopédiya*, published from 1926 to 1947. See more: *Schmidt 1927*

1929—California, USA—First rock art paintings in North America mistakenly interpreted as depicting sauropods
Havasupai Canyon contains some whimsical figures that some people interpret as sauropod dinosaurs, although that requires a stretch of the imagination, not to mention that they have the wrong proportions. See more: *Hubbard 1924; Senter 2012*

1929—Argentina—First sauropod skeleton illustrated in silhouette
Neuquensaurus australis (formerly *Titanosaurus*) was illustrated by German paleontologist Friedrich von Huene. See more: *Huene 1929*

1935—USA—First Cinderella stamps featuring a sauropod
The Sinclair Oil Corporation issued stamps with a logo featuring *Brontosaurus excelsus.* See more: *http://www.paleophilatelie.eu/ (Accessed December 31, 2018)*

1935—USA—First stamp album with sauropods
The Sinclair Oil Corporation released a stamp album of extinct animals, including a *Brontosaurus excelsus. Camarasaurus* was included in 1938. See more: *Moore 2014*

1947—USA—Largest mural featuring sauropods
The mural *The Age of Reptiles* by artist Rudolph Franz Zallinger (made from 1943 to 1947) features two *Brontosaurus excelsus*: one on land and the other in a swamp. The mural is almost 34 m long and 4.9 m high. See more: *Volpe 2001*

1947—USA—Largest mural with sauropodomorphs
Two plateosaurs are shown eating plants in the mural *The Age of Reptiles* by artist Rudolph Franz Zallinger. See more: *Volpe 2001*

Sauropods with very flexible necks

Popular illustrations often depict dinosaurs with snake-like necks. Actually, sauropod necks had relatively limited flexibility, like those of giraffes, as they had rigid ribs that kept them from bending when they were at rest.

1958—China—First postage stamp featuring a sauropodomorph
A postage stamp designed by Wu Jiankun shows a living *Lufengosaurus huenei*, along with a complete skeleton. See more: *Dodson et al. 1993*

1965—Poland—First postage stamps to feature sauropods
These collectible stamps created by A. Heindrich include one of *Brontosaurus excelsus* and another of *Giraffatitan brancai* (formerly *Brachiosaurus*), based on reconstructions by illustrator Zdenek Burian. See more: *http://www.paleophilatelie.eu/ (Accessed December 31, 2018)*

1966—Democratic Republic of the Congo—First mistaken photograph of a sauropod
Photographer Yvan Ridel took a photo of an enormous footprint in a swamp sometime in August or September 1966. As he did not know what had made the print, he attributed it to the mythological sauropod *Mokèle-mbèmbé*. The print was unlike that of a hippopotamus, as it had three toes instead of four, and the toes were pointed rather than rounded, as in elephants; however, the description is coherent with the type of print left by a rhinoceros. Furthermore, it does not look like a sauropod print. See more: *Mackal 1987*

1968—USA—First illustration showing a sauropod not dragging its tail
Researchers believed that sauropod tails floated in the water or were dragged along the ground; however, a series of anatomical analyses proposed that they did not actually touch the ground. This sketch showed two *Barosaurus lentus*, previously considered aquatic, walking on dry land. See more: *Bakker 1968, 1971; Anonymous 1971*

1968—Chile—First professional illustration of a sauropod footprint
Iguanodonichnus frenkii (now *Parabrontopodus*) were considered possible ornithopod footprints apparently produced by a bipedal animal, but 24 years later they were recognized as sauropod prints by several authors. See more: *Casamiquela & Fasola 1968; Dos Santos et al. 1992; Farlow 1992; Sarjeant et al. 1998; Moreno & Pino 2002; Rubilar-Rogers 2003; Moreno & Benton 2005*

1968—Chile—First photograph of a sauropod print in a formal scientific publication
Iguanodonichnus frenkii found in Chile, was believed to be an ornithopod print but is now considered a diplodocoid sauropod from the icthnogenus *Parabrontopodus. Breviparopus taghbaloutensis* was the first print that was recognized as that of a sauropod. It was published and presented in photographs in 1980 (present-day Morocco). See more: *Casamiquela & Fasola 1968; Dutuit & Ouazzou 1980*

1987—Iraq—First painting in Asia mistakenly interpreted as depicting sauropods
The Ishtar Gate, a segment of an interior mural created in Babylonia around 600 B.C., features several images of a "sirrush," a dragon-like creature with the head and neck of a snake and the body of a lion. The figures were discovered in 1902 and 85 years later were described as sauropods, which is highly doubtful, unless they were based on fossil skeletons. See more: *Koldewey 1902; Mackal 1987; Coleman 2007*

1987—Zimbabwe—First mistaken interpretation of rock art paintings in Africa featuring sauropods
Some rock paintings found in a series of grottoes depict animals typical of the region, including some simple shapes that some people have interpreted as sauropods. Given the short neck, curved trunk, and overall proportions, however, it is apparent they are monitor lizards. See more: *Clark 1959; Mackal 1987; Senter 2012*

1989—USA—First controversy over sauropod postage stamps
A major dispute arose when the US Postal Service launched a series of four "dinosaur" stamps, including one named *Brontosaurus*, instead of *Apatosaurus*, its official name at the time. The complaint argued that the use of the incorrect name encouraged scientific ignorance; it also challenged the collection's inclusion of *Pteranodon*, which is a pterosaur and not a dinosaur. See more: *Anonymous 1989*

1993—Democratic Republic of the Congo—First mistaken photograph of a sauropod
The photograph, which shows a strange shape at Télé Lake that supposedly belonged to the mythical *Mokèle-mbèmbé*, is doubtful. See more: *Nugent 1933*

1993—USA—Sauropod vertebral engineering compared to that of a suspension bridge
Sauropod mechanics were compared to that of suspension bridges. See more: *Lambert 1993*

2016—USA—Book with the most primitive sauropodomorph skeletal reconstructions
The second edition of *The Princeton Field Guide to Dinosaurs* by Gregory Paul includes 17 reconstructions of different sauropodomorph species. In the book, Eoraptor appears similar to a theropod. See more: *Paul 2016*

2016—USA—Book with the most sauropod skeletal reconstructions
The second edition of *The Princeton Field Guide to Dinosaurs* by Gregory Paul includes more than 40 reconstructions of different sauropod species. See more: *Paul 2016*

SAUROPODS AND SAUROPODOMOPHS IN THE MOVIES

1914—USA—First animated film featuring a sauropod shown in a cinema
The first animated film with the *Diplodocus* "Gertie" was created by Winsor McCay and lasted five minutes. However, it was so popular it was expanded to twelve minutes to be screened in a cinema. See more: *Canemaker 2005*

1915—USA—First film in which a sauropod kills a human
The silent film *The Dinosaur and the Missing Link: A Prehistoric Tragedy* was animated by Willis O'Brien. In the film, a sauropod kills a hominid similar to *Australopithecus*, and a cave man takes credit for the killing to win the heart of a woman. Some sources date it to 1917, the date of its premiere. See more: *Merkl 2015*

1915—USA—First film featuring a domesticated sauropod
The Dinosaur and the Missing Link: A Prehistoric Tragedy features a sauropod pulling a cart driven by a cave man. See more: *Merkl 2015*

1919—USA—First dinosaur film with 3-D puppets
Animator Tony Sarg used cutout silhouettes in the film *Adam Raises Cain* to represent a sauropod that cares for and entertains a small child. See more: *Bendazzi 2015*

1925—USA—First film portraying a fight between a sauropod and a theropod
The Lost World, directed by Harry O. Hoyt with animated special effects by Willis O'Brien, shows a fight between an *Allosaurus* and a *Brontosaurus*. See more: *Glut & Brett-Surman 1997*

1925—USA—First film with a sauropod skeleton
The Lost World includes a montage of a *Brontosaurus* skeleton. See more: *Moore 2014*

1925—USA—First dinosaur film character to cause panic in a city
In the film *The Lost World*, a *Brontosaurus* causes panic in the streets of London. See more: *Glut & Brett-Surman 1997*

1933—USA—First sound film involving sauropods
A carnivorous sauropod appears in the movie *King Kong*. See more: *Cooper & Schoedsack 1933; Pettigrew 1999*

1935—USA—First animated film with a sauropod skeleton
The first scene of the animated short *Buddy's Lost World*, by Jack King, includes a *Brontosaurus* skeleton. It was a Looney Tunes film produced by Warner Brothers. See more: *Maltin 1980*

1939—USA—First animated film with talking sauropods
Daffy Duck and the Dinosaur, by Chuck Jones, was part of the Merry Melodies series. In the film, the *Apatosaurus* Fido goes duck hunting with the caveman Casper. See more: *Jones 1939*

1940—USA—First animated film featuring a sauropodomorph
In "The Rite of Spring," part IV of the film *Fantasia*, a group of *Plateosaurus* individuals digs for clams. See more: *Culhane 1999*

1940—USA—First animated color film featuring sauropodomorphs
The first animated *Plateosaurus* appeared in color in the film *Fantasia*. The creatures were two-toned, with a light-colored belly. See more: *Culhane 1999*

1940—USA—First animated film with sauropods in color
Several animated *Apatosarus* and *Diplodocus* were depicted in brown, gray, and purple in the film *Fantasia*. See more: *Culhane 1999*

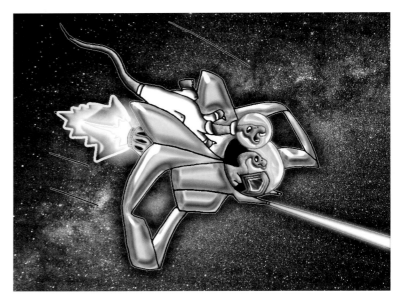

Galactic vertebrae

David Hobbins and Russell G. Chong designed the Umbaran battleships for the *Star Wars* film *The Clone Wars* based on the cervical vertebrae of *Apatosaurus*.

1951—USA—First film with an island-dwelling sauropod
The film *Lost Continent*, directed by Sam Newfield, features bulletproof *Brontosaurus* individuals that attack people. See more: *Berry 2005*

1975—Japan—First sauropod name given to a monster
In the film *Terror of Mechagodzilla*, an aquatic creature that fights Godzilla was called *Titanosaurus*. The monster is more like a theropod, however, with a long neck and adaptations for swimming. See more: *Barr 2016*

1998—USA—Most successful animated film with a sauropod protagonist
The Land Before Time was produced by Don Bluth. It earned more than US$48 million when it premiered and more than US$84 million worldwide. See more: *http://www.boxofficemojo.com/movies/?id=landbeforetime. htm (Accessed December 31, 2018)*

1998—USA—Most award-winning animated film featuring a sauropod
The Land Before Time was nominated for Best Family Animation or Fantasy Motion Picture at the 10th Young Artist's Awards and Best Fantasy Film at the 16th annual Saturn Awards in 1990. See more: *http:// youngartistawards.org/pastnoms10.htm (Accessed December 31, 2018*

1998—USA—Most critically acclaimed animated film with a sauropod protagonist
The Land Before Time (written by Judy Freudberg and Tony Geiss and directed by Don Bluth, achieved the highest scores from critics, reaching 6.5 on Filmaffinity, 7.4 on IMDb, and 71% on Rotten Tomatoes' tomatometer, with an Audience Score of 78%. See more: *https://www.filmaffinity.com/us/main.html; https:// www.imdb.com/; https://www.rottentomatoes.com/ (Accessed December 31, 2018)*

SAUROPODOMORPHS AND SAUROPODS IN THE THEATER, ON TELEVISION, AND IN OTHER MEDIA

1914—USA—First cartoon sauropod
Winsor McCay presented "Gertie," a charismatic *Diplodocus*, in a five-minute keyframe animation film. See more: *Canemaker 2005*

1914—USA—First animated sauropod to appear with real humans
Animator Winsor McCay appears in a scene with "Gertie," ordering her to do circus tricks. See more: *Canemaker 2005*

1915—USA—First plagiarized sauropod animation
Another "Gertie" cartoon was fraudulently presented as having been produced by Winsor McCay. Bray Productions was suspected of having made it. See more: *Crafton 1982*

1921—USA—First abandoned animated film with a sauropod
A second animated "Gertie" short, tentatively named *Gertie on Tour*, was left unfinished, leaving only some sketches and short animated segments. See more: *Canemaker 2005*

1932—USA—First mechanical sauropod created for the cinema
A mechanized *Diplocodus* 15 m long appeared in a scene in which it ate some dancers. See more: *Rious 1932*

1956—USA—First documentary involving sauropods
The show *The Animal World* featured different species from the past and present, including a female *Apatosaurus* with her calves. See more: *Webber 2004*

1960—USA—Most famous invented sauropod meat dish
The TV series *The Flintstones,* by William Hanna and Joseph Barbera, popularized the Bronto Burger. See more: *Klossner 2006*

1960—USA—Longest-appearing sauropodomorph in a television series
"Dino," a "snorkasaurus" sauropodomorph, appears in 166 episodes, specials, feature films, and other spinoffs of *The Flintstones*, one of the most popular TV series of all time. See more: *Klossner 2006*

1960—USA—Most popular fictitious sauropodomorph
"Dino" is a pet dinosaur of the "snorkosaurus" species that appeared in the animated TV series *The Flintstones*. He appears in episode 18, "The Snorkasaurus Hunter," as a blue creature that was intelligent and could also speak, in contrast to the similar-looking pink Flintstones' pet that acted like a dog. The creature's name is revealed in chapter 4, entitled "No Help Wanted." See more: *Klossner 2006*

1962—USA—First offspring of two saurischian species in the media
"Snorky" seems to be a sauropod, although on the show the script says it had a *Tyrannosaurus* father and *Brontosaurus* mother. Bob Clampett's short film was shown on the *Beany and Cecil Show*. See more: *Narváez**

1967—Russia—First animated political film with a sauropodomorph
A blue sauropodomorph is the protagonist of *Gora Dinozavrov* ("Dinosaur Mountain") written by Arkadiy Snesarev and directed by Rasa Strautmane. In the film, hatchling dinosaurs are enclosed in their shells, which represent the oppressive, overprotective Soviet regime that prevents them from being free. See more: *Narváez**

1977—France—First series comparing the largest sauropods
In chapter 1, "Et la terre fût" (And Earth Was Created), of the animated series *Il était une fois … l'Homme* (Once Upon a Time … Man) by Albert Barillé, the sauropods *Apatosaurus*, *Diplodocus*, and *Giraffatitan* (formerly *Brachiosaurus*) enter the scene and take their places from third to first place. See more: *Klossner 2006*

1998—USA—First animated series with a sauropod protagonist
The *Apatosaurus* (*Brontosaurus*?) "Littlefoot" is the main character in the series *The Land Before Time*. See more: *Lenburg 2009*

1998—USA—Most famous animated sauropod
"Littlefoot," from the series *The Land Before Time*, is an *Apatosaurus* calf who has adventures accompanied by other young dinosaurs and a pterosaur in search of an oasis known as the "Great Valley." See more: *Lenburg 2009*

1998—USA—Most successful series with a sauropod protagonist
The Land Before Time franchise, produced by Don Bluth, released 13 direct-to-video films from 1988 to 2007 and a 14th in 2016. See more: *Lenburg 2009*

2011—Brazil—Sauropods in a TV series
The children's series *Morde & Assopra* ("Dinosaurs & Robots") was produced and broadcast by Rede Globo in the 7 p.m. time slot from March 21 to October 14, 2011. It was written by Walcyr Carrasco, Claudia Souto, and others and directed by Pedro Vasconcelos and collaborators. The protagonist is a paleontologist who studies sauropods and, at one point in the episode, exclaims "Don't get in the way of my titanosaur excavation!" See more: *Teledramaturgia.com.br (Accessed December 31, 2018)*

2011—USA—First spaceship designed with sauropod vertebrae
The design of the Umbaran Starfighters in the *Star Wars* animated series *The Clone Wars* was inspired by a vertebra of a *Diplodocus*, maybe an *Apatosaurus ajax*. Designer David Hobbins based the model on photos he took at an exhibition in California. The ships were 10.4 m long and 12.5 m high, and appeared in season 4, episode 7. On the other hand, the *Barosaurus lentus* YPM 429 vertebrae shaped like a spaceship was informally called "Astrolembospondylus." See more: *Taylor & Wedel**

2015—Sauropod with the most hits on the Internet
According to Google search engine, the term "Brontosaurus" has almost 4 million results, far more than any other sauropod, despite being considered invalid for being a synonym of *Apatosaurus*. See more: *www.google.com (Accessed December 31, 2018)*

2015—Sauropodomorph with the most hits on the Internet
According to Google, the term "Plateosaurus" obtains 280,000 results. See more: *www.google.com (Accessed December 31, 2018)*

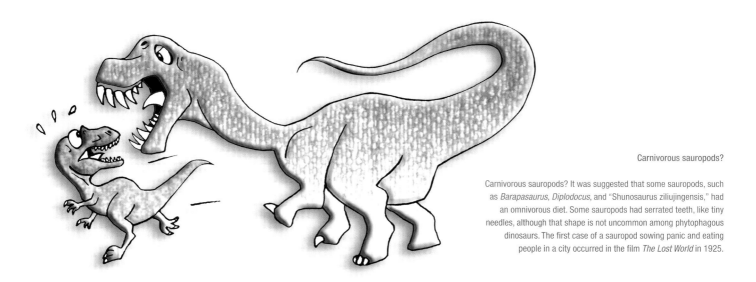

Carnivorous sauropods?

Carnivorous sauropods? It was suggested that some sauropods, such as *Barapasaurus*, *Diplodocus*, and "Shunosaurus ziliujingensis," had an omnivorous diet. Some sauropods had serrated teeth, like tiny needles, although that shape is not uncommon among phytophagous dinosaurs. The first case of a sauropod sowing panic and eating people in a city occurred in the film *The Lost World* in 1925.

SAUROPODOMORPHS AND SAUROPODS IN MUSIC

1990—England—First amateur singer with a sauropod name
Dan Booth, known as "Dan Diplo" or "Danny Diplo," gave some impromptu concerts at university before he formed the band Diplodocus Squad. See more: *https://www.diplo.co.uk*

1999—China—First professional singer with a sauropod name
The leader of the rock group Second Hand Rose is a singer known as Diplodocus. See more: *Narváez**

2003—USA—First DJ with a sauropod name
Thomas Wesley Pentz, best known as Diplodocus in 2003 and Diplo a year later, worked in musical genres such as EDM, moombahton, trap, dancehall, electro house, and hip-hop. His nickname derives from his fascination with *Diplodocus*. See more: *Narváez**

2005—USA—First album referring to dinosaur footprints
Fourth Grade Security Risk released the disc *Dinosaur Tracks* onto the market.

2005—USA—First song with the name of a sauropod
On its CD *Dinosaur Tracks*, Fourth Grade Security Risk included the song "For God's Sake," also known as "The Brontosaurus Song." The tune tells of how *Brontosaurus* was thought to be *Apatosaurus*, repeating the phrase "There was never a Brontosaurus."

2006—England—First European rock band named after a sauropod
Brontosaurus Chorus, consisting of vocalist Jodie Lowther and bassist Dominic Green, was active until 2011. See more: *https://www.discogs.com (Accessed December 31, 2018)*

2006—Louisiana, Massachusetts, USA—First North American rock band with a sauropod name
B for Brontosaurus was an Indie pop band that disbanded three years later. See more: *http://www.bfor-brontosaurus.com/ (Accessed December 31, 2018)*

2008—Massachusetts, USA—First song about fossil plants
The symphonic rock group Birdsongs of the Mesozoic recorded the song "Dawn of the Cycads." See more: *Strong 2003*

2009—USA—First music CD with a sauropod on the cover
The cover of B for Brontosaurus's EP *Home* includes a green *Brontosaurus*. See more: *http://www.bforbron-tosaurus.com/ (Accessed December 31, 2018)*

2009—Australia—First sauropod named after a song
Diamantinasaurus matildae is nicknamed Matilda, after the song "Waltzing Matilda." See more: *Hocknull et al. 2009*

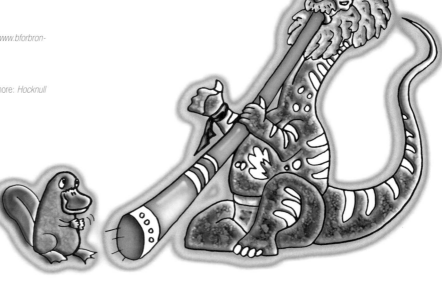

Folkloric dinosaur

The folkloric dinosaur *Diamantinasaurus matildae* was discovered in the Winton Formation, in Queensland, and nicknamed Matilda after the song "Waltzing Matilda," a traditional Australian song that has even been proposed as the national anthem.

OTHER CULTURAL RECORDS OF SAUROPODOMORPHS AND SAUROPODS

1879—USA—The most famous sauropod name
Although *Brontosaurus* became a synonym of *Apatosaurus* 24 years after being created, the name never lost its place in popular culture. It became a valid genus once again 112 years later and would never again be eclipsed by any other species. See more: *Marsh 1879; Riggs 1903; Tschopp, Mateus & Benson 2015*

1907—USA—Most famous rivalry between a sauropod and a theropod
It all began when a *Brontosaurus* vertebra was found with tooth marks of a theropod, seemingly an *Allosaurus fragilis*. The scene was reconstructed at the American Museum of Natural History in a display organized by Hermann and his assistants Falkenbach, Lang, and Schlosser. It inspired the animated film *The Lost World* (1925), which includes a battle between the two species, complete with magnificent special effects by Willis O'Brien. Renowned, award-winning illustrators Charles Knight, Rudolph Franz, and Rudolph Zallinger recreated the scene in their artworks. See more: *Beasley 1907; Glut & Brett-Surman 1997; Bakker 1998*

1916—USA—First company with a sauropod on its logo
The Sinclair Oil Corporation, founded by Harry F. Sinclair, used a green *Apatosaurus* as the company logo from 1916 to 1969. The logo was discontinued when the company was acquired by the Atlantic Richfield Company. See more: *Merkl 2015*

1918—Egypt, Iraq—Oldest objects on which sauropods were mistakenly identified
A cylindrical Mesopotamian seal discovered in 1969 in Iraq and the Narmer Palette, identified in 1898 in Hierakonpolis in Egypt, both approximately 3100–3300 years old, bear a similar image that some people have identified as a dinosaur, maybe a sauropod, while others believe it may have been an *Iguanodon*. The creature has the body of a dog and an extremely long, flexible neck, and represented the mythical creature Mushussu or Sirrush. See more: *Quilbell & Green 1902; Moortgart 1969; Mackal 1987*

1990—Chile—First asteroid named after a sauropod
On November 15, asteroid 9949 was discovered by E. W. Elst at La Silla Observatory and baptized *Brontosaurus*. Other asteroids discovered later were also given sauropod names, including 9954 (*Brachiosaurus*, April 8, 1991) and 58671 (*Diplodocus*, August 12, 1994). See more: *Minor planet center*

2002—USA—Most successful business with a sauropod corporate logo
Bronto Software is a marketing platform for online multichannel retailers that currently manages more than 1300 brands globally. It has more than 300 employees and on two occasions (2009 and 2010) won the prize for best Customer Service Department at the American Business Awards. It was also ranked one of the best workplaces by *Triangle Business Journal* in 2010, 2011, 2012, and 2014, has been a finalist for similar awards, and is also one of the fastest-growing companies in North America. See more: *Bronto Software 2012*

2004—Argentina—Wine with a sauropod on the logo
The wine Saurus Malbec, produced by Schroeder Winery, received a gold medal for quality. The image was used because a specimen of *Aeolosaurus rionegrinus* was found when one of the company's wineries was being built. The brand is a sponsor of the Saurus Cup, a tennis open held in Patagonia. See more: *Powell 1987*

2008—Binary prefix that uses the term "Bronto"
In the standardized IT measurement system, a byte (b) to the 10th power = 1 Kbyte (KB), since 210 bytes = 1,024, and the prefix kilo means 1000; 220 bytes (1048,576) make a megabyte, and so on, through gigabyte, terabyte, petabyte, exabyte, zettabyte, and yottabyte (280). For the next level, 290, the prefix Brontobyte (BB) has been suggested, equal to 1237,9400,3928,5380,2748,9912,4224,1027 bytes, although the term is not official.

2018—Iowa, USA—Tiniest sauropod form
Anatomist Nathan Swailes showed how some of the whimsical forms produced by organic tissue when viewed under a microscope can appear like dinosaurs. One such figure was similar to a toy *Diplodocus*. See more: *http://www.ihearthisto.com/tagged/Diplodocus (consultado el 31 de Diciembre de 2018)*

MYTH: Petroleum comes from dinosaurs

Actually, petroleum is formed from the decomposition of plankton (microscopic plants and animals), single-celled organisms that populate the oceans. However, it remains a popular idea that toy dinosaurs are made of a substance derived from dinosaurs themselves.

AUTHORS OF FORMAL PUBLICATIONS ABOUT SAUROPODOMORPHS

Authors Under the Microscope

The achievements and work of a dinosaur paleontologist are not measured by the quantity of dinosaurs they name throughout their career, but rather on their knowledge, based on investigation, reflection, experiments, and comparisons to present-day animals. The tendency to name incomplete or doubtful remains has gradually diminished over time, reducing the creation of problematic name proposals and unnecessary synonyms. There are more scientists today than at all other historical periods combined. See more: *Asimov 1979*

1699—England—First invalid sauropod name
A sauropod tooth was named "Rutellum implicatum" more for descriptive than taxonomical reasons, as it predates the Linnean system. The meaning of the name is unknown, but it may have come from someone named Rutell. See more: *Lhuyd 1699*

1841–1884—England—Paleontologist who named sauropods over the longest period
Richard Owen named sauropods for 43 years, from 1841 (*Cardiodon*) to 1884 (*Dinodocus mackesoni*). See more: *Owen 1841, 1884; Benton 2008*

1855—Germany—First invalid sauropodomorph name
Paleontologist Hermann von Meyer mentions the name "Riesensaurus" for some very large specimens of *Plateosaurus engelhardti*, the same species that he himself named 18 years before. See more: *Meyer 1855*

1899—USA—Paleontologist who has named the most sauropods
Othniel Charles Marsh named eight valid species: *Apatosaurus ajax, A. grandis* (now *Camarasaurus*), *Barosaurus lentus, Brontosaurus excelsus, Diplodocus longus, Morosaurus agilis, M. lentus* (now *Camarasaurus*), and *Pleurocoelus nanus;* five doubtful species: *Atlantosaurus immanis, Barosaurus affinis, Diplodocus lacustris, Pleurocoelus montanus,* and *Titanosaurus montanus;* and five synonyms: *Apatosaurus laticollis, Brontosaurus amplus, Morosaurus impar, M. robustus,* and *Pleurocoelus altus,* for a total of eighteen. See more: *Benton 2008*

1905–1932—Germany—Paleontologist who named sauropodomorphs for the longest period of time
Friedrich von Huene named sauropodomorphs from 1905 (*Plateosaurus erlenbergiensis*) to 1932 (*Pachysaurus giganteus, P. wetzelianus, P. fraasianus,* and the name change of *Yaleosaurus*), a period of 27 years, although he also unintentionally created "Pachysaurops" by mistakenly referring to *Pachysaurus* (*Pachysauriscus*) by that name, increasing his naming period to 56 years. See more: *Huene 1905, 1932, 1961; Benton 2008*

1932—Germany—Paleontologist who has named the most sauropodomorphs
Friedrich von Huene named a currently valid species, *Sellosaurus gracilis* (now *Plateosaurus*) and 11 possible synonyms — *Gresslyosaurus robustus, Pachysaurus ajax, P. giganteus, P. magnus, Plateosaurus erlenbergiensis, P. fraasianus, P. ornatus P. quenstedti, P. reinigeri, Sellosaurus fraasi,* and *Teratosaurus trossingensis.* See more: *Huene 1905, 1908, 1932*

1932—USA—Paleontologist who has named the most sauropod species
Friedrich von Huene made three name changes: *Cetiosauriscus leedsii* (Woodward 1905) Huene 1927, *Macrurosaurus platypus* (Seeley 1871) Huene 1932, and *Magyarosaurus dacus* (Nopcsa 1915) Huene 1932. See more: *Huene 1927, 1932*

1932—Germany—Paleontologist who has renamed the most sauropodomorph species
Friedrich von Huene made seven such name changes: *Plateosaurus poligniensis* (Pidancet & Chopard 1862) Huene 1932, *Plateosaurus cullingworthi* (Haughton 1924) Huene 1932, *Plateosaurus plieningeri* (Huene 1907-08), *Plateosaurus quenstedti* (Koken 1900) Huene 1932, *Plateosaurus reiningeri* (Huene 1905) Huene 1932, *Plateosaurus robustus* (Huene 1908) Huene 1932, and *Yaleosaurus colurus* (Marsh 1891) Huene 1932. See more: *Huene 1927, 1932; Weishampel & Chapman 1990*

1972—France, Lesotho—Paleontologist who has named the most sauropodomorph prints
Paul Ellenberger created several species, including these that may belong to sauropodomorphs: *Cridotrisauropus cruentus, C. unguiferus, Kalosauropus masitisii, K. pollex* (var. minor, minusculus, and victor), *Pseudotetrasauropus actunguis, P. bipedoida, P. jaquesi* (now *Lavinipes*), *P. mekalingensis, Senqutrisauropus priscus, Tetrasauropus unguiferus, Trisauropodiscus aviforma* (var. columba, merula, passer, and turtur), *T. galliforma, T. levis, T. phasianiforma, T. popompoi, T. superaviforma, T. superavipes,* and *Trichristolophus dubius.* See more: *Ellenberger 1965, 1970, 1972*

1985—China—Paleontologist who has named the most invalid sauropods
X. Zhao named *Chinshakiangosaurus zhongheensis* (now *C. chunghoensis*), "Damalasarus laticostalis," "D. magnus," "Kumingosaurus utingensis" ("K. utingi" or "K. wudingi"), *Lancangosaurus* (with numerous variants, "Lancanjiangosaurus," "Lancangjiangosaurus," "Lancanjiangosaurus," "Lancanjiangosaurus," or "Lanchangjiangosaurus"), "Megacervixosaurus tibetensis," and "Microdontosaurus dayensis." "Oshanosaurus youngi" was considered a sauropod; however, it could be *Eshanosaurus deguchianus,* a probable sauropodomorph or a therizinosaur theropod. See more: *Zhao 1983, 1985; Dong 1992; Xu et al. 2001; Barrett 2009; Mortimer**

1986—China—First sauropod named by an anonymous author
"Shunosaurus ziliujingensis," from the Lower Jurassic, was mentioned as a carnivore, unlike the previous *S. lii,* as the former has denticles on its teeth; however, this feature is found in several phytophagous sauropods. See more: *Anonymous 1986*

2006–2007—China, Italy—Paleontologists most honored in sauropod names
Paleontologists Dong Zhiming and Giancarlo Ligabue have each had two sauropods named after them: *Dashanpusaurus dongi* and *Dongbeititan dongi* for the former, and *Agustia ligabuei* (now *Agustinia*) and *Ligabuesaurus leanzai* for the latter. See more: *Peng et al. 2005; Bonaparte 1999, Bonaparte et al. 2006; Wang et al. 2007*

2007—China—Paleontologist most honored in sauropodomorph names
Paleontologist Chung-Chien Young has had three sauropodomorphs named after him: *Fulengia youngi, Yimenosaurus youngi,* and *Yunnanosaurus youngi.* See more: *Carroll & Galton 1977; Bai et al. 1990; Lu et al. 2007*

2014—India—Paleontologist who has named the most sauropod eggs
Ashu Khoslaha and his team have named eight species of oolites: *Fusioolithus berthei, Megaloolithus baghensis* (now *Fusioolithus*), *M. cylindricus, M. dholiyaensis, M. jabalpurensis, M. mohabeyi, M. padiyalensis,* and *M. walpurensis.* See more: *Khosla & Sahni 1995; Fernández & Khosla 2014*

2015—China, USA—Paleontologist who has named the most sauropod footprints
Martin G. Lockley participated in the creation of *Barrancapus cresapi, Brontopodus pentadactylus, Eosauropus cimarronensis, Liujianpus shunan,* and *Parabrontopodus mcintoshi* with different investigative teams. See more: *Hunt et al. 1993; Lockley et al. 1994, 2006; Kim & Lockley 2012; Xing et al. 2015*

ADDITIONAL AUTHORS INVOLVED IN THE DESCRIPTION AND NOMINATION OF SAUROPODOMORPH AND SAUROPOD SPECIES

Sauropodomorphs

First sauropodomorph named by one author
Plateosaurus engelhardti Meyer 1837

First sauropodomorph named by two authors
Thecodontosaurus antiquus Riley & Stutchbury 1836; Morris 1843

First sauropodomorph named by three authors
Yimenosaurus youngi Bai, Yang & Wang 1990

First sauropodomorph named by four authors
Eoraptor lunensis Sereno, Forster, Rogers & Monetta 1993

First sauropodomorph named by five authors
Aardonyx celestae Yates, Bonnan, Neveling, Chinsamy & Blackbeard 2009

First sauropodomorph named by seven authors
Yunnanosaurus youngi Lu, Li, Zhong, Azuma, Fujita, Dong & Ji 2007

First sauropodomorph named by twelve authors
Buriolestes schultzi Cabreira, Armin-Kellner, Dias-Da-Silva, Da Silva, Bronzati, de Almeida-Marsola, Temp-Muller, de Souza-Bittencourt, Batista, Raugust, Carrilho, Brodt & Cardoso-Langer 2016

Sauropodomorph footprints

First primitive sauropodomoroh footprint named by a single author
Otozoum moodii *Hitchcock 1847*

First primitive sauropodomorph footprint named by two authors
Evazoum sirigui *Nicosia & Loi 2003*

First primitive sauropodomorph footprint named by three authors
Lavinipes cheminii *Avanzini, Leonardi & Mietto 2003*

First primitive sauropodomorph footprint named by four authors
Pseudotetrasauropus grandcombensis *Gand, Vianey-Liaud, De-mathieu & Garric 2000*

First primitive sauropodomorph footprint named by five authors
Trisauropodiscus moabensis *Lockley, Yang, Matsukawa, Fleming & Lim 1992*

Sauropods

First sauropod named by a single author
Cardiodon rugolosus *Owen 1841, 1844*
Cetiosaurus brevis (in part), *C. epioolithicus, C. hypoolithicus, C. longus* (now *Cetiosauriscus*), and *C. medius Owen 1841; 1842*

First sauropod named by two authors
Elosaurus parvus *Peterson & Gilmore 1902*

First sauropod named by three authors
Asiatosaurus kwangshiensis *Hou, Yeh & Zhao 1975*

First sauropod named by four authors
Barapasaurus tagorei *Jain, Kutty, Roy-Chowdhury & Chatterjee 1975*

First sauropod named by five authors
Lirainosaurus astibiae *Sanz, Powell, Le Loeuff, Martinez & Suberbiola 1999*

First sauropod named by six authors
Tehuelchesaurus benitezii *Rich, Vickers-Rich, Gimenez, Cúneo, Puerta & Vacca 19*

First sauropod named by seven authors
Gongxianosaurus shibeiensis *He, Wang, Liu, Zhou, Liu, Cai & Dai 1998*

First sauropod named by eight authors
Chuanjiesaurus anaensis *Fang, Pang, Lu, Zhang, Pan, Wang, Li & Cheng 2000*

First sauropod named by ten authors
Chebsaurus algeriensis *Mahammed, Lang, Mami, Mekahli, Benhamou, Bouterfa, Kacemi, Cherief, Chaouati, & Taquet 2005*

First sauropod named by eleven authors
Jobaria tiguidensis *Sereno, Beck, Dutheil, Larson, Lyon, Moussa, Sadleir, Sidor, Varricchio, Wilson & Wilson 1999*
Nigersaurus taqueti *Sereno, Beck, Dutheil, Larson, Lyon, Moussa, Sadleir, Sidor, Varricchio, Wilson & Wilson 1999*

First sauropod named by twelve authors
Tangvayosaurus hoffeti *Allain, Taquet, Battail, Dejax, Richir, Veran, Limon-Duparcmeur, Vacant, Mateus, Sayarath, Kehenthavong & Phouyavong 1999*

First sauropod named by seventeen authors
Dreadnoughtus schrani *Lacovara, Lamanna, Ibiricu, Poole, Schroeter, Ullman, Voegele, Boles, Carter, Fowler, Egerton, Moyer, Coughenour, Schein, Harris, Martínez & Novas 2014*

Sauropod footprints

First sauropod footprints named by a single author
Rotundichnus muenchehagensis *Hendriks 1981* (originally *Iguanodonichnus*)

First sauropod footprints named by two authors
Elephantopoides barkhausensis *Kaever & Lapparent 1974*

First sauropod footprints named by three authors
Brontopodus birdi *Farlow, Pittman & Hawthorne 1989*

First sauropod footprints named by four authors
"Ophysthonyx portucalensis" *Santos, Moratalla, Rodrigues & Sanz 2004* (invalid)
"Polyonyx gomesi" *Santos, Moratalla, Rodrigues & Sanz 2004* (invalid)

First sauropod footprints named by eight authors
Liujianpus shunan *Xing, Lockley, Zhang, Klein, Li, Miyashita, Li & Kümmell 2015*

Sauropod eggs

First sauropod egg named by a single author
Megaloolithus matleyi *Mohabey 1996*

First sauropod egg named by two authors
Faveoloolithus ningxiaensis *Zhao & Dong 1976*

First sauropod egg named by three authors
Parafaveoloolithus guoqingsiensis *Fang, Wang & Jiang 2000*

First sauropod egg named by four authors
Megaloolithus aurelinesis, M. mammilare, M. petralta & M. siruguei *Vianey-Liaud, Mallan, Buscali & Montgelard 1994*

First sauropod egg named by five authors
Stromatoolithus pinglingensis *Zhao, Ye, Li, Zhao & Yan 1991*

SCIENTIFIC ARTICLES ABOUT SAUROPODO-MORPHS AND SAUROPODS

1699—England—First publication of a sauropod tooth
"Rutellum implicatum" was illustrated in Lhuyd (1699). *Lithophylacii Britannici Ichnographia, sive lapidium aliorumque fossilium Britannicorum singulari figura insignium.* Gleditsch and Weidmann: London.

1818—England—First publication of a Jurassic sauropodomorph
Smith 1818. Fossil bones found in red sandstone. *American Journal of Science and Arts* 2(1): 146–147.

1822—England—First publication of a Jurassic sauropod
Owen 1841. *Odontography; or, A Treatise on the Comparative Anatomy of the Teeth, Their Physiological Relations, Mode of Development, and Microscopic Structure in the Vertebrate Animals.* Volume I. Hippolyte Bailliere Publishers, London 1–655..

1836—France—First publication of a Triassic sauropodomorph
Riley & Stutchbury 1836. A description of various fossil remains of three distinct saurian animals discovered in the autumn of 1834, in the Magnesian Conglomerate on Durdham Down, near Bristol. *Proceedings of the Geological Society of London.* 2:397–399.

1842—England—First publication of a Cretaceous sauropod
Owen 1842. Report on British Fossil Reptiles. Part II: *Report of the British Association for the Advancement of Science*, vol. 11, p. 60–204.

1852—England—First publication of preserved sauropod skin
Mantell 1852. On the structure of the Iguanodon, and on the fauna

and flora of the Wealden Formation. *Notices of the Proceedings at the Meetings of the Members of the Royal Institution* 1:141–146.

1859—France—First publication on sauropod eggshells
Pouech 1859. Mémoire sur les terrains tertiaires de l'Ariège, rapportés à une coupe transversale menée de Fossat à Aillères, passant par le Mas d'Azil, et projetée sur le méridien de ce lieu. *Bulletin de la Société géologique de France*, 16, pp. 381–411.

1859—France—First publication on sauropod eggs
Matheron 1869. Notice sur les reptiles fossiles des dépôts fluvio-lacustres crétacés du bassin à lignite de Fuveau. *Mémoires de l'Académie Impériale des Sciences, Belles-Lettres et Arts de Marseille*, pp. 345–379.

1883—USA—First publication to estimate a sauropod weight
Marsh 1883. Principal characters of American Jurassic dinosaurs. Pt. VI. Restoration of Brontosaurus. *American Journal of Science*, Series 3, 26, 81–85 (plate 1).

1906—USA—First publication on sauropod gastroliths
Cannon 1906. Sauropoda Gastroliths. *Science*. Vol. 24:116.

1908—USA—First publication on bite marks on a sauropod
Matthew 1908. Allosaurus, a carnivorous dinosaur and its prey. *American Museum Journal*. 8:3–5.

1920—USA—First article about sauropod blood
Moodie 1920. Concerning the fossilization of blood corpuscles. *The American Naturalist*, vol. 54, pp. 460–464.

1929—Argentina—Longest sauropod article
This analysis of titanosaurs of Argentina is 200 pages long and has an additional 67 pages of plates. Huene 1929. Los saurisquios y ornitisquios del Cretacéo Argentino. *Anales del Museo de La Plata* (series 3) 3:1–196.

1932—Germany—First publication on sauropodomorph gastroliths
Huene 932. Die fossile Reptil-Ordnung Saurischia, ihre Entwicklung und Geschichte. *Monographien zur Geologie und Paläontologie* (in German) 4:1–361.

1932—Germany—Longest sauropodomorph article
Most of this review of saurishchian dinosaurs focuses on sauropodomorphs. It is 361 pages long, with an additional 56 illustrations on 113 pages, for a total of 474 pages.

1956—France—First publication on a Triassic sauropod
Ellenberger & Ellenberger 1956. Le gisement de dinosauriens de Maphutseng (Basutoland, Afrique du Sud) [The Maphutseng dinosaur locality (Basutoland, South Africa)]. *Comptes Rendus de la Société géologique de France* 1956:99–101.

1964—USA—First publication on sauropod stomach contents
Stokes 1964. Fossilized stomach contents of a sauropod dinosaur. *Science*. Feb. 7. 143(3606):576–577.

1968—Chile—First publication on sauropod footprints
Casamiquela & Fasola 1968. *Sobre pisadas de dinosaurios del Cretácico inferior de Colchagua (Chile).* Universidad de Chile, Departamento de Geología y Geofísica, 164 pp.

1968—USA—First publication on possible endothermy in sauropods
Bakker 1968. The superiority of dinosaurs. *Discovery* 3(2):11–22.

1979—South Africa—First publication on sauropodomorph eggs
Kitching 1979. Preliminary report on a clutch of six dinosaurian eggs from the Upper Triassic Elliot Formation, northern Orange Free State. *Palaeontologia Africana* 22:41–45.

1993—India—First publication on sauropod coprolites
Mohabey, Udhoji & Verma 1993. Palaeontological and sedimentological observations on non-marine Lameta Formation (Upper Cretaceous) of Maharashtra, India: their palaeoecological and palaeoenvironmental significance. *Palaeogeography, Palaeoclimatology, Palaeoecology* 105:83–94.

1999—USA—Longest book on a specific sauropod
Seismosaurus: The Earth Shaker, by David D. Gillette, is 495 pages long. See more: *Gillette 1999*

2004—USA—Longest thesis on sauropods
The thesis by Jarald D. Harris is 562 pages long and offers an analysis of *Suuwassea emilieae*. See more: *Harris 2004*

2005—USA—Longest book on sauropods
Thunder Lizards: The Sauropodomorph Dinosaurs by Virginia Tidwell & Kenneth Carpenter is 495 pages long. See more: *Tidwell & Carpenter 2005*

2007—Canada—Longest thesis on a primitive sauropodomorph
Timothy J. Fedak's doctoral thesis presents the species "Fendusaurus eldoni" and is 268 pages long. See more: *Fedak 2007*

2016—Spain—First sauropod name honoring a fictional character
Lohuecotitan pandafilandi is named after Pandafilando de la Fosca Vista (Pan Philanderer of the Menacing Gaze) from the novel *Don Quixote* (1605) by Cervantes. See more: *Cervantes Saavedra 1605; Díez Diaz et al. 2016*

BIBLIOGRAPHY OF PUBLICATIONS ON SAUROPODOMORPHS AND SAUROPODS, FROM A TO Z

Paleontologist names from A to Z
Alphabetical listings of sauropodomorph and sauropod paleontology citations would begin and end as follows:

Authors of publications on primitive sauropodomorphs from A to Z

Abel 1935. *Vorzeitliche Lebensspurren*. Gustav Fischer Verlag. Jena. 644 pp.
Zittel 1932. *Textbook of Paleontology* (translated by Eastman, revised 2nd edition by Woodward). MacMillan & Co., London: xvii + 464pp.

Authors of publications on sauropods from A to Z

Abel 1910. Die Rekonstruktion des Diplodocus. *Abh. Zool. Bot. Ges.* Wien. 5 Heft 3:1–60.
Zou, Wang & Wang 2013. A new oospecies of parafaveoloolithids from the Pingxiang Basin, Jiangxi Province, China. *Vertebrata PalAsiatica.* Vol. 51 (2):102–106.

Authors of publications on sauropodomorph footprints from A to Z

Abel 1935. *Vorzeitliche Lebenspuren*. Gustav Fischer Verlag. Jena. 644 pp.
Wright 1997. Connecticut River Valley. 143–147. In Currie & Padian (eds). *Encyclopedia of dinosaurs*. Academic Press, San Diego. 869 pp.

Authors of publications on sauropod footprints from A to Z

Antunes 1976. Dinosaurios eocretácicos de Lagosteiros. Universidad Nova de Lisboa, Ciencias da Terra. 33 pp.
Yoon & Soh 1991. Traces of Time Past: Footprints of Dinosaurs and Primitive Birds. *Seoul: The monthly magazine of Korea illustrated*, Jan: 6–11.

Authors of publications on primitive sauropodomorph eggs from A to Z
Bonaparte & Vince 1979. El hallazgo del primer nido de dinosaurios Triasicos, (Saurischia, Prosauropoda), Triásico superior de Patagonia, Argentina. *Ameghiniana* 16:173–182. (It turned out to be an egg-shaped geological concretion.)
Kitching 1979. Preliminary report on a clutch of six dinosaurian eggs from the Upper Triassic Elliot Formation, Northern Orange Free State. *Palaeontologia africana* 22:41–45.
Zelenitsky & Modesto 2002. Re-evaluation of the eggshell structure of eggs containing embryos from the Lower Jurassic of South Africa. *South African Journal of Science* 98:407–409.

Authors of publications on sauropod eggs from A to Z

Calvo, Englland, Heredia & Salgado 1997. First record of dinosaur eggshells (?Sauropoda – Megaloolithidae) from Neuquen, Patagonia, Argentina. *Gaia.* No. 14: 23–32.
Zou, Wang & Wang 2013. A new oospecies of parafaveoloolithids from the Pingxiang Basin, Jiangxi Province, China. *Vertebrata PalAsiatica.* Vol. 51 (2):102–106.

Authors of publications on sauropodomorph pathologies from A to Z

Apaldetti, Pol & Yates 2013. The postcranial anatomy of *Coloradisaurus brevis* (Dinosauria: Sauropodomorpha) from the Late Triassic of Argentina and its phylogenetic implications. *Palaeontology.* Vol. 56 (2): 277–301.
Xing, Rothschild, Randolph-Quinney, Wang, Parkinson & Ran 2018. Possible bite-induced abscess and osteomyelitis in *Lufengosaurus* (Dinosauria: sauropodomorph) from the Lower Jurassic of the Yimen Basin, China. *Scientific Reports* volume 8, Article number: 5045.

Authors of publications on sauropod pathologies from A to Z

Albritton 1989. *Catastrophic Episodes in Earth History.* Chapman & Hall, London, xvii + 221 pp.
Zhuo 2000. Do We know Anything about the Kinds of Diseases that Affected Dinosaurs? Found on Internet on Dec. 1, 2000 on the *Scientific American* website at: http://www.sciam.com/askexpert/rnedic

Authors of publications naming a sauropodomorph from A to Z

Agassiz 1846. Nomenclatoris zoologici index universalis : continens nomina systematica classium, ordinum, familiarum et generum animalium omnium, tam viventium quam fossilium, secundum ordinem alphabeticum unicum disposita, adjectis homonymiis plantarum, nec non variis adnotationibus et emendationibus. p. 393. (proposed name change)
Apaldetti, Martínez, Alcober & Pol 2011. A new basal sauropodomorph (Dinosauria: Saurischia) from Quebrada del Barro Formation (Marayes-El Carrizal Basin), Northwestern Argentina. *PLoS ONE* 6(11):e26964:1–194.
Zhang & Yang 1994. A new complete osteology of Prosauropoda in Lufeng Basin Yunnan China, *Jingshanosaurus:* Yunnan Publishing House of Science and Technology, Kunming, China. 1–100.

Authors of publications in which a sauropod was named from A to Z

Alifanov & Averianov 2003. *Ferganasaurus verzilini* gen. et sp. nov., a new neosauropod (Dinosauria, Saurischia, Sauropoda) from the Middle Jurassic of Fergana Valley, Kirghizia: *Journal of Vertebrate Paleontology.* Vol. 23 (2): 358–372.
Zhao 1993. A new Mid-Jurassic Sauropod (*Klamelisaurus gobiensis* gen. et sp. nov.) from Xinjiang, China: *Vertebrata PalAsiatica.* Vol. 31 (4): 132–138.
Zhao & Tan 2004. Citation lost ("Otogosaurus sarulai" is an invalid name).

Authors of publications in which a sauropodomorph footprint was named from A to Z

Avanzini, Leonardi & Mietto 1993. *Lavinipes cheminii* ichnogen. ichnosp. nov., a possible sauropodomorph track from the Lower Jurassic of the Italian Alps. *Ichnos.* Vol. 10: 179–193.
Young & Young 1987. Dinosaur Footprints of Sichuan Basin. Sichuan Science and Technology Publications, Chengdu, China, 30 pp. (also translated as Yang & Yang 1987)

Authors of publications naming a sauropod footprint from A to Z

Antunes 1976. Dinosaurios eocretácicos de Lagosteiros. Universidad Nova de Lisboa, *Ciencias da Terra.* 33 pp.
Xing, Lockley, Zhang, Klein, Li, Miyashita, Li & Kümmell 2015. A new sauropodomorph ichnogenus from the Lower Jurassic of Sichuan, China fills a gap in the track record. *Historical Biology.* Vol. 28 (7):1–15.

Authors of publications in which a sauropod egg was named from A to Z

Carpenter & Alf 1994. Global distribution of dinosaur eggs, nests and babies. In Carpenter, Hirsch & Horner (eds.) *Dinosaur Eggs and Babies.* 15–30. New York: Cambridge University Press. (proposed name change)
Fernández & Khosla 2014. Parataxonomic review of the Upper Cretaceous dinosaur eggshells belonging to the oofamily Megaloolithidae from India and Argentina. *Historical Biology.* 27:158–180.
Zhao, Ye, Li, Zhao & Yan 1991. Extinctions of the dinosaurs across the Cretaceous-Tertiary boundary in Nanxiong Basin, Guangdong Province: *Vertebrata PalAsiatica,* vol. 29:1–20.

This work includes a compilation of more than 600 possible sauropod species, including valid species and specimens for which the age, locality, or anatomical feature suggests they are likely sauropod species.

Complete list of valid primitive sauropodomorphs and sauropods

The graphic tables that follow present the different species of sauropodomorphs named as of January 1, 2019. These are divided into different phylogenetic groups or assigned to the closest one possible.

Estimations of body mass and length are calculated using one or more volumetric models, extrapolating from very similar specimens to the most incomplete. As many of the bone remains are far from complete (e.g., single teeth), in order to avoid overestimating, the lowest estimate is used in all cases.

Bibliographic citations do not always refer to the author who created the genus; they sometimes refer to the author who described the largest (or record) specimen of a species.

The following abbreviations are used in this book:

LT = Lower Triassic
MT = Middle Triassic
UT = Upper Triassic
LJ = Lower Jurassc
MJ = Middle Jurassic
UJ = Upper Jurassic
eLC = Early Lower Cretaceous
lLC = Late Lower Cretaceous
eUC = Early Upper Cretaceous
lUC = Early Upper Cretaceous

WNA = western North America
ENA = eastern North America
CA = Central America
ANT = The Antilles
WE = western Europe
EE = eastern Europe
WA = western Asia
EA = eastern Asia
CIM = Cimmeria
ME = Middle East
IND = Hindustan
NSA = northern South America
SSA = southern South America
NAf = northern Africa
SAf = southern Africa
Ma = Madagascar
OC = Oceania
AN = Antarctica

(n.d.) = Doubtful name
(n.n.) = Invalid name

Note: The estimated body sizes are approximate, with the significant +/- factors inherent to biology.

Sample graphics used in the tables:

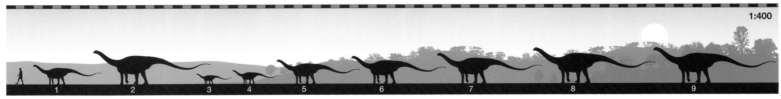

1:400

All primitive sauropodomorphs and sauropods are represented by silhouettes scaled down as indicated in the upper right of the table. Each bar at the top is equal to a meter in length. Human beings measure 1.8 meters in height.

SAUROPODOMORPHA

Primitive sauropodomorphs similar to *Buriolestes* - Bipedal, light-bodied, with serrated ziphodont teeth; hunted small prey.

Nº	Genus and species	Largest specimen	Material and data	Size	Mass
1	*Buriolestes schultzi* UT, SSA (southern Brazil)	ULBRA-PVT280 Indeterminate age	Skull and partial skeleton - *Cabreira et al. 2016* Specimen CAPPA/UFSM 0179 likely belongs to an individual 1.8 m long and weighing 7.4 kg. *Müller et al. 2017, 2018*	Length: **1.6 m** Hip height: **45 cm**	**5 kg**

Primitive sauropodomorphs similar to *Guaibasaurus* - Bipedal, light-bodied; hunted small prey, or may have been omnivorous.

Nº	Genus and species	Largest specimen	Material and data	Size	Mass
2	cf. *Agnosphitys cromhallensis* UT, WE (England, UK)	VMNH 1751 Indeterminate age	Incomplete jaw with teeth - *Fraser et al. 2002* The holotype is a dinosauromorph, and the referent is a guaibasaurid. *Langer et al. 2013*	Length: **1 m** Hip height: **30 cm**	**1.3 kg**
3	*Guaibasaurus candelariensis* UT, SSA (southern Brazil)	MCN-PV Indeterminate age	Metacarpal - *Bonaparte, et al. 2007* Sauropodomorph? *Baron et al. 2017a, 2017b; Langer et al. 2017; Parry et al. 2017*	Length: **3 m** Hip height: **90 cm**	**35 kg**

Primitive sauropodomorphs similar to *Panphagia* - Bipedal, with semi-robust bodies, serrated lanceolate-foliodont teeth; hunted small prey, or may have been omnivorous.

Nº	Genus and species	Largest specimen	Material and data	Size	Mass
4	*Alwalkeria maleriensis* UT, IND (India)	ISI R 306 Indeterminate age	Femur and vertebrae - *Chatterjee 1987* Other remains do not belong to this animal. *Remes & Rauhut 2005*	Length: **1.3 m** Hip height: **38 cm**	**2 kg**
5	*Eoraptor lunensis* UT, SSA (Argentina)	PVSJ 559 Adult	Skull and partial skeleton - *Sereno et al. 2013* Sauropodomorph or basal saurischian? *Martinez et al. 2011; Otero et al. 2015*	Length: **1.75 m** Hip height: **50 cm**	**5 kg**
6	"*Massospondylus*" sp. UT, IND (India)	ISI R277 Indeterminate age	Partial skeleton - *Kutty et al. 1987* More recent than *Alwalkeria*. *Novas et al. 2011*	Length: **1.95 m** Hip height: **60 cm**	**7.3 kg**
7	*Panphagia protos* UT, SSA (Argentina)	PSVJ-874 Subadult	Skull and partial skeleton - *Martínez & Alcober 2009* It had a more elongated neck than its close relatives.	Length: **2 m** Hip height: **60 cm**	**7.8 kg**

Primitive sauropodomorphs similar to *Pampadromaeus* - Bipedal, light-bodied, with serrated lanceolate-foliodont teeth; omnivorous hunters of small prey.

Nº	Genus and species	Largest specimen	Material and data	Size	Mass
8	*Pampadromaeus barberenai* UT, SSA (southern Brazil)	ULBRA-PVT016 Indeterminate age	Partial skeleton - *Cabreira et al. 2011* The teeth of type specimen ULBRA-PVT016 indicate that it was carnivorous.	Length: **1.4 m** Hip height: **28 cm**	**3 kg**
9	cf. *Pampadromaeus barberenai* UT, SSA (southern Brazil)	CAPPA/UFSM 0027 Indeterminate age	Femur - *Muller et al. 2016* *Pampadromaeus barberenai*?	Length: **1.65 m** Hip height: **45 cm**	**4.8 kg**

Primitive sauropodomorphs similar to *Saturnalia* - Bipedal, light-bodied, with serrated lanceolate-foliodont teeth; omnivorous hunters of small prey.

Nº	Genus and species	Largest specimen	Material and data	Size	Mass
10	*Saturnalia tupiniquin* UT, SSA (Argentina)	MCP 3844-PV Indeterminate age	Skull and partial skeleton - *Langer et al. 1999* It is named after the ancient Roman Sarturnalia festival.	Length: **1.7 m** Hip height: **45 cm**	**6 kg**
11	*Chromogisaurus novasi* UT, SSA (Argentina)	PVSJ 845 Indeterminate age	Partial skeleton - *Ezcurra 2010* The name refers to Valle Pintado, where it was found.	Length: **1.9 m** Hip height: **60 cm**	**12 kg**
12	cf. *Saturnalia* sp. UT, SAf (Zimbabwe)	Uncatalogued Indeterminate age	Incomplete femur - *Raath 1996* It may have been an indeterminate saurischian. *Ezcurra 2012*	Length: **2.5 m** Hip height: **65 cm**	**16 kg**

Primitive sauropodomorphs similar to *Thecodontosaurus* - Bipedal, light-bodied, serrated lanceolate-foliodont teeth; omnivorous hunters of small prey.

Nº	Genus and species	Largest specimen	Material and data	Size	Mass
13	*Pantydraco caducus* UT, WE (Wales, UK)	BMNH P24 o P65/24 Juvenile	Skull and partial skeleton - *Yates 2003* Discovered in 1952. *Galton et al. 2007*	Length 85 m Hip height: **21 cm**	**760 g**
14	*Pantydraco* sp. UT, WE (Wales, UK)	P65/42 Juvenile	Skull and partial skeleton - *Kermack 1984* *Pantydraco caducus*?	Length: **1.1 m** Hip height: **26 cm**	**1.5 kg**
15	*Thecodontosaurus minor* LJ, SAf (South Africa)	Uncatalogued Adult	Partial skeleton - *Haughton 1918* It has fused neurocentral sutures. *Yates*°	Length: **1.45 m** Hip height: **36 cm**	**3.8 kg**
16	*Asylosaurus yalensis* UT, WE (England, UK)	YPM 2195 Adult	Partial skeleton - *Riley & Stutchbury 1836a, 1836b* The associated bones may be from the same species. *Galton 2007*	Length: **2.25 m** Hip height: **57 cm**	**14 kg**
17	*Agrosaurus macgillivrayi* (n.d.) UT, WE (England, UK)	SMNS collection Indeterminate age	Partial skeleton - *Seeley 1891* *Thecodontosaurus antiquus*? *Huene 1906; Vickers-Rich et al. 1999*	Length: **2.25 m** Hip height: **57 cm**	**14 kg**
18	*Bagualosaurus agudoensis* UT, SSA (southern Brazil)	UFRGS-PV-1099-T Indeterminate age	Skull and partial skeleton - *Pretto et al. 2018* It displays intermediate characteristics between *Saturnalia* and *Thecodontosaurus*.	Length: **2.3 m** Hip height: **58 cm**	**15.5 kg**
19	*Thecodontosaurus antiquus* UT, WE (England, UK)	SMNS uncat Indeterminate age	Partial skeleton - *Carrano 2005* The holotype was destroyed in 1940. *Galton 2007*	Length: **3 m** Hip height: **75 cm**	**34 kg**

1:100

Primitive sauropodomorphs similar to *Efraasia* - Bipedal, with semi-robust bodies, serrated lanceolate-foliodont teeth; omnivorous hunters of small prey.

Nº	Genus and species	Largest specimen	Material and data	Size	Mass
1	*Arcusaurus pererabdalorum* LJ, SAf (South Africa)	BP/1/6235 Juvenile	Incomplete skull - *Yates et al. 2011* Similar to *Efraasia*?	Length: **2.3 m** Hip height: **60 cm**	**42 kg**
2	*Nambalia roychowdhurtii* UT, IND (India)	ISI R273/4 Indeterminate age	Partial hind limb - *Novas et al. 2011* Similar to *Efraasia*?	Length: **3.7 m** Hip height: **85 cm**	**125 kg**
3	*Xixiposaurus suni* LJ, EA (China)	ZLJ0108 Indeterminate age	Partial skeleton - *Sekiya 2010* Toe IV was slightly longer than toe III, making its feet different from those of other sauropodomorphs.	Length: **4.3 m** Hip height: **1 m**	**200 kg**
4	*Efraasia minor* UT, WE (Germany)	SMNS 12843 Adult	Skull and partial skeleton - *Huene 1932* The femur was mistakenly measured at 627 mm long; it actually was 527 mm. *Yates 2003, 2004*	Length: **5.3 m** Hip height: **1.2 m**	**365 kg**

1:100

1   2   3   4

PLATEOSAURIA

Primitive Plateosauria similar to *Plateosaurus* - Bipedal, with semi-robust bodies, serrated lanceolate-foliodont teeth; omnivorous hunters of small prey.

Nº	Genus and species	Largest specimen	Material and data	Size	Mass
1	*Unaysaurus tolentinoi* UT, SSA (southern Brazil)	UFSM11069 Adult	Partial skeleton - *Leal et al. 2004* Smallest plateosaur.	Length: 2.9 m Hip height: 65 cm	60 kg
2	*Macrocollum itaquii* UT, SSA (southern Brazil)	CAPPA/UFSM 0001b Indeterminate age	Partial skeleton - *Temp-Muller et al. 2018* Its neck was disproportionately long.	Length: 3.4 m Hip height: 74 cm	95 kg
3	*Plateosaurus sp.* UT, WE (Norway)	PMO 207.207 Indeterminate age	Indeterminate bone - *Hurum et al. 2006* Dinosaur fossil found at the greatest depth.	Length: 4 m Hip height: 90 cm	175 kg
4	*Jaklapallisaurus asymmetrica* UT, IND (India)	ISI R277 Indeterminate age	Incomplete pelvis - *Novas et al. 2011* Its talus was very asymmetrical.	Length: 4.5 m Hip height: 1.05 m	237 kg
5	*Orosaurus capensis* (n.d.) UT, SAf (South Africa)	BM(NH) R 1626 Indeterminate age	Partial skeleton - *Huxley 1867* It was mistakenly renamed *Orinosaurus*. *Lydekker 1889*	Length: 4.9 m Hip height: 1.15 m	310 kg
6	*Plateosaurus gracilis* UT, WE (Germany)	SMNS 17928 Adult	Partial skeleton - *Galton 1985* Better known by the name *Sellosaurus*. *Yates 2003*	Length: 5 m Hip height: 1.15 m	330 kg
7	*Palaeosaurus fraserianus* UT, ENA (Pennsylvania, USA)	AMNH 1861 Indeterminate age	Tooth - *Cope 1878* Sauropodomorph or phytosaur?	Length: 5.8 m Hip height: 1.35 m	500 kg
8	*Gresslyosaurus ingens* UT, WE (Switzerland)	NMB NB1582 Indeterminate age	Incomplete tibia - *Rütimeyer 1856* The remains of *G. ingens*, from Germany, may belong to *Plateosaurus engelhardti*. *Huene 1932*	Length: 6.3 m Hip height: 1.45 m	640 kg
9	*Plateosaurus cf. longiceps* UT, WE (Switzerland)	Uncatalogued Adult	Tibia - *Klein & Sander 2007* Smaller adults than those found in Germany.	Length: 6.6 m Hip height: 1.5 m	755 kg
10	*Euskelosaurus africanus* UT, SAf (South Africa)	SAM 3608 Indeterminate age	Ischium and vertebrae - *Haughton 1924* *Euskelosaurus brownii*?	Length: 6.7 m Hip height: 1.55 m	800 kg
11	*Plateosaurus cf. longiceps* UT, ENA (Greenland)	Uncatalogued Indeterminate age	Femur - *Jenkins et al. 1995* More recent than *Plateosaurus longiceps*. *Clemmensen et al. 2015*	Length: 6.9 m Hip height: 1.6 m	875 kg
12	*Ruehleia dedheimensis* UT, WE (Germany)	MB RvL I Indeterminate age	Partial skeleton - *Galton 2001* The most primitive Plateosauria.	Length: 7.65 m Hip height: 1.75 m	1.2 t
13	*Plateosaurus cf. plieningeri* UT, WE (France)	POL 74 Indeterminate age	Femur - *Gaudry 1890* Similar to *Ruehleia dedheimensis*.	Length: 7.7 m Hip height: 1.8 m	1.3 t
14	*"Thecodontosaurus" sp.* UT, WE (France)	Uncatalogued Indeterminate age	Tooth - *Gervais 1861* EA similar report also exists. *Tomasset 1930*	Length: 8 m Hip height: 1.85 m	1.3 t
15	*"Megalosaurus" obtusus* UT, WE (France)	Uncatalogued Indeterminate age	Teeth - *Henry 1876* Sauropodomorph?	Length: 8.2 m Hip height: 1.9 m	1.45 t
16	*Plateosauravus cullingworthi* UT, SAf (South Africa)	Uncatalogued Indeterminate age	Femur - *Huene 1932* *Euskelosaurus brownii*?	Length: 8.3 m Hip height: 1.9 m	1.5 t
17	*Gigantoscelus molengraaffi* (n.d.) UT, SAf (South Africa)	MT 65 Indeterminate age	Incomplete femur - *Hoepen 1916* *Plateosauravus stormbergensis*?	Length: 8.7 m Hip height: 2 m	1.65 t
18	*Plateosauravus stormbergensis* UT, SAf (South Africa)	Uncatalogued Indeterminate age	Incomplete femur - *Broom 1915* *Euskelosaurus brownii*?	Length: 8.75 m Hip height: 2 m	1.7 t
19	*Euskelosaurus brownii* (n.d.) UT, SAf (South Africa)	Uncatalogued Adult	Incomplete femur - *Durand 2001* Also known as *E. browni*. *Huxley 1866; Yates & Kitching 2003; Yates 2004*	Length: 9.1 m Hip height: 2.1 m	1.9 t
20	*Gresslyosaurus robustus* (n.d.) UT, WE (Germany)	GPTI B Indeterminate age	Partial skeleton - *Huene 1907–1908* *Plateosaurus*?	Length: 9.25 m Hip height: 2.15 m	2.1 t
21	*Plateosaurus longiceps* UT, WE (Germany, France, Switzerland)	SMNS 80664 Adult	Partial skeleton - *Fraas 1896* Sauropodomorph with the most conserved skeletons. More recent than *Plateosaurus engelhardti*.	Length: 9.3 m Hip height: 2.15 m	2.1 t
22	*Plateosaurus engelhardti* UT, WE (Germany, France)	IFG Uncatalogued Adult	Partial skeleton - *Wellnhofer 1993; Moser 2003; Sander & Klein 2005* Type species of the *Plateosaurus* genus. Its tail was proportionately shorter than the tail of *P. longiceps*. There was an attempt to change the name to "Playsaurus" ("broad lizard") as the original meaning of *Plateosaurus* ("flat lizard") was unclear. *Meyer 1837; Agassiz 1846; Paul 2010*	Length: 9.4 m Hip height: 2.3 m	2.6 t

Primitive Plateosauria similar to *Massospondylus* - Bipedal, with semi-robust bodies, serrated lanceolate-foliodont teeth; omnivorous hunters of small prey.

Nº	Genus and species	Largest specimen	Material and data	Size	Mass
23	*Ignavusaurus rachelis* LJ, SAf (Lesotho)	BM HR 20 Juvenile	Partial skeleton - *Knoll 2010* It was less than a year old.	Length: 1.45 m Hip height: 37 cm	9 kg
24	*Massospondylus sp.* UT, IND (India)	K. 33/621b Indeterminate age	Thoracic vertebra - *Huene 1940* Older than *Massospondylus hislopi*.	Length: 2.3 m Hip height: 53 cm	28 kg
25	*Leyesaurus marayensis* LJ, SSA (Argentina)	PVSJ 706 Indeterminate age	Partial skeleton - *Apaldetti et al. 2011* The name honors the Leyes family, who discovered and reported it.	Length: 2.4 m Hip height: 55 cm	31 kg
26	*Adeopapposaurus mognai* LJ, SSA (Argentina)	PVSJ568 Indeterminate age	Partial skeleton - *Martinez 2009* Some markings suggest there was a keratin beak present.	Length: 2.95 m Hip height: 68 cm	60 kg
27	*Massospondylus sp.* UT, SAf (South Africa)	SAM-PK-K5135 Indeterminate age	Skull and partial skeleton - *Haughton 1924* Older than *M. carinatus*. *Weishampel et al. 2004; Ford*	Length 3.6 m Hip height: 83 cm	120 kg
28	*Sarahsaurus aurifontanalis* LJ, WNA (Arizona, USA)	TMM 43646-2 Indeterminate age	Partial skeleton - *Rowe et al. 2011* MCZ 8893 is another specimen of the same size.	Length: 4.3 m Hip height: 1 m	193 kg
29	*Gryponyx transvaalensis* (n.d.) LJ, SAf (South Africa)	Uncatalogued Indeterminate age	Partial skeleton - *Broom 1912* Doubtful species. *Galton & Upchurch 2004*	Length: 4.5 m Hip height: 1.05 m	220 kg

Nº	Genus and species	Largest specimen	Material and data	Size	Mass
30	*Massospondylus hislopi* (n.d.) *UT, IND (India)*	Uncatalogued Indeterminate age	Thoracic vertebrae - *Lydekker 1890* The first sauropodomorph described from Hindustan.	Length: **4.8 m** Hip height: **1.1 m**	280 kg
31	*Massospondylus kaalae* *LJ, SAf (South Africa)*	SAM-PK-K7904 Indeterminate age	Tooth - *Barrett 2004* The holotype material SAM-PK-K1325 is a skull.	Length: **5.2 m** Hip height: **1.2 m**	360 kg
32	*Gryphonyx taylori* (n.d.) *LJ, SAf (Lesotho)*	SAM 3453 Indeterminate age	Partial skeleton - *Haughton 1924* *Massospondylus? Galton & Cluver 1976*	Length: **5.5 m** Hip height: **1.25 m**	410 kg
33	*Massospondylus carinatus* *LJ, SAf (Lesotho, South Africa, Zimbabwe)*	BP/1/4934 Adult	Partial skeleton - *Gow et al. 1990* The smallest calves are 13 cm long and weigh 7 g, 2.3% as long and 0.15% the weight of the largest known specimen. *Chinsamy 1991, 1992; Reisz et al. 2005; Paul**	Length: **5.7 m** Hip height: **1.3 m**	450 kg
34	*Gryponyx africanus* *LJ, SAf (South Africa)*	Uncatalogued Indeterminate age	Incomplete pelvis - *Broom 1911* More primitive than *Massospondylus. Vasconcelos & Yates 2004*	Length: **5.85 m** Hip height: **1.35 m**	485 kg
35	*Pradhania gracilis* *LJ, IND (India)*	ISI R265 Adult	Jaw and partial skeleton - *Kutty et al. 2007* Similar to *Massospondylus. Novas et al. 2007*	Length: **6.9 m** Hip height: **1.6 m**	830 kg
	Primitive Plateosauria similar to _Lufengosaurus_ - Bipedal, with semi-robust bodies, serrated lanceolate-foliodont teeth; omnivorous hunters of small prey.				
36	*Lufengosaurus* sp. *LJ, EA (China)*	Uncatalogued Juvenile	Femur - *Reisz et al. 2013* The smallest was 16 cm long and weighed 8 g.	Length: **23 cm** Hip height: **5 cm**	50 g
37	*Gripposaurus sinensis* *LJ, EA (China)*	IVPP V.27 Indeterminate age	Incomplete femur - *Young 1941* *Gyposaurus* cf. *sinensis* IVPP V277 was a similar size. Synonym of *Lufengosaurus huenei?. Young 1948; Barrett et al. 2007*	Length: **2.9 m** Hip height: **60 cm**	58 kg
38	cf. *Lufengosaurus huenei* *LJ, EA (China)*	IVPP V9069 Indeterminate age	Ungual phalange - *Dong et al. 1983* More recent than *Lufengosaurus huenei. Dong 1984*	Length: **4.5 m** Hip height: **95 cm**	217 kg
39	"*Fendusaurus eldoni*" (n.n.) *LJ, ENA (eastern Canada)*	FGM998GF 9 Indeterminate age	Partial skeleton - *Fedak 2007* Named and described in a thesis.	Length: **5.1 m** Hip height: **1.1 m**	315 kg
40	*Coloradisaurus brevis* *UT, SSA (Argentina)*	PVL field 6 Indeterminate age	Tibia - *Ezcurra & Apaldetti 2012* Originally named *Coloradia. Bonaparte 1978*	Length: **6.25 m** Hip height: **1.3 m**	590 kg
41	*Glacialisaurus hammeri* *LJ, AN (Antarctica)*	FMNH PR1822 Indeterminate age	Partial skeleton - *Hammer & Hickerson 1994, 1996* The piece was discovered in 1990–1991. *Smith & Pol 2007*	Length: **6.25 m** Hip height: **1.3 m**	590 kg
42	*Lufengosaurus huenei* *LJ, EA (China)*	GSC V15 LVP Adult	Partial skeleton - *Young 1942* Its calves were thought to be lizards (*Fulengia*) or Ornithischians (*Tawasaurus*). *Carroll & Galton 1977; Young 1982*	Length: **8.9 m** Hip height: **1.9 m**	1.75 t

1:250

SAUROPODIFORMES

Primitive sauropodiforms similar to _Jingshanosaurus_ - Bipedal, with semi-robust bodies, triangular-crowned spatulate-foliodont teeth, phytophagous.

Nº	Genus and species	Largest specimen	Material and data	Size	Mass
1	*Xingxiulong chengi* *LJ, EA (China)*	LFGT-D0002 Adult	Partial skeleton - *Wang et al. 2017* Like primitive sauropods, it had 4 sacral vertebrae.	Length: **6 m** Hip height: **1.3 m**	460 kg
2	*Jingshanosaurus xiwanensis* *LJ, EA (China)*	LV003 Indeterminate age	Skull and partial skeleton - *Zhang & Yang 1994* An intermediate between *Chuxiongosaurus* and *Yunnanosaurus*.	Length: **9.2 m** Hip height: **1.95 m**	1.6 t
3	*Pachysuchus imperfectus* (n.d.) *LJ, EA (China)*	IVPP V 40 Indeterminate age	Incomplete skull - *Young 1951* It was thought to be a phytosaur. *Barrett & Xing 2012*	Length: **10.1 m** Hip height: **2.15 m**	2.1 t
4	"*Sinosaurus triassicus*" *LJ, EA (China)*	IVPP V21 Indeterminate age	Sacrum and pelvis - *Young 1948* Some specimens were theropods, while others were sauropodomorphs. *Walker 1964; Galton 1999; Mortimer**	Length: **10.3 m** Hip height: **2.2 m**	2.3 t
5	"*Dachongosaurus yunnanensis*" (n.n.) *LJ, EA (China)*	Uncatalogued Subadult	Partial skeleton - *Zhao 1985* *Jingshanosaurus xiwanensis?*	Length: **10.7 m** Hip height: **2.3 m**	2.6 t

Primitive sauropodiforms similar to *Anchisaurus* - Bipedal, with semi-robust bodies, serrated lanceolate-foliodont teeth; omnivorous hunters of small prey.

#	Taxon / Locality	Specimen / Age	Material & Notes	Dimensions	Weight
6	*Anchisaurus polyzelus* LJ, ENA (Connecticut, Massachusetts, USA)	YPM 1883 Indeterminate age	Partial skeleton - *Marsh 1891* The differences in hips and legs from *Ammosaurus* may have been ontogenic in origin, but YPM 1883 was an adult. *Yates 2004, 2010*	Length: 2.4 m Hip height: 47 cm	25 kg
7	*Ammosaurus major* LJ, ENA (Connecticut, USA)	YPM 208 Adult	Partial skeleton - *Marsh 1889* Was *Ammosaurus major* an adult *Anchisaurus polyzelus*? *Yates 2004*	Length: 3.15 m Hip height: 63 cm	55 kg
8	*Ammosaurus* cf. *major* LJ, WNA (Arizona, USA)	MNA G2 7233 Indeterminate age	Partial skeleton - *Brady 1935, 1936* It was believed to be from the Middle Jurassic, but actually dates to the Lower Jurassic. *Galton 1971; Peterson & Pipiringos 1979; Weishampel et al. 2004*	Length: 3.5 m Hip height: 68 cm	73 kg
9	cf. *Ammosaurus* sp. LJ, ENA (eastern Canada)	VPPU 022196 Indeterminate age	Partial skeleton - *Olsen et al. 2015* First reported in Olsen, McCune & Thomson 1982.	Length: 4.55 m Hip height: 90 cm	160 kg

Primitive sauropodiforms similar to *Riojasaurus* - Semi-quadrupeds or quadrupeds, with robust bodies, type-O or slightly serrated cylindrodont teeth, phytophagous.

#	Taxon / Locality	Specimen / Age	Material & Notes	Dimensions	Weight
10	cf. *Riojasaurus* UT, SSA (Argentina)	ULR 56 Juvenile	Skull and partial skeleton - *Bonaparte & Pumares 1995* It may not belong to *Riojasaurus*. *McPhee & Choiniere 2017*	Length: 5.2 m Hip height: 1 m	370 kg
11	*Eucnemesaurus entaxonis* UT, SAf (South Africa)	BP/1/6234 Indeterminate age	Partial skeleton - *McPhee et al. 2015* Close to Sauropodiformes or to *Riojasaurus*? *McPhee & Choiniere 2017*	Length: 6 m Hip height: 1.2 m	560 kg
12	*Riojasaurus insertus* UT, SSA (Argentina)	PVL 3808 Indeterminate age	Partial skeleton - *Bonaparte 1969* Semi-quadruped or obligate quadruped? *Hartman**	Length: 6.8 m Hip height: 1.4 m	800 kg
13	*Eucnemesaurus fortis* UT, SAf (South Africa)	NMW 1889-XV-39 Indeterminate age	Incomplete femur - *Hoepen 1920* Specimen NMW 1876-VII-B124 was believed to be the large carnivor *Aliwalia rex*. *Galton 1985; Yates 2003*	Length: 7.8 m Hip height: 1.6 m	1.2 t

Primitive sauropodiforms similar to *Yunnanosaurus* - Bipedal, with semi-robust bodies, triangular-crowned spatulate-foliodont teeth, phytophagous.

#	Taxon / Locality	Specimen / Age	Material & Notes	Dimensions	Weight
14	*Seitaad ruessi* LJ, WNA (Utah, USA)	UMNH VP 18040 Indeterminate age	Partial skeleton - *Sertich & Loewen 2010* It was buried beneath a collapsed sand dune.	Length: 3.5 m Hip height: 75 cm	100 kg
15	*Yunnanosaurus huangi* LJ, EA (China)	Uncatalogued Indeterminate age	Femur - *Young 1942* A second specimen, larger than the holotype.	Length: 5 m Hip height: 1.05 m	255 kg
16	*Yunnanosaurus robustus* LJ, EA (China)	IVPP V94 Indeterminate age	Partial skeleton - *Young 1951* *Yunnanosaurus huangi*?	Length: 5.9 m Hip height: 1.25 m	430 kg
17	*Chuxiongosaurus lufengensis* LJ, EA (China)	LT9401 Indeterminate age	Skull - *Lu et al. 2010* Most primitive among the Anchisauria.	Length: 8.2 m Hip height: 1.75 m	1.1 t
18	*Yunnanosaurus youngi* MJ, EA (China)	CXMVZA 185 Indeterminate age	Partial skeleton - *Lu et al. 2007* Most recent of the Anchisauria.	Length: 10.8 m Hip height: 2.3 m	2.6 t
19	cf. *Yunnanosaurus* LJ, EA (China)	ZLJ 0035 Indeterminate age	Partial skeleton - *Xing et al. 2013* A colony of insects nested in the fossil.	Length: 12 m Hip height: 2.55 m	3.6 t

Primitive sauropodiforms similar to *Aardonyx* - Bipedal or quadrupedal, with semi-robust bodies, triangular-crowned spatulate-foliodont teeth, phytophagous.

#	Taxon / Locality	Specimen / Age	Material & Notes	Dimensions	Weight
20	*Sefapanosaurus zastronensis* LJ, SAf (South Africa)	BP/1/7409-7455 Subadult	Partial skeleton - *Otero et al. 2015* The first remains were discovered between 1936 and 1946.	Length: 6 m Hip height: 1.35 m	555 kg
21	cf. *Gresslyosaurus ingens* UT, WE (Switzerland or Germany)	HMN Fund XVIII Indeterminate age	Incomplete hind limb - *Heune 1932?* It may be a new species.	Length: 7.8 m Hip height: 1.75 m	1.2 t
22	*Lamplughsaura dharmaramensis* LJ, IND (India)	ISI R258 Adult	Caudal vertebra - *Kutty et al. 2007* The claws on its forefeet were straight.	Length: 7.8 m Hip height: 1.75 m	1.2 t
23	*Mussaurus patagonicus* UT, SSA (Argentina)	PVL uncat (4) (1971) Adult	Partial skeleton - *Casamiquela 1980; Carrano 1998; Otero & Pol 2013* Holotype PVL 4068 was a calf 28 cm long and weighing 60 g. *Bonaparte & Vince 1979; Otero et al. 2019*	Length: 8 m Hip height: 1.8 m	1.35 t
24	*Yizhousaurus sunae* LJ, EA (China)	LFGT ZLJ0033 Indeterminate age	Skull and partial skeleton - *Zhang et al. 2018* The name had been previously published informally. *Chatterjee et al. 2010*	Length: 8.25 m Hip height: 1.85 m	1.5 t
25	*Aardonyx celestae* LJ, SAf (South Africa)	BP/1/6254 Subadult	Partial skeleton - *Yates et al. 2009* They may be the remains of another kind of theropod.	Length: 8.7 m Hip height: 1.95 m	1.7 t
26	*Yimenosaurus youngi* LJ, EA (China)	YXV8702 Indeterminate age	Partial skeleton - *Bai et al. 1990* This specimen was not described.	Length: 8.9 m Hip height: 2 m	1.8 t

Primitive sauropodiforms similar to *Melanorosaurus* - Quadrupedal, with semi-robust bodies, triangular-crowned spatulate-foliodont teeth, phytophagous.

#	Taxon / Locality	Specimen / Age	Material & Notes	Dimensions	Weight
27	*Meroktenos thabanensis* UT, SAf (Lesotho)	MNHN LES-16 Adult	Partial skeleton - *Gauffre 1993* It was believed to be from the Lower Jurassic. *Peyre de Fabrègues & Allain 2016*	Length: 4.8 m Hip height: 1.1 m	300 kg
28	*Melanorosaurus readi* UT, SAf (South Africa)	NM QR1551 Indeterminate age	Partial skeleton - *Kitching & Raath 1984* A skull was found 83 years after it was first described. *Haughton 1924; Yates 2007*	Length: 6.5 m Hip height: 1.45 m	700 kg
29	*Camelotia borealis* UT, WE (England, UK)	BMNH R2870-R2874 Indeterminate age	Partial skeleton - *Galton 1985* Similar to the first sauropods.	Length: 10.2 m Hip height: 2.3 m	2.75 t

Primitive sauropodiforms similar to *Antetonitrus* - Quadrupedal, with robust bodies, triangular-crowned spatulate-foliodont teeth, phytophagous.

#	Taxon / Locality	Specimen / Age	Material & Notes	Dimensions	Weight
30	*Leonerasaurus taquetrensis* LJ, SSA (Argentina)	MPEF-PV 1663 Adult	Skull and partial skeleton - *Pol et al. 2011* Its teeth are directed forward.	Length: 3 m Hip height: 70 cm	70 kg
31	*Blikanasaurus cromptoni* UT, SAf (South Africa)	SAM K403 Indeterminate age	Partial hind limb - *Galton & Heerden 1985* The smallest of the sauropods?	Length: 5.4 m Hip height: 1.25 m	420 kg
32	*Ingentia prima* UT, SSA (Argentina)	PVSJ 1086 Indeterminate age	Partial skeleton - *Apaldetti et al. 2018* It was presented at a conference. *Apaldetti et al. 2016*	Length: 6.8 m Hip height: 1.6 m	850 kg
33	*Antetonitrus ingenipes* UT, SAf (South Africa)	BP/1/4952 Subadult	Partial skeleton - *Yates & Kitching 2003* It could hold things in its hands.	Length: 7.8 m Hip height: 1.8 m	1.25 t
34	*Lessemsaurus sauropoides* UT, SSA (Argentina)	CRILAR-PV 302 Adult	Ilium and ischium - *Martínez et al. 2004; Apaldetti et al. 2018* Its weight was calculated as up to 10 t.	Length: 10.3 m Hip height: 2.4 m	2.9 t
35	*Ledumahadi mafube* UT, SAf (South Africa)	BP/1/7120 Adult	Partial skeleton - *McPhee et al. 2018* The specimen was 14 years old. Its weight was calculated to be 12 t.	Length: 10.8 m Hip height: 2.5 m	3.4 t
36	"*Thotobolosaurus mabeatae*" (n.n.) UT, SAf (Lesotho)	Uncatalogued Indeterminate age	Ilium - *Ellenberger & Ellenberger 1956; Charig et al. 1965; Gauffre 1996* "Maphutsent sauropod" was named informally by Ellenberger 1970.	Length: 11 m Hip height: 2.45 m	3.6 t

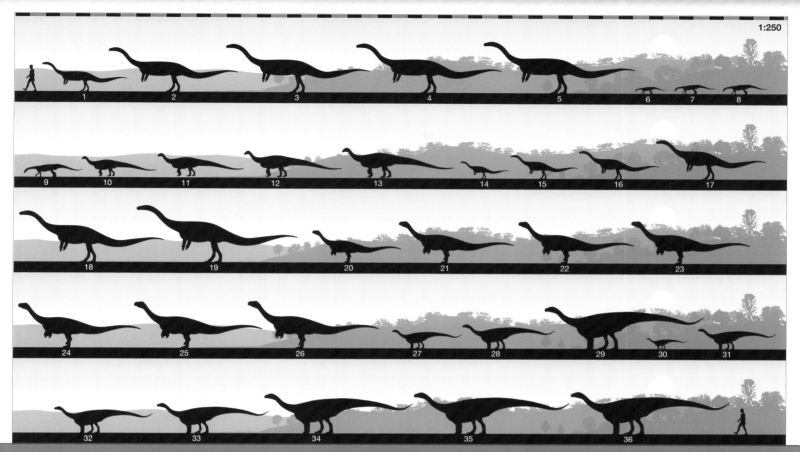

SAUROPODA

Primitive sauropods similar to *Gongxianosaurus* - Quadrupedal, with robust bodies, triangular-crowned spatulate-foliodont teeth, phytophagous.

Nº	Genus and species	Largest specimen	Material and data	Size	Mass
1	*Pulanesaura eocollum* LJ, SAf (South Africa)	BP/1/6210 Adult	Incomplete ulna - *McPhee et al. 2015* Smallest primitive sauropod? *McPhee & Choiniere 2017*	Length: **8 m** Hip height: **1.8 m**	**1.1 t**
2	*Chinshakiangosaurus chunghoensis* LJ, EA (China)	IVPP V14474 Indeterminate age	Partial skeleton - *Ye 1975* Basal sauropod or sauropodiform? *Becerra et al. 2017*	Length: **10.1 m** Hip height: **2.3 m**	**2.75 t**
3	"Yibinosaurus zhoui" (n.n.) LJ, EA (China)	Uncatalogued Indeterminate age	Partial skeleton - *Ouyang 2003* Described in a thesis, but it had been published two years earlier in a museum guide.	Length: **12.4 m** Hip height: **2.8 m**	**4 t**
4	*Gongxianosaurus shibeiensis* LJ, EA (China)	Uncatalogued Indeterminate age	Partial skeleton - *He et al. 1998* Basal sauropod or sauropodiform? *McPhee & Choiniere 2017*	Length: **12.5 m** Hip height: **2.8 m**	**4 t**

Indeterminate primitive sauropods - Quadrupedal, with robust bodies, triangular-crowned spatulate-foliodont teeth, phytophagous.

Nº	Genus and species	Largest specimen	Material and data	Size	Mass
5	*Isanosaurus attavipachi* UT, CIM (Thailand)	CH4-1 Subadult	Partial skeleton - *Buffetaut et al. 2000* Oldest sauropod of Cimmeria.	Length: **8.3 m** Hip height: **1.8 m**	**1.3 t**
6	*Amygdalodon patagonicus* MJ, SSA (Argentina)	MLP 46-VIII-21-1/8 Indeterminate age	Dentary and thoracic vertebra - *Cabrera 1947* It was more primitive than *Vulcanodon*. *Rauhut 2003; Becerra et al. 2017*	Length: **12 m** Hip height: **2.7 m**	**4.3 t**
7	*Kotasaurus yamanpallienis* LJ, IND (India)	S1Y col. Indeterminate age	Partial skeleton - *Yadagiri 1986* Its ilium was unusually elongated.	Length: **12.4 m** Hip height: **2.7 m**	**4.5 t**
8	*Isanosaurus sp.* UT, CIM (Thailand)	MH 350 Indeterminate age	Humerus - *Buffetaut et al. 2002* *Isanosaurus attavipachi?*	Length: **13.8 m** Hip height: **3 m**	**6 t**
9	*Protognathosaurus oxyodon* MJ, EA (China)	Uncatalogued Indeterminate age	Partial skeleton - *Zhang 1988* Its strange shape is similar to that of some therizinosaurs or *Archaeodontosaurus*.	Length: **14 m** Hip height: **3.1 m**	**6.3 t**
10	*Archaeodontosaurus descouensis* MJ, MA (Madagascar)	MHNDPal 2003-396 Indeterminate age	Incomplete dentary - *Buffetaut 2005* Teeth similar to those of primitive sauropodomorphs.	Length: **14.9 m** Hip height: **3.25 m**	**7.5 t**

Primitive sauropods similar to *Vulcanodon* - Quadrupedal, with robust bodies, triangular-crowned spatulate-foliodont teeth, phytophagous.

Nº	Genus and species	Largest specimen	Material and data	Size	Mass
11	"Yunnanosaurus" sp. LJ, EA (China)	FMNH CUP 2042 Indeterminate age	Tooth - *Simmons 1965* It was mistaken for *Y. robustus*. *Barrett 1999*	Length: **6.5 m** Hip height: **1.55 m**	**900 kg**
12	*Sanpasaurus yaoi* LJ, EA (China)	IVPP V156A Subadult?	Partial skeleton - *Young 1944* The remains were mixed with those of an ornithopod. *Upchurch 1995; McPhee et al. 2016*	Length: **7.2 m** Hip height: **1.7 m**	**1.1 t**
13	cf. *Sanpasaurus yaoi* LJ, EA (China)	Cat. No. V715 Subadult?	Radius, incomplete ulna, and thoracic vertebrae - *Young & Chow 1953* It is not certain whether or not it belongs to *S. yaoi*. *McPhee et al. 2016*	Length: **7.5 m** Hip height: **1.8 m**	**1.3 t**
14	*Nebulasaurus taito* MJ, EA (China)	LDRC-v.d.1 Indeterminate age	Incomplete skull - *Xing et al. 2015* It displays both primitive and advanced features.	Length: **8 m** Hip height: **1.95 m**	**1.7 t**
15	*Kunmingosaurus wudingensis* LJ, EA (China)	IVPP coll. Syntipes Indeterminate age	Partial skeleton - *Dong 1984; Zhao 1985* It was deemed to be the remains of *Lufengosaurus magnus*.	Length: **8.8 m** Hip height: **2.1 m**	**2.3 t**
16	*Vulcanodon karibaensis* LJ, SAf (Zimbabwe)	QG 24 Indeterminate age	Partial skeleton - *Bond et al. 1970* Specimen GC 152 was the same size. *Raath 1972*	Length: **11 m** Hip height: **2.65 m**	**4.3 t**

#	Taxon / Location	Specimen / Age	Description / Citation	Dimensions	Weight
17	Tazoudasaurus naimi LJ, NAf (Morocco)	To 2000–3 Indeterminate age	Incomplete forelimb - *Peyers & Allain 2010* Oldest sauropod of northern Africa. *Allain et al. 2004*	Length: **12.4 m** Hip height: **3 m**	6 t

Primitive sauropods similar to *Spinophorosaurus* - Quadrupedal, with robust bodies, triangular-crowned spatulate-foliodont teeth, phytophagous.

#	Taxon / Location	Specimen / Age	Description / Citation	Dimensions	Weight
18	Spinophorosaurus nigeriensis MJ, SAf (Niger)	NMB-1698-R Indeterminate age	Partial skeleton - *Remes et al. 2009* The supposed osteoderm on the tail was actually sternal bones.	Length: **13.8 m** Shoulder height: **3.6 m**	8.5 t

Primitive sauropods similar to *Barapasaurus* - Quadrupedal, with robust bodies, triangular-crowned spatulate-foliodont teeth, phytophagous.

#	Taxon / Location	Specimen / Age	Description / Citation	Dimensions	Weight
19	Ohmdenosaurus liasicus LJ, WE (Germany)	Hauff Museum Indeterminate age	Partial skeleton - *Wild 1978* GG411 are contemporary remains that are not comparable. *Stumpf et al. 2015*	Length: **7 m** Hip height: **1.8 m**	1.1 t
20	Zizhongosaurus chuangchengensis LJ, EA (China)	IVPP V9067 Indeterminate age	Thoracic vertebra - *Dong et al. 1983* Similar to *Barapasaurus*.	Length: **8.4 m** Shoulder height: **2.2 m**	1.8 t
21	"Damalasaurus laticostalis" (n.n.) LJ, EA (China)	Uncatalogued Indeterminate age	Partial skeleton - *Zhao 1985* It was mistakenly dated to the Middle Jurassic. *Glut 1997*	Length: **14 m** Shoulder height: **3.7 m**	8.5 t
22	Barapasaurus tagorei LJ, IND (India)	ISIR Col. Indeterminate age	Ulna - *Bandyopadhyay et al. 2010* The femur was reported as being 1.7 m long, but was actually 1.37 m. *Jain et al. 1975*	Length: **14 m** Shoulder height: **3.7 m**	8.5 t
23	Rhoetosaurus brownei MJ, OC (Australia)	QM F1659 Indeterminate age	Partial skeleton - *Longman 1926* Oldest sauropod of Oceania.	Length: **14.2 m** Shoulder height: **3.75 m**	9 t

Primitive eusauropods similar to *Shunosaurus* - Quadrupedal, with robust bodies, triangular-crowned spatulate-foliodont teeth, phytophagous or omnivorous?

#	Taxon / Location	Specimen / Age	Description / Citation	Dimensions	Weight
24	"Shunosaurus ziliujingensis" (n.n.) LJ, EA (China)	Uncatalogued Indeterminate age	Partial skeleton - *Anonymous 1986* Its teeth had denticles, unlike *S. lii*, and it is uncertain whether it belongs to this genus.	Length: **8.7 m** Shoulder height: **2.5 m**	2.5 t
25	Shunosaurus lii MJ, EA (China)	ZG65430 Subadult	Skull - *Chatterjee & Zheng 2002* The name derives from the Sotho word meaning "rainmaker."	Length: **12.5 m** Shoulder height: **3.3 m**	7 t

Primitive sauropods similar to *Patagosaurus* - Quadrupedal, with robust bodies, triangular-crowned spatulate-foliodont teeth, phytophagous.

#	Taxon / Location	Specimen / Age	Description / Citation	Dimensions	Weight
26	Patagosaurus fariasi MJ, SSA (Argentina)	PVL 4076 Adult	Partial skeleton - *Bonaparte 1979* Several individuals of varying sizes are known. *Coria 1994*	Length: **18.6 m** Shoulder height: **3.9 m**	12.3 t

Primitive sauropods similar to *Cetiosaurus* - Quadrupedal, with robust bodies, triangular-crowned spatulate-foliodont teeth, phytophagous.

#	Taxon / Location	Specimen / Age	Description / Citation	Dimensions	Weight
27	cf. Cetiosaurus oxoniensis MJ, WE (England)	Uncatalogued Indeterminate age	Partial skeleton - *Platt 1758* More recent than *C. oxoniensis*	Length: **8.1 m** Shoulder height: **2 m**	1.4 t
28	Chebsaurus algeriensis MJ, NAf (Morocco)	D001–01-78 Juvenile	Partial skeleton - *Mahammed et al. 2005* *Cheb* is a colloquial word used to refer to young people in Arabic.	Length: **8.2 m** Shoulder height: **2.05 m**	1.45 t
29	Cetiosaurus medius (n.d.) MJ, WE (England)	OUMNH J13693–13703 Indeterminate age	Partial skeleton - *Owen 1841* More recent than *Cetiosaurus* sp. A775.	Length: **10.8 m** Shoulder height: **2.7 m**	3.3 t
30	Cetiosaurus mogrebiensis MJ, NAf (Morocco)	No. 3 Indeterminate age	Femur - *Lapparent 1955* Specimen No. 8 was the same size.	Length: **16 m** Shoulder height: **4 m**	10.7 t
31	Cetiosaurus oxoniensis MJ, WE (England, UK)	OUMNH J13605-13613, J13615-13616, J13619- 13688, J13899 Indeterminate age	Partial skeleton - *Phillips 1871* The genus *Cetiosaurus* was created in 1841, while the species *C. oxoniensis* was created after other new species were already assigned to this genus. It is, however, the type species. *Owen 1841*	Length: **16.1 m** Shoulder height: **4 m**	11 t
32	Cetiosaurus sp. MJ, WE (France)	A775 Indeterminate age	Chevron - *Buffetaut et al. 2011* Older than *C. oxoniensis*.	Length: **16.8 m** Shoulder height: **4.2 m**	12.5 t
33	Cetiosaurus sp. MJ, WE (England, UK)	SDM 44.30-40 Adult	Partial skeleton - Reynolds 1939 *Cetiosaurus oxoniensis?*	Length: **19.5 m** Shoulder height: **4.8 m**	19.5 t

Primitive sauropods similar to *Datousaurus* - Quadrupedal, with robust bodies, triangular-crowned spatulate-foliodont teeth, phytophagous.

#	Taxon / Location	Specimen / Age	Description / Citation	Dimensions	Weight
34	"Lancangosaurus cachuensis" (n.n.) MJ, CIM (Tibet, China)	Uncatalogued Indeterminate age	Skull and partial skeleton - *Zhao 1985* Other names assigned include "Lancanjiangosaurus," "Lancangjiangosaurus," and "Lanchangjiangosaurus." *Mortimer**	Length: **13 m** Shoulder height: **3.8 m**	8 t
35	Datousaurus bashanensis MJ, EA (China)	CV00740 Indeterminate age	Incomplete skull - *Cao & You 2000* It had a disproportionately large head.	Length: **13.9 m** Shoulder height: **4.05 m**	10 t

1:400

MAMENCHISAURIDAE

Mamenchisaurids similar to *Omeisaurus* - Quadrupedal, with very long necks and semi-robust bodies, triangular-crowned spatulate-foliodont teeth, phytophagous.

Nº	Genus and species	Largest specimen	Material and data	Size	Mass
1	cf. *Omeisaurus junghsiensis* UJ, EA (China)	IVPP V.240 Indeterminate age	Teeth - *Young 1942* More recent than *Omeisaurus junghsiensis*.	Length: **9 m** Shoulder height: **2.1 m**	1.5 t
2	*Tonganosaurus hei* LJ, EA (China)	MCDUT 14454 Indeterminate age	Partial skeleton - *Li et al. 2010* The oldest mamenchisaurid.	Length: **11 m** Shoulder height: **2.3 m**	2 t
3	*Eomamenchisaurus yuanmouensis* MJ, EA (China)	IVPP V9067 Indeterminate age	Partial skeleton - *Lu et al. 2008* The mamenchisaurid with the longest name.	Length: **15.5 m** Shoulder height: **3 m**	4.5 t
4	*Huangshanlong anhuiensis* MJ, EA (China)	Uncatalogued Indeterminate age	Partial front limb - *Huang et al. 2014* It was the only described sauropod for Anhui province until *Anhuilong* was discovered.	Length: **16 m** Shoulder height: **3.2 m**	4.9 t
5	*Omeisaurus junghsiensis* MJ, EA (China)	IVPP Indeterminate age	Skull and partial skeleton - *Young 1939* In the original description, it is referred to as *O. yunghsiensis*.	Length: **16.5 m** Shoulder height: **3.25 m**	6 t
6	*Anhuilong diboensis* MJ, EA (China)	AGB 5822 Indeterminate age	Partial front limb - *Ren et al. 2018* Its name means "Dragon of Anhui Province."	Length: **17.5 m** Shoulder height: **3.35 m**	6.3 t
7	*Omeisaurus changshouensis* UJ, EA (China)	IVPP V930 Indeterminate age	Partial skeleton - *Young 1958* The most recent species of *Omeisaurus*.	Length: **18 m** Shoulder height: **3.45 m**	6.9 t
8	*Omeisaurus tianfuensis* MJ, EA (China)	ZDM T5701 Indeterminate age	Skull and partial skeleton - *He et al. 1984* Other specimens have a club on the tail. *Dong et al. 1989*	Length: **18.5 m** Shoulder height: **3.55 m**	7.4 t
9	*Omeisaurus luoquanensis* MJ, EA (China)	V 21501 Indeterminate age	Partial skeleton - *He 1988* Specimen V 21502 did not consist of the same bones, so the two could not be compared.	Length: **19 m** Shoulder height: **3.6 m**	8 t
10	*Omeisaurus jiaoi* MJ, EA (China)	ZDM 5050 Indeterminate age	Partial skeleton - *Jiang 2011* The last *Omeisaurus* species described to date.	Length: **20 m** Shoulder height: **3.8 m**	9 t

Mamenchisaurids similar to *Chuanjiesaurus* - Quadrupedal, with very long necks and robust bodies, triangular-crowned spatulate-foliodont teeth, phytophagous.

Nº	Genus and species	Largest specimen	Material and data	Size	Mass
11	*Cetiosauriscus glymptonensis* MJ, WE (England, UK)	Uncatalogued Indeterminate age	Tooth - *Phillip 1871* *Cetiosauriscus glymptonensis?*	Length: **9 m** Shoulder height: **2.3 m**	2.3 t
12	*Tienshanosaurus chitaiensis* UJ, EA (China)	IVPP AS 40002-3 Indeterminate age	Partial skeleton - *Young 1937* Mistakenly referred to in some publications as "Teishanosaurus."	Length: **10 m** Shoulder height: **2.55 m**	3.3 t
13	*Zigongosaurus fuxiensis* UJ, EA (China)	C.1042 Indeterminate age	Tooth - *Hou 1976* It may be a valid genus. *Valérie 1999*	Length: **11.5 m** Shoulder height: **2.7 m**	3.8 t
14	*Tienshanosaurus* sp. UJ, EA (China)	Uncatalogued Indeterminate age	Partial skeleton - *Young 1954* *Tienshanosaurus chitaiensis?*	Length: **12 m** Shoulder height: **2.8 m**	4.4 t
15	*Qijianglong guokr* UJ, EA (China)	QJGPM 1001 Subadult	Skull and partial skeleton - *Xing et al. 2015* Guokr is a mobile and web-based science education community.	Length: **13.2 m** Shoulder height: **3 m**	5.2 t
16	"*Omeisaurus*" *maoianus* MJ, EA (China)	ZNM N8510 Indeterminate age	Skull and partial skeleton - *Tang et al. 2001* Smallest *Omeisaurus* species.	Length: **13.8 m** Shoulder height: **3.1 m**	5.9 t
17	"*Omeisaurus*" *fuxiensis* UJ, EA (China)	CV00267 Indeterminate age	Dentary - *Dong 1983* *Zigongosaurus fuxiensis?*	Length: **14.8 m** Shoulder height: **3.3 m**	7.4 t
18	*Barosaurus affinis* (n.d.) UJ, WNA (Utah, USA)	YPM 419 Indeterminate age	Partial skeleton - *Marsh 1899* Similar to *Cetiosauriscus stewarti*. *Tschopp et al. 2015*	Length: **15.5 m** Shoulder height: **3.45 m**	8.4 t
19	*Gigantosaurus megalonyx* (n.d.) UJ, WE (England, UK)	IVPP Indeterminate age	Partial skeleton - *Seeley 1869* The name was reused in the original name *Janenschia* and *Tornieria*. *Fraas 1908*	Length: **16.1 m** Shoulder height: **3.6 m**	9.5 t
20	cf. *Mamenchisaurus hochuanensis* MJ, EA (China)	ZDM 0126 Indeterminate age	Thoracic vertebra - *Ye 2001* More recent than *M. hochuanensis*, it had a club on its tail. *Sekiya 2011*	Length: **16.3 m** Shoulder height: **3.65 m**	9.8 t
21	*Cetiosauriscus stewarti* MJ, WE (England, UK)	NHMUK R.3078 Indeterminate age	Partial skeleton - *Charig 1980* It was believed to be from the Lower Cretaceous and is not a diplodocoid. *Wilson 2002; Whitlock 2011*	Length: **16.8 m** Shoulder height: **3.75 m**	10.8 t
22	*Yuanmousaurus jiangyiensis* MJ, EA (China)	YMV 601 Indeterminate age	Partial skeleton - *Fu & Zhang 2004; Li et al. 2006* It was knwon as *Shunosaurus jiangyiensis*. Similar to *Chuanjiesaurus*. *Sekiya 2011*	Length: **16.9 m** Shoulder height: **3.8 m**	11 t
23	*Chuanjiesaurus anaensis* MJ, EA (China)	LFCH 1001 Indeterminate age	Partial skeleton - *Fang et al. 2000* Originally named *Chuanjiesaurus a'naensis*. Specimen LCD9701-I is slightly smaller. *Sekiya 2011*	Length: **17 m** Shoulder height: **3.8 m**	11.1 t
24	*Cetiosauriscus glymptonensis* MJ, WE (England, UK)	OUMNH J13750–13758 Indeterminate age	Caudal vertebrae - *Phillips 1871* Probable mamenchisaurid. *Whitlock 2011*	Length: **20.6 m** Shoulder height: **4.6 m**	20 t
25	cf. *Ornithopsis leedsi* UJ, WE (England, UK)	BMNH R1984 Indeterminate age	Thoracic vertebra - *Hulke 1887* A new species. *Upchurch & Martin 2003*	Length: **21.7 m** Shoulder height: **4.9 m**	23 t
26	*Xinjiangtitan shanshaensis* MJ, EA (China)	SSV12001 Indeterminate age	Skull and partial skeleton - *Wu et al. 2013* It has the longest neck relative to its body length. *Zhang et al. 2018*	Length: **27 m** Shoulder height: **4.85 m**	25 t

Nº	Genus and species	Largest specimen	Material and data	Size	Mass
27	"Cetiosaurus epioolithicus" (n.n.) MJ, WE (England, UK)	SCAWM 4G Indeterminate age	Metatarsal - *Owen 1842* Mamenchisaurid or Turiasauria? *Upchurch 1995; Upchurch & Martin 2003*	Length: **24 m** Shoulder height: **5.4 m**	**32 t**

Mamenchisaurids similar to *"Mamenchisaurus"* - Quadrupedal, with very long necks and robust bodies, triangular-crowned spatulate-foliodont teeth, phytophagous.

Nº	Genus and species	Largest specimen	Material and data	Size	Mass
28	"Mamenchisaurus guangyuanensis" (n.n.) UJ, EA (China)	CUT unnumbered Indeterminate age	Partial skeleton - *Zhang et al. 1998* It was not formally described.	Length: **7.1 m** Shoulder height: **1.85 m**	**1.2 t**
29	"Mamenchisaurus yunnanensis" (n.n.) MJ, EA (China)	IVPP V932 Indeterminate age	Partial skeleton - *Fang et al. 2004* Oldest species assigned to *Mamenchisaurus*. *Huang et al. 2005*	Length: **9.4 m** Shoulder height: **2.6 m**	**2.7 t**
30	"Mamenchisaurus" youngi UJ, EA (China)	ZDM 0083 Indeterminate age	Skull and partial skeleton - *Pi et al. 1996* Includes a preserved skin impression. *Christian et al. 2013*	Length: **16.4 m** Shoulder height: **2.9 m**	**7 t**
31	"Mamenchisaurus" anyuensis UJ, EA (China)	AL 001 Indeterminate age	Partial skeleton - *Young 1958* Frequently referred to as "M. anyeensis."	Length: **23 m** Shoulder height: **4.1 m**	**21 t**

Mamenchisaurids similar to *Mamenchisaurus* - Quadrupedal, with very long necks and robust bodies, triangular-crowned spatulate-foliodont teeth, phytophagous.

Nº	Genus and species	Largest specimen	Material and data	Size	Mass
32	aff. *Mamenchisaurus* sp. UJ, EA (Mongolia)	AL Col. Indeterminate age	Partial hind limb - *Graham et al. 1997* First Jurassic sauropod reported from Mongolia. *Gubin & Sinitza 1996*	Length: **8.7 m** Shoulder height: **1.6 m**	**1 t**
33	*Mamenchisaurus constructus* UJ, EA (China)	IVPP V.948 Indeterminate age	Caudal vertebra - *Young 1954* The type species of *Mamenchisaurus*.	Length: **20 m** Shoulder height: **3.6 m**	**12 t**
34	*Mamenchisaurus hochuanensis* UJ, EA (China)	IVPP 3 Indeterminate age	Partial skeleton - *Paul et al.1997* The second author's name was translated as Chao or Zhao. *Young & Zhao 1972*	Length: **21 m** Shoulder height: **3.8 m**	**14 t**
35	*Mamenchisaurus sinocanadorum* UJ, EA (China)	IVPP V10603 Indeterminate age	Lower jaw and cervical vertebrae - *Russell & Zheng 1994* It was an estimated 35 m long and weighed 75 t. *Paul 2010*	Length: **25 m** Shoulder height: **4.6 m**	**24 t**
36	*Mamenchisaurus* sp. UJ, EA (China)	PMOL-SGP 2006 Adult	Teeth and partial skeleton - *Wing et al. 2007* A histological study revealed that it was 31 years old when it died. *Griebeler et al. 2013*	Length: **27.5 m** Shoulder height: **5 m**	**31 t**
37	*Mamenchisaurus* sp. UJ, EA (China)	SGP 2006 Indeterminate age	Partial skeleton - *Wing et al. 2011* The size of the humerus was exaggerated at 1.8 m; it was approximately 1.42 m long.	Length: **28 m** Shoulder height: **5.1 m**	**33 t**
38	*Mamenchisaurus* sp. UJ, CIM (Thailand)	SM MD3–54 Indeterminate age	Tooth - *Suteethorn et al. 2013* Some vertebrae from a smaller individual also exist. *Buffetaut et al. 2005*	Length: **29 m** Shoulder height: **5.2 m**	**35 t**
39	*Hudiesaurus sinojapanorum* UJ, EA (China)	IVPP V. 11120 Indeterminate age	Thoracic vertebra - *Dong 1997* It may be a cervical, making the animal in this case 32 m long, with a weight of 55 t. *Taylor*	Length: **30.5 m** Shoulder height: **5.5 m**	**44 t**
40	*Mamenchisaurus jingyanensis* UJ, EA (China)	JV002 Indeterminate age	Femur - *Zhang et al. 1998* This piece is 2 m long.	Length: **31 m** Shoulder height: **5.6 m**	**45 t**

1:700

TURIASAURIA

Turiasauria similar to *Janenschia* - Quadrupedal, with robust bodies, oval-crowned spatulate-foliodont teeth, phytophagous.

Nº	Genus and species	Largest specimen	Material and data	Size	Mass
1	*Haestasaurus becklesii* eLC, WE (England, UK)	NHMUK R1868-1870 Indeterminate age	Partial skeleton - *Mantell 1852* Similar to *Janenschia*. *Upchurch et al. 2015*	Length: **9 m** Shoulder height: **2.3 m**	**2.9 t**
2	*Janenschia robusta* UJ, SAf (Tanzania)	HMN P Indeterminate age	Femur - *Fraas 1908* It has been considered a Titanosauria or similar to *Camarasaurus*. *Wild 1991; Upchurch et al. 2015*	Length: **15.3 m** Shoulder height: **3.8 m**	**14 t**

Nº	Genus and species	Largest specimen	Material and data	Size	Mass
3	Tehuelchesaurus benitezii UJ, SSA (Argentina)	MFEF-PV 1125 Indeterminate age	Partial skeleton - *Vickers-Rich et al. 1999* It was covered with flat, hexagonal scales. It was an extremely robust animal.	Length: **16 m** Shoulder height: **4 m**	**16 t**

Turiasauria similar to *Turiasaurus* - Quadrupedal, with robust bodies, heart-crowned spatulate-foliodont teeth, phytophagous.

Nº	Genus and species	Largest specimen	Material and data	Size	Mass
4	"Pelorosaurus" sp. UJ, WE (France)	Uncatalogued Indeterminate age	Tooth - *Cuny et al. 1991* Turiasauria?	Length: **5.4 m** Shoulder height: **1.55 m**	**600 kg**
5	"Ornithopsis" greppini UJ, WE (Switzerland)	MH 342 Adult	Partial skeleton - *Huene 1922* Specimen MH 260 had evidence of cartilage. *Schwarz et al. 2007*	Length: **6.3 m** Shoulder height: **1.8 m**	**1 t**
6	cf. Cardiodon rugolosus MJ, WE (Scotland, UK)	Uncatalogued Indeterminate age	Tooth - *Barrett 2006* A fossil mammal was called *Cardiodon* (now *Cardiatherium*). *Ameghino 1885,1883*	Length: **10 m** Shoulder height: **2.6 m**	**3.3 t**
7	Neosodon sp. UJ, WE (France)	Uncatalogued Indeterminate age	Caudal vertebra - *Le Loeuff et al. 1996* More recent than *Neosodon praecursor*.	Length: **11.4 m** Shoulder height: **3 m**	**4.8 t**
8	cf. Cetiosauriscus leedsi MJ, WE (England, UK)	NHMUK R3377 Indeterminate age	Tooth - *Martill 1988* Previously registered as BMNH R3377.	Length: **12.6 m** Shoulder height: **3.3 m**	**6.5 t**
9	Macrurosaurus sp. UJ, WE (France)	Uncatalogued Indeterminate age	Caudal vertebra - *Sauvage 1880* Mistakenly referred to as "Macrourosaurus."	Length: **16.3 m** Shoulder height: **4.25 m**	**14 t**
10	Losillasaurus giganteus UJ, WE (Spain)	Lo Col. Subadult	Partial skeleton - *Casanovas et al. 2001* It was considered a giant diplodocoid.	Length: **17.5 m** Shoulder height: **4.6 m**	**17 t**
11	Zby atlanticus UJ, WE (Portugal)	ML 368 Indeterminate age	Partial skeleton - *Mateus et al. 2014* Sauropod with the shortest genus name.	Length: **18 m** Shoulder height: **4.7 m**	**19 t**
12	Cardiodon rugolosus MJ, WE (England, UK)	BMNH R1527 Indeterminate age	Tooth - *Owen 1841, 1844* It received a species name 3 years later.	Length: **18.1 m** Shoulder height: **4.75 m**	**19.5 t**
13	Turiasaurus riodevensis UJ, WE (Spain, Portugal)	CPT-1195 & 1210 Indeterminate age	Partial skeleton - *Royo-Torres et al. 2006* The specimen from Portugal is ML 368. *Mateus 2009*	Length: **21 m** Shoulder height: **5.5 m**	**30 t**
14	cf. "Pelorosaurus" humerocristatus UJ, WE (Portugal)	Uncatalogued Indeterminate age	Tooth - ? *Neosodon praecursor?*	Length: **21 m** Shoulder height: **5.5 m**	**30 t**
15	cf. "Pelorosaurus" humerocristatus UJ, WE (England, UK)	NHMUK R2565 Indeterminate age	Tooth - *Lydekker 1893* It was a Turiasauria. *Mocho et al. 2013*	Length: **21.5 m** Shoulder height: **5.7 m**	**32 t**
16	Neosodon praecursor (n.d.) UJ, WE (France, Portugal)	BHN2R 113 Indeterminate age	Tooth - *Sauvage 1888, 1896; Moussaye 1885* The tooth is 6% larger than the largest in *Turiasaurus*. *Royo-Torres et al. 2006*	Length: **22.5 m** Shoulder height: **5.9 m**	**35 t**

Turiasauria similar to *Mierasaurus* - Quadrupedal, with robust bodies, triangular-crowned spatulate-foliodont teeth, phytophagous.

Nº	Genus and species	Largest specimen	Material and data	Size	Mass
17	"Hoplosaurus armatus" UJ, WE (England, UK)	NHMUK R2565 Indeterminate age	Skull and partial skeleton - *Woodward 1895* The teeth were believed to be from carnivorous dinosaurs.	Length: **9 m** Shoulder height: **2.4 m**	**2.5 t**
18	Mierasaurus bobyoungi eLC, WNA (Utah, USA)	UMNH.VP.26004 Subadult	Teeth and partial skeleton - *Royo-Torres et al. 2017* The oldest Turiasauria of North America.	Length: **11.5 m** Shoulder height: **3 m**	**4.8 t**
19	Moabosaurus utahensis ILC, WNA (Utah, USA)	Uncatalogued Indeterminate age	Teeth and partial skeleton - *Britt et al. 2017* It was reconstructed by comparing it to *Camarasaurus*. *Anonymous 2006; Kirkland et al. 1997*	Length: **12 m** Shoulder height: **3.15 m**	**5.7 t**
20	Oplosaurus armatus (n.d.) ILC, WE (Spain, England, UK)	NHMUK R964 Indeterminate age	Tooth - *Gervais 1852* Also referred to as *Hoplosaurus armatus*. *Lydekker 1893; Royo-Torres & Cobos 2007*	Length: **15.5 m** Shoulder height: **4 m**	**12.4 t**
21	cf. "Pelorosaurus" conybearei eLC, WE (England, UK)	NHMUK R1610 Indeterminate age	Tooth - *Lydekker 1889* It was a Turiasauria. *Mocho et al. 2013*	Length: **17 m** Shoulder height: **4.4 m**	**16.5 t**

Turiasauria similar to *Tendaguria* - Quadrupedal, with robust bodies, oval-crowned spatulate-foliodont teeth, phytophagous.

Nº	Genus and species	Largest specimen	Material and data	Size	Mass
22	Tendaguria tanzaniensis UJ, SAf (Tanzania)	MB.R.2092.1, NB4 Indeterminate age	Thoracic vertebrae - *Janensch 1929* They were believed to be the remains of *Janenschia*. *Bonaparte et al. 2000*	Length: **16 m** Shoulder height: **3.8 m**	**12 t**

1:600

NEOSAUROPODA

Primitive neosauropods similar to *Jobaria* - Quadrupedal, with robust bodies, triangular-crowned spatulate-foliodont teeth, phytophagous.

Nº	Genus and species	Largest specimen	Material and data	Size	Mass
1	Ferganasaurus verzilini MJ, WA (Kyrgyzstan)	PIN N 3042/1 Indeterminate age	Teeth and partial skeleton - *Alifanov & Averianov 2003* The name had existed informally 34 years before. *Rozhdestvensky 1969*	Length: **9.1 m** Shoulder height: **2.8 m**	**3.6 t**
2	Abrosaurus dongpoi MJ, EA (China)	ZDM5038 Indeterminate age	Skull - *Ouyang 1989* Before being corrected, the original name was *A. dongpoensis*. *Peng & Shu 1999*	Length: **9.5 m** Shoulder height: **2.9 m**	**4.1 t**
3	Jobaria tiguidensis MJ, NAf (Niger)	MNN TIG3 Indeterminate age	Skull and partial skeleton - *Sereno et al. 1994,1999* It was thought to be from the early Lower Cretaceous. *Rauhut & Lopez-Arbarello 2009*	Length: **15.2 m** Shoulder height: **4.7 m**	**17 t**

Primitive neosauropods similar to *Atlasaurus* - Quadrupedal, with short, robust bodies, triangular-crowned spatulate-foliodont teeth, phytophagous.

Nº	Genus and species	Largest specimen	Material and data	Size	Mass
4	*Volkheimeria chubutensis* LJ, SSA (Argentina)	PVL 4077? Indeterminate age	Femur - *Ogier 1975; Bonaparte 1986* The same code refers to the holotype specimen that measured 5.4 m in length and weighed some 700 kg.	Length: **8.7 m** Shoulder height: **3.2 m**	4 t
5	*Lapparentosaurus madagascariensis* MJ, MA (Madagascar)	D001–01-78 Adult	Femur - *Ogier 1975; Bonaparte 1986* *Bothriospondylus madagascariensis?*	Length: **12.3 m** Shoulder height: **4.4 m**	10.5 t
6	*Bothriospondylus madagascariensis* (n.d.) MJ, MA (Madagascar)	Uncatalogued Indeterminate age	Tooth - *Thevenin 1907* Not a titanosauriform, it was similar to *Turiasaurus* and to *Atlasaurus*. *Mannion 2010*	Length: **14 m** Shoulder height: **5.1 m**	16 t
7	*Atlasaurus imelakei* MJ, NAf (Morocco)	Uncatalogued Indeterminate age	Skull and partial skeleton - *Monbaron & Taquet 1981; Monbaron et al. 1999* Turiasauria?. *Mocho et al. 2013; Xing et al. 2015*	Length: **15.5 m** Shoulder height: **5.6 m**	21 t

Indeterminate primitive neosauropods - Quadrupedal, with robust bodies, triangular-crowned spatulate-foliodont teeth, phytophagous.

Nº	Genus and species	Largest specimen	Material and data	Size	Mass
8	"Northampton sauropod" MJ, WE (England, UK)	Uncatalogued Adult	Incomplete pelvis - *Reid 1984* It is similar to "*Apatosaurus*" *minimus*. The oldest of the neosauropods.	Length: **11 m** Shoulder height: **3 m**	5.7 t
9	"*Apatosaurus*" *minimus* UJ, WNA (Wyoming, USA)	AMNH 675 Indeterminate age	Incomplete pelvis - *Mook 1917* It had 6 sacral vertebrae.	Length: **12.4 m** Shoulder height: **3.4 m**	8 t

Primitive neosauropods similar to *Klamelisaurus* - Quadrupedal, with robust bodies, triangular-crowned spatulate-foliodont teeth, phytophagous.

Nº	Genus and species	Largest specimen	Material and data	Size	Mass
10	*Bellusaurus sui* MJ, EA (China)	IVPP V.8300 Juvenile	Skull and partial skeleton - *Dong 1990* Some 17 juvenile skeletons are known.	Length: **5 m** Shoulder height: **1.4 m**	450 kg
11	*Daanosaurus zhangi* UJ, EA (China)	ZDM0193 Juvenile	Skull and partial skeleton - *Ye et al. 2005* It was considered a brachiosaurid.	Length: **6.9 m** Shoulder height: **1.9 m**	1.2 t
12	*Bashunosaurus kaijiangensis* MJ, EA (China)	CUT unnumbered Indeterminate age	Partial skeleton - *Li et al.1998* Similar to *Datousaurus* or *Abrosaurus*?	Length: **13.3 m** Shoulder height: **3.1 m**	4.6 t
13	*Dashanpusaurus dongi* MJ, EA (China)	ZDM 5027 Indeterminate age	Partial skeleton - *Peng et al. 2005* It has been identified as a camarasaurid.	Length: **13.8 m** Shoulder height: **3.2 m**	5.2 t
14	*Klamelisaurus gobiensis* UJ, EA (China)	IVPP V.9492 Adult	Partial skeleton - *Zhao 1993* It was considered an adult *Bellusaurus*, but is more recent.	Length: **14.5 m** Shoulder height: **3.4 m**	6 t

1:500

DIPLODOCOIDEA

Primitive Diplodocoidea similar to *Haplocanthosaurus* - Quadrupedal, with robust bodies, type-O cylindrodont teeth, phytophagous.

Nº	Genus and species	Largest specimen	Material and data	Size	Mass
1	*Haplocanthosaurus* sp. UJ, WNA (Colorado, USA)	CMNH 10380 Indeterminate age	Partial skeleton - *Foster & Wedel 2014* *Haplocanthosaurus priscus* or *H. delfsi*?	Length: **5.6 m** Hip height: **1.7 m**	900 kg
2	*Haplocanthosaurus* sp. UJ, WNA (Utah, USA)	FHPR 1106 Adult	Partial skeleton - *Bilbey et al. 2000* It was an estimated 2.25 m high at the pelvis.	Length: **9.1 m** Hip height: **2.45 m**	3 t
3	*Ischyrosaurus manseli* UJ, WE (England, UK)	BMNH R41626 Indeterminate age	Incomplete humerus - *Hulke 1869; Hulke in Lydekker 1888* Rebbachisaurid or titanosauriform? *Barrett et al. 2010*	Length: **10.1 m** Hip height: **2.8 m**	4.5 t
4	*Haplocanthosaurus priscus* UJ, WNA (Colorado, USA)	CM 572, CM 33995 Indeterminate age	Partial skeleton - *Hatcher 1903* It was mistakenly changed from *Haplocanthus* to *Haplocanthosaurus*. It has been considered variously a neosauropod, macronarian, or Diplodocoidea. *Tschopp et al. 2015*	Length: **10.5 m** Hip height: **2.9 m**	5 t
5	*Haplocanthosaurus* sp. UJ, WNA (Wyoming, USA)	SMM P90.37.10 Indeterminate age	Partial skeleton- *Erickson 2014* *Haplocanthosaurus priscus*? *Ford**	Length: **12.7 m** Hip height: **3.5 m**	9 t
6	"*Haplocanthosaurus*" *delfsi* UJ, WNA (Colorado, USA)	CMNH 10380 Indeterminate age	Partial skeleton - *McIntosh & Williams 1988* It may be a different genus.	Length: **14.5 m** Hip height: **4 m**	13 t

Primitive Diplodocoidea similar to *Maraapunisaurus* - Quadrupedal, with semi-robust bodies, type-O cylindrodont teeth, phytophagous.

Nº	Genus and species	Largest specimen	Material and data	Size	Mass
7	*Amphicoelias* sp. UJ, SAf (Zimbabwe)	Uncatalogued Indeterminate age	Thoracic vertebra - *Bertram 1971* Known only from a photograph.	Length: **13 m** Hip height: **3.3 m**	5.3 t
8	*Maraapunisaurus fragillimus* UJ, WNA (Colorado, USA)	AMNH 5777 Adult	Thoracic vertebra and incomplete femur - *Cope 1878* Its estimated size has been highly contested. *Carpenter 2006, 2018; Woodruff & Forster 2014*	Length: **35 m** Hip height: **7.7 m**	70 t

Indeterminate primitive Diplodocoidea - Quadrupedal, with semi-robust bodies and high backs, type-O cylindrodont teeth, phytophagous.

Nº	Genus and species	Largest specimen	Material and data	Size	Mass
9	*Nopcsaspondylus alarconensis* eUC, SSA (Argentina)	Uncatalogued Juvenile	Thoracic vertebra - *Nopcsa 1902* Named 105 years after it was first published. *Apesteguía 2007*	Length: **3.6 m** Hip height: **1 m**	120 kg
10	*Algoasaurus bauri* eLC, SAf (South Africa)	5631 Juvenile	Partial skeleton - *Broom 1904* Diplodocoid? *Canudo & Salgado 2003; Ibicuru et al. 2012; Canudo & Salgado 2003*	Length: **4.8 m** Hip height: **1.3 m**	285 kg
11	*Lavocatisaurus sagrioensis* ILC ,SSA (Argentina)	MOZ-Pv 1232 Adult	Partial skeleton - *Salgado et al. 2012* More recent than *Zapalasaurus bonapartei*.	Length: **10.2 m** Hip height: **2.5 m**	2.3 t
12	*Zapalasaurus bonapartei* ILC, SSA (Argentina)	Pv-6127-MOZ Indeterminate age	Partial skeleton - *Salgado et al. 2006* It had a tail similar to that of Flagelicaudata. Rebbachisaurid? *Whitlock 2011*	Length: **10.2 m** Hip height: **2.5 m**	2.3 t
13	*Amazonsaurus maranhensis* ILC, NSA (Brazil)	MN 4560-V; UFRJ-DG 58-R Indeterminate age	Partial skeleton - *Carvalho et al. 2003* The fossil is highly fragmented.	Length: **10.5 m** Hip height: **2.55 m**	2.5 t

Nº	Genus and species	Largest specimen	Material and data	Size	Mass
14	Histriasaurus boscarollii eLC, EE (Croatia)	WN-V6 Indeterminate age	Thoracic vertebra - Dalla Vecchia 1998, 1999 The easternmost primitive diplodocoid.	Length: 11.5 m Hip height: 2.8 m	3.3 t
15	"Titanosaurus" rahioliensis (n.d.) IUC, IND (India)	GSI 20005 Indeterminate age	Teeth - Mathur & Srivastava 1987 It displays some similarities to Diplodocoides. Wilson & Upchurch 2003	Length: 13.5 m Hip height: 3.3 m	5 t
16	Comahuesaurus windharseni ILC, SSA (Argentina)	MOZ-PV-06741 Indeterminate age	Chevron - Carballido et al. 2012 It is more recent than Limaysaurus tessonei.	Length: 14 m Hip height: 3.4 m	5.8 t
17	Xenoposeidon proneneukos eLC, WE (England, UK)	BMNH R2095 Indeterminate age	Thoracic vertebra - Lydekker 1893 Named 114 years after first published. Taylor & Naish 2007; Taylor*	Length: 14.8 m Hip height: 3.6 m	7 t

Primitive Diplodocoidea similar to *Limaysaurus* - Quadrupedal, with semi-robust bodies and high backs, type-O cylindrodont teeth, phytophagous.

Nº	Genus and species	Largest specimen	Material and data	Size	Mass
18	cf. Rebbachisaurus sp. eUC, NAf (Morocco)	NMC 50890 Juvenile	Thoracic vertebra - Russell 1996 Rebbachisaurus garasbae?	Length: 1.9 m Hip height: 50 cm	20 kg
19	Katepensaurus goicoecheai eUC, SSA (Argentina)	UNPSJB-PV 1007 Indeterminate age	Vertebrae - Ibiricu et al. 2013 Katepenk means "needle" in the Tehuelche language.	Length: 12.9 m Hip height: 3.15 m	4.7 t
20	Rayososaurus agrioensis ILC, SSA (Argentina)	MACN-N 41 Indeterminate age	Partial skeleton - Bonaparte 1996 A doubtful species? Calvo & Salgado 1996; Bonaparte 1997	Length: 13.1 m Hip height: 3.2 m	4.9 t
21	Cathartesaura anaerobica eUC, SSA (Argentina)	MPCA- 232 Indeterminate age	Teeth and partial skeleton - Gallina & Apesteguía 2005 The name is a wordplay between the vulture Cathartes aura and the feminine form "saura."	Length: 14.8 m Hip height: 3.6 m	7 t
22	Limaysaurus tessonei eUC, SSA (Argentina)	MUCPv-205 Adult	Partial skeleton - Calvo & Salgado 1995 Gastroliths were found in association with the fossil.	Length: 15 m Hip height: 3.7 m	7.5 t
23	Rayososaurus sp. eUC, NSA (Brazil)	UFMA 1.20.418 Indeterminate age	Tooth - Carvalho et al. 2007 UFMA 1.10.283, 10.5 m tall and weighing 5.8 t, has been identified as Rayoso-saurus sp. Medeiros & Schultz 2004	Length: 21 m Hip height: 5.2 m	20 t
24	Rebbachisaurus garasbae eUC, NAf (Morocco)	NMC 41809 Adult	Tooth - Russell 1996 The first sauropod known to have a high back, considered a "sail," although it was actually a hump. Lavocat 1954; Bailey 1997; Wilson & Allain 2015	Length: 26 m Hip height: 6.5 m	40 t

Primitive Diplodocoidea similar to *Nigersaurus* - Quadrupedal, with semi-robust bodies and low backs, type-O cylindrodont teeth, phytophagous.

Nº	Genus and species	Largest specimen	Material and data	Size	Mass
25	Nigersaurus taqueti ILC, NAf (Niger)	MNN GAD517 Adult	Skull and partial skeleton - Sereno et al. 1999 Specimens MNN GAD513 and MNN GAD514 were the same size.	Length: 10 m Hip height: 2.15 m	1.9 t
26	Demandasaurus darwini ILC, WE (Spain)	MPS-RV II Indeterminate age	Skull and partial skeleton - Torcida Fernández-Baldor et al. 2011 It lacked the kind of dental batteries found in Nigersaurus. Torcida Fernández-Baldor 2012	Length: 10.8 m Hip height: 2.3 m	2.4 t
27	Tataouinea hannibalis ILC, NAf (Tunisia)	ONM DT 1-36 Indeterminate age	Partial skeleton - Fanti et al. 2013 Its pneumatized ischium is unique among dinosaurs.	Length: 15 m Hip height: 3.2 m	6.4 t

1:500

FLAGELLICAUDATA

Indeterminate Flagellicaudata - Quadrupedal, with semi-robust bodies and high backs, type-O cylindrodont teeth, phytophagous.

Nº	Genus and species	Largest specimen	Material and data	Size	Mass
1	"Megapleurocoelus menduckii" eUC, NAf (Morocco)	JP Cr376 Indeterminate age	Thoracic vertebra - Singer 2015* Dicraeosaurid or diplodocid? Mortimer*	Length: 13 m Hip height: 3 m	3.85 t

Primitive Flagellicaudata similar to *Dicraeosaurus* - Quadrupedal, with semi-robust bodies and high backs, robust type-O cylindrodont teeth, phytophagous.

Nº	Genus and species	Largest specimen	Material and data	Size	Mass
2	"Dicraeosaurus" sp. eUC, NAf (Sudan)	Vb-856, 857, 892, 884, 879 Indeterminate age	Partial skeleton - Rauhut 1999 The most recent.	Length: 6.7 m Hip height: 1.6 m	600 kg
3	cf. Dicraeosaurus sp. eUC, NAf (Egypt)	Uncatalogued Indeterminate age	Partial skeleton - Stromer 1934; El-Khashab 1977 Too recent to be Dicraeosaurus	Length: 9.3 m Hip height: 2.1 m	1.2 t
4	Brachytrachelopan mesai UJ, SSA (Argentina)	MPEF-PV 1716 Adult	Partial skeleton - Rauhut et al. 2005 Attempts have been made to change the name to "B. mesaorum." Martinelli et al. 2010; Ford*	Length: 8.5 m Hip height: 2.45 m	3 t
5	Dicraeosaurus sp. UJ, SAf (Tanzania)	MOZ-PV-06741 Indeterminate age	Chevron - Janensch Dicraeosaurus hansemanni or D. sattleri?	Length: 14.5 m Hip height: 3.2 m	5 t
6	Dicraeosaurus sattleri UJ, SAf (Tanzania)	HMN M Indeterminate age	Incomplete skull - Janensch 1961 Some characteristics are similar to Amargasaurus	Length: 14.8 m Hip height: 3.25 m	5.3 t
7	Dicraeosaurus hansemanni UJ, SAf (Tanzania)	HMN m 3 Indeterminate age	Fibula - Janensch 1961 The genus type species. Janensch 1914	Length: 15.5 m Hip height: 3.4 m	6 t
8	Dicraeosaurus sp. UJ, SAf (Zimbabwe)	QG69 Indeterminate age	Femur - Raath & McIntosh 1987 It was found in what was Rhodesia at the time.	Length: 15.6 m Hip height: 3.5 m	6.3 t

9	Suuwassea emilieae UJ, WNA (Montana, USA)	ANS 21122 Indeterminate age	Skull and partial skeleton - Harris & Dodson 2004 Primitive dicraeosaurid. Whitlock 2011; Tschopp et al. 2015	Length: 16.2 m Hip height: 3.6 m	6.9 t
10	Dyslocosaurus polyonichius UJ, WNA (Wyoming, USA)	AC 663 Indeterminate age	Partial hind limb - McIntosh et al. 1992 It was believed to be from the late Upper Cretaceous. Tschopp et al. 2015	Length: 16.6 m Hip height: 3.7 m	7.5 t
11	Lingwulong shenqi LJ, EA (China)	IVPP V23704 Indeterminate age	Teeth and partial skeleton - Xu et al. 2018 The oldest dicraeosaurid.	Length: 17 m Hip height: 3.8 m	8 t
12	Dystrophaeus viaemalae (n.d.) UJ, WNA (Utah, USA)	USNM 2364 Indeterminate age	Partial skeleton - Cope 1877 The oldest dicraeosaurid. Gillette 1996a, 1996b; Tschopp et al. 2015	Length: 18.7 m Hip height: 4.1 m	10.5 t
13	Morinosaurus typus UJ, WE (France)	MPEF-PV 1716 Indeterminate age	Tooth - Sauvage 1874 The first dicraeosaurid described, but the piece was lost. Upchurch et al. 2004	Length: 19 m Hip height: 4.2 m	11 t
14	"Morosaurus" agilis UJ, WNA (Colorado, USA)	USNM 5371 Indeterminate age	Metacarpal - Marsh 1889; Gilmore 1907 It was probably a dicraeosaurid. Whitlock & Wilson 2015, 2018	Length: 22 m Hip height: 4.8 m	17 t

Primitive Flagellicaudata similar to *Amargasaurus* - Quadrupedal, with semi-robust bodies and high backs, type-O cylindrodont teeth, phytophagous.

15	Amargatitanis macni ILC, SSA (Argentina)	MACN PV N51 53 Indeterminate age	Partial skeleton - Apesteguía 2007 It was considered a titanosaur. Gallina 2016	Length: 12 m Hip height: 2.65 m	3.1 t
16	Amargasaurus cazaui ILC, SSA (Argentina)	MACN-N 15 Indeterminate age	Skull and partial skeleton - Salgado & Bonaparte 1991 Some of its vertebrae were very high.	Length: 13.5 m Hip height: 3 m	3.5 t
17	Pilmatueia faundezi eLC, SSA (Argentina)	MLL-Pv-009 Subadult	Vertebrae - Coria et al. 2018 Dicraeosaurid remains were reported years earlier in the same locality. Coria et al. 2010, 2012	Length: 14.5 m Hip height: 3.2 m	4.2 t

1:500

DIPLODOCIDAE

Primitive Diplodocoides similar to *Amphicoelias* - Quadrupedal, with semi-robust bodies, type-O cylindrodont teeth, phytophagous

Nº	Genus and species	Largest specimen	Material and data	Size	Mass
1	Amphicoelias altus UJ, WNA (Colorado, USA)	AMNH 5764A Subadult	Scapulocoracoid - Cope 1877 It is much larger than the holotype. Osborn & Mook 1921	Length: 25 m Hip height: 5.5 m	26 t

Primitive Diplodocoides similar to - Quadrupedal, with semi-robust bodies, type-O cylindrodont teeth, phytophagous

2	Apatosaurus sp. UJ, WNA (South Dakota, USA)	DSM 25345 Juvenile	Caudal vertebra - Foster 1996 The most recent Apatosaurinae.	Length: 9.9 m Hip height: 2.4 m	2.4 t
3	Brontosaurus parvus UJ, WNA (Oklahoma, Utah, Wyoming, USA)	UWGM 15556 Indeterminate age	Partial skeleton - Wedel & Taylor 2013 Hototype specimen BYU 1252-18531 was a juvenile. Peterson & Gilmore 1902	Length: 19 m Hip height: 4.1 m	14 t
4	Brontosaurus yahnahpin UJ, WNA (Wyoming, USA)	TATE 001 Indeterminate age	Partial skeleton - Filla & Redman 1994 It was considered the most primitive. Bakker 1998; Tschopp, Mateus & Benson 2015	Length: 19 m Hip height: 4.1m	14 t
5	Brontosaurus excelsus UJ, WNA (Colorado, Wyoming, USA)	YPM 1981 Indeterminate age	Partial skeleton - Marsh 1881 It was thought to be of the Apatosaurus genus, but the name Brontosaurus is so popular that it has never been forgotten.	Length: 21 m Hip height: 4.2 m	16 t
6	Brontosaurus excelsus? UJ, WNA (Utah, USA)	FMNH P25112 Indeterminate age	Partial skeleton - Riggs 1903; Bertog et al. 2005 It may have been a B. excelsus or an entirely new genus. Tschopp et al. 2015	Length: 22 m Hip height: 4.6 m	17 t
7	Apatosaurus louisae UJ, WNA (Utah, Wyoming, USA)	CMNH 3018 (CM 3018) Adult	Partial skeleton - Gilmore 1936 It was the most robust species and the first with preserved skull.	Length: 23.5 m Hip height: 4.5 m	20 t
8	Atlantosaurus immannis (n.d.) UJ, WNA (Colorado, USA)	YPM 1840 Adult	Incomplete femur - Marsh 1878 It is not a synonym of Apatosaurus ajax. Tschopp et al. 2015	Length: 23 m Hip height: 4.75 m	20 t
9	"Titanosaurus" montanus (n.d.) UJ, WNA (Colorado, USA)	YPM 1835 Indeterminate age	Incomplete sacrum - Marsh 1877 Apatosaurus ajax? Taylor 2010	Length: 23 m Hip height: 4.75 m	20 t
10	Apatosaurus ajax UJ, WNA (Colorado, USA)	YPM 1860 Adult	Partial skeleton - Marsh 1877 Ajax or Ayante is a hero of Greek mythology.	Length: 23 m Hip height: 4.75 m	20 t
11	Apatosaurus sp. ("Camarasaurus" sp.) UJ, WNA (Oklahoma, USA	OMNH 1670 Adult	Thoracic vertebra - Stovall 1938 OMNH 1329 is another very large subadult. Wedel 2013	Length: 30 m Hip height: 6 m	33 t

Diplodocids similar to *Supersaurus* - Quadrupedal, with semi-robust bodies, type-O cylindrodont teeth, phytophagous.

12	Leinkupal laticauda eLC, SSA (Argentina)	MMCH-Pv 63-1-8 Indeterminate age	Partial skeleton - Gallina et al. 2014 The most recent diplodocid of South America. Gianechini et al. 2011	Length: 11 m Hip height: 2 m	1.65 t
13	Supersaurus lourinhanensis UJ, WE (Portugal)	ML 414 Indeterminate age	Partial skeleton - Bonaparte & Mateus 1999 A second species of Supersaurus. Mannion et al. 2012; Tschopp et al. 2015	Length: 21 m Hip height: 3.4 m	8.8 t
14	Tornieria africana UJ, SAf (Tanzania)	A4 Adult	Scapula - Janensch 1961 Barosaurus gracilis is an invalid name as the specimen was not properly analyzed. Remes 2006	Length: 24 m Hip height: 3.95 m	13.5 t
15	Tornieria sp. UJ, SAf (Zimbabwe)	QG68 Indeterminate age	Humerus - Raath & McIntosh 1987 Tornieria africana?	Length: 24.5 m Hip height: 4 m	14.5 t
16	cf. "Brachiosaurus" nougaredi UJ, NAf (Algeria)	Uncatalogued Indeterminate age	Incomplete sacrum - Lapparent 1960 It is too narrow to be a titanosauriform.	Length: 29.5 m Hip height: 5 m	25 t

| 17 | *Supersaurus vivianae*
UJ, WNA (Colorado, Wyoming, USA) | WDC DMJ-021
Indeterminate age | Scapula - *Lovelace et al. 2007*
The name "Supersaurus" was created in 1972 but was not formalized until 13 years later. WDC DMJ-021 specimen known as *Jimbo*, was a animal somewhat smaller with a length of 31 m and a weight of 29 t. *Jensen 1985; Lovelace et al. 2007* | Length: **33 m**
Hip height: **5.4 m** | **35 t** |

Diplodocids similar to *Diplodocus* - Quadrupedal, with light bodies, type-O cylindrodont teeth, phytophagous.

18	*Kaatedocus siberi* UJ, WNA (Wyoming, USA)	SMA 0004 Adult	Skull and partial skeleton - *Tschopp & Mateus 2013* The smallest diplodocid.	Length: **13 m** Hip height: **2.15 m**	**1.9 t**
19	*Diplodocus* cf. *carnegii* UJ, WNA (Wyoming, USA)	WDC-FS001A Indeterminate age	Partial skeleton - *Bedell & Trexler 2005* A new genus and species. *Tschopp et al. 2015*	Length: **18 m** Hip height: **2.9 m**	**5 t**
20	*Galeamopus pabsti* UJ, WNA (Wyoming, USA)	SMA 0011 Subadult	Skull and partial skeleton – *Tschopp & Mateus 2017* It was not an adult specimen but was sexually mature.	Length: **18.2 m** Hip height: **2.95 m**	**5.1 t**
21	"*Amphicoelias brontodiplodocus*" (n.n.) UJ, WNA (Wyoming, USA)	DQ-BS Indeterminate age	Partial skeleton - *Galiano & Albersdörfer 2010* It was not formally described.	Length: **22 m** Hip height: **3.75 m**	**8 t**
22	*Galeamopus hayi* UJ, WNA (Wyoming, USA)	HMNS 175 Indeterminate age	Partial skeleton - *Holland 1924* It was previously classified as CM 662. *Tschopp et al. 2015*	Length: **23 m** Hip height: **3.6 m**	**10 t**
23	*Diplodocus lacustris* (n.d.) UJ, WNA (Colorado, USA)	YPM 1922 Indeterminate age	Incomplete skull - *Marsh 1884* It may be a specimen of *D. longus* or another species. *Upchurch et al. 2004*	Length: **24 m** Hip height: **3.7 m**	**10.5 t**
24	*Barosaurus* sp. UJ, WNA (Utah, USA)	CM 11984 Indeterminate age	Partial skeleton - *McIntosh 2005* An uncertain specimen of *Barosaurus lentus*. *Tschopp et al. 2015*	Length: **26 m** Hip height: **3.75 m**	**12.2 t**
25	*Diplodocus longus* UJ, WNA (Colorado, Utah, Wyoming, USA)	YPM 1920 Indeterminate age	Partial skeleton - *Marsh 1878* Also known as USNM 2672. *Ford**	Length: **26 m** Hip height: **4.1 m**	**13 t**
26	*Diplodocus carnegii* UJ, WNA (New Mexico, Wyoming, USA)	AMNH 588 Indeterminate age	Partial forelimb - *Osborn 1899; Osborn & Granger 1901* It is frequently referred to as *D. carnegiei*. *Hatcher 1901, 1906*	Length: **26 m** Hip height: **4.1 m**	**13.5 t**
27	*Galeamopus* sp. UJ, WNA (Colorado, USA)	USNM 2673 Indeterminate age	Skull - *Holland 1906* A probable new species. *Tschopp et al. 2015*	Length: **28 m** Hip height: **4.4 m**	**17.5 t**
28	*Diplodocus* sp. UJ, WNA (USA)	AMNH 585 Indeterminate age	Tibia and fibula - *Wilhite 2003* It may be an older specimen of an already named species.	Length: **29.5 m** Hip height: **4.6 m**	**20 t**
29	*Diplodocus hallorum* UJ, WNA (New Mexico, Utah, Wyoming, USA)	NMMNH 3690 Adult	Partial skeleton - *Gillette 1991; Lucas et al. 2004, 2006* Poor arrangement of the caudal vertebrae led to the mistaken length of 52 m. *Gillette 1991*	Length: **30 m** Hip height: **4.6 m**	**21 t**
30	*Barosaurus lentus* UJ, WNA (South Dakota, Utah, Wyoming, USA)	YPM 429 Indeterminate age	Partial skeleton - *Marsh 1890; Lull 1919* The appendicular skeleton may belong to a different individual than the axial skeleton. *McIntosh 1981*	Length: **37 m** Hip height: **5.1 m**	**31 t**
31	cf. *Barosaurus lentus* UJ, WNA (Colorado, USA)	BYU 9024 Indeterminate age	Cervical vertebra - *Jensen 1985, 1987* The piece was believed to be from a *Supersaurus*. The cervical position is between C9 and C11. If it was a C9, its size should have exceeded 80 t. *Lovelace et al. 2007; Taylor & Wedel 2016; Taylor**	Length: **45 m** Hip height: **6.4 m**	**60 t**

1:700

MACRONARIA

Indeterminate macronarians - Quadrupedal, with robust bodies, oval-crowned robust spatulate-foliodont teeth, phytophagous.

Nº	Genus and species	Largest specimen	Material and data	Size	Mass
1	*"Bothriospondylus" suffossus* (n.d.) UJ, WE (England, UK)	NHM 44589–44595 Indeterminate age	Thoracic vertebra - *Owen 1875* Doubtful identification. *Mannion 2010*	Length: **7.9 m** Shoulder height: **2.25 m**	2.1 t
2	*"Bothriospondylus" robustus* (n.d.) MJ, WE (England, UK)	NHM 22428 Indeterminate age	Thoracic vertebra - *Owen 1875* Frequently mistakenly written as "B. suffosus." *Mannion 2010*	Length: **11.5 m** Shoulder height: **3.3 m**	6.5 t

Primitive macronarians similar to *Camarasaurus* - Quadrupedal, with robust bodies, robust oval-crowned spatulate-foliodont teeth, phytophagous.

Nº	Genus and species	Largest specimen	Material and data	Size	Mass
3	*Camarasaurus* sp. UJ, SAf (Zimbabwe)	QG59 Indeterminate age	Femur - *Raath & McIntosh 1987* Most recent *Camarasaurus*.	Length: **12.9 m** Shoulder height: **3.2 m**	7.5 t
4	*Cathetosaurus lewisi* UJ, WNA (Colorado, USA)	BYU 9047 Indeterminate age	Partial skeleton - *Jensen 1988* From a genus other than *Camarasaurus. Mateus & Tschopp 2013*	Length: **13.3 m** Shoulder height: **3.3 m**	8.3 t
5	*Camarasaurus grandis* UJ, WNA (Colorado, New Mexico, Wyoming, USA)	GMNH-PV 101 Adult	Partial skeleton - *Tidwell et al. 2005* Although grandis means "big," this is the smallest *Camarasaurus. Tschopp et al. 2014*	Length: **14.9 m** Shoulder height: **3.65 m**	11.5 t
6	*Camarasaurus* sp. UJ, WE (Germany)	Breitkreutz col. 2002/1510 Indeterminate age	Ungual phalange - *Diedrich 2011* Similar to *Camarasaurus*.	Length:**14.9 m** Shoulder height: **3.7 m**	11.7 t
7	*Camarasaurus lentus* UJ, WNA (Colorado, Utah, Wyoming, USA)	CM 11069 Indeterminate age	Vetebrae - *Holland 1924* This species migrated some 300 km in a 4–5 month cycle. *Fricke et al. 2008*	Length: **16 m** Shoulder height: **4 m**	14.5 t
8	*Lourinhasaurus alenquerensis* UJ, WE (Portugal)	MIGM Indeterminate age	Partial skeleton - *Lapparent & Zybszewski 1957* Its name is very similar to that of the theropod *Lourinhanosaurus. Mateus 1998*	Length: **17.5 m** Shoulder height: **4.4 m**	19 t
9	*Camarasaurus supremus* UJ, WNA (Colorado, USA)	AMNH 5760 Adult	Tibia- *Cope 1877; Osborn & Mook 1921* The catalog number AMNH 5760 includes several individuals. The largest is a tibia.	Length: **20 m** Shoulder height: **5 m**	30 t

Primitive macronarians similar to *Aragosaurus* - Quadrupedal, with robust bodies, oval-crowned spatulate-foliodont teeth, phytophagous.

Nº	Genus and species	Largest specimen	Material and data	Size	Mass
10	*Aragosaurus ischiaticus* eLC, WE (Spain)	MMG-SS Indeterminate age	Femur - *Sanz et al. 1987* A vertebrate research group at Zaragoza University is called "Aragosaurus."	Length: **14.2 m** Shoulder height: **3.55 m**	7.9 t
11	*"Cetiosaurus"* sp. ILC, WE (Spain)	MNCN Col. Indeterminate age	Incomplete femur - *Royo-Gomez 1927* Too recent to be *Cetiosaurus*. Macronaria?	Length: **14.7 m** Shoulder height: **3.75 m**	8.8 t
12	*Galvesaurus herreroi* UJ, WE (Spain)	MPG CLH-1-16 Adult	Partial skeleton - *Barco et al. 2005; Sanchez-Hernandez 2005* The name "Galveosaurus" was originally used in the Municipal Paleontolology Museum of Galve.	Length: **17 m** Shoulder height: **4.25 m**	13.9 t

1:500

TITANOSAURIFORMES

Primitive titanosauriforms similar to *Europasaurus* - Quadrupedal, with robust bodies, oval-crowned spatulate-foliodont teeth, phytophagous.

Nº	Genus and species	Largest specimen	Material and data	Size	Mass
1	*Europasaurus holgeri* UJ, WE (Germany)	DFMMh/FV 157 Adult	Fibula - *Sander et al. 2006* Smallest titanosauriform. *Windolf 1998; D'Emic 2012; Mannion et al. 2013*	Length: **6 m** Shoulder height: **1.7 m**	800 kg

Primitive titanosauriforms similar to *Padillasaurus* - Quadrupedal, with robust bodies, oval-crowned spatulate-foliodont teeth, phytophagous.

Nº	Genus and species	Largest specimen	Material and data	Size	Mass
2	*Brohisaurus kirthari* UJ, IND (Pakistan)	MSM-86-106-K Indeterminate age	Partial skeleton - *Malkani 2003* Titanosauriform or basal Titanosauria? *Mannion et al. 2013*	Length: **8 m** Shoulder height: **2.4 m**	1.5 t
3	*Vouivria damparisensis* UJ, WE (France)	NHM R2598 Subadult	Partial skeleton - *Lapparent 1943* A different genus than *"Bothriospondylus" madagascariensis. Mannion 2010*	Length: **14.6 m** Shoulder height: **4.4 m**	9.2 t
4	*Bothriospondylus elongatus* (n.d.) eLC, WE (England, UK)	NHM R2239 Indeterminate age	Thoracic vertebra - *Owen 1875* Identity in doubt. *Mannion 2010*	Length: **15.5 m** Shoulder height: **4.6 m**	11 t
5	*Padillasaurus leivaensis* ILC, NSA (Colombia)	JACVM 0001 Indeterminate age	Vertebrae - *Carballido et al. 2015* First named sauropod from Colombia.	Length: **16.1 m** Shoulder height: **4.8 m**	12.3 t
6	*"Brachiosaurus" nougaredi* UJ, NAf (Algeria)	Uncatalogued Indeterminate age	Metacarpal - *Lapparent 1960* A enormous sacrum assigned to this species was actually another kind of sauropod. *Salgado & Calvo 1997*	Length: **16.1 m** Shoulder height: **4.8 m**	12.3 t
7	*Ornithopsis hulkei* (n.d.) ILC, WE (England, UK)	BMNH 28632 Indeterminate age	Thoracic vertebra - *Seeley 1870* Believed to be a giant pterosaur.	Length: **17.4 m** Shoulder height: **5.2 m**	15.5 t
8	cf. *Ornithopsis leedsii* MJ, WE (England, UK)	BMNH R1716 Indeterminate age	Thoracic vertebra - *Martill & Clarke 1994* Different species than *Ornithopsis leedsii*	Length: **18.7 m** Shoulder height: **5.6 m**	19 t
9	*"Rebbachisaurus" tamesnensis* (n.d.) ILC, NAf (Algeria, Niger, Tunisia)	Uncatalogued Indeterminate age	Caudal vertebra - *Lapparent 1960* Believed to be a synonym of *Nigersaurus* but was a titanosauriform. *Weishampel et al. 2007*	Length: **19 m** Shoulder height: **5.7 m**	20 t

Primitive titanosauriforms similar to *Giraffatitan* - Quadrupedal, with robust bodies, oval-crowned spatulate-foliodont teeth, phytophagous.

#	Taxon / Locality	Specimen / Age	Material - Reference / Notes	Size	Mass
10	*Chondrosteosaurus gigas* ILC, WE (England, UK)	NHMUK 46869 Indeterminate age	Incomplete cervical vertebra - *Owen 1876* Brachiosaurid? *Upchurch 1993, 1995; Wedel 2003*	Length: **7.6 m** Shoulder height: **2.1 m**	1.4 t
11	*Pelorosaurus* sp. UJ, WE (France)	Uncatalogued Indeterminate age	Scapulocoracoid - *Huene 1929* Illustrated from a photogram sent by Franz Nopcsa.	Length: **8.5 m** Shoulder height: **2.4 m**	1.9 t
12	*"Cetiosaurus"* sp. eLC, WE (England)	NHMUK 24814 Indeterminate age	Caudal vertebra - *Delair 1959* They are likely from a titanosauriform. *Barrett et al. 2010*	Length: **8.6 m** Shoulder height: **2.4 m**	2 t
13	cf. *Duriatitan humerocristatus* UJ, WE (Portugal)	MG 4976 Indeterminate age	Incomplete humerus - *Mocho et al. 2016* *Duriatitan humerocristatus?*	Length: **10.6 m** Shoulder height: **2.9 m**	3.8 t
14	*Soriatitan golmayensis* eLC, WE (Spain)	MNS 2001 Indeterminate age	Tooth and partial skeleton - *Royo-Torres et al. 2017* Similar to *Abydosaurus*, *Cedarosaurus* and *Venenosaurus*	Length: **10.9 m** Shoulder height: **2.95 m**	4 t
15	*Chondrosteosaurus magnus* (n.d.) ILC, WE (England, UK)	NHMUK R98 Indeterminate age	Incomplete dorsal vertebra - *Owen 1876* Doubtful species. *Upchurch 1993*	Length: **12.4 m** Shoulder height: **3.35 m**	6 t
16	*Ornithopsis eucamerotus* (n.d.) ILC, WE (England, UK)	BMNH R97 Indeterminate age	Pubis and ischium - *Hulke 1882* Somphospondylian? *Upchurch et al. 2004*	Length: **13.3 m** Shoulder height: **3.6 m**	7.4 t
17	*Venenosaurus dicrocei* ILC, WNA (Utah, USA)	DMNH 40932 Adult	Partial skeleton - *Tidwell et al. 2001* Its tail displayed convergent features with *Aeolosaurus*.	Length: **13.6 m** Shoulder height: **3.7 m**	8 t
18	*"Pelorosaurus" leedsi* UJ, WE (England, UK)	BMNH R1984-8 Indeterminate age	Partial skeleton - *Hulke 1887* Different from cf. *Ornithopsis leedsi*. *Noè et al. 2010*	Length: **13.9 m** Shoulder height: **3.8 m**	8.6 t
19	*Eucamerotus foxi* ILC, WE (England, UK)	BMNH R2522 Indeterminate age	Thoracic vertebra - *Hulke 1871* The species was proposed 124 years later. *Blows 1995*	Length: **13.9 m** Shoulder height: **3.8 m**	8.6 t
20	*Cetiosaurus brevis* eLC, WE (England, UK)	BMNH 28626 Indeterminate age	Humerus - *Melville 1849; Mantell 1850* Somphospondylian? *Taylor & Naish 2007; Upchurch, Mannion & Barrett 2011*	Length: **14.1 m** Shoulder height: **3.85 m**	9 t
21	*Duriatitan humerocristatus* UJ, WE (England, UK)	BMNH R44635 Indeterminate age	Incomplete humerus - *Hulke 1874* Originally called "Ceteosaurus"	Length: **14.4 m** Shoulder height: **3.9 m**	9.5 t
22	*Dinodocus mackensoni* (n.d.) ILC, WE (England, UK)	BMNH R14695 Indeterminate age	Humerus - *Owen 1884* A doubtful brachiosaurid. *Upchurch et al. 2004*	Length: **14.8 m** Shoulder height: **4 m**	10.3 t
23	*Cedarosaurus weiskopfae* ILC, WNA (Texas, Utah, USA)	FMNH PR977 Indeterminate age	Metatarsal - *Jacobs & Winkler 1998* Identified as *Cedarosaurus*. *D'Emic 2012*	Length: **14.9 m** Shoulder height: **4.1 m**	10.6 t
24	*Brachiosaurus* sp. UJ, WE (Germany)	Uncatalogued Indeterminate age	Tooth - *Diedrich 2011* Similar to *Giraffatitan*.	Length: **15.8 m** Shoulder height: **4.3 m**	12.6 t
25	*Sonorasaurus thompsoni* ILC, WNA (Arizona, USA)	ASDM 500 Indeterminate age	Partial skeleton - *Ratkevich 1998* The name had been informally presented two years earlier. *Thayer et al. 1996*	Length: **17.8 m** Shoulder height: **4.8 m**	18 t
26	cf. *Giraffatitan brancai* UJ, SAf (Tanzania)	F 2 Indeterminate age	Partial skeleton - *Janensch 1961* Older than *Giraffatitan brancai*.	Length: **20 m** Shoulder height: **5.4 m**	25 t
27	cf. *Morosaurus marchei* UJ, WE (Portugal)	Uncatalogued Indeterminate age	Tooth - *Sauvage 1897/1898* The holotype material was from theropods. *Lapparent & Zbyszewski 1957*	Length: **20.6 m** Shoulder height: **5.6 m**	27.5 t
28	*"Brachiosaurus"* sp. UJ, SAf (Zimbabwe)	QG54 Indeterminate age	Partial skeleton - *Bond, Wilson & Raath 1970; Raath & McIntosh 1987* *Giraffatitan brancai?*	Length: **20.7 m** Shoulder height: **5.6 m**	28 t
29	*Giraffatitan* sp. UJ, SSA (Argentina)	MPEF PV 3099 Indeterminate age	Partial skeleton - *Rauhut 2006* First South American brachiosaurid.	Length: **22 m** Shoulder height: **6 m**	33 t
30	*"Brachiosaurus"* sp. UJ, SAf (Tanzania)	BMNH R5937 Indeterminate age	Partial skeleton - *Migeod 1927a, 1927b, 1930* Known as "The Archbishop," it is different than *Giraffatitan*. *Taylor 2005*	Length: **22.6 m** Shoulder height: **6.2 m**	35 t
31	*Giraffatitan brancai* UJ, SAf (Tanzania)	HMN XV2 Indeterminate age	Fibula - *Janensch 1914* *Giraffatitan* is the genus upon which the popular model of *Brachiosaurus* is based.	Length: **25 m** Shoulder height: **6.8 m**	48 t

Primitive titanosauriforms similar to *Abydosaurus* - Quadrupedal, with robust bodies, type-D cylindrodont teeth, phytophagous.

#	Taxon / Locality	Specimen / Age	Material - Reference / Notes	Size	Mass
32	*Abydosaurus mcintoshi* iLC, WNA (Utah, USA)	DINO 17849 Subadult	Partial skull - *Chure et al. 2010* Its teeth were different from those of other titanosauriforms.	Length: **20 m** Shoulder height: **5.45 m**	26 t

Primitive titanosauriforms similar to *Brachiosaurus* - Quadrupedal, with robust bodies, robust oval-crowned spatulate-foliodont teeth, phytophagous.

#	Taxon / Locality	Specimen / Age	Material - Reference / Notes	Size	Mass
33	*Brachiosaurus* sp. UJ, WNA (Wyoming, USA)	SMA 0009 Juvenile	Partial skeleton - *Foster 2005* It was considered a diplodocoid. *Schwarz et al. 2007; Carballido et al. 2012*	Length: **2.4 m** Shoulder height: **70 cm**	45 kg
34	*"Biconcavoposeidon"* UJ, WNA (Wyoming, USA)	AMNH FARB 291 Juvenile	Thoracic vertebrae - *Taylor & Wedel 2017* The vertebral centra were not completely ossified, which is rare for an animal of this size.	Length: **14.7 m** Shoulder height: **3.7 m**	8.7 t
35	*Brachiosaurus* sp. UJ, WNA (Colorado, USA)	BYU 9462 Indeterminate age	Scapulocoracoid - *Jensen 1985* It may belong to another genus. *Curtice et al. 1996*	Length: **23 m** Shoulder height: **5.8 m**	32 t
36	*Lusotitan atalaiensis* UJ, WE (Portugal)	MIGM Col. Indeterminate age	Partial skeleton - *Lapparent & Zbyszewski 1957* Basal macronarian or brachiosaurid? *Mannion et al. 2013; D'Emic et al. 2016; Poropat et al. 2016*	Length: **24 m** Shoulder height: **5.9 m**	34 t
37	*Brachiosaurus* sp. UJ, WNA (Oklahoma, USA)	BYU 725 Indeterminate age	Cervical vertebrae - *Wedel 1997* A metacarpal was reported. *Bonnan & Wedel 2004*	Length: **24 m** Shoulder height: **6.1 m**	37 t
38	*Brachiosaurus altithorax* UJ, WNA (Colorado, USA)	FMNH P25107 Indeterminate age	Partial skeleton - *Riggs 1903* A contemporary skull is known as *Brachiosaurus* sp. *Carpenter & Tidwell 1998*	Length: **24.5 m** Shoulder height: **6.2 m**	40 t
39	*Brachiosaurus* sp. UJ, WNA (Utah, USA)	Uncatalogued Indeterminate age	Incomplete femur - *Jensen 1985* It may have belonged to a gigantic *Camarasaurus*. *Taylor**	Length: **26.5 m** Shoulder height: **6.7 m**	50 t

1:700

1:700

SOMPHOSPONDYLI

Primitive somphospondylans similar to *Chubutisaurus* - Quadrupedal, with robust bodies, oval-crowned spatulate-foliodont teeth, phytophagous.

Nº	Genus and species	Largest specimen	Material and data	Size	Mass
1	cf. *Astrodon* sp. ILC, WNA (Utah, USA)	Uncatalogued Juvenile	Tooth - *Kirkland et al. 1995* Most recent *Astrodon* of North America.	Length: 3.1 m Shoulder height: **94 cm**	135 kg
2	*Astrodon* sp. ILC, NAf (Niger)	Uncatalogued Juvenile	Thoracic vertebra - *Lapparent 1960*	Length: 3.1 m Shoulder height: **95 cm**	135 kg
3	*Pleurocoelus valdensis* ILC, WE (England, UK)	BMNH R1730 Indeterminate age	Tooth - *Lydekker 1889* Believed to be the teeth of *Hylaeosaurus*. *Owen 1853*	Length: 5.9 m Shoulder height: **1.5 m**	615 kg
4	cf. *Pleurocoelus* sp. eLC, WE (Denmark)	Uncatalogued Juvenile	Tooth - *Bonde & Christiansen 2003* Contemporary with *Dromaeosauroides*. *Christiansen & Bonde 2003*	Length: 6 m Shoulder height: **1.6 m**	680 kg
5	*Astrodon* sp. eLC, WE (Spain)	CBH3 Juvenile	Tooth - *Sanz et al. 1987, 1990* Assigned to *Pleurocoelus* sp. *Weishampel 1990; Ruiz-Omeñaca & Canudo 200*5	Length: 8.6 m Shoulder height: **2.05 m**	1.4 t
6	*Astrodon* sp. eUC, NSA (northern Brazil)	UFMA 1.20.472 Indeterminate age	Caudal vertebra - *Candeiro et al. 2011* Brazil Cenomanian Alcántara Formation.	Length: 8.8 m Shoulder height: **2.1 m**	1.5 t
7	*Pleurocoelus* sp. ILC, WNA (Texas, USA)	USNM 187535 Juvenile	Tooth - *Langston 1974* SMU 72146 may have been 2 m long and weighed 30 kg, but the piece may belong to an ornithischian. *Winkler et al. 1990*	Length: 10 m Shoulder height: **2.35 m**	2.2 t
8	"*Pleurocoelus*" *valdensis* ILC, WE (Portugal)	Uncatalogued Juvenile	Tooth - *Sauvage 1897–98* The same species as MMM815/99? *Ruiz-Omeñaca & Canudo 2005*	Length: 10 m Shoulder height: **2.35 m**	2.2 t
9	"*Pleurocoelus*" cf. *valdensis* ILC, WE (Spain)	MMM815/99 Indeterminate age	Tooth - *Ruiz-Omeñaca & Canudo 2005* A possible valid species.	Length: 10.4 m Shoulder height: **2.4 m**	2.4 t
10	*Astrophocaudia slaughteri* ILC, WNA (Texas, USA)	SMU 61732 & 203/73655 Indeterminate age	Teeth and partial skeleton - *Langston 1974* Identified as a new species 39 years after its discovery. *D'Emic 2013*	Length: 10.9 m Shoulder height: **2.55 m**	2.85 t
11	*Astrodon* sp. eLC, SAf (South Africa)	SAM K6137 Indeterminate age	Tooth - *Forster 1996* The southernmost *Pleurocoelus*.	Length: 11.4 m Shoulder height: **2.65 m**	3.3 t
12	"*Pleurocoelus nanus* (n.d.) ILC, ENA (Maryland, USA)	USNM 4971 Adult	Partial hind limb - *Marsh 1888* *P. altus* and *P. nanus* are probably juvenile *Astrodon johnsoni*. *Carpenter & Tidwell 2005*	Length: 11.7 m Shoulder height: **2.7 m**	3.6 t
13	*Angolatitan adamastior* eUC, NAf (Angola)	MGUANPA-003 Indeterminate age	Partial skeleton - *Mateus et al. 2011* The first named dinosaur found in Angola.	Length: 13.9 m Shoulder height: **3.25 m**	6 t
14	*Rugocaudia cooneyi* ILC, WNA (Montana, USA)	MOR 334 Indeterminate age	Caudal vertebrae - *Woodruff 2012* The vertebrae's posterior part is very rough.	Length: 14.1 m Shoulder height: **3.3 m**	6.3 t
15	*Wintonotitan wattsi* eUC, OC (Australia)	QMF 7292 Indeterminate age	Partial skeleton - *Coombs & Molnar 1981* The remains were donated to a museum in 1974. *Hocknull et al. 2009*	Length: 14.7 m Shoulder height: **3.45 m**	7 t
16	*Tastavinsaurus sanzi* eLC, WE (Spain)	CT-19 Indeterminate age	Partial skeleton - *Royo-Torres et al. 2011* The informal name was in use years before. *Canudo et al. 2008*	Length: 15 m Shoulder height: **3.5 m**	7.5 t
17	*Austrosaurus mckillopi* (n.d.) ILC, OC (Australia)	QM F2316 Indeterminate age	Thoracic vertebra - *Longman 1933* A doubtful species. *Hocknull et al. 2009*	Length: 18.1 m Shoulder height: **4.25 m**	13.2 t
18	*Chubutisaurus insignis* eUC, SSA (Argentina)	MACN 18222 Indeterminate age	Partial skeleton - *del Corro 1974* Its age is in doubt, somewhere between the late Lower and late Upper Cretaceous. *Carballido et al. 2011; Ford*; Holtz**	Length: 18.5 m Shoulder height: **4.3 m**	14 t
19	*Ligabuesaurus leanzai* ILC, SSA (Argentina)	MCF-PVPH-233 Indeterminate age	Partial skeleton - *Bonaparte et al. 2006* Its front limbs were relatively high.	Length: 18.7 m Shoulder height: **4.4 m**	14.5 t
20	*Austrosaurus* sp. ILC, OC (Australia)	DGBU-1973 Indeterminate age	Humerus - *Longman 1926* More recent than *Austrosaurus mckillopi*.	Length: 19 m Shoulder height: **4.4 m**	15.2 t
21	*Austrosaurus* sp. eUC, OC (Australia)	Uncatalogued Indeterminate age	Femur and ribs - Undescribed Known as "George." More recent than *Austrosaurus mckillopi*.	Length: 19.6 m Shoulder height: **4.6 m**	17 t
22	*Australodocus bohetii* UJ, SAf (Tanzania)	G66–67 Indeterminate age	Ischium? - *Remes 2007* It was considered a diplodocoid. *Whitlock 2011*	Length: 20.1 m Shoulder height: **4.7 m**	18 t
23	*Europatitan eastwoodi* ILC, WE (Spain)	MDS-OTII 1-32 Adult	Teeth and partial skeleton - *Torcida Fernández-Baldor et al. 2017* The species name pays homage to actor and director Clint Eastwood.	Length: 21.4 m Shoulder height: **5 m**	22 t
24	*Astrodon johnsoni* ILC, ENA (Maryland, USA)	Uncatalogued Adult	Teeth and incomplete femur - *Kranz 2004* The species name was created 6 years after the genus. *Johnston 1859; Leidy 1865*	Length: 21.7 m Shoulder height: **5.1 m**	23 t
25	*Astrodon* sp. ILC, WNA (Texas, USA)	FM 214-50 Adult	Ischium - *Gallup 1975* The largest *Pleurocoelus*.	Length: 23.8 m Shoulder height: **5.6 m**	30 t
26	"*Francoposeidon charantensis*" (n.n.) eLC, WE (France)	Uncatalogued Indeterminate age	Partial skeleton - Unpublished ANG 10-400 is the longest dinosaur bone in Europe, measuring 2.2 m long. *Néraudeau et al. 2012*	Length: 28 m Shoulder height: **6.5 m**	47 t

Nº	Genus and species	Largest specimen	Material and data	Size	Mass
27	*Brontomerus mcintoshi* ILC, WNA (Utah, USA)	OMNH 27761 Indeterminate age	Partial skeleton - *Taylor et al. 2011* The pelvis was very developed.	Length: **13.2 m** Shoulder height: **3.2 m**	6.9 t

Primitive somphospondylans similar to *Sauroposeidon* - Quadrupedal, with robust bodies, type-D cylindrodont teeth, phytophagous.

Nº	Genus and species	Largest specimen	Material and data	Size	Mass
28	cf. *Sauroposeidon proteles* ILC, WNA (Wyoming, USA)	YPM 5451 Indeterminate age	Incomplete femur - *Ostrom 1970; D'Emic & Foreman 2012* More recent than *Sauroposeidon proteles*.	Length: **18.8 m** Shoulder height: **4.2 m**	10.7 t
29	*Paluxysaurus jonesi* (n.d.) ILC, WNA (Texas, USA)	FWMSH 93B-10-18 Indeterminate age	Incomplete skull - *Rose 2007* A juvenile *Sauroposeidon?* *D'Emic & Foreman 2012*	Length: **19.7 m** Shoulder height: **4.4 m**	12.5 t
30	"Angloposeidon" (n.n.) ILC, WE (England, UK)	MIW07306 Indeterminate age	Cervical vertebra - *Naish et al. 2004* Similar to *Sauroposeidon*.	Length: **22 m** Shoulder height: **4.9 m**	17 t
31	*Sauroposeidon proteles* ILC, WNA (Texas, Oklahoma, USA)	OMNH 53062 Indeterminate age	Vertebrae and cervical ribs - *Wedel et al. 2000* The fossil was thought to be petrified wood.	Length: **29 m** Shoulder height: **6.5 m**	40 t

Primitive somphospondylans similar to *Ruyangosaurus* - Quadrupedal, with robust bodies, oval-crowned spatulate-foliodont teeth, phytophagous.

Nº	Genus and species	Largest specimen	Material and data	Size	Mass
32	*Dongbeititan dongi* ILC, EA (China)	D2867 CMI Indeterminate age	Partial skeleton - *Wang et al. 2007* Titanosauriform? *Mannion et al. 2013*	Length: **13.9 m** Shoulder height: **3.3 m**	5.9 t
33	"Brachiosaurus" sp. ILC, EA (South Korea)	KS 7002 Indeterminate age	Tooth - *Lim et al. 2001* There is insufficient evidence of brachisaurids in Asia. *Ksepka & Norell 2010*	Length: **14 m** Shoulder height: **3.3 m**	6 t
34	*Huanghetitan liujiaxaensis* ILC, EA (China)	GSLTZP02-001 Indeterminate age	Partial skeleton - *You et al. 2006* More recent than originally thought.	Length: **18 m** Shoulder height: **4.3 m**	12.5 t
35	"Nurosaurus qaganensis" (n.n.) ILC, EA (China)	Uncatalogued Indeterminate age	Partial skeleton - *Dong & Li, 1991; Dong 1992* Not yet described, but a reconstructed skeleton is on display in a museum exhibit. A preserved scapula and femur also exist.	Length: **20.4 m** Shoulder height: **4.9 m**	18.5 t
36	*Sibirotitan astrosacralis* ILC, EA (eastern Russia)	LMCCE 108/4 Indeterminate age	Tooth - *Averianov et al. 2017* Skeleton PM TGU 120 is a smaller specimen.	Length: **21.4 m** Shoulder height: **5 m**	21.5 t
37	*Ultrasaurus tabriensis* ILC, EA (South Korea)	DGBU-1973 Indeterminate age	Incomplete humerus - *Kim 1981,1983* It was thought to be an ulna. *Paul 1988; Barrett et al. 2002*	Length: **22.5 m** Shoulder height: **5.4 m**	25 t
38	"Huanghetitan" ruyangensis eUC, EA (China)	41HIII-0001 Indeterminate age	Partial skeleton - *Lu et al. 2007* A genus distinct from *H. liujiaxaensis*. *Mannion et al. 2013*	Length: **24 m** Shoulder height: **5.7 m**	30 t
39	*Ruyangosaurus giganteus* eUC, EA (China)	41HIII-0002 Subadult	Partial skeleton - *Lu et al. 2009* Its femur is estimated to be about 2.07 m long.	Length: **24.8 m** Shoulder height: **5.8 m**	34 t
40	*Fusuisaurus zhaoi* ILC, EA (China)	NHMG 6729 Indeterminate age	Partial skeleton - *Mo et al. 2006* Very similar to titanosauriforms, but the latter are absent in Asia. *Ksepka & Norell 2010*	Length: **25.2 m** Shoulder height: **6 m**	35 t

1:700

EUHELOPODIDAE

Euhelopodids similar to *Euhelopus* - Quadrupedal, with robust bodies, oval-crowned spatulate-foliodont teeth, phytophagous.

Nº	Genus and species	Largest specimen	Material and data	Size	Mass
1	cf."*Camarasaurus*" sp. MJ, EA (eastern Russia)	PIN 4874/7 Indeterminate age	Incomplete tooth - *Kurzanov et al. 2003* The oldest euhelopodid.	Length: **9.5 m** Shoulder height: **2.1 m**	1.7 t
2	*Chiayusaurus lacustris* (n.d.) ILC, EA (China)	Uncatalogued Indeterminate age	Tooth - *Bohlin 1953* Originally known as *Chiayüsaurus*. It is identical to *Euhelopus*. *Barrett et al. 2002*	Length: **11 m** Shoulder height: **2.75 m**	3.9 t
3	*Chiayusaurus* sp. eLC, EA (South Korea)	KPE 8001 Indeterminate age	Partial skeleton - *Park 2000* *Pukyongosaurus milleniumi?* *Dong et al. 2001*	Length: **12.1 m** Shoulder height: **3 m**	5.2 t
4	"Moshisaurus" (n.n.) ILC, EA (Japan)	NSMN PV17656 Indeterminate age	Incomplete humerus - *Hisa 1985* It has been referred to as *Mamenchisaurus* but is much more recent and may be a Euhelopodid. *Hasegawa et al. 1991; Ford**	Length: **12.1 m** Shoulder height: **3 m**	5.2 t

#	Name / Age / Location	Catalog	Material / Notes	Dimensions	Weight
5	*Euhelopus zdanskyi* eLC, EA (China)	GSC Indeterminate age	Humerus - *Carrano 2005* The holotype PMU R234 is the most complete euhelopodid; it was 11 m long and weighed 3.4 t. *Wiman 1929*	Length: **12.9 m** Shoulder height: **3.2 m**	**6.2 t**
6	cf. *Euhelopus* sp. ILC, EA (China)	IVPP V15010.3 Indeterminate age	Tooth - *Amiot et al. 2010* More recent than *Euhelopus zdansyi*.	Length: **13.6 m** Shoulder height: **3.35 m**	**7.3 t**
7	*Chiayusaurus* sp. ILC, EA (Mongolia)	Uncatalogued Indeterminate age	Tooth - Undescribed to date.	Length: **13.6 m** Shoulder height: **3.35 m**	**7.3 t**
8	*Pukyongosaurus milleniumi* (n.d.) eLC, EA (South Korea)	PKNU-G.102 Indeterminate age	Partial skeleton - *Dong et al. 2001* The diagnostic features are insufficient, so the assigned name is doubtful. *Park 2016*	Length: **14.3 m** Shoulder height: **3.55 m**	**8.6 t**
9	*Chiayusaurus asianensis* (n.d.) eLC, EA (South Korea)	KPE 8001 Indeterminate age	Tooth - *Lee et al. 1997* Euhelopodid? *Barrett et al. 2002*	Length: **14.5 m** Shoulder height: **3.6 m**	**9 t**
10	cf. *Chiayusaurus* sp. ILC, EA (eastern Russia)	ZIN PH 4/13 Adult	Tooth - *Nesov & Starkov 1992; Nesov 1995* Described in Averianov et al. 2003	Length: **16.3 m** Shoulder height: **4.1 m**	**12.5 t**
11	aff. *Chiayusaurus* ILC, EA (China)	Uncatalogued Indeterminate age	Tooth - *Bohlin 1953* Larger than, and different from, *Chiayusaurus lacustris*.	Length: **18.7 m** Shoulder height: **4.7 m**	**19 t**

Euhelopodids similar to *Asiatosaurus* - Quadrupedal, with robust bodies, oval-crowned spatulate-foliodont teeth, phytophagous.

#	Name / Age / Location	Catalog	Material / Notes	Dimensions	Weight
12	"*Oharasisaurus*" (n.n.) ILC, EA (Japan)	Uncatalogued Juvenile	Tooth - *Matsuoka 2000* The origin of the name is unknown.	Length: **4.5 m** Shoulder height: **1 m**	**160 kg**
13	*Fukuititan nipponensis* ILC, EA (Japan)	FPDM-V8468 Indeterminate age	Teeth and partial skeleton - *Azuma & Shibata 2010* The specimen known as "Sugiyamasaurus" was about 9 m and 1.2 t. *Lambert 1990*	Length: **16.1 m** Shoulder height: **3.15 m**	**5.75 t**
14	cf. *Asiatosaurus mongoliensis* ILC, EA (China)	IVPP V 4021 Indeterminate age	Thoracic vertebra - *Dong 1973* More recent than *Asiatosaurus mongoliensis*.	Length: **20.5 m** Shoulder height: **3.95 m**	**11.5 t**
15	*Asiatosaurus mongoliensis* ILC, EA (Mongolia)	AMNH 6296 Indeterminate age	Tooth - *Osborn 1924* The holotype specimen would have been 20 m long and weighed 12.5 t.	Length: **31 m** Shoulder height: **6 m**	**45 t**

Euhelopodids similar to *Huabeisaurus* - Quadrupedal, with robust bodies, type-D cylindrodont teeth, phytophagous.

#	Name / Age / Location	Catalog	Material / Notes	Dimensions	Weight
16	cf. *Nemegtosaurus* sp. eUC, EA (Japan)	IMCF 959 Indeterminate age	Tooth - *Tanimoto & Suzuki 1997* Similar to *Huabeisaurus* and *Borealosaurus*. *Saegusa & Tomida 2011*	Length: **12.4 m** Shoulder height: **2.5 m**	**3 t**
17	*Borealosaurus wimani* ILC, EA (China)	LPM0169 Indeterminate age	Tooth - *You et al. 2004* Similar to *Huabeisaurus* or basal Titanosauria? *D'Emic et al. 2013; Averianov & Sues 2017*	Length: **15 m** Shoulder height: **3 m**	**5.5 t**
18	"*Xinghesaurus*" (n.n.) ILC, EA (China)	Uncatalogued Indeterminate age	Partial skeleton - *Hasegawa et al. 2009* Undescribed, the reconstructed material resembles *Huabeisaurus*.	Length: **15.4 m** Shoulder height: **3.1 m**	**6 t**
19	*Mongolosaurus haplodon* ILC, EA (China)	AMNH 6710 Indeterminate age	Axis - *Gilmore 1933* Serrated teeth. Euhelopodid or basal Titanosauria? *D'Emic et al. 2013; Mannion et al. 2013*	Length: **16 m** Shoulder height: **3.2 m**	**6.9 t**
20	*Phuwiangosaurus sirinhornae* ILC, CIM (Thailand)	PC.DMR KD2-1 Adult	Humerus - *Klein et al. 2009* Named after Princess Maha Chakri Sirindhorn for her interest in geology and paleontology. *Martin et al. 1994*	Length: **18.7 m** Shoulder height: **3.75 m**	**11 t**
21	*Huabeisaurus allocotus* eUC, EA (China)	HBV-20001 Indeterminate age	Partial skeleton - *Pang & Cheng 2000* It was considered similar to Saltasauroides, but was closer to euhelopodids. *D'Emic et al. 2013*	Length: **21 m** Shoulder height: **4.2 m**	**15.5 t**

Indeterminate euhelopodids - Quadrupedal, with robust bodies, unknown tooth type, phytophagous.

#	Name / Age / Location	Catalog	Material / Notes	Dimensions	Weight
22	*Erketu ellisoni* eUC, EA (Mongolia)	IGM 100/1803 Adult	Partial skeleton - *Ksepka & Norell 2006* Its neck was longer in proportion to its size than any other sauropod.	Length: **16 m** Shoulder height: **3.1 m**	**5.6 t**
23	*Jiutaisaurus xidiensis* ILC, EA (China)	CAD-02 Indeterminate age	Caudal vertebrae and chevrons - *Wu et al. 2006* Euhelopodidae?	Length: **16.3 m** Shoulder height: **3.15 m**	**5.9 t**
24	cf. "*Mamenchisaurus*" sp. eLC, EA (Japan)	Uncatalogued Indeterminate age	Tibia - *Tanimoto 1998* Mamenchisaurid or euhelopodid?	Length: **16.3 m** Shoulder height: **3.15 m**	**5.9 t**
25	*Erketu* sp. IUC, EA (China)	PMU 24707 Adult	Cervical vertebra - *Tan 1923* It was similar to *Erketu*. *Poropat 2013*	Length: **16.8 m** Shoulder height: **3.25 m**	**6.5 t**
26	cf. *Camarasaurus* sp. ILC, EA (eastern Russia)	PM TGU 16/0–80/88 Indeterminate age	Metatarsals and phalanges - *Averianov et al. 2002* Euhelopodid?	Length: **16.8 m** Shoulder height: **3.3 m**	**6.5 t**
27	"*Otogosaurus sarulai*" (n.n.) IUC, EA (China)	Uncatalogued Indeterminate age	Partial skeleton - *Zhao 2004; Zhao & Tan 2004* Some sources attribute the reference to Zhao 2004, others to Zhao & Tan 2004.	Length: **16.9 m** Shoulder height: **3.3 m**	**6.7 t**
28	*Gobititan shenzhouensis* ILC, EA (Mongolia)	IVPP 12579 Indeterminate age	Partial hind limb I - *You et al. 2003* Similar to *Huabeisaurus*? *Mocho et al. 2016*	Length: **17.6 m** Shoulder height: **3.4 m**	**8 t**
29	*Tambatitanis amicitiae* ILC, EA (Japan)	MNHAH D-1029280 Indeterminate age	Partial skeleton - *Saegusa & Ikeda 2014* It had chevrons disproportionately large for its size.	Length: **17.8 m** Shoulder height: **3.45 m**	**8.1 t**
30	"*Tobasaurus*" (n.n.) eLC, EA (Japan)	MPMF 0014 Indeterminate age	Partial skeleton - *Tomida et al. 2001* Discovered in 1996. *Tomida & Tsumura 2006*	Length: **19.8 m** Shoulder height: **4.1 m**	**11.2 t**
31	*Qiaowanlong kangxii* ILC, EA (China)	FRDC GJ 07-14 Indeterminate age	Partial skeleton - *You & Li 2009* Similar to *Tangvayosaurus*. *Mannion et al. 2013; D'Emic et al. 2016; Poropat et al. 2016*	Length: **20.7 m** Shoulder height: **4.3 m**	**13 t**
32	*Tangvayosaurus hoffeti* ILC, CIM (Laos)	TV4-1 Indeterminate age	Femur - *Allain et al. 1999* It was very robust.	Length: **22.8 m** Shoulder height: **4.7 m**	**17.5 t**
33	"*Titanosaurus*" *falloti* (n.d.) ILC, CIM (Laos)	T.1 Indeterminate age	Femur - *Hoffett 1942* It is not certain whether it is a *Tangvayosaurus*. *Pang & Cheng 2000; Upchurch et al. 2004*	Length: **24.7 m** Shoulder height: **5.1 m**	**22 t**
34	*Daxiatitan biblingi* eLC, EA (China)	GSLTZP03-001 Indeterminate age	Partial skeleton - *https://www.dailynews.co.th/regional/602555* Primitive Titanosauria? *Poropat et al. 2016*	Length: **25 m** Shoulder height: **5.2 m**	**23 t**
35	*Gannansaurus sinensis* IUC, EA (China)	GMNH F10001-2 Indeterminate age	Thoracic and caudal vertebrae - *Lu et al. 2013* The most recent euhelopodid. Similar to *Asiatosaurus* or to *Euhelopus*?	Length: **25.8 m** Shoulder height: **5.3 m**	**25 t**
36	*Liubangosaurus hei* ILC, EA (China)	NHMG8152 Indeterminate age	Thoracic vertebrae - *Mo et al. 2010* Basal euhelopodid? *Mocho et al. 2016*	Length: **26 m** Shoulder height: **5.4 m**	**26 t**
37	*Yunmenglong ruyangensis* ILC, EA (China)	KLR-07-50 Indeterminate age	Partial skeleton - *Lu et al. 2013* Also identified with the catalog number 41HIII-0006.	Length: **27 m** Shoulder height: **5.6 m**	**29 t**

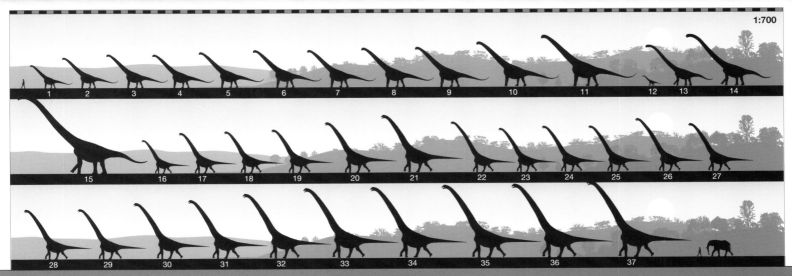

TITANOSAURIA

Primitive Titanosauria similar to *Andesaurus* - Quadrupedal, with robust bodies, oval-crowned spatulate-foliodont teeth, phytophagous.

N°	Genus and species	Largest specimen	Material and data	Size	Mass
1	*Clasmodosaurus spatula* (n.d.) IUC, SSA (Argentina)	MACN A-IOR63 Indeterminate age	Teeth - *Ameghino 1898* A probable primitive Titanosauria. *Bonaparte 1996*	Length: 7.6 m Shoulder height: 1.8 m	900 kg
2	*Campylodoniscus ameghinoi* (n.d.) IUC, SSA (Argentina)	Uncatalogued Indeterminate age	Maxillary and teeth - *Huene 1929* The name was already in use. *Haubold & Kuhn 1961*	Length: 8.7 m Shoulder height: 2.05 m	1.5 t
3	"Sousatitan" (n.n.) eLC, NSA (northern Brazil)	DGEO-CTG-UFPE 7517 Subadult	Fibula - *Ghilardi et al. 2016* The adult was estimated to have been 40–50% larger.	Length: 8.8 m Shoulder height: 2.05 m	1.5 t
4	*Aepisaurus elephantinus* (n.d.) ILC, WE (France)	Uncatalogued Indeterminate age	Incomplete humerus - *Gervais 1852* The classification is doubtful, and the piece was lost. *Le Loeuff 1993*	Length: 12.3 m Shoulder height: 2.7 m	3.5 t
5	*Andesaurus* sp. eUC, SSA (Argentina)	UNPSJB Pv 595 Indeterminate age	Caudal vertebra - *Powell et al. 1989* It is referred to as *Andesaurus* sp. in Casal et al. 2016.	Length: 13 m Shoulder height: 2.85 m	4.2 t
6	"Acantopholis" platypus" (n.d.) ILC, WE (England)	CAMSM B55454-55461 Indeterminate age	Metatarsal - *Seeley 1871* It was considered to be remains of an ankylosaur.	Length: 13.5 m Shoulder height: 2.95 m	4.6 t
7	*Aegyptosaurus baharijensis* eUC, NAf (Egypt)	BSP 1912 VIII 61 Indeterminate age	Partial skeleton - *Stromer 1932* The most complete titanosaur was destroyed.	Length: 15.9 m Shoulder height: 3.45 m	7.6 t
8	*Savannasaurus elliottorum* eUC, OC (Australia)	AODF 836 Indeterminate age	Incomplete skull - *Poropat et al. 2016* The holotype specimen is a skeleton similar in size.	Length: 16.7 m Shoulder height: 3.65 m	8.8 t
9	cf. *Aegyptosaurus baharijensis* ILC, NAf (Niger)	Uncatalogued Indeterminate age	Caudal vertebra - *Greigert et al. 1954; Lapparent 1960* More recent than *Aegyptosaurus baharijensis*.	Length: 17.5 m Shoulder height: 3.8 m	10 t
10	*Malarguesaurus florenciae* eUC, SSA (Argentina)	IANIGLA-PV 110 Indeterminate age	Partial skeleton - *González-Riga et al. 2008* Titanosauria or titanosauriform?	Length: 20.4 m Shoulder height: 4.5 m	16 t
11	*Triunfosaurus leonardii* eLC, NSA (northern Brazil)	UFRJ-DG 498 Indeterminate age	Cervical vertebra - *de Souza-Carvalho et al. 2017* More derived than *Andesaurus*.	Length: 20.8 m Shoulder height: 4.55 m	17 t
12	*Andesaurus delgadoi* eUC, SSA (Argentina)	MUCPv-271 Indeterminate age	Partial skeleton - *Salgado & Bonaparte 2007* Holotype MUCPv 132 was 19 m long and weighed about 13 t. *Calvo & Bonaparte 1991*	Length: 22 m Shoulder height: 4.8 m	20 t
13	*Bruhathkayosaurus matleyi* (n.d.) IUC, IND (India)	Uncatalogued Indeterminate age	Fibula? - *Yadagiri & Ayyasami 1989* The piece was thought to be a tibia but actually appears to be a fibula. Some researchers have speculated that they are fossil tree trunks. *Krause et al. 2006*	Length: 37 m? Shoulder height: 8 m?	95 t?

Primitive Titanosauria similar to *Xianshanosaurus* - Quadrupedal, with robust bodies, oval-crowned spatulate-foliodont teeth, phytophagous.

N°	Genus and species	Largest specimen	Material and data	Size	Mass
14	*Liaoningotitan sinesis* ILC, EA (China)	PMOL-AD00 112 Indeterminate age	Skull and partial skeleton - *Zhou et al. 2018* The name was known informally years before.	Length: 13.3 m Shoulder height: 3.15 m	4.5 t
15	*Dongyangosaurus sinensis* eUC, EA (China)	DYM 04888 Indeterminate age	Partial skeleton - *Lu et al. 2008* Basal Titanosauria or Eutitanosauria? *Poropat et al. 2016*	Length: 14.9 m Shoulder height: 3.55 m	6.3 t
16	*Xianshanosaurus shijiangouensis* eUC, EA (China)	KLR-07 Indeterminate age	Partial skeleton - *Lu et al. 2009* Titanosauria? *Poropat et al. 2016*	Length: 15.5 m Shoulder height: 3.7 m	7.1 t
17	"Poekilopleuron" schmidti ILC, WA (eastern Russia)	Uncatalogued Indeterminate age	Metacarpal - *Kiprijanow 1883* A chimera, with bones of a theropod and a titanosaur sauropod. *Mortimer**	Length: 15.7 m Shoulder height: 3.75 m	7.2 t
18	*Apatosaurus* sp. eLC, EA (Japan)	NSM-PV 20375 Indeterminate age	Partial skeleton - *Tomida et al. 2001* There were no diplodocids in Asia. A titanosaur? *Tomida & Tsumura 2006*	Length: 17.9 m Shoulder height: 4.25 m	10.8 t
19	"Asiatosaurus" kwangshiensis ILC, EA (China)	Uncatalogued Indeterminate age	Tooth and partial skeleton - *Hou et al. 1975* It was not a euhelopodid. *Barrett et al. 2002*	Length: 20.3 m Shoulder height: 4.8 m	16 t
20	*Baotianmansaurus henanensis* eUC, EA (China)	41HIII-0200 Indeterminate age	Thoracic vertebrae - *Zhang et al. 2009* Titanosauria? *Poropat et al. 2016*	Length: 22.5 m Shoulder height: 5.3 m	21 t

Primitive Titanosauria similar to *Diamantinasaurus* - Quadrupedal, with robust bodies, oval-crowned spatulate-foliodont teeth, phytophagous.

N°	Genus and species	Largest specimen	Material and data	Size	Mass
21	*Diamantinasaurus matildae* eUC, OC (Australia)	AODF 603 Indeterminate age	Partial skeleton - *Hocknull et al. 2009* Titanosauria or saltasaurid? *Mannion 2013; Poropat et al. 2016*	Length: 16 m Shoulder height: 3.5 m	10 t
22	"Bananabendersaurus" (n.n.) ILC, OC (Australia)	Uncatalogued Indeterminate age	Humerus - Undescribed The piece is 1.5 m long and is very robust.	Length: 21.5 m Shoulder height: 4.7 m	24 t

Primitive Titanosauria similar to *Yongjinglong* - Quadrupedal, with robust bodies, oval-crowned spatulate-foliodont teeth, phytophagous.

| 23 | *Yongjinglong datangi*
eUC, EA (China) | GSGM ZH(08)-04
Indeterminate age | Partial skeleton - *Saegusa & Ikeda 2014*
A probable basal Titanosauria. *Averianov & Sues 2016* | Length: **12 m**
Shoulder height: **3.2 m** | **7.5 t** |

1:1000

LITHOSTROTIA

Primitive lithostrotians similar to *Malawisaurus* - Quadrupedal, with robust bodies, type-D cylindrodont teeth, phytophagous.

Nº	Genus and species	Largest specimen	Material and data	Size	Mass
1	"*Titanosaurus*" *lydekkeri* (n.d.) (*Titanosaurus* sp.) eUC, WE (England, UK)	BMNH 32390 Indeterminate age	Caudal vertebrae - *Lydekker 1888; Huene 1929* It is named after the person who discovered it, Richard Lydekker.	Length: **4.3 m** Shoulder height: **95 cm**	**200 kg**
2	cf. *Macrurosaurus* sp. IUC, SSA (Argentina)	Av. 1005 Indeterminate age	Caudal vertebra - *Huene 1929* More recent than *Macrurosaurus semnus*.	Length: **6.6 m** Shoulder height: **1.5 m**	**800 k**
3	"*Domeykosaurus chilensis*" (n.n.) IUC, SSA (Chile)	Uncatalogued Juvenile	Partial skeleton - *Iriarte et al. 1999* As yet undescribed.	Length: **8.8 m** Shoulder height: **1.75 m**	**1.45 t**
4	*Macrurosaurus semnus* ILC, WE (England, UK)	SMC B55630 Indeterminate age	Caudal vertebrae - *Seeley 1876* The two parts considered a single specimen were two different-sized individuals. *Le Loeuff 1993*	Length: **10.1 m** Shoulder height: **2 m**	**2.2 t**
5	*Iuticosaurus valdensis* (n.d.) (*Titanosaurus* sp.) ILC, WE (England, UK)	BMNH 151 Indeterminate age	Caudal vertebra - *Huene 1929* Titanosauria? *Upchurch et al. 2012*	Length: **10.5 m** Shoulder height: **2.1 m**	**2.5 t**
6	*Malawisaurus dixeyi* ILC, SAf (Malawi)	Mal-201 Indeterminate age	Incomplete femur - *Haughton 1928* The species is known to have had osteoderms.	Length: **11 m** Shoulder height: **2.2 m**	**2.8 t**
7	cf. "*Titanosaurus indicus*" IUC, WE (France)	Uncatalogued Indeterminate age	Caudal vertebra - *Déperet 1899* It is highly doubtful it is *Titanosaurus indicus*.	Length: **11.6 m** Shoulder height: **2.3 m**	**3.3 t**
8	"Taxon A" eUC, SSA (Argentina)	UNPSJB-Pv 1010 Indeterminate age	Thoracic vertebra - *Ibiricu et al. 2011* More primitive than *Epachthosaurus*.	Length: **12.3 m** Shoulder height: **2.5 m**	**3.9 t**
9	*Titanosaurus* sp. ILC, WE (England, UK)	BMNH 1886 Indeterminate age	Caudal vertebra - *Lydekker 1890* Other remains are described in Blows 1998.	Length: **12.5 m** Shoulder height: **2.5 m**	**4.1 t**
10	*Atacamatitan chilensis* IUC, SSA (Chile)	SGO-PV-961 Indeterminate age	Partial skeleton - *Kellner et al. 2011* It is predated by other reports from the same locality. *Chong 1985; Iriarte et al. 1998*	Length: **12.8 m** Shoulder height: **2.55 m**	**4.4 t**
11	*Titanosaurus* sp. IUC, NSA (northern Brazil)	DGM 311-R Indeterminate age	Incomplete femur - *Huene 1931; Price 1951* First report of a sauropod from northern South America. *Kellner & Campos 2000; Peyerl et al. 2015*	Length: **15.3 m** Shoulder height: **3.05 m**	**7.6 t**
12	*Agustinia ligabuei* (*Augustia ligabuei*) ILC, SSA (Argentina)	MCF-PVPH-110 Indeterminate age	Partial skeleton - Bonaparte 1999 The "long osteoderms" may be poorly preserved bones. *Mannion et al. 2013; Bellardini & Cerda 2016*	Length: **16.7 m** Shoulder height: **3.3 m**	**9.8 t**
13	"*Titanosaurus* cf. *indicus*" IUC, WE (Spain)	Uncatalogued Indeterminate age	Femur - *Lapparent & Aguirre 1956* Its identification as *Titanosaurus indicus* is uncertain.	Length: **18.5 m** Shoulder height: **3.7 m**	**13.5 t**
14	aff. *Malawisaurus* sp. eUC, NSA (northern Brazil)	UFMA 1.20.473 Indeterminate age	Tooth - *Carvalho et al. 2007* It was much larger than *Austroposeidon magnificus*.	Length: **22.5 m** Shoulder height: **4.5 m**	**24 t**

1:500

Primitive lithostrotians similar to *Rapetosaurus* - Quadrupedal, with robust bodies, type-D cylindrodont teeth, phytophagous.

1	*Magyarosaurus dacus* IUC, EE (Hungary, Romania)	FGGUB R.1992 Adult	Femur - *Nopcsa 1915* It was confirmed as a dwarf species. *Stein et al. 2010*	Length: **5.55 m** Shoulder height: **1.2 m**	**520 kg**
2	*Titanosaurus* sp. IUC, IND (India)	K27/619 Indeterminate age	Incomplete femur - *Huene & Matley 1933* *Titanosaurus indicus* or *Jainosaurus septentrionalis*?	Length: **7 m** Shoulder height: **1.55 m**	**1.1 t**
3	*Hypselosaurus priscus* IUC, SSA (Argentina)	Uncatalogued Indeterminate age	Partial skeleton - *Matheron 1846, 1869* The fossil eggs *Megaloolithus* were attributed to this species. *Gervais 1846*	Length: **9 m** Shoulder height: **1.8 m**	**1.7 t**
4	*Karongasaurus gittelmani* ILC, SAf (Malawi)	Mal-36 Indeterminate age	Tooth - *Gomani 2005* First sauropod formally published in an electronic document.	Length: **9.4 m** Shoulder height: **1.85 m**	**1.95 t**
5	*Sarmientosaurus musacchioi* eUC, SSA (Argentina)	CNRST-SUNY-196 Indeterminate age	Skull - *Martínez et al. 2016* Less derived than *Tapuiasaurus*.	Length: **9.7 m** Shoulder height: **1.9 m**	**2 t**
6	*Titanosaurus* sp. IUC, SSA (Argentina)	MPCA-Pv 33 Indeterminate age	Femur - *García & Salgado 2013* A contemporary of *Rocasaurus muniozi*.	Length: **10 m** Shoulder height: **2 m**	**2.3 t**
7	*Tapuiasaurus macedoi* ILC, NSA (northern Brazil)	MZSP-PV 807 Indeterminate age	Skull and jaw - *Zaher et al. 2011* Named in a journal the previous year. *Carvalho 2010*	Length: **10.8 m** Shoulder height: **2.3 m**	**2.8 t**

#	Taxon	Specimen / Age	Material & Notes	Length / Shoulder height	Weight
8	Rinconsaurus caudamirus IUC, SSA (Argentina)	MRS-Pv Col. Indeterminate age	Teeth and partial skeleton - *Calvo & Riga 2003* All of the pieces described may belong to a single individual.	Length: 11.1 m Shoulder height: 2.4 m	3.2 t
9	Magyarosaurus hungaricus IUC, EE (Hungary, Romania)	MAFI Ob.3104 Adult	Incomplete humerus - *Huene 1932* Variation in large *Magyarosaurus dacus* individuals? *Stein et al. 2010*	Length: 11.3 m Shoulder height: 2.6 m	3.3 t
10	cf. Laplatasaurus madagascariensis IUC, IND (India)	K27/498-500 Indeterminate age	Caudal vertebrae - *Huene & Matley 1933* They are remains belonging to a different species. *Wilson & Upchurch 2003*	Length: 11.9 m Shoulder height: 2.75 m	3.9 t
11	Shingopana songwensis ILC, SAf (Tanzania)	RRBP 02100 Indeterminate age	Partial skeleton - *Gorscak et al. 2017* It had a thick neck.	Length: 11.9 m Shoulder height: 2.75 m	3.9 t
12	Tengrisaurus starkovi ILC, EA (eastern Russia)	ZIN PH 7/13 Indeterminate age	Vertebrae - *Averianov & Skutschas 2017* The oldest saltasaurid of Asia.	Length: 12.3 m Shoulder height: 2.8 m	4.2 t
13	cf. Magyarosaurus sp. IUC, EE (Romania)	NVM1-3 Indeterminate age	Caudal vertebra - *Codrea et al. 2008* It was more recent than *Magyarosaurus dacus*.	Length: 12.5 m Shoulder height: 2.85 m	4.4 t
14	cf. Normanniasaurus genceyi ILC, WE (France)	MHNR-coll. Indeterminate age	Partial skeleton - *Buffetaut 1984* More recent than *Normanniasaurus genceyi*, but identical in size. *Le Loeuff, Suteethorn & Buffetaut 2013*	Length: 12.5 m Shoulder height: 2.85 m	4.4 t
15	Normanniasaurus genceyi ILC, WE (France)	MHNH-2013.2.1.1-12 Indeterminate age	Partial skeleton - *Le Loeuff et al. 2013* One specimen attributed to this species was described 29 years earlier. *Buffetaut 1984*	Length: 12.5 m Shoulder height: 2.85 m	4.4 t
16	"Titanosaurus" madagascariensis (n.d.) IUC, MA (Madagascar)	FSL 92827 Indeterminate age	Incomplete humerus - *Deperet 1896* *Rapetosaurus kausei* or *Vahiny depereti*?	Length: 13.4 m Shoulder height: 3.1 m	5.5 t
17	Muyelensaurus pecheni eUC, SSA (Argentina)	MRS-PV 259 Indeterminate age	Incomplete scapula - *Calvo et al. 2007* It presents lonkosaurian and Aeolosaurini traits. *Poropat et al. 2016*	Length: 13.4 m Shoulder height: 3.1 m	5.5 t
18	Vahiny depereti IUC, MA (Madagascar)	UA 9940 Indeterminate age	Incomplete skull - *Rogers & Wilson 2014* Pronounced "va-heenh."	Length: 13.7 m Shoulder height: 3.15 m	5.8 t
19	cf. Laplatasaurus sp. IUC, SSA (Argentina)	Uncatalogued Indeterminate age	Metacarpal - *Huene 1929* Different than *Laplatasaurus araukanicus*.	Length: 14 m Shoulder height: 3.2 m	6.4 t
20	Khetranisaurus barkhani IUC, IND (Pakistan)	MSM-27-4 Indeterminate age	Caudal vertebra - *Malkani 2004* Smallest nemegtosaurid of Hindustan.	Length: 14.2 m Shoulder height: 3.25 m	6.5 t
21	cf. Antarctosaurus sp. IUC, IND (India)	K22/754 Indeterminate age	Incomplete femur - *Huene & Matley 1933* Diffferent than *Titanosaurus indicus*.	Length: 14.7 m Shoulder height: 3.3 m	6.9 t
22	Titanosaurus indicus (n.d.) IUC, IND (India)	K20/315-6 Indeterminate age	Partial skeleton - *Lydekker 1877* Holotype specimen K20/315-6 was lost but then found again. A synonym of *Jainosaurus septentrionalis*? *Jain & Bandhyopadhay 1997; Mohabey et al. 2012; Sen & Wilson 2013*	Length: 15.1 m Shoulder height: 3.55 m	7.8 t
23	cf. Hypselosaurus priscus IUC, WE (France)	MNHN Indeterminate age	Metatarsal - *Lapparent 1947* It is not certain whether it is *H. priscus*.	Length: 15.8 m Shoulder height: 3.65 m	8.1 t
24	Rapetosaurus kausei ("Titanosaurus" madagascariensis) IUC, MA (Madagascar)	MAD 93-18 Adult	Femur - *Curry-Rogers 2001; Curry-Rogers et al. 2011* Its teeth were similar to those of Aeolosaurini teeth. Eutitanosauria or saltasauroid? *Poropat et al. 2014; Bandeira et al. 2016; França et al. 2016; Otero & Gasparini 2016*	Length: 16.5 m Shoulder height: 3.8 m	10.3 t
25	cf. Titanosaurus indicus IUC, IND (India)	K22/488 Indeterminate age	Partial skeleton - *Lydekker 1921* *Titanosaurus indicus*? *Huene & Matley 1933*	Length: 17.2 m Shoulder height: 3.95 m	11.5 t
26	Titanosaurus blandfordi (n.d.) IUC, IND (India)	K27/501 Indeterminate age	Caudal vertebra - *Lydekker 1879* A doubtful species. *Wilson & Upchurch 2003*	Length: 18 m Shoulder height: 4.05 m	13.3 t
27	Barrosasaurus casamiquelai IUC, SSA (Argentina)	MCF-PVPH-447/1–3 Indeterminate age	Thoracic vertebrae - *Salgado & Coria 2009* It was an estimated 30 m long, according to the popular press.	Length: 18 m Shoulder height: 4.15 m	13.5 t
28	Volgatitan simbirskiensis eLC, EE (European Russia)	UPM 976/1–7 Indeterminate age	Caudal vertebrae - *Averianov & Efimov 2018* Its caudal vertebrae are very procoelous. It was estimated to be 17.3 t in weight.	Length: 20 m Shoulder height: 4.5 m	15 t
29	Jainosaurus septentrionalis IUC, IND (India)	UGSI K27 Indeterminate age	Partial skeleton - *Huene 1932; Huene & Matley 1933* Similar to "Malagasy Taxon B", *Muyelensaurus* and *Pitekunsaurus*. *Wilson et al. 2009, 2011*	Length: 20 m Shoulder height: 4.6 m	18 t
30	cf. Hypselosaurus sp. IUC, WE (Spain)	IPSN-19 Indeterminate age	Caudal vertebra - *Casanovas et al. 1987* It was more recent than *H. priscus*. *Lapparent 1947*	Length: 22.8 m Shoulder height: 5.2 m	25 t

1:800

Primitive lithostrotians similar to *Aeolosaurus* - Quadrupedal, with robust bodies, type-D cylindrodont teeth, phytophagous.

#	Taxon	Specimen / Age	Material & Notes	Length / Shoulder height	Weight
1	Overosaurus paradasorum IUC, SSA (Argentina)	MAU-Pv-CO-439 Indeterminate age	Partial skeleton - *Coria et al. 2013* The most complete and most basal Aeolosaurini.	Length: 8.5 m Shoulder height: 2 m	1.8 t
2	Gondwanatitan faustoi eUC, NSA (northern Brazil)	MN 4111-V Indeterminate age	Partial skeleton - *Kellner & Azevedo 1999* Its name is a reference to the Gondwana paleocontinent.	Length: 10 m Shoulder height: 2.15 m	2.5 t
3	Aeolosaurus sp. IUC, SSA (Argentina)	MPCA-Pv 27177 Indeterminate age	Femur - *Salgado & Coria 1993* Found in the Allen Formation.	Length: 11.3 m Shoulder height: 2.45 m	3.6 t
4	Pitekunsaurus macayai IUC, SSA (Argentina)	MAU-Pv-AG-446 Indeterminate age	Partial femur - *Filippi & Garrido 2008* It had a very small head in proportion to its size.	Length: 11.8 m Shoulder height: 2.55 m	4 t
5	Gondwanatitan sp. IUC, NSA (northern Brazil)	MP 286 Indeterminate age	Incomplete tibia - *Kellner et al. 1995* More recent than *Gondwanatitan faustoi*.	Length: 12.4 m Shoulder height: 2.7 m	4.7 t
6	cf. Aeolosaurus sp. IUC, NSA (southern Brazil)	LGP-D0001-5 Indeterminate age	Partial skeleton - *Pereia & Sekwiguchi de Carvalho 2008* The most recent Aeolosaurini.	Length: 14.8 m Shoulder height: 3.2 m	8 t

#	Species / Location	Specimen / Age	Description	Size	Mass
7	*Panamericansaurus schroederi* IUC, SSA (Argentina)	MUCPv-417 Indeterminate age	Partial skeleton - *Calvo & Porfiri 2010* The Pan American company financed the research.	Length: **15.4 m** Shoulder height: **4 m**	12 t
8	*Aeolosaurus maximus* eUC, SSA (southern Brazil)	MPMA 12-0001-97 Indeterminate age	Partial skeleton - *Santucci & de Arruda-Campos 2011* The oldest *Aeolosaurus*.	Length: **17 m** Shoulder height: **3.7 m**	12.3 t
9	*Aeolosaurus colhuehuapensis* IUC, SSA (Argentina)	UNPSJB-PV 959/1-27 Indeterminate age	Caudal vertebrae - *Casal et al. 2007* From the Lago Colhué Huapi Formation.	Length: **17.5 m** Shoulder height: **3.8 m**	13.3 t
10	*Aeolosaurus* sp. IUC, NSA (southern Brazil)	UFRI-DG 270-R Indeterminate age	Caudal vertebra - *Santucci 2002; Almeida et al. 2014* A contemporary of *Adamantisaurus mezzariai*.	Length: **17.8 m** Shoulder height: **3.85 m**	14.2 t
11	*Adamantisaurus mezzariai* IUC, NSA (southern Brazil)	MUGEO 1282 Indeterminate age	Caudal vertebrae - *Mezzalira 1959* It was named 47 years after being reported. *Santucci & Bertini 2006*	Length: **18 m** Shoulder height: **3.9 m**	14.4 t
12	*Aeolosaurus rionegrinus* IUC, SSA (Argentina)	MPCA 27174 Indeterminate age	Skeleton - *Powell 1987* *Aeolosaurus* type species.	Length: **18.1 m** Shoulder height: **3.9 m**	14.7 t

Primitive lithostrotians similar to *Bonitasaura* - Quadrupedal, with short, robust bodies, square jaws, type-D cylindrodont teeth, phytophagous.

#	Species / Location	Specimen / Age	Description	Size	Mass
13	*Laplatasaurus* sp. IUC, SSA (Argentina)	MCF-PVPH-272 Embryo	Skull - *Chiappe et al. 2001* The skull has an "egg tooth," a protuberance that helped the hatchling break out of its shell. *García 2007; García et al. 2010*	Length: **39 cm** Shoulder height: **10 cm**	230 g
14	*Uberabatitan riberoi* IUC, SSA (northern Brazil)	CPP-UrHo Specimen A Indeterminate age	Partial skeleton - *Salgado & Carvalho 2008* It lived in an extremely hot, dry climate.	Length: **8.1 m** Shoulder height: **2.25 m**	2.65 t
15	*Laplatasaurus araukanicus* IUC, SSA (Argentina, Uruguay)	MLP CS 1316 Indeterminate age	Caudal vertebra - *Huene 1929* Similar to *Bonitasaura* and *Uberatitan*. *Gallina & Otero 2015*	Length: **9.9 m** Shoulder height: **2.8 m**	4.9 t
16	*Antarctosaurus* sp. IUC, SSA (Argentina)	PVL. 3670 X 1/10 Indeterminate age	Partial skeleton - *Bonaparte & Bossi 1967* More recent than *A. wichmannianus*.	Length: **10 m** Shoulder height: **2.8 m**	5 t
17	cf. *Bonitasaura* sp. IUC, SSA (Argentina)	Av. 1046 Indeterminate age	Incomplete humerus - *Huene 1929* Previously considered *Laplatasaurus araukanicus* *Gallina & Otero 2015*	Length: **10.3 m** Shoulder height: **2.9 m**	5.5 t
18	*Brasilotitan nemophagus* IUC, NSA (southern Brazil)	MPM 125R Indeterminate age	Teeth and partial skeleton - *Machado et al. 2013* Some authors consider the antiquity of eUC (Turonian-Santonian) and other IUC (Campanian).	Length: **10.3 m** Shoulder height: **2.9 m**	5.5 t
19	*Bonitasaura salgadoi* IUC, SSA (Argentina)	HOS 9 Juvenile	Skull and partial skeleton - *Apesteguía 2003* It had a keratin beak high up on the snout. The adult would have been 15.5 m long and weighed 19 t. *Gallina 2012*	Length: **10.3 m** Shoulder height: **2.9 m**	5.5 t
20	*Baalsaurus mansillai* eUC, SSA (Argentina)	MUCPv-1460 Indeterminate age	Incomplete dentary - *Calvo & Riga 2018* The skull was an estimated 40 cm long.	Length: **10.7 m** Shoulder height: **3 m**	6 t
21	*Antarctosaurus wichmannianus* IUC, SSA (Argentina, Uruguay)	MACN 6804 Indeterminate age	Partial skeleton - *Huene 1929; Huene 1929b* Reported the same year in Argentina and Uruguay. Giant specimens FMNH P13019 and P13020 do not belong to this species. *Mannion & Otero 2012*	Length: **12.5 m** Shoulder height: **3.5 m**	9.5 t
22	*Antarctosaurus brasiliensis* IUC, NSA (southern Brazil)	FFCL-GP-RD 3 Indeterminate age	Partial skeleton - *Arid & Vizotto 1971* Titanosauria. *Bonaparte 1996*	Length: **13.5 m** Shoulder height: **3.8 m**	12 t
23	*Antarctosaurus* cf. *wichmannianus* IUC, SSA (Chile)	SGO.PV Indeterminate age	Partial skeleton - *Casamiquela et al. 1969* *Antarctosaurus wichmannianus?*	Length: **14 m** Shoulder height: **3.9 m**	13.3 t

Primitive lithostrotians similar to *Argyrosaurus* - Quadrupedal, with robust bodies, type-D cylindrodont teeth, phytophagous.

#	Species / Location	Specimen / Age	Description	Size	Mass
24	*Trigonosaurus pricei* IUC, NSA (northern Brazil)	MCT 1488-R Indeterminate age	Partial skeleton - *Campos et al. 2005* Known for a long time as the "titanosaur of Peiròpolis." *Powell 2003*	Length: **12.5 m** Shoulder height: **2.6 m**	6.5 t
25	*Elaltitan lilloi* IUC, SSA (Argentina)	PVL 4628 Indeterminate age	Femur - *Huene 1929* The remains were mistaken for those of *Argyrosaurus*. It has been dated to the Cenomanian or the Campanian. *Powell 2003; Mannion & Otero 2012*	Length: **20 m** Shoulder height: **4.3 m**	23 t
26	*Argyrosaurus superbus* IUC, SSA (Argentina, Uruguay)	MLP 77-V-29-1 Indeterminate age	Partial skeleton - *Lydekker 1893* It was believed to be older, from the early Upper Cretaceous. *Mannion & Otero 2012*	Length: **21 m** Shoulder height: **4.7 m**	26 t
27	*Argyrosaurus* cf. *superbus* IUC, SSA (Argentina)	MLP 27 Indeterminate age	Incomplete femur - *Huene 1929* Older than *Argyrosaurus*, its identification is problematic. *Mannion & Otero 2012, Mortimer**	Length: **22 m** Shoulder height: **4.7 m**	29 t

1:700

Saltasauroidea similar to *Epachthosaurus* - Quadrupedal, with robust bodies, type-D cylindrodont teeth, phytophagous.

Nº	Genus and species	Largest specimen	Material and data	Size	Mass
1	*Mansourasaurus shahinae* IUC, NAf (Egypt)	MUVP 200 Juvenile	Skull, partial skeleton, and osteoderms - *Sallam et al. 2018* It is unknown whether specimen MUVP 201 belongs to this species. This specimen was about 14.3 m long and weighed 6 t.	Length: **8.5 m** Shoulder height: **1.7 m**	1.25 t
2	*Paludititan nalatzensis* IUC, EE (Romania)	UBBNVM1 Indeterminate age	Partial skeleton - *Csiki et al. 2010* A contemporary of *Magyarosaurus*.	Length: **8.6 m** Shoulder height: **1.7 m**	1.3 t
3	*Lohuecotitan pandafilandi* IUC, WE (Spain)	HUE-EC-11 Subadult	Partial skeleton and osteoderms - *Ortega et al 2015; Diez Díaz et al. 2016* Dedicated to the character "Pandafilando de la Fosca Vista." *Cervantes Saavedra 1605*	Length: **11 m** Shoulder height: **2.2 m**	3.2 t
4	*Narambuenatitan palomoi* IUC, SSA (Argentina)	MAU-Pv-N-425 Subadult	Skull and partial skeleton - *Filippi et al. 2011* Similar to *Epachthosaurus*.	Length: **12.5 m** Shoulder height: **2.5 m**	4.1 t
5	*Maxakalisaurus topai* IUC, NSA (southern Brazil)	MBC-42-PV Juvenile	Jaw and teeth - *França et al. 2016* The slightly smaller holotype, MN 5013-V, was not an adult. *Kellner et al. 2006*	Length: **12.6 m** Shoulder height: **2.5 m**	4.2 t
6	*Epachthosaurus sciuttoi* eUC, SSA (Argentina)	UNPSJB-PV 920 Indeterminate age	Partial skeleton - *Martínez et al. 2004* The name was mentioned 4 years before its formal presentation. *Martinez et al 1986; Powell 1990*	Length: **12.7 m** Shoulder height: **2.55 m**	4.3 t
7	*Rukwatitan bisepultus* ILC, SAf (Tanzania)	RRBP 07409 Indeterminate age	Thoracic vertebrae - *Gorscak et al 2014* Its discovery was reported in O'Connor et al. 2003, 2006.	Length: **16.2 m** Shoulder height: **3.5 m**	7.9 t
8	*Epachthosaurus* sp. eUC, SSA (Argentina)	UNPSJB-PV 1006 Adult	Thoracic vertebra - *Casal & Ibiricu 2010* *Epachthosaurus sciuttoi?*	Length: **19 m** Shoulder height: **3.8 m**	14.7 t
9	*Paralititan stromeri* eUC, NAf (Egypt)	CGM 81119 Indeterminate age	Partial skeleton - *Smith et al. 2001* First sauropod proven to have lived in a mangrove swamp.	Length: **27 m** Shoulder height: **5.4 m**	30 t

Saltasauroidea similar to *Patagotitan* - Quadrupedal, with robust bodies, type-D cylindrodont teeth, phytophagous.

Nº	Genus and species	Largest specimen	Material and data	Size	Mass
10	"Taxon B" eUC, SSA (Argentina)	UNPSJB-Pv 581 Indeterminate age	Incomplete thoracic vertebra - *Sciutto & Martínez 2001; Ibiricu et al. 2011* Similar to *Argentinosaurus*, it is considered more derived than *Epachthosaurus*.	Length: **6.8 m** Shoulder height: **1.4 m**	790 kg
11	*Choconsaurus baileywillisi* eUC, SSA (Argentina)	MMCh-PV 44 Indeterminate age	Partial skeleton - *Simón et al. 2017* Specimen MMCh-PV 80-92, 111-112 has cylindrical teeth.	Length: **21.5 m** Shoulder height: **4 m**	18 t
12	*Traukutitan eocaudata* IUC, SSA (Argentina)	MUCPv 204 Indeterminate age	Femur - *Salgado & Calvo 1993* It was named 18 years after being described. *Juárez Valieri & Calvo 2011*	Length: **24.2 m** Shoulder height: **4.5 m**	26 t
13	*Mendozasaurus neguyelap* eUC, SSA (Argentina)	IANIGLA-PV 084 Indeterminate age	Femur - *Riga & Astini 2007* The Longkosauria may belong to the Saltasauroidea. *Tykoski & Fiorillo 2016; de Souza-Carvalho et al. 2017*	Length: **24.7 m** Shoulder height: **4.6 m**	28 t
14	"Sauropodus" (n.n.) eUC, SSA (Argentina)	Uncatalogued Indeterminate age	Partial skeleton - *Simón 2001; Simon & Calvo 2002* The name was erroneously created in a newspaper. *Anonymous 2001*	Length: **26 m** Shoulder height: **4.8 m**	33 t
15	*Patagotitan mayorum* ILC, SSA (Argentina)	MPEF PV 3399 Subadult	Partial skeleton - *Carballido et al. 2017* There is a skeletal reconstruction 37.2 m in length.	Length: **31 m** Shoulder height: **6 m**	55 t

Saltasauroidea similar to *Argentinosaurus* - Quadrupedal, with very robust bodies, type-D cylindrodont teeth, phytophagous.

Nº	Genus and species	Largest specimen	Material and data	Size	Mass
16	*Argentinosaurus huinculensis* eUC, SSA (Argentina)	PVPH-1 Indeterminate age	Partial skeleton - *Mazzetta et al. 2004* The fibula was thought to be a tibia, owing to its enormous size and girth.	Length: **35 m** Shoulder height: **6.8 m**	75 t
17	cf. *Argentinosaurus* eUC, SSA (Argentina)	MLP-DP 46-VIII-21-3 Indeterminate age	Incomplete femur - *Mazzetta et al. 2004* The incomplete piece is 1.75 m long and would have been 2.7 m in all. It is more recent than *A. huinculensis*. *Paul in press.*	Length: **36 m** Shoulder height: **7 m**	80 t

Saltasauroidea similar to *Futalognkosaurus* - Quadrupedal, with very robust bodies, type-D cylindrodont teeth, phytophagous.

Nº	Genus and species	Largest specimen	Material and data	Size	Mass
18	*Quetecsaurus rusconii* eUC, SSA (Argentina)	UNCUYO-LD-300 Indeterminate age	Partial skeleton - *González-Riga & Ortiz 2014* The best-conserved sauropod from the Cerro Lisandro Formation.	Length: **14.8 m** Shoulder height: **3.2 m**	7 t
19	*Austroposeidon magnificus* IUC, NSA (Brazil)	MCT 1628-R Indeterminate age	Vertebrae and cervical rib - *Bandeira et al. 2016* It was believed to be the largest sauropod in Brazil.	Length: **16.5 m** Shoulder height: **3.6 m**	10 t
20	*Drusilasaura deseadensis* eUC, SSA (Argentina)	MPM-PV 2097/1-19 Indeterminate age	Partial skeleton - *Martínez et al. 1989; Navarrete et al. 2011* The oldest Longkosauria.	Length: **18 m** Shoulder height: **3.95 m**	13 t
21	*Futalognkosaurus dukei* eUC, SSA (Argentina)	MUCPv-323 Indeterminate age	Partial skeleton - *Calvo 2000; Calvo et al. 2007* It was considered the same size as *Argentinosaurus*. *Calvo et al. 2008; Paul 2010*	Length: **24 m** Shoulder height: **5.2 m**	30 t
22	*Puertasaurus reuili* IUC, SSA (Argentina)	MPM 10002 Indeterminate age	Vertebrae - *Novas et al. 2005* The 2.2-m-long femur MPM-Pv.39 may belong to this species. *Lacovara et al. 2004*	Length: **28 m** Shoulder height: **6 m**	50 t

Saltasauroidea similar to *Notocolossus* - Quadrupedal, with semi-robust bodies, type-D cylindrodont teeth, phytophagous

Nº	Genus and species	Largest specimen	Material and data	Size	Mass
23	*Notocolossus gonzalezparejasi* eUC, SSA (Argentina)	UNCUYO-LD-301 Indeterminate age	Partial skeleton - *Gónzalez-Riga et al. 2016* The claws on its feet were truncated.	Length: **28 m** Shoulder height: **5.9 m**	40 t

Saltasauroidea similar to *"Antarctosaurus"* - Quadrupedal, with semi-robust bodies, type-D cylindrodont teeth, phytophagous.

Nº	Genus and species	Largest specimen	Material and data	Size	Mass
24	*"Antarctosaurus" giganteus* eUC, SSA (Argentina)	MLP 26-316 Indeterminate age	Partial skeleton - *Huene 1929* It had an estimated length of 40 m and weighed up to 80 t. *Paul 2010*	Length: **30.5 m** Shoulder height: **6.5 m**	45 t

1:1000

SALTASAURIDAE

Indeterminate saltasaurids - Quadrupedal, with robust bodies, type-D cylindrodont teeth, phytophagous.

Nº	Genus and species	Largest specimen	Material and data	Size	Mass
1	Bonatitan reigi IUC, SSA (Argentina)	MACN RN 821 Adult	Partial skeleton - *Martinelli & Forasiepi 2004* It was not a saltasaurine. *Gallina & Carabajal 2015*	Length: 6 m Shoulder height: **1.35 m**	**600 kg**
2	Nicksaurus razashahi IUC, IND (Pakistan)	MSM-190-4n Indeterminate age	Partial skeleton - *Malkani 2014, 2015* Smallest Cretaceous sauropod of Hindustan.	Length: 9.6 m Shoulder height: **2.2 m**	**2 t**
3	Baurutitan britoi IUC, NSA (northern Brazil)	MCT 1490-R Indeterminate age	Vertebrae - *Kellner et al. 2005* It was named after the Bauru Geological Group.	Length: 11.4 m Shoulder height: **2.65 m**	**3.5 t**
4	"Baguasaurus" (n.n.) IUC, NSA (Peru)	Uncatalogued Indeterminate age	Caudal vertebra - *Mourier et al. 1986* A larger unpublished individual is mentioned, with a humerus of 90 cm. *Salas-Gismondi unpublished*	Length: 11.9 m Shoulder height: **2.75 m**	**3.9 t**
5	Saraikimasoom vitakri IUC, IND (Pakistan)	Uncatalogued Indeterminate age	Incomplete skull - *Malkani 2014, 2015* The forehead had a 40° slope.	Length: 12.4 m Shoulder height: **2.85 m**	**4.4 t**
6	Balochisaurus malkani IUC, IND (Pakistan)	MSM-37-4 Indeterminate age	Caudal vertebrae - *Malkani 2006* It has been suggested that it belongs to the balochisaurid family.	Length: 13.7 m Shoulder height: **3.15 m**	**5.9 t**
7	Pellegrinisaurus powelli IUC, SSA (Argentina)	MPCA 1500 Indeterminate age	Partial skeleton - *Salgado 1996* Its length has been calculated as 25 m.	Length: 15.3 m Shoulder height: **3.5 m**	**8.1 t**
8	Gspsaurus pakistani IUC, IND (Pakistan)	MSM-79-19 Indeterminate age	Incomplete skull - *Malkani 2014, 2015* Slightly recurved teeth.	Length: 17 m Shoulder height: **3.9 m**	**11 t**
9	Marisaurus jeffi IUC, IND (Pakistan)	MSM-37-4 Indeterminate age	Caudal vertebra - *Malkani 2006* Specimens MSM-79-19 and MSM-80-19 consist of a skull and teeth.	Length: 17.1 m Shoulder height: **3.9 m**	**11.2 t**
10	Petrobrasaurus puestohernandezi IUC, SSA (Argentina)	MAU-Pv-PH-449/1-32 Indeterminate age	Teeth and partial skeleton - *Filippi et al. 2011* Derived saltasauroid. *Coria et al. 2013*	Length: 17.8 m Shoulder height: **4.1 m**	**13 t**
11	Maojandino alami IUC, IND (Pakistan)	Uncatalogued Indeterminate age	Partial skeleton - *Malkani 2014, 2015* Largest sauropod of Pakistan.	Length: 19.2 m Shoulder height: **4.4 m**	**16.5 t**

Saltasaurids similar to *Dreadnoughtus* - Quadrupedal, with robust bodies, type-D cylindrodont teeth, phytophagous.

Nº	Genus and species	Largest specimen	Material and data	Size	Mass
12	Dreadnoughtus schrani IUC, SSA (Argentina)	MPM-PV 1156 Subadult	Skull and partial skeleton - *Lacovara et al. 2014* It weighed an estimated 59 t. *Bates et al. 2015*	Length: 24 m Shoulder height: **5 m**	**35 t**

Saltasaurids similar to *Alamosaurus* - Quadrupedal, with robust bodies, type-D cylindrodont teeth, phytophagous.

Nº	Genus and species	Largest specimen	Material and data	Size	Mass
13	Jiangshanosaurus lixianensis ILC, EA (China)	M1322 Indeterminate age	Partial skeleton - *Tang et al. 2001* Similar to *Alamosaurus*?	Length: 18 m Shoulder height: **4.1 m**	**12.5 t**
14	Alamosaurus sp. IUC, WNA (Mexico)	Uncatalogued Indeterminate age	Incomplete femur - *Rivera-Sylva et al. 2009* It was believed to be a tibia. *Ramírez-Velasco in press*	Length: 22.5 m Shoulder height: **5.2 m**	**24.5 t**
15	Alamosaurus sp. IUC, WNA (Arizona, USA)	Uncatalogued Indeterminate age	Radius - *Ratkevich & Duffek 1996* More recent than UALP 4005. *Ratkevich 1997*	Length: 24 m Shoulder height: **5.5 m**	**30 t**
16	Alamosaurus sp. IUC, WNA (New Mexico, USA)	NMMNH P-29722 Indeterminate age	Caudal vertebra - *Lucas & Sullivan 2000; Sullivan & Lucas 2000* Older than *Alamosaurus sanjuanensis*.	Length: 24.5 m Shoulder height: **5.6 m**	**31 t**
17	Alamosaurus sanjuanensis IUC, WNA (New Mexico, Texas, Utah, USA)	SMP VP-1850 Indeterminate age	Cervical vertebra - *Fowler & Sullivan 2011* Juveniles had cervical vertebrae different from those of adults. The huge anterior caudal SMP-2104 belonged to an animal of similar size. *Tykoski & Fiorillo 2016*	Length: 26 m Shoulder height: **6 m**	**38 t**

Saltasaurids similar to *Ampelosaurus* - Quadrupedal, with robust bodies, type-D cylindrodont teeth, or intermediate type-D foliodont teeth, phytophagous.

Nº	Genus and species	Largest specimen	Material and data	Size	Mass
18	Atsinganosaurus velauciensis IUC, WE (France)	MHN-Aix-PV.1999.48 Adult	Cervical vertebra - *Díez Díaz et al. 2013* The name means "gypsy lizard." *Garcia et al. 2010*	Length: 8.3 m Shoulder height: **2.1 m**	**2 t**
19	cf. Lirainosaurus astibiae IUC, WE (France)	C3-61 Indeterminate age	Femur - *Vila et al. 2012* The only dinosaur name in the Basque language (Euskara), it means "lean lizard." *Sanz et al. 1999*	Length: 9.7 m Shoulder height: **2.5 m**	**3.3 t**
20	Ampelosaurus sp. IUC, WE (Spain)	MCCM-HUE-1667 Indeterminate age	Skull and partial skeleton - *Knoll et al. 2015* *Lohuecotitan pandafilandi*?	Length: 11 m Shoulder height: **2.9 m**	**5 t**
21	Lirainosaurus astibiae IUC, WE (Spain)	MCNA 14474 Adult	Tooth and partial skeleton - *Sanz et al. 1999* It was reported in the popular press as 25 m long and weighing 25 t.	Length: 14.3 m Shoulder height: **3.7 m**	**10.7 t**
22	Ampelosaurus atacis IUC, WE (France)	MHN.Aix.PV.1996 Indeterminate age	Incomplete femur - *Vila et al. 2012* It had 4 types of osteoderms. *Le Loeuff 1995*	Length: 16 m Shoulder height: **4.2 m**	**15 t**

Saltasaurids similar to *Opisthocoelicaudia* - Quadrupedal, with robust bodies, type-D cylindrodont teeth, phytophagous.

Nº	Genus and species	Largest specimen	Material and data	Size	Mass
23	Yunxianosaurus hubeinensis IUC, EA (China)	SYH28 Juvenile	Partial skeleton - *Li 2001* "Yunxiansaurus hubei" is an erroneous reference. *Zhou 2005*	Length: 4.1 m Shoulder height: **95 cm**	**270 kg**
24	Arkharavia heterocoelica IUC, EA (eastern Russia)	AEHM 2/418 Indeterminate age	Caudal vertebra - *Alifanov & Bolotsky 2010* A mixture of sauropod and hadrosaurid bones. *Godefroit et al. 2012*	Length: 6.3 m Shoulder height: **1.45 m**	**1 t**
25	Zhuchengtitan zangjiazhuangensis IUC, EA (China)	ZJZ-57 Indeterminate age	Humerus - *Xu et al. 2006* The proximal part of the humerus is very broad.	Length: 8.3 m Shoulder height: **1.7 m**	**1.85 t**
26	Quaesitosaurus orientalis IUC, EA (Mongolia)	No. 3906/2 Indeterminate age	Incomplete skull - *Kurzanov & Bannikov 1983* Similar to *Opisthocoelicaudia skarzynskii*. *Curry-Rogers 2005*	Length: 9.4 m Shoulder height: **1.95 m**	**2.6 t**
27	Sonidosaurus saihangaobiensis IUC, EA (China)	LH V 0010 Indeterminate age	Partial skeleton - *Xu et al. 2006* Similar to *Opisthocoelicaudia*?	Length: 10.1 m Shoulder height: **2.1 m**	**3.3 t**
28	Nemegtosaurus mongoliensis IUC, EA (Mongolia)	Z. Pal. MgD-I/9 Indeterminate age	Skull - *Nowinski 1971* An *Opisthocoelicaudia* skull? *Paul 2010; Benton 2012; Currie et al. 2017*	Length: 11.4 m Shoulder height: **2.4 m**	**4.9 t**
29	Qinlingosaurus luonanensis IUC, EA (China)	NWUV 1112 Indeterminate age	Partial pelvis - *Xue et al. 1996* Titanosauria?	Length: 12 m Shoulder height: **2.5 m**	**5.7 t**
30	Qingxiusaurus youjiangensis IUC, EA (China)	NHMG 8499 Indeterminate age	Partial skeleton - *Mo et al. 2008* The most recent of the group.	Length: 12.5 m Shoulder height: **2.6 m**	**6.3 t**
31	Opisthocoelicaudia skarzynskii IUC, EA (Mongolia)	ZPAL MgD-I/48 Indeterminate age	Partial skeleton - *Borsuk-Białynicka 1977* The animal could probably have taken a tripod stance by using its tail.	Length: 14 m Shoulder height: **2.9 m**	**8.6 t**

32	*Nemegtosaurus pachi* (n.d.) IUC, EA (China)	IVPP V 4879 Indeterminate age	Tooth - *Dong 1977* Its placement in this genus is uncertain.	Length: **14.4 m** Shoulder height: **3 m**	**10 t**
33	*"Antarctosaurus" jaxarticus* eUC, WA (Kazakhstan)	Uncatalogued Indeterminate age	Femur - *Riabinin 1938* It is very unlikely that it belonged to the genus *Antarctosaurus*.	Length: **15 m** Shoulder height: **3.1 m**	**11 t**
34	cf. *Nemegtosaurus* ILC, EA (eastern Russia)	ZIN PH 2/112 Indeterminate age	Tooth - *Avenianov & Skutschas 2009* Older than *Nemegtosaurus mongoliensis*	Length: **16.3 m** Shoulder height: **3.4 m**	**14 t**

Saltasaurids similar to *Isisaurus* - Quadrupedal, with robust bodies, type-D cylindrodont teeth, phytophagous.

35	*Pakisaurus balochistani* IUC, IND (Pakistan)	MSM-11-4 to MSM-14-4 Indeterminate age	Tibia - *Malkani 2004* Represents the Pakisauridae family. *Malkani 2003*	Length: **9 m** Shoulder height: **3.2 m**	**6 t**
36	*Isisaurus colberti* IUC, IND (India)	ISI R335/1-65 Indeterminate age	Skull and partial skeleton - *Jain & Bandyopadhyay 1997* Its body proportions are among the strangest of all sauropods. *Wilson & Upchurch 2003*	Length: **11 m** Shoulder height: **3.9 m**	**11.5 t**

Saltasaurids similar to *Neuquensaurus* - Quadrupedal, with robust bodies, type-D cylindrodont teeth, phytophagous.

37	*"Carnosaurus"* (n.n.) IUC, SSA (Argentina)	SMP VP-1850 Indeterminate age	Metacarpal - *Huene 1929* *Neuquensaurus* or *Saltasaurus*?	Length: **6.3 m** Shoulder height: **1.4 m**	**1 t**
38	cf. *Rocasaurus* sp. IUC, SSA (Argentina)	MCPA-Pv 57 Indeterminate age	Caudal vertebrae - *Salgado & Azpilicueta 2000* *Rocasaurus muniozi*?	Length: **7.6 m** Shoulder height: **1.7 m**	**1.8 t**
39	*Rocasaurus muniozi* IUC, SSA (Argentina)	MPCA-Pv 46 Subadult	Femur - *Salgado & Azpilicueta 2000* The smallest Saltasaurinae.	Length: **7.9 m** Shoulder height: **1.75 m**	**1.9 t**
40	cf. *Neuquensaurus australis* IUC, SSA (Argentina)	Uncatalogued Adult	Sacral vertebra - *Huene 1929* It was more recent than *Neuquensaurus australis*. *Bonaparte & Powell 1980; Otero 2010; D'Emic & Wilson 2011*	Length: **8 m** Shoulder height: **1.8 m**	**2 t**
41	*Neuquensaurus australis* IUC, SSA (Argentina, Uruguay)	MCS-5/28 Adult	Femur - *Salgado et al. 2005* It had 7 sacral vertebrae, more than any other sauropod. *Bonaparte et al. 1977*	Length: **8.2 m** Shoulder height: **1.85 m**	**2.25 t**
42	*Neuquensaurus robustus* (n.d.) IUC, SSA (Argentina)	MLP CS 1265 Adult	Fibula - *Huene 1906; 1929* A doubtful species, possibly a different genus altogether. *Otero 2010*	Length: **8.5 m** Shoulder height: **1.9 m**	**2.55 t**
43	*Saltasaurus loricatus* IUC, SSA (Argentina)	PVL 4017-92 Adult	Ilium - *Bonaparte & Powell 1980* The first sauropod proven to be associated with osteoderms.	Length: **8.9 m** Shoulder height: **2 m**	**2.85 t**

1:1000

Glossary

Air sacs
Organs connected to the lungs of some dinosaurs, including birds, to store air.

Alismatales
A group of monocotyledon angiosperm plants that encompasses several kinds of terrestrial and aquatic plants, including the genus *Elodea*.

Allometric growth
Growth of an organism in which different parts develop at different rates, causing its appearance to change as it grows.

Amborellales
A group of angiosperm plants with only one surviving order: Amborella.

Angiosperms
A group of plants that produce flowers and fruit.

Apophysis
A bony protuberance that forms part of a joint or is used as a muscle anchor.

Austrobaileyales
Group of angiosperm plants that includes primitive lianas.

Avulsion
Severe detachment of a ligament.

Basal
Refers to an organism or feature that is phylogenetically primitive or ancient.

Basipodium
The area of the hand or foot that includes the carpals, tarsals, metacarpals, and metatarsals.

Bennettitales
Group of now-extinct gymnosperm plants resembling cycads that had flower-like structures with seeds and leaves.

Biomechanics
The scientific field focused on the study of mechanical structures in living beings.

Biped
Animal that uses its hind legs only to move around.

Caytoniales
A group of pteridospermatophytes (seed ferns) that had leaves like angiosperms, seeds housed in cupules, and did not develop flowers.

Ceratophyllales
Group of angiosperm plants that includes the hornworts.

Cetaceans
A group of marine mammals that includes whales, dolphins, and porpoises.

Chloranthales
Group of angiosperm plants that includes herbs, bushes, and trees with small flowers.

Clade
A group that includes various related organisms with a common ancestor.

Cladistics
A branch of biology that defines evolutionary relations among organisms on the basis of common derived characteristics.

Cololite
Fossilized stomach contents.

Commelinidas
Group of monocot angiosperm plants that includes bananas, grains, palms, and grasses.

Coniferales
Group of gymnosperm plants that includes pines, cypresses, and araucarias.

Convergence/Convergent evolution
The evolutionary process in which species of different lineages evolve similar characteristics.

Cordaitales
Extinct group of gymnosperm plants with heart-shaped seeds and small, broad leaves.

Corytospermales
Group of pteridospermatophytes (seed ferns) that includes the extinct genus *Dricroidium* and had fern-like leaves and seed clusters.

Cursorial
Animal adapted for running.

Cycads
Group of gymnosperm plants with a palm-like appearance that developed cones like pinecones.

Cylindrodont
Cylindrical tooth pattern.

Czekanowskiale
Extinct group of gymnosperm plants with fine, narrow leaves like pine needles and seed clusters.

Denticles

Small pointed structures that together form the serrated edges of some teeth.

Derived
Trait or organism possessing specialized or evolutionarily novel features.

Dermestids
A family of beetles that includes species that feed off carrion, excrement, and/or pollen.

Dinoturbation
Alteration of the substrate caused by dinosaur treading.

Diverticulum
Cavity shaped like a small pouch that can form naturally or as a pathology.

Egagropile (Pellet)
Balls containing bone and feathers or hair that some birds disgorge after eating their prey whole. When fossilized they are known as regurgitalith.

Epidermis
Outermost layer of the skin.

Equisetales
Group of sphenophyte plants known as equisets or "horsetails."

Eudicotyledoneae
Group of angiosperm plants with tricolpate (three-lobed) pollen.

Evolution
The process that gives rise to and transforms living beings over time.

Exostosis
An abnormal bone outgrowth.

Foliodont
Leaf-shaped tooth.

Fossil
Any naturally preserved evidence of life in the past.

Frontal (bone)
Bone located on the anterior dorsal part of the cranium.

Gastroliths
Stones ingested by certain animal species to help break down and mix food, as a mineral supplement, or to clean out the stomach.

Ginkgos
Group of ginkoal gymnosperms that includes only one extant species.

Gland
A group of cells that produce and expel liquid substances that are required by an organism to function.

Glossopteridales
Group of pteridospermatophyte plants (seed ferns), some with large trunks and long, broad tongue-like leaves.

Gnetales
Group of gymnosperm plants that includes melinjo.

Graviportal
A group of vascular, spermatophyte (seed-producing) plants that includes pines, cycads, gnetales, and other extinct groups.

Hadrosaurids
A family of phytophagous facultative bipeds commonly known as duck-billed dinosaurs.

Hemangioma
A benign tumor caused by the abnormal buildup of blood vessels.

Hiatus
Spatial or temporal interruption in the fossil record.

Hydrocarbon
Chemical compound formed of carbon and hydrogen.

Hyperostosis
Excessive bone growth.

Ichthyosaurs
A group of aquatic sauropods that lived in the Mesozoic Era, similar in appearance to dolphins.

Intraspecific
Describes biological interaction between members of the same species.

Isoetales
Group of lycophyte plants with one surviving genus: *Isoetes*.

Limulidae
A family of very primitive marine arthropods related to spiders and scorpions. The horseshoe crab is a living example.

List of fauna
List of species found in some region or locality.

Locomotion
The act of moving from one place to another.

Long bones

Elongated or cylindrical bones such as the femur, the phalanges, and the radius.

Lycopodiales
Group of lycophyte plants such as lycopodia, commonly known as "ground pines."

Malocclusion
Misalignment of the teeth.

Mammiferoid
A clade of (vertebrate) amniotes with attributes that situate them between "reptiles" and true mammals.

Mesaxonic
Having hands or feet in which the middle digit is longest.

Metabolism
The series of primordial chemical reactions that enable an organism to function properly.

Nymphaeaceae
Group of angiosperm plants that includes nenuphars.

Ontogeny
The history of the growth and development of an organism from embryo to adult.

Ornithischians
Herbivorous dinosaurs with horny beaks, such as ankylosaurs, stegosaurs, ceratopses, pachycephalosaurs, and ornithopods.

Osteoarthritis
An illness caused by the wearing down of the joints as a creature ages.

Osteoderm
An ossified portion of skin on some animals, such as the dorsal scales on a crocodile or the armor of an armadillo.

Osteomyelitis
Inflammation of the bone and bone marrow.

Osteophytes
Small tissue deposits near an inflamed joint.

Paleocene
Epoch of the Cenozoic Era that began 66 Ma and ended 55.8 Ma.

Paraphyletic
In cladistics, this refers to a group of organisms descended from a common ancestor but not including all of that ancestors' descendants.

Peltaspermales
Group of pteridospermatophyte plants (seed ferns) with umbrella-shaped culpules.

Perinatal neonate
A newborn.

Petroglyph
Human-made images carved on stone.

Phylogeny
Evolutionary history of a group of organisms.

Phytophagous
Refers to animals that eat plants.

Phytosaur
A primitive archosaur from the late Triassic, similar to a crocodile.

Plantigrade
Refers to an animal that walks entirely on the soles of its feet.

Pleuromeiales
Extinct group of lycophyte plants, some of them very large.

Pneumatic bones
Hollow bones with air chambers and respiratory tissue inside.

Postcrania
The parts of the skeleton that include the vertebrae and long bones but not the skull.

Quadruped
Animal that moves around on four legs.

Saurischia
A group of dinosaurs that includes theropods and sauropodomorphs.

Sauropodomorpha
A group of herbivorous dinosaurs that includes sauropods and their ancestors.

Sauropsids
A group of (vertebrate) amniotes that includes "reptiles" and birds, but not synapsids or mammiferoid reptiles.

Sexual dimorphism
A set of morphological and physiological variations that distinguish males and females of the same species.

Specific epithet
The second part of the binomial that comprises a species' scientific name.

Sphenophyllales
Extinct group of herbaceous, broad-leafed plants related to equisets.

Spondylitis
An infection of the vertebra.

Supernova
Explosion that occurs at the end of the life cycle of massive stars.

Taphonomy
The branch of paleontology that studies factors that influence the preservation or destruction of organic remains.

Taxonomy
The branch of biology concerned with the hierarchical classification of living things.

Tetrapods
Group of vertebrates with two pairs of limbs. It includes all vertebrates except fish.

Type specimen (holotype)
The principal specimen (complete organism or part thereof) used to represent a new species when first reported in a publication.

Vertebral arch
The upper half of a vertebra, comprising the neural arch and neural spine, more commonly known as a backbone.

Voltziales
Extinct group of coniferophyte gymnosperms that somewhat resemble cypresses but are not close relatives.

Taxonomic index

271

Bibliography

General

www.eofauna.com/en/appendix/sauropoda_ref.pdf

Scientific webpages

Databases
Taylor Mike, and Matt Wedel – SVPOW
www.svpow.com
Ford, Tracy – Paleofile
www.paleofile.com
www.dinohunter.info
Aragosaurus
www.aragosaurus.com
Stuchlik, Krzysztof – Tribute to Dinosaurs
www.dinoanimals.pl/pliki/Baza_Dinozaurow.xlsx
www.encyklopedia.dinozaury.com
Olshevsky, Jorge – Dinogenera
www.polychora.com/dinolist.html
Mortimer, Mickey – Theropod Database
www.theropoddatabase.blogspot.com

Reconstructions
Paul, Gregory – The Science and Art of Gregory S. Paul
www.gspauldino.com
Hartman, Scott – Skeletal Drawing
www.skeletaldrawing.com

Chronology and fossils
The Paleobiology Database
www.paleobiodb.org

Paleomaps
Scotese, Robert – Paleomap Project
www.scotese.com
Blakey, Ron – Colorado Plateau Geosystems, Inc
www.cpgeosystems.com

Blogs
Headden, Jaime A. – The Bite Stuff
www.qilong.wordpress.com
Cau, Andrea – Theropoda blog
www.theropoda.blogspot.com

Appendix

Statistics and other data

www.eofauna.com/en/appendix

Acknowledgments

First of all we would like to give our big thanks to Angel Alejandro Ramírez Velasco, UNAM Professor, for his careful review of this work. We also wish to thank everyone who helped in compiling the scientific documentation: Augusto Haro, Tracy Ford, Ignacio Díaz Martínez, René Hernández Rivera, Sue Turner, Tony Thulborn, José Rubén Guzmán Gutiérrez, Antonio Garcia Palmeiro, Francisco J. Vega Vera, Alexander Elistratov, Pedro de Luna, Krzysztof Rogoz, Octavio Mateus, Roman Ulansky, Richard Hofmann, and especially the Wikipaleo Facebook group. Special thanks are also due to Mike Taylor for his unflagging willingness to resolve concerns about sauropods and to David Alejandro Vouillat for his services during our visit to the museums of Argentina. We thank Gregory Paul for providing us with reconstructions of *Argentinosaurus* and *Patagotitan*. Our gratitude is also extended to Rafael Royo-Torres and to Jinyou Mo for sending us photos of the pedal phalange of *Turiasaurus* and the distal segment of the femur of *Fusuisaurus*, respectively. We also cannot fail to acknowledge Antonio Garcia Palmeiro, Matthew E. Clapham, Luis Rey, Abel Aldana, Antonio García Palmeiro, and Leví Bernardo Martínez Reza, who provided comments, inspiration, and information. Many thanks also to Jorge A. Ortiz Mendieta for his grayscale illustrations (pp. 99, 201, 233–238), and to Josefa I. Valdivia-Alcaino for her *Shunosaurus* art (pp. 124–125). We also thank Kamila L. N. Bandeira , Antonio Garcia Palmeiro and Krzysztof Stuchlik Shahen for their helpful remarks and comments. Lastly, we thank the entire editorial team at Princeton University Press for their assistance during the final preparation of this book. If we have inadvertently failed to mention anyone to whom thanks is also due, our sincere apologies.

Almodóvar

A Retrospective

'Luckily, nature has endowed me with
an irrational curiosity for even the
most trivial things. That saves me.
Curiosity is the only thing that keeps
me afloat. Oh, and vocation.'

Almodóvar
A Retrospective

Pau Gómez

Foreword by **Antonio Banderas**
Afterword by **Cecilia Roth**

First published in the United Kingdom in 2024 by
Thames & Hudson Ltd, 181A High Holborn,
London WC1V 7QX

ISBN 978-0-500-02856-8

Printed and bound in China

Be the first to know about our new releases, exclusive
content and author events by visiting
thamesandhudson.com
thamesandhudsonusa.com
thamesandhudson.com.au

MIX
Paper | Supporting
responsible forestry
FSC® C008047

CONTENTS

FOREWORD

In 2002, twelve years after our last collaboration on *Tie Me Up! Tie Me Down!*, Pedro and I had our first conversation about *The Skin I Live In* at the Cannes Film Festival. He told me that he had read Thierry Jonquet's novel and that he was going to start the process of adapting it to film, and that he was interested in me playing Doctor Ledgard. In all that time without working together, he had called me a couple of times, but I always had a contract that committed me for a long time to another film and it was impossible for me to dedicate myself to Pedro's project. Finally, one day in early 2010, he called me on the phone as I was leaving a rehearsal on Broadway, and he said, 'The time has come.'

I've always thought that the only time an actor is also a spectator is when he reads a script for the first time. *The Skin I Live In* had a huge impact on me, and I immediately felt that it was a project tailor-made for Almodóvar, because only he could tell that story and tell it the way that the script reflected, with such freedom, using the premise of the novel as an inspiration and a starting point from which to create something totally different and genuine. I was very clear that I had to approach my character from a gestural economy, that he should do everything he does with absolute naturalness and turn him into a blank screen where the audience could express their concerns. I soon realised that this was the right project for our reunion, and I knew that the long wait had been worth it.

I've had the good fortune to work with Pedro Almodóvar many times, with wonderful characters who somehow always had some particularity that made them strangely fascinating (in *Matador* my character, Ángel, suffered from a kind of vertigo that gave him visions of the future!). His system of work is long and complex, but it always manages to bring out the best in you, and that is something for which I am deeply grateful.

However, even if it had never been like that and our paths had never crossed, I would have to thank him for all the good he has done for cinema – in particular, for Spanish cinema, although sometimes it is hard to recognise it – and the enormous and well-deserved admiration he has all over the world. Fortunately for me, when we met in 1982 to shoot *Labyrinth of Passion*, Pedro told me that my real name – José Antonio Domínguez – sounded like a bullfighter to him, and that, if I agreed, he preferred to use my middle name and surname – Bandera – in the plural, because he liked it very much. 'They're the credits of your film, so go ahead,' I told him.

The rest... is history.

Antonio Banderas

INTRODUCTION
The Long and Painful Road to Glory

Few contemporary filmmakers have exposed and given so much of their emotional life to their art as Pedro Almodóvar. From his first film, *Pepi, Luci, Bom and Other Girls Like Mom* (1980) to the most recent, *Parallel Mothers* (2021), his cinema has evolved through various stages without ever losing sight of a series of common and universally constant themes, arising from a mixture of his own experiences, his cultural influences, and his very particular way of seeing and understanding the world. It is undeniable that the early wild and experimental works have given way to others that are more serene and introspective, a reasonable transition for an auteur whose filmmaking changes and adapts to the different tides in a life. But the amazing thing about Almodóvar is his ability to imbue films four decades apart with the same spirit. A spirit that continues to be inimitable, and thanks to which he has become one of the most important filmmakers of the last four decades.

Pedro Almodóvar's works have achieved worldwide recognition, based on universal stories with a strong influence of Spanish popular culture. The identity of his characters, the constant references to the rural environment and the recurrent use of iconographies and the traditions of his country – such as religious fervour or the world of bullfighting – are some of the most fascinating and attractive elements for foreign audiences. Today, there are many who, without knowing Spain, feel a strange closeness to the country thanks to Almodóvar's films. His vision, somewhat grotesque and disproportionate at times, is far removed from conservative circles and leans towards characters of low social status. It has been able to adapt to different periods – from glam and the Madrid *Movida* of the eighties to the social portrait and the critical sentiment of the twenty-first century – and which perfectly defines the style of the director from La Mancha. Perhaps this is why he has always refused, despite multiple offers, to set one of his films outside his own country and to work with crews and casts from other countries. Almodóvar's cinema and Spanish idiosyncrasy have been linked from the very first moment and will continue to be so until the last of his projects.

Almodóvar's tendency to exaggeration and the construction of extravagant characters has also allowed him to establish the archetype that gives meaning to his films: the strong, determined woman who manages to overcome the blows of fate and confronts the patriarchy, so present in the Spain of the Transition (the period from the mid-1970s to the early 1980s, during which Spain saw the end of Franco's regime, the introduction of democratic elections and the adoption of a new constitution) in which Almodóvar began shooting his first works. His ability to delve into such a complex female universe and extract extraordinary characters from it, as if he shares a sensibility alien to most men, is astonishing.

Born on 25 September 1949, in the small town of Calzada de Calatrava (Ciudad Real), in the heart of La Mancha, Pedro Almodóvar was accustomed from an early age to being

"

I LEARNED A LOT FROM MY MOTHER,
WITHOUT EITHER OF US BEING
AWARE OF IT.

"

surrounded almost exclusively by women. His father, Antonio, was a mule driver and spent prolonged periods of time away from home, leaving Pedro and his siblings – Antonia, María Jesús and Agustín – in the care of their mother, who was always surrounded by relatives and neighbours. He, meanwhile, observed them with affection and admiration: 'They were the secret power of Spain, a kind of communal force that had managed to survive the post-war period. It is true that, in my films, the women are very strong, with enormous moral independence and full of energy. And the fact is that, although we have all grown up in a very macho society, women have managed to exercise power in silence.'

Almodóvar continued to develop this special devotion when, at the age of nine, he moved with his family to Madrigalejo, a village in Extremadura. It was there that he began to focus his gaze on the figure of his mother, Francisca Caballero, a generous and tenacious woman who, soon after arriving in their new home, set up a small business reading and writing letters for illiterate neighbours, which she adorned with marvellous embroidery. 'Sometimes, I would listen to what my mother read, and I was astonished to hear that it did not match the content of the letter,' Almodóvar remembered in 2000, during his investiture as Doctor Honoris Causa by the University of Castilla-La Mancha. 'Back home, I reproached her for inventing part of the content, and she defended herself by saying to me: "but have you seen how happy Grandma was to hear that her granddaughter remembered her?"' Over time, Francisca would become a regular presence in his films ('although she never saw any of them, because she had the intuition that she would not like them') and a continuous source of inspiration for his stories, as shown by the unforgettable Jacinta, played by Chus Lampreave in *The Flower of My Secret* (1995). 'I learned a lot from my mother, without either of us being aware of it,' he wrote after her death in 1999. 'I learned something essential to my work, the difference between fiction and reality, and how reality needs to be supplemented by fiction to make life easier.'

The women created by Almodóvar are true cinematic icons, and it is no coincidence that his best and most awarded feature films – *Women on the Verge of a Nervous Breakdown* (1988), *All About My Mother* (1999) and *Volver* (2006) – feature these charismatic fighters based on his own mother, brought to life by magnificent actors who, over the decades, have confirmed themselves as colossal muses: Carmen Maura, Cecilia Roth, Victoria Abril, Marisa Paredes, Verónica Forqué, Penélope Cruz. Even in those films in which the central character is a man, such as *Labyrinth of Passion* (1982), *Matador* (1986), *Law of Desire* (1987), *Live Flesh* (1997), *Talk to Her* (2002) or *Pain and Glory* (2019), we find female characters that in many cases sustain the emotional stability of the male protagonist, someone much weaker and unstable by nature. This is due, in the director's eyes, to the fact that women possess a gift unattainable for any man: motherhood, undoubtedly one of his most recurring themes – because the memory of Francisca will always accompany him – and a feeling capable of oscillating between happiness and tragedy, with such representative examples as *What Have I Done to Deserve This?* (1984), *High Heels* (1991) or *Julieta* (2016).

Around the powerful figure of the woman, Almodóvar began to define a series of characteristic themes that would end up defining his personality. One of the most significant is his fervent rejection of clerical authoritarianism, the result of his student years spent with Salesian and Franciscan fathers at a school in Cáceres. 'Now I can say that there were three places where I was formed: the patios of La Mancha where the women made bobbin

lace, sang and criticised the whole town; the explosive and free-flowing nightlife of Madrid from '77 to '90, and the dark, religious education I received from the Salesians in the early sixties,' he stated in 2023 at the time of the publication of his first book of short stories.

The experience caused him to rebel and impregnate his films with criticism of ecclesiastical dogma, seen in the irreverence of *Dark Habits* (1983) or the autobiographical story of *Bad Education* (2004), in which he recalled the admiration his beautiful voice aroused among the religious or the terrible abuse suffered by some of his classmates. 'All the ceremonial was a theatrical experience that amazed me,' he confesses. 'But there came a moment when I saw that those hands holding the chalice had very recently been caressing things they shouldn't be caressing... At that moment I stopped having faith.' Alongside this controversial desire to confront the power of the Church, we can identify other equally important themes that have run through his work from the beginning: homosexuality and transsexuality as identity struggles, drug use as an escape route from physical and emotional pain, prostitution, and the 'cinema within the cinema', so present in *Law of Desire, Tie Me Up! Tie Me Down!* (1990), *Broken Embraces* (2009), *Pain and Glory* and *The Waning Lover*, the silent film included in the prologue of *Talk to Her*.

All of these themes are paraded before the camera either as drama or a comedy – and often both – the two genres that best suit his artistic vision. But while he has employed these for most of his films, there have been very successful forays into film noir during his more mature later years. In Almodóvar's films, genres never maintain their classic structure, but intermingle and enrich each other, giving rise to a unique, tragicomic and provocative brew. His lighter films always include heart-rending passages and situations, while the more dramatic works feature numerous shots of that dark humour so characteristic of his scripts. It is very likely that we will never see him directing a science fiction story or a musical, because the simple context would distort his universe.

Almodóvar has never hidden the multiple references in his films, from the more rowdy and politically incorrect John Waters of the early works to the irreverence of Billy Wilder, passing through the classic perspective of masters of melodrama such as Douglas Sirk or Howard Hawks in his most mature and relaxed stage, without forgetting the silent influence of Alfred Hitchcock – in practically all his films there is a murder or an accident that triggers the narrative – or the imprint of other great Spanish directors such as Luis Buñuel or Víctor Erice. He discovered all of them during the summers in Madrigalejo, when he and his brother, Agustín, attended the screenings that took place on the wall of an old building. 'Basically, they showed spaghetti westerns, although we also saw Bergman, Welles or Antonioni.'

During the rest of the year, while he attended his classes at the Catholic school, he repeated the ritual by escaping to a cinema in the same street: 'The priests tried to form my spirit, deforming it with religious tenacity. Engulfed in the cinema seat, I was reconciled with the world, with my world. Very soon, I was forced to choose, and I did so with that forcefulness of inexperience. If I deserved hell for watching *Johnny Guitar*, *Picnic*, *Splendor in the Grass*, and *Cat on a Hot Tin Roof*, I had no choice but to accept such a punishment. I did not know what genes were, but, without a doubt, in my genetic code I had the stigma of the provincial cinephile branded red hot.' During those sessions in Cáceres, the young Pedro discovered that films were not made by the stars, but that behind them there was

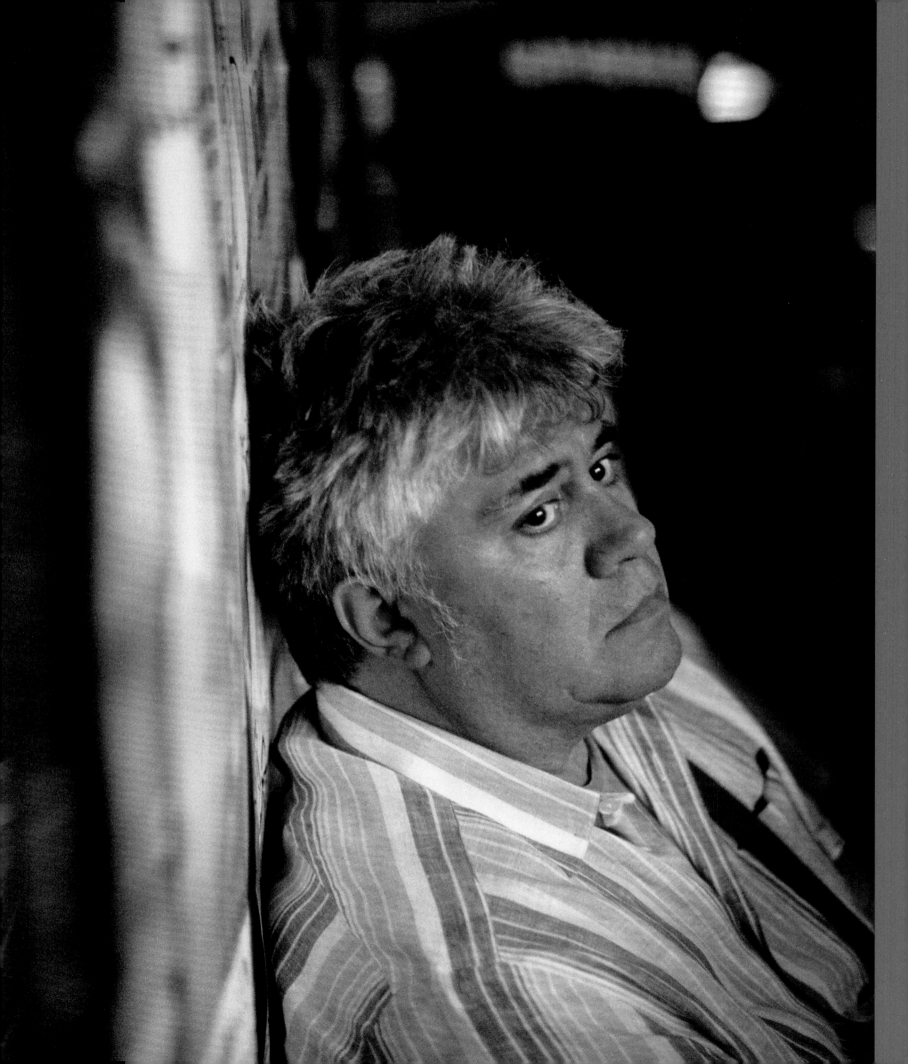

WE CAN RECOGNISE ANY OF HIS FILMS BY A SINGLE FRAME, STUNNED BY THE VISUAL IMPACT IT PRODUCES.

a scriptwriter who shaped the story and a director who gave instructions. And he immediately knew that he wanted to do both. So, when he returned to the village after finishing his studies in Cáceres, the first thing he did was to tell his parents that he was going to Madrid to pursue his dream. His father, he recalls, 'threatened to hand me over to the National Guard,' to which he replied: 'Do it. But I'm going.'

Almodóvar's catalogue of references encompasses other arts that go beyond the cinematographic, starting with music. He typically features songs, carefully selecting ones whose lyrics always help to describe an attitude or a state of mind, and continuing with literature, through authors as diverse as Jean Cocteau, Tennessee Williams or Mary Shelley, whose *Frankenstein* must have been a fundamental book for Almodóvar while he was preparing the asphyxiating *The Skin I Live In* (2011), his triumphant reunion with Antonio Banderas after twenty-one years without working together.

On the formal side, painters such as Andy Warhol and Salvador Dalí contributed, to give personality to the palette of primary colours in Almodóvar's films, where red, the symbol of passion, always occupies a predominant place in the sets, objects, and the costumes of the characters. We can recognise any of his films by a single frame, stunned by the visual impact it produces. So important and exquisite is it for Almodóvar to maintain the identifying aesthetic in his works that he has cast Rossy de Palma – an actor of overwhelming presence and genuine figure – on seven occasions without ever having to reserve a leading role for her.

For all these reasons, and for many more that we will have the opportunity to explore, Pedro Almodóvar is a master of contemporary cinema. Even his most misunderstood films, like *Kika* (1993) or *I'm So Excited!* (2013), have those flashes of genius that are only within the reach of the chosen ones. His list of accolades is virtually unmatched: two Oscars, two Golden Globes, four BAFTAs, Best Director at the Cannes Film Festival, four César Awards, a Golden Lion in Venice, five Goyas, National Film Award, Prince of Asturias Award of the Arts, Knight of the French Legion of Honour, Doctor *honoris causa* from the Universities of Oxford and Harvard... To speak about Almodóvar is to speak of a creator with an indisputable international dimension, someone who has been able to maintain the essence of his art through the intimacy of stories that are close, extreme and profoundly Spanish.

An author with an infinite imagination, creator of unforgettable characters, promoter of a challenging and captivating cinema.

LEFT: During his youth, Almodóvar represented the rebellious spirit of a society awakening from the nightmare of Franco's regime.

PEPI, LUCI, BOM AND OTHER GIRLS LIKE MOM

PEPI, LUCI, BOM AND OTHER GIRLS LIKE MOM

Pepi, Luci, Bom y otras chicas del montón (1980)

I n the late 1970s, a countercultural phenomenon began to take shape in Madrid. Over the following decade, the *Movida* challenged and removed the artistic constraints of a country silenced by Franco's dictatorship. Inspired by punk and new wave bands, the movement celebrated the arrival of democracy with an uncontrolled burst of creativity, which included everything from music to painting, photography, literature and fashion. Cinema, of course, was no stranger to this outpouring of freedom and provocation, consecrating such outstanding filmmakers as Fernando Colomo, Iván Zulueta and Fernando Trueba, and above them a young man from La Mancha who had arrived in Madrid at the tender age of eighteen trying to emulate his idols Federico Fellini, Ingmar Bergman and François Truffaut.

However, Pedro Almodóvar had to wait to realise his dream. The only film school in the city had closed its doors by order of Franco, who considered it a dangerous hotbed of communism. In 1969, after some sporadic jobs as a disc jockey and an extra in some movies (he always got brief roles as a hippie thanks to his looks and his characteristic long hair), he ended up getting a job as an administrative assistant at Telefónica, a position he would keep for twelve years. Despite everything, he always kept his aspirations intact and never stopped going to art and rehearsal halls. With the emergence of the *Movida*, Almodóvar became one of the most active figures in the movement: he was a member of the underground theatre group Los Goliardos; created the cult punk-glam duo Almodóvar & McNamara with Fabio McNamara; wrote short novels, newspaper stories and transgressive comics; and, despite a lack of resources, he began to make his own experimental works in Super 8 with the help of several friends.

'Super 8 was really my only school,' he confesses. 'It allowed me to touch all genres: musicals, biblical films, comedies. . . I wasn't aware of it, but those films show very clearly what I wanted to do in the cinema.' Little by little, short films such as *Dos putas o historia de amor que termina en boda* (1974), *La caída de Sódoma* (1975), *Sexo va, sexo viene* (1977) or *Salomé* (1978) consolidated Almodóvar as one of the leading figures of the Madrid phenomenon, thanks to his provocative, extreme and surrealist perspective. As none of the films had sound, during the screenings he gave for his friends, he himself was in charge of the soundtrack: 'I would stand in the middle of the audience, next to the projector, and I would do all the voices, explain, narrate the story, sing, sometimes even criticise the things I didn't like about the actors, and I had a small cassette where I would play music to accompany it.'

ABOVE: A moustachioed Almodóvar comments on a scene with Carmen Maura, the muse of his early films.

NEXT PAGE: The filmmaker soon became the creative and spiritual leader of each of his films.

In 1978, Almodóvar shot his first feature-length work, the experimental melodrama *Folle... Folle... Fólleme Tim!*, although his first commercial film did not arrive until two years later. Two friends and colleagues in Los Goliardos, Félix Rotaeta and Carmen Maura, convinced him to turn the story he had written for a photo novel entitled *Erecciones generales* (*General Erections*) – a play on words in reference to the first free elections in Spain in forty years – into a film script. 'I felt an absolute physical need to make the film,' he says. 'I really liked the script. But, as I didn't have any resources, I had to improvise the production.' Rotaeta and Almodóvar's generous friends raised the necessary funds – around half a million pesetas – to make *Pepi, Luci, Bom and Other Girls Like Mom* an unforgettable calling card for a filmmaker swimming against the tide, revealing the first daring brushstrokes of his art in which sex, masochism and even a mythical golden shower scene filmed with hot beer and an enema douche are all present.

Depicting the director – gender swapped – in practically all his early works, Carmen Maura plays Pepi, a young woman who grows cannabis on her terrace and who, in exchange for her silence, is raped by her policeman neighbour (Félix Rotaeta). Seeking revenge, Pepi meets Luci (Eva Siva), her attacker's wife and an extreme fan of pain, who pushes her

"SUPER 8 WAS REALLY MY ONLY SCHOOL."

into the arms of Bom (played by the singer Alaska, another of the undisputed icons of the *Movida*), a cursed punk artist with sadistic tendencies. The three women are just the spearhead of a gallery of bizarre and fascinating female characters, some of them played by key actors from Almodóvar's later films, such as Julieta Serrano, Kiti Mánver and Cecilia Roth.

LUCI: **What do you do for a living?**
PEPI: **Well, I'm a rich heiress and my parents give me money, but they've had enough, and they've told me to get by as best I can.**
LUCI: **And what are you going to do now?**
PEPI: **Well, I thought I'd start by selling my virginity, but the other day I was raped, and my plan was ruined.**

The scarcity of means and the meagre budget led to an endless and creative shoot. Production began in 1979 and had to be suspended on several occasions due to lack of money, not being completed until almost a year-and-a-half later. During this time, the crew alternated exhausting fifteen-hour filming days with long months without work, which meant that some roles had to be changed and actors replaced, as some were not available. The actors were responsible for providing their own wardrobe and often did each other's make-up, always ready in case the director called them to shoot a scene the following day. As if all this were not enough, Almodóvar had to combine the film with his work at Telefónica – he could only devote his full

I REALLY LIKED THE SCRIPT. BUT, AS I DIDN'T HAVE ANY RESOURCES, I HAD TO IMPROVISE THE PRODUCTION.

LEFT: Almodóvar reviews the script with his actresses and adjusts Eva Siva's hair before shooting.

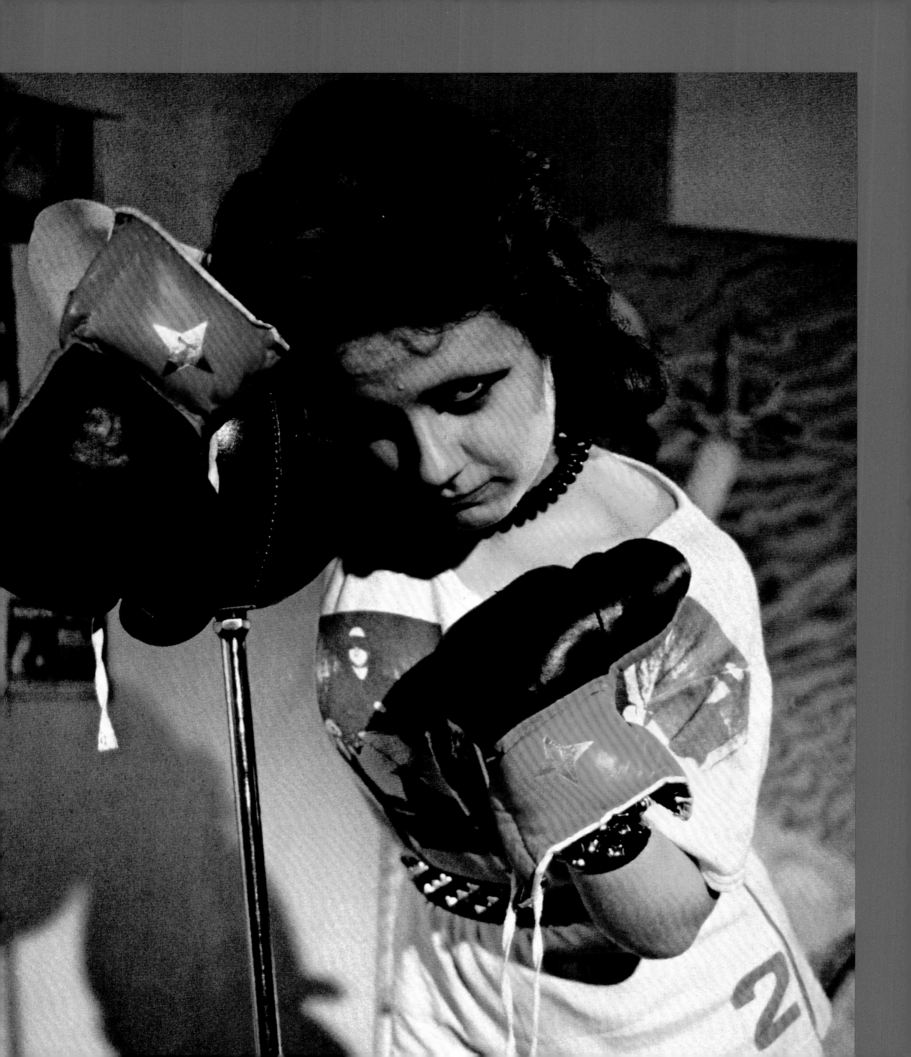

WHEN A FILM HAS ONLY ONE OR TWO FLAWS, IT IS CONSIDERED IMPERFECT, WHEREAS WHEN THE DEFECTS ARE SO PROFUSE, THEY CONSTITUTE A STYLE.

attention to it at weekends – and make sure he completed the exterior sequences in the shortest possible time, as they lacked permits to shoot on public roads.

There was even a moment when the director, tired of so many delays, thought of shooting a hasty ending and truncating the length of the film: 'At the beginning, Pepi opens the door to the policeman in June 1979, he sits in the living room in December of that same year and starts talking in June 1980,' Almodóvar himself would admit years later, and his main concern was 'to reach the *end* word.' Everything changed when the producer Pepón Coromina saw the material they had shot and decided to provide distribution advances in order to finish the film, which was completed with a final budget of around six million pesetas and was even presented out of competition at the San Sebastián Film Festival: 'I had to continually adapt to the lack of resources, which meant I had to give up some scenes and also meant that I could not replace fragments of the material shot at the beginning with scenes that, a year later, seemed more appropriate.'

Finally, on 27 October 1980, the film premiered at the legendary Alphaville cinema in Madrid, where it practically became a night-time emblem of the *Movida* and remained a midnight showing mainstay for almost four years, reaching a final box-office taking of close to forty million pesetas. Shortly before, Almodóvar had been able to fill the Carrión Theatre during the Valladolid Film Festival, after personally putting up posters all over the city with the slogan of his debut film. 'It's full of defects,' he acknowledged, while at the same time claiming the existence of his own spirit based on those same singularities. 'When a film has only one or two flaws, it is considered imperfect, whereas when the defects are so profuse, they constitute a style. That's what I jokingly said when I was promoting it, but I think it's pretty close to the truth. We made it with two coins, on handouts, passion, and unconsciousness, but I approached it as seriously as if I were shooting *Gone with the Wind*.'

It is paradoxical that, four decades later, a story like *Pepi, Luci, Bom and Other Girls Like Mom* is inconceivable in the current industry. The carefree vision of some particularly tricky subjects, the irresistible amateur aesthetics, and the firm commitment to incorrectness make it a rarity in which some of its creator's fundamental themes begin to be glimpsed. We can find the attraction to the female universe – with those stoic and charming women, the perfect counterweight to the clichés of toxic masculinity – or the representation of sex and passion in its freest and most diverse version, without limits or rules. A work impossible to classify, where the genres are confused and cinema is shown in its purest state, as a glorious explosion of creativity and bravery.

LABYRINTH OF PASSION

LABYRINTH OF PASSION
Laberinto de pasiones (1982)

The nightly pilgrimage of viewers to the Alphaville cinema to see *Pepi, Luci, Bom and Other Girls Like Mom* led its managing director, Javier de Garcillán, to design a budget plan with which to finance Pedro Almodóvar's second feature film. He himself decided to contribute seventy per cent of the twenty million pesetas that the film would cost, raising the rest through various private contributions. Aware of the complexity of the script and the numerous technical shortcomings of the director's previous film, Garcillán was determined to assemble a first-rate team, including the director of photography Ángel Luis Fernández – a benchmark of the period thanks to his contribution to such iconic works as *Ópera prima* and *Arrebato* – and the German Martin Müller, the regular sound designer for Wim Wenders's films. All of this was done with the intention of elevating the Almodóvarian gaze to a new formal and narrative dimension, much closer to professional cinema than the irregular – although captivating – *Pepi, Luci, Bom*. The filmmaker himself acknowledged that he was overcome by a clear aspiration: 'To say that it is a delicious and unclassifiable comedy is not enough, I know. But I can talk about my intentions. Well, here they are: my only intention with this film is to conquer the world, and by the way, to move house, to broaden the horizons of my private life and to convince myself that life is worth living.'

Labyrinth of Passion was not only filmed at the height of the *Movida*, but also represents the filmmaker's most complete homage to the spirit of that unrepeatable era. Its story full of subplots and its wide gallery of characters – no less than fifty – is directly reminiscent of the choral and sophisticated comedies directed by masters such as Billy Wilder or Richard Lester, two influences recognised by Almodóvar himself. 'I've always felt very close to the genre of delirious comedy,' acknowledges the director. 'When I wrote the script, my desire was to show that Madrid was the first city in the world, a

ABOVE: Fabio McNamara, half of the legendary musical duo Almodóvar & McNamara, was one of the most charismatic and uncontrollable presences on-set.

" MY ONLY INTENTION WITH THIS FILM IS TO CONQUER THE WORLD, AND BY THE WAY, TO MOVE HOUSE. "

LEFT: Almodóvar, who was thirty-two years old when the film was released, was already one of the most transgressive and admired artists of the emerging Spanish counter-cultural movement.

ABOVE: Cecilia Roth as the volcanic Sexilia, her first leading role under Almodóvar's direction.

place where all kinds of people came and where anything could happen. In fact, there was a version that featured Dalí and the Pope, who met there and had a great love story. This passage was deleted from the film, but it sums up its ironic nature very well.' Beyond these influences, *Labyrinth of Passion* is, above all, a wayward taboo-free version of the drama *Luna* (Bernardo Bertulocci, 1979), the harrowing story of a successful singer whose teenage son plunges into the world of drugs when he feels abandoned by his mother.

Almodóvar chose two young performers with barely any experience in front of the camera to play the main characters, and they later became big names in the industry. The Argentinian Cecilia Roth, established as a muse of the *Movida* thanks to her appearances in *Arrebato* and *Pepi, Luci, Bom and Other Girls Like Mom*, would play Sexilia, a singer with a wild personality who has sex with men compulsively to overcome a childhood trauma related to her father, a well-known gynaecologist who has developed a revolutionary fertility method. For his part, Imanol Arias would assume his first leading role as Riza Niro, an Arab prince who arrives in the city in search of new experiences after the fall of the despotic regime of his father, the Emperor of Tiran. Both will live a strange and passionate

love story in which they will have to face the different obstacles that prevent them from achieving happiness.

As he did in his first film, Almodóvar completed the cast with names as varied as the German actor Helga Liné, who plays the mother of the wayward prince (which was the director's first exploration of the maternal–filial conflict so characteristic of his later work). Also noteworthy are the performances of the excellent Marta Fernández Muro and a very young Antonio Banderas in his film debut, portraying a terrorist who tries to kidnap Riza and ends up falling madly in love with him. Alongside them is the presence of important musical figures from the *Movida*. The film is above all a pop celebration of its extravagant and legendary underground artists and bands, from the members of Radio Futura, trans-muted here into an emblematic group of Madrid partygoers, to the confrontational Fabio McNamara, so undisciplined during the filming that he had to be directed from inside the

ABOVE: The German actress Helga Liné had already appeared in more than a hundred films when she joined the cast.

shot, as he never remembered the marks and continually went off-camera. According to Almodóvar, 'Fabio has a very strong personality, so I directed him almost like an animal, in a very shocking and violent way. But, at the same time, I allowed him much more freedom than the other actors because what I wanted to get from him was the expression of his own character. Since I couldn't control him from behind the camera, I got inside the frame to tell him exactly the things he had to say and to keep him tied up.'

Almodóvar asked Telefónica for an unpaid leave of absence to shoot the film, which was produced between March and April 1982. On its tour of Madrid, *Labyrinth of Passion* visits venues closely linked to the artistic life of the time – and by extension to Almodóvar's – such as La Bobia, Tablada 25 and Sala Carolina, and draws on compositions by artists such as Alaska y los Pegamoides and Bernardo Bonezzi, known as 'the Mozart of the Movida', a precocious and unconventional genius who was barely eighteen years old when the film was shot. The author himself would admit that, beyond its classic boy-meets-girl approach, the film is a compendium of love stories that gravitate around urban music and opposing gangs, with obvious references to *West Side Story* (Robert Wise and Jerome Robbins, 1961) and *Quadrophenia* (Franc Roddam, 1979).

With *Labyrinth of Passion*, Almodóvar also inaugurates a very particular plot universe, in which the stories and characters from his different works appear connected in a particularly subtle and witty way. On this occasion, the self-referential figure is the star of porn novels Patty Diphusa, a sort of female alter ego that the filmmaker created in the early eighties on behalf of the art publication *La Luna*, and who is here quoted in an article in the magazine that Riza Niro leafs through. Her wild spirit would give rise over the years to a novel and even a theatrical adaptation in Mexico City, as well as being very present in titles of pure debauchery such as *I'm So Excited!*

Many critics received the film with some dismay. They were very curious to see Almodóvar's new work after *Pepi, Luci, Bom and Other Girls Like Mom*, which was quite acclaimed at the time. However, they found a frenzy of eccentric characters, multiple narrative lines and an exaltation of subjects that were still taboo for Spanish cinema, such as drugs or sexual freedom in all its expressions. Even Almodóvar himself has admitted on occasion that he was not prepared for a challenge of this magnitude, although the film, despite the lack of enthusiasm for it after the premiere has emerged as a brilliant and beautiful evocation of the freedom of the years of the *Movida*. The public adored it unreservedly: an audience of almost 400,000 and ten years of late-night screenings at the Alphaville attest to this.

"I'VE ALWAYS FELT VERY CLOSE TO THE GENRE OF DELIRIOUS COMEDY.

DARK
HABITS

DARK HABITS
Entre tinieblas (1983)

With his first two films, Pedro Almodóvar had shaken the artistic foundations of a country silenced for decades by dictatorship. Artists' yearning for freedom during the transition to democracy demanded a defiance towards everything established, including, of course, scrupulous respect for Catholicism. It was only a matter of time before such an unusual filmmaker decided to tackle the moral degradation hidden behind the doctrines of Francoism, although in his case it would be from an even more subversive perspective, using the crudest satire and parody. *Dark Habits* is, once again, the result of the riotous creativity of the *Movida*, 'a crazy, playful period, full of feverish nights, where Madrid was an explosion that left the world speechless,' as described by Almodóvar when the film was revived in 1996. 'That was the turbulent world to which I belonged, I don't understand where I found the time, but apart from going to Rock-Ola every night and getting high on substances, I was still working at Telefónica, shooting movies and singing.'

Although *Pepi, Luci, Bom and Other Girls Like Mom* and *Labyrinth of Passion* had received some curious financing, *Dark Habits* managed to get off the ground in an even more unusual way. Producer Luis Calvo was looking for a project to satisfy the ambitions of his wife, Cristina Sánchez Pascual, an actor of modest ability who was desperate to work with one of her three favourite Spanish directors: Luis García Berlanga, Iván Zulueta and Pedro Almodóvar. Determined to fulfil her wish, Calvo contacted each director and offered to finance any script if his wife could play the lead. Almodóvar, aware of the difficulties of starting a project about a drug addict and lesbian nuns, ended up being the most astute of the three and accepted the proposal, ahead of an indecisive Berlanga.

LEFT: With *Dark Habits*, Almodóvar turned his biting and provocative gaze on religion for the first time.

“ A CRAZY, PLAYFUL
PERIOD, FULL
OF FEVERISH
NIGHTS, WHERE
MADRID WAS AN
EXPLOSION THAT
LEFT THE WORLD
SPEECHLESS. ”

ABOVE: Almodóvar's main inspiration
for creating the troubled artist was
Marlene Dietrich's films of the 1930s.

Almodóvar had conceived *Dark Habits* as a drama about a powerful female character, a bolero singer who seeks refuge in a convent after the death of her boyfriend from a drug overdose. His main inspiration was the films directed by Josef von Sternberg in the 1930s starring Marlene Dietrich, in which the German actor gave fascinating performances thanks to the effect of her close-ups. However, after witnessing during rehearsals the acting limitations of the lead imposed on him, he decided to strengthen the film's comic component and divert the viewer's attention to the group of nuns who make up the community of the 'Humiliated Redeemers'. These include the Mother Superior, addicted to heroin and determined to give shelter to troubled young women with whom she ends up falling in love; Sister Damned, a cleanliness obsessive who takes care of the tiger that the nuns keep as a pet, feeding it and entertaining it with the bongos; Sister Manure, a fan of LSD and sadomasochism; and Sister Sewer Rat, a secretive nun who leads a double life as the author of pornographic bestsellers.

For these roles, Almodóvar chose, respectively, Julieta Serrano (whose career had been built playing in great theatrical dramas, and who almost turned down the offer because she did not trust her comedic skills), Carmen Maura, Marisa Paredes and Chus Lampreave,

and thanks to their combined talents, he discovered the possibilities and power of close-ups, which he considered 'a kind of X-ray of the character, because they offer no room for lying.' Leaving aside his inseparable Maura, this group of actors would become core cast members in many of Almodóvar's later films, especially Lampreave, who would appear in seven more until her death in 2016. 'He had already called me for his first film, and then for *Labyrinth of Passion*,' she said. 'But I didn't work because I was scared, I didn't feel like making movies. Then he kept insisting and told me that he would always call me with every new film, and he has done so.'

Sister Sewer Rat is probably the great revelation of *Dark Habits*. Almodóvar creates a character to match Lampreave's comic skill and gives her the most memorable lines; when the nun receives a visit from her sister Antonia (Eva Siva), who secretly publishes her novels and brings her literary magazines to the convent:

SISTER SEWER RAT: **Did you bring it?**

ANTONIA: **Yes, there's a review inside.**

SISTER SEWER RAT: **And what does it say?**

ANTONIA: **Not much. What did you expect? An article by Umbral?**

(Passing the magazine slyly under her habit)

ANTONIA: **Do you have any ideas? They're waiting for something new.**

SISTER SEWER RAT: **We're going through a bad time, you know. A new girl has come in, but I don't think it will solve anything. I don't know what's wrong with me, but sometimes I've thought about leaving all this and starting afresh.**

ANTONIA: **What are you saying? It's too late to change your life. Your place is here. Besides, where are you going to go when you're forty-eight years old?**

SISTER SEWER RAT: **Hey, no! Forty-seven, if you don't mind [. . .] Times have changed a lot, life isn't the same anymore.**

ANTONIA: **Come on, look. . . Those are nun's fantasies. You're all crazy, because, as you don't set foot on the street, you think that things happen in the street. Nothing happens in the street! Everything, everything, everything is exactly the same as when you came here.**

SISTER SEWER RAT: **Why?**

ANTONIA: **Because I'm telling you, I live outside, and I know!**

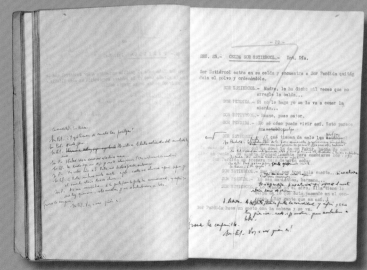

OPPOSITE and TOP: Mercedes (Cecilia Roth) the cabaret singer begs Mother Superior (Julieta Serrano) for forgiveness.

ABOVE: *Dark Habits* original script, with annotations and corrections by the director.

> # IT WAS THE FIRST FILM IN WHICH I BEGAN TO BECOME AWARE OF THE LANGUAGE, OF THE MEANING OF THE SHOTS.

ABOVE and LEFT: In *Dark Habits*, Almodóvar cast three of the most important actresses of his career: Julieta Serrano and Marisa Paredes (above), and Chus Lampreave (left with the filmmaker).

'It was a continuous joy to watch these four nuns work,' Almodóvar admits. 'The mixture of Chus, Carmen, Julieta and Marisa was marvellous. . . It was a shoot worth remembering, for that reason and because I have never again been more scared while filming one of my films.' The scare he refers to occurred when, before filming the confession scene, the tiger attacked a wardrobe assistant and bit her leg. 'It was stuffed with food, so it didn't tear the leg, but it took several crew members to open its mouth and free the girl.' Practically the entire film was shot in an old convent in Madrid, Santa María Magdalena, located at number 88 Hortaleza Street. Shortly afterwards, the building was acquired by the UGT trade union to house its new headquarters, although they soon decided to abandon it, claiming that it was haunted.

With *Dark Habits*, Almodóvar refined and built on the style of his previous films: formal splendour, marginal characters in search of redemption, and a refined direction of his performers. We also find an almost perfect fusion between the melodrama of Douglas Sirk or Rainer W. Fassbinder and the unbridled comedy of John Waters, sprinkled with the irreverent anticlericalism of Luis Buñuel's works such as *Viridiana* (1961) or *La Voie lactée* (1969). All of this was wrapped up in magnificent and unbridled provocation, still strange for a country in the midst of reconstruction, which, by tackling religious hypocrisy, laid the foundations for future projects, such as *Bad Education*, with the Church as the target. 'It was the first film in which I began to become aware of the language, of the meaning of the shots, of the significance of each shoot's size,' he says of his leap in maturity. 'I suppose that, having a unique scenario, a unique set, forced me to think a lot more about where to place the camera so as not to repeat myself.'

Dark Habits marked the beginning of Almodóvar's international recognition, although its controversial approach almost prevented it from being screened at the Venice Film Festival, the first foreign event he attended, on the recommendation of the Italian writer and critic – as well as a regular collaborator of Bernardo Bertolucci – Enzo Ungari. The festival director, Gian Luigi Rondi, opposed the film's inclusion in the official section as he branded it 'obscene,' but he could not prevent it from being screened out of competition, where it received one of the most enthusiastic and unexpected ovations of that year. The audience was delighted with its daring and sense of humour, and reviews in the press, such as *Corriere della sera*, described Almodóvar as 'the heir to Pier Paolo Pasolini,' while others referred to him as the 'Mediterranean Fassbinder.'

The film arrived in Spanish cinemas in October 1983 to mixed reviews from critics but public acclaim, while in France it attracted an audience of 54,000 in its first week of release. The influential Spanish newspaper *Diario 16* declared it 'the scandalous film of the year,' highlighting that 'its central story is that of a love affair between a heroin-addict convent superior and a whoremongering slut who ignores her completely.' Although many consider it the most rushed and least personal film of the director's early work, *Dark Habits* has become recognised as a significant cult piece of art, to the extent of being part of an exhibition at the Reina Sofía Museum in Madrid between 2018 and 2020.

WHAT HAVE I DONE TO DESERVE THIS?

ABOVE: Carmen Maura (right), accompanied here by a splendid Verónica Forqué (left), turned Gloria into one of her most long-suffering and celebrated characters.

WHAT HAVE I DONE TO DESERVE THIS?

¿Qué he hecho yo para merecer esto!! (1984)

Encouraged by the strong box-office performance of *Dark Habits*, Luis Calvo wanted to produce Almodóvar's next film. *What Have I Done to Deserve This?*, the film that marks the end of Almodóvar's early career, introduces some key themes of what is to come: frenzy and surrealism give way to a more mature portrait of the failures of post-Franco Spanish society, while the storytelling is tempered by a much more meticulous *mise-en-scène*. All this is done without giving up the usual flashes of black comedy or the gallery of over-the-top characters, each with their own quirks and traumas. The result was a work of early maturity that, even today, is among the director's best works.

The screenplay of *What Have I Done to Deserve This?* is partially based on *Lamb to the Slaughter*, a 1953 short story by British novelist Roald Dahl, popularised five years later by Alfred Hitchcock in his TV series *Alfred Hitchcock Presents* – it was one of the few episodes that the master of suspense directed himself. In it, a housewife who is devoted to her family murders her husband with a frozen leg of lamb, which she later ends up serving as dinner to the police officers investigating the case. Based on this premise – in the film, the lamb would be replaced by *jamón* – Almodóvar depicts the squalid life of Gloria (the amazing Carmen Maura), a woman addicted to amphetamines, who works as a cleaner and dedicates all her time to supporting her dysfunctional family. This gaudy group consists of her taxi driver husband, Antonio, her ungrateful mother-in-law, two children – one a drug dealer and the other in love with his best friend's father – and even a lizard they call Dinero (Money). Her only friend is her neighbour, Cristal, a naive and kind-hearted sex worker whose friendship keeps Gloria going.

Thanks to its extraordinary depiction of social reality in Spain in the mid-1980s, *What Have I Done to Deserve This?* is the Almodóvar film that comes closest to the raw, poignant and hopeful spirit of Italian neorealism. 'The critics started talking about me as a director because I was dealing with the tribulations of a poor housewife, and you could tell that my heart was very close to this character,' he said. 'And I, who was a very modern guy, very night owlish and all that, had no shame in saying that this is the social class I belong to. That neighbourhood and that building where the protagonist lives contain all the characters that are dear and familiar to me. In my cinema I move around clichés, by prototypes, I digest them and express them in my own way, but in the background, there is the Neorealism of Vittorio de Sica with Sophia Loren or Anna Magnani screaming, dishevelled… That's why I thought that this was my Italian film par excellence.' However, there is a distinction that sets Almodóvar apart from movements such as the postwar period in Italy or the Nouvelle Vague: 'They took the cameras out onto the streets because they wanted to film life honestly. And they achieved all the possible semblance of truth because cinema, including documentary, is full of tricks. I love both periods and they have produced dozens of masterpieces, but what interests me most about reality is its representation. I'm not interested in showing it as it is.'

Gloria is one of those Almodóvarian women who turns to legal drugs to escape their frustrations, loneliness and depressing lives. In one of the film's most memorable scenes, Gloria reveals her total anguish when she goes to the pharmacy – a recurring place for the director from a tragicomic perspective – in search of medicines to help her alleviate her despair:

ABOVE: The film's cast included two renowned Spanish directors: Gonzalo Suárez (with Almodóvar, right) and Jaime Chávarri.

PHARMACIST: **What do you want?**
GLORIA: **Good evening. I'd like Minilip.**
PHARMACIST: **That's not available without a prescription. Besides, it's been withdrawn.**
GLORIA: **Give me Bustaid then.**
PHARMACIST: **We have neither.**
GLORIA: **Well, they've always given it to me without a prescription!**
PHARMACIST: **Well, that's too bad.**
GLORIA: **Well, give me. . . Dexedrines, or something similar. . . I'm very nervous.**
PHARMACIST: **You must have the syndrome.**
GLORIA: **Syndrome? And what is that?**
PHARMACIST: **Look, madam. Go to the doctor, tell him you're a drug addict and have him write you a prescription.**
GLORIA: **I'm a drug addict? But. . . You're insulting me!**
PHARMACIST: **Ma'am, all you're asking me for is drugs.**
GLORIA: **Well, well. . . Well, I'm a drug addict. Drug addict! And what do you want me to do? Assault you and take you by force, or what?**
PHARMACIST: **I've already told you what the rules are.**
GLORIA: **And what are the rules when you must work all day and you can't keep your soul?**

Although the role of Gloria continues to be one of the professional highlights of Carmen Maura's career, Almodóvar found it hard to convince himself that she was the right actor for the part. 'He wanted a tougher woman,' the Madrid-born artist would admit years later. At the time, she had established herself as one of the great progressive voices of the post-Franco culture, thanks to the talk show she presented on Spanish television, *Esta noche*. Almodóvar thought it would be difficult for the audience to accept her as a cleaner on the verge of despair so had decided to offer the role first to two other veteran actors, Esperanza Roy and Concha Velasco, both of whom turned it down. His hand forced, the director went back to Maura, who returned his trust by giving one of the best performances of Spanish cinema in the eighties.

Almodóvar assembled a stellar cast of acting talent, both new and experienced, around his leading lady. On the one hand, he demonstrated his great intuition when casting new

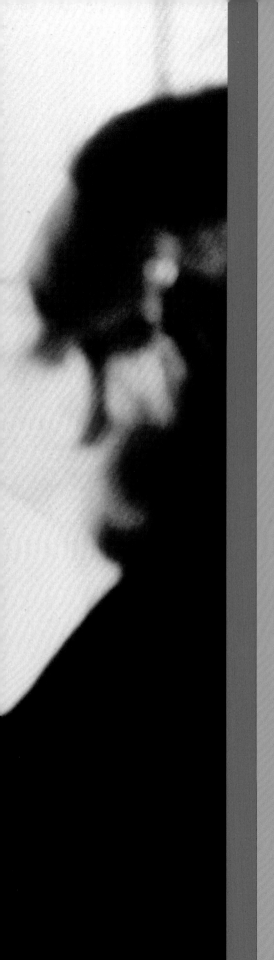

"

WHAT INTERESTS
ME MOST ABOUT
REALITY IS ITS
REPRESENTATION.
I'M NOT
INTERESTED IN
SHOWING IT AS
IT IS.

"

performers such as Ángel de Andrés López and the dazzling Verónica Forqué, whom he would collaborate with again in *Women on the Verge of a Nervous Breakdown* and *Kika*, respectively, while also relying on faces that were already regulars in his films, such as Kiti Mánver or Chus Lampreave, the latter's role as the Grandmother being the first of her many irreverent Almodóvarian matriarchs. Even his own mother, Francisca Caballero, appeared briefly in a clear reference to the role of motherhood and its different interpretations at play in the story. 'The film is a parade of monsters, a reflection on the institution of the family. I get on very well with my family, although I have put some distance between myself and them... I think that the family unit is very good for a society that tries to control and repress the individual,' Almodóvar declared.

Filming took place during the first months of 1984, in such symbolic locations as the Barrio de la Concepción in Madrid, a neighbourhood located next to the M-30 highway which, at that time, was home to the famous 'beehive buildings' where poor families from different parts of Spain lived on top of each other. However, most of the film was shot in a studio, where the flat in which Gloria lives with her family was recreated, and where Almodóvar shows a maturity unbecoming of a director with only three films to his credit. The use of the almost poetic fixed camera shots – another legacy of the neorealist masters – is splendid and captures the range of emotions of each character as they move between the pathetic and the sublime. 'The film is like the reverse of the comedies of Doris Day and Rock Hudson, in which the world of the home became a paradise where household appliances made them very happy,' the director says of the importance of the space in which most of the story takes place. 'Here, on the other hand, the fridges are dwarfed, they have almost no light and when you open them all you find is a can of out-of-date *sofrito*.'

The film received excellent reviews and was a notable success with audiences in Spain. It also became Almodóvar's first work to be commercially released in the United States. After the initial impact of the Venice screening of *Dark Habits*, *What Have I Done to Deserve This?* opened the doors of international cinema and announced him, in the eyes of the American press, as one of the most important European filmmakers of the time. *Los Angeles Weekly* defined his style as a perfect blend of Buñuel, Waters and Woody Allen, and *The New York Times* stated that the film was 'a wonderful black comedy, simply a small masterpiece.' But the strongest validation came from *Newsweek* magazine: 'After nearly fifty years of repression, the arts are finally reviving in Spain... A cultural renaissance the country has not seen since Picasso and Buñuel left for Paris at the turn of the century.' The world was beginning to take notice of Almodóvar, to revel in his unusual and exuberant cinema, as he prepared an unpredictable move and would succumb, once again, to the influence of his masters.

PREVIOUS PAGE: After the film, Maura and Forqué worked together again in various projects and developed a long and close friendship.

LEFT: Lucas Villalba (Suárez) and his wife Patricia (Amparo Soler Leal) hatch a plan to get money from his brother.

RIGHT: Chus Lampreave, here as the Grandmother, would become the quintessential Almodóvarian mother figure.

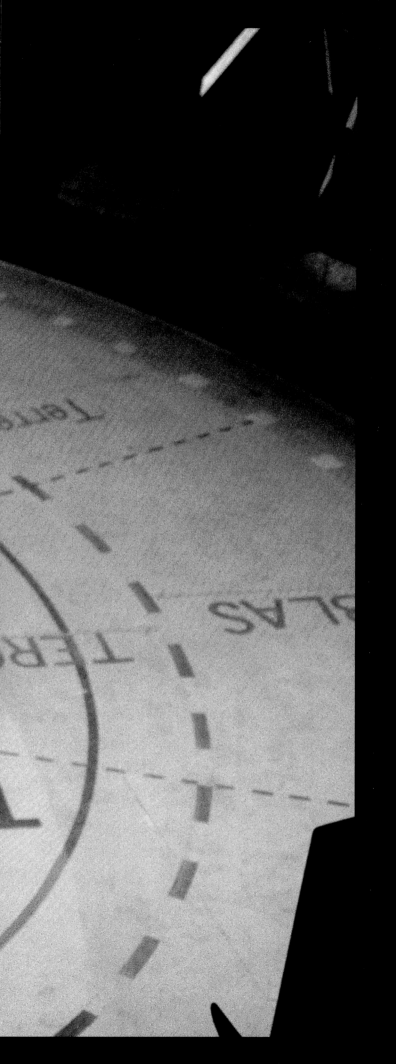

MATADOR

MATADOR (1986)

Spanish cinema has always been a magnificent exponent of European noir. In recent decades, directors such as Enrique Urbizu (*No Rest for the Wicked*, 2011), Mariano Barroso (*Washington Wolves*, 1999), Agustín Díaz Yanes (*Nobody Will Speak of Us When We're Dead*, 1995) and Alberto Rodríguez (*Marshland*, 2014) have lifted the genre to another level in Spain, though curiously, the contribution of Pedro Almodóvar tends to be overlooked. No one doubts that his work usually follows other narrative paths, although the criminal component has always played a leading role in his stories, not only in those films with a purer structure (*Live Flesh* and *The Skin I Live In*), but also in others framed as comedy or drama, such as *Women on the Verge of a Nervous Breakdown, Kika, Volver, Broken Embraces* or, as we have just seen, *What Have I Done to Deserve This?* Not surprisingly, Almodóvar has always been a lover of film noir, never hiding the fact that several of his favourite films are classics of the genre, such as *Night of the Hunter* (Charles Laughton, 1955), *Out of the Past* (Jacques Tourneur, 1947) or *Touch of Evil* (Orson Welles, 1958), to cite just a few examples.

With *Matador*, Almodóvar began a new artistic phase in which he opted for a greater formal perfectionism and for stories where sex and death are closely linked. Initially, the story was about a director in his twilight years who agrees to shoot a musical for the greater glory of a dwarf actor, whose closest friend is a murderer with multiple personalities. 'I started to feel more interested in that character than in the other two, so I decided that the script would revolve around him,' he said of this first foray into the world of erotic noir, starring two characters who find a morbid source of pleasure in the suffering of others. Diego (Nacho Martínez) is a retired bullfighter with a sexual fixation for slasher films, and whose obsession with death leads him to murder the women he makes love to. Meanwhile, María (Assumpta Serna) is a young lawyer who defends political prisoners and shares Diego's fondness for killing each of her lovers after sex. When the two meet, they begin a love-hate relationship that will inevitably bring tragic consequences.

The title of *Matador* was chosen by Almodóvar not only because it was short – *What Have I Done to Deserve This?* was so long that it was difficult to fit onto the promotional posters – but it was also a word that did not need to be translated internationally. '*Matador* contained the whole essence of the story because it refers to someone who kills, and this is a circumstance that affects the two protagonists. . . it's not a film about bullfighting,' Almodóvar said in 1986. 'It's about a character who is physiologically linked to death, and how that determines all his romantic relationships, especially the one he has with the lawyer played by Assumpta Serna. One is the bull and the other the bullfighter, and then they swap roles. In the film, bullfighting allows me to talk about pleasure, physical pleasure, and the relationship of both with death.'

In the mid-1980s, Serna was one of the most promising actors in the country after working with such prestigious filmmakers as Pilar Miró, Carlos Saura, Mario Camus and

BELOW: Almodóvar chose Assumpta Serna after Charo López and Ana Belén turned down the role of María.

MATADOR CONTAINED THE WHOLE ESSENCE OF THE STORY BECAUSE IT REFERS TO SOMEONE WHO KILLS . . . IT'S NOT A FILM ABOUT BULLFIGHTING.

Bigas Luna, and Almodóvar opted for her after being turned down by Charo López, first, and Ana Belén, later. Nacho Martínez had already appeared in *Tasio* (1984) and *Extramuros* (1985) and secured the role mainly because of his moody aura and his 'bullfighting bearing.' Almodóvar once again assembled a solid cast in which Antonio Banderas stood out, playing a young man from a well-to-do background, a student at the bullfighting school, who plunges into a spiral of confusion when he confesses to the police to the murders perpetrated by Diego. Alongside him, other important Almodóvarian figures stand out in secondary roles, such as Carmen Maura, Eusebio Poncela, Julieta Serrano and the already essential Chus Lampreave, transformed again into a stoic mother, Francisca Caballero's alter ego.

Almodóvar had by now become the visible head of a generation of filmmakers who symbolised freedom and artistic abundance, someone who, moreover, was beginning to shine at major international events. This allowed him to tackle *Matador* with an infrastructure far removed from the chaotic and unsophisticated filming of his early years. The budget of 120 million pesetas was supplemented with a grant from the Spanish Ministry of Culture and the support of Andrés Vicente Gómez, by then considered one of the most respected and prolific producers in the industry thanks to his collaborations with filmmakers of the calibre of Gonzalo Suárez, Fernando Trueba and Orson Welles. 'It is the first time that the Ministry has offered a film of mine a grant without stinginess,' said Almodóvar on a controversial issue, which even required the publication of an open letter by the Insituto Nacional de Cinematogafia y de las Artes Visuales (ICAA). 'Despite the fact that they like my films, more or less, they have verified that they are admired abroad and have given me the category of a cultural export. I think this is the most aggressive of my films, and if the others scared them, this one will scare them even more, so they must know they are subsidising my radicalism.'

After setting out to make a film full of brutal crimes in the style of *The Texas Chainsaw Massacre* (Tobe Hooper, 1974), Almodóvar opted instead to make a film that was 'elegant and exquisite, where violence was replaced by emotions and feelings.' In this sense, it is worth highlighting the magnificent cinematography by

"I THINK THIS IS THE MOST AGGRESSIVE OF MY FILMS, AND IF THE OTHERS SCARED THEM, THIS ONE WILL SCARE THEM EVEN MORE.

RIGHT: Actress Eva Cobo points a (fake) gun
directly at the camera during a break in filming.

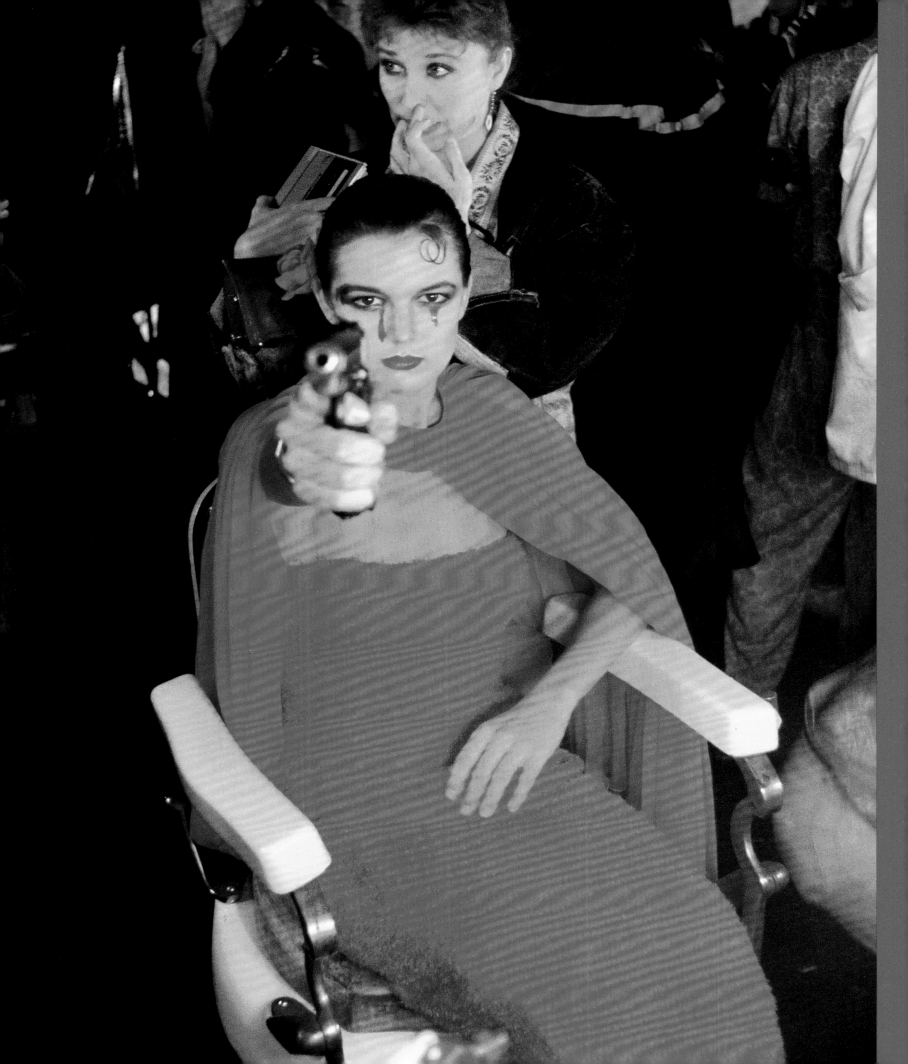

Ángel Luis Fernández based on a series of visual recommendations from Almodóvar. These included the melodramas of Douglas Sirk, the works of the Golden Age painter Francisco de Zurbarán, and the captivating Technicolor of the classic *Pandora and the Flying Dutchman* (Albert Lewin, 1951).

Surprisingly, audiences and critics did not embrace the change of direction that *Matador* represented. Despite its gripping plot and hypnotic *mise-en-scène*, the film was widely mis-understood at the time and was the first artistic setback for its director. At the first Goya Awards – created to recognise the best work in Spanish cinema – the film received only one nomination, in the supporting actor category (Antonio Banderas), and was ignored in the rest. As is usual in these cases, and especially in Almodóvar's work, *Matador* gained fans over time and has become one of his most loved pieces. One of these fans, Quentin Tarantino, has acknowledged that it was one of the films that encouraged him to become a filmmaker: 'That opening scene… There was nothing like it available in America. I thought I wanted to do shit like that, to always shoot whatever I wanted to do, and thanks to that we managed to change the cinema of the nineties.'

LEFT: *Matador* marked the second collaboration between Almodóvar and Antonio Banderas, four years after *Labyrinth of Passion*.

RIGHT: The relationship between Diego and Maria is inevitably scarred by perversion and death.

I THOUGHT I WANTED TO DO SHIT LIKE THAT, TO ALWAYS SHOOT WHATEVER I WANTED TO DO.

LAW OF
DESIRE

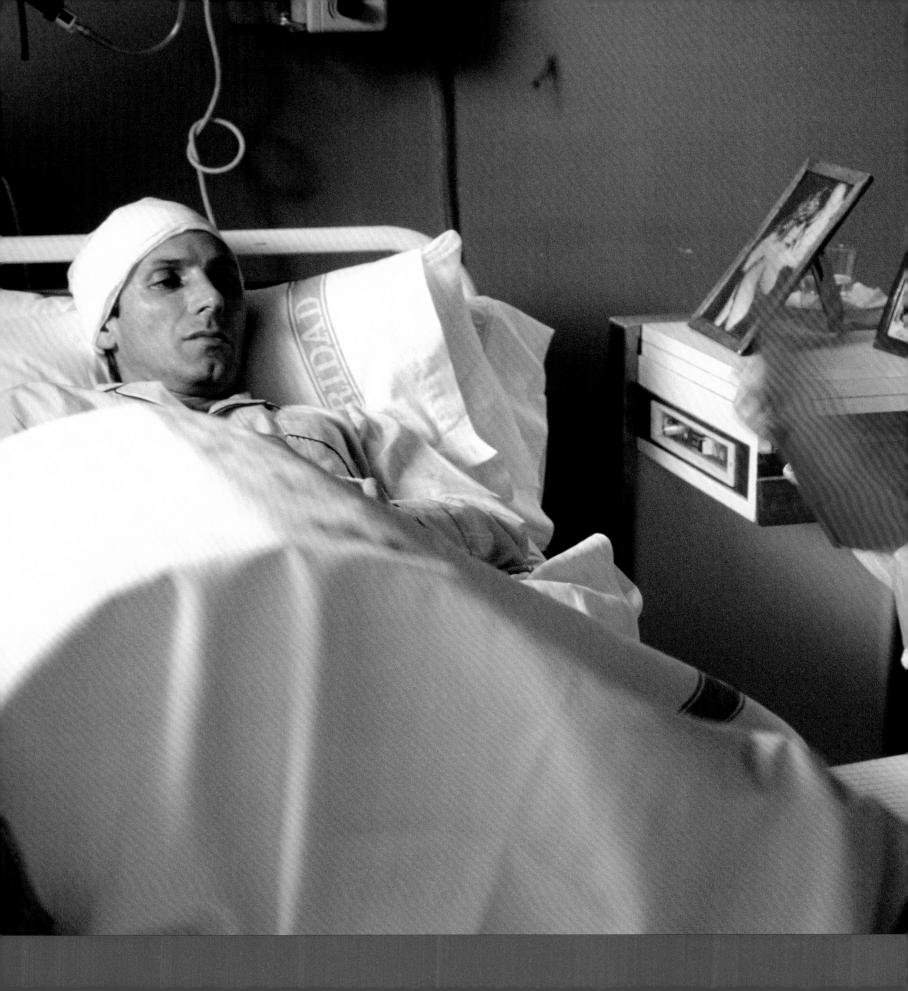

LAW OF DESIRE
La ley del deseo (1987)

While Pedro Almodóvar became one of the great figureheads of the cultural vibrancy of Madrid in the 1980s, his younger brother, Agustín, graduated in Chemistry and initially chose a profession in a very different area. However, fate, together with Pedro's bad experiences with the producers of his early films, would have the two brothers founding one of the most important production companies in contemporary Spanish cinema. Established at the beginning of 1986, El Deseo (Desire) was born of Almodóvar's need to control his works as much as possible, conveying to the public his uniquely personal vision untainted by the commercial interests of an external funder. One of the greatest privileges he gained from doing so would be to shoot his scripts in chronological order, a process that, at great expense, considerably enriches the actors' performances and that, even today, is within the reach of very few filmmakers.

'I have been lucky, because being a boy of my type, and in an industry like this, I have been able to make a film a year, jumping from one producer to another,' he recognised at the time. 'But there's something about me that doesn't work with them. . . I felt like I had five children with five different fathers, and I was always arguing with

> ## "IT'S A TRIBUTE, I ADORE HIM, AND I ALWAYS WANTED TO MAKE A FILM ABOUT BROTHERS."

them over custody. Producers are capable of all kinds of atrocities with negatives, and I wanted to be able to decide for myself. We were gambling everything; it was an all or nothing bet. But I believed in that film, and I took all the risks. That's why it is so fundamental in my career.' The film to which Almodóvar refers is *Law of Desire* – hence the name of the company – and it featured the first appearance of one of the recurrent alter egos in his career: the figure of a filmmaker, to be seen again in *Broken Embraces* and *Pain and Glory*. 'It was as if I were starting all over again, as if I were shooting my first film and it was about a character very close to me, who works in the same profession.'

That character is Pablo Quintero (the charismatic and elegant Eusebio Poncela), a successful film and theatre director who is in love with Juan (Miguel Molina), a much younger man who does not reciprocate with the same intensity, and whom Pablo will replace, fleetingly, with the attractive Antonio (Antonio Banderas) who is obsessive and potentially dangerous. Pablo is very close to his sister Tina (Carmen Maura), a transsexual actor who is dedicated to raising her ex-lover's daughter.

It seems far from coincidental that this brotherly bond is at the heart of the first film produced by El Deseo, as if Almodóvar wanted to vindicate the driving force that two brothers can generate; in fact, the name of Tina comes from *Tinín*, a diminutive Pedro uses to refer to Agustín. 'It's a tribute, I adore him, and I always wanted to make a film about brothers.'

Pablo and Tina, like the Almodóvars, share an artistic bond that sometimes leads to confrontations typical of two disillusioned and wounded people still searching for their place in the world.

PABLO: **As you're a bit paranoid, before you read it, I want to warn you so that you don't get upset.**
TINA: **What's going on? What's the script about?**
PABLO: **Do you see? You're already upset.**
TINA: **Tell me now, otherwise I'll get really upset.**
PABLO: **[. . .] Look, you see. . . Your role. . . It's not that it's inspired by you, but it has a certain affinity. . .**
TINA: **How much of an affinity?**
PABLO: **Well, when it comes to your problems with guys.**
TINA: **I don't have problems with guys, because for me they haven't existed for a long time.**
PABLO: **And that doesn't seem like much of a problem to you?**
TINA: **What's the matter? Are you going to treat me like I'm a freak too?**
PABLO: **Stop. . . I didn't say that.**
TINA: **Talk about your own problems with guys and leave me alone [. . .] I forbid you to discuss even the smallest details of my life! As ridiculous as it is, I have the right to be respected!**
PABLO: **But who said your life is ridiculous?**
TINA: **I don't need anyone to tell me. I know that [. . .] My failures with men are more than just the plot of a script. I won't allow you or anyone else to play with them!**

PREVIOUS PAGE: In one of his most personal films, Almodóvar pays tribute to his brother Agustín and to overcoming adversity with fraternal support.

ABOVE: In *The Law of Desire*, Almodóvar broke with all genre conventions to create a work totally ahead of its time.

The family, the gravitational axis without which it would be impossible to understand Almodóvar's cinema, is represented in his early films in a totally unusual way, challenging and dismantling all the patriarchal clichés imposed by the dictatorship. Although in his films from the nineties onwards they began to acquire a more classical structure, in the eighties the Almodóvarian families break away from traditional concepts and become a place of refuge for marginalised characters who seek – and need – to feel loved. Blood ties between parents and children are so flawed that they sometimes lead to traumatic episodes that drag on forever, and the family ends up being a matter of complicity and affinity, of a love built on acceptance. In *Pepi, Luci, Bom and Other Girls Like Mom*, the three protagonists establish a union with which to face – and lean against – the world, while in *What Have I Done to Deserve This?* the traditional family is so grotesque and suffocating that the closest thing to a *sister* that Gloria has in her life is her sex worker neighbour. In *Law of Desire*, Pablo, Tina and little Ada (Manuela Velasco) end up forming their own nucleus, one in which the role of father figure is occupied by a gay artist and the maternal figure by his transsexual sister. Undoubtedly, this is complex and dense terrain for any director, but Almodóvar navigates through it with mastery.

Law of Desire was filmed in Madrid during the sweltering summer of 1986. Almodóvar knew how to take advantage of the deserted and rundown appearance of the city during the holidays, offering the viewer an urban portrait of a place where the *Movida* was in its last throes and the bohemian atmosphere was about to succumb to the invasion of big business. 'The film is a complete celebration of Madrid, and more specifically of Madrid in the eighties. It was like *La La Land*, a city where dreams come true, at least for me. I remember how quickly and easily it was shot. Everything was light and simple, and there was an incredible rapport with the crew. A kind of miracle where everything happened in a harmonious and natural way. We did not stop laughing, it is something that is stuck in my memory.'

Especially distinctive was the moment, totally improvised, in which Tina asks a man who is washing down the streets with a hose to 'water' her as well. 'I asked Carmen if she minded if we watered her, because it is a wish that I have always had on hot nights in Madrid. The city hall employee who was holding the hose was freaked out, but he loved watering Carmen Maura.' The most curious thing was that, at first, the actor fell to the ground due to the force of the water, and she had to be taken to a nearby bar to dry her hair and make-up before filming again. 'It is a moment that for me identifies and represents the whole film, because, under that spontaneous watering, the character suddenly becomes an explosive image of desire.' Years later, the writer Susan Sontag – one of the cultural figures most admired by Almodóvar – would tell him that the powerful imagery of the scene was comparable to that of Marilyn Monroe's raised skirt in *The Seven Year Itch* (Billy Wilder, 1955).

Law of Desire became a key title for contemporary melodrama after its release. The frankness with which Almodóvar portrayed homosexuality within the framework of a tragic romance, at a time when not even *The New York Times* used the word *gay*, was nothing short of revolutionary, and even today its boldness and ability to build characters so full of life, passion and dreams is still surprising. It was recognised with the Teddy Award for best LGBT feature film at the Berlin Film Festival and won several other international awards, although in France its poster was censored because it showed two naked men in bed together. Sadly, but not surprisingly, it was ignored and at the Goya Awards, an omission that particularly annoyed Almodóvar, and precipitated his love-hate relationship with the awards: 'It hurt me, because at that time we did need a little support. But that absence didn't hurt me for me, but for my team. That Carmen and Antonio were not nominated seemed flagrant to me. It was a full-fledged grievance.'

> "EVERYTHING WAS LIGHT AND SIMPLE. A KIND OF MIRACLE WHERE EVERYTHING HAPPENED IN A HARMONIOUS AND NATURAL WAY."

PREVIOUS PAGE: A thoughtful and exhausted Almodóvar during a brief break in filming.

RIGHT: At the age of 23, Rossy de Palma was cast in the first of her eight films with Almodóvar.

WOMEN ON THE VERGE OF A NERVOUS BREAKDOWN

WOMEN ON THE VERGE OF A NERVOUS BREAKDOWN

Mujeres al borde de un ataque de nervios (1988)

In one of the most iconic scenes from *Law of Desire*, Carmen Maura's character, Tina, performs an excerpt from *The Human Voice*, the acclaimed 1930 play by Jean Cocteau about a woman who, abandoned by her lover, waits impatiently for a phone call to end her despair. Almodóvar had always had a fascination with Cocteau's monologue and conceived that moment in the film as his tribute. However, Maura's superb performance soon made him decide that he had to adapt the whole piece just for her.

Almodóvar's initial intention was to make a small, experimental film with a modest budget, and just the actor in front of the camera. However, when he realised that the text of *The Human Voice* was not long enough for a feature film, the filmmaker opted to reinvent the play's theme of abandonment and focus on the forty-eight hours prior to it, moving from a story with a single character to a festive parade of extravagant women and unreliable men. Many were surprised by this turn by the director, moving away from his usual agitating and daredevil cinema towards the sophisticated comedies of the fifties: 'The characters don't take drugs, they don't drink, they don't even smoke because the doctor advises against it. They don't have time to do dirty things either. It is my reunion with immaculate comedy,' he said shortly after filming commenced. *Women on the*

ABOVE: Lucía (Julieta Serrano) threatens Pepa (Carmen Maura) while she holds a glass of the famous gazpacho.

THE CHARACTERS DON'T TAKE DRUGS, THEY DON'T DRINK, THEY DON'T EVEN SMOKE BECAUSE THE DOCTOR ADVISES AGAINST IT.

RED ALWAYS APPEARS ... IN SPANISH CULTURE, IT IS ALSO THE COLOUR OF PASSION, BLOOD AND FIRE.

PREVIOUS PAGE: Marisa (Rossy de Palma) will be one of the first to be affected by the cocktail of sleeping pills.

LEFT: Almodóvar shows Carmen Maura how to spike the gazpacho with sleeping pills.

LEFT: As in *Dark Habits*, Julieta Serrano's character Lucía embodies the most genuine Almodóvarian humour.

Verge of a Nervous Breakdown would become a landmark film for Almodóvar, launching his international commercial career and confirming, in the eyes of the world, his status as a genuine artist.

In fact, Almodóvar's core themes were still very much present (female camaraderie versus male violence, unhealthy relationships, conflicts between parents and children) but this time from a completely light-hearted and derisive perspective. 'I didn't want to do something boring, quite the opposite,' he explained. 'You can tell the story of a woman torn apart by grief without having to frighten the audience as if the theatre was shaken by an earthquake. I had to find a way to make that pain recognizable, identifiable, and work like a magnet. Everything was going to depend on the tone, so I decided that high comedy was the most appropriate.' Almodóvar discarded the dramatic component and the structure of *The Human Voice*, but he would return to Cocteau's universe, showing a much more tragic abandonment in *The Flower of My Secret*, first, and turning the original piece into a short film, later. In this way, *Women on the Verge of a Nervous Breakdown* was nourished by the influence of masters such as Lubitsch, Sturges, Hawks, Wilder and even Hitchcock and *Rear Window* (1954), as it progressively became a crazed reflection on such complex themes as loneliness and lack of communication (that omnipresent telephone that never rings, a wink from the director to his years at Telefónica). The result is a wonderful tangle that turns suffering into laughter, and despair into hope.

Pepa (Carmen Maura) works as a dubbing actor, as does her lover, Iván (Fernando Guillén), a playboy who uses women and then abandons them. 'When thinking about *The Human Voice*, I suddenly came up with a natural medium, and that is that they were both dubbing actors,' explained the filmmaker. When Pepa discovers she is pregnant, Iván breaks off the relationship and disappears without a trace, leaving only an answering machine message asking her to put his things in a suitcase. She, who still dreams that Iván will reconsider his decision, rents out the penthouse they shared because she cannot bear to continue living there alone, and a parade of bizarre characters begins to populate the house: Iván's ex, who has just left the psychiatric hospital; their son Carlos and his girlfriend; Pepa's best friend, Candela, who is hiding from the police because her boyfriend is a terrorist. . . Almodóvar achieves in all of them a perfect cocktail of fun and pathos, as the women who arrive at the apartment are united by an anguish that makes them as vulnerable as they are reckless.

PEPA: **Where is Ivan?**
CARLOS: **Well. . . I don't know.**
PEPA: **Why doesn't he call me? I must talk to him.**
CARLOS: **I don't see him much, you know?**
PEPA: **Don't lie to me too. He's going on a trip with your mother.**
CARLOS: **With my mother? No way! But she thinks he's going with you!**
PEPA: **So, he's going with someone else? Of course. . . That's why he didn't spend the night in the studio.**
CARLOS: **And how can you be so sure?**
PEPA: **Because I've been up all night going from your house to the studio, and from the studio to your house. You'll think I'm crazy. . .**
CARLOS: **A bit nervous. . . But it's normal if you haven't slept. . .**
PEPA: **. . . At all.**
CARLOS: **Ivan never told you he had a son?**
PEPA: **Never. I had no idea. With your father it's impossible to know anything! I always find out everything by chance. Like last night. I was in the cabin, the suitcase fell, it opened, a portrait of you came out with a dedication: 'From your father, Ivan, who doesn't deserve you.' And that's how I found out. He never says anything. He never acknowledges anything. Not even a reproach comes out of his mouth.**

The cast, with the addition of Almodóvarian depth in Julieta Serrano, Antonio Banderas, Kiti Mánver and a hilarious Chus Lampreave, is simply unbeatable. Special mention should be made of two actors who significantly contributed to magnifying the film's mythology: Rossy de Palma, whose distinctive profile would become the most potent expression of the director's universe in another six films, and María Barranco, who was chosen for the role of Candela ahead of the original choice – Victoria Abril – just as the actor was considering leaving the profession due to a lack of opportunities (the director found her so nervous and overwhelmed during filming that he ordered her to clean the set 'so that she could blow off steam'). With all of them, and with Carmen Maura at the peak of her career, Almodóvar locked himself in a studio to shoot the bulk of the film in a set built for the occasion, although the address of the attic did correspond to a real place in Madrid: number 7 Montalbán Street.

Pepa's apartment perfectly represents in miniature Almodóvar's own obsessions, peculiarities and whims. From the flamenco dolls to the rubber flowers, the chicken coop, the deckchairs or the beach ball, all the elements seem out of place but, at the same time, are in perfect harmony with the surreal setting in which the story unfolds. The whole is saturated in red: Pepa's dress, the telephone, the *gazpacho* laced with sleeping pills, common in all of Almodóvar's work and especially visible here. 'Red always appears, but I don't know why,' he said. 'However, an explanation can be found. Red, in Chinese culture, is the colour of those condemned to death, which makes it a human colour. But, in Spanish culture, it is also the colour of passion, blood and fire.'

Since *Pepi, Luci, Bom and Other Girls Like Mom*, Almodóvar's films had enjoyed the support and complicity of the audience, but nothing compared to the critical and commercial noise generated by *Women on the Verge of a Nervous Breakdown* when it was released in March

1988. In Spain, it played in theatres for more than a year and was seen by 3.3 million people, with a final box office of 912 million pesetas. It also won five Goya Awards that, until now, had been elusive, receiving nominations in all categories and winning Best Film, Lead Actress (Carmen Maura), Supporting Actress (María Barranco), Original Screenplay and Editing.

Success was not just limited to Spain and Europe, though Cannes refused to accept it in its official section, considering it too commercial. It was chosen to open the New York Film Festival ahead of *The Last Temptation of Christ* (Martin Scorsese, 1988), where there were ten standing ovations from the audience during the screening. It was an enormous success in France and grossed over seven million dollars in the United States, an extraordinary figure for the time for a foreign production. It was nominated for Best Foreign Language Film at the Golden Globe, BAFTA and Academy Awards, marking Almodóvar's first encounters with the academies that, in the future, would recognise the global legacy of his work with statuettes in 1999 and 2002.

Sadly, while the film achieved commercial success, and garnered widespread critical and industry acclaim, a disagreement at the Oscars between Almodóvar and Carmen Maura, blamed on the wear and tear of their professional relationship and heated clashes during filming, saw their working relationship end for a decade. 'There are consequences of the intense work that I do with the actors,' he acknowledged. 'The relationship with Carmen stopped being strictly professional and that hurt both of us.' Decades after its premiere, the characters in *Women on the Verge of a Nervous Breakdown* have become icons of popular culture, revered by an audience that embraced their misfortunes and knew how to laugh at them by throwing their phone out of the window.

ABOVE: The film brings together one of the most brilliant casts of Almodóvar's career. Candela (María Barranco) and Carlos (Antonio Banderas) drink the gazpacho under the watchful eyes of Pepa and the flamboyant Lucía.

TIE ME UP! TIE ME DOWN!

TIE ME UP!
TIE ME DOWN!
¡Átame! (1990)

The idea for *Tie Me Up! Tie Me Down!* began to take shape during the filming of *Women on the Verge of a Nervous Breakdown*. In that excessive and deliberately artificial location, Almodóvar imagined a second story that would take place on a film set, which would give him the freedom to include in the shot all the paraphernalia that usually surrounds studio work: cameras, technical equipment, props. . . The intention, shared with his brother, Agustín, was to shoot two films almost consecutively on a single stage, spreading their budget resources and giving the production a 'Roger Corman' feel. The story would focus on three men who have escaped from a psychiatric hospital and hide on the set of a B-movie that is about to celebrate its end-of-filming wrap party. During it, they are mistaken for crew members until they decide to take the cast and crew hostage and ask the Ministry of Culture for an unlikely ransom. Meanwhile, one of them falls madly in love with the film's female lead actor, who also begins to develop a strange attraction to her captor.

Ultimately, the enormous demands of completing *Women on the Verge of a Nervous Breakdown* caused Almodóvar to discard this initial concept, although the love story that emerges from a kidnapping would remain at the heart of the eventual film. The new approach, reminiscent of *The Desperate Hours* (William Wyler, 1955) and Luis Buñuel's classic *El ángel exterminador* (1962), follows Ricki, a young orphan who has spent several years in a mental institution. When he is discharged, he begins to stalk Marina, a former actor and recovering drug addict with whom he is obsessed, until one day he

LEFT: The film presents an interpretation of Stockholm Syndrome from Almodóvar's unique perspective.

breaks into her apartment and kidnaps her with the hope that she will eventually fall in love with him. The victim's initial reluctance gradually gives way to an unsuspected tenderness towards Ricki, when he ends up badly injured after being beaten by some drug dealers. In the end, the two run away in pursuit of a life together with Marina's sister Lola, giving rise to another of Almodóvar's typically strong and bizarre families.

RICKI: (*Shortly after kidnapping Marina in her apartment*) I tried to talk to you, but you wouldn't let me. I had to kidnap you so that you could get to know me. I'm sure you'll fall in love with me then, as I am with you (*She looks at him incredulously*) I'm twenty-three years old and I have 50,000 pesetas, and I'm alone in the world. I'll try to be a good husband to you and a good father to your children.
MARINA: Are you the one who stole from the set?
RICKI: Yes [. . .] We met each other before. A year ago, in a bar called Lulú. Don't you remember? I had just escaped from the mental hospital. I met you by chance. Then we went to your apartment and had sex. You really don't remember? I promised I'd get you off the street and protect you.
MARINA: A lot of men have promised me that!
RICKI: But I've come back to prove it to you!

Ricki was the first character that the director wrote expressly for Antonio Banderas, and the first leading role for the actor from Malaga in an Almodóvar film after his four earlier supporting roles. Banderas was by now one of the great stars of Spanish cinema and about to make the leap to Hollywood with *The Mambo Kings* (Arne Glimcher, 1992). Victoria Abril had already had a long and successful career in Spain and France – between 1986 and 1991 she earned six consecutive Goya nominations as Lead Actress – and had been on the verge of working with Almodóvar on several occasions, which made her the ideal performer for the character of Marina. Aided by terrific performances, and with a stellar cast featuring Loles León, María Barranco and an immense Paco Rabal, who stood out in a sort of tribute to John Huston, Almodóvar delivers a film of overflowing imagination, in contrast to the struggles of *Women on the Verge of a Nervous Breakdown*. *Tie Me Up! Tie Me Down!* marked a return to the marginal and outsider characters of his early works, and to the defining elements of his storytelling: drugs, sex, brotherly complicity, strong women and film within film. 'It is a real love story, in which we shamelessly talk about the need we all have for someone to love us,' he declared at the premiere. '*Tie me up* is the equivalent of saying I love you, with all that it entails, all that part of relationships that we are not willing to accept but that we accept because we do not want to, nor can we, live without love.'

The film was shot over three months in Madrid and the town of Granadilla, in Cáceres, where the splendid denouement takes place. For both stars, *Tie Me Up! Tim Me Down!* was to be one of the most intense and demanding experiences of their careers, especially for Victoria Abril, who spent a good part of the shoot with her mouth covered and had to be able to convey her emotions with just her eyes; for this reason, Almodóvar considers her to be the actor who cries best on screen. As if this were not enough, the adhesive tape gave her cold sores, a situation that forced the director to improvise the comical scene in the

LEFT: For his next project after *Women on the Verge of a Nervous Breakdown*, Almodóvar chose a much darker and more unnerving story.

"IT IS A REAL LOVE STORY, IN WHICH WE SHAMELESSLY TALK ABOUT THE NEED WE ALL HAVE FOR SOMEONE TO LOVE US.

RIGHT: The excellent chemistry between Victoria Abril and Antonio Banderas was key to achieving the credibility demanded by the plot.

pharmacy. 'Victoria wasn't used to improvising so much on set,' said the director. 'She told me that she was not used to directors asking her for so many new things on the spot [. . .] Until she understood that she did not have to invent anything, but that I was going to invent everything for her and that what she needed was enormous flexibility to pick up everything that I suggested.' For Antonio Banderas, the sex scene was one of the most difficult to shoot, taking several hours and nine takes to complete because Almodóvar demanded the characters be tired and drenched in sweat; legendary filmmaker Elia Kazan said it was the best sex scene he had ever seen.

Tie Me Up! Tie Me Down! was Almodóvar's first film since *Labyrinth of Passion* not to feature a soundtrack by Bernardo Bonezzi. Instead, Almodóvar turned to one of the foremost composers in the history of cinema, Ennio Morricone, who at that time was enjoying one of his best creative periods thanks to titles such as *The Mission* (Roland Joffé, 1986), *The Untouchables* (Brian De Palma, 1987) and *Cinema Paradiso* (Giuseppe Tornatore, 1988). However, the relationship between the two artists was never smooth and their ways of working ended up being less than compatible. 'He had a method that didn't work for me,'

A FILM AS AUDACIOUS AS *TIE ME UP! TIE ME DOWN!*, WITH SUCH A CONTROVERSIAL PLOT, WOULD BE ALMOST IMPOSSIBLE TO MAKE IN THE FEBRILE, POLITICALLY CORRECT AND INTOLERANT WORLD OF TODAY.

"

LEFT: The iconic sex scene surprised even such major filmmakers as Elia Kazan, and was one of many that earned the film a NC-17 rating in the USA.

Almodóvar explained. 'I participate a lot in the music of my films, which is an essential element of the narrative. But Ennio would take the script, compose the soundtrack, and then give it to you in its entirety, and it is impossible for a first version of the soundtrack to seem totally valid to me. In the film, I kept what fitted for me, and what did not fit for me was left out. The music was much more conventional than the plot of the film [. . .] I listened to other themes of his and I realized that he did nothing but repeat himself: the central theme of Roman Polanski's *Frantic* was practically the same as that of *Tie Me Up! Tie Me Down!*' Morricone, wanting to keep all soundtrack royalties for himself, wouldn't agree to the inclusion of the Dúo Dinámico version of the song 'Resistiré'. After featuring in the film, it became a hymn to perseverance: 'I don't think he wanted to share the copyright, and that made me like him less.' Of course, the two geniuses never worked together again.

There is no doubt that a film as audacious as *Tie Me Up! Tie Me Down!*, with such a controversial plot, would be almost impossible to make in the febrile, politically correct and intolerant world of today. Even upon its release, Almodóvar had to deal with the wrath of feminist journalists at the Berlin Film Festival and with an incomprehensible X rating in the United States by the MPAA (Motion Picture Association of America), due to the infamous scene in which Marina masturbates in the bathtub with the help of a toy submarine (despite, or maybe because of, the controversy, the film grossed four million dollars at the North American box office). In Spain, both the audience and critics received it with relative enthusiasm, mainly because the huge success of *Women on the Verge of a Nervous Breakdown* had set an impossibly high bar. The film left no one indifferent and even set a record at the Goyas by failing to win any of its fifteen nominations, another sign of Almodóvar's tense and complex relationship with his homeland's most important awards.

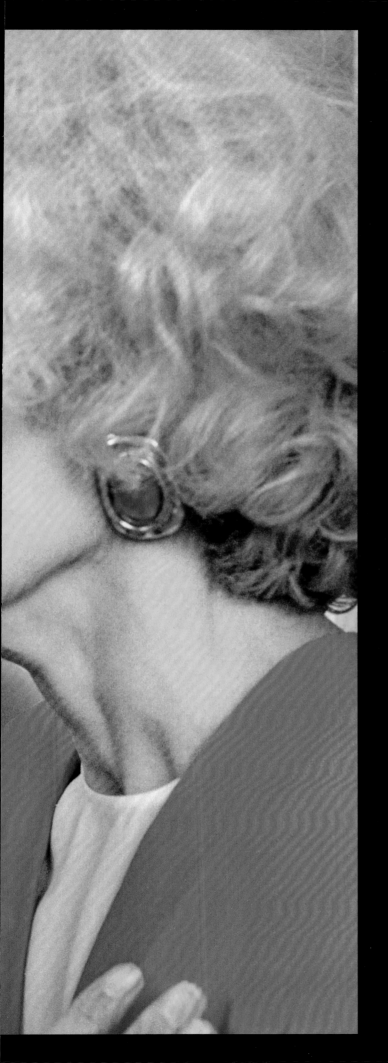

HIGH
HEELS

HIGH HEELS
Tacones lejanos (1991)

Like many other Almodóvar feature films, *High Heels* was conceived as a very different work from the one we all know today. The director himself has acknowledged that many of his best ideas come to him during the long sessions prior to shooting, as a way of escaping the anxious – and at times tedious – pre-production process. While he was preparing *Tie Me Up! Tie Me Down!*, a particularly powerful image began to take shape in his mind: a television presenter confesses to a murder in the middle of a live broadcast – the death of her husband and owner of the network, no less – and then collapses in front of the cameras, showing viewers a series of photographs of his clothes, his desk – their memories together – that she had taken after his death to fight her anguish. 'I was having a coffee near my house, and at that moment the light bulb went on. I dropped everything and went upstairs to start writing straight away,' he said.

The premise seized Almodóvar, who soon had a script ready to turn his idea into a short film that he would direct once he finished *Tie Me Up! Tie Me Down!* However, the presenter further aroused his curiosity, to the point of imagining all the events and reasons that preceded the television revelation, as well as its consequences. 'She was too big a character for such a short story,' he admitted. 'So, I started developing her story from both ends, leaving the confession right in the middle. And it wasn't easy, because I wanted the character to be neither a monster nor a psychopath. My intention was for the audience to be excited by her, to come to understand her without judging or sentencing. For a simple reason of length, the narrative of a short allows you to show the facts without the need to explain or get involved in them, but a feature film needs the author to provide a detailed description of the facts to find their place within the story. And I found mine at the beginning, very close to Rebeca. That was the main difficulty of writing, directing and performing this story:

LEFT: Contrasting emotions testifying before the judge, from the strained body language between Rebeca (Victoria Abril) and Becky (Marisa Paredes), to the naivety of Isabel (Miriam Diaz-Aroca).

not to make her a nasty killer, but an angry and wounded human being, the victim of her own fear.' Victoria Abril's extraordinary work in *Tie Me Up! Tie Me Down!*, where she played a character of enormous emotional complexity, made her the ideal actor for the role of this news anchor who is trapped by her past.

The director went so far into Rebeca Giner's backstory that he ended up finding in her childhood the reason for her deep unhappiness. While still very young, her mother, the well-known singer Becky del Páramo (a sublime Marisa Paredes), abandoned her to go to Mexico in search of fame and fortune. As a consequence, Rebeca feels an overwhelming need to recover the love and lost time, but she also hides a terrible resentment for being forced to live in the shadow of the myth.

BECKY: **Why did you do it?**

REBECA: **I didn't kill him, Mom.**

BECKY: **But you confessed it yourself. Nobody made you do it.**

REBECA: **Killing him would have been the legitimate thing to do. . . But since you wouldn't even let me do that, my only revenge was to confess it, even if it was a lie!**

BECKY: **Why are you tormenting me, Rebeca, for having slept with him? Is that why?**

REBECA: **Don't be silly, you weren't the only one [. . .] I've spent my life imitating you. Ever since we separated, I've tried to compete with you in everything. And without any success. Only once have I managed to beat you! Once! With Manuel!**

BECKY: **With Manuel we both lost.**

REBECA: **Yes, but it was me who married him, not you. But you had to come here to prove to me that you could take him away from me if you wanted to. I knew it, but you had to prove it to me!**

BECKY: **Forgive me, Rebeca. I know I've been very bad to you, but what can I do now?**

REBECA: **Now you can just listen to me.**

BECKY: **You tell me.**

REBECA: **Since I was little, I was only ever a nuisance to you. But, despite my insignificance, I tried hard to be useful to you. Because I adored you [. . .] I only wanted you to be in control of your life, and you promised me that we would enjoy it together, that we would never be separated. But you didn't keep your promise. And I don't think I'll ever forgive you for that.**

ABOVE: After Carmen Maura's estrangement, her casting in *High Heels* announced Victoria Abril as Almodóvar's new muse.

High Heels is Almodóvar's first great work about negligent motherhood, depicting how traumatic maternal separation from one's children can lead to reunion and redemption. Later films such as *Volver* or *All About My Mother* also explore the figure of the imperfect mother who manages to re-establish emotional ties – with her own family or with a new and unexpected one – to become, if only for an instant, the person she always should have been. Almodóvar's films are, above all, an ode to the strong and devoted mother, but also show empathy and compassion to those women who at some point have failed their children but find the integrity – and the love – to make amends.

The plot of *High Heels* includes a third character of some importance: Judge Domínguez, the investigating magistrate in charge of the case, whose split personality in different identities or 'disguises' allows him to go undercover to investigate possible suspects. His main alter ego, Femme Letal, a transvestite, is based on the style and look of Becky del Páramo. Antonio Banderas was to have played him, but the siren song of Hollywood led him to abandon the production just before it began and forced Almodóvar to postpone filming for six months to find a replacement. In a move not without risk, the director ended up choosing Miguel Bosé, son of the famous bullfighter Luis Miguel Dominguín, and one of the most successful singers in the country. Despite some debate about the choice, Bosé – who had been working in cinema since the mid-seventies with filmmakers such as Dario Argento and Fernando Colomo – knew how to give the character the enigmatic aura required and made Femme Letal one of the great Almodóvarian characters of the decade.

After the experience with Ennio Morricone in *Tie Me Up! Tie Me Down!*, Almodóvar turned for the score to the highly regarded Ryuichi Sakamoto, who had won an Oscar four years earlier for his work on *The Last Emperor* (Bernardo Bertolucci, 1987). However, Almodóvar ended up discarding most of the music created by Sakamoto, feeling that it did not fit the tone of the story, and did not correspond to his vision (years later, the composer would admit that he knew almost nothing about Spain and that Almodóvar did the right thing by removing his pieces). Instead, the director opted to include several songs from his personal miscellany, such as 'Soleá' and 'Saeta', by Miles Davis, 'C'est irreparable', by Nino Ferrer, and even a couple of compositions by George Fenton from *Dangerous Liaisons* (Stephen Frears, 1988). Despite this, it was the two songs interpreted expressly for the film by the Galician artist Luz Casal – the adaptation of 'Piensa en mí' by Agustín Lara and Chavela Vargas, and 'Un año de amor' by Gaby Verlor, with lyrics by the filmmaker himself – that turned the soundtrack into a bestseller and one of the musical highlights of Spanish cinema.

RIGHT ABOVE: The director rehearses with Miguel Bosé (Letal) for one of his extravagant musical performances.

RIGHT: Rebeca's live on-air murder confession was the first scene Almodóvar devised for the film.

IT WASN'T EASY, BECAUSE I WANTED THE CHARACTER TO BE NEITHER A MONSTER NOR A PSYCHOPATH.

ALMODÓVAR'S FILMS ARE, ABOVE ALL, AN ODE TO THE STRONG AND DEVOTED MOTHER.

Exhibiting a sure-footed maturity, *High Heels* showcases Almodóvar's ability to combine with surprising naturalness two seemingly contrary genres: melodrama and crime thriller. The shadow of Douglas Sirk hovers over the whole story, especially his classic *Imitation of Life* (1959), which narrated the stormy relationship between a movie star and her daughter. Almodóvar drew direct inspiration from Lana Turner's character in the film for Marisa Paredes's hairstyle. However, it is not the only film referenced by the director, who also made use of the maternal-filial conflicts of titles such as *Stella Dallas* (King Vidor, 1937), *Mildred Pierce* (Michael Curtiz, 1945), *Terms of Endearment* (James L. Brooks, 1983) and *Postcards from the Edge* (Mike Nichols, 1990) to shape the story of Becky and Rebeca. From all of them he extracted a dramatic potential which is omnipresent in the film, sitting happily alongside other genres ranging from film noir to comedy, including the musical through the iconic prison choreography.

While the critical reception was ambivalent, commercially it was one of the greatest successes of Almodóvar's career to date, attracting an audience of nearly two million in Spain. It was a blockbuster in France too, where it also won the César Award for Best Foreign Film of the year. In Chile, the reaction was more extreme; three men, belonging to a 'moralistic league' and determined to stop the film from being seen, stole the only copy after a preview in a cinema in the capital. It had a modest commercial run in the United States but did receive a Golden Globe nomination, prompting actors of the calibre of Jodie Foster, Glenn Close and Susan Sarandon to publicly express their desire to work with the director. Publications as prestigious as *Liberation*, *The Guardian* and *Vanity Fair* dedicated extensive features to a radiant Almodóvar. The international recognition once again had its strange counterpoint in a lack of success at the Goya Awards, the film not winning in any of the five technical categories it was nominated. Unfathomably, neither the director nor his two leading actors (whose performances are among the best in his filmography) received a nomination.

KIKA

KIKA (1993)

'**A**s always, I wrote it just for fun, to detox. Also, as always, at the beginning it was a translation of my needs. The world around me and my own world threatened to suffocate me, and I needed a good dose of optimism. I wanted to recover for my life and for my cinema the fresh breath of comedy.' When Pedro Almodóvar began to contemplate his next lead during the long promotional trips for *High Heels*, he found himself giving shape to a stunning character, a woman full of life, probably the most naive and charming of all his imagined characters. He saw her as an injection of positivity after the dramatic intensity of his most recent films, a perfect mix between Marilyn Monroe, the Audrey Hepburn of *Breakfast at Tiffany's* (Blake Edwards, 1961) and two of his own creations: the emblematic Patty Diphusa and Candela, played by María Barranco in *Women on the Verge of a Nervous Breakdown*. But, as the story progressed, much shadier characters began to break through until the film descended into an unexpected darkness, a spiral from which the director could not – nor wanted to – escape.

Almodóvar knew very well which actor he should cast for a character like Kika. In *What Have I Done to Deserve This?*, Verónica Forqué had already sketched a first outline of this make-up artist with an indelible smile: Cristal, the sex worker who was always positive no matter how hard life became. Almodóvar, though, links Cristal and Kika much more darkly; Cristal submits to men, sometimes violently, through her toil as a sex worker, while Kika has been the victim of rape by a porn actor; these are both women who suffer in a male world, where any ray of light can be easily extinguished.

In this way, a film that starts like a screwball comedy of contagious optimism (alongside Forqué, Rossy de Palma features once again, giving a hilarious performance as her assistant) is transformed into a dark and sinister thriller, loaded with fatalism and social commentary. *Kika* also features two of the most diabolical characters ever

ABOVE: In her third consecutive film with Almodóvar, Victoria Abril played the role of the unscrupulous television star Andrea.

KIKA HAS REMARKABLE ASPECTS THAT I'M PROUD OF, BUT IT WAS IMPOSSIBLE TO JUDGE THEM IN SUCH A TENSE ATMOSPHERE.

created by its director: the writer and serial killer Nicholas Pierce (Peter Coyote), and the ferocious and resentful Andrea Caracortada (Victoria Abril), creator and presenter of an outrageously exploitative reality television show. Almodóvar took the idea from a series of programmes he had seen on American television, as at that time, this type of unscrupulous reality TV had not yet arrived in Spain. Sometime later, the arrival of these formats on most of the country's channels would confirm, once again, the filmmaker's prophetic nature and his ability to intuit social transformations.

Since its premiere, *Kika* has had the aura of a cursed work among Almodóvar's films, an exaggerated and unfair label – it is neither a bad film, nor the worst made by the director – but the result of a particular moment in the country's history. In 1992, Spain had become the epicentre of world news thanks to the Olympic Games being staged in Barcelona, the Universal Exhibition in Seville – which, coincidentally, premiered Almodóvar's unreleased short film *Salomé* – and the fifth centenary of the discovery of America. This sudden international focus on the country translated into a period of (fleeting) economic growth and sociocultural optimism. As a result, the cultural spotlight shone on Spanish creators of all kinds who were feted with unbridled enthusiasm; that year, Spanish cinema won only its second Oscar with *Belle Époque*. Directed by Fernando Trueba, that brilliant and restrained period drama is a clear reflection of the kind of image that the industry tried to export to the rest of the world.

When *Kika* hit screens in 1993, there were many who were appalled by, as they saw it, its celebration of evil as a destructive force, of corrupting a comedy starring a forceful woman and transforming it into a dark reflection of real life. Critics circled and Almodóvar attracted the anger of many feminists who, when details of the film's story were leaked, criticised the comic treatment of rape in the film, which thankfully led him to discard the crass *An Inopportune Rape* as one of the film's possible titles (other titles that were considered were *The Eyes of Tamil*, *A Horrible Summer Day*, *The Murderer's Nails* and a female version of *The Good, the Bad and the Ugly*). '*Kika* has remarkable aspects that I'm proud of, but it was impossible to judge them in such a tense atmosphere because of political correctness,' recalls the director. 'I think we are now more aware that humour cannot aspire to be politically correct, and that it can serve to deal with the most serious and painful aspects of life, including rape.' Among the cited references for the justification of the controversial scene were *Torn Curtain* (Alfred Hitchcock, 1966) and *Blood Simple* (Joel Coen, 1984).

The critical and commercial success of his films to date had positioned Almodóvar at the peak of Spanish cinema. Few directors enjoyed his international prestige, and his stories exuded the mark of a pure and indomitable author. It is possible that, for all this, his expectations for *Kika* were overly ambitious: a 700 million pesetas budget and fourteen weeks of shooting, both the highest figures of his career. It included an exclusive wardrobe for Victoria Abril's character designed by Jean Paul Gaultier and another for Verónica Forqué by Gianni Versace, and the inclusion, for the first time in one of his films, of a Hollywood actor (Peter Coyote, fresh from filming *Bitter Moon* with Roman Polanski). These extremely high expectations were soon dashed by the bad smell that seemed to follow the film wherever it went. It received terrible reviews and a smear campaign that even spread abroad, where adverts for the film featuring Victoria Abril's fake breasts were banned on London's buses and in the pages of *The New York Times*, supposedly 'to avoid giving offence.'

Kika was a failure, not because of its disappointing – although by no means catastrophic – box office, the scant harvest of awards (despite everything, Forqué won a well-deserved Goya for Best Actress) or the disaffection it caused among Almodóvar's enthusiasts. What hurt the film, and its author, was the fierce campaign that, paradoxically, accused him of taking risks and entering uncomfortable terrain from a formal and narrative point of view. 'It's the closest my career has ever come to going bankrupt,' he admitted. 'There was an extraordinarily negative unanimity towards *Kika*. That's why I used the word lynching. I don't want to fall into the easy resource of talking about envy or settling scores, nor do I want to feel like a victim. I prefer to analyse everything calmly. Fortunately, the film has tremendous strength and will end up surviving, like Kika herself.'

RIGHT: The fabulous work of Verónica Forqué (Kika) and Rossy de Palma (Juana) creates the film's most hilarious moments.

THE
FLOWER
OF MY
SECRET

THE FLOWER OF MY SECRET
La flor de mi secreto (1995)

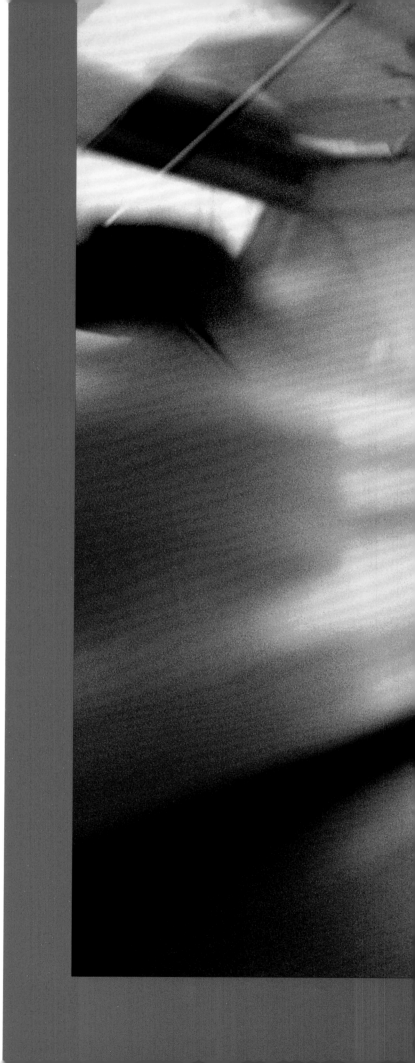

For Pedro Almodóvar, *The Flower of My Secret* was an exercise in reconciliation on all levels after the furore generated by *Kika*: with the public and critics, and of course, with the classic melodrama of his previous films. But, above all, his eleventh film represented a return to the major themes such as life at the crossroads and heartbreak, the suffering of female characters and the vindication of the mother as the driving force of the family. A story without villains – 'like Frank Capra's' – where pain is shown but also tenacity and hope, and in which Almodóvar pays tribute to his first love, storytelling.

'I wanted to be a writer from my earliest childhood, and when I was only eight years old, I was already writing my own fiction stories,' he recalls. 'My aspiration was to write a great novel, although, as time went by, reality showed me that what I wrote ended up becoming little films. I understood that those texts were not literary stories, but sketches of film scripts.' Little by little, Almodóvar knew that he had to express his inner world through the lens of a camera and not on the pages of a book: 'On more than one occasion I have been asked to write my autobiography and I have always refused; I have also been asked to have someone else write it, but I still feel a kind of allergy to seeing a book that talks entirely about me as a person.' By directly invoking such an intrinsic part of his personality, *The Flower of My Secret* can be seen as a very intimate process of affirmation (and healing) by a director who, for the first time in his very successful career, had looked into the abyss of failure.

As in *High Heels*, the genesis of *The Flower of My Secret* lies in a specific situation imagined by Almodóvar, and his deep desire to

RIGHT: Marisa Paredes is stunning in her role as a woman, Leo, in complete emotional breakdown.

"

I WANTED TO BE A WRITER FROM MY
EARLIEST CHILDHOOD.

"

see it projected on a screen. The scene involved a lonely woman who receives an unexpected visit from her husband, a high-ranking military officer deployed to Bosnia, and ends up being abandoned soon after. She refuses to accept that the love between them has ended and tries to win him back with a desperate question, which the filmmaker would eventually turn into the provisional title of his project: *Is there any possibility, however small, of saving what is ours?* Almodóvar began to develop the before and after of that moment, a process that entailed many revisions leading to eight different versions of the script, one of the most laborious writing processes of his career. The final script would feature a romance writer named Leo Macías, who, in the middle of a creative block due to the breakup with her husband, decides she needs to write a noir genre work. Marisa Paredes took the role of Leo (although Ana Belén was originally considered for the role), alongside Carme Elías as Betty, Leo's best friend, Juan Echanove as Ángel, an editor at *El País*, and Imanol Arias, who returned to the director's universe thirteen years after *Labyrinth of Passion*, as the absent husband.

In Almodóvar's films, colour evokes situations and emotions, portraying the inner journey of the main character, and has, without exception, a specific dramatic meaning. In *The Flower of My Secret*, it is used as a fundamental element to explore the confusing and changing personality of the protagonist, someone who dedicates herself to writing romantic, pink, novels under a pseudonym that refers, precisely, to an absence of colour: Amanda Gris (Amanda Grey). 'If a writer like Leo, out of absent-mindedness or pain, contemplates herself in the black mirror of reality, she will cross the border that divides two genres as opposite and neighbouring as Pink and Black,' explained the filmmaker. To further emphasise his point he borrowed one of his favourite phrases from *Casablanca* (Michael Curtiz, 1942) for the moment when Ángel (Juan Echanove) shares his feelings for Leo in the Plaza Mayor in Madrid, reminding her that she was wearing blue the day they met. 'Bogart was telling Ingrid Bergman that he remembered the day he saw her for the first

LEFT: After anticipating a loving reunion with her husband Paco (Imanol Arias), Leo is instead devastated when he ends their relationship.

RIGHT: Almodóvar and Marisa Paredes
rehearse the moment of Leo's passionate
confrontation with Paco.

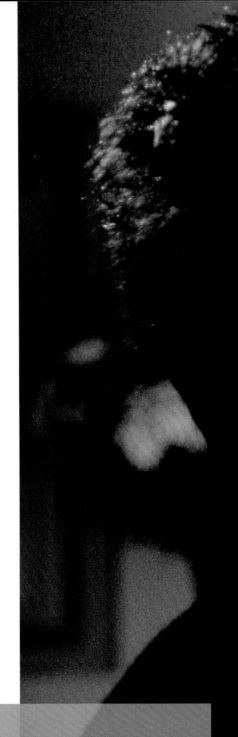

time, during the occupation of Paris, because the Germans were wearing grey, and she was wearing blue. It is impossible to express more emotion. . . And all that Bogart did was make a comment about clothes.'

The paths of Almodóvar and Leo run parallel; they are both artists who tell stories, have suffered a setback and are looking to rediscover their identity. While in pre-production, the director received a call from his sister telling him that his mother had asked to see a psychiatrist so she could talk to someone. Realising that his widowed mother must be intensely lonely, he planned a trip to see her and record their conversations on film. However, he was unable to take the trip, but he did plan one for Leo, who, in her moment of greatest despair, decides to seek solace with her mother (Chus Lampreave), who is eager to leave the city and return to her village home. 'From the beginning, Chus has officially represented my mother, because she knows it and because the three or four characters inspired by my mother have been made by her,' Almodóvar would admit years later. 'Of course, in *The Flower of My Secret*, absolutely all of the phrases that she says were said by my mother.'

It was in this way, with a return to one's roots through the mother, that Almodóvar and Leo find a way to recover their motivation and instinct. The scenes that take place in Almagro – located thirty kilometres from Calzada de Calatrava, Almodóvar's hometown in Ciudad Real – are like a breath of fresh air after the suffocation of the city and are wrapped in a distinct halo of poetry and simplicity. 'I photographed the fields of red earth, infinite, glued directly to the sky,' he said.

Lampreave hadn't worked with Almodóvar since *Women on the Verge of a Nervous Breakdown*, but she delivered one of the most famous and repeated lines of his films: *Cara de ladilla* (Crab face); a Spanish expletive that her character calls her youngest daughter every time she gets annoyed and fed up with her.

"I PHOTOGRAPHED THE FIELDS OF RED EARTH, INFINITE, GLUED DIRECTLY TO THE SKY."

MOTHER: **Oh, my daughter, what a pity. . . Your father must be turning in his grave!**

ROSA: **(Trying to take the phone away from her) Leo!**

MOTHER: **Shut up, crab face! Listen, I'm going back to the village and my house where I can get some peace.**

LEO: **I'm going with you. I'll pick you up right away and take you in the car.**

MOTHER: **You're coming with me? Oh, I'm so happy!**

ROSA: **Leo, don't listen to her! Nobody here has thrown her out of the house!**

MOTHER: **No? Your husband!**

ROSA: **My husband? Leo, Santiago didn't throw her out, all he told her is that no one must give him permission to drink in his house! What were you thinking, calling him a drunkard to his face?**

MOTHER: **Because he is!**

ROSA: **You don't know anything!**

MOTHER: **You're the one who doesn't know anything! What do you want me to do, stand here with my mouth shut? You treat me like a dog!**

The Flower of My Secret was the first collaboration between Almodóvar and the musician Alberto Iglesias, born in San Sebastián in 1955, a professional relationship that has been maintained ever since and has given rise to some of the best scores of his career. At that time, Iglesias was one of the most promising composers in Spanish cinema, thanks mainly to his work with Julio Medem in *Cows* (*Vacas*, 1991) and *The Red Squirrel* (*La ardilla roja*, 1993), two films in which he demonstrated his great ability to transmit very deep emotions using few resources, some as unusual as the *txalaparta*, a traditional Basque percussion instrument. Captivated by the composer's artistic personality, Almodóvar set him the challenge of creating music that would represent the intense pain that afflicts Leo, something that Iglesias achieved thanks to his impressive mastery of string instruments, in this case the viola, violin and cello. Despite this, the director – still bruised and wary from the disappointing experiences with Morricone and Sakamoto – decided to include only part of Iglesias's work in the film, completing the soundtrack with songs by Caetano Veloso, Bola de Nieve, and Chavela Vargas. But learning from his experience, Alberto Iglesias adapted to the style and requirements of Almodóvar, and the two have developed a very fruitful creative relationship.

Through the film, Almodóvar returned to his central theme of female redemption, depicting women who live subjugated to the archetype of the Iberian *macho*: selfish, unfaithful and dominant men who no longer love them. As part of their journey, they will lose their way, and may even mourn their loneliness, but they will receive the support of family, and discover that, far from those toxic male figures, they can be themselves, raise their voices, and live and love freely. For these reasons, *The Flower of My Secret* occupies a central position in Almodóvar's cinema, a title of enormous artistic depth where previous stories and the ideal of the feminine universe come to converge in glorious fullness.

ABOVE: Chus Lampreave (Leo's mother) and Rossy de Palma (Rosa) once again deliver superb comedy performances.

FAR LEFT: Leo is consumed by heartbreak.

LEFT: The director, ready to start shooting.

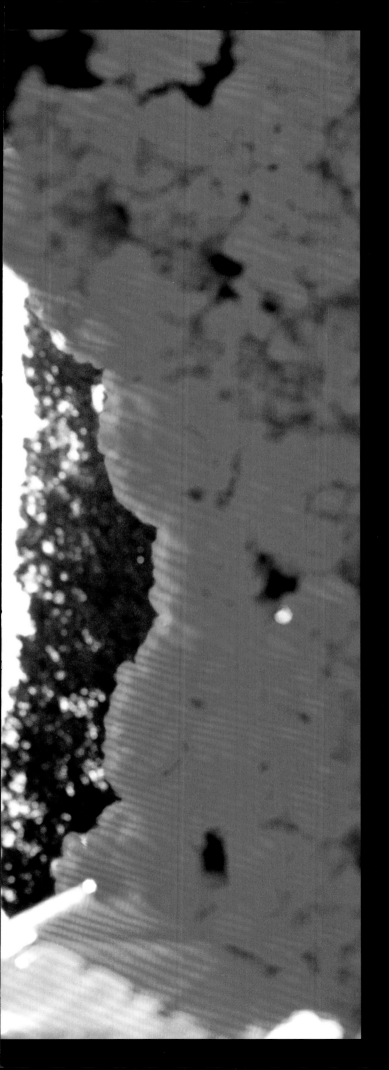

LIVE
FLESH

LIVE FLESH
Carne trémula (1997)

O nce Almodóvar regained his artistic pulse thanks to *The Flower of My Secret*, he began work on what would be his strangest and seemingly most alien film to date. *Live Flesh*, besides being his first pure noir without concessions to melodrama or comedy, is considered a rarity in Almodóvar's career for several reasons, most notably because it is the first feature film adapted from foreign material – in this case, a 1986 novel by the British mystery writer Ruth Rendell – and the first for which he shared screenplay credit. In an unusual six-handed exercise, that he would never repeat, Almodóvar turned to two young Spanish writing talents for his adaptation: the cult novelist Ray Loriga and the Asturian screenwriter Jorge Guerricaechevarría, the latter responsible for the script of one of the great successes of Spanish cinema of the nineties, *The Day of the Beast* (*El día de la bestia*, Álex de la Iglesia, 1995).

The approach to the story also presented two substantial variations. The first of these occurs in the prologue, set in 1970, during which a young woman gives birth on a bus while the Franco regime decrees the State of Exception, a crackdown on political protest and student revolts. This is the first explicit reference to the dictatorship that we find in a film by Almodóvar, who until then had always argued that the best revenge against Franco was to ignore him completely, as if he had never existed. After the opening sequence, the plot moves forward two decades and depicts the unhappy life of Víctor, the bus baby turned pizza delivery boy who is sent to prison for beating up a policeman named David, who was trying to intervene in a fight between Víctor and Elena, a young drug addict. During the confrontation, Víctor shoots David leaving him partially but severely paralysed. After he has served his sentence, Víctor tries to reconcile with Elena, but she is now married to David, now a famous wheelchair basketball player for the Spanish Olympic team, who tells

RIGHT: Victor (Liberto Rabal) threatens Elena (Francesca Neri) during the explosive beginning of the film.

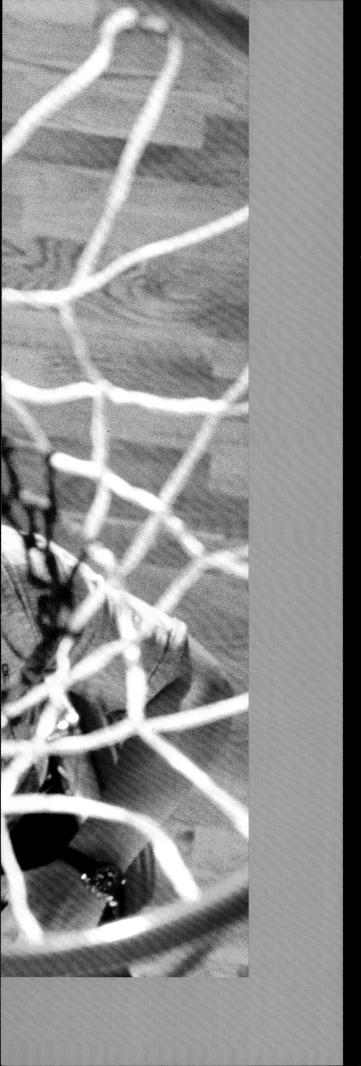

"

LIVE FLESH IS AN ANOMALY WITHIN ALMODÓVAR'S BODY OF WORK.

LEFT: True to his exhaustive preparation, Javier Bardem learned to play wheelchair basketball with amazing skill.

"

Víctor to keep away. In this way, *Live Flesh* is an anomaly within Almodóvar's body of work to date, since it is the first – though later films *Bad Education*, *The Skin I Live In* and *Pain and Glory* would follow suit – in which the male characters carry the weight of the story almost exclusively. Almodóvar's male characters tend to be erratic and immature, in stark contrast to the integrity and strength of his women: 'As a dramatic subject, I am much more interested in men when they start to be men, like Víctor. I don't see myself writing stories about forty-somethings who have problems with their love lives.'

As well as changing his working methods, the director dispensed with his usual stable of returning performers, thinking that perhaps they were too attached to a style from which *Live Flesh* was intentionally trying to escape. Of the main characters, only Javier Bardem (David), who had a very brief role in *High Heels*, had worked with the director before, with Jorge Sanz – then one of the most glittering stars in the Spanish industry – in the role of Víctor. The cast was rounded out with the Italian Francesca Neri (well known in Spain for her work with Bigas Luna in *The Ages of Lulu* and Carlos Saura in *Outrage*) as Elena, and the acclaimed José Sancho and Ángela Molina playing a married couple, Sancho and Clara, mired in obsession and jealousy. Almodóvar put his cast through four months of intense rehearsals, time that Bardem took advantage of to learn how to play wheelchair basketball with amazing skill.

Shooting began in early January 1997 – days before, the Christmas-decorated Arenal Street in Madrid was used for one scene – but soon disagreements arose between Almodóvar and Jorge Sanz, who openly challenged the director's methods in front of the rest of the crew. After a week of filming, both agreed that the best thing was to start again with a new actor: Sanz exited by mutual consent, receiving his full salary of ten million pesetas, and El Deseo began a frantic search for a replacement. On 1 February, Liberto Rabal, grandson of the legendary Paco Rabal (who had played a film director in *Tie Me Up! Tie Me Down!*), and a promising newcomer who had just starred in his first film, *Tramway to Malvarrosa* (*Tranvía a la Malvarrosa*, José Luis García Sánchez, 1997), for which he was nominated for a Goya as Best New Actor, was added to the cast. However, this was not to be Almodóvar's only headache, as he had to deal with one of the hottest and least rainy winters in Spain in living memory: 'For the location shooting, I had hoped to have those overcast skies, full of dark clouds like smoke, which are so typical of Madrid. But nature was not on my side, so instead of grey skies, we suffered insistently from blazing sun. I had no choice but to accept it as an imposition of fate.'

Fate, however, would also place before him the most important performer of his later career. When she first received Almodóvar's call, Penélope Cruz was twenty-two years old and was already regarded as one of the greatest actors in Spain. In *Live Flesh*, her role was limited to the prologue, in which she would play the young woman giving birth to her child on a lonely bus. 'As soon as we got to the set, Pedro and I would go into a room to practise animal moans, because he said that I was very fine and that I couldn't be that fine in the film,' recalled the Madrid-born actor. Despite the brevity of the role, Cruz began to establish herself as the quintessential representation of motherhood in the director's work – it was no accident that Almodóvar named her character Isabel Plaza Caballero, in clear reference

ABOVE: Francesca Neri enjoyed considerable popularity in Spain thanks to her previous work with Carlos Saura.

RIGHT: Victor, a character in constant search of redemption.

FAR RIGHT: The prologue, set in 1970, was the only reference to Francoism.

to his mother's surname – lauded over time for her extraordinary performances in *Volver*, *Pain and Glory* and *Parallel Mothers*.

Despite being unusual within the director's canon, *Live Flesh* is full of many familiar Almodóvarian themes: violence, resilience, redemption and obsessive love. That he was able to take another author's work, in another genre, and adapt it so successfully to his style demonstrated a previously untapped side of the director. He described it as 'an intense drama, baroque and sensual, totally independent of the Ruth Rendell novel that inspired it, which resides in the classic thriller and tragedy.' However, the film – which was seen by an audience of 1.4 million and was nominated for a BAFTA for Best Foreign Film – suffers at times from the inconsistency shown by Almodóvar throughout the decade, alternating passages of excellent cinematography and narrative pulse with others that are much more dispensable, mainly, in retrospect, due to some questionable casting decisions. Today, *Live Flesh* can be regarded as a *rara avis*, as curious as it is attractive, and as a precursor to the explosion that was about to take place.

"

I WOULD GO INTO A ROOM TO PRACTISE ANIMAL MOANS, BECAUSE HE SAID THAT I WAS VERY FINE AND THAT I COULDN'T BE THAT FINE IN THE FILM.

PENÉLOPE CRUZ

"

ALL
ABOUT
MY
MOTHER

ALL ABOUT MY MOTHER
Todo sobre mi madre (1999)

All About My Mother is a film born of enthusiasm. From the first stirrings of the story, Almodóvar was overtaken with a contagious passion for the magnitude of the project. 'I think it will be my most moving film,' he said shortly before production began.

The initial concept arose from the opening scenes of *The Flower of My Secret*, in which a nurse played by Kiti Mánver role-plays a mother's grief over the death of her son during a seminar on organ transplants. 'I had the idea of making a film about the acting ability of certain people who are not actors,' he explained, once again fascinated by the kaleidoscopic effect of watching someone play a role within a role. After drawing inspiration, once again, from his vast cinephile knowledge – Gena Rowlands in *Opening Night* (John Cassavetes, 1977) and Romy Schneider in *That Most Important Thing: Love* (*L'important c'est d'aimer*, Andrzej Żulawski, 1975) were cited references – Almodóvar developed 'a story of women with great conflicts,' two characters connected by the figure of Blanche DuBois, the maddened and tragic protagonist of Tennessee Williams's *A Streetcar Named Desire*.

Like the fleeting character in *The Flower of My Secret*, Manuela (Cecilia Roth) is a nurse who supervises donor organ transplants in a hospital in Madrid and who, at times, tries her luck as an amateur actor. Her teenage son Esteban (Eloy Azorín) longs to know more about his absent father, whose identity Manuela has never revealed. On the night of his seventeenth birthday, just as his mother has decided to tell him the whole truth, Esteban is run over and killed

RIGHT: Fifteen years after her last appearance in an Almodóvar film, Cecilia Roth (Manuela) is the driving force in this captivating story about loss and solidarity among women.

new, makeshift family includes Rosa (Penélope Cruz, pregnant again to illustrate the perfect image of motherhood), a giggly, HIV-infected nun, and Agrado (Antonia San Juan), a transsexual sex worker who brings a gallows humour to the darkest corners of life. Most memorable is the sequence in which Agrado delivers an improvised monologue about her life, which was inspired by the true story of the Argentinian actor Lola Membrives, who, after an electrical failure at the theatre she was performing in, told a story to the audience about her own experiences until the power returned.

> I THINK THE SUCCESS LIES PRECISELY IN THE FACT THAT, DESPITE THE WILDNESS OF THE STORY, THE PEOPLE WHO SEE THE FILM FEEL VERY CLOSE TO ITS PROFOUND IDEAS.

LEFT: The partnership between Almodóvar and Penélope Cruz, who plays the radiant Rosa, was already formidable.

AGRADO: My friend and I want to get off the street, but we have to work, don't we, Manolita? Whatever, even if it's cleaning stairs. We don't care.

ROSA: The truth is that there's not much else. . . Well, garbage collectors. . . Or learning how to make crafts here in the workshop, petit-point tablecloths, centrepieces of dried flowers. . .

AGRADO: Well, I'd almost prefer to be a garbage collector.

ROSA: And what do you know how to do, apart from the street?

MANUELA: I've worked as a cook in a restaurant.

AGRADO: She's half a surgeon. Look at my face. . . She did it to me [. . .] She's related to Lola.

ROSA: Oh yeah? And do you know what's happened to her?

MANUELA: I haven't seen her for more than eighteen years.

AGRADO: She robbed my house.

ROSA: Well, she was here, about four months ago. We helped her detox [. . .] If you see her, tell her I'd like to say goodbye before going to El Salvador.

AGRADO: You're going to El Salvador? Maybe I'll come too. . . I've always thought I could do well in the developing world [. . .] Here, the street is getting worse every day, sister. Even if we had little competition from the whores, the drags are sweeping us away. I can't stand the drags. They're a bunch of mamarrachas [. . .]

ROSA: In El Salvador I don't think there's much drag, but they're in full guerrilla mode.

AGRADO: Oh yeah? I didn't know that.

ROSA: I'm going to replace some nuns who were murdered.

AGRADO: Well, I don't know if the best thing for me right now is a guerrilla.

MANUELA: Oh, you're such a brute, Agrado.

RIGHT: The filmmaker with two of his most treasured collaborators, Cecilia Roth and Marisa Paredes, reunited for the first time since *Dark Habits*.

Cecilia Roth's powerful portrayal of Manuela is the soul of *All About My Mother*, or, as Almodóvar put it, 'the marrow, because she is the woman I follow with the camera and who takes us through the different stories of the film.' A cast regular in his early films, Roth had been absent from his universe for fifteen years; in that time, she had become one of the most respected Latin American actors worldwide, with acclaimed appearances in *A Place in the World* (*Un lugar en el mundo*, 1992) and *Martín (Hache)* (1997), both directed by Adolfo Aristarain. 'I don't know how, during the three months that the shooting lasted, she knew how to contain herself and be beyond pain, but always reflecting it,' Almodóvar commented on a role that earned Roth a dozen international awards. 'I loved Manuela a lot,' she recalled. 'Like me, she came from a faraway country, wanted to invent a life in another place and managed, putting one brick on top of another, to put together that life more or less similar to the one of her dreams.'

Undoubtedly, one of the most moving and powerful passages of the film is when we hear Manuela's voice-over, on board a train to Barcelona, explaining the reason for that journey to redemption. Accompanied by the chords of the song 'Tajabone', by the Senegalese musician Ismaël Lô, the city appears in all its grandeur before the viewer's eyes. After almost two decades of stories set in Madrid, Almodóvar found in Barcelona the ideal place to locate Manuela's emotional journey; somehow, the Mediterranean spirit and the modernist architecture of the city provided a balm to the suffering of his characters. Approximately eighty per cent of the scenes take place there, with locations as picturesque and representative as the Sagrada Familia, the Borne, the Gothic Quarter, the Plaza Real and the seaside district of La Barceloneta.

Surprisingly, a film directed by Pedro Almodóvar achieved both unanimous critical and public acclaim for the first time. *All About My Mother* became a resounding triumph practically from the moment of its release, reaching an audience of 2.5 million in Spain alone – where it played in theatres for sixty weeks – and winning a total of seven Goya Awards, including Best Film, Director and Lead Actress. Its international success was even more extraordinary, with a global gross of $68 million and more than fifty awards, including the award for Best Foreign Language Film at the Golden Globe, BAFTA, César and David di Donatello awards, plus the award for Best Director at the Cannes Film Festival. In the words of its author, 'I think the success lies precisely in the fact that, despite the wildness of the story, the people who see the film feel very close to its profound ideas.' The maelstrom of recognition reached its climax on 26 March 2000, at the Shrine Auditorium in Los Angeles, where Almodóvar picked up the Oscar for Best Foreign Language Film from Antonio Banderas and Penélope Cruz. That initial enthusiasm he felt while imagining the story had led to an undisputed masterpiece, a profoundly beautiful and inspiring artistic exaltation. The provocative and brazen young man from *La Movida* had become a revered filmmaker who, from that moment on, had earned his place in the history of cinema.

"

EVERYONE WANTS TO BE A MOTHER...
WE ALL WANT TO CONCEIVE.

TALK TO HER

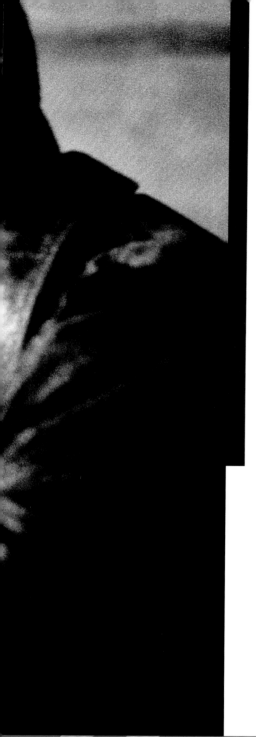

TALK TO HER
Hable con ella (2002)

I n 1989, during his first promotional visit to Los Angeles for the Oscar nomination for *Women on the Verge of a Nervous Breakdown*, Almodóvar had the opportunity to meet one of his great idols, Billy Wilder. During the meal they shared, the legendary filmmaker gave him a piece of advice that has never left him: 'Never come to Hollywood. It doesn't matter what they can offer you.' Throughout the following decade, Almodóvar had little trouble dodging the proposals that came to him from American cinema, mainly because their artistic value (the musical comedy *Sister Act*, for example) was dubious to say the least. However, after winning the Oscar for *All About My Mother*, the quality of the offers increased considerably, making it more difficult for the director to deny the Hollywood temptation. Even so, he decided to return to Spain with the firm conviction of maintaining his creative independence and continuing to bet on his scripts, born from his own perception and inexhaustible sharpness.

While he was still in the United States, Almodóvar began to develop his next project, based on a series of real incidents that captured his attention. The first was the story of an American woman who woke up after sixteen years in a coma that, according to doctors, was irreversible. The second was the return to life of a young Romanian woman who had been presumed dead after the morgue guard abused her supposed corpse. And the third was the mysterious pregnancy of a New York girl who had been in a coma for nine years, and who had been raped by a clinical assistant. 'Human acts have many readings, and these can be seen as a crime or as saving a life. I wanted to defend that dilemma,' said the director, for whom *Talk to Her* is, above all, 'a story about communication and non-communication, about the friendship between two men and the long convalescence caused by the wounds of passion. But also, about cinema as a subject of conversation, and about how a monologue in front of a person in silence can be an effective form of dialogue.'

Talk to Her is, in effect, the story of two lonely individuals whose destinies are intertwined by tragedy. Almodóvar wrote the character of Benigno, a nurse at a private clinic who lives hidden from others, with his friend Roberto Benigni in mind – hence the name – but he was unable to take on the role, leading the director to cast Javier Cámara, an immense and versatile actor who until then had only been cast in comic roles in film and television. Quite the opposite of Darío Grandinetti, a sober and prestigious Argentinian performer, who had worked with directors such as Juan Carlos Desanzo and Eliseo Subiela. Almodóvar cast him in the role of Marco, a writer who is in the same clinic as Benigno, watching over his beloved, Lydia (Rosario Flores), a bullfighter who remains in a state of unconsciousness after a serious injury. Meanwhile, Benigno is devoted to Alicia (Leonor Watling), a dancer who is also in a coma after a car accident. He shares with her a passion for literature and cinema, trapped by a love that cannot be reciprocated, but which he dreams of manifesting when she wakes up.

BENIGNO: **On my days off I started going to the ballet. I also go to the Film Archive. I watch all the silent films I can: German, American, Italian. . . Everything. Then I tell her everything I've seen. These last four years have been the richest of my life, taking care of Alicia, and doing the things she liked to do. Except travelling, of course.**

MARCO: **The opposite happens to me with Lydia [. . .] I can't even touch her. I don't recognise her body. I'm even incapable of helping the nurses turn her over in bed. And I feel very mean.**

BENIGNO: **Talk to her. Tell her.**

MARCO: **Yes, I'd like to, but she can't hear me.**

BENIGNO: **And how are you so sure they can't hear us?**

MARCO: **Because her brain is dead, Benigno.**

BENIGNO: **A woman's brain is a mystery. And in this state, even more so. You must take women into account, talk to them. To share a detail from time to time, to caress them suddenly. Remember that they exist, that they are alive, and that they matter to us. That's the only therapy, I can tell you from experience.**

MARCO: **And what experience do you have with women?**

BENIGNO: **Me? All of it. I've lived day and night with one for twenty years and I've been with Alicia for four years.**

As in *Kika*, the characters' futures will be changed by a rape. However, in this case, Almodóvar does not show the assault, but turns it, with all the terrible consequences that doing so entails, into a subtle demonstration of love. To illustrate this, he chooses a wonderful seven-minute piece entitled *El amante menguante* (*The Shrinking Lover*), in homage to the classic *The Incredible Shrinking Man* (Jack Arnold, 1957). This is a fake silent film that Benigno tells Alicia about on the night he decides to act on his desire for her, and in which a man (Fele

Martínez) shrinks after ingesting a potion and decides to give himself to the woman he loves (Paz Vega) in the only way physically possible: by entering her through her vagina and staying inside her forever. Through this passage inserted in the middle of the story, Almodóvar conveys the consummation of something dreadful from the beauty of images that show an impossible love, emphasizing the profoundly poetic personality of a film where everything, even the most atrocious event, is sublimated to the power of ingenuity.

After the rape, Alicia becomes pregnant and Benigno is imprisoned, unaware that she regains consciousness after childbirth. That manifestation of his feelings, the rape, although unforgivable, brings Alicia back to life and allows her to resume her career as a dancer. That is the great paradox of *Talk to Her*: that the most unhealthy and cruel love can make death – or something terribly similar – become life. The story is incredibly moving and Almodóvar triumphantly tackles the extraordinarily complex challenge. This is partly due to the delicacy and sobriety he exhibits when dealing with such an uncompromising subject, and because of his ability to stir the viewer's emotions – and also those of some characters who cry without blushing – from the most genuine artistic expressions.

Almodóvar started shooting at the Théâtre de la Ville in Paris in June 2001, with Javier Aguirresarobe, one of European cinema's most highly regarded cinematographers, behind the camera. For the choreographed scenes that top and tail the film, Almodóvar sought out the German choreographer Pina Bausch, whose piece *Café Müller* he was convinced was 'specially designed for *Talk to Her*.' By chance, her troupe was performing another of her pieces, *Masurca Fogo*, in Paris at the same time, so he took a unit to record a dance from it that would feature at the film's end. The production of *Talk to Her* continued for over three months in various locations, including the bullrings of Aranjuez (Madrid) and Brihuega (Guadalajara), and the Cordoba town of Lucena, which received the film crew during the shock of the September 11 terrorist attacks. Almodóvar also used his own house, located thirty kilometres from Madrid, to film the scenes in which the Brazilian musician Caetano Veloso performs his interpretation of Tomás Méndez's classic 'Cucurrucucú Paloma', and in which friends such as Marisa Paredes, Cecilia Roth and Manuel Bandera appear as extras.

Talk to Her premiered in March 2002 amidst unprecedented attention, the result of the high expectations generated by the worldwide triumph of *All About My Mother*. 'I only consider being a genius, not merely great or wonderful. I can only move on a thin line called perfection,' said Almodóvar, as he gladly accepted the pressure. In Spain, the press applauded it as one of the best films of the year and moviegoers filled the theatres, although the real recognition would come again from abroad, with more than $64 million in global box

COMBINES SENSUALITY, SPIRITUALITY AND PURE NARRATIVE JOY IN WONDERFULLY HARMONIOUS PROPORTIONS.

TIME OUT

ABOVE: Leonor Watling practised yoga to keep her body in a state of maximum relaxation, controlling her breathing and keeping her body inert.

office and enthusiastic reviews from *Time Out* ('combines sensuality, spirituality and pure narrative joy in wonderfully harmonious proportions'), *USA Today* ('warmly humanistic and boldly innovative') and *The New York Times* ('you can't get it out of your heart'). Particularly striking was the snub once again from the Spanish Academy of Cinema, which decided to award a single Goya for Best Original Soundtrack and to nominate Fernando León de Aranoa's *Mondays in the Sun* (*Los lunes al sol*) as the candidate for the Oscar for the Best Foreign Language Film. In a formidable example of poetic justice, *Talk to Her* received two Oscar nominations for Best Director and Original Screenplay – both for Almodóvar – winning in the latter category ahead of Todd Haynes (*Far from Heaven*), Steven Zaillian (*Gangs of New York*) and Alfonso Cuarón (*Y tu mamá también*).

BAD
EDUCATION

BAD EDUCATION
La mala educación (2004)

On occasions, Pedro Almodóvar has said that the script for *Bad Education* is the best he has ever written, and the one that took him the longest time to complete. At first it was a short story, 'full of adolescent fury' and written in the seventies from his own experiences as a child, when a student at the high school in Cáceres with Salesian and Franciscan fathers. In it, a transvestite returns to the school where he studied to blackmail the priests who assaulted him in his childhood: 'There was a lot of abuse, especially among the youngest children. I was ten years old. In the bedroom, at night, we would tell each other about our experiences. The rumours spread beyond the school walls, and, because there were so many cases, the school administration had to intervene. In the end, those responsible were sent, without punishment, to teach at a boarding school for adolescents.' Almodóvar took up the idea again in the 1990s, changing the vengeful tone of the initial draft in order to find a larger story that justified the whole tale. By then, the project had already become a feature film and was provisionally titled *La visita* (*The Visit*).

He planned to shoot the film right after *All About My Mother*, but, unable to find an actor for the lead who was equally attractive as a man and as a woman – Leonardo Sbaraglia and Eduardo Noriega were some of the names that paraded unsuccessfully through the casting – he decided to park it and concentrate on *Talk to Her* instead. After winning his second Oscar, Almodóvar was convinced that he had to turn the script – now called *Bad Education* – which had been in development for more than three decades, into a film: 'I had to make it, to get it out of me before it became a frustrating obsession.' More than just an autobiographical experience, it was a very intimate story which exposed and denounced the sexual abuse that took place in religious schools and community centres: 'I'm not just telling a story about my school days [. . .] My memories were important when writing it, because, after all, I lived in the scenarios and in the times in which it takes place. But it is not about a settling of scores with the priests who miseducated me, nor with the clergy in general.'

"

THERE WAS A LOT OF ABUSE, ESPECIALLY AMONG THE YOUNGEST CHILDREN.

"

More than a vengeful work, *Bad Education* represents the filmmaker's umpteenth twist on the original concept of film noir. What, mistakenly, may seem to be an anticlerical drama by way of confession, is an arduous and splendid criminal game where cinema, specifically the figure of the tortured director who seeks to redeem himself through his art – already appreciated in *Law of Desire* and revisited in *Pain and Glory* – once again plays an essential role. Enrique (Fele Martínez) is a famous filmmaker who, one day in 1980, receives a mysterious visit from Ignacio (Gael García Bernal), an actor looking for work who claims to be an old schoolmate with whom he fell in love. He proposes to shoot a script he has written – curiously titled *The Visit* – about their years at their Catholic school, where they discovered their passion for cinema and suffered the abuses of Father Manolo (Daniel Giménez Cacho). But Enrique distrusts his old friend and ends up finding out that it is Ignacio's younger brother, Juan. Despite this, he agrees to direct the film in order to discover the truth about the fate of the real Ignacio.

From here, Almodóvar masterfully and delicately constructs a plot marked by a terrible murder and the passions that led to it. *Bad Education* is sprinkled with glorious noir references to *La Bête Humaine* (Jean Renoir, 1938) and *The Adultress* (*Thérèse Raquin*, Marcel Carné, 1953) and features an elemental archetype of the genre: the man with a dark past who becomes a femme fatale (Juan, transformed into the disconcerting Zahara), almost an heir to the transvestite murderer in *Dressed to Kill* (Brian De Palma, 1980). In this sense, the return to the Almodóvarian canon of cinematographer José Luis Alcaine is decisive. His use of colour again accompanies the moods of the characters and manages to create a diffuse and sombre atmosphere with the predominance of black, the tone that distinguishes the cassocks of the 'bad educators'.

Bad Education extends the look of *Talk to Her*, and similarly, is based on the connection between two men who are united by a traumatic event. This is Almodóvar's most masculine work, in terms of story and cast, and would require an exhaustive search throughout the Spanish-speaking acting world to find his longed-for leading man. Gael García Bernal was considered an international star when he was chosen for the role. Despite being only twenty-five years old, his career already included the award-winning *Amores perros* (Alejandro González Iñárritu, 2000) and *Y tu mamá también* (Alfonso Cuarón, 2001). Even so, he could not have imagined the demands Almodóvar would make of him during the almost four months of filming, starting with the obligatory neutralisation of his Mexican accent. He also had to learn some of the characteristic body language of the Spanish, taking flamenco classes, and studying the films of the camp icon Sara Montiel, as well as thoroughly reviewing the work of Carmen Maura and Victoria Abril in the director's earlier films. Despite acquiring all of these desired characteristics, García Bernal and Almodóvar maintained a very tense relationship throughout the production, to the point of stopping filming for a week so that the actor could recover emotionally.

His relationship with his other lead, Fele Martínez, was much smoother. He arrived already endorsed by his work with Alejandro Amenábar, Julio Medem and Jaume Balagueró, not forgetting his memorable contribution to *Talk to Her* as the tiny man in the fake silent film, *The Shrinking Lover*. 'I made him lose weight and train for five months until he got another body,' recalled the director. 'We also worked on his tone of voice; I lowered his vocal range. He put his heart and skin into it.' For the rest of the male roles, Almodóvar

counted on experienced actors Daniel Giménez Cacho (a legend in Mexico thanks to his collaborations with Arturo Ripstein and Guillermo del Toro), Lluís Homar, who was reliably superb, and Javier Cámara, capable of bringing a touch of humour and tenderness to a tale of tragedy and doom.

Increasingly accustomed to shooting in places other than Madrid, Almodóvar moved his story to locations as diverse as Noia and the village of Ponte Nafonso (A Coruña), an impressive nineteenth-century neoclassical building in Alella (Barcelona), and the city of Valencia. In the latter city, several scenes were filmed in the neighbourhoods of El Carmen and Benimaclet, in addition to the legendary – but now defunct – Tyris cinema. In May 2004, *Bad Education* became the first Spanish film in history to open the Cannes Festival – a milestone that the filmmaker defined as 'the apogee of the honeymoon that I have been living with the French public for years' – just two months after its premiere in Spain, where it had a mixed reception, but ended up becoming a great box-office success, exceeding six million euros in earnings. Once again, the disconnect within the Spanish film industry when evaluating their most revered director (the film only received four Goya nominations, all without awards) would contrast with unanimous international acclaim, reflected in different nominations for the European Film Awards, the Césars, BAFTAs and the Independent Spirit Awards. Not even the protests of Catholic fundamentalists, who were consistently annoying and managed to stop the trailer for *Bad Education* from being screened in France before *The Passion of the Christ* (Mel Gibson, 2004), could overshadow its impressive reception.

ABOVE: Despite their reported differences, Almodóvar got Gael García Bernal to give one of the best and most disconcerting performances of his career.

RIGHT: Almodóvar demonstrates the position of a football goalkeeper to his young actor.

IT IS NOT ABOUT A SETTLING OF SCORES WITH THE PRIESTS WHO MISEDUCATED ME.

VOLVER

VOLVER (2006)

I n the first scene of *Bad Education*, Juan (Gael García Bernal) visits Enrique Goded's production company pretending to be his brother Ignacio. On the wall, next to the main door, there is a poster for a fictitious movie called *La abuela fantasma* (*The Ghostly Grandmother*), directed in the past by Enrique. What at first might seem to be just another element of the film's particular universe was in fact a foreshadowing from Almodóvar of his next project, which would end up being called *Volver* and would be, in effect, a return for the director to the common places of his cinema and his life: to the rural world of La Mancha, to comedy, to the indelible memory of his mother, to marginalized characters, to Penélope Cruz, to the cinema of fascinating women. A return even to Carmen Maura – the *ghostly grandmother* of this story – after eighteen years of personal and professional estrangement. 'It was very funny, because it had been a long time since we had seen each other,' recalled the actor. 'He called me and asked: "Do you mind playing a wreck?" And I told him: "What a question you are asking me. What's it going to matter to me?" Let's get along the way we get along; we both know the other one is doing well.'

Seen in perspective, *Volver* has become a work of key importance within Pedro Almodóvar's artistic output. It is a film full of warmth, tremendously tender and funny, in which the director presents some of his most unforgettable characters and illuminates them in a beautiful way. It is, in fact, a question of a continuous return, a reunion with his origins after a particularly intense dramatic journey. It is no coincidence that *Volver* is a film twinned with *The Flower of My Secret*, the 1995 title that Almodóvar wrote and shot to make up for such turbulent stories as *Tie Me Up! Tie Me Down!*, *High Heels* and *Kika*. In both we find a woman undergoing a vital transformation, let down once again by a man, who decides to return to her village home and reconnect with her mother to find a new meaning to her existence. Almodóvar himself acknowledges that the initial idea for *Volver* came from the crime novel written by *The Flower of My Secret*'s Leo Macías (Marisa Paredes), in which a woman murders her daughter's father to protect her and then hides the corpse in the cold storage room of a restaurant.

In Almodóvar's mind, there was never any other Raimunda than Penélope Cruz. The actor from Madrid gives a prodigious performance in *Volver* and becomes one of the bravest and most charming women in the filmmaker's imagination, inspired by the Sophia Loren of the early years, with Claudia Cardinale's hairstyle and the imposing physical presence and working-class beauty of Anna Magnani in Luchino Visconti's *Bellissima*. 'I wanted Penélope to be inspired by the great Mediterranean icons of acting, very physical, visceral women, with all the emotions on the surface, so obvious, vulgar and uninhibited. Fortunately for her, that's just the way she usually approaches and embodies her characters.'

Like Gloria in *What Have I Done to Deserve This?*, Raimunda lives on the outskirts of Madrid and works hard to provide for her daughter, Paula (Yohana Cobo), while her husband, Paco (Antonio de la Torre), dedicates himself to being lazy and feeding his vices and perversions.

LEFT: *Volver* was a glorious return to suburban comedy, to the traditions of La Mancha and, above all, to the stories of radiant, feisty women.

"

I WANTED PENÉLOPE TO BE INSPIRED BY THE GREAT MEDITERRANEAN ICONS OF ACTING, VERY PHYSICAL, VISCERAL WOMEN, WITH ALL THE EMOTIONS ON THE SURFACE.

LEFT: In her third film with Almodóvar, Penélope Cruz plays a woman of overflowing charisma, based on the great Italian actresses of the 1950s.

"

Like Gloria's character, her life is turned upside down when circumstances force Paula to kill her father to protect herself, and Raimunda must use her wits to get rid of the body. Because of this, she's unable to return to her childhood home for her aunt's funeral, but her sister, Sole (Lola Dueñas), is able to go. After the funeral, her aunt's neighbour, Agustina (Blanca Portillo), tells Sole that she overheard her aunt talking to her dead mother's ghost. When she returns to Madrid, Sole discovers that this ghost of her mother (Carmen Maura), who died in a fire years ago, is also travelling in her car. Rather than look for a logical explanation, Sole accepts that she must live with her, and even puts her to work in her lover's hairdressers, posing as a Russian tramp. 'I wanted the dead mother to be present in her daughters' lives as a physical ghost, with the same needs as a human being,' explained the director. 'Here, the ghost only shows herself to Sole, who is the most gullible and easily manipulated of the sisters. According to the traditional superstition of La Mancha, ghosts return to this world to solve things they left unfinished in life. That is the intention of the mother's ghost.'

Almodóvar sets up a brilliant conflict between the sisters and what they hide from each other. While Raimunda lies to hide Paco's death, Sole does the same to cover up the fact that her mother has come back to life.

HAIRDRESSER'S CLIENT: **Sole, what about the Russian?**

RAIMUNDA: **Who's the Russian?**

SOLE: **I have one here to help me.**

CLIENT: **Yes, well, I was just telling her about my Borja, who's been given another expulsion warning. What do you think? He's punctured the tyres of the priest who teaches him religion. . . Well, I'm telling her about it, and she leaves me there alone, talking, and with my hair half washed.**

SOLE: **She must have gone out.**

CLIENT: **It's not that she's gone out. . . She ran away.**

SOLE: **She suffers from claustrophobia, and sometimes the poor woman needs to go outside.**

RAIMUNDA: **Well, what a help. And you pay her for that?**

SOLE: **No. I keep her at home. She eats and sleeps here. I've given her Mum's clothes.**

RAIMUNDA: **I don't like you picking up people you don't know, Sole.**

CLIENT: **We've told her. . . That she's too nice and people take advantage of her. Look at the Russian. You can't imagine how she lives here. Like a queen.**

SOLE: **And Paco? How did it go the other night?**

RAIMUNDA: **Very bad. He came home to get his clothes. . . I think he's living with another woman now. But come on, I don't know where he is, and I don't care. Hey, why didn't you tell me you had a Russian woman here?**

SOLE: **I must have forgotten, I don't know.**

ABOVE LEFT: Carmen Maura and Penélope Cruz, the two great and undisputed muses of Almodóvar's cinema.

ABOVE RIGHT: The film was Maura's first work with the director since 1988.

LEFT: Lola Dueñas, in the centre of the picture, brings all her candour and comic talent to the character of Sole.

NEXT PAGE: The cemeteries of La Mancha are one of the most symbolic locations in the film.

As a child, Almodóvar was impressed by the traditional La Mancha ritual of women cleaning gravestones in the cemetery. Paradoxically, in *Volver* he chose it as the opening sequence. 'Now I look at death with less strangeness, in a more natural way, with more serenity. More than a film about death itself, *Volver* is about the rich culture that surrounds it in the place where I was born. It is about the way (not at all tragic) that several female characters, from different generations, must face this reality,' he said, about the way in which the film naturalises this issue until it is an accepted part of life, stripping it of any transcendence. 'When my grandfather died, he left many things unresolved. Then he appeared to a brother-in-law of his, who became ill from the apparitions. Until one day the women told him not to be afraid, to ask the ghost what he wanted. The thing is so incredible that eventually the whole town accompanied my grandfather's brother-in-law and my grandfather's spirit to the cemetery to say goodbye to him. I think that image of a procession accompanying a ghost is just great.'

In the case of these sisters, death arrives to provide solace to the empty and isolated Sole – her full name, appropriately enough, being Soledad, meaning loneliness – and as a motivator and self-affirmation for Raimunda, through getting a job at the same restaurant where she was forced to hide her husband's corpse. This is the main theme of the film – and a recurring one in many of Almodóvar's films, but by no means the only one: the importance of roots, the bond with the mother, the strength of character in the face of adversity, and female camaraderie (represented by the wonderful Agustina, the neighbour who is always there when needed) all make *Volver* a true celebration of the genius and passion of a filmmaker at the height of his powers.

Between July and September 2005, Almodóvar moved the production from the Madrid neighbourhoods of Tetuán and Vallecas to various towns and villages in his beloved Castilla-La Mancha: Granátula, Calzada and Valenzuela amongst them. But it was in Almagro, famous for its beautiful historic centre made up of palaces, churches, ancestral homes and the Corral de Comedias (built during the Spanish Golden Age), that the director found the traditional Manchegan home that would house Agustina (Blanca Portillo), not far from the location that a decade earlier had hosted several scenes in *The Flower of My Secret*. 'I love the austerity of its streets, the cobblestones, the black iron windows, without flowerpots, clean of any kind of ornamentation. The dark plinth. The intense daylight,' said Almodóvar during filming. Even the music composed by Alberto Iglesias is once again rich with that Hispanic nuance absent from the director's more recent films, resorting to a string quartet, Spanish guitar and a main theme that borrows pasodoble traits. Not forgetting, of course, the inclusion of Carlos Gardel's iconic tango from the sublime and deep voice of Estrella Morente.

Almost two decades after its release, *Volver* remains Almodóvar's biggest box-office success in Spain, with more than ten million euros grossed and an audience of almost two million. It was one of the rare instances in the director's career in which the audience, critics and academics were all in agreement: not even the reticent Goyas could resist its magnetism, awarding it a total of five awards, including Best Film, Director and Actress. Outside Spain, the reception was equally passionate, demonstrating that only Almodóvar could produce a film with such universal resonance from a story so intimate and rooted in a particular country and culture. With a global box office of $85 million, it is the second-highest-grossing film in Spanish history – only surpassed by the Mexican *Instructions Not Included* (*No se aceptan devoluciones*, Eugenio Derbez, 2013) – and its accolades included four European Film Awards, two awards at Cannes (Best Screenplay and Best Actress for the entire female ensemble) and an Oscar nomination for Penélope Cruz, the first Spanish actor to achieve this distinction.

MORE THAN A FILM ABOUT DEATH ITSELF, *VOLVER* IS ABOUT THE RICH CULTURE THAT SURROUNDS IT.

BROKEN EMBRACES

BROKEN EMBRACES
Los abrazos rotos (2009)

Pedro Almodóvar's seventeenth film is the story of two embraces, one real and furtive, the other cinematographic. The first was captured by the director's own camera in 1999, in Lanzarote's Playa del Golfo, during a vacation on the island shortly after the death of his mother. 'That visit happened at a very special time,' he recalled. 'My spirit, still in mourning, found a reflection and a comfort in the blackness of the island, like a kind of energy shot.' One day, he decided to photograph the immense black volcanic sands of a beach without noticing that, hidden in the distant landscape, a couple were passionately embracing. When he saw the developed image, Almodóvar began to imagine their lives, trying to find out the reasons for that fleeting gesture. He tried to find them, without success, but from then, he knew he would make a film about an almost secret embrace, in that same place, surrounded by the dramatic and captivating nature of the island.

The filmmaker returned to the dramatic landscape of Lanzarote several times, trying to find the inspiration to finish the story, but none of the ideas met his expectations. However, in the early months of 2007, a succession of severe migraines forced him to cancel a trip to New York to write a script with Paul Auster, and to lock himself in a darkened room for several days. It was in this blackness that Almodóvar discovered the way to tell the story that had proved so elusive to him: through the figure of a blind director, someone who was once immensely happy but whose embraces were cut short by a fateful destiny.

'I felt that it is the first time that I had made such an express declaration of love for cinema, not with a specific scene, but with

RIGHT: Almodóvar's irresistible metacinema: Carmen Machi and Penélope Cruz in a scene from *Chicas y maletas*, the film within the film.

the whole film,' explained Almodóvar. The film once again centres around a film director, played by Lluís Homar – the third film director, though not the last, to feature in one of Almodóvar's films, after *Law of Desire* and *Bad Education*. 'It is a statement about something that, even if you can make a living from it, is not just a profession, but an irrational passion.' Indeed, *Broken Embraces* is probably his most kaleidoscopic work as far as the device of 'cinema within cinema' is concerned, and the one that focuses most clearly on the gaze of the filmmaker, marked by tragedy. Everything, from the photograph on the beach to the darkness of blindness, is part of a unique and particular perspective in which Almodóvar makes the viewers participants.

The second embrace references, once again, a cinematic memory. There is a scene where Mateo Blanco (Lluís Homar) and Lena (Penélope Cruz) watch *Journey to Italy* (*Viaggio in Italia*, Roberto Rossellini, 1954) on television, one of the masterpieces of neorealism. In that film, a couple, played by Ingrid Bergman and George Sanders, visit Pompeii and come across a shocking scene: the petrified bodies of a woman and a man, immortalised by the lava of Vesuvius while they slept two thousand years ago. In that instant, Bergman's character, and by extension Penélope's, are moved by this demonstration of a love so strong it is capable of resisting death itself. Lena feels the urge to embrace Mateo, to hold him close to her in the face of adversity and decides to preserve that moment with a photograph that, shortly afterwards, will end up broken into a thousand pieces.

LEFT: Almodóvar makes the final adjustments to a shot of Penélope Cruz in front of a mirror...

RIGHT: ... and runs through some dialogue with Tamar Novas and Lluís Homar.

LENA: **What are you writing?**
MATEO: **'The secret of Playa del Golfo.' When I took the photo,**
       I didn't see the couple kissing.
LENA: **And what is their secret?**
MATEO: **I don't know. I have to write it down to find out.**
LENA: **That couple is us.**

Broken Embraces is one of the most complex stories to emerge from Almodóvar's mind. A challenge that the director felt he could only take on based on the artistic recognition that had accompanied him during the last decade, and that placed him, on his own merits, in a privileged situation from which to face such a risky project. At any other stage in his career, or in the hands of any other author, a film so marked by fatality, so intricate and demanding on the page, would have been a leap into the void with unpredictable consequences. Instead, Almodóvar masterfully solves the challenge and creates a labyrinthine plot in which the characters, and the narrative itself, develop a constant duplicity: two eras (1994

IT IS THE FIRST TIME THAT I HAD MADE SUCH AN EXPRESS DECLARATION OF LOVE FOR CINEMA, NOT WITH A SPECIFIC SCENE, BUT WITH THE WHOLE FILM.

ABOVE: Lena (Penélope Cruz) feels
trapped in a life she no longer wants.

and the present), a lead character split into two personalities (Mateo Blanco, the brilliant
filmmaker, and Harry Caine, the disgraced screenwriter, blind after the car accident that
killed his beloved), two Ernesto Martels (father and son, one arrived to destroy and the
other to rebuild) and even two different plot lines, that of the story itself – the reality – and
that of the film shot by the director – the fiction.

Almodóvar loved filming the scenes for this fake film, titled *Chicas y maletas* (*Girls and
Suitcases*) and inspired by the frenetic surrealism of *Women on the Verge of a Nervous
Breakdown*: 'We shot it in the exact same spot in the studio where we made the original,
twenty years earlier. I had a lot of fun adapting myself, it was a very inspiring experience.'
This is a new and splendid demonstration of cinematographic metalanguage by the director, probably the only one capable of extracting a passage full of sublime comedy – where
neither the suitcase nor the *gazpacho* so characteristic of the 1988 film are missing – from
such a decidedly cruel and stormy context. Undoubtedly, the great attraction of *Girls and
Suitcases* is the conservative-minded council member, Chon, played by Carmen Machi, a
cyclonic woman fond of sex, drugs and cannibalism. Almodóvar was so taken with the character that he ended up shooting more scenes than the film required, which gave rise to an
eight-minute short film, *La concejala antropófaga* (*The Cannibalistic Councillor*), in which the

A TRUE POET OF CINEMA, SOMEONE WHO CREATES TERRIBLE AND HEALING IMAGES THAT LIVE IN YOUR HEAD AS IF IN A WAKING DREAM.

ROLLING STONE

LEFT: Except for her brief appearance in *I'm So Excited!*, *Broken Embraces* is the only Almodóvar film in which Penélope Cruz's character does not have to deal with problematic motherhood.

origin of her depraved dietary habits is riotously disclosed.

Almodóvar began production of *Broken Embraces* in Lanzarote at the end of May 2008. The crew stayed for two weeks, working in various locations: Famara beach, the volcanic and vineyard area of La Geria, Charco de Los Clicos, Timanfaya National Park and the village of Tahíche, which was chosen for the car accident scenes and where, in 1992 (in a coincidence unknown to Almodóvar), the admired Canarian artist César Manrique had died. Filming continued at Madrid's Barajas studios and at other locations around the city, such as an apartment on Cuenca Street, owned by the director's sister, which had already been used for several scenes for *The Flower of My Secret*. The shoot – one of the most arduous and ambitious of Almodóvar's career – was supported by one of the best cinematographers in the world, the Mexican Rodrigo Prieto, used regularly by Alejandro González Iñarritu and Martin Scorsese, and a specialist in achieving textures shrouded in darkness. In addition, the filmmaker brought together a cast made up of many of his usual accomplices: Blanca Portillo, Ángela Molina, Kiti Mánver and Lola Dueñas. However, his relationship with his lead actor Lluís Homar was tense throughout, with the actor claiming to have felt insecure in such a demanding role and due to the director's apparent disappointment in his performance. The fall-out was such that he was totally ignored by Almodóvar after shooting and had no role in the promotion of the film. The film was released in Spain in March 2009, with Almodóvar buoyed by a succession of triumphant works and Penélope Cruz having just won an Oscar for her performance in *Vicky Cristina Barcelona* (Woody Allen, 2008), but the unexpected happened. At the box office, its gross was less than half that of *Volver*, with only a third of the audience, and it received scathing reviews from some critics. It even underperformed in those countries – France and the USA – usually so loyal to the director, although internationally it ended up garnering endless praise from the most prestigious publications. While *The Wall Street Journal* spoke of a 'totally delicious' film, *Variety* highlighted 'the extraordinary strength of the cinematic personality' of its director, who was described by *Rolling Stone* magazine as 'a true poet of cinema, someone who creates terrible and healing images that live in your head as if in a waking dream.'

THE
SKIN
I LIVE
IN

ABOVE: Elena Anaya (Vera) and Antonio Banderas (Ledgard) listen to Almodóvar's instructions before shooting one of the most powerful scenes in the film.

THE SKIN I LIVE IN
La piel que habito (2011)

Like many projects in Almodóvar's career, *The Skin I Live In* underwent a long development period and multiple transformations. At the beginning of the twenty-first century, fresh from the international success of *All About My Mother*, the director had been fascinated by the 1984 novel *Tarantula*, by the great French master of noir literature Thierry Jonquet. After acquiring the film rights through El Deseo, Almodóvar began writing nearly twenty versions of the script, none of which convinced him. 'I worked on the story for nine years,' he says, of a process full of uncertainties during which he even considered shooting a silent, black-and-white adaptation, as a kind of tribute to his idols Fritz Lang and F. W. Murnau, with cards on which the key plot elements and dialogue would appear. 'After hesitating for months, I decided to go my own way and let myself be carried away by intuition – which after all is what I have always done – without the shadow of the masters of the genre and renouncing my own cinematographic memory.'

The fact that the script didn't adhere to any one specific genre – it lies somewhere between noir, science fiction and horror – was a headache for Almodóvar when defining the film's approach. 'I wrote it many times because, when I got to the end, there was always something I didn't like. To tell the truth, the most sensible thing would have been to abandon it. When a script gives you so many problems that you always seem to get stuck, maybe it's because it has no solution. But, as I was still very interested in the central situation of the story, I kept thinking about it until I finally found the solution.' Finally, the only element that Almodóvar kept from Jonquet's novel was the protagonist's desire for revenge. Robert Ledgard is a renowned plastic surgeon obsessed with the tragic death of his wife after suffering severe burns in an accident, and so invents an artificial skin incapable of being damaged.

Back on his own creative terrain, the La Mancha-born filmmaker knew how to imbue the story with his unmistakable stamp. As had already happened with his previous literary adaptation (*Live Flesh*), he made so many modifications that his personality ended up absorbing the original material almost in its entirety. Thus, the viewer is reunited with entirely identifiable Almodóvarian archetypes, from the two-faced psychopath of *Matador* to the love-blinded kidnapper (and his captive victim) of *Tie Me Up! Tie Me Down!*, touching on characteristic themes of his universe such as transsexuality, self-destruction, atonement and loss. While the representation of motherhood acquires the tragic component of titles such as *High Heels* or *All About My Mother*, the character of Marilia (the superb Marisa Paredes) must deal with a suffocating sense of guilt, and with the certainty of having given birth to two very different incarnations of evil, Ledgard and Zeca, while hoping for a spiritual redemption that never arrives. As in *Bad Education*, the shadow of Cain and Abel hovers over the brothers, and one of them even appears dressed as a tiger, giving rise to a

contrast as trashy and grotesque as that which, three decades earlier, was caused by the presence of that same animal among the nuns of *Dark Habits*.

The Skin I Live In marked Almodóvar's reunion with the crime genre, and with Antonio Banderas, twenty-one years after their last collaboration (which, coincidentally, also revolved around an unstable individual who holds a young woman against her will in his home). It feels fitting that their paths should meet again at the height of their careers, one as the director revered around the world, the other as an undisputed star of Hollywood. 'I was eager to work with Antonio again, but we had to wait for the right vehicle,' said the director, who during rehearsals had to ask his leading man to shed his acting tics, as he was looking for a very restrained character, while Banderas initially planned to tackle the role of Dr. Robert Ledgard as a stereotypical film psychopath. 'He was very prepared, but I explained to him that, although I like very baroque characters, the story was so fantastical that even with the slightest hint of over-acting we would go too far. So, I insisted until I emptied his face of any emotion.' For the actor, the experience meant a return to Almodóvar's discipline after two decades of very different jobs in the United States: 'When it comes to Pedro, the shortest distance between two points is never a straight line. Shooting with him is anything but boring. In America we actors enjoy a lot of freedom, but this is unthinkable in his cinema. He directs you in a very specific way, he doesn't allow ideas. But when you let him guide you, everything goes very well.'

Almodóvar contrasts Ledgard's implacable voracity with the apparent fragility and subtlety of his victim, Lena, a young woman who has been trapped for six years for an unknown reason, beyond serving as a human guinea pig for her captor's terrible experiments.

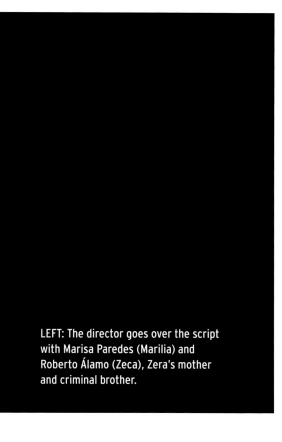

LEFT: The director goes over the script with Marisa Paredes (Marilia) and Roberto Álamo (Zeca), Zera's mother and criminal brother.

LENA: **Do you like what you see?**
LEDGARD: **What do you mean?**
LENA: **Is there something you want to improve?**
LEDGARD: **No. I don't want to improve anything.**
LENA: **Then I can consider myself complete?**
LEDGARD: **Yes. And you can boast of having the best skin in the world.**
LENA: **What now?**
LEDGARD: **Now I'm going to light this opium ball, and I'm going to smoke it.**
LENA: **I mean us. I mean me. If I'm finished. . . What are you going to do with me?**
LEDGARD: **I don't know. I'll think about it.**
LENA: **When?**
LEDGARD: **If you keep asking, I'm leaving.**
LENA: **Don't you think the simplest thing would be to live? To live together?**
LEDGARD: **Live together? How?**
LENA: **Like everybody else.**
LEDGARD: **You and I are not like everybody else.**
LENA: **Look at it as another one of your experiments. . . Living together as equals [. . .] I'm yours. I'm tailor-made for you. And you just told me you like me.**
LEDGARD: **Did I say that?**
LENA: **I know you look at me. Since you brought me here, we practically live in the same room.**

Although Penélope Cruz was originally attached to play Lena, the role was eventually given to Elena Anaya, a wonderful dramatic actor who had previously worked with the director in a small role in *Talk to Her*. 'Pedro is very affectionate, obsessive about perfection and detail-oriented,' she said. 'It is true that he directs the actors a lot, but he also gives you the key you need and that, in turn, coincides with what he is looking for in each shot.' Lena is the great mystery of *The Skin I Live In*, someone who hides a devastating secret and has a special bond with her fellow captive Vicente (Jan Cornet), who was involved long ago in the tragic death of Ledgard's daughter. To strengthen their characters' chemistry, Anaya and Cornet began spending time off-set together without Almodóvar's knowledge, and even went jogging at the same time so that their bodies would naturally synchronise. Their efforts were rewarded when, during filming, the director noticed that both walked in a very similar way and congratulated them on it.

"PEDRO IS VERY AFFECTIONATE, OBSESSIVE ABOUT PERFECTION AND DETAIL-ORIENTED.

ELENA ANAYA

ABOVE: Elena Anaya's extraordinary and highly complex performance brought her several awards, including the Goya Award for Best Actress.

BELOW: After several unsuccessful attempts, Banderas and Almodóvar returned to work together, ending a long hiatus of more than two decades.

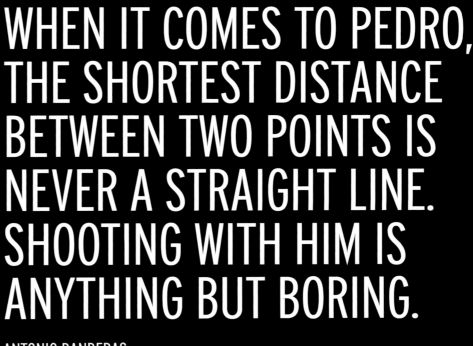

"WHEN IT COMES TO PEDRO, THE SHORTEST DISTANCE BETWEEN TWO POINTS IS NEVER A STRAIGHT LINE. SHOOTING WITH HIM IS ANYTHING BUT BORING.

ANTONIO BANDERAS

"

The film had a budget of ten million euros and was shot mainly in an eighteenth-century manor house in Toledo, with some scenes set in Santiago de Compostela and the Pazo de Oca (Pontevedra). As he had done on other occasions (remember, for example, the extraordinary fusion of film, literature and dance in *The Flower of My Secret*), Almodóvar gave free rein to his artistic spirit with a dazzling combination of disciplines, from the sculptures of Louise Bourgeois – Lena's great inspiration during her confinement – to the multitude of art distributed throughout the house – Titian, Juan Gatti and Guillermo Pérez Villalta, among others – passing through the different versions of *Frankenstein* and *Pygmalion*. Alberto Iglesias based his majestic score on the ballet piece *Cautiva*, composed by himself for the film *¡Dispara!* (Carlos Saura, 1993) and with clear references to the work of masters such as Bernard Herrmann or Jerry Goldsmith. Not to mention the film influences, which include gems of the calibre of *The Invisible Man* (James Whale, 1933), *Rebecca* (Alfred Hitchcock, 1940), *Eyes Without a Face* (Georges Franju, 1960) and even *The Silence of the Lambs* (Jonathan Demme, 1991), where a psychopath creates a second skin, flayed from his victims, to satisfy his need to change sex.

Like *Broken Embraces*, *The Skin I Live In* was received rapturously by critics but with a certain lack of enthusiasm by the public, who were disconcerted by the oppressive and dark tone of Almodóvar's latest work. In Spain, the film barely grossed more than four million euros. Time, however, has been kind to the film, which is now considered an exquisite and sombre rarity.

I'M SO EXCITED!

I'M SO EXCITED!
Los amantes pasajeros (2013)

I'm So Excited! came about as a reaction to a debt Almodóvar felt he owed to his audience. 'When I walked down the street, they would always tell me the same thing: that they loved my latest films, how much I had matured with those dramas. . . But then they would remind me how much they had laughed with me, and I felt a huge responsibility.' Aware that his fans had long been calling for a return to his irreverent and crazy comedies of the eighties, he decided to give in to their wishes and dusted off a half-written script about a group of quirky characters travelling on a flight between Madrid and Mexico City. The grotesque characters include a corrupt businessman, a VIP dominatrix, a hired killer, a psychic, a failed actor, an engaged couple and a peculiar trio of cabin crew with a liking for narcotics. 'Many of the plots of my films, or new ideas that break a narrative logjam if that's the case, have occurred to me while travelling by plane, surrounded by strangers,' Almodóvar said, of the inspirational role that these journeys have always played in his films.

'The idea came to me very early on, and I wrote the first half feverishly, as a comic whim,' he recalls. 'What I found difficult was to finish it off so that it wouldn't turn out to be a banal exercise, funny but superfluous. Comedy demands a certain reflection of reality, even if it is hidden among the humour of the situations.' That *reality* of which Almodóvar spoke referred to the protest movement known as 15-M, initiated in May 2011 in Spain by different social organisations that demanded a profound change in a system marked by political corruption and an unsustainable economic situation. *I'm So Excited!* was a response to the need felt by the director to raise his voice in solidarity with the protests in his own way. The passengers represent a microcosm of society, with all of its lies, divisions and moral degradation, with the masses represented in the anaesthetised tourist class, while the middle classes sit in business unable to give up their privileges. In this way, a film initially conceived as a broad comedy becomes, against the odds, a paradigm of social awareness: 'I don't want to say that it is prophetic, but when there are social upheavals – and we are now living through the strongest I can remember since democracy – films can become old or, on the contrary, acquire

ABOVE: With *I'm So Excited!*, Almodóvar returned to the ensemble and crazed comedy of *Women on the Verge of a Nervous Breakdown*.

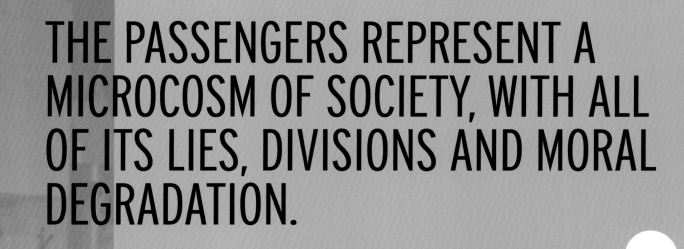

"THE PASSENGERS REPRESENT A MICROCOSM OF SOCIETY, WITH ALL OF ITS LIES, DIVISIONS AND MORAL DEGRADATION."

a dimension in an unconscious way, a meaning that was not in the director's head.'

It is not difficult to draw a clear comparison between a country on the brink of revolution and a faulty aeroplane: both seem doomed to crash due to their own negligence. When a technical problem forces a Peninsula Airbus to circle over Spain awaiting an emergency landing, the passengers and crew believe they are about to die and decide to indulge in their innermost confessions and their most unattainable fantasies. 'During the gestation of the film there was no conscious cinematic reference; in fact, theatre, television, and my own claustrophobia are more present than cinema. To tell the truth, my films owe a lot to theatre, they are full of scenes with two performers, sometimes of undisguised monologues,' admitted Almodóvar, who was especially seduced by the idea of having a group locked up and devoid of any technology, whose only recourse is the words they share with each other. 'They relate to one another, they unburden themselves, lie, assume they have lied, seduce and are seduced, and thus they can fight against fear, loneliness and the idea of death.'

Only an artist of the magnitude and confidence of Almodóvar could enclose some of the most renowned performers of Spanish cinema – none with a leading role in such a choral story – to film in a single and very limited space, during the summer months and with temperatures that, at times, approached fifty degrees due to the heat of the spotlights. There, in complete harmony, we find old acquaintances of the director, such as Javier Cámara, Lola Dueñas, Antonio de la Torre and Cecilia Roth, who received the script shortly before embarking on a theatrical tour of Argentina, which she hastily gave up for the opportunity to work with Almodóvar again, fourteen years after *All About My Mother*. Alongside them are new additions: Hugo Silva, Miguel Ángel Silvestre, Guillermo Toledo, José María Yazpik, José Luis Torrijo, Raúl Arévalo and Carlos Areces, whose instinct for comedy turned his character, Fajas, into someone much more Machiavellian than the script

LEFT: The director, pictured here with Javier Cámara (Joserra) and Carlos Areces (Fajas), faced the logistical challenge of shooting on a set that reproduced the interior of an aeroplane.

suggested, a development that pleased the director enormously. The few scenes that take place outside the aircraft featured brief but stellar appearances by Paz Vega, Carmen Machi and Blanca Suárez, as well as two Almodóvarian icons, Antonio Banderas and Penélope Cruz, together for the first time in one of his films.

With *I'm So Excited!*, Almodóvar decided to shoot the film in Castilla-La Mancha, not because he wanted once again to show the traditions and idiosyncrasies of its inhabitants, but because the local airport, Ciudad Real, was then disused and had all the necessary infrastructure for filming. Inside a huge warehouse, the film crew took thirteen weeks to build a full-scale aircraft, which could be disassembled to facilitate camera movements, with parts acquired on the second-hand market and imported from Germany.

Once the sets were built, the technicians, actors and the director filmed for almost two months in the confined space offered by the cabin, while cinematographer José Luis Alcaine battled to keep the lights out of shot. In order to encourage the cast to bond under the harsh conditions of the production, El Deseo built a colourful little village next door, which they called Little Miami. There, the stars of the film each had a dressing room, a communal rest area with a ping-pong table, and an impressive catering service to help them cope with the long work sessions. 'We were all very

attentive to our colleagues, and in the end, we formed a real group of people supporting each other,' said Lola Dueñas. 'Even if we didn't have to be in the shot, we were always there to give feedback.'

For its international distribution, the film changed its title to *I'm So Excited!* – the Spanish title was a pun on *Passing Lovers* and *Loving Passengers* – in reference to the song by the Pointer Sisters that led to one of the film's funniest scenes, in which the three cabin crew perform a flamboyant dance to the track. In Spain, the film got off to a flying start, with the best opening weekend figures ever for an Almodóvar film: an audience of 250,000 and a gross of €1.86 million. However, mixed reviews caused a fifty-five per cent drop in its second week, leaving the final box office at just over €5 million, far from the numbers achieved by earlier films such as *Volver*, *All About My Mother* or *Talk to Her*. Something similar happened in most foreign markets too, where audience opinions were divided, leading to a commercial performance below expectations, except in France.

JULIETA

JULIETA (2016)

When Almodóvar filmed the scene in *The Skin I Live In* in which Marilia (Marisa Paredes) puts a copy of *Runaway* on her prisoner's breakfast tray, he was already working on the adaptation of three short stories from the book, written by Canadian author and Nobel Prize laureate Alice Munro. Although these stories, entitled 'Chance', 'Soon' and 'Silence', were independent of each other, they had the same protagonist and a series of common themes (love, the passage of time, separation) that, in a way, grouped them together. An accurate portraitist – like Munro herself – of female idiosyncrasy, Almodóvar acquired the rights to the book in 2009 and turned the three narratives into a single story that straddled two eras: 'They were not consecutive, but I wanted to unify them by inventing whatever was necessary.'

It was to be the first film that Almodóvar would write and shoot entirely in English, having previously declined proposals as seductive as *Brokeback Mountain* – turned into a contemporary classic by Ang Lee – or an adaptation of Irène Némirovsky's novel *Suite française*. Feeling an affinity to the American way of life rather than to the Canadian one, he relocated the action of Munro's book from Vancouver to Boston first, and then to New York, delving into a family model unknown to him but very similar in both countries, where parents and children separate at very early ages and the distance between them, in most cases, is not only emotional but also geographical. However, with pre-production already underway and Meryl Streep lined up to play the lead, the director decided to back out and put the project on hold. 'I was defeated by uncertainty. I didn't feel confident about the script or my ability to work in English; I speak it well enough to direct the actors, but I'm referring to the *idea*. I feared having to change language, culture and country. So, I kept the first draft, which I had written in Spanish, without any specific plan for it.'

In 2014, a year after the premiere of *I'm So Excited!*, Almodóvar travelled to the Algarve in Portugal, accompanied by two of his closest collaborators, with the intention of mapping out what his next project would be. They reminded him how much they had liked that initial adaptation of Munro's book and suggested that he move the story to Spain. The director loved the idea and soon had a new version ready, in which the author's original concept was diluted in a typically Spanish and Almodóvarian context: 'I chose to follow my own way and

RIGHT: In *Julieta*, Adriana Ugarte took on a huge dramatic commitment, and put herself completely in Almodóvar's hands to build the character.

forget about Munro. I had to fly with my own wings. It was like the moment when teenagers leave their parents behind and take charge of their own lives.' In the end, Almodóvar had introduced so many changes – especially in the denouement – and had integrated the story into his universe in such a meticulous way, that what began as a free adaptation ended up becoming a tribute where the initial inspiration almost vanished. As in his previous literary translations (*Live Flesh* and *The Skin I Live In*), only the original concept was retained. This time not even the reference remained, since Almodóvar had chosen to use the title of one of the three stories ('Silence') but was forced to change it when he discovered that Martin Scorsese was working on a film with the same name, also scheduled for release in 2016.

Its stark exploration of loneliness and loss and the conflict between mothers and daughters makes *Julieta* the filmmaker's most painful film, and the only one in which he does not resort to humour as a palliative element. Nor is there a mix of genres: everything is pure drama, with Bergman as an invisible guest. 'It's a very different movie from the rest,' he says. 'I imposed sobriety and restraint during each day of the shoot. It was deliberate.' Unlike *Broken Embraces*, in which Lluís Homar played both a young and mature version of

"

ITS STARK EXPLORATION OF LONELINESS AND LOSS AND THE CONFLICT BETWEEN MOTHERS AND DAUGHTERS MAKES *JULIETA* THE FILMMAKER'S MOST PAINFUL FILM.

"

his character, Almodóvar wanted two different actors to represent the different stages of Julieta's life. Emma Suárez would play her in the present, when the character's hidden suffering reappears due to an encounter with an old friend of her daughter's from whom she has been estranged for years. We then meet the Julieta from 1985 (Adriana Ugarte), see her fiery encounter on a train with a fisherman named Xoan (Daniel Grao) and the tragic event that will forever change the lives of Julieta and her little girl, Antía.

XOAN (After seeing a deer through the window of the train's restaurant car): I hope it doesn't come too close to the train. . .
YOUNG JULIETA: It's not afraid of the train. It's looking for a female. It smells her in the air.
XOAN: Would you like a drink?
JULIETA (Narrating the encounter from the present): Xoan told me his name was Xoan, and I told him mine was Julieta. He told me he was married and that Ana, his wife, had been in a coma for five years. I told him that I was teaching Classical Philology, and that I was substituting for a teacher who was ill. Xoan told me that he was a fisherman, that he had three gamelas. He was going to Madrid to buy an engine for one of them. He also told me that all his life he had lived by the sea, in the house his grandfather bought when he came from Cuba.

The actors approached the character of Julieta in completely opposite ways. Emma Suárez personified the Julieta wounded by time and circumstances, someone whose emotional armour was cracking under the weight of guilt. To prepare for the role, the actor immersed herself in the work of authors such as Emmanuel Carrère, Marguerite Duras and Michael Cunningham. She studied the paintings of Gerhard Richter, analysed films by Bergman, Malle and Polanski and studied the behaviour of Almodóvar's female characters, in addition to spending many hours in self-imposed solitude. Ugarte, meanwhile, preferred to approach the naivety of the young Julieta from a blank canvas, allowing herself be guided only by the director's instructions. They did not even meet on the set, as Suárez only began filming her scenes once Ugarte had already completed hers. The only time they worked together, at Almodóvar's request, was to rehearse the way they walked so that each one could assimilate and match the other's step.

The result in both cases was a dazzling and delicate performance, brimming with feeling whilst being subtle and concise. The film's contrasts are exemplified by the cinemaphotography of the French Jean-Claude Larrieu which wonderfully merges the muted tones of the night, rain and death, with garments full of bright colours and a predominance of red, present in practically every shot of the film, to emphasise love and blood. Even the settings chosen by Almodóvar evoke different emotions: the Estudio school in Madrid houses the young and dreamy Julieta who begins her work as a teacher, while the Aragonese Pyrenees symbolise the loneliness and helplessness of her older self. The exuberance of the Andalusian estate where the protagonist's parents live reflects the strength of the

family bond, and the Galician coast accompanies the sense of freedom and well-being that envelopes Julieta and Xoan at the beginning of their relationship. 'The landscapes of the film are characters with a dramatic entity,' acknowledged the director, who also had the opportunity to fulfil his long-held wish to shoot on a train – where several reference works of his cinephile repertoire take place, such as *Strangers on a Train* (Alfred Hitchcock, 1951) or *Human Desire* (Fritz Lang, 1954) – and to vindicate its metaphorical power through elements such as snow, isolation and unbridled passion.

Julieta served to reconcile Almodóvar with the critics after the relative disappointment of *I'm So Excited!*, although viewers, especially in Spain, were more sceptical (in France, the film grossed twice as much as in its country of origin, and the reception in Italy was excellent as well). Beyond its repercussions and the different interpretations, what is certain is that Pedro Almodóvar's twentieth feature film was a decisive turning point in his work, a gateway to a much more introspective and serene phase, populated by characters who resurrect the pending accounts of the past and survive in the face of anguish without the balm of humour.

PAIN
AND
GLORY

BELOW: Antonio Banderas received his first Academy Award nomination for his evocative portrayal of Salvador Mallo.

PAIN AND GLORY
Dolor y gloria (2019)

Pain and Glory begins with a man submerged at the bottom of a swimming pool. Salvador Mallo (Antonio Banderas) remains motionless and thoughtful underwater, while we observe the scar that runs along his back as if it were a war wound. Minutes later, a brilliant succession of drawings created by Juan Gatti introduce us to the multiple ailments that afflict the character, who we soon recognise as a successful film director. Among his afflictions, we see tinnitus – an annoying and persistent noise in the ears – powerful migraines and excruciating lower back pain. All conditions that Pedro Almodóvar also suffered from, with a long confinement after back surgery leading him to fear for his ability to continue directing. His therapy in the face of such tremendous pain and debilitating isolation was to write a film that more than any other was inspired by his own experiences: 'The script would not have been possible without knowing the pain that forced me to stay at home. It was born out of that isolation and physical suffering, especially the headaches and back pain. Because once they open you up you are never the same again. . . I didn't want the film to be a whimper, and that's why I resorted to Juan's drawings, a playful way of giving viewers a lot of information and putting them in a situation in a short time.'

Almodóvar has insisted that it is not an autobiographical story, although he acknowledges that he used himself as a model to create his protagonist and those around him. During this period of personal and professional uncertainty, Mallo reunites with an actor

> **BEYOND ITS CHARACTERS, *PAIN AND GLORY* IS A DELICIOUS COMPENDIUM OF ALMODÓVARIAN ELEMENTS.**

with whom he has had a complicated relationship (Asier Etxeandia), is visited by a former lover (Leonardo Sbaraglia) and receives advice from a compassionate and loyal friend (Nora Navas), all characters based on real figures from the filmmaker's life. And there is, of course, the evocation of the maternal ideal, that cheerful, loving woman, this time played in her youth by Penélope Cruz and in her later years by Julieta Serrano. 'That mother has to do with mine, it's obvious, but on this occasion, I separated myself a little from her by approaching her cinematographically when she gets older. However, there are moments of the character that are taken directly from my own reality, such as when she talks to her son about how he should shroud her when she dies, a moment that comes from the conversations my mother had with my sister on that subject, which they always treated with absolute naturalness.'

Beyond its characters, *Pain and Glory* is a delicious compendium of Almodóvarian elements. Everything, from the filming process seen from the perspective of the creator himself, to the appearance of his own father (representing Mallo's father) in a photomontage with Julieta Serrano, including the mention of Chavela Vargas, the delirious proliferation of taxis or the street where Salvador Mallo lives, all refer to the very intimacy of the director. Production Designer Antxón Gómez oversaw the recreation of the apartment that Almodóvar has in Paseo Rosales in Madrid, down to the very last detail. He built a kitchen almost exactly like the original and adapted the hallway, the lobby and the rest of the spaces to the needs of the production. Even the paintings that Antonio Banderas's character owns – and the odd piece of furniture, such as an armchair or a sideboard – belong to the filmmaker. 'Everything was brought directly from my house, which was very convenient for the production,' he says. 'In fact, I think it was that comfort that made me, for the first time in my career, finish filming ahead of schedule.'

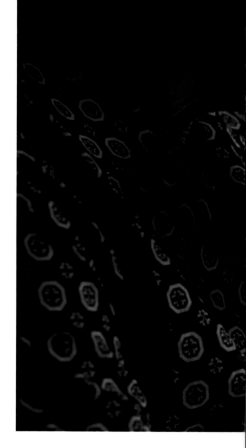

The highest representation of Almodóvar in *Pain and Glory* is found, naturally, in the character of Salvador Mallo. Their hairstyles are almost identical, they are both passionate about tea, and every stitch of the wardrobe worn by Antonio Banderas is an exact replica of the director's own clothes (even the shoes he wears are Almodóvar's own). Despite the personal and artistic relationship that unites them, Banderas was not the first choice for the role. In fact, there was a prolonged casting process with many actors, but none of them convinced the director. In the end, he decided to forget about the search and send the script to Banderas, who accepted the challenge and ended up delivering one of the most brilliant performances of his lengthy career.

'It's the best performance he's ever given in his life,' Almodóvar stated emphatically. 'When we started, Antonio was a passionate animal, who swept everyone away with his mere presence. But now he is different, because he is in maturity and because he has undergone surgery three times [...] The Antonio Banderas of today is in a different position: his gestures are very subtle, small... And with the film finished, it seems entirely right that it was him who took on my role. Because Antonio is the legitimate protagonist, he is Fellini's Mastroianni in *Eight and a Half*, for many reasons: for having lived hand in hand with me in the eighties, for having worked together, for everything we have done.' The director even told him that, in case of doubt or need, he could imitate him without any problem, but Banderas preferred to create his own portrait of the character, from a very personal perspective. His way of approaching this alter ego comes from wisdom and passion.

Banderas's colossal work is evident in Salvador Mallo's journey through the hells of heroin. The actor gives an overwhelming performance as someone who takes refuge in addiction, only to silence the physical pain of his illnesses and the emotional suffering that comes from not being able to direct the films he writes. During a conversation with his faithful assistant Mercedes, we discover that his desire to forget has even led him to neglect his loved ones, and the character reveals himself to the audience as someone deeply disoriented, lost in the melancholy of his past:

MERCEDES: I'm separating from Luis.

SALVADOR (High on heroin): I didn't know you were having problems.

MERCEDES: I didn't want to bother you. It started a long time ago, and now that I have to spend so much time at home. . . I couldn't keep fooling myself.

SALVADOR: I'm sorry.

MERCEDES: So, if you don't mind, I'd like to keep taking care of your mail. People like to get answers.

SALVADOR: But it's always no. . .

MERCEDES: Well, you should do something. You have too much free time to think about your ailments. Give your brain something to entertain itself, Salvador.

SALVADOR: I'd like to do more things too, Mercedes, but. . .

MERCEDES: You could write. You've got a pile of pages full of ideas you could develop. Shall I make you a list?

SALVADOR: No, I don't want to write if I can't shoot it afterwards. And you know better than anyone that I can't face shooting in these conditions. . . Without shooting, my life has no meaning. But that's the way things are.

ABOVE: Nora Navas, Antonio Banderas and Pedro Almodóvar rehearse the scene in which her character Mercedes shares her marital problems with a heroin-fuelled Salvador.

On several occasions, Almodóvar has described the shoot as the most idyllic and happy of his career. The scenes that take place during Mallo's childhood were filmed in the Valencian town of Paterna, in some caves of Moorish origin where, after the Civil War, poor families like his own lived. Most of the scenes were filmed on location, with the interior of one of the caves reproduced in the studio in Madrid. The filmmaker fell in love with this area fifteen years earlier, while he was looking for locations for *Bad Education*, and had always wanted to include them in one of his films because of how much they reminded him of 'the precariousness' with which he grew up in Calzada de Calatrava. Nearby, in Moral de Calatrava, there were houses like those in Paterna, and when at the age of eight he moved with his family to Orellana la Vieja, in Extremadura, he ended up living in a house made of adobe, in a neighbourhood that seemed to him 'out of the Wild West.'

The film had a painless and glory-filled international tour. *Time* magazine chose it as its best movie of 2019, and it was nominated for Best International Feature Film at the Academy Awards, along with a first nomination for the Best Actor Award for Antonio Banderas, though he lost out to Joaquin Phoenix for *Joker* (Todd Phillips, 2019). The reception was so enthusiastic that even Spanish critics, rather circumspect about Almodóvar's most recent works, were ecstatic at such a return to form for the director. *Pain and Glory* emerged as the great winner at the Goya Awards with five wins, including Best Film, Best Director and Best Actor in a Leading Role, and garnered passionate reviews such as that of Luis Martínez in *El Mundo*: 'It reaches a level of perfection that is hard to surpass. The very complicated structure of overlapping times flows without interruption or fissure. Once all the unnecessary elements of folkloric style have been discarded, there remains a sense of purification and clarity very close to the sublime.'

" IT REACHES A LEVEL OF PERFECTION THAT IS HARD TO SURPASS. "

EL MUNDO

PARALLEL
MOTHERS

PARALLEL MOTHERS
Madres paralelas (2021)

I n March 2020, the Covid-19 pandemic brought the world to a complete standstill. On the 13th, the Spanish government, like others around the world, declared a state of emergency, requiring citizens to confine themselves to their homes due to the unstoppable advance of the disease. Almodóvar was alone in his Madrid apartment, finalising the details for *The Human Voice*, the short film he was about to shoot with Tilda Swinton in early April. The sudden confinement, together with the impossibility of interacting face-to-face with anyone, caused the director great uncertainty and he was so discouraged that he stopped writing for nine days. After that time, he began to capture his thoughts in different articles for the press, in which he narrated how he tried – unsuccessfully – to ignore the growing number of deaths by immersing himself in books, in his memories of Chavela and in James Bond movies. 'If I stop in front of reality, I think I will die. And I don't want to,' he said.

As the days went by, Almodóvar adjusted to the situation, but his mind became progressively more agitated out of sheer boredom. His brother, Agustín, had managed to reschedule the shooting of *The Human Voice* and slowly he found the strength again to develop new ideas, and to revisit some incomplete projects forgotten on his computer. One of these was *Parallel Mothers*, which told the story of the complicity between two single women, of different ages, who meet in a hospital shortly before giving birth. Almodóvar had begun working on the script in the early 2000s, and even visited a maternity ward to investigate the pre-birth ritual and the relationships established between pregnant women. However, some narrative obstacles ended up frustrating his creative impulse and forced him to abandon the story for a period. Until, one day during lockdown, he decided to revisit it. 'When I reviewed it, it seemed different,' he explained. 'Because of the opportunity to concentrate, because no one was going to distract me, I was not going anywhere. I corrected half of the script, and, at that moment, the pieces started to fit.'

Almodóvar found the key to unlocking the plot in an issue that had long troubled him: the murders of men and women during the Spanish Civil War, perpetrated primarily by the Francoist side extrajudicially, or after cursory trials. Many of these victims were buried in mass graves and their families never found their bodies. In recent years, different political

LEFT: Janis, a woman of unbreakable will, who is confronted with a hidden past and unplanned motherhood, is one of the artistic highlights of Penélope Cruz's career.

and legal initiatives in Spain, with the 2007 Historical Memory Law most prominent, had sought restorative judicial measures in favour of those who were persecuted during the conflict and the subsequent dictatorship, although the text exempted the government from the responsibility of exhuming the bodies as stipulated by international law. The issue struck a chord with Almodóvar, who, despite having deliberately ignored the nightmare of Franco's regime in his films, felt a special empathy with those people who struggled to find their disappeared ancestors. 'I felt somehow morally obligated to deal with it. Out of sheer empathy for the relatives of the victims, and because I also believe that this subject would end the Spanish war once and for all. It will remain there until those dead are honoured and that debt is settled.'

The key to unlocking the script was drawing a parallel between motherhood and the search for a missing great-grandfather. Janis (Penélope Cruz), a fashion photographer, becomes pregnant after an affair with a married man, Arturo, a forensic archaeologist, and has invited him to her home village to open a mass grave in which she believes her great-grandfather is buried along with other disappeared villagers. Almodóvar was inspired by a case he had read about of a ten-year-old girl, whose house was taken by three Falangists. Shortly after arriving, they took her father, who was a teacher, to dig his own and other Republican comrades' graves. On the third night, he did not return. 'I chose that little girl to have a very clear memory of the moment when she stopped seeing her father, and I put her in Janis as a grandmother.' Up to that point, the filmmaker had only tackled the dictatorship years in the prologue of *Live Flesh*, also featuring Penélope Cruz and imminent childbirth. With *Parallel Mothers*, he would produce what is undoubtedly his most committed film, focusing as it does on the tragic past of his country.

Almodóvar wrote the character with Penélope Cruz in mind, something he had only done three times in his career: with Carmen Maura in *Women on the Verge of a Nervous Breakdown*, with Antonio Banderas in *Tie Me Up! Tie Me Down!* and with Cruz herself in *Volver*. 'I think it's the most difficult role she's ever played in her life,' confessed the director. 'She has grown hugely as an actress, because she suffers every single thing she does, but establishing enough distance to know that, although she is giving all her soul, it is a recreation, a representation.' Almodóvar rehearsed for months with her and with Milena Smit (who plays Ana, a single teenage mother), a young actor from Alicante who, just two years earlier, was alternating jobs as a waitress, sales clerk, babysitter and information assistant in the subway due to the lack of acting opportunities. Her lucky debut as the femme fatale in *Cross the Line* (*No matarás*, David Victori, 2020) opened wide the doors of the Almodóvarian universe and allowed her to take a very different role, that of a teenager paralysed by uncertainty and fear, a very complex challenge to which she rose admirably. The relationship between the two characters – clear models of the independent and tenacious woman that the director likes so much – is marked by an accidental and traumatic event that takes place shortly after giving birth, while both are still in hospital.

ABOVE: Rossy de Palma (Elena), Israel Elejalde (Arturo), Penélope Cruz and Milena Smit (Ana), in one of the most revealing moments of the film.

“

UNDOUBTEDLY HIS MOST COMMITTED FILM, FOCUSING AS IT DOES ON THE TRAGIC PAST OF HIS COUNTRY.

”

SHE HAS GROWN HUGELY AS AN ACTRESS, BECAUSE SHE SUFFERS EVERY SINGLE THING SHE DOES.

ANA: How's your baby?

JANIS: Fine. She's under observation. They only left her with me for a little while. Isn't it wonderful to hear her beating over your heart?

ANA: I can't wait to have her back.

JANIS: Is yours under observation too?

ANA: Yes.

JANIS: Well, that must be normal. . . Mine was born with extrauterine inadaptation, the doctor told me. 'Well, that's a good way to start,' I said. Because that's the life that awaits her, the extrauterine life.

ANA (smiles): Well, yes.

JANIS: But apparently, it's nothing. The poor thing had trouble controlling her breathing outside the womb. What's wrong with yours?

ANA: She seems to have a little low blood sugar. But I've also been told it's nothing.

JANIS: Sure, sure. I'll give you my number if you want to call me.

ANA: OK.

JANIS: Since we're in the same situation, let's talk about it. When do you get the baby?

ANA: Tonight, I think. Or this afternoon.

JANIS: Me too.

RIGHT: If there is one actress who embodies the meaning of motherhood in Almodóvar's work, it is, without a doubt, Penélope Cruz.

When *Parallel Mothers* began filming at the end of March 2021, Spain had recorded more than three million cases of Covid-19 since the beginning of the pandemic, and in Madrid a curfew was still in force every night from 11pm onwards. Making a film in such conditions might have seemed impossible, but the Almodóvar brothers fought fervently to make theirs a reality. They hired nursing staff, conducted thousands of medical tests, and ensured that every member of cast and crew complied with Covid safety restrictions both on and off set.

Production was concentrated in Madrid and its near surroundings, mainly in the town of Torrelaguna, where Janis's emotional journey ends. Two months after the first take, the film completed its principal photography without major complications, in a remarkable display of control and foresight on the part of the professionals at El Deseo. Once the health threat was under control, Almodóvar strove to extract from his story the artistic excellence that characterises his work: exquisite performances (we must not forget the work of Aitana Sánchez-Gijón and Israel Elejalde), warmth and formal splendour, and a beautifully poetic reference to Federico García Lorca and the unhealed wounds of Spain's fascist past.

The post-production process was one of the fastest in the director's filmography. With its premiere set for early October, *Parallel Mothers* arrived in time to be screened at the Mostra di Venezia with overwhelming success, winning a well-deserved Volpi Cup for Best Actress for Penélope Cruz. The film also received several nominations at the Golden Globe, BAFTA and European Film awards, garnering some of the most glowing reviews of Almodóvar's career and topping the French box office in its first weekend, the director's best result in the country since *Volver*. Nor did the Oscars forget the film, awarding it nominations for Best Original Score – Alberto Iglesias here completes a prodigious composition, always linked to the inner world of the protagonist – and for Best Actress, the fourth for Cruz in her career.

EPILOGUE

EPILOGUE
An Artist for the World

We have already seen how, for decades, Pedro Almodóvar was able to resist the temptation of Anglo-Saxon cinema and the big Hollywood stars. Although he was widely recognised by the industry and received a multitude of stimulating proposals, he always remained faithful to the Spanish idiosyncrasy of his stories. However, after *Pain and Glory*, something changed. In a way, that exercise of personal and professional atonement represented the culmination of a dazzling introspective peri-od, a settling of accounts where the roots and traces of the past formed an indissoluble part of the characters' souls. After that film, Almodóvar felt ready to explore the unknown and adapt his artistic personality to the universal language of cinema. He had been hesitating for some time about whether or not to take the plunge into shooting in English, with an international cast and a much deeper thematic and geographic scope. 'I wanted to experience how I moved within the language, how I saw myself directing in En-glish,' he said, 'although I preferred to do it as a short, because in a long film I didn't dare.' The decision was made: Almodóvar would shoot for the first time in a foreign language, and he would do it through an old acquaintance – the short film – as a dress rehearsal to tackle a longer story in the future. In the end, due to the pandemic (or thanks to it), he still had time to approach for one last time the history and context of his country with the wonderful and overwhelming *Parallel Mothers*.

RIGHT: In *The Human Voice*, Tilda Swinton became the first actress with whom Almodóvar filmed entirely in English.

"I WANTED TO EXPERIENCE HOW I MOVED WITHIN THE LANGUAGE, HOW I SAW MYSELF DIRECTING IN ENGLISH."

The chosen text was also particularly familiar to him. It is worth remembering that *The Human Voice*, the 1930 monologue by Jean Cocteau, written for the greater glory of Edith Piaf, was one of Almodóvar's favourite pieces and an essential reference point in his films, present in titles such as *Law of Desire*, *The Flower of My Secret* and, above all, *Women on the Verge of a Nervous Breakdown*. Faced with the experience of working in English, the director needed a terrain on which to move with total confidence, and this story about a woman abandoned by her lover, which he had so often analysed and reinterpreted, was perfect for it. 'It proposes a female character in a situation that I like very much or, at least, in which I manage very well as a writer. The grieving woman is a subject that I find very inspiring,' he acknowledged. 'However, when faced with the original text, I realised that I did not identify with that woman. With the pain, yes, but not with that part of submission. I made her more mine, more contemporary, more in control of herself.' To play her, Almodóvar turned to Tilda Swinton, one of the most fascinating actors of recent times, Oscar winner for *Michael Clayton* (Tony Gilroy, 2007) and muse of such sublime filmmakers as Jim Jarmusch, Wes Anderson and the Coen brothers.

The Human Voice condenses in twenty-eight minutes the entire essence of its director's tragic tale: a woman who is a victim of despair, self-imposed solitude as a way of escape, baroque colours, homicidal impulse, sudden rebellion against the harmful man. Swinton amazingly composes a character on the edge of her own destruction, wounded and mis-guided, who finds the only way to freedom is through revenge. Almodóvar also surrounds

THIS IS A QUEER WESTERN, IN THE SENSE THAT THERE ARE TWO MEN, AND THEY LOVE EACH OTHER.

LEFT: Almodóvar was able to subvert the rules of the western – a genre that always appealed to him as a viewer – in his masterful short film *Strange Way of Life*.

himself with his trusted artistic circle (José Luis Alcaine in photography, Teresa Font in editing, Alberto Iglesias in composition) and offers one of his most vigorous and melodramatic works, where even the sobriety of this new language is imbued with unbridled passion, with that suggested and invisible blood, and even with a purifying fire.

Filming took place over twelve days in July 2020, amid strict security measures due to the Covid-19 pandemic. A little over a month later, on 3 September, *The Human Voice* was screened at the Mostra di Venezia to the delight of a devoted public, despite the restrictions and extreme control of seating capacity. Precisely in this very Kafkaesque context for theatres, Almodóvar was able to release the film at the end of October of that cursed year. While the big studios were cancelling one after another their main bets for the big screen, he achieved the unusual feat of programming a short film in more than a hundred Spanish cinemas and made it the highest grossing in the history of the country.

In early 2022, three months after the premiere of *Parallel Mothers*, the long-awaited announcement arrived: Almodóvar would shoot his first film in English, adapting five of the forty-three stories that make up *A Manual for Cleaning Women*, a sensational anthology in which writer Lucia Berlin turned her own experiences – full of humour and emotion – into a survival notebook for women from around the world. Leading the cast, and as producer, would be two-time Oscar winner Cate Blanchett. 'I'm so excited that we finally get to make it,' the Australian actor declared shortly after the news broke. 'No one can create roles as moving as Pedro. . . Women talking to women about surreal things that on the surface are bizarre, but at the same time are very realistic.' However, nine months later Almodóvar unexpectedly announced his departure from the project: 'It has been a very painful decision for me. I have dreamed of working with Cate for a long time. But unfortunately, I no longer feel capable of making this film in its entirety.'

Among the reasons that led to his withdrawal, the director acknowledged that he did not feel physically prepared for a shoot that would take place in several countries, and also that he was going to need a time for rehearsals that a cast of this calibre, so much in demand with different projects around the world, could not guarantee. 'The problem would be me with my back and so many locations. And I would also have problems with the actors, who were all stars. There were a lot of new things: everything was period, and everything was on a set, and everything was made in a factory. I'm very obsessive about that. . . Everything that appears in my films has passed through my hands and has been selected from a lot of options,' he confessed months after the cancellation of the film, which he had intended to shoot mainly in Alicante's Ciudad de la Luz. 'It was scheduled to start in January 2022, but Cate told me that I had to wait because she had projects throughout the year. So I sat on my hands and had a whole year to think about it.'

The disappointment of his failed project with Cate Blanchett did not prevent Almodóvar from continuing with the plan initiated with *The Human Voice*. In fact, the filmmaker's next step in this process of idiomatic and narrative adaptation was going to be a challenge of imposing proportions: nothing less than a western, undoubtedly the quintessential North American genre and a cinematographic model in complete opposition to his films, always so intimate and geographically defined. Almodóvar wrote the script for *Strange Way of Life* during lockdown, just after completing that of *Parallel Mothers*, and conceived the story as a medium-length film that would completely reverse the idea of masculinity in western films, always linked to a heterosexual and conservative context. 'My cowboys say things that have never been heard in this genre. . . This is a queer western, in the sense that there are two men, and they love each other, but they live that situation in opposite ways,' the director pointed out, in reference to the protagonists, two former hired gunslingers who meet again twenty-five years after seeing each other for the last time. One works as a rancher and the other as a sheriff in the town of Bitter Creek. However, beneath this old friendship hides a feeling that time has not been able to attenuate, and that will once again come between the two characters and their respective passions.

Strange Way of Life owes its title to the famous fado by singer Amália Rodrigues, whose lyrics suggest that there is no stranger existence than that which is lived with one's back to one's own desire (the song can be heard at the beginning of the film in a version by Caetano Veloso). Almodóvar completed filming in August 2022 in the desert of Tabernas, in Almería – specifically in the cowboy village built by Sergio Leone in the 1960s to shoot his legendary *Dollars Trilogy* with Clint Eastwood, and which Almodóvar found 'full of rust and dust that had eaten the sets but made them look less artificial' – with a cast headed by the undisputed icon of indie cinema Ethan Hawke and Pedro Pascal, star of TV series *Narcos*, *The Mandalorian* and

HIS STORIES ARE UNIVERSAL BECAUSE THEY SPEAK OF EMOTIONS, OF PEOPLE WHO SUFFER AND LOVE.

The Last of Us. Despite the peculiarity of the genre, the filmmaker was able to convey not only the plot premise but also the aesthetic line of his films, and decided to call on Anthony Vaccarello, creative director of Saint Laurent, for the costume design and the accessories that appear on the screen.

Strange Way of Life, like *The Human Voice* before it, was the necessary preparation to the inevitable. In the early months of 2024, Almodóvar began filming his first English-language feature, *The Room Next Door*, between New York and Madrid and starring Tilda Swinton and Julianne Moore. The plot revolves around the relationship between a war reporter and an autofiction novelist, and the progressive emotional bond they establish as writers. A situation that the author himself defines as "extreme and strangely sweet", and which stands as the central axis of a film that also speaks about "the limitless cruelty of wars, death, friendship and sexual pleasure as the best allies in the fight against horror". *The Room Next Door* is the definitive demonstration that Pedro Almodóvar's art is not limited to a specific area and audience but can be experienced from multiple perspectives.

Almodóvar's stories do not belong to anyone. They move without distinction. They do not understand ideologies, gender, race or borders. They are not even his own, because, once shared, they accompany us forever.

They belong to the world.

BELOW: The director poses with one of his cowboys, Pedro Pascal (Silva).

ABOVE: Cecilia Roth's natural magnetism and beauty made her the perfect choice for the lead role in *Labyrinth of Passion*.

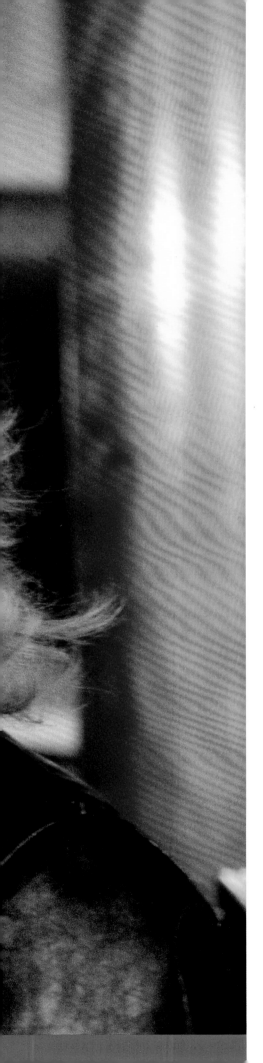

AFTERWORD

When I think about how I met Pedro, memories come flooding back. Actually, I have several perspectives regarding that meeting.

The first has to do with some friends in common, starting with Gustavo Pérez de Ayala. I was eighteen or nineteen, and one fine day Gustavo told me that, every Friday, a friend of his organised a meal at a trendy restaurant in Madrid. I was invited to one and there I was introduced to Pedro, who seemed as lost as me. I was immediately attracted by his humour, his grace, and his very relaxed attitude. It was not something that was common in Spain at that time.

The second memory takes me to the San Sebastián Festival in 1977. Although I was still very young, that year there were two of my films in the official section: *De fresa, limón y menta*, directed by Miguel Ángel Díez, and another Argentinian film entitled *No toquen a la nena*, by Juan José Jusid. At that time, all the films were screened at the Maria Cristina, next to the Reina Victoria, the hotel where we stayed. On the same street, on the corner, there was a tapas bar where absolutely everyone went. That was where they did the interviews, always with lots of curious people around. Among all of them, my attention was always drawn to Pedro, who was extremely enthusiastic about film and never missed a single edition of the festival.

And there is still a third way to explain how we met. Shortly after arriving in Spain, I got close to a group of people in an almost natural way, for purely temporal and geographical reasons. I mean people like Iván Zulueta, Eusebio Poncela, Will More, Marta Fernández-Muro, Laura García Lorca. . . And Pedro, of course. I was the youngest, and for me they were my teachers of cinema, literature and life.

Pepi, Luci, Bom was like a game for me. The camera was Pedro's, and Pepón Coromina, I think his first producer, believed in his talent. The script was marvellous, very daring for that time in Spain. Finding something like this was totally unusual. . . There was an advertisement for 'Bragas Ponte,' which served all kinds of feminine needs. Over time, that phrase has become a kind of advice to never forget what is essential. *'Hagas lo que hagas, Ponte bragas'* ('Whatever you do, put on panties').

I was very amused by everything Pedro invented about my participation in the film. I had a lot of fun. We shot on weekends because Pedro was loyal to Telefónica during the week. I think that, for that reason, I was never too conscious of making a film. For me it was like filming a piece of life, like when your parents film you blowing out your birthday candles. And in relation to Pedro, I knew I would do anything he could ask of me. He trusted me more than I trusted myself.

Labyrinth of Passion was another movie so irreverent that I find it hard to believe it could be filmed in present-day Spain. I doubt very much that his way of making humour, of interpreting reality, could be understood today as irony. Pedro was ahead of his time, for what he told, for the characters he invented (which we eventually saw in real life. . . ahead of time), and because of him I had a great time filming again. However, now I was aware of being inside a movie. When I saw it again after almost thirty years, I discovered extraordinary and unthinkable characters for the time, such as the psychologist or the doctor played by Fernando Vivanco. That is something that Pedro has always had: he can see something possible in the smoke, for in his head there is no situation that cannot happen. The coincidences in his films are so plausible that although in real life they would be improbable, in his films they take on the certainty that needs a truth to settle in, and you believe that the son of the Emperor of Tiran lives in Madrid (which is the most modern city in the world) during his exile, and that there he meets exactly who he needs to meet.

Then came small appearances in *Dark Habits* and *What Have I Done to Deserve This?*, until in 1986 I returned to Buenos Aires. I planned to stay only twenty days (I had to return to Spain to shoot *Lulú de noche* with Emilio Martínez-Lázaro), but I decided to stay indefinitely because I felt that, at that moment, that was my place.

During all the time I spent in Argentina, I distanced myself from Spanish cinema. Despite this, I never stopped thinking about working with Pedro again. I went to Madrid two or three times a year to see my friends, and even shot a series or a film from time to time. Until *Martín* (*Hache*) arrived, and I imagine that Pedro wanted us to shoot together again. We were very close when the film was released. In fact, I remember perfectly when we were doing our make-up together with Bibi in a room at the Palace Hotel. That night I won the Goya and a new panorama opened up for me in Spanish cinema. Months later, it was summer in Argentina and the phone started ringing. It was the unmistakable voice of Pedro, who told me that he was preparing a film about women, and that he wanted me to play the main character. I remember hanging up and in seconds going through all kinds of emotions possible in such a short time: I was laughing, jumping, screaming, crying. . . I was in a state of adrenalin-fuelled excitement. I would never have imagined that he would call me right then and there, that he would call me for a film like *All About My Mother*, and that he would then go through everything we went through with it. When he sent me the script, I connected at once and understood Manuela, her journey, that wonderful empathy between female characters. The help that these women give each other is so moving, so brutal, that it alleviates what is impossible to alleviate, which is the death of a child. Pedro manages to keep the character in a very particular state, flooded with all the love she has been able to receive. Instead of becoming resentful, Manuela understands that life is suffering, also love and stumbles, but never evil. The possibility of a generous life, despite the pain of losing her son, still seems to me something very complex from a rational point of view.

After Manuela came other characters of Pedro's that I adore, like the ones he entrusted to me in films such as *I'm So Excited!* and *Pain and Glory*, although neither he nor I are the same as we were in those early years. Everything we did then was full of joy and future, and the idea that it might end at some point never crossed our minds. However, the things that happen to us now are different, and I think that Pedro has had the enormous courage to always shoot what he needs to tell at that moment. . . And not only in that: he has also been brave, as always, making decisions within each of his films.

I feel very close to his sensitivity, and I know that we can share similar views on many things. I still have a deep feeling of enormous affection for and curiosity about him, and I consider him to have been one of the people who have most influenced me in many aspects of my life. Because there are people who, for some reason, can touch deep fibres of your biology, of your organism.

Pedro Almodóvar is one of them.

Cecilia Roth

TOP: Almodóvar, during the filming of *Julieta*.

ABOVE: The filmmaker with Cecilia Roth and Rosa Maria Sardà on the set of *All About My Mother*.

RIGHT: Reunited on *I'm So Excited!* fourteen years after the film that led them to Oscar glory.

FILMOGRAPHY

FEATURE FILMS

PEPI, LUCI, BOM AND OTHER GIRLS LIKE MOM
(Pepi, Luci, Bom y otras chicas del montón)
(Fígaro Films)
80 minutes
Writer: Pedro Almodóvar
Director of Photography: Paco Femenía
Cast: Carmen Maura (Pepi), Félix Rotaeta (The Policeman), Alaska (Bom), Eva Siva (Luci).
Release Date: 27 October 1980

LABYRINTH OF PASSION
(Laberinto de pasiones)
(Musidora / Alphaville)
100 minutes
Writer: Pedro Almodóvar
Director of Photography: Ángel Luis Fernández
Cast: Cecilia Roth (Sexilia), Imanol Arias (Riza Niro), Helga Liné (Toraya), Marta Fernández-Muro (Queti), Fernando Vivanco (Doctor), Antonio Banderas (Sadec).
Release Date: 7 September 1982

DARK HABITS
(Entre tinieblas)
(Tesauro)
110 minutes
Writer: Pedro Almodóvar
Director of Photography: Ángel Luis Fernández
Cast: Cristina S. Pascual (Yolanda Bel), Julieta Serrano (Mother Superior), Marisa Paredes (Sister Manure), Mari Carrillo (Marchioness), Lina Canalejas (Sister Snake), Manuel Zarzo (Chaplain), Carmen Maura (Sister Damned), Chus Lampreave (Sister Rat).
Release Date: 3 October 1983

WHAT HAVE I DONE TO DESERVE THIS?
(¿Qué he hecho yo para merecer esto!!)
(Tesauro / Kaktus Producciones Cinematográficas)
100 minutes
Writer: Pedro Almodóvar
Director of Photography: Ángel Luis Fernández
Cast: Carmen Maura (Gloria), Luis Hostalot (Polo), Gonzalo Suárez (Lucas Villalba), Ángel de Andrés López (Antonio), Verónica Forqué (Crystal), Kiti Manver (Juani), Chus Lampreave (Grandmother), Juan Martínez (Toni), Emilio Gutiérrez Caba (Pedro), Amparo Soler Leal (Patricia).
Release Date: 25 October 1984

MATADOR
(Compañía Iberoamericana de TV / Televisión Española)
110 minutes
Writer: Pedro Almodóvar
Director of Photography: Ángel Luis Fernández
Cast: Assumpta Serna (María Cardenal), Nacho Martínez (Diego), Antonio Banderas (Ángel), Eva Cobo (Eva), Julieta Serrano (Berta), Chus Lampreave (Pilar), Carmen Maura (Julia), Eusebio Poncela (Superintendent Del Valle).
Release Date: 7 March 1986

THE LAW OF DESIRE
(La ley del deseo)
(El Deseo / Lauren Films)
102 minutes
Writer: Pedro Almodóvar
Director of Photography: Ángel Luis Fernández
Cast: Eusebio Poncela (Pablo Quintero), Carmen Maura (Tina Quintero), Antonio Banderas (Antonio Benítez), Miguel Molina (Juan Bermúdez), Fernando Guillén (Police Inspector), Manuela Velasco (Ada).
Release Date: 7 February 1987

WOMEN ON THE VERGE OF A NERVOUS BREAKDOWN
(Mujeres al borde de un ataque de nervios)
(El Deseo / Lauren Films)
88 minutes
Writer: Pedro Almodóvar
Director of Photography: José Luis Alcaine
Cast: Carmen Maura (Pepa), Antonio Banderas (Carlos), Julieta Serrano (Lucía), María Barranco (Candela), Rossy de Palma (Marisa), Guillermo Montesinos (Taxi Driver), Kiti Manver (Paulina Morales), Chus Lampreave (The Concierge), Loles León (Cristina), Fernando Guillén (Iván).
Release Date: 23 March 1988

TIE ME UP! TIE ME DOWN!
(¡Átame!)
(El Deseo)
111 minutes
Writer: Pedro Almodóvar
Director of Photography: José Luis Alcaine
Cast: Victoria Abril (Marina Osorio), Antonio Banderas (Ricki), Loles León (Lola), Julieta Serrano (Alma), María Barranco (Doctor), Francisco Rabal (Máximo Espejo), Rossy de Palma (Woman on Vespa).
Release Date: 22 January 1990

HIGH HEELS
(Tacones lejanos)
(El Deseo / TF1)
113 minutes
Writer: Pedro Almodóvar
Director of Photography: Alfredo Mayo
Cast: Victoria Abril (Rebeca), Marisa Paredes (Becky del Páramo), Miguel Bosé (Judge Domínguez), Ana Lizarán (Margarita), Cristina Marcos (Paula), Féodor Atkine (Manuel).
Release Date: 23 October 1991

KIKA
(El Deseo / TF1)
114 minutes
Writer: Pedro Almodóvar
Director of Photography: Alfredo Mayo
Cast: Verónica Forqué (Kika), Peter Coyote (Nicholas Pierce), Victoria Abril (Andrea Caracortada), Álex Casanovas (Ramón), Rossy de Palma (Juana), Santiago Lajusticia (Paul Bazzo), Anabel Alonso (Amparo), Bibiana Fernández (Susana).
Release Date: 25 October 1993

THE FLOWER OF MY SECRET
(La flor de mi secreto)
(El Deseo / TF1)
103 minutes
Writer: Pedro Almodóvar
Director of Photography: Affonso Beato
Cast: Marisa Paredes (Leo Macías), Juan Echanove (Ángel), Carmen Elías (Betty), Rossy de Palma (Rosa), Chus Lampreave (Mother), Imanol Arias (Paco), Joaquín Cortés (Antonio), Manuela Vargas (Blanca).
Release Date: 20 September 1995

LIVE FLESH
(Carne trémula)
(El Deseo / France 3 Cinéma)
100 minutes
Writers: Pedro Almodóvar, Jorge Guerricaechevarría and Ray Loriga, based on the novel by Ruth Rendell
Director of Photography: Affonso Beato
Cast: Javier Bardem (David), Francesca Neri (Elena), Liberto Rabal (Víctor), Ángela Molina (Clara), José Sancho (Sancho), Penélope Cruz (Isabel), Pilar Bardem (Miss Centro de Mesa).
Release Date: 9 October 1997

ALL ABOUT MY MOTHER
(Todo sobre mi madre)
(El Deseo / Renn Productions / France 2 Cinéma)
101 minutes
Writer: Pedro Almodóvar
Director of Photography: Affonso Beato
Cast: Cecilia Roth (Manuela), Marisa Paredes (Huma Rojo), Antonia San Juan (Agrado), Penélope Cruz (Rosa), Candela Peña (Nina), Rosa María Sardà (Rosa's Mother), Fernando Fernán Gómez (Rosa's Father), Toni Cantó (Lola), Eloy Azorín (Esteban).
Release Date: 16 April 1999

TALK TO HER
(Hable con ella)
(El Deseo)
109 minutes
Writer: Pedro Almodóvar
Director of Photography: Javier Aguirresarobe
Cast: Javier Cámara (Benigno Martín), Darío Grandinetti (Marco Zuluaga), Leonor Watling (Alicia), Rosario Flores (Lydia González), Mariola Fuentes (Rosa), Geraldine Chaplin (Katerina Bilova), Paz Vega (Amparo), Fele Martínez (Alfredo).
Release Date: 15 March 2002

BAD EDUCATION
(La mala educación)
(El Deseo)
109 minutes
Writer: Pedro Almodóvar
Director of Photography: José Luis Alcaine
Cast: Gael García Bernal (Ángel / Juan / Zahara), Fele Martínez (Enrique Goded), Daniel Giménez Cacho (Father Manuel), Lluís Homar (Manuel Berenguer), Javier Cámara (Paquito), Francisco Maestre (Father José), Francisco Boira (Ignacio).
Release Date: 19 March 2004

VOLVER
(El Deseo)
110 minutes
Writer: Pedro Almodóvar
Director of Photography: José Luis Alcaine
Cast: Penélope Cruz (Raimunda), Carmen Maura (Irene), Lola Dueñas (Sole), Blanca Portillo (Agustina), Yohana Cobo (Paula), Chus Lampreave (Aunt Paula), Antonio de la Torre (Paco).
Release Date: 16 March 2006

BROKEN EMBRACES
(Los abrazos rotos)
(El Deseo)
125 minutes
Writer: Pedro Almodóvar
Director of Photography: Rodrigo Prieto

Cast: Penélope Cruz (Lena), Lluís Homar (Mateo Blanco / Harry Caine), Blanca Portillo (Judit García), José Luis Gómez (Ernesto Martel), Rubén Ochandiano (Ernesto Martel Jr. / Ray X), Tamar Novas (Diego), Ángela Molina (Lena's Mother).
Release Date: 18 March 2009

THE SKIN I LIVE IN
(La piel que habito)
(El Deseo)
118 minutes
Writer: Pedro Almodóvar, based on the novel *Tarantula* by Thierry Jonquet
Director of Photography: José Luis Alcaine
Cast: Antonio Banderas (Dr. Robert Ledgard), Elena Anaya (Vera), Marisa Paredes (Marilia), Jan Cornet (Vicente), Roberto Álamo (Zeca), Eduard Fernández (Fulgencio), Blanca Suárez (Norma), Bárbara Lennie (Cristina).
Release Date: 2 September 2011

I'M SO EXCITED!
(Los amantes pasajeros)
(El Deseo)
90 minutes
Writer: Pedro Almodóvar
Director of Photography: José Luis Alcaine
Cast: Antonio de la Torre (Álex Acero), Hugo Silva (Benito Morón), Javier Cámara (Joserra), Carlos Areces (Fajas), Raúl Arévalo (Ulloa), José María Yazpik (Infante), Cecilia Roth (Norma Boss), Lola Dueñas (Bruna), Guillermo Toledo (Ricardo Galán), José Luis Torrijo (Sr. Más), Miguel Ángel Silvestre (Groom), Laya Martí (Bride), Paz Vega (Alba), Blanca Suárez (Ruth), Antonio Banderas (León), Penélope Cruz (Jessica).
Release Date: 8 March 2013

JULIETA
(El Deseo)
96 minutes
Writer: Pedro Almodóvar, based on the short stories "Chance", "Soon" and "Silence" by Alice Munro
Director of Photography: Jean-Claude Larrieu
Cast: Emma Suárez (Julieta), Adriana Ugarte (Young Julieta), Daniel Grao (Xoan), Inma Cuesta (Ava), Darío Grandinetti (Lorenzo), Michelle Jenner (Beatriz), Pilar Castro (Claudia), Nathalie Poza (Juana), Susi Sánchez (Sara).
Release Date: 8 April 2016

PAIN AND GLORY
(Dolor y gloria)
(El Deseo)
113 minutes
Writer: Pedro Almodóvar
Director of Photography: José Luis Alcaine
Cast: Antonio Banderas (Salvador Mallo), Asier Etxeandia (Alberto Crespo), Leonardo Sbaraglia (Federico Delgado), Nora Navas (Mercedes), Julieta Serrano (Jacinta), Penélope Cruz (Young Jacinta), César Vicente (Eduardo), Asier Flores (Young Salvador), Cecilia Roth (Zulema), Raúl Arévalo (Venancio Mallo).
Release Date: 22 March 2019

PARALLEL MOTHERS
(Madres paralelas)
(El Deseo)
123 minutes
Writer: Pedro Almodóvar
Director of Photography: José Luis Alcaine
Cast: Penélope Cruz (Janis), Milena Smit (Ana), Israel Elejalde (Arturo), Aitana Sánchez-Gijón (Teresa), Rossy de Palma (Elena), Julieta Serrano (Brígida).
Release Date: 8 October 2021

AMATEUR & SHORT FILMS

Film político
4 minutes
Writer: Pedro Almodóvar
1974

Dos putas, o historia de amor que termina en boda
10 minutes
Writer: Pedro Almodóvar
1974

Blancor
5 minutes
Writer: Pedro Almodóvar
1975

La caída de Sodoma
10 minutes
Writer: Pedro Almodóvar
1975

Homenaje
10 minutes
Writer: Pedro Almodóvar
1975

El sueño, o la estrella
12 minutes

Writer: Pedro Almodóvar
1975

Muerte en la carretera
(Ajax Films)
8 minutes
Writer: Pedro Almodóvar
Director of Photography: Roberto Gómez
Cast: Paloma Hurtado, Juan Lombardero, Pepe Maya, Miguel Ángel Requejo.
1976

Sea caritativo
5 minutes
Writer: Pedro Almodóvar
1976

Tráiler de Who's Afraid of Virginia Woolf?
5 minutes
Writer: Pedro Almodóvar
1976

Sexo va, sexo viene
17 minutes
Writer: Pedro Almodóvar
1977

Las tres ventajas de Ponte
5 minutes
Writer: Pedro Almodóvar
1977

Complementos
10 minutes
Writer: Pedro Almodóvar
1977

Salomé
(Manuela Films)
12 minutes
Writer: Pedro Almodóvar, based on the play by Oscar Wilde
Director of Photography: Luciano Berriatúa
Cast: Isabel Mestres (Salomé), Fernando Hilbeck (Abraham), Agustín Almodóvar (Isaac), Juan Lombardero (Voice of God).
1978

Folle… Folle… Fólleme Tim!
90 minutes
Writer: Pedro Almodóvar
Cast: Eva Siva, Carmen Maura, Kiti Mánver, Pedro Almodóvar.
1978

Tráiler para amantes de lo prohibido
(RTVE)
17 minutes

Writer: Pedro Almodóvar
Cast: Josele Román (Wife), Bibiana Fernández (Lili Put), Sonia Hoffman (Daughter), Pau Poch (Husband).
1985

Pastas Ardilla
1 minute
Writer: Pedro Almodóvar
Cast: Rossy de Palma, Chus Lampreave.
1996

THE CANNIBALISTIC COUNCILLOR
(La concejala antropófaga)
(El Deseo)
8 minutes
Writer: Pedro Almodóvar (as Harry "Huracán" Caine)
Director of Photography: Joaquín Manchado
Cast: Carmen Machi (Chon), Penélope Cruz (Pina), Marta Aledo (Maribel).
2009

THE HUMAN VOICE
(La voz humana)
(El Deseo)
28 minutes
Writer: Pedro Almodóvar, based on the play *La voix humaine*, by Jean Cocteau
Director of Photography: José Luis Alcaine
Cast: Tilda Swinton, Agustín Almodóvar, Miguel Almodóvar, Pablo Almodóvar.
2020

STRANGE WAY OF LIFE
(Extraña forma de vida)
31 minutes
Writer: Pedro Almodóvar
Director of Photography: José Luis Alcaine
Cast: Pedro Pascal (Silva), Ethan Hawke (Jake), Manu Ríos (Singer), Jason Fernández (Young Jake), Pedro Casablanc (Carpenter), Sara Sálamo (Conchita), José Condessa (Young Silva).
2023

MUSIC DEPARTMENT

Labyrinth of Passion (Writer / Performer)
'Suck It to Me', 'Gran Ganga'

Dark Habits (Writer / Performer)
'Suck It to Me'

The Law of Desire (Writer / Performer)
'Voy a ser mama', 'Susan Get Down', 'Satanasa'

Tie Me Up! Tie Me Down! (Writer /

Performer)
'Satanasa'

High Heels (Lyrics)
'Un año de amor'

The L Word (TV Series)
(Anonymous Content / Dufferin Gate
Productions / Showtime Networks /
Viacom Production)
Episode *L'Ennui* (Lyrics)
'Un año de amor'
2004

Bad Education (Soundtrack)
'Torna a Surriento'

El Calentito
(Vértice 360 / Estudios Picasso / Canal+
España)
90 minutes
Director: Chus Gutiérrez
Writers: Chus Gutiérrez, Juan Carlos
Rubio
Director of Photography: Kiko de la Rica
Songs: 'Suck It to Me' (Perfomer /
Writer)
Cast: Verónica Sánchez, Macarena
Gómez, Juan Sanz.
2005

Cuéntame cómo pasó (TV Series)
(Grupo Ganga Producciones / TVE)
Episode *La movida y mucho más*
(Performer / Writer)
'Suck It to Me'
2013

El Ministerio del Tiempo (TV Series)
(Cliffhanger / Netflix / Onza Partners)
Episode *El laberinto del tiempo*
(Performer / Writer)
'Suck It to Me'
2020

ACTOR

Film político (Self)

A Man Called Autumn Flower
(Un hombre llamado Flor de Otoño)
(José Frade Producciones
Cinematográficas / Panorámica)
100 minutes
Director: Pedro Olea
Writers: Pedro Olea, Rafael Azcona
Director of Photography: Fernando
Arribas
Cast: José Sacristán, Francisco Algora,
Carmen Carbonell, Roberto Camardiel,
Carlos Piñeiro, Pedro Almodóvar (Lola
Nicaragua).
1978

Times of the Constitution
(Tiempos de Constitución)
(Rafael Gordon Producciones)
101 minutes
Director: Rafael Gordon
Writer: Rafael Gordon
Director of Photography: Miguel Ángel
Martín Sánchez
Cast: Francisco Algora, Verónica
Forqué, Héctor Alterio, José Bódalo,
Kiti Mánver, Alfonso del Real, Pedro
Almodóvar.
1978

What's a Girl Like You Doing in a Place
Like This?
(¿Qué hace una chica como tú en un
sitio como este?)
(La Salamandra Producciones
Cinematográficas)
85 minutes
Director: Fernando Colomo
Writers: Fernando Colomo, Jaime
Chávarri
Director of Photography: Javier
Aguirresarobe

Cast: Carmen Maura, Félix Rotaeta,
Héctor Alterio, José Lage, Pedro
Beltrán, Tony Canal, Marta Fernández
Muro, Mercedes Sampietro, Pedro
Almodóvar (Spectator).
1978

Folle… Folle… Fólleme Tim! (Man)

Rapture
(Arrebato)
(Nicolás Astiarraga P.C.)
Director: Iván Zulueta
Writer: Iván Zulueta
Director of Photography: Ángel Luis
Fernández
Cast: Eusebio Poncela, Cecilia Roth,
Will More, Marta Fernández Muro,
Helena Fernán-Gómez, Carmen Giralt,
Pedro Almodóvar (Gloria's Voice).
1979

Pepi, Luci, Bom & Other Girls Like Mom
(Master of Ceremonies)

Labyrinth of Passion (Singer and Photo
Novel Director)

Dark Habits (Bus Passenger)

What Have I Done to Deserve This?
(Singer)

La bola de cristal (TV Series)
(TVE)
Season 1 – Episode 10 (Self)
1984

Matador (Francisco Montesinos)

The Law of Desire (Hardware Store
Clerk / Journalist's Voice)

Delirios de amor (TV Series)
(TVE)

Episode *El eterno adolescente*
1989

La mujer de tu vida (TV Series)
(Fernando Trueba PC / TVE)
Episode *La mujer feliz* (Self)
1990

Bad Education (Swimming Pool
Cleaner)

Vanity Fair: Killers Kill, Dead Men Die
(Vanity Fair)
6 minutes
Director: Annie Leibovitz
Director of Photography: David
Schisgall
Cast: Pedro Almodóvar (The Club
Owner), Amy Adams, Ben Affleck,
Penélope Cruz, Judi Dench, Robert de
Niro, Robert Downey Jr., Kirsten Dunst,
Tobey Maguire, Helen Mirren, Julianne
Moore, Jack Nicholson, Edward Norton,
Sylvester Stallone, Sharon Stone, Naomi
Watts, Bruce Willis, Kate Winslet.
2007

Alaska y Mario (TV Series)
(El Terrat / MTV España)
Episodes *Ibiza Mix* and *Huracán Maletas*
(Self)
2011-2018

Maricón perdido (TV Series)
(WarnerMedia / El Terrat / Codetma
Producciones)
Episode *Recuerda* (Self)
2021

BIBLIOGRAPHY

BOOKS

Acevedo-Muñoz, Ernesto, *Pedro Almodóvar*, London,
British Film Institute, 2019.
Allison, Mark, *Un laberinto español: Las películas de Pedro
Almodóvar*, Madrid, Ocho y Medio, 2003.
Almodóvar, Pedro, *El último sueño*, Barcelona,
Reservoir Books, 2023.
Camarero Gómez, Gloria, *Madrid en el cine de Pedro
Almodóvar*, Madrid, Akal, 2019.
Castro, Antonio, *Las películas de Pedro Almodóvar*,
Madrid, Ediciones JC, 2010.

D'Lugo, Marvin & Vernon, Kathleen M., *A Companion
to Pedro Almodóvar*, Chichester, Blackwell Publishing
Ltd., 2013.
Duncan, Paul & Peiró, Bárbara, *The Pedro Almodóvar
Archives*, London, Taschen, 2021.
García, Ladis, *Pedro Almodóvar: La película de su vida*,
Madrid, Letrame, 2019.
Holguín, Antonio, *Pedro Almodóvar*, Madrid, Cátedra,
2006.
Kercher, Dona, *Latin Hithcock. How Almodóvar,
Amenábar, De la Igesia, Del Toro and Campanella Became
Notorius*, London, Wallflower Press, 2015.

Levy, Emanuel, *Gay Directors, Gay Films?*, New York,
Columbia University Press, 2015.
Lowenstein, Stephen (Ed.) *Mi primera película*,
Barcelona, Alba, 2001.
Markus, Sasa, *La poética de Pedro Almodóvar*, Barcelona,
Littera Books, 2001.
Martínez-Carazo, Cristina, *Almodóvar en la prensa de
Estados Unidos*, Valencia, Universitat de València, 2017.
Mejean, Jean-Max, *Almodóvar, les femmes et les chan-
sons*, Paris, L'Harmattan, 2011.
Sánchez-Arce, Ana María, *The Cinema of Pedro
Almodóvar*, Manchester University Press, 2020.

Sánchez Noriega, José Luis, *Universo Almodóvar: Estética de la pasión en un cineasta posmoderno*, Madrid, Alianza, 2017.

Shulman, Liliana, *Los films de Almodóvar: Un entramado de evocaciones, autobiografía y emociones*, Buenos Aires, Biblos, 2020.

Smith, Paul Julian, *Desire Unlimited: The Cinema of Pedro Almodóvar (Third Edition)*, London, Verso, 2014.

Sotinel, Thomas, *Maestros del cine: Pedro Almodóvar (Spanish Edition)*, Paris, Cahiers du Cinéma, 2010.

Strauss, Frédéric, *Conversaciones con Pedro Almodóvar*, Madrid, Akal, 2001.

Urios-Aparisi, Eduardo, *Puro teatro: Metáfora y espacio en el cine de Pedro Almodóvar*, San Lorenzo de El Escorial, Madrid, Libertarias, 2010.

Vidal, Nuria, *El cine de Pedro Almodóvar*, Madrid, Ministerio de Cultura-ICAA, 1988.

FEATURES AND INTERVIEWS

Almodóvar, Pedro, 'El director cumple diez años', *El Mundo*, 30 October 1989.

Almodóvar, Pedro, 'Génesis de *Kika*', *El País*, 11 May 1993.

Almodóvar, Pedro, 'Epílogo', from the book *Almodóvar: El cine como pasión*, Cuenca, University of Castilla-La Mancha, 2005.

Almodóvar, Pedro, 'El largo viaje hacia la noche', *El Diario.es*, 30 March 2020.

Alonso Franch, Eduardo, 'Medicina, médicos y hospitales en el cine de Almodóvar', *Journal of Medicine and Movies*, University of Salamanca, January-March 2022.

Alonso G., Agustín, 'Desnudando a Pedro Almodóvar: El Making Of de *Los abrazos rotos*', *Informe Semanal*, RTVE, 12 March 2009.

Álvarez, Juan Francisco, 'La música en el cine de Almodóvar', *Encadenados*, 17 March 2013.

Ander, Álex, 'Pedro me pidió que, con los ojos cerrados, una furtiva lágrima saliera de un ojo para meterse en el otro', *Vanity Fair*, 19 April 2020.

Ander, Álex, 'Historia oral de *Pepi, Luci, Bom...*', *Vanity Fair*, 29 November 2020.

Aparicio, Enrique P., 'Infinitas curiosidades: Julieta Serrano y Benedicta Sánchez', *Academia de Cine*, 25 March 2020.

Bescós, María, 'Ethan Hawke comparte una imagen con Pedro Pascal anunciando el final del rodaje de *Extraña forma de vida*', *Hobby Consolas*, 3 September 2022.

Bonet Mojica, Lluís, 'Pedro Almodóvar desarrolla en su última película una historia de risas y lágrimas, con Carmen Maura', *La Vanguardia*, 20 July 1984.

Cabrera, Daniel, 'Viaje mitómano a La Mancha de Almodóvar', *El País*, 8 April 2006.

Calvo, Alejandro G., 'Pedro Almodóvar en SensaCine: Del *tacaño* de Ennio Morricone, a su primera vez con Penélope y las escenas míticas que improvisó Carmen Maura', *SensaCine*, 18 October 2021.

Casas, Quim, 'Reencuentro en Bitter Creek', *Dirigido por 540*, June 2023.

Castilla, Amelia, 'Liberto Rabal será el protagonista de la nueva película de Almodóvar', *El País*, 1 February 1997.

Claros, Isabel, '*El matador*, una historia de amor y muerte', *La Vanguardia*, 1 November 1985.

Cobos, Juan, & Marías, Miguel, 'Almodóvar secreto', *Nickel Odeon* 1, Winter 1995.

Crespo, Irene, '*Madres paralelas*: el viaje emocional de Pedro Almodóvar', *Traveler*, 8 October 2021.

Davis, Edward, 'Cate Blanchett says Todd Field's *TAR* is about a fall from grace & talks finally working with Almodóvar', *The Playlist*, 28 April 2022.

De Lucas, Gonzalo, 'El deseo de la actriz. Estética del proceso creativo en los filmes de Almodóvar', from the book *El cine de Almodóvar: Una poética de lo trans*, Sevilla, Universidad Internacional de Andalucía, 2015.

De Pablos, Juan, 'Los cortometrajes de Pedro Almodóvar', *Encadenados*, 12 March 2009.

De Prado, Claudio M., 'Pedro Almodóvar y Tilda Swinton presumen de nueva normalidad en la primera foto del rodaje de *La voz humana*', *GQ*, 16 July 2020.

Del Corral, Pedro, 'Pedro Almodóvar y el pueblo que salvó *Volver*', *La Razón*, 25 July 2019.

Devís, Álvaro, 'El primer largometraje de Almodóvar en inglés, el proyecto frustrado de la nueva Ciudad de la Luz', *Valencia Plaza*, 6 June 2023.

Fernández Rubio, Andrés, '*Átame equivale a Te quiero*, dice Almodóvar de su última película', *El País*, 13 December 1989.

Fernández-Santos, Elsa, 'Pedro Almodóvar rueda *Todo sobre mi madre*, su historia más femenina', *El País*, 24 September 1998.

Fernández-Santos, Elsa, 'La muerte en La Mancha está llena de vida y de gracia', *El País*, 26 June 2005.

Ferrando, Carlos, 'Pedro Almodóvar lleva a cabo su antigua aspiración de hacer un film de hermanos', *Diario 16*, 1 September 1986.

Ferrández Sampietro, Lara, 'La representación de la madre en el cine de Pedro Almodóvar', University of Zaragoza, 2016.

Fiestas, Jorge, & Ferrando, Carlos, '*Entre tinieblas* será la película escándalo del 83', *Diario 16*, 7 March 1983.

Galán, Diego, 'Un País de Cine: ¿Qué he hecho yo para merecer esto!!', *El País*, 6 February 2004.

García, Rocío, 'Almodóvar reclama la intimidad del dolor', *El País*, 27 October 1993.

García, Yago, 'Los rodajes más conflictivos del cine español', *Cinemanía*, 25 October 2011.

García, Yago, '¿Por qué es *La voz humana* tan importante para Almodóvar?', *Cinemanía*, 12 February 2020.

Gómez Gómez, Agustín, 'Del autorretrato a una cierta autobiografía', from the book *El cine de Almodóvar: Una poética de lo trans*, Sevilla, Universidad Internacional de Andalucía, 2015.

González Miranda, Carolina, 'Dónde se rodó *Julieta*, de Almodóvar', *Traveler*, 8 April 2016.

Guerra, María; Martínez, Luis & Alegre, Luis, 'Encuentro con el público de Pedro Almodóvar en Zaragoza con motivo del Premio Audi Feroz de Honor 2023', 27 January 2023. https://www.youtube.com/watch?v=XSz0oR0LXZ0.

Guzmán, Almudena, 'Penélope Cruz: Soy actriz, no carne de cañón de la prensa rosa', *ABC*, 14 December 1997.

Hernando, Alberto, 'Quién es Milena Smit, la nueva chica Almodóvar', *Esquire*, 27 July 2021.

Herrero, Nacho, 'Días de gloria en Paterna gracias a Pedro Almodóvar', *El Periódico*, 26 January 2020.

Iturribarria, Fernando, '*Hable con ella* es un filme brutalmente lírico y romántico', *Diario 16*, 9 June 2001.

Lázaro, Margarita, '23 datos curiosos que seguro que no conocías de *Dolor y gloria*', *The Huffington Post*, 5 September 2019.

López, Ianko, '*Entre tinieblas*, o cómo Almodóvar finalizó la transición con una historia de monjas, drogas y lesbianismo', *Vanity Fair*, 26 January 2019.

López García, Raquel, '*Los abrazos rotos* es un drama con tintes de cine negro', *Interfilms*, June 2008.

Losa, David, 'Los escenarios de película de Pedro Almodóvar por España', *The Huffington Post*, 16 February 2016.

Madrid, José, '*Volver*, 15 años de la película que reconcilió a Almodóvar y Carmen Maura (y gustó incluso a Boyero)', *Vanitatis / El Confidencial*, 19 March 2021.

Maíllo, J.A., 'Chus Lampreave: Me asusta la vida y hacer cine, por eso solo trabajo con mis amigos', *Diario 16*, 3 February 1986.

Martí, Octavi, 'Almodóvar conquista a Pina Bausch', *El País*, 8 June 2001.

Martínez, Beatriz, '10 curiosidades de *La ley del deseo*, por Pedro Almodóvar', *Fotogramas*, 6 March 2017.

Martínez, Luis, 'Ryuichi Sakamoto: Me arrepiento de lo que hice con Pedro Almodóvar', *El Mundo*, 5 September 2017.

Martínez, Luis, '*Dolor y gloria*: La fiebre del cine perfecto', *El Mundo*, 13 January 2020.

Martínez, Luis, 'Mis vaqueros dicen cosas que nunca se han escuchado en un *western*', *El Mundo*, 27 January 2023.

Medina, Marta, 'Almodóvar en corto: *La voz humana*, una anomalía del cine español', *El Confidencial*, 23 October 2020.

Mengual, Elena, 'Pedro Almodóvar regresa con *Volver*, una comedia en la que mira a la muerte con naturalidad', *El Mundo*, 14 March 2006.

Montano, Alicia G., & Guerra, Manolo, 'Almodóvar: Regreso a la adolescencia', *Informe Semanal*, RTVE, 6 March 2004.

Montano, Alicia G., '*Los amantes pasajeros*: Para mayores sin reparos', *Informe Semanal*, RTVE, 26 February 2013.

Montano, Alicia G., 'Pedro Almodóvar nos habla de *Dolor y gloria*, su película más íntima', *Fotogramas*, 22 March 2019.

Morán López, Ángela, 'Pedro Almodóvar como caso de cine posmoderno a través de seis películas', University of Sevilla, July 2022.

Muñoz, Diego, 'Nuevo Almodóvar, con Carmen Maura transexual y Eusebio Poncela como *alter ego* del director', *La Vanguardia*, 24 August 1986.

Murillo, Noelia, 'Pedro Almodóvar abandona la adaptación de *Manual para mujeres de la limpieza*', *Woman Magazine*, 14 September 2022.

Noriega, David, & Morales, Clara, 'Pedro Almodóvar: Utilizar la pandemia para atacar al gobierno es el peor uso posible de la democracia', *El Diario.es*, 19 October 2020.

Núñez Jaime, Víctor, 'La creación literaria en Almodóvar', *Milenio*, 28 December 2019.

Ortiz, Francisco J., '*Noir Almodovariano. A propósito de Carne trémula y La piel que habito*', University of Alicante, 2021.

Padalino, Leah, '*La piel que habito*: un thriller *almodovariano*', *La mente es maravillosa*, 7 November 2022.

Pagani, Malcom, 'Pedro Almodóvar: Tutto so di me. I trauma, i vizi, i miei 70 anni, la mia vita', *Vanity Fair Italia*, 15 May 2019.

Parrado, Diego, 'Mujeres al borde de un Stendhalazo', *Revista AD*, 23 March 2018.

Pereira Zazo, Oscar, 'Reseña de *La flor de mi secreto*: Relevancia de la feminidad en la identidad masculina', University of Nebraska-Lincoln, May 2007.

Pinedo, Lucio V., 'Las influencias de Almodóvar', *El Ciudadano*, 2016.

Ponga, Paula, 'No sé cuántas películas me quedan por hacer, noto el paso del tiempo', *Fotogramas*, 4 October 2021.

Porcel, María, 'Emma Suárez y Adriana Ugarte son *Julieta*: sus sorprendentes formas de prepararse para Almodóvar', *The Huffington Post*, 8 April 2016.

Ricci Anduaga, Aníbal, '*Hable con ella*: La ética de un acto de amor', *Cine y Literatura*, 27 May 2020.

Rosado, Ricardo, 'La película de Pedro Almodóvar que inspiró a Quentin Tarantino para cambiar el cine de los 90', *Fotogramas*, 11 August 2022.

Sánchez Alcolea, Marina, 'Risas y lágrimas en *Tacones lejanos*, de Pedro Almodóvar', *RTVE*, 24 July 2021.

Sánchez-Mesa, Domingo, 'Plasticidad de la identidad ciborg en *La piel que habito*', from the book *El cine de Almodóvar: Una poética de lo trans*, Sevilla, Universidad Internacional de Andalucía, 2015.

Sancho Cardiel, Mateo, 'El avión de *Los amantes pasajeros* es una muestra de la España de hoy', *20 Minutos*, 18 February 2013.

Sardá, Juan, 'Las madres de Almodóvar o el amor puro', *El Cultural*, 8 October 2021.

Sartori, Beatriz, 'Esta película me representa por entero', *El Mundo*, 2 February 2002.

Silvestre, Juan, 'Pedro Almodóvar nos da las 8 claves de *Dolor y gloria*', *Fotogramas*, 13 March 2019.

Silvestre, Juan, '12 razones por las que seguimos amando *La mala educación*', *Fotogramas*, 18 March 2019.

Silvestre, Juan, '*Todo sobre mi madre* en 9 curiosidades', *Fotogramas*, 16 April 2019.

Silvestre, Juan, '*La flor de mi secreto*: 10 curiosidades en su 25 aniversario', *Fotogramas*, 22 September 2020.

Silvestre, Juan, 'Fotogramas de Plata 2019: Pedro Almodóvar en *Qué película la de aquel rodaje*', *Fotogramas*, 20 November 2020.

Silvestre, Juan, 'Pedro Almodóvar: Amar en el lejano Oeste', *Fotogramas* 2.156, June 2023.

Sisí Sánchez, Alberto, '*Extraña forma de vida*: Un western en Almería producido por Saint Laurent, el nuevo proyecto de Almodóvar', *Vogue*, 17 August 2022.

Tena, Agustín, 'Pedro Almodóvar dirige en *Laberinto de pasiones* una alta comedia de ficción histórica', *El País*, 25 April 1982.

Tessé, Jean-Philippe, 'Des douleurs, del couleurs, entretien avec Pedro Almodóvar', *Cahiers du Cinéma*, 722, May 2016.

Valdés, Marcela, 'Pedro Almodóvar Is Still Making Movies That Shock', *The New York Times Magazine*, 18 December 2021.

Vallín, Pedro, 'Lo más sensato era abandonar este guion': El director de cine manchego Pedro Almodóvar estrena este viernes su último trabajo, *La piel que habito*', *La Vanguardia*, 29 August 2011.

Varderi, Alejandro, 'Familias al borde: El cine de Pedro Almodóvar 40 años después', *Viceversa Magazine*, 24 November 2014.

Vega, Cristina, '*Julieta*: La recaudación de lo nuevo de Almodóvar en Francia duplica la taquilla española', *Sensacine*, 14 June 2016.

Vegas, Valeria, 'Las 20 revelaciones de Pedro Almodóvar que hace sobre sí mismo en *Dolor y gloria*', *El Mundo*, 30 March 2019.

Vilar, Màrius, 'El cine de Almodóvar en la taquilla mundial', *Industrias del Cine*, 21 March 2019.

Ximénez, Mario, 'Pedro Almodóvar: Mi vida en 35 milímetros', *Vogue*, 21 March 2019.

ACKNOWLEDGMENTS

The author would like to thank the following people for their invaluable help:

To Rob Nichols and Caterina Favaretto, for entrusting me with such a challenging and exciting project.
To Adelle Mahoney and the Palazzo team, for creating a book beyond all my expectations.
To Antonio Banderas and Cecilia Roth, for sharing their memories and experiences with Pedro.
To Lola García and Sergio Rey, for making the treasures of El Deseo available to me.
To Manuel Outumuro, for sharing with us his fascinating vision of Almodóvar.
To Annabelle Sandwith and María Puchol, for solving all my doubts with the English version.
To Trini Solano and Goyo Ramos, for making possible what seemed impossible.
And, of course, to my wife and children, for the time not shared during all these months. I love you all.

PICTURE CREDITS